MILITARY WEAPONS AND ENVIRONMENT

MILITARY WEAPONS AND ENVIRONMENT

DR U. C. JHA

KNOWLEDGE WORLD
KW Publishers Pvt Ltd
New Delhi

ISBN 978-93-86288-94-3 Hardback
ISBN 978-93-86288-95-0 ebook

Published in India by Kalpana Shukla

KNOWLEDGE WORLD

KW Publishers Pvt Ltd
4676/21, First Floor, Ansari Road
Daryaganj, New Delhi 110002
Phone: +91 11 23263498/43528107
Marketing: kw@kwpub.com
Editorial: jose@kwpub.com
Website: www.kwpub.com

Printed and Bound in India.

CONTENTS

PREFACE

This is an enlarged and updated version of the text published under the title, "Weapons of War: Environmental Impact" in the year 2013. Since then there have been many changes and armed conflicts have become more complicated, with the emphasis shifting towards new weapons such as drones, cyber and autonomous weapons. However, discussions on the devastating effects of the use of conventional and nuclear weapons continue. In July 2017, the UN General Assembly adopted the Treaty on the Prohibition of Nuclear Weapons. This treaty is the first multilateral legally-binding instrument for nuclear disarmament to have been negotiated in the last two decades. It prohibits a full range of nuclear-weapon-related activities, such as undertaking to develop, test, produce, manufacture, acquire, possess or stockpile nuclear weapons or other nuclear explosive devices, as well as the use or threat of use of these weapons. The treaty will be open for signature to all States at the UN Headquarters in New York in September 2017. Once 50 States have ratified the treaty, nuclear weapons which pose the single biggest threat to the environment will be illegal.

The ongoing conflicts have shown that the consequences of the use of explosive weapons are not limited to death, physical injury and disability, but also include long-term impacts on mental well-being. The use of improvised weapons by States and non-State actors is an area of concern for the environment. It has been reported, for example, that Syrian regime helicopters dropped 12,958 barrel bombs in 2016. A barrel bomb is an improvised explosive device, typically made from a large barrel-shaped metal container that has been filled with high explosives, shrapnel and chemicals. Due to the large amount of explosives (up to 1,000 kg), the resulting detonations have been devastating. In 2016 alone, barrel-bombs were responsible for the deaths of 653 civilians, including 166 children and 86 women in Syria. It is difficult to assess the environmental harm that such weapons would cause in the long run.

The testing of weapons, military training exercises and military activity during armed conflict have devastating effects on the environment. War not only destroys homes and infrastructure, and causes the displacement of people, but also has a long-term impact on the lives of people. For instance, the consequences of landmines are felt years after hostilities cease. Other than causing human casualties, landmines are a significant contributor to such global environmental crises as deforestation, soil erosion, water pollution and declining biodiversity. They also render fertile farmland unusable, leading to food shortages and malnutrition. Evidence suggests that during the first Gulf War, the US bombed Iraq with 340 tonnes of missiles containing depleted uranium. Researchers have suggested that radiation from these weapons has poisoned the soil and water of Iraq, making the environment carcinogenic. Today, nearly 50 million people are affected by urban armed conflict, leading to mass displacement, destruction of critical infrastructure and interrupted or inadequate provision of basic public services.

Every State must, therefore, ensure that weapons used by their armed forces are explicitly adjudged under international humanitarian law (IHL) and human rights law. While reviewing a new weapon, the States must adopt multilateral approaches, drawing upon relevant legal, health, environmental and military expertise.

This book describes the environmental effects of eight weapons and explosive remnants of war that have caused extensive environmental harm in the recent past. It also makes specific recommendations addressed to the international community and the States for protecting the natural environment from the impact of weapons of war. I hope this edition of the book will contribute to a better understanding of the environmental harm caused by military weapons. I thank KW Publishers Pvt Ltd for their assistance in bringing out this edition.

U C Jha

ABBREVIATIONS

AXO	Abandoned Ordnance
BWC	Biological Weapons Convention
BTWC	Biological and Toxin Weapons Convention
CBM	Confidence-Building Measure
CBU	Cluster Bomb Unit
CBW	Chemical and Biological Weapons
CCM	Convention on Cluster Munitions
CCW	Convention on Certain Conventional Weapons
CD	Conference on Disarmament
CTBT	Comprehensive Nuclear-Test-Ban Treaty
CTBTO	Comprehensive Nuclear-Test-Ban Treaty Organization
CTR	Cooperative Threat Reduction
CWC	Chemical Weapons Convention
DU	Depleted Uranium
ERW	Explosive Remnants of War
EXO	Explosive Ordnance
FAO	Food and Agriculture Organization
FMCT	Fissile Material Cut-Off Treaty
HEU	Highly Enriched Uranium
HRW	Human Rights Watch
IAEA	International Atomic Energy Agency
ICBM	Intercontinental Ballistic Missile

ICBL	International Campaign to Ban Landmines
ICJ	International Court of Justice
ICRC	International Committee of the Red Cross
IED	Improvised Explosive Devices
INF	Intermediate-Range Nuclear Forces (Treaty)
LEU	Low-Enriched Uranium
MAD	Mutual Assured Destruction
NATO	North Atlantic Treaty Organization
NBC	Nuclear/Biological/Chemical
NGO	Non-Governmental Organisation
NNWS	Non-Nuclear-Weapon State
NPT	Non-Proliferation Treaty
NSG	Nuclear Suppliers Group
NWFZ	Nuclear-Weapon-Free Zone
NWS	Nuclear-Weapon State
MBT	Mine Ban Treaty
OPCW	Organisation for the Prohibition of Chemical Weapons
P5	Five permanent members of the United Nations Security Council
PTBT	Partial Test-Ban Treaty (Treaty Banning Nuclear Weapon Tests in the Atmosphere, in Outer Space and Under Water)
SARS	Severe Acute Respiratory Syndrome
SIPRI	Stockholm International Peace Research Institute
SLBM	Submarine-Launched Ballistic Missile
SORT	Strategic Offensive Reductions Treaty

SSOD	Special Session on Disarmament (of the UN General Assembly)
START	Strategic Arms Reduction Treaty
UAV	Unmanned Aerial Vehicle or drones
UN	United Nations
UNDC	United Nations Disarmament Commission
UNDDA	United Nations Department for Disarmament Affairs
UNDP	United Nations Development Programme
UNGA	United Nations General Assembly
UNHCR	United Nations High Commissioner for Refugees
UNICEF	United Nations Children's Fund
UNIDIR	United Nations Institute for Disarmament Research
UNMOVIC	United Nations Monitoring, Verification and Inspection Commission
UNSC	United Nations Security Council
UNSCOM	United Nations Special Commission on Iraq
UXO	Unexploded Ordnance
WHO	World Health Organization
WMD	Weapons of Mass Destruction
WMDC	Weapons of Mass Destruction Commission

1

INTRODUCTION

Armed conflict between nations or between opposing factions within a nation can have grave consequences.[1] The impact of military weaponry and tactics extends beyond military targets to affect civilian populations and the natural environment. The main impacts of armed conflict on the environment are habitat destruction and loss of wildlife, over-exploitation and degradation of natural resources, and pollution. Armed forces may directly target forests and other ecosystems in order to deprive enemy troops of cover, shelter, and food. Mass movements of people and other disruptions caused by armed conflict can deplete forest cover, timber and wildlife. During non-international armed conflict (NIAC)[2] in a weak State, lawlessness can make it difficult to prevent illegal logging, mining, and poaching. Even peacetime military activities and preparation for war can be extraordinarily harmful to the environment.

Although wartime environmental damage is as old as war itself, the technological advancement in weapon systems and modern tactics have raised the scale of destruction of ecosystems. From the use of poison gases in World War I and atomic bombs in World War II to the use of chemical defoliants in Vietnam, the laying of landmines in numerous NIAC,[3] and the burning of oil wells in the Gulf War, war has left a legacy that extends far beyond the battlefield and long past the duration of the original conflict. The Gulf War zone is still littered with tonnes of depleted uranium and unexploded military ordnance left by the coalition forces.[4] The US military forces based in Afghanistan since 2001 have generated a huge quantity of toxic chemicals and hazardous radioactive waste; when they withdraw, the waste they leave behind will continue to pollute Afghanistan for centuries.

It was after the Vietnam War that the world first isolated the environmental consequences of war as a separate legal issue. The 1990 Gulf War created such severe environmental devastation that the international community was compelled to create an institution to enforce legal norms. The 1999 Kosovo conflict raised further environmental issues. Serbian forces and militias poisoned wells and allegedly engaged in scorched earth tactics to spur Kosovar Albanians to leave their homes. NATO's 78-day bombing campaign caused severe damage to certain areas, particularly around the oil refinery, and petrochemical and fertiliser plants complex at Pancevo and at the industrial facilities of Novi Sad.[5] More recently, a United Nations Environment Programme (UNEP) report has alleged serious environmental damages in the Gaza Strip following a 23-day conflict between Israel and Palestinians.[6] Non-state armed conflicts may also cause depletion of natural resources and biodiversity. This may weaken the chances of lasting peace to find sustainable livelihoods. Thus, whatever may be the cause of a conflict, environmental degradation and resource depletion can drag it into a vicious circle of poverty, further political instability, more armed conflict, greater environmental degradation, and even greater poverty.

The Environment

The word "environment" derives from the verb "environ," which means to surround or encircle.[7] Broadly speaking, the term includes water, air, soil, flora and fauna. Dictionaries define "environment" as "the surroundings or conditions in which a person, animal, or plant lives or operates."[8] Accordingly, the term encompasses the features and the products of the natural world as well as those of human civilisation. It refers to the conditions under which any organism or thing lives or is developed and the sum total of the influences which modify and determine the development of life or character or more generally, that which surrounds and influences. This vision of the environment as the external surroundings that determine the development of life is applied broadly to living beings inclusive of humans. The environment could also be defined as the sum total of the components of the atmosphere, biosphere, geosphere, hydrosphere, and lithosphere. Another definition is that the environment is anything not made by humans.

The legal definition of "environment" is important; however, many treaties on environmental law do not define the term. States have been reluctant to expand the definition of the environment to include such things as natural resources, climate modification, biodiversity, and ecosystems for fear of limiting their military options. The US Council on Environmental Quality's definition of the environment is "the natural and physical environment and the relationship of people with that environment." This definition illustrates the problems of breadth, ambiguity, and circularity that plague this most basic question, namely, exactly what we are attempting to protect.[9] It seems safe to say that the environment comprises abiotic and biotic components including air, water, soil, flora, fauna and the ecosystems formed by their interaction.[10]

The Environment Act of India states that the environment includes water, air and land and the interrelationship which exists among and between water, air and land, and human beings, other living creatures, plants, micro-organisms and property.[11] The UK's Environmental Protection Act 1990, provides that the "environment" consists of all, or any, of the following media, namely, the air, water and land; and the medium of air includes the air within buildings and the air within other natural or man-made structures above or below ground. The legal definition of "environment" is notable at two levels. At the general level, it defines the scope of the legal subject and the competence of international organisations.[12] More specifically, it is crucial to efforts at establishing rules to prevent damage to the environment by hostile activities and the liability for such damage.[13] The meanings of the term "environment" are multiple and contested in contemporary usage. The terms "nature," "wilderness," "ecosphere,"[14] and "ecosystem,"[15] in common parlance are used synonymously with "natural environment." The distinction between "natural" and "man-made" has also become blurred in recent scholarly works of political ecologists and bio-geographers which highlight the long history of human alteration of nearly every environment on Earth, and the continual alteration and management of pristine natural environments by rural and indigenous peoples.[16] The distinction becomes foggier in the categorisation of genetically modified organisms.

The environment has an independent, truly unique and intrinsic value—value that often exceeds that of human artefacts. It is interconnected within itself in a way that is very different from the way people are connected. Thus, when a combatant poisons the water of an enemy's river, for example, he harms all the riparian states, not simply the target state. Recent history demonstrates that even in its just and lawful forms, armed conflict has become increasingly destructive[17] and is likely to become more so in the future, given the technological advancement in weaponry. The environment has been described as the silent casualty of armed conflict. The governments involved in armed conflict honour the fallen soldiers and acknowledge the "collateral damage" of civilians injured and killed. However, they treat impact on the environment as the necessary cost of armed conflict and disregard any responsibility for environmental contamination.

Classification of Environmental Damage

Though an armed conflict is synonymous with environmental damage, systematic analysis about the effects of conflict on the environment is rare to find in literature. Dahl (1992) has classified environmental destruction into six categories based on the intention of the attacker:[18]

(a) Destruction of the human environment
(b) Destruction of the cultivated environment
(c) Destruction of the natural environment of economic importance

(d) Destruction of the natural environment of non-economic categories
(e) General environmental degradation
(f) Environmental manipulation as a tool of war

In an armed conflict, the opposing forces may legally cause (a) and (b) only. Causing (c) to (f) would be unlawful, as this would affect civilians and other protected persons. However, Dahl's classification is not useful when one is interested in the effects of war on nature per se.

Lanier-Graham (1993) has proposed three categories of environmental harm: (i) Intentional direct destruction of the environment during war, (ii) Incidental direct destruction, that is, collateral environmental destruction incidental to war aims, and (iii) Indirect or induced destruction, that is, medium or long-term consequences directly attributable to war. The first category refers to deliberate attacks on cultivated and uncultivated lands and natural resources with the objective of environmental destruction for its own sake. The setting of oil wells on fire during the 1991 Gulf War serves as an example of this category.[19] An example of the second category includes soil disturbance when troops dig trenches or when heavy equipment and battle tanks are driven across fragile surfaces. Riding heavy war machines on desert surfaces can break the desert's thin sheet of encrusted sand. Damage in the third category includes destruction which may occur as a result of the migration of human population, for example, Afghans fleeing to Iran and Pakistan. Such migration can result in an enormous amount of untreated trash, due to the lack of sanitation and proper waste disposal, and large-scale deforestation due to the lack of shelter and fuel.

Indirect or induced destruction, Lanier-Graham's third category, refers to habitat denial to non-human species and addresses mostly long-term wildlife consequences of war, such as species depletion and extinction. This is probably the most important category in terms of damage done and occurs in a large part because war induces human population shifts and thereby brings resource pressures to marginal lands.[20] This category of war-induced effects includes crude and subtle effects.[21] Induced damage, i.e., alteration of the natural environment *after* war—possibly irreversible alteration—thus emerges as the most important category of the effect of armed conflict on the natural environment.

Levy and others (1997: 52) have classified the natural environment into physical, chemical, and biological components.[22] The physical environment includes aspects of the natural environment, such as weather and climate, soil conditions and vegetation, water sources, as well as human infrastructure, such as water supply and sanitation, and transportation and communication networks. The chemical environment refers to things affecting air, land, and water quality, and the biological environment refers to micro- and macro-organisms and their ecological interactions in and over time and space. Thus, specialists such as marine biologists, atmospheric climate researchers, ornithologists, organic chemists, geochemists and geophysicists could in principle make valuable contributions to the assessment of damage to the natural environment from armed conflict. The approach could be useful for those recording war-related environmental damage, but does not provide an integrated and ecological assessment of the damage.

Schwartz (1998: 489),[23] has categorised environmental destructions into eight categories:

1. Deliberate, "primary symbolism," peacetime, e.g., Galapagos Islands incident[24]
2. Deliberate, "primary symbolism," wartime, no current examples
3. Deliberate, "secondary symbolism," peacetime, e.g., manipulation of chemical and biological agents
4. Deliberate, "secondary symbolism," wartime, e.g., oil spill and oil well sabotage during Gulf War
5. Deliberate, not symbolic, peacetime, e.g., nuclear testing by France in the Pacific Ocean
6. Deliberate, not symbolic, wartime, e.g., environmental damage during the Vietnam War

7. Unintentional, not symbolic, peacetime, e.g., nuclear accident (Chernobyl)
8. Unintentional, not symbolic, wartime, e.g., collateral effects of conventional warfare

Machlis (2006) has used the term "warfare ecology" for environmental damage during war. Ecology in this context includes both biophysical and socio-economic systems. All three stages of war (preparation, war, post-war) have significant ecological consequences. Modern warfare preparation requires research, weapons testing, training and associated facilities. Training activities often lead to residual unexploded ordnance, chemical contamination, craters, noise pollution, removal of vegetation, soil erosion, and economic disruption.[25] The ecology of war itself is largely distinguished by immense and concentrated energy flows, severe disturbances, and habitat destruction. Post-war conditions include intense pollution, unexploded ordnance, damaged and destroyed infrastructure, degraded landscapes, economic disruption, refugee populations, and long-term illness.[26]

Environmental disturbance occurs when armies intentionally eliminate the forest cover or resource base of an enemy, or more commonly, as an unintentional consequence associated with war efforts. Based on this premise, Hupy (2008: 406) divided the environmental disturbance associated with war into three general categories: (i) Environmental disturbance and destruction from weaponry; (ii) Direct consumption of resources such as timber, water and food to support armies; and (iii) Indirect consumption of resources by the military industrial complex that supplies the war effort.[27]

Irrespective of how we classify it, the scope of environmental disturbance has continually and significantly increased in scale. The term "scale," according to Hupy, refers not only to the spatial extent, or geographical scale, but also to the temporal scale. Human technological innovations from one war to the next have not only increased the level of harm inflicted upon the enemy, but also upon the environment. Every aspect of modern armed conflict is of greater magnitude than that of armed conflict prior to the industrial age; armies and battlefields are larger, munitions are more powerful, casualty rates are higher, battles and wars are fought longer, and the environmental harm is more widespread.[28]

The authors have also attempted to classify environmental harms based on ecological severity. According to them environmental harm can be classified as "degradation," "depletion" and "destruction" in ascending order of severity. If full natural or human-assisted reconstitution can be expected then the damage is time-limited and we can refer to it as environmental degradation. Where only partial reconstitution is possible or expected, we might refer to it as environmental depletion. The absence of any possible reconstitution may be termed as environmental destruction.[29] Environmental degradation, depletion, and destruction need be viewed in the ecological context of the affected physical entity. For example, a war-degraded coral reef may take thousands of years to redevelop. On the other hand, the killing of a large number of camels during the Gulf War would be classified as "degradation" since camel herds surely would be expected to regrow.[30]

Environmental Impact of Warfare

The well-being of the human race depends upon the care with which it treats the environment. This environment shared with all other living beings is beginning to suffer the strains of pollution and other destructive human activities. In peacetime, the ramifications of military activities are virtually endless. Military activities can disrupt the environment both in peace and during armed conflict, on the battlefield and off it. Such disruption has in the past often been the incidental by-product of a military activity, but is increasingly becoming the result of specific intent. The environment may suffer from: (i) Incidental or indirect effects of warfare; (ii) Direct or intentional effects of warfare; and (iii) Effects of non-hostile military activities.[31]

(i) *Incidental or indirect environmental effects*

The use of force is accepted in international law in the case of legitimate self-defence, in so far as it is directed at the military forces of the enemy. However, when such attack is carried out with modern weapons and techniques it is likely to indiscriminately affect the civil population and to cause widespread, long-lasting and severe damage to the environment. Thus, in spite of the continuing efforts in international law and national regulations to circumscribe the effects of such attacks, they may result in substantial incidental environmental damage.

Front-line troops of the major powers today have about 25 times the firepower of their predecessors in World War II. Today, cluster munitions can be disseminated in large numbers by aircraft, artillery or rockets. Huge quantities can be delivered either on the battlefield to impede an advancing enemy, or in rear areas to harass the enemy, which may pose a grave danger to the civil population and to the environment. Environmental dangers of delayed-action munitions have been compounded by the unreliability of the fuses used, with the result that they can remain a hazard for a long time into the future.

(ii) *Direct or intentional environmental effects*

Certain methods of warfare seek to weaken the military forces of an enemy by intentionally destroying or denying their means of existence, usually including those of the civil population, which is thereby prevented from supporting the military forces. These techniques include: blockade; the destruction of water supplies; the destruction of forest sanctuary or cover; the driving of pastoral communities into inhospitable terrain lacking grazing land for their livestock; other forced relocation of populations; the destruction of housing, communication and health facilities; and actions that result in the deterioration of the weather. Techniques in which the environment of the enemy nation, rather than its military forces, is the direct object of attack, are referred to as environmental warfare.[32]

(iii) *Effects of non-hostile military activities*

There are a variety of military activities that are not intentionally directed either at an enemy force or at the environment, but which nevertheless cause injury to the environment. Impacts of this kind include environmental pollution resulting from the production of munitions (both conventional and nuclear) and other military equipment; land use and the consumption of raw materials for military purposes; and damage to the environment resulting from the testing of conventional and nuclear weapons, from the training of troops and from accidents involving military forces.

Cohan (2003: 483) has advanced six main sources of environmental harm in times of war: (i) Direct attacks upon the environment so as to achieve a military advantage (such as earth-scorching, deforestation to prevent enemies from hiding, and blowing up caves in Afghanistan to weed out terrorists); (ii) Direct manipulations of the natural environment as a mode of warfare in order to inflict damage on military targets (the use of environmental modification techniques, which has received increased attention in international law); (iii) Attacks on installations such as dams, dykes or power plants, which results in flooding and other environmental havoc in the region; (iv) Conventional attacks against enemy targets that, in addition to destroying the military targets, produce foreseeable collateral damage to the environment (such as deploying uranium shells against enemy tanks, with the depleted uranium creating an environmental hazard to civilians after the conflict terminates); (v) Unforeseeable environmental harms that result from military battles, sometimes not discovered until many years later (e.g., systematic oil discharge from US and Japanese warships sunk during World

War II are claimed to have produced consequential depletion of natural resources of the Solomon Islands in recent times); and (vi) Environmental damage from military operations other than war (MOOTW).[33]

According to Rafael (2010) warfare significantly affects the environment, but the sizes of these effects depend on the environmental attribute (whether the conflict is IAC or NIAC) and development (whether the fighting country is developed or less developed).[34] Warfare reduces CO_2 emissions, but the effect is weaker in less developed countries (LDCs) than in developed countries (DCs). Warfare increases deforestation during the NIAC. Warfare at home reduces NOX emissions for LDCs and increases them for DCs; warfare abroad increases NOX emissions for both DCs and LDCs. Finally, warfare increases aggregated environmental stress, particularly for LDCs when fought at home and for DCs when fought abroad.

According to Al-Azzawi (2008), military operations in Iraq have resulted in the following environmental damages:[35]

- Excessive release of nitrogen, sulfur and carbon oxides from explosions of conventional weapons.
- Soot and hydrocarbon plumes from burning thousands of barrels of oil from oil wells and pits surrounding Baghdad and other cities. Smoke and soot from burning crude petroleum generates toxic and carcinogenic substances like polycyclic aromatic hydrocarbons or PAH's, dioxins, furan, mercury and sulfur. Black soot plumes covered Baghdad and other cities for more than weeks during the invasion operations.
- Thermal heat and pollution as a result of using Napalm and other heat generating weapons.
- Noise pollution from the "shock and awe" attack on the civilian population of the major Iraqi cities where noise intensity exceeded 130db, close to the threshold of pain to human beings.
- Increase of total suspended solids (TSP) in the air due to the invading forces' heavy artilleries traffic and deep earth

bombardment using Bunker Buster bombs and other earth penetrating missiles.

- Electromagnetic pollution from the use of laser guided missiles, radars and advanced electronic devises. Increase of electromagnetic energy in the atmosphere cause the ionization of the atmosphere. Ionization of atmosphere generates free oxygen radicals. Formation of these radicals can cause serious related diseases like anxiety, depression, and pregnancy problems. Higher rates of cardiovascular disease and cancer were diagnosed in areas of early radar systems.
- Ionized radiation from the use of DU weapons in highly populated areas like Baghdad, Smawa, Basra and other cities.
- Surface and ground water pollution as a result of: (i) Fuel and toxic chemicals under storage tanks rupture as a result of bombing and explosions, looting of industrial complexes, and Iraqi military camps and bases; (ii) Sewage water accumulation as a result of sewer network destruction; it percolated to shallow ground water then to nearby water courses; (iii) Polluted rain storms and runoff as a result of dissolution of previously mentioned air pollutants; and (iv) Contamination of fresh water supply with the sewage.
- Land and soil degradation as a result of explosions and heavy artilleries traffic and sewage flooding of large areas of Baghdad and other major cities in addition to the accumulation of garbage.
- Contamination of Al-Tuwaitha (Iraqi Atomic Commission complex) where about 600 Tons of natural Uranium and Cobalt 60 containers were looted after spilling this radioactive waste on the ground of the complex and surrounding areas.
- Radiological contamination of parts of Al-Jazeera high land of Mosul Uranium Extraction site. The looters took highly contaminated Uranium extraction instruments and destroyed the radioactive waste ponds causing serious ground water contamination in the area.

The armed forces may destroy their own environment, or the opposition's, as a strategy to win a war. For example, forests may be destroyed to deny timber or hiding places, and oil wells, freshwater sources, crops, land, and animals may be damaged to prevent their use by a foe. Both sides may intensify the exploitation of their own resources or the commandeered resources of the other side. Damage may also be indirect: troop movement may degrade arable land and vegetation; fighting and arms production may increase pollution and waste; provisions for troops may intensify pressures on resources; norms in favour of environmental protection may deteriorate; and war refugees may dump waste and damage ecosystems in pursuit of food, land, and firewood.[36]

Conversely, war may reduce ordinary activities that harm the environment. For example, industrial facilities and motor vehicles may be destroyed, reducing production and transportation and, therefore, the associated pollution and waste. Indirectly, a rise in fish stocks could occur if fewer fishing boats go to sea because fishermen are enlisted or avoid combat locations. Biodiversity may increase as the military often designates some zones as "off-limits" to people. As more fossil fuels are shipped to the front and more labourers are enlisted in the military, ordinary economic activities may decline, reducing environmental pressure, emissions, and waste.

Environmental Impact of Weapons

The use of a weapon to kill or injure fellow man, unfortunately, is a characteristic of man. At an early age man used simple tools for hunting. These tools became potential weapons of war. In the course of evolution, man started using simple hand-held weapons and projectiles made from wood and stones. Sticks and clubs used for hand-to-hand fighting evolved into maces and axes with stone, bronze or iron heads. Clubs and axes were later replaced by swords. The production of steel from iron made it possible to hone the blade of a sword to a fine edge. The sword remained an important weapon of war until the nineteenth century when the development of the high-powered rifle, the machine-gun and quick firing artillery converted warfare from a contest between groups of armed men to a contest between manned arms. The twentieth century introduced military aircraft, armoured vehicles, self-propelled guns, rockets and missiles on the battlefield. The inventions of the present century that could be added to the list of weapons of war[37] are drones—unmanned aircraft. Over the years, there has also been an enormous increase in the firepower available to combating troops.[38]

Military power is no longer measured by the possession of territory, the number of armed men, and the number of weapons available, but by the scientific breakthroughs and the technological innovations in the weaponry. Advancements in science and technology have resulted in the production of weapons of mass destruction that have the potential to wipe out entire cities, contaminate the environment, and even threaten the survival of future generations. In addition, the destruction of the natural environment has itself become a tactic of war. Considering the consequences of the use of such weapons, the UN General Assembly adopted a resolution in 1982 on the "Renunciation of the Use of Scientific Achievements for Military Purposes."[39] The resolution called on all States to undertake efforts to ensure that in the future scientific and technological achievements may be used solely for peaceful purposes.

Humankind has always counted its war casualties in terms of dead and wounded soldiers and civilians, destroyed cities and livelihood. The environment has always been an unpublicised, unnoticed victim of war. It is not only the use of weapons in war but also weapons tests that can have disastrous consequences for the natural environment. The storage, deployment, and disposal of weapons, all have an impact on the environment. What is more, it is often impossible to reverse these effects.

The use of over 19 million gallons of Agent Orange by the US military in Vietnam, between 1962 and 1971, not only caused serious health problems for soldiers and civilians, but also affected the wildlife and contaminated the soil and rivers and, through the food chain, passed into fish—a staple of the Vietnamese diet.

The consequences of landmines are felt years after hostilities cease. Besides causing human casualties, landmines are a significant contributor to such global environmental crises as deforestation, soil erosion, water pollution and declining biodiversity. They also render fertile farmland unusable, creating food shortages and malnutrition. As landmines are planted just below the surface of the land, their most direct impact is upon soil quality and composition. When a landmine explodes it destroys surrounding vegetation and shatters and displaces the soil, making it vulnerable to water and wind erosion. If landmines explode on cultivated land, levels of agricultural production are dramatically reduced. In many countries, landmines have reduced harvest yields by as much as 50%. Even the reclamation of landmines has a detrimental effect on soil productivity as it gets contaminated by toxic substances. They are long-lasting and can easily penetrate the food chain.

The use of biological weapons is not only a threat to humans; it is also a serious threat to agricultural ecosystems, wildlife and their habitats. Of all the weapons of mass destruction, biological weapons are the easiest and cheapest to produce. They are the hardest to detect, and can cause disastrous epidemics. A bioterrorist attack on a nation's livestock could have a devastating effect on that nation's agricultural industry in terms of economic loss.

The destructive potential of nuclear weapons is unparalleled in human experience. The impact of such weapons cannot be limited in either space or time; the radiation released can affect health, agriculture, and natural resources over a very wide area and poses a serious danger for future generations. The use of nuclear weapons would affect the environment for many years and render agriculture impossible in vast areas, most likely causing mass starvation and disruption of the global food distribution.

The types of weapons, the extent to which they are used, the duration and intensity of armed conflict, are major determinants of the total environmental damage caused in war. While all weapons systems present threats to environmental integrity, they vary in the effects they cause. Three categories of weapons that have serious consequences on human beings as well as the environment have been discussed in this book. Weapons of mass destruction (WMD), namely, nuclear, chemical and biological weapons, have been discussed in Chapter II. Designed to terrify as well as destroy, these weapons can cause destruction on a vastly greater scale than any conventional weapons, and their impact is far more indiscriminate and long-lasting.[40] Chapter III covers three conventional weapons that can cause serious harm to civilians as well as the natural environment: depleted uranium (DU), high-explosives (HEW), and incendiary weapons such as napalm and white phosphorus. Radioactive substances too can be intentionally scattered by the use of conventional explosives (dirty-bomb),[41] to expose populations and the environment to radiation. Virtually any State or non-State actor can build and detonate a "dirty-bomb," as explosive material is widely available and radioactive materials have become more plentiful throughout the world.

Certain conventional weapons, considered inhumane and indiscriminate, have been banned through international agreements. However, a larger number of countries have not signed or ratified these weapons-ban treaties. Three such weapons, viz., anti-personnel landmines, cluster munitions and the explosive remnants of war (ERW)[42] have been discussed in Chapter IV. Chapter V highlights international humanitarian law relating to weaponry, the necessity of legal review before a State acquires a new weapon and the responsibility of a military commander in the selection and the use of a weapon in warfare. In the concluding chapter, certain recommendations have been made for the protection of civilians and the environment from the scourge of armed conflict.

Notes

1. According to the Uppsala Conflict Data Programme (UCDP), an armed conflict is "a contested incompatibility which concerns government and/or territory where the use of armed force between two parties, of which at least one is the government of a state, results in at least 25 battle-related deaths in one calendar year." Available at: http://www.pcr.uu.se/research/ucdp/definitions/definition_of_armed_conflict/, accessed August 12, 2012.
2. A non-international armed conflict (NIAC) is a confrontation between the existing governmental authority and groups of persons subordinate to this authority or between different groups none of which act on behalf on the government, which is carried out by force of arms within national territory and reaches the magnitude of an armed confrontation or a civil war. An international armed conflict (IAC) exists if one State uses force of arms against another State. This also applies to all cases of total or partial military occupation, even if this occupation meets with no armed resistance (Article 2, para 2 common to the Geneva Conventions of 1949). Dieter Fleck (ed.), *The Handbook of International Humanitarian Law* (Oxford: Oxford University Press, 2008), pp. 45-55. The study conducted by the International Committee of the Red Cross (ICRC) of customary international humanitarian law (IHL) indicates that the line between IACs and NIACs is on the verge of disappearing. For further details see: Dabone Zakaria, "International Law: Armed Groups in a State-centric System," vol. 93, no. 882, *International Review of the Red Cross*, June 2011, pp. 395-424.
3. A. A. Berhe, "The Contribution of Landmines to Land Degradation," vol. 18, *Land Degradation & Development*, 2007, pp. 1-15.
4. As in most conflicts, the environmental damage in the 1990 Gulf War was not unilateral. The region is now littered with as much as 300 tons of armour-piercing depleted uranium (DU) ammunition used by Coalition (largely US) forces. The Coalition forces dropped a total of 88,500 tons of ordnance during the forty-three days of the Gulf War, much of which targeted environmental infrastructure, such as sewage treatment plants, and some of which remained on the ground unexploded. No objective study of the ecological, health or economic effects of these actions is available. Jay E. Austin and Carl E. Bruch (eds.), *The Environmental Consequences of War: Legal, Economic and Scientific Perspectives* (Cambridge: Cambridge University Press, 2000), p. 3.
5. Nicholas G. Alexander, "Airstrikes and Environmental Damage: Can the United States Be Held Liable for Operation Allied Force?" vol. 11, no. 2, *Colorado Journal of International Environmental Law and Policy*, 2000, pp. 471-98; Ida L. Bostian, The Environmental Consequences of the Kosovo Conflict and the NATO Bombing of Serbia, *Colorado Journal of International Environmental Law and Policy: 1999 Year Book* (2000), pp. 230-40.
6. Environmental Assessment of the Gaza Strip: following the escalation of hostilities in December 2008-January 2009, United Nations Environment Programme (UNEP) 2009, available at: http://www.unep.org/PDF/dmb/UNEP_Gaza_EA.pdf, accessed September 30, 2012.
7. *Webster's II, New College Dictionary* (1995, 2nd edition), p. 377.
8. *The Concise Oxford Dictionary,* Judy Pearsall, (ed.) (1999, 2nd impression), p. 477.
9. Parson Rymn James, "The Fight to Save the Planet: US Armed Forces, 'Green-keeping,' and Enforcement of the Law Pertaining to Environmental Protection During Armed Conflict," vol. 10, *Geo. Int'l Envtl L. Rev.* (1998), pp. 441-42.

10. The UN Security Council Resolution 687 (1991) established Iraqi liability for damage, including environmental damage, arising from the 1990 Iraqi invasion and occupation of Kuwait. The Working Group of Experts established for the purpose, concluded this definition of the term "environment." *Report of the United Nations Environment Programme (UNEP) Working Group of Experts on Liability and Compensation for Environmental Damage Arising from Military Activities*, May 17, 1996, para 42.
11. Section 2 (a), The Environment (Protection) Act, 1986. The scope of Environmental Protection Act is broad, with "environment" defined to include water, air and land and the interrelationship which exists among water, air and land, and human beings and other living creatures, plants, micro-organisms and property. The New Zealand Environment Act, 1986, defines environment as including: (a) ecosystems and their constituent parts; (b) all natural and physical resources; and (c) the social, economic, aesthetic and cultural conditions which affect the environment or which are affected by changes to the environment.
12. Legal definitions of the "environment" reflect scientific categorisations and groupings, as well as political acts which incorporate culture and economic considerations. A scientific approach will divide environmental issues into "compartments." These include the atmosphere, atmospheric depositions, soils and sediments, water quality, biology and humans. Scientific definitions are transformed by political process into legal definitions found in treaties; although "environment" does not have a generally accepted usage as a term of art under international law, recent agreements have consistently identified the various media included in the term. Philippe Sands, *Principles of International Environmental Law* (New York: Cambridge University Press, 2003), p.16. The 1982 World Charter for nature does not define the "environment," but addresses the need to respect nature through principles which are applicable to all life forms, habitats, all areas of the earth, ecosystems and organisms, and land, marine and atmospheric resources.
13. The environment is not merely a collection of fauna and flora, or simply an organism's surroundings, but the natural environment acts upon an organism to the extent that it determines that organism's fate. This biological interdependence is of fundamental importance with regard to the severity of environmental damage. It is not just the environmental components that are connected to each other; people are a part of the environment and are dependent on a healthy and viable environment in which they live. Karen Hulme, *War Torn Environment: Interpreting the Legal Threshold* (Leiden: Martinus Nijhoff Publishers, 2004), pp.12-13.
14. Nature: the phenomenon of the physical world collectively, including plants, animals, the landscape, and the other features and products of the earth, as opposed to humans or human creations. Wilderness: an uncultivated, uninhibited and inhospitable region. Ecosphere: the biosphere of the earth, especially when the interaction between the living and non-living components is emphasised. Judy Pearsall (ed.), *The New Oxford Dictionary of English* (New Delhi: Oxford University Press, 2000).
15. Ecosystem is a unit of "ecology," which includes the plants and animals occurring together plus that part of their environment over which they have an influence. Ecology is the study of the interrelationships of living organisms and, especially, of groups of living organisms among themselves and between them and the non-living (or physical) environment. These interrelationships are unified within the framework of an ecological system—or ecosystem—that is

comprised of the entire community of interacting living things together with the non-living environment with which they come in contact. Such an ecosystem is considered to be a self-sustaining life-support system that is self-sufficient with the exception of a continuing need for an external source of energy, usually the sun. The living community of the ecosystem, that is, its entire biotic component, is comprised of many populations, each of which is an interacting group of individuals of a separate species of plant or animal. Each of these populations is considered to play some role in maintaining the ecosystem. *Threat of modern warfare to man and his environment: An Annotated Bibliography*, UNESCO Reports and Papers in Social Sciences—SS/CH 40, p. 7. Available at: http://unesdoc.unesco.org/images/0003/000357/035791eo.pdf, accessed August 11, 2012.

16. William Cronon, *Changes in the Land: Indians, Colonists, and the Ecology of New England* (New York: Hill and Wang, 1983); James Fairhead and Melissa Leach, "False forest history, complicit social analysis: Rethinking some West African environmental narratives," vol. 23, no. 6, *World Development* (1995), pp. 1023-26.
17. Damage to the environment is defined in the instruments of environmental law, and includes all adverse effects on man, his artefacts and the environment. Compensable damage is defined in schemes of restitution and liability, and embraces only economic losses, or rather harm expressed in economic terms. Marie-Louise Larsson, *Legal Definitions of the Environment and of Environmental Damage*, Stockholm Institute for Scandinavian Law, p. 159. Available at: http://www.scandinavianlaw.se/pdf/38-7.pdf, accessed May 20, 2011.
18. Arne Willy Dahl, "Environmental Destruction in War," vol. XV, no. 2, *Disarmament*, 1992, pp. 113-27.
19. An intentional direct destruction refers primarily to the destruction of cultivated environments with the intent to affect habitat-denial to its human occupants. Thus, crops and fields and fruit-bearing trees are considered favoured targets for destruction. For instance, during the 1779 American Revolutionary War, General George Washington directed his troops to destroy entire corn crop and fruit orchards were cut down. Susan D. Lanier-Graham, *The Ecology of War: Environmental Impacts of Weaponry and Warfare* (New York: Walker and Company, 1993), p. 13.
20. For example by 1983, Vietnam had lost half of the forests standing only 40 years before. The displacement resulting from this environmental holocaust brought suffering to entire populations of animals and humans. An ecological domino effect took place when starving hill tribes were forced to turn from chemically contaminated rice fields to the forests for survival. Logging for cash and land clearing accelerated, as did subsistence killing. William Thomas, *Scorched Earth: The Military's Assault on the Environment* (Philadelphia, PA: New Society Publishers, 1995), p. 113.
21. For example during the 1990-91 Gulf War, non-recyclable ready-to-eat food containers, plastic water bottles, aluminium soft-drink cans, and cellophane-packaged junk food might have been buried by allies in the desert along with spoilage from fuel-leaks and spills, solvents, paints, lubricants, acids, and other potentially toxic materials.
22. Barry Levy, G. Shahi, and Chen Lee, "The Environmental Consequences of War," in Barry S. Levy and Victor W. Sidel (eds.), *War and Public Health* (New York: Oxford University Press, 1997), pp. 51-62.
23. Daniel M. Schwartz, "Environmental Terrorism: Analysing the Concept," vol. 35, no. 4, *Journal of Peace Research* (1998), pp. 483-96.
24. In January 1995, a small group of armed fishermen took over the Darwin Research Station in the Galapagos Islands, Ecuador. The fishermen—irate

over a recently imposed limit on sea-cucumber harvesting (a highly lucrative trade)—held the station workers hostage and threatened to kill several rare and endangered species of tortoises, including the last known survivor of a Pinta Island sub-species. Although the Ecuadorian marines recaptured the station without loss of human life, it was later discovered that 81 Galapagos Island tortoises had been killed—mostly by way of torture, mutilation, and hanging. In this case, the environment was a victim because the tortoises were threatened and killed by the local fisherman in order to instil fear in the larger audience over the ecological consequences of their act. Constance Casey, "The Survival of the Slowest," *The Globe and Mail*, October 19, 1996: D6.

25. The effects of training activity on wildlife appear to be case specific. Investigations of mass whale strandings during naval exercises in the Bahamas and the Canary Islands suggest that high-intensity sonar can cause erratic behaviour, internal tissue damage, and mortality in cetaceans. M. Schrope, "Whale deaths caused by US Navy's sonar," vol. 415, *Nature* (2002), p. 106; P. D. Jepson, et al., "Gas-bubble lesions in stranded cetaceans," vol. 425, *Nature* (2003), pp. 575-76.
26. Gary E. Machlis, "The Ecology of Warfare," Paper presented at the Frontiers in Forest and Rangeland Ecosystems Seminar, December 1, 2006, Moscow. Warfare ecology can help develop ecosystem monitoring tools useful for policy and decision making by the network of humanitarian organisations that includes United Nations agencies, the International Committee of the Red Cross and other aid organisations, host governments, and military services. Gary E. Machlis and Thor Hanson, "Warfare Ecology," vol. 58, no. 8, *BioScience*, September 2008, pp. 729-36.
27. Joseph Hupy, "The Environmental Footprint of War," vol. 14, no. 3, *Environment and History* (August 2008), pp. 405-21.
28. Ibid., p. 407.
29. Jurgen Brauer, *The Effect of War on the Natural Environment*, August 2000, p. 6. Available at: https://el.trc.gov.om/htmlroot/K12/tcolon/grade7/Social%20Studies/Geography/Our%20Environment%20Natural%20and%20Human/Notes/The%20Effect%20of%20War%20on%20the%20Natural%20Environment.pdf, accessed August 10, 2012.
30. For instance, during the German occupation of Norway during World War II, German troops destroyed about half of the then 95,000 strong reindeer population. By 1960, the reindeer population regrew to 90,000 heads. Susan D. Lanier-Graham, *The Ecology of War: Environmental Impacts of Weaponry and Warfare* (New York: Walker and Company, 1993), p. 23.
31. *Threat of modern warfare to man and his environment: An Annotated Bibliography*, UNESCO Reports and Papers in Social Sciences—SS/CH 40, pp. 9-10. Available at: http://unesdoc.unesco.org/images/0003/000357/035791eo.pdf, accessed August 11, 2012.
32. The environment in the form of weather, climate, terrain, soil, and vegetation has played an important and sometime crucial role in combat. Harold A. Winters, with General Galloway, William Reynolds, and David Rhyne, *Battling the Elements: Weather and Terrain in the Conduct of War* (Baltimore: John Hopkins University Press, 1998), pp. 1-4.
33. John Alan Cohan, "Modes of Warfare and Evolving Standards of Environmental Protection under International Law of War," vol. 15, *Fla. J. Int'l L.* (2002-3), p. 483.
34. Rafael Reuveny, Andreea S. Mihalache-O'Keef and Quan Li, "The Effect of Warfare on the Environment," vol. 47, no. 6, *Journal of Peace Research* (2010), pp. 749-60.

35. Al-Azzawi Souan N., Crimes of the Century: Occupation & Contaminating Iraq with Depleted Uranium, Associate Professor in Environmental Engineering, 15 June 2008, available at:. http://www.brusselstribunal.org/pdf/DU-Azzawi.pdf.
36. Rafael Reuveny, Andreea S. Mihalache-O'Keef and Quan Li, "The Effect of Warfare on the Environment," vol. 47, no. 6, *Journal of Peace Research* (2010), p. 750.
37. A concise and satisfactory definition of "weapon of war" is not easy to formulate. Some dictionaries are content merely to describe it as an instrument used in combat: "A thing designed or used for inflicting bodily harm or physical damage," [Judy Pearsall (ed.), *The New Oxford Dictionary of English* (2000), p. 2091], but without further qualification this could apply to almost anything with the remotest of military applications, from a motorcycle to a pair of binoculars. On the other hand, to restrict the use of the term to devices specifically employed to kill or wound a combatant would be to exclude both battleships and warplanes, whose main function is essentially that of a carrier. P. E. Cleator, *Weapons of War* (London: Robert Hale, 1967), p. 15.
38. In the last 60 years, the US has dropped 15,000,000 tons of bombs on the Earth's ecosystems along with 1,000,000 tons of napalm, with at least 20,000,000 gallons of defoliants sprayed on rainforests and crops with the intention of destroying them. The irony is that the life sustaining qualities of the earth are the very source of human life. Dana Visalli, "War, Ecology, and Emerging Intelligence," available at: http://www.opednews.com/articles/War-Ecology-and-Emerging-by-Dana-Visalli-110104-115.html, accessed January 25, 2013.
39. The UN General Assembly resolution 37/189 (December 18, 1982).
40. *Weapons of Terror: Freeing the World of Nuclear, Biological and Chemical Arms*. 2006. The Weapons of Mass Destruction Commission (WMDC), final report, Stockholm, Sweden, June 1, 2006.
41. A "dirty-bomb" combines radioactive materials with conventional explosives to scatter radioactive particles into the environment. No nuclear fission reaction takes place as would occur with a nuclear weapon. Almost any radioactive material can be used to construct a radiological dispersal device (RDD), including spent fuel from nuclear reactors and radioactive substances used for medical or industrial purposes, though only a handful of materials are considered optimal. Weapons grade materials (i.e., highly enriched uranium or plutonium) are not needed, but could be used. The RDD threat is fourfold: (i) the blast and fragmentation effects from the conventional explosive, (ii) the radiation exposure from the radioactive material used, (iii) the fear and panic that would spread among the target group or population, and (iv) the economic dislocation and mitigation costs that could result. A passive, non-explosive source can also be used to disperse radiation.
42. The term "Explosive Remnants of War" (ERW) does not denote a typical military weapon, it includes unexploded military ordnance. The 2003 Protocol V to the UN Convention on the Prohibition or Restrictions on the Use of Certain Conventional Weapons Which May be Deemed to Be Excessively Injurious or to Have Indiscriminate Effects (CCW) defines ERW as "unexploded ordnance and abandoned explosive ordnance." The examples of abandoned and unexploded weapons that could be considered ERW include aircraft bombs, anti-tank ammunition, artillery shells, ballistic missiles, mortar rounds, cluster bomb units, and cannon ammunition, etc.

2

WEAPONS OF MASS DESTRUCTION

Weapons of mass destruction (WMD)[1] are designed to terrorise as well as destroy. They have the potential to kill several thousand of people in a single attack, and their effects may persist in the environment and in our bodies, in some cases indefinitely. WMD are not a new phenomenon. They have been used from ancient times through the medieval era into the modern age. It is only twentieth-century science and industrialisation that has given rise to weapons that pose a threat to human beings and the environment on a scale never seen before.[2]

The first known use of the term "weapons of mass destruction" dates back to the December 1937 Christmas address on "Christian Responsibility" delivered by the Archbishop of Canterbury, William Cosmo Gordon Lang:

> Take, for example, the question of peace. Who can think without dismay of the fears, jealousies, and suspicions which have compelled nations, our own among them, to pile up their armaments? Who can think at this present time without a sickening of the heart of the appalling slaughter, the suffering, the manifold misery brought by war to Spain and to China? Who can think without horror of what another widespread war would mean, waged as it would be with all the new weapons of mass destruction?[3]

While the Archbishop's remarks gave no clear indication of what he meant by WMD, few believed that he was thinking only of aerial bombardment and explosive weapons.[4]

The term, "weapons capable of mass destruction," appears in the very first resolution passed by the UN General Assembly in 1946.[5] In 1948, the UN Commission on Conventional Armaments (CCA) generated the first authoritative definition of "weapons of mass destruction" (WMD): "WMD are ... atomic explosive weapons, radioactive material weapons, lethal chemical and biological weapons, and any weapons developed in the future which have characteristics comparable in destructive effect to those of the atomic bomb or other weapons mentioned above." Starting in the 1950s, the Soviet military adopted the term "weapon of mass destruction," in their military doctrine to denote nuclear, chemical, and biological weapons.

However, it was only in 1977 that the UN formally accepted the 1948 definition finalised by the CCA.[6] This led the UN General Assembly to adopt Resolution 32/84, formally accepting the CCA definition for use in disarmament diplomacy:

> Reaffirms the definition of weapons of mass destruction, contained in the resolution of the Commission for Conventional Armaments of August 12, 1948, which defined weapons of mass destruction as atomic explosive weapons, radioactive material weapons, lethal chemical and biological weapons and any weapons developed in the future which might have characteristics comparable in destructive effect to those of the atomic bomb or other weapons mentioned above.[7]

General Assembly resolutions related to the "prohibition of the development and manufacture of new types of weapons of mass destruction and new systems of such weapons" mentioned the CCA definition in 1996, 1999, 2002, 2006, and 2009.[8] A review of disarmament documents indicates that the international community believes that the CCA definition now incorporates all chemical, biological, radiological, and nuclear (CBRN) weapons, despite its stated limitation to "lethal" chemical and biological weapons. There are three treaties that place limitations generally on WMD (rather than specifically on nuclear, chemical, or biological weapons): the 1967 Outer Space Treaty,[9] the 1972 Seabed Treaty,[10] and the 1991 Strategic Arms Reduction Treaty.[11] Additionally, the term WMD appears in the preambles of at least three other treaties: the 1967 Treaty for the Prohibition of Nuclear Weapons in Latin America, the 1972 Biological Weapons Convention, and the 1993 Chemical Weapons Convention. In contrast, the 1968 nuclear Non-Proliferation Treaty (NPT) does not use the term. In the wake of the World Trade Centre attacks, the term WMD has come to include any means capable of inflicting mass casualties.

Researchers have identified more than 50 definitions of WMD issued by various governments and international organisations. The compilation is not comprehensive, although it incorporates the most significant alternatives from the perspective of US Government policy.[12] Despite the relative clarity of the CCA definition used in disarmament diplomacy, multiple definitions have appeared over the years. These define WMD as:

- nuclear, biological, and chemical weapons (NBC)
- chemical, biological, radiological, and nuclear weapons (CBRN)
- CBRN and high explosive weapons (CBRNE)
- CBRN weapons capable of causing mass destruction or mass casualties
- including some CBRN weapons but not limited to CBRN, capable of causing mass destruction or mass casualties
- weapons of mass effect capable of causing mass destruction or mass casualties or that cause mass disruption.[13]

A United Nations study has compared the hypothetical results of an attack carried out by one strategic bomber using nuclear, chemical or biological weapons.[14] The study found that a one-megaton nuclear bomb, might kill 90% of unprotected people over an area of 300 sq km. A chemical weapon of 15 tons might kill 50% of the people in a 60 sq km area. A 10-ton biological weapon could kill 25% of the people, and make 50% ill, over an area of 100,000 sq km. These estimates assume that chemical and biological agents can be delivered over a large surface and reach the ground level, whereas nuclear weapons can be exploded at any predetermined altitude or on ground level with the desired efficiency.

In this chapter the focus will be on nuclear, biological and chemical weapons.[15]

Notes

1. The meaning and definition of "weapons of mass destruction" (WMD) continues to evolve over time and with technology. Though the phrase was first used in a *Times* article in 1937, referring to a saturation bombing during the Spanish Civil War. Originally referring only to atomic weapons, through treaties and international conventions WMD has come to include all types of nuclear, biological, chemical, and toxic weapons. Today an exact definition of WMD is non-existent, varying by place and policy. However, in general WMD are broken down into the following four categories of weaponry: nuclear, biological, chemical, and radiological. A. M. Mannion, 2003. *The Environmental Impact of War and Terrorism*, Geographical Paper No. 169. Available at: http://www.reading.ac.uk/web/FILES/geog/GP169.pdf, accessed March 9, 2012.
2. Paul I. Bernstein, *Weapons of Mass Destruction: A Primer*, October 31, 2006, available at: http://www.fas.org/irp/agency/dod/dtra/wmd-primer.pdf, accessed September 14, 2012.
3. Archbishop's Appeal: "Individual Will and Action; Guarding Personality," *The Times* (London), December 28, 1937.
4. The reference to the wars in Spain and China certainly suggests that the Archbishop had concerns about the widely publicised 1937 bombings of cities by the Fascists in Spain and the Japanese in China. However, the Archbishop was gravely concerned about the dangers of chemical weapons, having addressed the subject during a Parliamentary debate following the initial reports of the 1936 Italian chemical attacks in Abyssinia. W. Seth Carus, "Defining 'Weapons of Mass Destruction,'" Centre for the Study of Weapons of Mass Destruction, Occasional Paper, no. 8, Washington, DC: National Defence University Press, January 2012.
5. The UN General Assembly adopted its first resolution on January 24, 1946, which established a "Commission to Deal with the Problem Raised by the Discovery of Atomic Energy." The General Assembly directed that the Commission "make specific proposals ... for the elimination from national armaments of atomic weapons and of all other *major weapons adaptable to mass destruction*." General Assembly resolution A/RES/1(I) of January 24, 1946 on the Establishment of a Commission to Deal with the Problems Raised by the Discovery of Atomic

Energy, available at: http://daccess-dds-ny.un.org/doc/UNDOC/GEN/NL4/602/91/PDF/NL460291.pdf?OpenElement, accessed October 15, 2012.

6. W. Seth Carus, op. cit.
7. The General Assembly reaffirmed its adherence to this definition in 1999: "Determined to prevent the emergence of new types of weapons of mass destruction that have characteristics comparable in destructive effect to those of weapons of mass destruction identified in the definition of weapons of mass destruction adopted by the United Nations in 1948." UN General Assembly Resolution A/RES/54/44, "Prohibition of the development and manufacture of new types of weapons of mass destruction and new systems of such weapons," December 23, 1999.
8. UN General Assembly Resolution A/RES/51/37, "Prohibition of the development and manufacture of new types of weapons of mass destruction and new systems of such weapons," December 10, 1996; UN General Assembly Resolution A/RES/54/44, "Prohibition of the development and manufacture of new types of weapons of mass destruction and new systems of such weapons," December 23, 1999; UN General Assembly Resolution A/RES/57/50, "Prohibition of the development and manufacture of new types of weapons of mass destruction and new systems of such weapons," December 30, 2002; UN General Assembly Resolution A/RES/60/46, "Prohibition of the development and manufacture of new types of weapons of mass destruction and new systems of such weapons: report of the Conference on Disarmament," January 6, 2006; UN General Assembly Resolution A/RES/63/36, "Prohibition of the development and manufacture of new types of weapons of mass destruction and new systems of such weapons: report of the Conference on Disarmament," January 13, 2009.
9. Article IV of the 1967 Treaty on Principles Governing the Activities of States in the Exploration and Use of Outer Space, including the Moon and Other Celestial Bodies (The Outer Space Treaty) provides: "States Parties to the Treaty undertake not to place in orbit around the earth any objects carrying nuclear weapons or any other kinds of weapons of mass destruction, install such weapons on celestial bodies, or station such weapons in outer space in any other manner."
10. Article I of the Treaty on the Prohibition of the Emplacement of Nuclear Weapons and Other Weapons of Mass Destruction on the Seabed and the Ocean Floor and in the Subsoil (The Seabed Treaty), imposes restrictions on the geographic placement of WMD: "The States Parties to this Treaty undertake not to implant or emplace on the seabed and the ocean floor and in the subsoil thereof beyond the outer limit of a seabed zone, as defined in article II, any nuclear weapons or any other types of weapons of mass destruction as well as structures, launching installations or any other facilities specifically designed for storing, testing or using such weapons."
11. The 1991 Strategic Arms Reduction Treaty (START) reiterated the prohibitions contained in the Seabed and Outer Space Treaties. Article V, paragraph 18 of the START provides: Each Party undertakes not to produce, test, or deploy: … launchers of ballistic or cruise missiles … all areas of the ocean floor and the seabed, including the seabed zone referred to in Articles I and II of the Seabed and Outer Space Treaties; (c) systems, including missiles, for placing nuclear weapons or any other kinds of weapons of mass destruction into Earth orbit or a fraction of an Earth orbit.

12. W. Seth Carus, "Defining 'Weapons of Mass Destruction,'" Centre for the Study of Weapons of Mass Destruction, Occasional Paper, no. 8, Washington, DC: National Defence University Press, January 2012, p. 35.
13. Ibid., p. 6.
14. K. K. Clements and Malcolm Dando, "A Wall against These Living Weapons," *International Herald Tribune*, September 3, 1993.
15. The term Weapons of Mass Destruction (WMD), used to encompass nuclear, biological, and chemical weapons, is misleading, politically dangerous, and cannot be justified on grounds of military efficiency. Chemical weapons have shown to be largely ineffective in warfare; biological weapons have never been deployed on any significant scale. Both types should be better designated as weapons of terror against civilians and weapons of intimidation for soldiers. Gert G. Harigel, "Chemical and Biological Weapons: Use in Warfare, Impact on Society and Environment," 2001, http://www.wagingpeace.org/articles/2001/11/00_harigel_cbw.htm, accessed June 20, 2011.

2 A

NUCLEAR WEAPONS

On July 16, 1945, the United States conducted the world's first nuclear weapon test at Alamogordo, New Mexico. The primary purpose of the test was to check the reliability and effectiveness of nuclear weapons. In August 1945, the United States dropped two atomic bombs over Japan: the first bomb was dropped over Hiroshima,[1] at 8:15 am (local time) on August 6, 1945; while the second was dropped over Nagasaki, at 11:02 am on August 9, 1945.[2] Both the Hiroshima and Nagasaki nuclear explosions were airbursts, at elevations of 580 m and 500 m, respectively.[3] Ground temperatures in the two cities reached 7,000°C, and black radioactive rain poured down. In Hiroshima, an urbanised area of approximately 13 sq km was laid to waste, while in Nagasaki, an area of approximately 7 sq km was destroyed. In central Hiroshima, only the hulks of the most resilient steel-reinforced concrete buildings were left standing. About 270,000 people were killed in the two cities by the end of 1945, and the rates of cancer and chronic disease increased among the survivors, and continues to be higher than the average rates 68 years later.

Nuclear weapons are potentially the most destructive weapons ever invented. In the year 2000, former Soviet Union leader Mikhail S. Gorbachev observed, "Models made by Russian and American scientists showed that a nuclear war would result in a nuclear winter that would be extremely destructive to all life on earth; the knowledge of that was a great stimulus to us, to people of honour and morality, to act."[4]

Kinds of Nuclear Weapons

There are two basic types of nuclear weapons. (i) In an A-bomb (atomic or fission bomb), the atoms of heavy elements (uranium-235[5] or plutonium-239[6]) break up (fission) into lighter elements and an enormous amount of energy is released in the process; (ii) In an H-bomb (hydrogen, fusion, or thermonuclear bomb), atoms of the lightest element (hydrogen) fuse to form a heavier element (usually helium, the next lightest) and produce an enormous amount of energy.[7] Several variations of these two bombs exist. In a more important variant, the H-bomb's core is surrounded by a shell of uranium-238. This enhances explosive power. The result is a four-layered series of explosions: conventional, fission of uranium-235 (or of plutonium-239), fusion of hydrogen isotopes, and fission of uranium-238.

For any given weight, the yield of nuclear bombs is roughly 3.5 million times greater than the yield of conventional explosives. In the 1980s, the average American nuclear warhead weighed about 100 kg and had an equivalent yield of some 350,000,000 kg (or 350,000 metric tons) of TNT. Such enormous amounts of energy can be more conveniently expressed in thousands of metric tons of TNT (kilotons, abbreviated as kt), or in millions of tons (megatons, or Mt).[8] Thus, nuclear bombs produce far more destructive blasts per unit of weight than conventional bombs, in addition to devastatingly high temperatures (similar to those at the centre of the sun) and high radiation levels.

Nuclear Weapons Arsenal

As of early 2017 nine states—the United States, Russia, the United Kingdom, France, China, India, Pakistan, Israel and the Democratic People's Republic of Korea (North Korea)—together possess a total of approximately 14,900 nuclear weapons. Of these, roughly 9,400 are in the military stockpiles and the rest are awaiting dismantlement. At present 4,110 warheads are deployed with operational forces in the US, Russia, Britain and France and are on high alert and ready for use on short notice.[9] Approximately 93 percent of all nuclear warheads are owned by Russia and the United States; no other nuclear-armed state sees a need for more than a few hundred nuclear weapons for national security. An estimate about the size and composition of the world nuclear weapons stockpiles is shown in the table.

Table: Estimated Global Nuclear Warhead Inventories, 2017[10]

Country	**Total**	**Military Stockpile**	**Deployed Weapons**	**Reserve/ Non-deployed**
Russia	7,000	4,300	1,910	2,390
United States	6,800	4,000	1,800	2,200
France	300	300	280	20
China	270	270	-	270
United Kingdom	215	215	120	95
Israel	80	80	-	80
Pakistan	120-130	120-130	-	120-130
India	110-120	110-120	-	110-120
North Korea	10	10	-	10
Total	14,925	9,425	4,110	5,315

Global nuclear weapon inventories have been declining. The decline has been due primarily to cuts made in the Russian and US nuclear forces as a result of three arms limitation treaties since 1991 as well as unilateral force reductions. However, the pace of their reductions appears to be slowing compared with a decade ago, and neither Russia nor the USA has made significant reductions in its deployed strategic nuclear forces.

The world's nine nuclear-armed States – the United States, the Russian Federation, China, France, the United Kingdom, India, Pakistan, Israel and North Korea – are each making significant investments in maintaining and modernizing and increasing nuclear military capabilities. China, Pakistan, India, and North Korea, are even increasing the sizes of their nuclear arsenals. In addition to reaffirming their intention to retain nuclear weapons, the nuclear-armed States and many of their allies frequently emphasize the importance of nuclear weapons to national and international security. To maintain and demonstrate this role, nuclear weapon systems are periodically test-launched and nuclear exercises are frequently conducted in order to practice offensive strike plans against potential adversaries.[11]

Faced with growing threats of nuclear weapons and missile capabilities from North Korea, South Korea clearly needs reliable means to deter the North's nuclear weapons and effective responses if deterrence fails. The South Korean political leaders and defence planners are cognizant that worsening security in Northeast Asia could lead to the country to consider and even develop nuclear weapons. Although a surprise nuclear first strike is highly unlikely, the US, Russia, UK and France keep large numbers of nuclear warheads on alert, capable of being launched on short notice. Maintaining nuclear forces on alert increases the risk of accidents and incidents. The highly alerted nuclear postures of these states may encourage smaller nuclear-armed States to increase the readiness level of their nuclear forces, thus increasing nuclear risks for everyone.

Five European nations host US nuclear weapons on their soil as part of a NATO nuclear-sharing arrangement. These are Belgium, Germany, Italy, the Netherlands and Turkey. Another 23 nations claim to rely on US nuclear weapons for their security. An estimated 50 countries in the world have weapons grade uranium;[12] while more than 40 countries have nuclear power or research reactors capable of producing nuclear weapons. The spread of nuclear know-how has increased the risk of more nations developing nuclear weapons.

Destructive Power

Nuclear bombs owe their greater destructive power to immediate blast, heat and radiation, and the lingering effects of radioactive fallout.[13] A single nuclear bomb dropped on a large city could kill millions of people. The physical characteristics and effects of a single nuclear explosion are determined by many variables, including the type of bomb used, its yield, the height at which the detonation occurs, weather conditions, and the type of target.[14] Since our experience with nuclear explosions over cities has been limited, only a rough sketch of the effects of a single nuclear explosion can be drawn.[15]

Ultraviolet Pulse: For a person standing outdoors some distance from ground zero, the first indication that a nuclear explosion has occurred is a blinding flash of intense ultraviolet radiation. The duration of this flash depends, among other things, on the explosion's yield. In a 1-Mt detonation, this flash lasts about a tenth of a second and can dazzle observers miles away (especially if they happen to look in the direction of ground zero) and blind them temporarily.

Electromagnetic Pulse (EMP): Although this pulse is similar in character to the waves which transmit radio and television signals, it is millions of times stronger and is of a very short duration—less than one-thousandth of a second. Wherever this pulse occurs, it can be absorbed by power lines, antennae, long wires, and other collectors, and carried to the electrical and electronic devices to which these collectors are attached. EMP can therefore lead to temporary interference in communication and power systems, and it can disable electric power supplies, telephones, telegraphs, radars, radios, computers, and other electronic devices. In the event of an all-out war, EMP could incapacitate or severely cripple a nation's military and civilian power and communication systems, thereby complicating retaliation and recovery in the affected area. EMP's direct effects on people are negligible: only the few people who happen to hold a pipe, long wire, or similar collector at the moment of explosion could die of severe shock.[16]

Heat: About 25% of the bomb's energy is given off as heat (thermal radiation).[17] At the moment of explosion, the bomb itself becomes as hot as the sun. Within a fraction of a second, a fireball—a luminous spherical mass of air and the bomb's residues—is formed. The diameter of a 1-Mt bomb's fireball at its most luminous stage is about 1.5 miles.[18] The diameter of the fireball of a bomb one-fortieth that yield (12.5 kt, the yield of the Hiroshima bomb) is a quarter of a mile. A fireball can be seen from a great distance. A 1-Mt high-altitude explosion can be seen from as far away as 700 miles. The fireball rises fast, like a hot air balloon, grows in size, and cools off. In just one minute after the explosion, it assumes the familiar shape of a mushroom cloud, some 4.5 miles above the point at which the explosion has taken place.[19]

The heat pulse given off by the fireball starts fires over a large area. Fires may also start as an indirect result of the blast. These fires increase the number of casualties. Under certain conditions, for example during a clear, dry, summer day, these small fires might coalesce into larger fires, rage hours after the explosion and burn or asphyxiate everything in their path, including human beings still alive in their homes or in underground shelters.[20]

Blast: About 50% of the bomb's energy is taken up by the blast, which could last for a few seconds. Its severity and physical characteristics depend on the bomb's yield. The main direct effect of the blast is overpressure, which is experienced by human beings in its path as a sudden, shattering blow immediately followed by hurricane-like winds. The direct effects on the human body of the overpressure created by nuclear explosions are comparatively mild. However, it may damage lungs and rupture eardrums. The winds following the blast, on the other hand, can kill or injure human beings by sweeping them off their feet, tossing them about, or hurling them into solid objects. The winds accompanying a 1-Mt air burst would kill most people in the open up to a distance of 3.3 miles from ground zero.

The combined impact of overpressure and strong winds of a 1-Mt bomb would demolish most buildings within a range of 2.5 miles from ground zero and break most windows within a range of 13 miles. The collapsed buildings, uprooted trees, overturned cars, and flying objects would take a heavy toll on human lives. Some of the flying and overturned objects (such as ovens or wood stoves) may start fires. Most human beings within a distance of one mile from ground zero of an explosion as small as the Hiroshima bomb would die from the effects of the blast alone; crushed in collapsed buildings, knocked out by flying objects, hurled by the winds, or incinerated.[21]

Ionising Radiation: About 15% of the bomb's energy is taken up by ionising radiation. This radiation is perhaps the most frightening direct effect of nuclear explosions. Unlike fire and blast, ionising radiation not only damages our health, but, through its potential impact on foetuses and on reproductive cells, it may damage the health of our descendants. Though the heat and the blast wreak incredible havoc, their direct effects are gone within seconds, or, in the case of the fires they cause, within hours or days. In contrast, poisonous radioactivity may linger for years.[22]

Initial radiation is released within the first minute of an explosion.[23] It accounts for about 5% of the bomb's energy. The initial radiation of a 12.5-kt explosion will knock unconscious people standing in the open within half a mile from ground zero. These people would die from radiation sickness within two days (even if they somehow manage to escape the heat and blast). People standing in the open three-quarters of a mile away would die within one month.

Given these three powerful effects—blast, heat, initial radiation—the chances of survival are slim for anyone within a one-mile radius of a small nuclear explosion. Besides, in the event of a nuclear attack, medical infrastructure would be destroyed and no effective humanitarian response would be possible. The lingering effects of radiation on human beings would cause suffering and death many years after the initial explosion. Those in the vicinity who survive the blast would suffer from extreme dehydration and diarrhoea, as well as life-threatening infections and severe bleeding. They would also have a significantly increased risk of developing cancers and passing on genetic damage to future generations.

Radioactive fallout (residual radiation) accounts for some 10% of the bomb's energy. Fallout is emitted by fission products such as radioactive iodine, weapon residues such as plutonium and radioactive hydrogen, and substances in the vicinity of the explosion which become radioactive as a result of exposure to the bomb's initial radiation.[24] Although both global and local fallout are generated by every nuclear explosion, their relative proportions depend on several conditions. For example, because rain washes down some radioactive particles, there would be more local fallout and less global fallout when an explosion is followed by heavy rain.[25]

Environmental Impact

Nuclear weapons are a serious threat to human beings and environment during all the stages of their development, use, dismantling, and disposal. The complete production cycle comprises a number of operations. These operations, many of which are common to the civilian use of nuclear energy, include mining, milling of uranium, uranium enrichment, reactor fuel fabrication, operation of reactors for plutonium production, spent fuel reprocessing, weapons manufacture, handling of weapons, dismantling of weapons and final disposal of waste. Most of these operations are associated with possible risks to the personnel involved and to the environment. Accidental releases of radioactive substances and chemicals during ongoing processes or transport, and resulting from mismanagement of waste may cause environmental damage.[26]

A. Weapons Testing

Of all the activities connected with nuclear weapons, testing has been the most destructive of human health and the environment. China, France, India, Pakistan, Russia, the US and the UK have collectively conducted over 2,000 nuclear explosions for testing purposes— approximately 600 above ground,[27] underwater or in space; and the remaining 1,400 underground. The largest US and Soviet nuclear tests were, respectively, a 15-megaton test in 1954, and a 50-megaton test in 1961.[28] Radioisotopes, such as carbon-14, caesium-137, strontium-90 and plutonium-239 (half-lives 5,730 years, 30 years, 28 years and 24,400 years respectively), produced by nuclear tests, pose risks to the environment, and to current and future generations through ingestion, inhalation and absorption of external radiation.

Nuclear weapons tests and their results remain state secrets and the information is controlled by a select few in the government. Many aspects of nuclear weapons testing have been characterised by a disregard, sometimes wilful, of public health and the environment. Test sites around the world are contaminated. It has been estimated that the radiation exposure from carbon-14 (integrated over infinity) would result in over 2.4 million human cancer deaths.[29]

Between 1952 and 1963, the UK tested a total of 10 nuclear weapons in Australia. One of these tests was done in the Monte Bello islands off the northern coast of Western Australia, and the other nine took place near Maralinga and Emu Junction, in South Australia. Though the British government claimed that the tests were done safely, the radiation from these tests affected villagers living 100 miles away from the nuclear test sites, causing diarrhoea, skin rashes, and blindness.[30]

In the US, in 1997, the National Cancer Institute revealed that atmospheric tests at the Nevada site resulted in significant contamination of the nation's milk supply with iodine-131, with an estimated 11,000 to –12,000 thyroid cancers in excess of the normal.[31] The Soviet Union's development programmes for nuclear weapons were conducted with little regard for human health or natural resources. Residents of the Western Siberian town of Altay, located near the nuclear test site of Semipalatinsk, showed evidence of damaged immune systems from long-term exposure to radiation.[32] The environmental effects of French underground nuclear weapons testing have been reported as: (i) physical damage to the reef, (ii) major underwater landslides of about one million cubic metres of coral and rock, (iii) venting of gaseous and volatile fission products, (iv) medium- and long-term leakage of fission products into the biosphere, and (v) ciguatera fish poisoning.[33]

B. Weapons Facilities and Surrounding Areas

There is evidence of major health, safety and environmental problems at nuclear weapons complexes around the world. This is most apparent in the US and Russia, which hold approximately 93% of the world's nuclear weapons. Accidental leakage of liquid radioactive waste at Hanford, the former plutonium production complex in Washington, has contaminated soil and underground water resources.[34] The US Department of Energy has estimated that minimal remediation of the nuclear weapons complex will cost $230 billion over 75 years. Even at this level of expenditure, many sites and buildings will remain out-of-bounds for humans for the foreseeable future. The situation in Russia is even worse.

While the US and the former Soviet Union, due to the sheer number of nuclear weapons produced, present by far the most disturbing pictures of radioactive contamination from weapons facilities, the problem is not confined to those two countries alone. Radioactive contamination from nuclear weapons facilities across the world will take an incalculable but heavy human and environmental toll for a very long time. As the nuclear power reactors and weapons facilities age they will get more and more contaminated, releasing greater amounts of long-lasting, active radioactive materials to the biosphere, increasing the radiation to human beings and the environment.

Radiation affects all living things—genetic material, cells, individual animals and plants, biological systems and the environment in general. When radiation hits a tissue or cell, it can kill the cell or damage it. If damaged, the cell can repair correctly; it can repair incorrectly but not reproduce; or it can repair incorrectly and reproduce. If a damaged cell reproduces it passes on the defects to future generations of cells. Furthermore, radiation can reduce immunity, making the animal more susceptible to other diseases that would have been fended off. Studies on both plants and animals have repeatedly shown that exposure to ionising radiation causes genetic mutations. It can also lead to cancer in humans and animals.

However, attributing with certainty a specific cancer to a specific episode of radiation exposure may not be possible because: (i) cancers may occur decades after the exposure; (ii) there is no way of distinguishing a cancer caused by radiation from any other cancer; (iii) cancer is a common illness, with many other possible triggers; (iv) there are a number of difficulties in assessing the biological effects of low-level radioactivity; and (iv) radiation can spread over large distances, depending on weather patterns, and be dispersed in such a fashion that determining the dose received by specific people or animals is very difficult.[35] Relatively recent research indicates that radiation behaves in unexpected ways. Some radiation effects are not immediately visible and thus cannot be observed or quantified as indicators of damage.[36]

Animals in the vicinity of nuclear facilities unavoidably take up some radioactivity through water and nutrient cycles. The continuous creation and release of radioactive materials into the air, water, food webs, organisms and gene pools of our planet are a dangerous experiment by the nuclear power and weapons industry. The result of these continuous releases is what has been called "a thickening of the radiation environment." Ionising radiation effects are multiple, additive, cumulative and synergistic. They impact the present and future generations, but no major efforts have been made to assess these effects. Radioactive contamination of the environment and the organisms in it is a double whammy. It weakens the gene pool, thus reducing the ability of organisms to prevent or overcome environmental threats, and simultaneously increases the environmental stresses to which the organisms are exposed. This is especially disturbing when we realise that all future generations of species are in the genetic material of this generation of organisms.

C. Impact of Weapons

Nuclear weapons have been used only once, however, their future use in armed conflicts cannot be ruled out with certainty. The environmental damage resulting from the use of nuclear weapons would be catastrophic. Hypothetically, if enough nuclear weapons are detonated at approximately the same time a "nuclear winter" could result. Also, there is a good chance that no life forms would survive such an event. The following figures apply to air and surface bursts of various yields. The blast wave of an 18-kt air burst would blow down most trees within an area of 565 ha[37] and most vertebrates would be killed within an area of 43 ha; the blast wave of a 0.91-Mt air burst would blow down most trees within an area of 14,100 ha and kill most vertebrates within an area of 591 ha; and the blast wave of 9.1-Mt air burst would blow down most trees within an area of 82,000 ha and kill most vertebrates within an area of 2,740 ha. For surface bursts these numbers would be lower: most trees would be blown down within an area of 362 ha (18 kt), 9,040 ha (0.9 Mt) and 52,500 (9.1 Mt); and most vertebrates would be killed within an area of 24 ha (18 kt); 332 ha (0.91 Mt); and 1,540 (9.1 Mt) respectively.[38]

The damage to the environment from thermal radiation would be significant.[39] Damage to organisms depends upon the species, since different organisms have different sensitivities to nuclear radiation. Generally, the higher the species is on the evolutionary scale, the greater is the sensitivity. Mammals are the most sensitive, followed by birds; plants; fish; amphibians; reptiles; insects; crustaceans; molluscs; moss; lichen; algae; bacteria; protozoan; and viruses. For amphibians, the lethal dose appears to be about three times that for mammals. The lethal dose levels for higher plants spans the mammalian and reptilian ranges. All higher plants are more resistant to radioactive damage during their dormant periods. Insects for the most part are about a hundred times as resistant as are mammals. However, social insects, such as honey bees, important as pollinators, are destroyed by 5-kR of radiation. Many bacteria, algae and fungi can withstand doses that are a thousand times greater than doses that would kill mammals.[40]

The following tables show the damage that would be wreaked by radiation and bursts.

Table 1: Damage to biota from a nuclear bomb exploded in the troposphere[41]

S. No.	Type of damage	Area affected (ha)	Area affected (ha)	Area affected (ha)
		Bomb size: 18 kt	Bomb size: 0.91Mt	Bomb size: 9.1 Mt
1.	Craterisation by blast wave	0	0	0
2.	Trees blown down by blast wave	565	14,100	82,000
3.	Trees killed by nuclear radiation	129	648	1,250
4.	All vegetation killed by nuclear radiation	18	312	759
5.	Dry vegetation ignited by thermal radiation	1,170	33,300	183,000
6.	Vertebrates killed by blast wave	43	591	2,740
7.	Vertebrates killed by nuclear radiation	318	1,080	1,840
8.	Vertebrates killed by thermal radiation	1,570	42,000	235,000

Table 2: Damage to biota from a nuclear bomb exploded at the surface[42]

S. No.	Type of damage	Area affected (ha)	Area affected (ha)	Area affected (ha)
		Bomb size: 18 kt	Bomb size: 0.91Mt	Bomb size: 9.1 Mt
1.	Craterisation by blast wave	1	12	57
2.	Trees blown down by blast wave	362	9,040	52,500

3.	Trees killed by nuclear radiation	148	12,800	63,800
4.	All vegetation killed by nuclear radiation	43	2,830	12,100
5.	Dry vegetation ignited by thermal radiation	749	21,300	117,000
6.	Vertebrates killed by blast wave	24	332	1,540
7.	Vertebrates killed by nuclear radiation	674	36,400	177,000
8.	Vertebrates killed by thermal radiation	1,000	26,900	150,000

The combined effects of the Hiroshima bomb killed over half of the city's residents, turned the lives of many survivors into a lifelong nightmare, and levelled the entire city. Owing to its greater yield, the effects of a typical contemporary bomb are expected to be greater. Although the aftermath of an all-out nuclear war among major nuclear powers cannot be described with certainty, it would surely be the greatest catastrophe in recorded history. In any combatant country, it may kill millions of people, afflict many survivors with a variety of radiation-induced diseases, destroy industrial and military capabilities, and contaminate vast tracts of land. Such a war might also lower the quality of the human genetic pool, damage the biosphere, cause a breakdown of national and international economic systems, destroy the health care and prevention system, and move surviving societies in unpredictable directions.

Dr. Marcel Junod, an ICRC delegate, was the first foreign doctor in Hiroshima to assess the effects of the atomic bombing and to assist its victims. He described the havoc caused as: "We ... witnessed a sight totally unlike anything we had ever seen before. The centre of the city was a sort of white patch, flattened and smooth like the palm of a hand. Nothing remained. The slightest trace of houses seemed to have disappeared. The white patch was about two kilometres in diameter. Around its edge was a red belt, marking the area where houses had burned, extending quite a long way further … covering almost all the rest of the city." In a few seconds after the blast "thousands of human beings in the streets and gardens in the town centre, struck by a wave of intense heat, died like flies. Others lay writhing like worms, atrociously burned. All private houses, warehouses, etc., disappeared as if swept away by a supernatural power. Trams were picked up and hurled yards away, as if they were weightless; trains were flung off the rails. … Every living thing was petrified in an attitude of acute pain."[43] The atomic explosions in Japan in 1945 offer several clear lessons: (i) The destructive power of nuclear weapons is immense and a single bomb can destroy an entire city in a matter of seconds; (ii) This is particularly true since the yield of a typical strategic warhead is now at least ten times greater than the Hiroshima or Nagasaki bombs; (iii) Nuclear weapons are efficient long-range incendiary devices—all of the area subject to blast damage is susceptible to burnout in conflagrations; (iv) The atmosphere over a large region is affected by a nuclear explosion: smoke and dust are lofted, clouds form, precipitation may occur, and radioactive debris is dispersed through the environment; and (v) The human impacts of nuclear explosions can be enormous—physical injuries from the blast, severe burns from the heat rays, exposure to radiation, psychological trauma—in addition to the long-term effects.[44]

The impact of a global nuclear war involving multiple nuclear exchanges and possibly leading to a nuclear winter would be tremendous. Apart from the expected short-term atmospheric and climatic changes, there would be a long-term impact on the biosphere.[45] A study on the "Long-term Biological Consequences of Nuclear War" concludes: "subfreezing temperatures, low light levels, and high doses of ionizing and ultraviolet radiation extending for many months after a large-scale nuclear war could destroy the biological systems of civilizations." Those plants that survive will experience a severe decrease in productivity as a result of reduced photosynthesis and will be exposed to damaging radioactivity, solar ultraviolet radiation, smog and acid rain. As far as the surviving animals and humans are concerned, the severe cold and continuous darkness, in combination with widespread death and destruction, would cause severe distress and mortality. Reduced crop yields, loss of agricultural production material, loss of eatable vegetation and livestock, and lack of clean water will lead to severe competition amongst survivors for the remaining products and could lead to widespread epidemic disease, malnutrition, famine and mass starvation and account for an increasing number of casualties.[46] Many life-forms may cease to exist and the extinction of the human species itself cannot be excluded.[47]

It has been estimated that a war between India and Pakistan in which each uses weapons with total yield of 0.74-Mt could lead to about 44 million casualties and produce about 7.6 trillion grams (Tg) of soot. A relatively modest 5 Tg of soot would be sufficient to produce the lowest temperatures the Earth has experienced in the past 1,000 years—lower than that during the post-medieval Little Ice Age or in 1816,[48] the so-called year without summer. With 75 Tg soot, the temperature would correspondent to that during the last full Ice Age, and precipitation would decline by more than 25 per cent globally. The soot would rise to much higher altitudes, and the greenhouse gases would alter the climate. The duration of forcing will be different: the radioactive forcing by nuclear-weapons-generated soot might persist for a decade, while that from the greenhouse gases is expected to last for a century or more, allowing time for the climate system to respond to forcing. An indirect effect of war could result in the loss of one to several billion humans.

Models made by Russian and American scientists have shown that a nuclear war would be extremely destructive to all life on the earth. An attack by the US on Russia and China with 2,200 weapons could produce 86.4 Tg of soot, enough to create Ice Age conditions, affecting agriculture worldwide, and possibly lead to mass starvation. In any nuclear conflict, nuclear winter would seriously affect non-combatant countries. A regional war between India and Pakistan, for example, has the potential to dramatically damage Europe, the US, and other regions through global ozone loss and climate change.[49]

Other world-wide effects of a major nuclear exchange are difficult to examine and assess. However, the fact that today's world is characterised by a large, intricate and increasing international interdependence in all aspects of life strongly suggests that significant global economic and social disruptions would be an unavoidable consequence of such an exchange. In the first place, all countries in the world, combatants as well as non-combatants, would suffer a drastic reduction of foreign trade. This would be due to factors such as a decrease in the production volume of both essential commodities and raw materials, disruption of services and breakdown of the organisation of world commerce and communications. The world food supply and production would also be imperilled by trade disruptions. It is also expected that climatic perturbations would have some impact on agriculture in any major war scenario.[50]

Disposal of Excess Military Nuclear Material

Military stockpiles contain the largest amount of nuclear fissile material produced in the world. The global stockpile of highly enriched uranium (HEU) and plutonium is about 2,000 tons. This is equivalent to more than 55,000 nuclear weapons.[51] After the end of the cold war, the US and Russia, the two States with the largest stockpiles of military fissile materials, declared more than 700 tons of HEU and 100 tons of weapons-grade plutonium as excess to military requirements. They also made progress in setting up programmes to eliminate the excess material.[52] The UK is the only other State that has declared some of its military material as excess to national security needs. However, unlike the US and Russia, it has not yet made arrangements for the elimination of this material. The experience of the US–Russian programmes on elimination of nuclear weapons[53] has demonstrated the difficulty of disposing of such material in an environmentally safe and economically efficient way.

In the US, the elimination of the excess HEU is carried out by down-blending it with natural or low-enriched uranium (LEU) and then using it to fuel power, research or special-purpose reactors. The elimination of HEU is scheduled to be completed by 2050. The current blend-down rate is about 3-4 tonnes annually, which corresponds to the rate of dismantlement of weapon components. The US had invited the International Atomic Energy Agency (IAEA) to monitor parts of its HEU elimination programme. The IAEA has conducted a verification experiment that monitored down-blending of about 50 tonnes of HEU at two US facilities. This arrangement, however, has not been made permanent. The IAEA also had no access to the US Department of Energy facilities that carry out most of the current down-blending activities.[54]

Russia's only declaration of excess HEU was made as part of the US–Russia HEU-LEU deal, also known as the "Megatons to Megawatts" programme. In this arrangement of 1993, Russia designated 500 tonnes of its HEU of military origin for down-blending to LEU for the purpose of producing fuel for US civilian power reactors. The first shipment of LEU to the US took place in 1995 and by the end of 2011 the programme had eliminated 442.5 tonnes of HEU.[55] While the elimination of HEU is technically straightforward, the disposition of plutonium presents a serious technical challenge. The process selected by the US and Russia—burning plutonium in power reactors—is rather controversial from the point of view of economics and long-term security.[56]

Dismantling of Surplus Weapons

The dismantling of surplus weapons will generate large quantities of plutonium and highly enriched uranium (HEU), the two key ingredients of nuclear bombs. Both pose a hazard to human health, the environment and international security. Keeping these materials from contaminating the environment and from being used in future weapons poses a great challenge. Of the two, plutonium poses a greater problem[57] because of the relative ease with which it can be used in weapons, the severe biological (one-millionth of an ounce can cause cancer if inhaled) and environmental hazard it poses, and its radioactive decay half-life of 24,000 years.[58] Because it is less radioactive than plutonium, HEU poses less severe health and environmental hazards. However, it has a half-life[59] of more than 700 million years.[60]

Activities relating to the dismantling of nuclear warheads are ongoing at several sites in the US and Russia. There has been repeated criticism of the lack of line management attention to environmental safety, and health issues at these sites. Though widespread environmental contamination with nuclear materials during dismantling is considered highly unlikely by the governments, an inadvertent nuclear detonation, an accident, or the scatter of nuclear materials from an explosion cannot be ruled out. The dismantling of nuclear warheads generates parts that contain chemical explosives, special nuclear and hazardous materials, and classified components. There is a possibility of exposure to hazardous material during the packaging, storage and transportation of these materials, as the dismantling facilities still employ inefficient processes/technologies and create large amounts of waste.[61]

The clean-up of contaminated sites, disposition of excess fissile material and dismantling of nuclear weapons contaminate the environment and threaten human health. The cleaning up and containment of radioactive products presents the biggest challenge, though there are risks involved in the dismantling of nuclear weapons too. These include hazards to workers and environmental risks associated with non-nuclear aspects, such as missile destruction. For example, pursuant to the Intermediate Range Nuclear Forces Treaty, hundreds of Pershing missiles were burned in the open air or exploded on a test stand at the Pueblo Army Depot in Colorado, United States. Such procedures release clouds of toxic hydrochloric acid when the missiles' solid fuel combines with moisture.[62]

Nuclear Waste

There is no country in the world which has a satisfactory long-term solution to the problem of nuclear waste. The disposal of defence and civil nuclear wastes in an environmentally friendly manner is a formidable task. Unless a solution is found, future generations will inherit this problem. In the US alone, nuclear waste has accumulated at 120 sites around the country. This includes approximately 55,000 tons of waste from civilian reactors, and 15,000 tons from nuclear weapons production. All the existing sites and methods of nuclear waste disposal are temporary.

Some of the environmentally unsatisfactory practices that have been employed in the past comprise: (i) direct disposal of unconditioned raw wastes in liquid or other inadmissible form; (ii) discharge to waterways or sewer systems before evaluating the potential danger and harmful environmental effects; (iii) deep injection of liquid waste into porus strata without proven barrier efficiency of the surrounding strata; (iv) disposal of sludge and slurries in landfills where leachate may contaminate ground water; (v) disposal on-site without proper precautions to avoid ground water and surface water contamination; and (vi) incineration without controlled emission of toxic or corrosive gases to the environment.[63]

The disposal of radioactive waste is not always carried out within a State's borders. Many governments have chosen to dump their nuclear waste into the oceans rather than to build treatment and storage facilities. Since 1946, when the US began dumping, at least one nuclear nation has been dumping radioactive waste into the sea.[64] The Russian Federation's dumping of 237,000 gallons (900 tons) of low-level nuclear waste into the Sea of Japan in October 1993 caused worldwide criticism of this practice. Although several nuclear nations claim that the dumping of low-level radioactive waste into the oceans is the safest and the most economical method of disposal, few governments are unwilling to admit this option today due to the negative public perception of ocean dumping.

The increase in the number of shipments has given rise to the problem of international transportation and immersion of radioactive wastes in areas beyond national jurisdiction. Several international conventions contain provisions aimed at preventing the dumping of radioactive waste. The London Convention on the Prevention of Marine Pollution by Dumping of Wastes and Other Matter of December 29, 1972 forbids the immersion of "high-level radioactive wastes or other high-level radioactive matter ... as unsuitable for dumping at sea."[65] A non-binding Resolution adopted by the Consultative Meeting of the State Parties in 1985, established a moratorium on all dumping at sea of radioactive materials pending scientific studies, but several States publicly opted not to comply, including most States possessing nuclear weapons.[66] In 1994, the International Maritime Organisation made the ban on sea-dumping of nuclear wastes obligatory.[67] All state parties, with the exception of Russia, accepted this ban, which is subject to a 25 years review.[68]

Vast quantities of radioactive waste from Soviet and Russian nuclear powered ships and submarines were dumped into the Pacific and Arctic Oceans.[69] The Mayak complex in the eastern Ural mountains (also called Chelyabinsk-65, or Kyshtym), covering an area of 2,700 sq km, is the largest of the former Soviet Union's three plutonium production centres. The highly contaminated site lies in a region of interconnecting lakes, marshes and waterways at the headwaters of the Techa River. Between 1948 and 1956 radioactive waste from the Mayak complex was poured straight into the river, the source of drinking water for many villages. The liquid radioactive waste, including caesium and strontium, that had been dumped was detected in the Arctic Ocean nearly 1,000 miles away. The waste discharge point at Lake Karachay in the Ural Mountains remains excessively radioactive. It has been reported that a person standing near it would receive a lethal dose of radiation in less than one hour.[70]

The dumping was mainly done in three ways: (1) direct dumping of uncontained high-, medium- and low-level liquid radioactive waste; (2) direct dumping of thousands of tons of solid, high-level radioactive waste in various forms of containment; and (3) direct dumping of 16 to 18 nuclear submarine reactors—six or seven with all of their fuel—reportedly after the submarines had met with accidents of varying severity.[71] The Arctic is an important global ecosystem,[72] part of the marine food chain, and the feeding and breeding ground of many migratory fish, birds, and mammals. It provides an important habitat for many migratory species such as the Canadian goose, the killer whale, and the reindeer. It is also a nursery to many animals, especially birds and fish. These migratory species have the capacity to carry radioactive contamination back to less contaminated lands. Thus damage to the Arctic habitat could result in serious ecological consequences.[73] Because of its unique ecology, the Arctic terrestrial ecosystem is more vulnerable to radioactive contamination than other regions. The efficient uptake of radio-nuclides by Arctic plants and their transport to grazing animals, such as caribou and reindeer, leads to Arctic inhabitants receiving higher radiation doses than inhabitants of other regions of the world.[74]

Russia lacks a comprehensive, "cradle-to-grave" system for decommissioning its nuclear-powered submarines and warships. Between 1959 and 1991, for example, the Soviet Union disposed of its high-, intermediate- and low-level radioactive waste in the Arctic Ocean and the seas adjacent to the Far East. Although Russia suspended ocean dumping in 1993, it has not substantially expanded its capacity to manage nuclear waste, and the influx of material stemming from its fleet reductions has overwhelmed its existing capacity.[75] Given its weak economy and unstable social and political systems, Russia currently lacks the capacity to create an adequate system of waste disposal within a reasonable time frame. The situation has given rise to concern over the potential threat this material poses to people, the environment, property and economic activity. The US is also facing a problem with 52,000 tons of dangerously radioactive spent fuel from commercial and defence nuclear reactors.[76]

Non-strategic Nuclear Weapons

During the Cold War, the US and Soviet Union both deployed non-strategic (tactical) nuclear weapons[77] for use in the field during a conflict. Analysts consider non-strategic weapons to be shorter-range delivery systems with lower yield warheads that might be used to attack troops or facilities on the battlefield. They may include nuclear mines; artillery; short-, medium-, and long-range ballistic missiles; cruise missiles; and gravity bombs. In contrast with the longer-range "strategic" nuclear weapons, the non-strategic nuclear weapons had a lower profile in policy debates and arms control negotiations, because they did not pose a direct threat to the continental United States. At the end of the 1980s, each nation had thousands of these weapons deployed with their troops in the field, aboard naval vessels, and on aircraft.[78]

In April 2011 Pakistan conducted a test of a new tactical nuclear missile the HAFT IX (Nasr). Pakistan described the Nasr as a quick response weapon designed to support full spectrum deterrence by countering India's growing conventional force advantages. It has been reported that four missile canisters are contained on each transporter erector launcher (TEL). The missile has a range of 60 kilometers and equipped with terminal guidance system for improved accuracy. There are possibilities that the development of short-range, nuclear capable systems might entail parallel efforts to build small nuclear warheads that could be employed by a variety of new and existing platforms against advancing Indian conventional forces.[79] With increasing political instability prevailing in Pakistan there is a constant fear for the international community that Islamabad's nuclear weapons might fall into the hands of terrorists.[80]

Low-Yield Earth-Penetrating Nuclear Weapons

Earth-penetrating weapons (EPW), or "bunker busters" are designed to hit the earth at high speed and to penetrate the ground before exploding. Earth penetration increases the damage to underground targets by "coupling" the energy of the explosion to the ground.

The US currently deploys both conventional and nuclear EPWs.[81] Proponents of a new generation of low-yield nuclear EPWs (such as the B61 modification 11, currently in the US stockpile) claim that such weapons could be used against deeply buried and hardened underground bunkers with "minimal collateral damage."

A missile made of the hardest of steel cannot survive severe ground impact stresses at velocities greater than about 900 metres per second without destroying itself. This limits the maximum possible penetration depth of the missile into reinforced concrete to about four times the missile length; approximately twelve metres for a missile three metres long. Even for the strongest of materials, impact velocities much greater than one kilometre per second will crumple and destroy the penetrator and its warhead.[82] At this relatively shallow depth, the explosion will inevitably breach the ground surface and throw out radioactive dirt and debris. The resulting base surge of radioactive fallout will extend over an area of several square kilometres. Anyone remaining in this area for more than a few hours would receive a fatal dose of radiation and shorter exposure would cause significant injury.[83] In addition to the risk of radiation exposure, analysis of the effects of EPWs used on underground storage sites indicates that all the hazardous stored materials are unlikely to be incinerated by an EPW. Instead, some may be disseminated to the ground surface and to the atmosphere.

Even a very-low-yield nuclear EPW exploded in or near an urban environment will cause radioactive dirt and debris and other radioactive material to be thrown out over several square kilometres. A nuclear EPW with a yield less than one-tenth of that of the nuclear weapon used on Hiroshima or Nagasaki could result in fatal doses of radiation to tens of thousands of victims. Biological and chemical agents stored in targeted bunkers may be dispersed into the atmosphere without being destroyed by an EPW, potentially injuring or killing unprotected civilians. A very-low-yield nuclear weapon used in an urban environment would have the potential of producing tens of thousands of civilian radiation casualties. The number of casualties from a nuclear EPW attack would depend on the location of the target, the density of the population in the surrounding area, the extent of debris dispersal, and the possibility of escape or evacuation.[84]

In view of the complexity and interdependence of ecological systems, efforts to forecast the effects of nuclear war on particular ecosystems and on the biosphere as a whole are plagued by uncertainties and controversies. The radiation effects of the Hiroshima and Nagasaki bombs, the subsequent atmospheric nuclear tests and the Chernobyl accident give an indication of the scale of environmental damage that would ensue from even a limited use of nuclear weapons. The damage to the earth's ecosystem would be severe, and the economic and human impact huge. Ecological destruction would be complete and limit the chances of continued life on Earth. Even the detonation of a single nuclear weapon would have a devastating impact on the environment.[85] Some commentators attribute the fact that nuclear weapons have not been used since 1945, to the role of "deterrence," the notion that nuclear devastation is so unthinkable, and the threat of nuclear retaliation so unacceptable, that the weapons will remain forever unused. These assumptions are flawed, as political or military leaders working under extreme pressure may not care about their own country and its population. There have been well-documented instances where the world has come frighteningly close to nuclear conflict. The assumption that no major accident will take place,[86] and no errors of judgement will be made in the monitoring and overseeing of nuclear weapons, may not be true.[87] This is contrary to what we know of human nature, which is that people make errors, especially when working under intense pressure.[88]

Nuclear Weapons: Legal Regulation

For more than 150 years, humanity has sought to outlaw weapons and methods of war with indiscriminate or particularly cruel effects. The St. Petersburg Declaration of 1868 outlawed the use of certain projectiles which uselessly aggravated the suffering of disabled men, or rendered their death inevitable. The first Hague Peace Conference, held in 1899, also adopted several rules for this purpose. After the extensive use of gas during World War I, the 1925 Geneva Protocol sought to prohibit the use of both chemical and biological weapons. In the closing days of World War II, Hiroshima and Nagasaki were incinerated with nuclear weapons. Since then, there have been worldwide efforts to control the number of nuclear weapons, prevent their spread, prohibit their use and eliminate them.[89] However, international law does not prohibit the possession or the use of nuclear weapons. This raises the question that can the use of such weapons be compatible with the dictates of human conscience and with international humanitarian law (IHL)?

The UN General Assembly has, on numerous occasions, condemned the use of nuclear weapons as illegal under IHL and a violation of the UN Charter. However, some nuclear weapons States are of the view that nuclear weapons are not specifically prohibited by any international treaty, hence they are not illegal. In 1994, the General Assembly sought an Advisory Opinion from the International Court of Justice (ICJ)[90] on: "Is the threat or use of nuclear weapons in any circumstance permitted under international law?"[91] In its reference to the ICJ the General Assembly expressed its conviction that the complete elimination of nuclear weapons was the only guarantee against the threat of nuclear war.

ICJ Opinion

In 1996, the ICJ issued an opinion on the legality of the threat or use of nuclear weapons that includes significant points on the protection of the environment.[92] It concluded that the threat or use of nuclear weapons,

> ... would generally be contrary to the rules of international law applicable in armed conflict, and in particular the principles and rules of humanitarian law;

> However in view of the current state of international law, and of the elements of fact at its disposal, the Court cannot conclude definitively whether the threat or use of nuclear weapons would be lawful or unlawful in an extreme circumstance of self-defence, in which the very survival of a State would be at stake.[93]

The ICJ acknowledged the "unique characteristics of nuclear weapons, and in particular their destructive capacity, their capacity to cause untold human suffering, and their ability to cause damage to generations to come."[94] It stated that the survivors of the initial blast and heat would be exposed to the resulting effects of nuclear winter. Nuclear winter would be an ecological disaster of the same ... magnitude as the [one that occurred] ... 65 million years ago. The initial blast and the scourging fires thereafter would emit huge amounts of dust and smoke into the air. The dust and smoke would circle the northern hemisphere quickly and the temperature at the surface would be low [while] the temperature of the upper part of the troposphere would rise because the sunlight would be absorbed by the smoke. This drastic temperature change would destroy crops and bring about global starvation.

The ICJ provided a broad framework for the application of the rules of IHL to nuclear weapons, but left certain questions open. The court basically said that the use of nuclear weapons is subject to IHL and would be generally unlawful under such law. It emphasised the wide scope of humanitarian law:

> The cardinal principles contained in the texts constituting the fabric of humanitarian law are the following. The first is aimed at the protection of the civilian population and civilian objects and establishes the distinction between combatants and non-combatants; States must never make civilians the object of attack and must consequently never use weapons that are incapable of distinguishing between civilian and military targets. According to the second principle, it is prohibited to cause unnecessary suffering

> to combatants: it is accordingly prohibited to use weapons causing them such harm or uselessly aggravating their suffering. In application of that second principle, States do not have unlimited freedom of choice of means in the weapons they use.
>
> The Court would likewise refer, in relation to these principles, to the Martens Clause, which was first included in The Hague Convention II with Respect to the Laws and Customs of War on Land of 1899 and which has proved to be an effective means of addressing the rapid evolution of military technology. A modern version of that clause is to be found in Article 1, paragraph 2, of Additional Protocol I of 1977, which reads as follows: "In cases not covered by this Protocol or by other international agreements, civilians and combatants remain under the protection and authority of the principles of international law derived from established custom, from the principles of humanity and from the dictates of public conscience."
>
> In conformity with the aforementioned principles, humanitarian law, at a very early stage, prohibited certain types of weapons either because of their indiscriminate effect on combatants and civilians or because of the unnecessary suffering caused to combatants, that is to say, a harm greater than that unavoidable to achieve legitimate military objectives. If an envisaged use of weapons would not meet the requirements of humanitarian law, a threat to engage in such use would also be contrary to that law.[95]

The ICJ went on to find the use of nuclear weapons "scarcely reconcilable" with IHL:

> The principles and rules of law applicable in armed conflict—at the heart of which is the overriding consideration of humanity—make the conduct of armed hostilities subject to a number of strict requirements. Thus, methods and means of warfare, which would preclude any distinction between civilian and military targets, or which would result in unnecessary suffering to combatants, are

> prohibited. In view of the unique characteristics of nuclear weapons, to which the Court has referred above, the use of such weapons in fact seems scarcely reconcilable with respect for such requirements.[96]

The ICJ further stated:

> A threat or use of nuclear weapons should ... be compatible with the requirements of the international law applicable in armed conflict, particularly those of the principles and rules of international humanitarian law, as well as with specific obligations under treaties and other undertakings which expressly deal with nuclear weapons.[97]

Referring to the contrasting contentions presented, the Court concluded that it did not have the necessary facts to determine the likely effects of the limited use of low-yield nuclear weapons or of escalation. It first addressed the contentions of the United Kingdom:

> The reality ... is that nuclear weapons might be used in a wide variety of circumstances with very different results in terms of likely civilian casualties. In some cases, such as the use of a low-yield nuclear weapon against warships on the High Seas or troops in sparsely populated areas, it is possible to envisage a nuclear attack which caused comparatively few civilian casualties. It is by no means the case that every use of nuclear weapons against a military objective would inevitably cause very great collateral civilian casualties.[98]

The Court then summarised the diametrically opposite contentions of certain other States:

> Recourse to nuclear weapons could never be compatible with the principles and rules of humanitarian law and is therefore prohibited. In the event of their use, nuclear weapons would in

> all circumstances be unable to draw any distinction between the civilian population and combatants, or between civilian objects and military objectives, and their effects, largely uncontrollable, could not be restricted, either in time or in space, to lawful military targets. Such weapons would kill and destroy in a necessarily indiscriminate manner, on account of the blast, heat and radiation occasioned by the nuclear explosion and the effects induced; and the number of casualties which would ensue would be enormous. The use of nuclear weapons would therefore be prohibited in any circumstance, notwithstanding the absence of any explicit conventional prohibition.[99]

While finding itself unable to resolve these competing factual contentions, the Court did conclude that the proponents of the lawfulness of the use of nuclear weapons had failed to substantiate their position as to the possibility of limited use, without escalation, of low-yield nuclear weapons or even of the potential utility of such use if it were possible:

> None of the States advocating the legality of the use of nuclear weapons under certain circumstances, including the "clean" use of smaller, low-yield, tactical nuclear weapons, has indicated what, supposing such limited use were feasible, would be the precise circumstances justifying such use; nor whether such limited use would not tend to escalate into the all-out use of high-yield nuclear weapons. This being so, the Court does not consider that it has a sufficient basis for a determination of the validity of this view.[100]

The Court noted at the outset that, ostensibly based on the advisory nature of its task, it did not intend to descend into the minute details of the facts:

> The Court does not consider that, in giving an advisory opinion in the present case, it would necessarily have to write "scenarios,"

> to study various types of nuclear weapons and to evaluate highly complex and controversial technological, strategic and scientific information. The Court will simply address the issues arising in all their aspects by applying the legal rules relevant to the situation.[101]

Similarly, in discussing proportionality, the court stated that it did "not find it necessary to embark upon the quantification" of risk factors surrounding the use of nuclear weapons and did not "need to enquire into the question whether tactical nuclear weapons exist which are sufficiently precise to limit those risks."[102] As to the limits on a State's right of self-defence, the court, after noting that a State's exercise of the right of self-defence must comply, inter alia, with the principle of proportionality, specifically stated that a "use of force that is proportionate under the law of self-defence, must, in order to be lawful, also meet the requirements of the law applicable in armed conflict which comprise in particular the principles and rules of humanitarian law."[103] The court also referred to the contentions of the UK: "Assuming that a State's use of nuclear weapons meets the requirements of self-defence, it must then be considered whether it conforms to the fundamental principles of the law of armed conflict regulating the conduct of hostilities."[104]

The ICJ noted that under the UN Charter, the threat or use of force is prohibited except in individual or collective self-defence in response to armed attack or in instances of military enforcement measures undertaken by the Security Council,[105] and stated that under customary international law the right of self-defence is subject to the conditions of necessity and proportionality. The court quoted its decision in *Military and Paramilitary Activities in and against Nicaragua*: "There is a 'specific rule whereby self-defence would warrant only measures which are proportional to the armed attack and necessary to respond to it, a rule well established in customary international law.'"[106] It observed, "The destructive power of nuclear weapons cannot be contained in either space or time."[107] Because their effects are uncontrollable, nuclear weapons cannot be used in such a way as to limit their effects to those permitted under the rules of distinction, proportionality, and necessity.

The ICJ opined that certain fundamental principles of the Stockholm and Rio Declaration are now a part of customary international law, specifically, "the existence of the general obligation of the States to ensure that activities within their jurisdiction and control respect the environment of the other States or of areas beyond national control is now a part of the corpus of international law relating to the environment." The ICJ also held that the natural environment enjoys the protection given by IHL to civilian objects. In other words, the elements of the natural environment cannot be made the object of attack, unless their destruction would give direct military advantage in the particular circumstances in question; and an attack cannot be made if the risk of collateral damage to the environment is disproportionate to the direct military advantage of the attack. These principles apply to both nuclear and conventional attacks that may cause environmental damage.[108]

In conclusion, the ICJ gave a strong presumption of illegality. Of the fourteen Judges sitting, ten determined that the use of nuclear weapons would generally be unlawful. Further, six judges were of the view that all uses of nuclear weapons would be unlawful *per se*.

ICJ: Dissenting Opinion of Judge Weeramantry

According to Justice Weeramantry:[109]

> Humanitarian law and custom have a very ancient lineage. They reach back thousands of years. They were worked out in many civilisations—Chinese, Indian, Greek, Roman, Japanese, Islamic, modern European, among others. Through the ages many religious and philosophical ideas have been poured into the mould in which modern humanitarian law has been formed. They represented the effort of the human conscience to mitigate in some measure the brutalities and dreadful sufferings of war. In the language of a

notable declaration in this regard (the St. Petersburg Declaration of 1868) international humanitarian law is designed to "conciliate the necessities of war with the laws of humanity." In recent times, with the increasing slaughter and devastation made possible by modern weaponry, the dictates of conscience have prompted ever more comprehensive formulations.

My considered opinion is that the use or threat of use of nuclear weapons is illegal *in any circumstances whatsoever*. It violates the fundamental principles of international law, and represents the very negation of the humanitarian concerns which underlie the structure of humanitarian law. It offends conventional law and, in particular, the Geneva Gas Protocol of 1925, and Article 23*(a)* of the Hague Regulations of 1907. It contradicts the fundamental principle of the dignity and worth of the human person on which all law depends. It endangers the human environment in a manner which threatens the entirety of life on the planet.

The extent of damage to the environment, which no other weapon is capable of causing, has been summarised in 1987 by the World Commission on the Environment and Development in the following terms: "The likely consequences of nuclear war make other threats to the environment pale into insignificance. Nuclear weapons represent a qualitatively new step in the development of warfare. One thermonuclear bomb can have an explosive power greater than all the explosives used in wars since the invention of gunpowder. In addition to the destructive effects of blast and heat, immensely magnified by these weapons, they introduce a new lethal agent—ionizing radiation—that extends lethal effects over both space and time."[110]

Nuclear weapons have the potential to destroy the entire ecosystem of the planet. Those already in the world's arsenals have the potential of destroying life on the planet several times over. Nuclear weapons: (i) cause death and destruction; (ii) induce cancers, leukaemia, keloids and related afflictions; (iii) cause gastrointestinal, cardiovascular and related afflictions; (iv)

> continue for decades after their use to induce the health-related problems mentioned above; (v) damage the environmental rights of future generations; (vi) cause congenital deformities, mental retardation and genetic damage; (vii) carry the potential to cause a nuclear winter; (viii) contaminate and destroy the food chain; (ix) imperil the ecosystem; (x) produce lethal levels of heat and blast; (xi) produce radiation and radioactive fallout; (xii) produce a disruptive electromagnetic pulse; (xiii) produce social disintegration; (xiv) imperil all civilization; (xv) threaten human survival; (xvi) wreak cultural devastation; (xvii) span a time range of thousands of years; (xviii) threaten all life on the planet; (xix) irreversibly damage the rights of future generations; (xx) exterminate civilian populations; (xxi) damage neighbouring States; (xxii) produce psychological stress and fear syndromes, *as no other weapons do.*
>
> There is now a consensus that the climatic effects of a nuclear winter and the resulting lack of food aggravated by the destroyed infrastructure could have a greater overall impact on the global population than the immediate effects of the nuclear explosions. The evidence is growing that in a post-war nuclear world *Homo sapiens* will not have an ecological niche to which he could flee. It is apparent that life everywhere on this planet would be threatened.[111]

Justice Weeramantry commented, "Nuclear war has the potential to destroy all civilisation. Such a result could be achieved through the use of a minute fraction of the weapons already in existence in the arsenals of the nuclear powers."

Judge Shahabuddeen noted the extreme and indiscriminate effects of nuclear weapons:

> To classify these effects as being merely a by-product is not to the point; they can be just as extensive as, if not more so than, those immediately produced by blast and heat. They cause unspeakable

> sickness followed by painful death, affect the genetic code, damage the unborn, and can render the earth uninhabitable. These extended effects may not have military value for the user, but this does not lessen their gravity or the fact that they result from the use of nuclear weapons. This being the case, it is not relevant for present purposes to consider whether the injury produced is a by-product or secondary effect of such use. Nor is it always a case of the effects being immediately inflicted but manifesting their consequences in later ailments; nuclear fallout may exert an impact on people long after the explosion, causing fresh injury to them in the course of time, including injury to future generations. The weapon continues to strike for years after the initial blow, thus presenting the disturbing and unique portrait of war being waged by a present generation on future ones—on future ones with which its successors could well be at peace.
>
> The preamble to the 1967 Treaty of Tlatelolco, Additional Protocol II of which was signed and ratified by the five [nuclear weapons States], declared that the Parties were convinced that the incalculable destructive power of nuclear weapons has made it imperative that the legal prohibition of war should be strictly observed in practice if the survival of civilisation and of mankind itself is to be assured. Also, nuclear weapons, whose terrible effects are suffered, indiscriminately and inexorably, by military forces and civilian population alike, constitute, through the persistence of the radioactivity they release, an attack on the integrity of the human species and ultimately may even render the whole earth uninhabitable.[112]

Judge Koroma noted, with respect to the atomic attacks on Hiroshima and Nagasaki, "Over 320,000 people who survived but were affected by radiation still suffer from various diseases caused by radiation, including leukaemia, thyroid cancer, breast cancer, lung cancer, gastric cancer and cataracts. More than half a century after the disaster, they are still said to be undergoing medical examinations and treatment."[113]

The ICJ's opinion in *Legality of the Threat or Use of Nuclear Weapons* has implications for international environmental law and IHL. The duty not to cause trans-boundary harm is clearly stated by the Court to be part of international law. The Court's recognition of environmental concerns as a factor in necessity and proportionality analysis continues the trend towards recognizing the importance of environmental issues in the law of armed conflict. The Court appropriately balanced the independent legal doctrines of respect for the environment and self defence through the limiting principles of necessity and proportionality. The Court erroneously opened the door for a similar balancing approach when it failed to recognize that humanitarian principles and self-defence are not independent legal doctrines.[114]

The ICJ's Advisory Opinion[115] makes it quite clear that nuclear weapons would generally breach all of the following:

- The Declaration of St. Petersburg, 1868, because unnecessary suffering would be caused;[116]
- The Martens Clause, 1899, because humanity would not remain under the protection and authority of the principles of international law derived from established custom, the principles of humanity and the dictates of public conscience;
- The Hague Conventions, 1907, because unnecessary suffering would be caused and there would be no guarantee of the inviolability of neutral nations;[117]
- The UN Charter;[118]
- The Universal Declaration of Human Rights, 1948, because long-lasting radioactive contamination would interfere with innocent people's inherent right to life and health;
- The Geneva Conventions, 1949, because the protection of the wounded, the sick, the infirm, expectant mothers, civilian hospitals and health workers would not be ensured; and
- The Protocols Additional to the Geneva Conventions, 1977, because there would be massive incidental loss of civilian lives and widespread, long-term and severe damage to the environment.[119]

In addition, the Non-Proliferation Treaty (NPT), 1968, is being violated by all the nuclear weapons states, as they are not fulfilling their obligation to negotiate in good faith a nuclear disarmament.[120] Serious violations of these treaties and declarations are defined as criminal acts under the Nuremberg Principles. Specifically, Nuremberg Principle VI (a) defines crimes against peace as: "Planning, preparation, initiation or waging of ... a war in violation of international treaties, agreements or assurances. ... Participation in a common plan or conspiracy for the accomplishment of any of the acts mentioned." Nuremberg Principle VI (b) defines war crimes as "violations of the laws or customs of war" and Nuremberg Principle VI (c) defines crimes against humanity as "murder, extermination ... and other inhumane acts done against any civilian population ... when ... carried on in execution of, or in connection with any crime against peace or any war crime."

Customary Law

The customary rules of IHL applicable to nuclear weapons are distinction/discrimination, proportionality, and military necessity. The rule of distinction prohibits the use of a weapon that cannot discriminate between military targets and non-combatant persons and objects. It is unlawful to use weapons whose effects are incapable of being controlled and therefore cannot be directed against a military target. If the State cannot maintain such control over the weapon, it cannot ensure that such use will comply with the rule of discrimination and may not lawfully use the weapon.

The rule of proportionality prohibits the use of a weapon whose potential collateral effects upon non-combatant persons or objects would likely be disproportionate to the value of the military advantage anticipated by the attack. The rule of proportionality requires that a State using a weapon be able to control the effects of the weapon. If the state cannot control such effects, it cannot ensure that the collateral effects of the attack will be proportional to the anticipated military advantage.

The rule of necessity provides that a State may only use such a level of force as is necessary to achieve the military objective of the particular strike. Any additional level of force is unlawful. The corollary rule of controllability provides that a State may not use a weapon if its effects cannot be controlled because, in such circumstances, it would be unable to ensure that the particular use of the weapon would comply with the rules of distinction, proportionality, or necessity. International law on reprisals provides, at a minimum, that a State may not engage in even limited violations of the law of armed conflict in response to an adversary's violation of such law, unless such acts of reprisal meet the requirements of necessity and proportionality and be solely intended to compel the adversary to adhere to the law of armed conflict. The reprisal must be necessary to achieve that purpose and proportionate to the violation against which it is directed.

A State's right of self-defence is subject to the requirements of necessity and proportionality under customary international law and the Charter of the United Nations. A State's use of force in the exercise of self-defence is also subject to the requirements of IHL, including the requirements of distinction, proportionality and necessity, and the corollary requirement of controllability. International law as to individual and command liability provides that military, government, and even private industrial personnel are subject to criminal conviction for violation of the law of armed conflict if they knowingly or recklessly participate in or have supervisory responsibility over violators of the law of armed conflict. Such potential criminal liability of commanders extends not only to what the commanders knew but also to what they "should have known" concerning the violation of law.

A customary obligation to employ means and methods of warfare with due regard to the protection and preservation of environment is contained in Rules 43 to 45 of the ICRC's Customary Rules of IHL.[121] These provisions are not weapon specific and are also applicable to nuclear weapons.

There is a persistent and growing interest worldwide to ensure that nuclear weapons are subject to the rule of law, the constraints of IHL, and the fundamental norms of human rights.[122] In the absence of any general prohibition of nuclear weapons, IHL is of fundamental importance in moderating States' behaviour regarding nuclear weapons. The 1977 Additional Protocol I (AP I) prohibits indiscriminate attacks on civilian populations, including the use of technology where its scope of destruction cannot be limited. Therefore, an armed conflict that does not distinguish between civilian and military targets would be in violation of IHL. AP I also prohibits means of warfare that "cause widespread, long-term, and severe damage to the natural environment." The ICJ in the *Nuclear Weapons Case* identified the principles of distinction and unnecessary suffering as cardinal principles of the law of armed conflict. The former protects civilians from direct attack, while the latter prohibits weapons that cause unnecessary suffering to combatants.[123] It is therefore, difficult to see how the use of nuclear weapons—the ultimate weapon of mass destruction—could ever be consistent with the customary principles of IHL. Relevant considerations include: (i) the destructive power of even "small" nuclear weapons; (ii) the deliberate targeting of cities (which are described as "counter value" targets); (iii) the inevitable spread of radioactive contamination; and (iv) the prospect of nuclear winter.

Elimination of Nuclear Weapons

The first attempt to eliminate nuclear weapons had failed in the late 1940s. The UN General Assembly's first resolution (January 24, 1946) established the UN Atomic Energy Commission to address "the problems raised by the discovery of atomic energy." The Commission was to make proposals for the elimination of atomic weapons from national armaments. The US made a proposal to the Commission for abandoning its monopoly on nuclear weapons and share nuclear secrets with the Soviet Union, in exchange for: (i) an agreement against developing further nuclear weapons; (ii) establishment of an inspections system; and (iii) punishment for violations, not subject to Security Council veto. In response, the Soviet Union contended that the US should eliminate its nuclear weapons before controls and inspections could be considered.

The Nuclear Non-Proliferation Treaty (NPT)

Following the Soviet Union's first nuclear test in 1949, attention turned to how to stop the further proliferation of nuclear weapons. These efforts eventually led to the negotiation of the Nuclear Non-Proliferation Treaty (NPT), which was opened for signature in 1968. By that time the number of nuclear-weapons States had grown to five, namely, the US, the UK, Soviet Union, France and China.

The NPT[124] obligates the five acknowledged nuclear-weapons states (NWS)—the US, the UK, Russian Federation, France, and China—not to transfer nuclear weapons, other nuclear explosive devices, or their technology to any non-nuclear-weapons state (NNWS).[125] The NWS are also obligated, under Article VI, to "pursue negotiations in good faith on effective measures relating to the cessation of the nuclear arms race at an early date and to nuclear disarmament, and on a treaty on general and complete disarmament under strict and effective international control." The NNWS are obliged not to acquire or produce nuclear weapons or nuclear explosive devices. They are also required also to accept inspections to detect diversions of nuclear materials from peaceful activities, such as power generation, to the production of nuclear weapons or other nuclear explosive devices.[126]

The ICJ in its 1996 advisory opinion had unanimously held: "There exists an obligation to pursue in good faith and bring to a conclusion negotiations leading to nuclear disarmament in all its aspects under strict and effective international control." Endorsed by every judge on the Court, this statement on the disarmament obligation is now the authoritative interpretation of Article VI of the NPT, which requires States to achieve nuclear disarmament through negotiations in good faith. It is clear that the obligation applies to all

States, and not only those who are party to the NPT, thus binding the nuclear-armed, non-NPT party States India, Israel, and Pakistan.[127]

The disarmament obligation stated by the ICJ and Article VI need to be interpreted in the light of the commitments to disarmament made in the 2000 NPT Review Conference. These commitments include: (i) Reduction and elimination of nuclear arsenals to be accomplished pursuant to principles of verification, transparency, and irreversibility; and (ii) Implementation of the disarmament obligation facilitated by a diminishing role of nuclear weapons in security policies and the reduction of their operational status. It was felt that the process of nuclear disarmament must involve the reduction and elimination of nuclear arsenals and related measures taken by the NWS as well as multilateral deliberations and negotiations involving NNWS. The obligation is to achieve the complete elimination of nuclear weapons, without any precondition of comprehensive demilitarisation.

The Comprehensive Test Ban Treaty (CTBT)

The Comprehensive Nuclear Test Ban Treaty (CTBT) was negotiated in 1996[128] and prohibits all nuclear tests for military or civilian purposes, underground and above the surface, underwater and in outer space. So-called peaceful nuclear tests above specified yields were prohibited under the Peaceful Nuclear Explosions Treaty of 1976, and are forbidden altogether under the CTBT. The CTBT established an extensive international monitoring system and allows for short-notice inspections of nuclear and research facilities.[129]

The CTBT had not entered into force, though it has achieved near universal adherence. It will enter into force 180 days after the 44 States listed in Annex 2 of the treaty have ratified it. These are States that participated in the CTBT's negotiations between 1994 and 1996 and possessed nuclear power reactors or research reactors at that time. Eight of the States had not ratified the treaty as of March 31, 2013. China, Egypt, Iran, Israel and the US have signed but not ratified the Treaty; whereas India,[130] North Korea and Pakistan have not signed it.[131]

The preamble to the CTBT makes its purpose clear: "... the cessation of all nuclear weapon test explosions and all other nuclear explosions, by constraining the development and qualitative improvement of nuclear weapons and ending the development of advanced new types of nuclear weapons, constitutes an effective measure of nuclear disarmament and non-proliferation in all its aspects." The obligations under the CTBT are contained in Article I, which states: (1) Each State Party undertakes not to carry out any nuclear weapon test explosion or any other nuclear explosion, and to prohibit and prevent any such nuclear explosion at any place under its jurisdiction or control; (2) Each State Party undertakes, furthermore, to refrain from causing, encouraging, or in any way participating in the carrying out of any nuclear weapon test explosion or any other nuclear explosion."

The CTBT was meant to contribute effectively to the prevention of the proliferation of nuclear weapons in all its aspects, to the process of nuclear disarmament and therefore to the enhancement of international peace and security. After signing the treaty, then US President Clinton said before the UN General Assembly: "This Comprehensive Test Ban Treaty will help prevent the nuclear powers from developing more advanced and more dangerous weapons. It will limit the ability of other States to acquire such devices themselves. It points us towards a century in which the roles and risks of nuclear weapons can be further reduced and ultimately eliminated."

General Assembly Resolutions

The General Assembly has on several occasions declared that the use of nuclear weapons is against IHL, starting most explicitly with the adoption of Resolution 1653 of 1961, which stated that any such use would be, "contrary to the spirit, letter and aims of the United Nations, and, as such, a direct violation of the Charter while also being contrary to the rules of international law and to the laws of humanity."[132] Four General Assembly resolutions have declared any use of nuclear weapons as a crime against humanity,[133] and various additional resolutions have re-affirmed or recalled previous non-use resolutions.

Since the ICJ issued its Advisory Opinion in 1996, the General Assembly has adopted annual resolutions calling on all States to commence multilateral negotiations leading to the early conclusion of a nuclear weapons convention. The resolution 65/80 reaffirmed that any use of nuclear weapons would be a violation of the Charter of the UN and a crime against humanity. It stressed that an international convention on the prohibition of the use of nuclear weapons would be an important step in a phased programme towards the complete elimination of nuclear weapons, with a specified time frame. In 2010, twelve General Assembly resolutions, dealing mostly with nuclear weapons, identified humanity or humanitarian aims as their goals. In its resolution 66/45, the General Assembly called upon the NWS to further diminish the role and significance of nuclear weapons in all military and security concepts, doctrines and policies. It urged them to reduce and ultimately eliminate all types of nuclear weapons, deployed and non-deployed, through unilateral, bilateral, regional and multilateral measures.[134]

In July 2017 the General assembly has adopted the Treaty on the Prohibition of Nuclear Weapons, the first multilateral legally-binding instrument for nuclear disarmament to have been negotiated in the last two decades. The treaty – adopted by a vote of 122 in favour to one against (Netherlands), with one abstention (Singapore) – prohibits a full range of nuclear-weapon-related activities, such as undertaking to develop, test, produce, manufacture, acquire, possess or stockpile nuclear weapons or other nuclear explosive devices, as well as the use or threat of use of these weapons. However, a number of countries stayed out of the negotiations, including the United States, Russia and other nuclear-weapon States, as well as many of their allies.

Security Council Resolutions

In 2004, the UN Security Council adopted resolution 1540, which obliged all States to enact legislation to prevent the proliferation of weapons of mass destruction or their acquisition by non-state actors.[135] At its 6191st meeting, on September 24, 2009, the Security Council affirmed its commitment to the goal of a world free of nuclear weapons and established a broad framework for reducing global nuclear dangers.

The Security Council Resolution 1887 (2009) deals with four basic issues: (i) Combating nuclear proliferation and strengthening the nuclear Non-Proliferation Treaty; (ii) Ensuring peaceful uses of nuclear energy and supporting the work of the International Atomic Energy Agency (IAEA); (iii) Controlling and safeguarding nuclear exports; and (iv) Combating nuclear terrorism and securing vulnerable nuclear stocks globally.[136] The resolution is broad in scope—covering a range of non-proliferation issues—and general in terms—offering no time frame and delineating few concrete steps toward achieving its goals.[137] It calls on States to refrain from nuclear testing and to sign and ratify the CTBT. It also calls on the Conference on Disarmament to negotiate a treaty banning the production of fissile material.

Resolution 1887 represents a potential shift in emphasis. Unlike the NPT, it focuses on disarmament as its primary mission, though it also continues to reaffirm the principle of non-proliferation. The Security Council's unanimous adoption of the resolution indicates a willingness by international leaders to fully eliminate global nuclear stockpiles. The resolution also recognises that disarmament will limit regional proliferation fears and diminish the threat from terrorists.[138] However, it has three major flaws that prevent it from becoming an ideal regime for nuclear disarmament. It remains attached to the problem-laden NPT regime, does not exclusively focus on disarmament, and lacks concrete benchmarks and enforcement procedures.[139]

Reaffirming that proliferation of weapons of mass destruction, and their means of delivery, threatens international peace and security, the Security Council adopted a resolution on 23 September 2016 urging all States who have not done so to sign the CTBT. The CTBT bans all nuclear explosions for both civilian and military purposes.[140]

Human Rights Treaties

Nuclear weapons violate the fundamental principles of IHL, as well as treaties protecting human rights and the natural environment.[141] A single nuclear bomb, if detonated over a large city, could kill millions of people. No effective humanitarian response would be possible, since most medical infrastructure in the city would be destroyed and external relief efforts would be severely hampered by high levels of radioactivity. The Advisory Opinion of the ICJ in the *Nuclear Weapons Case* did not produce a clear and unambiguous ruling on the threat or use of nuclear weapons. However, the Court declared that the protections contained within the International Covenant on Civil and Political Rights (ICCPR) does not cease during the armed conflict. While reviewing IHL with respect to nuclear weapons, the ICJ declared that the non-derogable human rights obligations continued to apply in a time of armed conflict. It specifically identified the right to life within Article 6 of the ICCPR[142] as having continuing legal effect in an armed conflict. The Court stated:

> The Court observes that the protection of the International Covenant on Civil and Political Rights does not cease in times of war, except by operation of Article 4 of the Covenant whereby certain provisions may be derogated from in a time of national emergency. Respect for the right to life is not, however, such a provision. In principle, the right not arbitrarily to be deprived of one's life applies also in hostilities. The test of what is an arbitrary deprivation of life, however, then falls to be determined by the applicable *lex specialis*, namely, the law applicable in armed conflict which is designed to regulate the conduct of hostilities.[143]

In acknowledging the non-derogable provisions of the ICCPR that applied during the armed conflict, the Court specifically highlighted the right to life, as the most basic or fundamental of all human rights.[144] The right to life is universally acknowledged in national constitutions and expressed in both regional and international law.

In addition to the ICCPR, the 1948 Universal Declaration of Human Rights, the European Convention on Human Rights, the American Convention on Human Rights, and the African Charter on Human and People's Rights all proclaim the right to life.

The UN's efforts to advance human rights are carried out through the Economic and Social Council (ECOSOC), the Human Rights Council, the General Assembly's Third Committee, the Office of the High Commissioner for Human Rights, and nine treaty-based committees, in addition to numerous other UN entities that directly or indirectly promote human rights. Some of these institutions have shown an interest in advancing disarmament goals. The Human Rights Committee reported in 1985 that threats posed by nuclear weapons were amongst the greatest threats to the right to life which confront mankind today.[145] In 2002, the UN's former Sub-Commission on the Promotion and Protection of Human Rights produced a detailed working paper on the human rights impacts of WMD.[146] Para 41 of the Report stated:

> Nuclear weapons (NWs) are explosive devices whose energy results from the fusion or fission of the atom. The process releases huge amounts of heat and energy and also powerful and prolonged radiation causing superfluous injury and unnecessary suffering to victims. The destructive powers of NWs cannot be contained in either space or time and are indiscriminate. The effects of NWs are catastrophic and have the potentiality of annihilating the whole mankind and the entire ecosystem of the planet. NWs therefore infringe humanitarian and human rights law.

Regional Nuclear Weapon Free Zones

Nuclear weapon free zones (NWFZs) are regions in which the manufacture, production, possession, testing, acquisition, receipt, and deployment of nuclear weapons are prohibited. NWS are barred from deployment of nuclear weapon in these zones. Such zones contribute to confidence-building and consensus in a region. There are presently eight treaties relating to the concerned zones: the 1959 Antarctic Treaty; the 1967 Outer Space Treaty; the 1967 Treaty of Tlatelolco (Latin America); the 1971 Seabed Arms Control Treaty; the 1985 Raratonga Treaty (South Pacific); the 1995 Bangkok Treaty (South East Asia); the 1996 Pelindaba Treaty (Africa); and the 2006 Semipalatinsk Treaty (Central Asia). In addition, Mongolia in 1992 declared itself a single-State nuclear-weapon free zone.

The Role of the International Committee of the Red Cross

The International Committee of the Red Cross (ICRC), which has a special responsibility in the field of IHL, has repeatedly voiced its concerns about the use of nuclear weapons. In response to the ICJ's Advisory Opinion, the ICRC made a statement to the 51st session of the UN General Assembly:[147]

> We were pleased to see the reaffirmation of certain rules which the Court defined as "intransgressible," in particular the absolute prohibition of the use of weapons that are by their nature indiscriminate as well as the prohibition of the use of weapons that cause unnecessary suffering. We also welcome the Court's emphasis that humanitarian law applies to all weapons without exception, including new ones. In this context we would like to underline that there is no exception to the application of these rules, whatever the circumstances. International humanitarian law is itself the last barrier against the kind of barbarity and horror that can all too easily occur in wartime, and it applies equally to all parties to a conflict at all times.
>
> Turning now to the nature of nuclear weapons, we note that, on the basis of the scientific evidence submitted, the Court found that "... The destructive power of nuclear weapons cannot be contained in either space or time ... the radiation released by a nuclear explosion would affect health, agriculture, natural

> resources and demography over a very wide area. Further, the use of nuclear weapons would be a serious danger to future generations ..." In the light of this, the ICRC finds it difficult to envisage how a use of nuclear weapons could be compatible with the rules of international humanitarian law.
>
> We are convinced that because of their devastating effects no one ever wants to see these weapons used. It is the ICRC's earnest hope that the opinion of the Court will give fresh impetus to the international community's efforts to rid humanity of this terrible threat.

The President of the ICRC has summed up the uniqueness of nuclear weapons in his speech delivered in April 2010 in advance of the five-yearly NPT Review Conference: "Nuclear weapons are unique in their destructive power, in the unspeakable human suffering they cause, in the impossibility of controlling their effects in space and time, in the risks of escalation they create, and in the threat they pose to the environment, to future generations, and indeed to the survival of humanity."[148]

In the view of the ICRC, preventing the use of nuclear weapons requires the fulfilment of the existing legal obligations to pursue negotiations aimed at prohibiting and completely eliminating such weapons through a legally binding international treaty. It also means preventing their proliferation and controlling access to materials and technology that can be used to produce them. Referring to the five new IHL treaties adopted in the previous fifteen years, an October 2010 ICRC statement to the United Nations General Assembly concluded that:

> States can and must set the limits at which "the necessities of war ought to yield to the requirements of humanity," in the words of the 1868 St. Petersburg Declaration. These treaties demonstrate that humanity is not powerless in the face of the harmful effects of the technologies it creates. ... they can inspire and guide us together

in pursuing the objective of a world without nuclear weapons and with standards for the responsible transfer of conventional arms.

During an armed conflict or an accident where chemical, biological, radiological or nuclear (CBRN) weapons are released,[149] the lives and well-being of a large number of people would be affected. This affect could be from direct exposure and/or indirectly after the release and dispersal of the agent, such as through cross-contamination. Recognizing the above, in 2007, the ICRC undertook a global risk assessment with respect to the use of CBRN weapons and assessment of the capacity of other agencies or coordination mechanisms to respond. The conclusion drawn was that an effective international assistance response which would be of direct benefit to surviving or potential victims and which provides adequate security for staff is not possible at present. Further, no government, international organization (including the ICRC), NGOs or collaborative body has either realistic plans or the capacity to mount such an international response. The ICRC does not have a stand-by capacity to provide effective assistance to victims of CBRN events, especially involving large-scale use of CBRN weapons. The ICRC may also have to reduce or abandon its humanitarian activities because of the nature of a CBRN event in order to minimize risks to health, safety and security of its staff.[150]

There has been an increased focus on the question of a ban on the *use* of nuclear weapons considering the devastation that it is bound to cause. In November 2011, the Council of Delegates of the International Red Cross and Red Crescent Movement adopted a resolution that "emphasises the incalculable human suffering that can be expected to result from any use of nuclear weapons, the lack of any adequate humanitarian response capacity and the absolute imperative to prevent such use." In view of the virtually limitless destructive power of nuclear weapons the ICRC has appealed to all States to ensure that such weapons are never used again, regardless of the views of individual States on the legality of such use.

A few States consider that nuclear weapons could be used in certain very specific circumstances without necessarily violating IHL while others believe that any use of nuclear weapons would necessarily violate the provisions of IHL. The British Government on December 4, 2006 published a White Paper on "The Future of the United Kingdom's Nuclear Deterrent." Paragraph 2-11 of the White Paper, speaks about the UK's obligations under IHL: "In 1996 the ICJ delivered an Advisory Opinion which confirmed that the use, or threat of use, of nuclear weapons is subject to the laws of armed conflict, and rejected the argument that such use would necessarily be unlawful. The threshold for the legitimate use of nuclear weapons is clearly a high one. We would only consider using nuclear weapons in self-defence (including the defence of our NATO allies), and even then only in extreme circumstances. The legality of any such use would depend upon the circumstances and the application of the general rules of international law, including those regulating the use of force and the conduct of hostilities."[151]

The 2015 US Manual on Laws of War declares that there is no general prohibition in treaty or customary international law on the use of nuclear weapons. The US has not accepted a treaty rule that prohibits the use of nuclear weapons *per se*, and thus nuclear weapons are lawful weapons for the United States. The law of war governs the use of nuclear weapons, just as it governs the use of conventional weapons. For example, nuclear weapons must be directed against military objectives. In addition, attacks using nuclear weapons must not be conducted when the expected incidental harm to civilians is excessive compared to the military advantage expected to be gained. Accordingly, the principles of distinction and proportionality will be followed to minimize collateral damage to civilian populations and civilian objects. The US will not intentionally target civilian populations or civilian objects.

The US has developed national policy on the use of nuclear weapons. For example, the US has stated that it would only consider the use of nuclear weapons in extreme circumstances to defend the vital interests of the United States or its allies and partners. In addition, the US will not use or threaten to use nuclear weapons against non-nuclear weapons States that are party to the Nuclear Non-Proliferation Treaty and in compliance with their nuclear nonproliferation obligations. Nuclear weapons are regulated by a number of arms control agreements restricting their development, testing, production, proliferation, deployment, use, and, with respect to specific types, possession. Some of these agreements may not apply in times of war. Under the US military doctrine, authority to launch nuclear weapons is restricted to the highest levels of government.[152]

Other than the devastation that nuclear weapons would cause if used in armed conflict, the very existence of nuclear weapons carries several risks to global security. Inherent in a State possessing nuclear weapons is the risk of an accidental launch or of nuclear technology reaching a rogue state or terrorist organisation. The international community has not yet developed a regulatory regime capable of handling modern nuclear threats. Several bodies of international law currently regulate nuclear weapons, promoting the goals of non-proliferation and disarmament. In 1996, the International Court of Justice opined that the threat or use of nuclear weapons was not illegal under international law in extreme circumstances. There is neither binding international law nor customary *opinio juris* to justify an absolute ban on the possession and the use of nuclear weapons. The survival of humanity depends on how threats posed by nuclear weapons are addressed by the present generation. As the non-proliferation regime has proved ineffective, complete disarmament should be the goal of any future international regime regulating nuclear weapons.[153]

In 2009, the International Commission on Nuclear Non-Proliferation and Disarmament, jointly organised by Australia and Japan, issued a massive study containing a detailed step-by-step proposal for achieving global nuclear disarmament.[154] This was followed by a demand made by over 200 international political, military, business, and faith leaders in Paris for the Global Zero Summit to launch the next phase of the Global Zero Campaign focused on the phased elimination of all nuclear weapons. A compilation of a large volume of laws, treaties, regulations, and resolutions, no matter how thorough and exhaustive, from which the illegality of the threat and use of nuclear weapons can be deduced, will not necessarily bring about a nuclear-weapons-free world. Indeed, what is required is a clear, absolute, and enforceable mandate, similar to the biological and chemical weapons conventions.[155] The Model Nuclear Weapon Convention, circulated by the governments of Malaysia and Costa Rica, which was drafted by non-governmental experts, is a laudable step towards disarmament. It is a bold and imaginative initiative designed to show that if diplomats and bureaucrats will not tackle the job, civil society will, as it has done with the mine-ban treaty and the cluster-bomb treaty.[156] A new vigorous initiative from individuals, members of civil society and senior Statesmen is required to achieve a nuclear-weapons-free world.[157]

Three international conferences on the humanitarian impact of nuclear weapons held in 2013 and 2014 in Oslo (Norway), Nayarit (Mexico) and Vienna (Austria), discussed the consequences of nuclear weapons solely in humanitarian terms. The main conclusions drawn from these conferences were: (a) The use of nuclear weapons, even on a limited scale, could have severe and potentially long-lasting consequences for human health and well-being, the environment, the climate, food production and socioeconomic development; (b) The health effects can last for decades and even impact the children of survivors through genetic damage to their parents; (c) There is no effective or feasible means of assisting a substantial portion of survivors in the immediate aftermath of a nuclear detonation, while adequately protecting those delivering assistance in most countries or at the international level; (d) Accidental nuclear weapon detonations remain a very real danger. Malfunctions, mishaps, false alarms and misinterpreted information have nearly led to the intentional or accidental detonation of nuclear weapons on numerous occasions since 1945; and (e) The effects of a nuclear detonation, irrespective of the cause, would not be constrained by national borders and could have regional and even global consequences.[158]

The detonation of a single nuclear weapon has potential to cause over a million casualties, and significant environmental damage, including the depletion of the ozone layer. Although the effects on the ozone layer cannot be calculated with certainty, it can be estimated that the reduction in the ozone layer could be 50%-70% over the whole northern hemisphere. In three billion years of evolution, the earth has not been exposed to radiation of that percentage. Once the ozone layer has been reduced, if not eliminated completely, drastic changes in temperature may expedite the process of nuclear winter. Thus the effects of nuclear weapons cannot be confined within national boundaries. These weapons cannot discriminate between combatants and non-combatants, children and adults, humans and any other species, or according to any other criteria.

The existing nuclear weapons in the world have a combined destructive force equivalent to approximately 150,000 Hiroshima bombs. Around 4,100 of them are maintained on launch-ready alert at all times. Nine countries possess nuclear weapons. In addition, five European nations host nuclear weapons on their territory as part of a NATO nuclear sharing arrangement. More than twenty other countries maintain military doctrines that rely on nuclear weapons.[159]

The existing knowledge about the effects of the use of nuclear weapons on humans and the environment is far from complete. The studies on the effects of a nuclear war are generally based on data from Hiroshima and Nagasaki, nuclear-weapon testing and extrapolations or scientific hypotheses that by definition cannot be verified. The outcome of these explosions has been meticulously investigated, yet considerably different data are given by different sources, in particular, the number of casualties and the environmental harm that may be caused. The reason being that the studies have used different war scenarios and applied different assumptions. Irrespective of the sophistication of the models applied in these studies, it must be clearly understood that no desk calculations could give a true picture of the consequences of the use of nuclear weapons in armed conflict.

Nuclear weapons represent humankind's ultimate confrontation with the natural environment that sustains us. The purpose of these weapons is wholesale destruction on a massive scale. No other single human creation has such potential for harm.[160] Such is the threat to life posed by nuclear weapons that the International Court of Justice, in its 1996 landmark ruling on the general illegality of these weapons, stated that the destructive power of nuclear weapons cannot be contained in either space or time. What we must understand is that a nuclear war cannot be won. Even a "first strike" would be suicidal. Likewise, a "limited" nuclear war could cause severe effects if targeted at cities and industrial areas, and it is doubtful that a nuclear war could ever be limited. Future nuclear arms treaties need to address the environmental consequences posed by the potential use of the total number of weapons they allow to remain in the world's arsenals.

The General Assembly's first resolution of 1946 identified the goal of the elimination from the national armaments of atomic weapons and all other weapons adaptable to mass destruction. There is a need to outlaw and eliminate all nuclear weapons.[161]

Notes

1. Hiroshima was selected because of the large port used by the Japanese Army, its Army headquarters with 25,000 troops in garrison and its large industrial complex; Nagasaki was selected because it was one of the cities that had yet not been bombed, it was a major port and one of the largest shipbuilding and repair cities. L. G. Groves, *Now it can be Told: The Story of Manhattan Project* (London: Andre Deutsch Publishers, 1963).
2. The Hiroshima bomb (Little Boy) had an energy yield of about 15±3 kilotons (kt; a one kt explosion is equivalent in energy release to the detonation of about 1,000 tons of TNT; one megaton, Mt, equals 1,000 kT). The Nagasaki bomb (Fat Man) had an energy yield of 21±2 kilotons. A. B. Pittock, T. P. Ackerman and P. J. Crutzen, *Environmental Consequences of Nuclear War, Volume I: Physical and Atmospheric Effects* (SCOPE: John Wiley & Sons Ltd., 1986), p. 1.
3. These heights are near optimal for thermal irradiation and blast damage, but produce relatively little radioactive fallout because the fireball does not touch the ground. The most immediate consequence was the intense thermal irradiation "pulse," which caused serious skin burns and primary fire ignitions at distances of up to several kilometres from the hypocentre. A. B. Pittock, T. P. Ackerman and P. J. Crutzen, *Environmental Consequences of Nuclear War, Volume I: Physical and Atmospheric Effects* (SCOPE: John Wiley & Sons Ltd., 1986), p. 1.

4. O. B. Toon, A. Robock and Richard P. Turco, "Environmental Consequences of Nuclear War," *Physics Today*, December 2008, pp. 37-42. Recent studies have resurrected the "nuclear winter" fears of the 1980s. It is estimated that the use of just 100 Hiroshima-sized weapons in urban areas, for example a war between India and Pakistan where each side used 50 weapons, could cause severe global climatic consequences. Fires ignited would release copious amounts of light-absorbing smoke and debris into the upper atmosphere, causing persistent surface cooling even a decade later. In such a scenario, there would be decreases in growing seasons in many of the most important grain producing parts of the world, with severe reductions in food production. A scenario of this magnitude could lead to a total global death toll of one billion from starvation alone, major epidemics of infectious disease, and immense potential for war and civil conflict. I. Helfand, "An Assessment of the Extent of Projected Global Famine Resulting from Limited, Regional Nuclear War," presented at "Nuclear Weapons: The Final Pandemic" conference at London, October 2007, pp. 3-4, available at: http://www.psr.org/assets/pdfs/helfandpaper.pdf, accessed October 4, 2012.
5. The enriched uranium is fabricated into fuel that goes into either nuclear power or weapons reactors. In the reactor core the fuel is bombarded with neutrons. The uranium either splits giving off its binding energy to heat water, make electricity and form other radioactive elements or the uranium absorbs the neutron, gives off electrons, and forms plutonium which can be used to make nuclear weapons. The fuel is millions of times more radioactive when it comes out of the reactor than when it goes in. Some of the materials formed will be radioactive for literally millions of years. At every link of this fuel chain, and in the transport from step to step, nuclear wastes are created and radioactive emissions are released into the air, water and environment, inevitably adding to the natural background radiation and increasing exposures to living things in that environment.
6. Plutonium, a synthetic element, is created by nuclear reactors. Spent reactor fuel contains a mixture of uranium, plutonium and highly radioactive "fission products." In order for the plutonium to be used in weapons, it must first be separated from spent fuel through a chemical or electrochemical process. That is why civilian spent fuel does not pose a proliferation danger as long as the plutonium in it is not separated. It has been estimated that there are about 400 metric tonnes of separated plutonium in the world today, most of it in the US and former Soviet military stockpiles. The high cost of producing the plutonium in nuclear weapons does not imply that it has any economic value. In fact, it would cost more to process existing plutonium for use in reactors than simply by uranium fuel. The ample known reserves of inexpensive uranium make plutonium's economic prospects very dim for at least another century. Its human health, environmental and proliferation hazards are additional reasons to treat plutonium as a dangerous waste. Arjun Makhijani, "Warhead Dismantlement and Material Disposition: Environment, Safety and Health," in *Facing Reality: Beyond the Bomb; Dismantling Nuclear Weapons and Disposing of their Radioactive Wastes*, Peter Gray (ed.), the Council on the Department of Energy's Nuclear Weapons Complex of the tides Foundation's Project for Participatory Democracy, 1996, available at: http://www.ananuclear.org/Portals/0/Facing_Reality_Beyond_the_Bomb.pdf, accessed October 3, 2012.
7. Fusion bombs, also called thermonuclear of H-bombs, derive their energy from a process which is reverse of that of fission, namely the formation of heavier nuclides from higher ones. The only element which has so far been used for

this purpose is hydrogen. Joseph Rotblat, "Digest of Nuclear Weaponry," in Christine Cassel, Michael McCally and Henry Abraham (ed.), *Nuclear Weapons and Nuclear War* (New York: Praeger, 1984), p. 81.

8. The energy released in a nuclear explosion (yield) is usually measured in kilotons (kt) or megatons (Mt) corresponding to the energy released by a thousand or a million metric tons of the conventional explosive TNT (trinitrotoluene).
9. Kristensen Hans M. and Robert S. Norris, Status of World Nuclear Forces, Federation of American Scientists, available at: https://fas.org/issues/nuclear-weapons/status-world-nuclear-forces/, accessed 30 June 2017.
10. The exact number of nuclear weapons in each country's possession is a closely held national secret. These estimates are based on publicly available information, analysis of historical records, and occasional leaks in media. North Korea maintains an active but highly opaque nuclear weapon programme. It is estimated that North Korea may have built up to 10 nuclear warheads, although there is no open-source evidence that it has produced or deployed operational weapons. The estimate is based primarily on calculations of the amount of plutonium that may have been produced by the graphite-moderated reactor located at the Yongbyon nuclear centre. Kile Shannon N. and Kristensen Hans M., Trends in World Nuclear Force, 2016, SIPRI, Factsheet June 2016.
11. Kristensen H.M. and McKinzie M.G., Nuclear arsenals: Current developments, trends and capabilities, *International Committee of the Red Cross*, Vol. 97, No. 899, 2015, p. 563-599.
12. David Albright and Kimberly Kramer, *Global Stocks of Nuclear Explosive Materials*, Institute for Science and International Security, August 2005.
13. The damage resulting from a nuclear blast wave is much larger than from a conventional blast due to the combination of high peak overpressure, drag winds and duration. Most buildings and structures will be demolished or heavily damaged, many people will be killed. Casualties will result from two different type of blast injuries: (i) direct (or primary) injuries associated with exposure of the body to the environmental pressure variations accompanying a blast wave, and (ii) indirect injuries resulting from impact of penetrating and non-penetrating missiles on the body or as the consequences of displacement of the body as a whole. Erik Koppe, *The Use of Nuclear Weapons and the Protection of Environment During International Armed Conflict* (USA, Oregon: Oxford and Portland, 2008), p. 72.
14. According to McNaught, "the type of burst is classified by the position of the fireball at its maximum diameter in relation to the ground." Based on this definition, one could distinguish three main categories, namely air, surface, and sub-surface burst. The type of explosion that is eventually chosen for depends on the nature of the target and the seriousness and magnitude of the damage that needs to be inflicted. L. W. McNaught, *Nuclear Weapons and Their Effects* (London: Brassey's Defence Publishers, 1984), p. 26; S. Glasstone and J. Dolan (eds.), *The Effects of Nuclear Weapons* (Washington DC: US Department of Defence and the US Department of Energy, 1977), p. 9.
15. Percy Shelley, "Consequences of Nuclear War," available at: http://www.is.wayne.edu/mnissani/pagepub/CH2.html, accessed March 9, 2012.
16. Charles S. Grace, *Nuclear Weapons: Principles, Effects and Survivability* (London: Brassey's, 1994), pp. 91-105.
17. The energy released from a nuclear weapon detonated in the troposphere can be divided into four basic categories: (i) Blast—50 to 60% of total energy; (ii) Thermal radiation—35 to 45% of total energy; (iii) Ionising radiation—5% of

total energy; and (iv) Residual radiation—5 to 10% of total energy. Depending on the design of the weapon and the environment in which it is detonated the energy distributed to these categories can be increased or decreased. Available at: http://nuclearweaponarchive.org/Nwfaq/Nfaq5.html, accessed October 7, 2012.

18. The fireballs effects depend on distance, the bomb's yield, and weather conditions. Everything within the fireball, or close by, evaporates or melts. On a clear day, a direct exposure to the brief heat pulse given off by the fireball of a 1-Mt explosion can cause severe (third degree) burns as far as 5 miles away from ground zero. For a 12.5 kt explosion, the corresponding distance is some 1.3 miles.
19. Former CIA Director Stansfield Turner described the actual effects of one bomb: "The fireball created by a nuclear explosion will be much hotter than the surface of the sun for fractions of a second and will radiate light and heat, as do all objects of very high temperature. Because the fireball is so hot and close to the earth, it will deliver enormous amounts of heat and light to the terrain surrounding the detonation point, and it will be hundreds or thousands of times brighter than the sun at noon. If the fireball is created by the detonation of a 1-MT (megaton) nuclear weapon, for example, within roughly eight- to nine-tenths of a second, each section of its surface will be radiating about three times as much heat and light as a comparable area of the sun itself. The intense flash of light and heat from the explosion of a 550-KT weapon can carbonize exposed skin and cause clothing to ignite. At a range of three miles, for instance, surfaces would fulminate and recoil as they emanate flames, and even particles of sand would explode like pieces of popcorn from the rapid heating of the fireball. At three and a half miles, where the blast pressure would be about 5 psi, the fireball could ignite clothing on people, curtains and upholstery in homes and offices, and rubber tires on cars. At four miles, it could blister aluminium surfaces, and at six to seven miles it could still set fire to dry leaves and grass. This flash of incredibly intense, nuclear-driven sunlight could simultaneously set an uncountable number of fires over an area of close to 100 square miles." Stansfield Turner, *Caging the Nuclear Genie: An American Challenge for Global Security* (1997), pp. 127-28.
20. Charles S. Grace, *Nuclear Weapons: Principles, Effects and Survivability* (London: Brassey's, 1994), pp. 36-46; L. W. McNaught, *Nuclear Weapons and Their Effects* (London: Brassey's Defence Publishers, 1984), pp. 37-48.
21. L. W. McNaught, op. cit., pp. 73-87.
22. Human tissue is damaged by the ionisation resulting from exposure to radiation. Growth in all animals is achieved by the multiplication of cells which results from the process of cell division. This process is called mitosis. Radiation may damage a cell nucleus so that the ability to the cell to divide is impaired. This inability to undergo normal mitosis may eventually cause death of the cell. Another form of damage can result in alteration of a gene but the cell is still capable of undergoing mitosis. Such damage can have important consequences if the cell is a reproductive (germ) cell. Due to repair mechanisms which operate in cells, the damage due to radiation depends not only on the total radiation dose but also on the rate at which it is received. L. W. McNaught, op. cit., p. 57.
23. For military purposes the radiation emitted by a nuclear explosion in considered under the headings of Immediate and Residual Radiation. Immediate radiation is defined as that emitted within one minute of the burst. Residual radiation is defined as that emitted more than one minute after the burst and generally from

fallout. L. W. McNaught, op. cit., p. 50.

24. Radioactive fallout is usually classified into two components, early and delayed. Early fallout reaches the ground within 24 hours of the explosion. Delayed fallout reaches the ground after 24 hours. Early fallout is also called local fallout because it tends to remain in the vicinity of the explosion site. Delayed fallout is also called global fallout because it can take months or years to come down to earth, during which time it can be carried to all corners of the globe. The medical effects of ionising radiation depend on the dose. A strong dose (over 5,000 rads) of radiation, such as the initial radiation given off near ground zero, can knock people unconscious on the spot and kill them within a day or two. In contrast, the health of people receiving a weak dose (less than 100 rads) will be little affected in the near term (although years later they will be a bit more likely to suffer cancer, vision impairment, and other long-term effects of radiation). Intermediate doses (100-500 rads) would cause radiation sickness. The severity of this sickness and the chances of surviving it depend, among other things, on the total radiation dose accumulated (the higher the dose, the more severe the symptoms and the lower the probability of survival), and on the age of the victim (the very young and very old are especially vulnerable). Within this intermediate range of exposure, a victim may develop a variety of symptoms, including loss of appetite, nausea, vomiting, intestinal cramps, diarrhoea, apathy, fever, and headache.
25. Charles S. Grace, op. cit., pp. 64-90.
26. Ibid., pp. 62-64.
27. From 1945 to 1980, nearly 600 nuclear weapons tests were conducted in the atmosphere at a number of locations around the world. These tests resulted in the release of substantial quantities of radioactive debris to the environment. Local, intermediate, and global fallout deposition densities downwind from test sites depended on the heights of bursts, the yields, and the half-lives and volatilities of the particular fission or activation products, as well as on the meteorological conditions. The impact of weapons fallout will continue to be felt for years to come since a contaminant baseline has been imposed on the ambient radiation environment that will be an important factor in the assessment of past and future releases of radioactive materials into the biosphere. Harold L. Beck and Burton G. Bennett, "Historical overview of atmospheric nuclear weapons testing and estimates of fallout in the continental United States," vol. 82 (5), *Health Physics*, May 2002, pp. 591-608.
28. The Soviet Union produced a fifty-megaton-nuclear bomb in 1961, an equivalent of 5,000 Hiroshima. Charles J. Moxley, John Burroughs, and Jonathan Granoff, "Nuclear Weapons and Compliance with International Humanitarian Law and the Nuclear Non-Proliferation Treaty," vol. 34, *Fordham International Law Journal*, p. 599.
29. *Radioactive Heaven and Earth: The health and environmental effects of nuclear weapons testing in, on and above the earth*, 1991, International Physicians for the Prevention of Nuclear War and the Institute for Energy and Environmental Research (New York: Apex Press, and London: Zed Books).
30. "Blinded by the Bomb: The Story of Yami Lester," *International Humanitarian Law Magazine*, Issue 2, 2011, Australian Red Cross, pp. 14-15.
31. Steven L. Simon, Andre Bouville and Charles E. Land, "Fallout from Nuclear Weapons Tests and Cancer Risks," vol. 94 (1), *American Scientist Online*, p. 48.
32. Valentin Pavlov, Immune Systems damaged, JPRS-TAC-92-023, August 7, 1992, p. 41. Quoted in Butts Kent Hughes, "Why Military Is Good for the

Environment," in Jyrki Kaukonen (ed.), *Green Security or Militarized Environment* (USA: Dartmouth).

33. The first French nuclear tests were conducted in Algeria between 1960 and 1965, when Algeria was still a colony. A total of 14 nuclear weapons tests were conducted at the two Algerian locations, four atmospheric and 10 underground. The French moved the nuclear testing to its colony Polynesia after Algeria won its independence. From 1966 to 1990, 167 nuclear test explosions have been performed in the Pacific at Moruroa and Fangataufa Atolls. These tests were used for the development of at least eight types of nuclear warheads. These tests are shrouded in extreme secrecy and all the information is controlled by the French military and nuclear establishment. Measurements of radiation exposure of armed forces personnel have never been made available to the scientists or the public. At least two hot spots in the South Pacific have been identified by radiation measurements. The total amount of plutonium-239 dispersed as a result of the 45 announced French atmospheric tests, including the four in Algeria, would be about 6,750 curies, assuming 150 curies per test. *Environmental Effects of French Nuclear Testing*, International Physicians for the Prevention of Nuclear War and the Institute for Energy and Environmental Research, available at: http://cyberplace.org.nz/peace/nukenviro.html, accessed October 4, 2012.
34. At Hanford, the former plutonium production complex in Washington, approximately 800 billion litres of low-level liquid radioactive waste were discharged directly into the soil over a 50-year period. Groundwater at Hanford has been contaminated with caesium-137, iodine-129, plutonium-239, heavy metals and other radioactive or toxic substances. High-level radioactive waste at Hanford is stored in 177 underground tanks, 70 of which have leaked. Hanford is possibly the most contaminated site in the US nuclear weapons complex. Sue Wareham, "Nuclear weapons, nature and society, Medical Association for Prevention of War (Australia)," November 2008, available at: http://www.icanw.org/files/NSF%20nuclear%20weapons%20Nov08.pdf, accessed October 2, 2012.
35. Hard statistical evidence of genetic damage from radiation exposure being passed on to progeny in humans has long been lacking, despite overwhelming evidence of radiation-induced mutations in plant and animal experiments. Specifically, such damage in the descendants of Hiroshima and Nagasaki survivors has not been demonstrated thus far. However new evidence from New Zealand on survivors of the 1957-58 UK Operation Grapple nuclear tests in the Pacific shows three times the frequency of total chromosome changes (translocations) in the test veterans as in a control group. R. E. Rowland, et al., "Elevated chromosome translocation frequencies in New Zealand nuclear test Veterans," vol. 121, *Cytogenetics and Genome Research*, 2008, pp. 79-87.
36. Examples are cancer with a latency period that makes it difficult or impossible to attribute the cause. In addition, the mechanisms that cause cancer are multiple and interdependent. Radiation exposure to an organism that has already been exposed and stressed could be the final straw to result in a cancer. If an organism has greater immunity or few other factors present that cause cancer it might not get cancer, at that point. Diane D'Arrigo, "Ionising Radiation from Nuclear Power and Its Impact on Animals," June 2004, p. 3, available at: http://www.nirs.org/radiation/radstds/radiationandanimals.pdf, accessed October 2, 2012.
37. 1 ha equals 10,000 square metres.
38. *Weapons of Mass Destruction and the Environment*, Stockholm International Peace Research Institute (SIPRI), 1977 (London: Taylor & Francis Ltd.), pp. 16-17,

Tables 1.12 and 1.13.

39. The surface area within which the most (dry) vegetation is ignited by thermal radiation in case of an air burst is 1,170 ha (18 kt yield), 33,300 ha (0.91 Mt yield), and 183,000 ha (9.1 Mt yield); and in case of surface burst 749 ha (18 kt yield), 21,300 ha (0.91 Mt yield), and 117,000 ha (9.1 Mt yield). The surface area within which most vertebrates will be killed after an air burst is 1,570 ha (18 kt yield), 42,000 ha (0.91 Mt yield), and 235,000 ha (9.1 Mt yield); and for a surface burst 1,000 ha (18 kt yield), 26,900 ha (0.91 Mt yield), and 150,000 ha (9.1 Mt yield). Stockholm International Peace Research Institute (SIPRI), *Weapons of Mass Destruction and the Environment* (London: Taylor & Francis Ltd., 1977), pp. 16-17, Tables 1.12 and 1.13.
40. Stockholm International Peace Research Institute (SIPRI), *Weapons of Mass Destruction and the Environment* (London: Taylor & Francis Ltd., 1977), p. 11.
41. Stockholm International Peace Research Institute (SIPRI), *Weapons of Mass Destruction and the Environment* (London: Taylor & Francis Ltd., 1977), p. 16.
42. Ibid., p. 17.
43. Extracts from the book, *The Hiroshima disaster—a doctor's account* written by Dr. Marcel Junod. Dr. Junod, the new head of the ICRC's delegation in Japan, arrived in Tokyo on August 9, 1945, the day the US dropped the second atomic bomb on Nagasaki. Available at: http://www.icrc.org/eng/resources/documents/misc/hiroshima-junod-120905.htm, accessed March 4, 2012.
44. A. B. Pittock, T. P. Ackerman and P. J. Crutzen, *Environmental Consequences of Nuclear War, Volume I: Physical and Atmospheric Effects* (SCOPE: John Wiley & Sons Ltd., 1986), p. 5.
45. A. B. Pittock et al., *Environmental Consequences of Nuclear War, Vol. I: Physical and Atmospheric Effects*, chapter 5, pp. 149-214. Available at: http://dge.stanford.edu/SCOPE/SCOPE_28_1/SCOPE_28-1_1.6_Chapter5_149-214.pdf, accessed July 22, 2011.
46. A very small decline in agricultural output could have devastating effects. At the time of the Great Bengal Famine in 1943, food production fell by only five per cent from the average of the five preceding years, but that was enough to cause panic, hoarding, and a five-fold increase in food prices. As a result, more than 3 million people starved to death. Erik Koppe, *The Use of Nuclear Weapons and the Protection of Environment During International Armed Conflict* (USA, Oregon: Oxford and Portland, 2008), pp. 104-5.
47. P. R. Ehrlich, "Long-term Biological Consequences of Nuclear War," vol. 222, *Science*, 1983, p. 1293.
48. In 1816 North America and Europe experienced "The year without a summer," following the 1815 eruption of the Indonesian volcano Tambora, the largest volcanic eruption in recorded history. The average global deviation in temperature was -0.7°C, and there was significant shortening of the growing season. In north-eastern US and eastern Canada, which were particularly hard hit, temperatures were actually above average during the early part of the year, and even during the summer months there were a number of periods with average or above average temperatures. But four severe cold waves, June 6-11, July 9-11, and August 21, and August 30, brought killing frosts as far south as the Mid Atlantic States, and in New England and Quebec there was even significant snowfall in June. These periods of frost caused extensive damage to crops, particularly to the most important crop, corn, much of which was destroyed. The crop failures were mainly due to cooling and lower precipitation. The resulting shortages led to the extensive slaughter of livestock which could

not be fed, and to a doubling in grain prices throughout the area. I. Helfand, "An Assessment of the Extent of Projected Global Famine Resulting from Limited, Regional Nuclear War," presented at "Nuclear Weapons: The Final Pandemic" conference at London, October 2007, p. 2, available at: http://www.psr.org/assets/pdfs/helfandpaper.pdf, accessed October 4, 2012.

49. O. B. Toon, A. Robock and Richard P. Turco, "Environmental Consequences of Nuclear War," *Physics Today*, December 2008, pp. 37-42.

50. *Nuclear Weapons: A Comprehensive Study*, UN Document: A/45/373, Department for Disarmament Affairs, Report of the Secretary-General, 1991, United Nations.

51. In 2012 the global stockpile of highly enriched uranium (HEU) was estimated to be about 1,440±125 tons and of separated plutonium 495±10 tons. Most of this material was produced as part of military programmes and a large fraction of it remains available for military purposes. About 940 tonnes of HEU and almost 140 tonnes of plutonium are in nuclear weapons or weapon components or available for warhead production. International Panel on Fissile Materials, *Global Fissile Material Report 2011: Nuclear Weapon and Fissile Material Stockpiles and Production*, 2012, pp. 2-3; Pavel Podvig, *Disposition of Excess Military Nuclear Material*, February 2012, The United Nations Institute for Disarmament Research (UNIDIR) Publication.

52. Since 1987 the US and countries of the former USSR have signed a series of disarmament treaties to reduce the nuclear arsenals by about 80 per cent. Weapons-grade uranium and plutonium surplus to military requirements in the US and Russia is being made available for use as civil fuel. Weapons-grade uranium is highly enriched, to over 90 per cent U-235 (the fissile isotope). Weapons-grade plutonium has over 93 per cent Pu-239 and can be used, like reactor-grade plutonium, in fuel for electricity production. Highly-enriched uranium from weapons stockpiles is displacing some 10,600 tons of U3O8 production from mines each year, and meets about 13 per cent of world reactor requirements through to 2013. Highly-enriched uranium in US and Russian weapons and other military stockpiles amounts to about 2,000 tons, equivalent to about twelve times annual world production. Military plutonium can blended with uranium oxide to form mixed oxide (MOX) fuel. Military Warheads as a Source of Nuclear Fuel, available at: http://www.world-nuclear.org/info/inf13.html, accessed October 2, 2012.

53. The Strategic Offensive Reduction Treaty (SORT) of 2002 calls for the US and Russia each to limit their operationally deployed warheads to 1,700-2,200 by December 2012. The treaty has many unusual features: warheads, rather than delivery systems, are limited; verification measures are not specified; permanent arsenal reductions are not required; warheads need not be destroyed; either side may quickly withdraw; and the treaty expires on the same day that the arsenal limits are to be reached. O. B. Toon, A. Robock, and Richard. P. Turco, Environmental Consequences of Nuclear War, *Physics Today*, December 2008, pp. 37-42.

54. International Panel on Fissile Materials, *Global Fissile Material Report 2011: Nuclear Weapon and Fissile Material Stockpiles and Production*, 2012, p. 9; International Panel on Fissile Materials, *Global Fissile Material Report 2007: Developing the Technical Basis for Policy Initiatives to Secure and Irreversibly Reduce Stocks of Nuclear Weapons and Fissile Materials*, 2007, p. 30.

55. As part of the US–Russian umbrella agreement that regulates the HEU-LEU deal, the US monitors the key stages of the process during regular visits to the facilities that are involved in the programme. Russia also conducts visits to the US fuel fabrication facilities to ensure that the LEU is not diverted from

civilian use. The IAEA is not involved in the transparency and verification activities. International Panel on Fissile Materials, *Global Fissile Material Report 2011: Nuclear Weapon and Fissile Material Stockpiles and Production*, 2012, p. 8; Oleg Bukharin, "Understanding Russia's Uranium Enrichment Complex," vol. 12 (3), *Science & Global Security*, 2004, pp. 193-214.

56. Pavel Podvig, *Disposition of Excess Military Nuclear Material*, February 2012, The United Nations Institute for Disarmament Research (UNIDIR) Publication, p. 6.
57. Radioactive materials in nuclear warheads require measures to control health risks from occupational or environmental exposures for thousands of years. The radioactive half-lives (i.e., the time required for one-half of the material to undergo radioactive decay) of uranium-235 (the principal isotope in highly enriched uranium), plutonium-239, and plutonium-240 (the principal isotopes of plutonium in weapons) are approximately 700 million, 24 thousand, and 6.5 thousand years, respectively. The actual risk posed by a radioactive material is a combination of the material's half-life, the radiation emitted during decay, and its quantity. If ingested with food or water, most plutonium is poorly absorbed by the stomach and excreted. If inhaled, the amount remaining in the lungs depends on the particle size and form. Forms that dissolve easily may be absorbed and move to other parts of the body. Forms that dissolve less easily are often coughed up and possibly swallowed. Plutonium may remain in the lungs or move to the bones, liver, or other organs. It generally stays in the body for decades and continues to expose the surrounding tissues to radiation, which may eventually cause cancer. Cancer risks due to enriched uranium are not known; however, there is some evidence that very long-term, low-level exposure to insoluble uranium causes increased risk of lung cancer. The chemical toxicity of uranium is a health concern, especially for soluble compounds that can cause kidney damage. Diane D'Arrigo, "Ionising Radiation from Nuclear Power and Its Impact on Animals," June 2004, p. 3, available at: http://www.nirs.org/radiation/radstds/radiationandanimals.pdf, accessed October 2, 2012.
58. In November 1993, the RAND National Defence Research Institute study, funded by the US Department of Defence for processing and disposition options for plutonium and HEU made their assessment of plutonium's value: "We found that military plutonium is a liability rather than an asset." The RAND analysis predicted that plutonium fuel will not be economical for at least 50-100 years, and advised against storing plutonium in reactor- or weapon-usable forms. Quoted in Peter Gray (ed.), *Facing Reality: Beyond the Bomb; Dismantling Nuclear Weapons and Disposing of Their Radioactive Wastes*, the Council on the Department of Energy's Nuclear Weapons Complex of the Tides Foundation's Project for Participatory Democracy, 1996, available at: http://www.ananuclear.org/Portals/0/Facing_Reality_Beyond_the_Bomb.pdf, accessed October 3, 2012.
59. The radioactive half-life of the substance is the period of time over which the number of radioactive nuclei decreases by a factor of one-half.
60. Peter Gray (ed.), *Facing Reality: Beyond the Bomb; Dismantling Nuclear Weapons and Disposing of their Radioactive Wastes*, the Council on the Department of Energy's Nuclear Weapons Complex of the Tides Foundation's Project for Participatory Democracy, 1996, available at: http://www.ananuclear.org/Portals/0/Facing_Reality_Beyond_the_Bomb.pdf, accessed October 3, 2012.
61. US Congress, Office of Technology Assessment, *Dismantling the Bomb and Managing the Nuclear Materials, OTA-O-572*, Washington, DC: US Government Printing Office, September 1993, pp. 45-60, available at: http://www.fas.org/ota/reports/9320.pdf, accessed October 3, 2012.

62. "Health and Environmental Effects of the Production and Testing of Nuclear Weapons," available at: http://www.nuclearfiles.org/menu/key-issues/nuclear-weapons/issues/effects/effects-of-nuclear-weapons.htm, accessed October 2, 2012.
63. Erich P. Merz, "Multi-barrier Effectiveness as the Expedient Measure for Selecting the Appropriate Stabilization and Immobilizing Procedure for the Various Waste Categories," in M. J. Stenhouse and V. I. Kirko (eds.), *Defence Nuclear Waste Disposal in Russia: International Perspective*, NATO ASI Series, Disarmament Technologies, vol. 18 (London: Kluwer Academic Publishers, 1996), p. 20.
64. Steven D. Lavine, "Russian Dumping in the Sea of Japan," vol. 24 (2), *The Denver Journal of International law and Policy* (1996) pp. 417-50.
65. Convention on the Prevention of Marine Pollution by Dumping of Wastes and other Matter, Annex I (6), December 29, 1972 (London Dumping Convention). The objective of the treaty is to prevent the pollution of the sea by dumping waste and other matters that is liable to create hazard to human health, to harm living resources and marine life.
66. Resolution LDC 21 (9) of 1985; the Parties agreed to a suspension of all dumping at sea of radioactive waste until the completion of studies and assessment required by the resolution. See earlier resolution: International Maritime Organisation [IMO], *Disposal of Radio-Active Wastes And Other Radio-Active Matter at Sea*, Seventh Consultative Meeting, IMO Doc. LDC 7/12, Annex 3 Resolution LDC 14(7) (February 1983); Steven D. Lavine, "Russian Dumping in the Sea of Japan," vol. 24, *Denv J. International Law and Policy* (1996), pp. 417-27.
67. *Amendments to the Annexes to the Convention on the Prevention of Marine Pollution by Dumping of Wastes and other Matter*, Sixteenth Consultative Meeting, IMO Doc. LC 16/14, Annex 5, Resolution LDC 51(16) (1993). The prohibition entered into force on February 20, 1994.
68. Annex I, paragraph 9 of the London Dumping Convention now provides that materials containing more than *de minimis* levels of radioactivity shall not be considered eligible for the dumping.
69. Russian nuclear submarines remain a significant source of pollution. The fleet of over 140 retired nuclear submarines moored in the Russian naval graveyard ports of Murmansk, in the Barents Sea of the Arctic Ocean, and Vladivostok, in the Sea of Japan in the Pacific Ocean, are of particular concern. These shipyards do not have safe facilities for storing the spent nuclear waste generated by nuclear submarines. It has been reported that they are not managed according to recognised international standards. Lakshman D. Guruswamy and Jason B. Aamodt, "Nuclear Arms Control: The Environmental Dimension," vol. 10 (2), *Colo. J. Int'l Envtl. L. & Pol'y*, 1999, pp. 267-318, at p. 270, available at: http://www.cjielp.org/documents/cjielp_art2.pdf, accessed October 4, 2012.
70. Arjun Makhijani, Howard Hu and Katherine Yih, *Nuclear Wastelands: A Global Guide to Nuclear Weapons Production and Its Health and Environmental Effects* (MIT Press, 1995), p. 2.
71. The Yablokov Report, written after the Fifteenth Consultative Convention on the Prevention of Marine Pollution by Dumping of Wastes and Other Matter, has documented the frightening extent to which dumping of various kinds took place between 1958 and 1992. The report recounts how the huge Russian nuclear fleet, the largest in the world, used the shallow Barents and Kara Seas of the Arctic Ocean to dispose of its nuclear waste, including unsafe reactors. Lakshman D. Guruswamy and Jason B. Aamodt, "Nuclear Arms Control: The

Environmental Dimension," vol. 10 (2), *Colo. J. Int'l Envtl. L. & Pol'y*, 1999, p. 277, available at: http://www.cjielp.org/documents/cjielp_art2.pdf, accessed October 4, 2012.

72. A number of physical, topographical, and oceanographic features of the Arctic Ocean give rise to deep concern about the dangers presented by increasing nuclear pollution: (i) the Arctic is almost completely surrounded by the continental land masses of Eurasia, North America, and Greenland, with very little circulation between itself and the Atlantic or Pacific Ocean; (ii) the Eurasian side of the Arctic Ocean, where radioactive dumping and land-based pollution has occurred, consists of shallow waters that lie over continental shelves ranging from 300 to 1,100 miles in length; and (iii) while the Arctic does contain deep basins, the shallow waters in which the Soviet dumping took place are connected because the Arctic contains a high ratio of freely connected shallow seas to deep basins. This means that pollution can become concentrated in shallow waters, rendering dilution of such wastes impossible; thus threatening the marine ecosystem.
73. Lakshman D. Guruswamy and Jason B. Aamodt, "Nuclear Arms Control: The Environmental Dimension," vol. 10 (2), *Colo. J. Int'l Envtl. L. & Pol'y*, 1999, pp. 267-318, at p. 272, available at: http://www.cjielp.org/documents/cjielp_art2.pdf, accessed October 4, 2012.
74. Steven G. Sawhill and Anne-Kristin Jorgensen, "Military Nuclear Waste and International Cooperation in Northwest Russia," Fridtjof Nansen Institute, Norway, FNI report 12/2001, available at: http://www.fni.no/doc&pdf/FNI-R1201.pdf, accessed April 5, 2012.
75. As a result of disarmament and naval force reductions in Russia, scores of nuclear-powered submarines have been decommissioned resulting in large quantities of fissile material and radioactive waste. Though Russia had initially maintained that it had never dumped radioactive waste at sea, the Soviet nuclear pollution of the Arctic is now well-documented. Steven D. Lavine, "Russian Dumping in the Sea of Japan," vol. 24, *Denv J. Int'l L. & Pol'y*, (1996), p. 417; James R. McCullagh, "Russian Dumping of Radioactive Wastes in the Sea of Japan: An Opportunity to Evaluate the Effectiveness of the London Convention 1972," vol. 5, *Pac. Rim L. & Pol'y J.*, 1996, p. 399.
76. By the mid-1960s, the height of the Cold War, the US had stockpiled around 32,000 nuclear warheads, as well as mountains of radioactive garbage from the production of plutonium for these weapons. A long-deferred clean-up is now under way at 114 of the nation's nuclear facilities, which encompass an acreage equivalent to Rhode Island and Delaware combined. Michael E. Long, "Half Life," *National Geographic Magazine*, July 2002.
77. The tactical use of nuclear weapons is defined as "the use of nuclear weapons by land, sea, or air forces against opposing forces, supporting installations or facilities, in support of operations that contribute to the accomplishment of a military mission of limited scope, or in support of the military commander's scheme of maneuver, usually limited to the area of military operations." Woolf Amy F, Non-strategic Nuclear Weapons, Congressional Research Service, February 23, 2015, p.6.
78. In 1991, the US and Soviet Union both withdrew from deployment most and eliminated from their arsenals many of their nonstrategic nuclear weapons. The United States now has approximately 760 nonstrategic nuclear weapons, with around 200 deployed with aircraft in Europe and the remaining stored in the US. Experts believe Russia still has between 1,000 and 6,000 warheads

for non-strategic nuclear weapons in its arsenal. Some analysts are of the view that Russia has backed away from its commitments from 1991 and may develop and deploy new types of nonstrategic nuclear weapons. Woolf Amy F., Non-strategic Nuclear Weapons, Congressional Research Service, February 23, 2015.

79. Pakistan's efforts to develop and produce short range nuclear-capable systems will seriously undermine deterrence stability and escalation control on the subcontinent. Despite economic catastrophe, Pakistan is producing nuclear weapons at a faster rate than any other country in the world. The danger posed by Pakistan's growing nuclear arsenal, especially short-range systems, is amplified by its growing weaknesses in governance and persistent internal instability. McCausland Jeffery D., Pakistan'sTactical Nuclear Weapons: Operational Myths and Realities, available at: https://www.stimson.org/content/pakistans-tactical-nuclear-weapons-operational-myths-and-realities, accessed 10 June 2017.
80. Terrorist or organized crime groups are not expected to be able to produce nuclear weapons material themselves; the concern is their direct acquisition of nuclear materials by theft or through a state sponsor. Ansolabehere Stephen, et. al, *The Future of Nuclear Power: An Interdisciplinary MIT Study*, Massachusetts Institute of Technology, 2003, p. 65-66; Kazi Reshmi. 2013. *Nuclear Terrorism: The New Terror of the 21st Century*, Institute for Defence Studies and Analyses, New Delhi, p. 56-57.
81. The largest and most effective conventional systems (the GBU-28 and the GBU-37) are designed to be dropped from an aircraft, have about 630 lb of high explosive, and during tests have been able to penetrate up to 6 metres in concrete or 30 metres of earth. The United States also has about 50 nuclear-tipped EPWs (the "B61 modification 11") which are designed to be dropped from aircraft. Tests indicate the current design penetrates 2-3 metres in frozen soil. The yield of these warheads is reported to be between 0.3 kilotons and 340 kilotons. Victor W. Sidel, Geiger H. Jack, Herbert L. Abrams, Robert W. Nelson and John Loretz, "The Threat of Low-Yield Earth-Penetrating Nuclear Weapons to Civilian Populations: Nuclear 'Bunker Busters' and Their Medical Consequences," International Physicians for the Prevention of Nuclear War, pp. 1-7, March 2003, available at: http://www.ippnw.org/pdf/IPPNWEPWReport.pdf, accessed March 11, 2012.
82. American air force has found that its 2,000 lb (about a ton) bunker-busters were incapable of piercing some Iraqi bunkers. The US bomb designers have developed 13 tons Massive Ordnance Penetrator (MOP) to be dropped from B-52 bombers. It can reportedly break through over 60 metres of concrete. "Bunker-busting: Smart Concrete," *The Economist*, March 3-9, 2012, pp.75-76.
83. R. W. Nelson, "Low-yield earth-penetrating nuclear weapons," vol. 10 (1), *Science and Global Security* (2002), pp. 1-20.
84. Victor W. Sidel, Geiger H. Jack, Herbert L. Abrams, Robert W. Nelson and John Loretz, "The Threat of Low-Yield Earth-Penetrating Nuclear Weapons to Civilian Populations: Nuclear 'Bunker Busters' and Their Medical Consequences," International Physicians for the Prevention of Nuclear War, pp. 1-7, March 2003, available at: http://www.ippnw.org/pdf/IPPNWEPWReport.pdf, accessed March 11, 2012. Also see Brian L. Bengs, "Legal Constraints upon the Use of a Tactical Nuclear Weapon Against the Natanz Nuclear Facility in Iran," vol. 40, *The Geo. Wash. Int'l L. Rev.* (2008), pp. 323-99.
85. A. M. Mannion. 2003. "The Environmental Impact of War and Terrorism." Geographical paper no. 169, available at: http://www.reading.ac.uk/web/FILES/geog/GP169.pdf, accessed March 9, 2012.

86. In 1950 a US Air Force, B-29 bomber carrying a nuclear bomb crashed on takeoff. In 1961, a B-52 with two nuclear bombs crashed near Yuba City, California. In the same year, another B-52 with two nuclear bombs went out of control near Goldsboro, North Carolina. When the air force bomb experts reached the scene of the accident, they found that five of the six safety interlocks on one of the weapons had been set off by the force of the crash; only one remaining switch prevented the 24-megaton bomb from detonating and spreading destruction. In 1966 a B-52 crash near Palomares, Spain, resulted in dispersal of plutonium over an extensive agriculture area. The US cleaned up the damage at a cost of $50 million. In 1968, a B-52 bomber crashed and burned near Thule Air Force base in Greenland. The bomber carried four nuclear weapons, all of which were destroyed by fire. During a four-month operation 237,000 cubic feet of radioactively contaminated ice, snow and water were removed to an approved storage site in the US. Arthur Macy Cox, "Accidental Nuclear War," in Christine Cassel, Michael McCally and Henry Abraham (eds.), *Nuclear Weapons and Nuclear War* (New York: Praeger, 1984), pp. 27-28.
87. On August 31, 2007, a US Air Force B-52 plane with the call sign "Doom 99" took off from Minot AFB, North Dakota, inadvertently loaded with six Advanced Cruise Missiles loaded with nuclear warheads and flew to Barksdale AFB, Louisiana. After landing, "Doom 99" sat on the tarmac at Barksdale unguarded for nine hours before the nuclear weapons were discovered. While the US Air Force was reeling from the investigations of the unauthorised movement of nuclear weapons, it was revealed that Taiwan received classified forward sections used on the Minuteman III intercontinental ballistic missile rather than the helicopter batteries it had ordered from the US, bringing to light a second nuclear-related incident. The error was noted by the Taiwanese government in January 2007. However, only after repeated requests by Taiwan, the US government acknowledged the error 14 months later. Michelle Spencer, Aadina Ludin and Heather Nelson, *The Unauthorized Movement of Nuclear Weapons and Mistaken Shipment of Classified Missile Components: An Assessment*, The Counterproliferation Papers, Future Warfare Series no. 56, January 2012; The USAF Counterproliferation Centre, Maxwell Air Force Base, Alabama. Available at: http://cpc.au.af.mil/pdf/monograph/unauthmovementnuclear.pdf, accessed February 11, 2013.
88. The 1996 report of the Canberra Commission on the Elimination of Nuclear Weapons stated that the proposition that nuclear weapons can be retained in perpetuity and never used—accidentally or by decision—defies credibility. Jonathan Schell reminds us that our past need not determine our future: "Whether [nuclear weapons] are merely a monstrous leftover from a frightful era that has ended, and will soon follow it into history, or whether, on the contrary, they are seeds of a new, more virulent era, in which nuclear weapons are held more widely and rooted more deeply, is not a matter of prediction; it is a matter of choice." Sue Wareham, "Nuclear weapons, nature and society," Medical Association for Prevention of War (Australia), November 2008, p. 6, available at: http://www.icanw.org/files/NSF%20nuclear%20weapons%20Nov08.pdf, accessed October 2, 2012.
89. *Weapons of Terror: Freeing the World of Nuclear, Biological and Chemical Arms*. 2006. The Weapons of Mass Destruction Commission (WMDC), final report, Stockholm, Sweden, June 1, 2006, p. 32.
90. The International Court of Justice (ICJ) is the judicial branch of the UN, and the highest court in the world on general questions of international law. Article 65

of the Statute of the ICJ states that the Court may give an Advisory Opinion on any legal question at the request of whatever body may be authorised by or in accordance with the Charter of the United Nations to make such a request. Article 96 (2) of the UN Charter states that, in addition to the General Assembly or the Security Council, "other organs of the United Nations and specialized agencies, which may at any time be so authorized by the General Assembly, may also request Advisory Opinion of the Court." Dino Kritsiotis, "The fate of nuclear weapons after the 1996 advisory opinions of the world court," *Journal of Armed Conflict Law* (1996), pp. 95-119. Available at: https://hypercontent.hull.ac.uk/short_loan_collection/Law_Modules/22130/Kritsiotis_22130_453.pdf, accessedJuly 22, 2012.

91. There were two cases referred to the ICJ for an advisory opinion as to the lawfulness of the use and threat of use of nuclear weapons: one referred by the World Health Organisation (WHO) in 1993 and the other by the UN General Assembly in 1995. The ICJ ultimately found that the WHO did not to have standing to assert such a claim but proceeded to hear the case presented by the General Assembly. Y. K. J. Yeung Sik Yuen, "Human rights and weapons of mass destruction, or with indiscriminate effect, or of a nature to cause superfluous injury or unnecessary suffering," Working Paper, E/CN.4/Sub.2/2002/38, Commission on Human Rights, Sub-Commission on the Promotion and Protection of Human Rights (UN: ECOSOC, June 27, 2002), paragraph 43.
92. Legality of the Threat or Use of Nuclear Weapons (Request for Advisory Opinion by the General Assembly of the United Nations), ICJ Communique, No. 96/23, July 8, 1996. The ICJ's opinion is "advisory" in that it is not legally binding, but such opinions can still be of considerable importance in the development of international law and its acceptance by states. Michael J. Matheson, "The Environmental Effects of Nuclear Weapons and the 1996 World Court Opinion," vol. 25, *Vt. L. Rev.*, (2000-2001), pp. 773-78.
93. *Legality of the Threat or Use of Nuclear Weapons*, ICJ Advisory Opinion, July 8, 1996, I.C.J. 226, para 105 (2) E and para 97.
94. Nuclear weapons are explosive devices whose energy results from the fusion or fission of the atom. By its very nature, that process, in nuclear weapons as they exist today, releases not only immense quantities of heat and energy, but also powerful and prolonged radiation. According to the material before the Court, the first two causes of damage are vastly more powerful than the damage caused by other weapons, while the phenomenon of radiation is said to be peculiar to nuclear weapons. These characteristics render the nuclear weapon potentially catastrophic. The destructive power of nuclear weapons cannot be contained in either space or time. They have the potential to destroy all civilisation and the entire ecosystem of the planet. The radiation released by a nuclear explosion would affect health, agriculture, natural resources and demography over a very wide area. Further, the use of nuclear weapons would be a serious danger to future generations. Ionising radiation has the potential to damage the future environment, food and marine ecosystems, and to cause genetic defects and illness in future generations.
95. Legality of the Threat or Use of Nuclear Weapons, ICJ Advisory Opinion, July 8, 1996, I.C.J. 226, para 78.
96. Ibid., para 95.
97. Ibid., para 105 (2) D.
98. Legality of the Threat or Use of Nuclear Weapons, ICJ Advisory Opinion, July 8, 1996, I.C.J. 226 (quoting Written Statement of the Government of the United Kingdom), para 91.

99. Legality of the Threat or Use of Nuclear Weapons, ICJ Advisory Opinion, July 8, 1996, I.C.J. 226, para 92.
100. Ibid., para 94.
101. Ibid., para 15.
102. Ibid., para 43.
103. Legality of the Threat or Use of Nuclear Weapons, ICJ Advisory Opinion, July 8, 1996, I.C.J. 226, para 42.
104 Legality of the Threat or Use of Nuclear Weapons, ICJ Advisory Opinion, July 8, 1996, I.C.J. 226 (quoting Written Statement of the Government of the United Kingdom), para. 91.
105. Legality of the Threat or Use of Nuclear Weapons, ICJ Advisory Opinion, July 8, 1996, I.C.J. 226, para 38 (citing UN Charter Article 51).
106. Legality of the Threat or Use of Nuclear Weapons, ICJ Advisory Opinion, July 8, 1996, I.C.J. 226, para 41 (quoting Military and Paramilitary Activities in and against Nicaragua [*Nicaragua v. US*], June 27, 1986 ICJ 14, para 176).
107. Legality of the Threat or Use of Nuclear Weapons, ICJ Advisory Opinion, July 8, 1996, I.C.J. 226, para 35.
108. Michael J. Matheson, "The Environmental Effects of Nuclear Weapons and the 1996 World Court Opinion," vol. 25 (3), *Vermont Law Review* (2000-2001), p. 776.
109 Available at: http://www.icj-cij.org/icjwww/icases/iunan/iunan_judgment_advisory%20opinion_199607, accessed March 8, 2012.
110 World Commission on Environment and Development (the Brundtland Commission), *Our Common Future* (1987), p. 295.
111. Legality of the Threat or Use of Nuclear Weapons (separate opinion by Justice Weeramantry), July 8, 1996, I.C.J. 226, para 21.
112. Legality of the Threat or Use of Nuclear Weapons, 1996, I.C.J. 226, at 382-84 (J. Shahabuddeen, dissenting).
113. Legality of the Threat or Use of Nuclear Weapons, 1996, I.C.J. 226, at 567 (J. Koroma, dissenting).
114. Timothy J. Heverin, Legality of the Threat or Use of Nuclear Weapons: Environmental and Humanitarian Limits on Self-Defence, *Notre Dame L. Rev.* , Vol. 72, 1997, p-1277-1308.
115. There are views that the ICJ's Nuclear Weapons Opinions highlight the shortcomings of judicial intervention into a politically-charged domain. In terms of substance, the ICJ pitched its tent in the middle ground of international opinion, formulating a compromise that affords no viewpoint, neither absolute victory nor absolute defeat. Liz Heffernan, "The Nuclear Weapons Opinion: Reflections on the Advisory Procedure on the International Court of Justice," vol. XXVIII, *Stetson Law Review* (1998), p. 169.
116. For example, the Declaration of St. Petersburg of 1868 proclaimed "that the only legitimate object which States should endeavour to accomplish during war is to weaken the military force of the enemy."
117. The Hague Convention IV of 1907 reminds belligerents that their right to adopt means of injuring the enemy is not unlimited. The Convention also proclaimed occupying forces to be no more than "administrators and usufructuaries of public buildings, real estate, forest, and agricultural estates belonging to the hostile State, and situated in the occupied country." Johan D. van der Vyver, "The Environment: State Sovereignty, Human Rights and Armed Conflict," vol. 23, no. 1, *Emory International Law Review* (2009), p. 98.
118. In international law, the *use of force* and the *threat of use of force* appear together under the general prohibition of use of force against other states as laid down in

Article 2.4 of the Charter of the United Nations. Hence, if possession (and thus deterrence) of nuclear weapons is deemed to constitute *threat of use*, one could conclude that the mere possession of nuclear weapons constitutes a breach of the UN Charter.

119. Since the use of nuclear weapons would violate IHL, especially because their destructive power cannot be contained in either space or time, their threatened use is likewise illegal. Under Article 51(2) of AP I acts or threats of violence, the primary purpose of which is to spread terror among the civilian population, are prohibited.
120. The Nuclear Non-Proliferation Treaty goes part way towards this goal. When the NPT was introduced as international law, five nuclear-weapon states existed: the United States, the Soviet Union (today Russia), the United Kingdom, France and China. Since then India, Pakistan, Israel and North Korea have developed nuclear weapons. The first three of these states have never been NPT members, while North Korea was a member but withdrew from the treaty in 2003. The NPT is the only legally binding instrument that establishes an obligation for nuclear disarmament, defined in Article VI. In the NPT, nuclear-weapon states also make a commitment not to assist in the transfer of nuclear weapons to non-nuclear-weapon states. The non-nuclear-weapon states commit not to acquire nuclear weapons. The NPT has three related objectives: eliminating nuclear weapons, preventing the proliferation of nuclear weapons, and facilitating the use of nuclear technology for peaceful
121. Henckaerts Jean-Marie and Louise Doswald-Beck, *Customary International Humanitarian Law*, Volume I: Rules, Cambridge University Press/International Committee of the Red Cross, 2005, p. 147-148. purposes.
122. This is not intended to minimise the importance of contributions from the legal profession, as exemplified by Charles J. Moxley, Jr., John Burroughs, and Jonathan Granoff, "Nuclear Weapons and Compliance with International Humanitarian Law and the Nuclear Non-Proliferation Treaty," vol. 34, no. 4, *Fordham International Law Journal* (April 2011), pp. 595-696, available at http://lcnp.org/wcourt/Fordhamfinaljoint.pdf, accessed October 23, 2012.
123. Dale Stephens, "Human Rights and Armed Conflict—The Advisory Opinion of the International Court of Justice in the Nuclear Weapons Case," vol. 4, *Yale Human Rights and Development L. J.*, 2001, pp. 1-24.
124. The Treaty on the Non-Proliferation of Nuclear Weapons, also referred to as the Nuclear Non-Proliferation Treaty (NPT), was opened for signature on July 1, 1968, and signed on that date by the US, the UK, the Soviet Union, and 59 other countries. The Treaty entered into force with the deposit of US ratification on March 5, 1970. China acceded to the NPT on March 9, 1992, and France acceded on August 3, 1992. In 1996, Belarus joined Ukraine and Kazakhstan in removing and transferring to the Russian Federation the last of the remaining former Soviet nuclear weapons located within their territories, and each of these nations has become a State Party to the NPT, as a non-nuclear-weapon state. In June 1997 Brazil became a State Party to the NPT. The NPT is the most widely accepted arms control agreement; only Israel, India, and Pakistan have never been signatories of the Treaty, and North Korea withdrew from the Treaty in 2003.
125. The NPT divides the world into nuclear-weapons states (NWS) and non-nuclear-weapons states (NNWS) and places obligations on both parties. NWS—Russia, the United States, France, the United Kingdom, and China—undertake not to transfer nuclear weapons to NNWS and not to "assist, encourage, or induce"

NNWS to develop their own nuclear weapons. NNWS agree to refuse any such transfers and "not to manufacture or otherwise acquire nuclear weapons or other nuclear explosive devices." The NPT also authorises the International Atomic Energy Agency (IAEA) to monitor the "flow of all nuclear material in a country." The main stipulation of the NPT is that in exchange for NNWS forgoing their pursuit of nuclear weapons, NWS will move towards disarmament. The only real movement towards disarmament has occurred largely outside the framework of the NPT. As a result of the bilateral Strategic Arms Reduction Treaties (START), signed outside the NPT framework, Russia and the United States have reduced their weapons stockpiles since the Cold War. Usman Ahmed and Raghav Thapar, "Security Council Resolution 1887 and the Quest for Nuclear Disarmament," vol. 33, *Michigan Journal of International Law*, Spring 2012, pp. 587-625.

126. This must be done in accordance with an individual safeguards agreement, concluded between each non-nuclear-weapons State Party and the International Atomic Energy Agency (IAEA). Under these agreements, all nuclear materials in peaceful civil facilities under the jurisdiction of the State must be declared to the IAEA, whose inspectors have routine access to the facilities for periodic monitoring and inspections. If information from routine inspections is not sufficient to fulfil its responsibilities, the IAEA may consult with the State regarding special inspections within or outside declared facilities. In 1994, the United States and North Korea signed an "Agreed Framework" bringing North Korea into full compliance with its non-proliferation obligations under the NPT. In 2003 North Korea announced it was withdrawing from the Treaty effective immediately, and on October 9, 2006 became the eighth country to explode a nuclear device.
127. John Burroughs, "The Legal Framework for Non-Use and Elimination of Nuclear Weapons," Briefing Paper for Greenpeace International, February 2006, Lawyers' Committee on Nuclear Policy, New York, USA.
128. The Treaty was adopted by the UN General Assembly on September 10, 1996. It opened for signature in New York on September 24, 1996, when it was signed by 71 States, including five of the eight then nuclear-capable states. As of March 31, 2013, 159 states have ratified the CTBT and another 24 states have signed but not ratified it.
129. The CTBT comprises a preamble, 17 articles, two annexes and a protocol. The preamble of the treaty lays down that the objective of the treaty is to "contribute effectively to the prevention of the proliferation of nuclear weapons in all its aspect, to the process of nuclear disarmament and therefore to the enhancement of international peace and security." Article I refers to the basic obligations of all signatory members whereby each member must abjure nuclear weapon test explosion or any other nuclear explosion no matter how small in yield on its territory and prevent any such occurrence under its jurisdiction.
130. In 1998 India said it would only sign the treaty if the United States presented a schedule for eliminating its nuclear stockpile, a condition the United States rejected. India has refused to be a signatory member to the CTBT from the very beginning. The main arguments against the treaty in the Indian circle are the following. First, the treaty proposes to impose ban on nuclear weapon testing but it is not linked to a time-bound schedule for global disarmament. Thus this treaty in its present form would create two types of nations for all time to come—one belonging to nuclear haves and the other the nuclear have-nots. This type of global dichotomy will not be in the interest of international peace. Second, the CTBT, being a child of the NPT is discriminatory in character. Third,

it is decisively flawed because in its present form it allows sub-critical testing by the nuclear weapon states; does not prevent advances in computer simulation techniques; and allows research and development of direct fusion weapons to continue through such institutions as the planned National Ignition Facility in the US and the laser Megajoule facility in France.

131. So far only 35 of these states have signed and ratified the treaty. Although the CTBT has not yet entered into force, the United States, Russia, the United Kingdom, France and China are adhering to voluntary moratoria on nuclear testing. India and Pakistan, which have refused to sign the CTBT, said they would no longer test after their 1998 nuclear tests. Israel, which has not acknowledged that it possesses nuclear weapons and has not ratified the CTBT, has not tested. North Korea has not signed the CTBT, and tested nuclear weapons in 2006, 2009 and 2013. A preparatory commission for the Comprehensive Nuclear Test Ban Treaty Organisation has been established to prepare for the entry into force of the treaty and to provide details on its status. Pending entry into force, the CTBT Organisation is already functioning and operates the international monitoring system.
132. Resolution 1653 (XVI): Declaration on the prohibition of the use of nuclear and thermonuclear weapons, November 24, 1961. Resolution 1653 declared that: "The use of nuclear and thermonuclear weapons is contrary to the spirit, letter and aims of the United Nations and, as such, a direct violation of the Charter of the United Nations."
133. The UN General Assembly Resolutions 1653 (XVI) of November 24, 1961, 33/71B of December 14, 1978, 34/83G of December 11, 1979, 35/152D of December 12, 1980, 36/921 of December 9, 1981.
134. UN General Assembly Resolution A/RES/66/45 of December 2, 2011.
135. Security Council Resolution 1540, UN Doc. S/RES/1540 dated April 28, 2004.
136. The UN Security Council Resolution S/RES/1887 of 2009, dated September 24, 2009.
137. The main focus of the resolution is on preventing the spread of nuclear weapons, while relatively little is said about eliminating such weapons from the arsenals of the world's nuclear weapons states. Indeed, the latter is dealt with in a single paragraph which echoes article VI of the NPT, calling on parties to that treaty to "undertake to pursue negotiations in good faith on effective measures relating to nuclear arms reduction and disarmament ..." No timetable is set out, nor does the resolution call for achieving the goal of a nuclear-weapon-free world. Significantly the resolution also does not call for reducing the role of nuclear weapons in the arsenals of those States that possess them, nor does it call for taking nuclear weapons off high alert status.
138. Resolution 1887, however, has several problems. It tries to salvage the framework of the NPT when it could have served well as a starting point for a new international regime. The resolution also should call for a stronger enforcement mechanism—specifically targeted, automatic sanctions. To address these problems, Resolution 1887 needs some amendment in its scope to effectively address the threat of nuclear weapons. Usman Ahmed and Raghav Thapar, "Security Council Resolution 1887 and the Quest for Nuclear Disarmament," vol. 33, *Michigan Journal of International Law*, Spring 2012, pp. 587-625, at pp. 590-91.
139. Usman Ahmed and Raghav Thapar, "Security Council Resolution 1887 and the Quest for Nuclear Disarmament," vol. 33, *Michigan Journal of International Law*, Spring 2012, p. 612.

140. Under the Nuclear Non-Proliferation Treaty (NPT), the five permanent members of the Security Council are legally enabled to have nuclear weapons. So the Security Council cannot act assertively to prevent proliferation, because its most powerful members are all implicated, in one way or another. While some of the permanent five may be reducing number of their nuclear arsenals, but all five are always upgrading their weapons and discarding those that are obsolete. In this two-tier world set up by the NPT, we cannot expect the Security Council to take effective and even-handed action. Lucy Webster, Program Coordinator, Global Education Associates, Former Political Affairs Officer, UN Office of Disarmament.
141. Malcolm Fraser, "The Illegality of Nuclear Weapons," *Nuclear Abolition Forum*, Issue no. 1, p. 36.
142. International Covenant on Civil and Political Rights (ICCPR), Article 6(1): "Every human being has the inherent right to life. This right shall be protected by law. No one shall be arbitrarily deprived of his life."
143. "Legality of the Threat or Use of Nuclear Weapons," 1996, I.C.J., 226, at para 25.
144. Dale Stephens, Human Rights and Armed Conflict—The Advisory Opinion of the International Court of Justice in the Nuclear Weapons Case," vol. 4, *Yale Human Rights and Development L. J.*, 2001, pp. 1-24, at p. 6.
145. Report of the Human Rights Committee, Official Records of the General Assembly, 40th Session, no. 40, document A/40/40 of 1985; cited by Peter Weiss and John Burroughs, "Weapons of Mass Destruction and Human Rights," Disarmament Forum, vol. 3, 2004, p. 29.
146. Y. K. J. Yeung Sik Yuen, "Human rights and weapons of mass destruction, or with indiscriminate effect, or of a nature to cause superfluous injury or unnecessary suffering," Working Paper, E/CN.4/Sub.2/2002/38, Commission on Human Rights, Sub-Commission on the Promotion and Protection of Human Rights (UN: ECOSOC, June 27, 2002), para 41.
147. ICRC statement to the 51st United Nations General Assembly on the Advisory Opinion of the International Court of Justice on the legality of the threat or use of nuclear weapons, 1996, available at: http://www.icrc.org/web/eng/siteeng0.nsf/html/57JNFU, accessed October 12, 2012.
148. Statement of ICRC President Jakob Kellenberger to Geneva Diplomatic Corps, Geneva, April 20, 2010. ICRC Vice-President Christine Beerli in an address to the 19th World Congress of International Physicians for the Prevention of Nuclear War in August 2010 stated: "the debate about nuclear weapons must be conducted not only on the basis of military doctrines and power politics but also on the basis of public health and human security. The existence of nuclear weapons poses some of the most profound questions about the point at which the rights of States must yield to the interests of humanity, the capacity of our species to master the technology it creates, the reach of IHL, and the extent of human suffering that people are willing to inflict, or to permit, in warfare." Available at: http://www.ippnw2010.org/fileadmin/user_upload/Plenary_presentations/Plen1_Beerli_Eliminating_Nuclear%20Weapons_a%20Humanitarian%20Imperative.pdf, accessed February 23, 2012.
149. CBRN agent release and dispersal may be: (i) Unintentional – for example, natural disease outbreak, natural disaster, accident in transport or at an industrial facility, collateral damage in armed conflict, remnants/contaminants from past agent use; or (ii) Intentional – for example, targeted or indiscriminate

military action or attacks by individuals or groups using purpose-built or improvised devices to cause injuries or deaths, temporarily incapacitate, or terrorize. Malich Gregor, Robin Coupland, Steve Donnelly and Johnny Nehme, Chemical, biological, radiological or nuclear events: The humanitarian response framework of the International Committee of the Red Cross, *International Review of the Red Cross*, Vol. 97, No. 899, 2015, p. 651.

150. Malich Gregor, Robin Coupland, Steve Donnelly and Johnny Nehme, Chemical, biological, radiological or nuclear events: The humanitarian response framework of the International Committee of the Red Cross, *International Review of the Red Cross*, Vol. 97, No. 899, 2015, pp. 647-661.

151. The British Government White Paper: The Future of the United Kingdom's Nuclear Deterrent, dated December 4, 2006, paragraphs 2-11. Available at: https://www.gov.uk/government/uploads/system/uploads/attachment_data/file/27378/DefenceWhitePaper2006_Cm6994.pdf, accessed February 13, 2013.

152. According to the US, state parties to AP I have expressed the understanding that the rules relating the use of weapons introduced by AP I were intended to apply exclusively to conventional weapons. Thus, parties to AP I have understood AP I provisions not to regulate or prohibit the use of nuclear weapons. Although the US is not a party to AP I, the US participated in the diplomatic conference that negotiated AP I based upon this understanding. Department of Defence Law of War Manual, June 2015, Paragraph 6.18, p. 393-395.

153. For instance, as long as the US maintains its nuclear stockpile, its major geopolitical rivals, China and Russia, will continue to keep their arsenals as well. As long as China maintains its arsenal, India will keep an arsenal to counter the perceived threat posed by its neighbour. As long as India has weapons, Pakistan will keep developing weapons to compete with its main international rival. Until these States all agree to disarm, there can be no downward pressure on proliferation. Usman Ahmed and Raghav Thapar, "Security Council Resolution 1887 and the Quest for Nuclear Disarmament," vol. 33, *Michigan Journal of International Law*, Spring 2012, pp. 587-625 at p. 611.

154. Gareth Evans et al., "International Communication on Nuclear Non-Proliferation and Disarmament," *Eliminating Nuclear Threats: A Practical Agenda for Global Policymakers* (2009), available at: http://www.icnnd.org/reference/reports/ent/pdf/icnnd-report-eliminatingnuclearthreats.pdf, accessed September 13, 2012.

155. Peter Weiss, "Taking the Law Seriously: The Imperative Need for a Nuclear Weapons Convention," vol. 34, *Fordham International Law Journal* (2011), pp. 776-87.

156. A revised version of the Model Nuclear Weapons Convention was published in 2007. In launching it as a UN document, the two sponsoring countries, Costa Rica and Malaysia, stated, "This revised model takes into account relevant technical, legal and political developments since 1997 … It is submitted as a work in progress setting forth legal, technical and political elements for the establishment and maintenance of a nuclear-weapons-free world." Model Nuclear Weapons Convention, Letter dated December 17, 2007 from the Permanent Representative of Costa Rica and Malaysia to the United Nations Addressed to the Secretary-General, Annex, U.N. Doc. A/62/650 (January 18, 2008). *See also* Peter Weiss, "Taking the Law Seriously: The Imperative Need for a Nuclear Weapons Convention," vol. 34, *Fordham International Law Journal* (2011), pp. 776-87.

157. Sergio Duarte, "Nuclear weapons and the Rule of Law," vol. 33, issue 2, *Fordham International Law Journal* (2010), pp. 573-84.
158. Mitchell Eleanor and Maresca Louse, The human costs and legal consequences of nuclear weapons under international humanitarian law, *International Committee of the Red Cross*, Vol. 97, No. 899, 2015, p. 612-645.
159. International Humanitarian Law Magazine, issue 2, 2011, Australian Red Cross, p. 3.
160. Sue Wareham, "Nuclear weapons, nature and society," Medical Association for Prevention of War (Australia), November 2008, available at: http://www.icanw.org/files/NSF%20nuclear%20weapons%20Nov08.pdf, accessed October 2, 2012.
161. David S. Jonas, "General and Complete Disarmament; Not Just for Nuclear Weapons States Anymore," vol. 43, *Georgetown Journal of International Law*, Spring 2012, pp. 587-634.

2 B

BIOLOGICAL WEAPONS

The history of warfare and the history of disease are intertwined. Attempts at warfare with biological weapons[1] date back to antiquity.[2] It was recognised by warring tribes and nations that, although not without risk to their own armies, the spread of infectious diseases to enemies often resulted in their destruction with little or no cost or effort. Biological warfare has evolved from the crude use of cadavers to contaminate water supplies to the development of specialised munitions for battlefield and covert use.[3] With the continuous developments in science and technology, the threat posed by biological weapons is different from what it was 50 years ago.

As early as the sixth century BC, the Assyrians poisoned enemy wells with rye ergot and Solon of Athens used skunk cabbage to poison the water supply during his siege of Krissa. In 400 BC, Scythian archers dipped their arrows in blood and manure, attempting to cause illness among their enemies. The Greeks polluted their enemy's wells and drinking water supplies with animal corpses in 300 BC; a strategy which, the Romans and Persians adopted later.[4] Hannibal, the great Carthaginian leader, who, in preparation for a naval battle against King Eumenes of Pergamum in 184 BC, ordered that earthen pots be filled with "serpents of every kind." During the heat of battle, these earthen pots were hurled onto the decks of the Pergamene warriors, who faced a new enemy—serpents crawling on their ships. The battle was won by Hannibal's forces, as the Pergamene soldiers battled two enemies.[5]

Military leaders during the Middle Ages recognised that victims of infections could become weapons in themselves. At the battle of

Tortona, Italy, in 1155, Barbarossa put human corpses in his enemy's water supply. The best known example of biological warfare has been the Tartar attack on the city of Caffa (now Feodosia in Ukraine) in 1346, when corpses infected with bubonic plague were catapulted into the city in an attempt to break resistance.[6] The city surrendered and an epidemic of plague followed, forcing the Genoese forces to retreat.[7] The exported disease continued to spread in Europe.[8] During the Black Plague, which killed 25 million Europeans in the fourteenth and fifteenth centuries, the bodies of dead soldiers and "2,000 cartloads of excrement" were hurled into the ranks of the enemy at Carolstein in 1422. In 1485, near Naples, the Spanish supplied their French enemies with wine laced with leprosy patients' blood.

In 1710, Russian troops battling Swedish forces in Reval resorted to throwing plague victims over the city walls.[9] On several occasions, smallpox has been used as a biological weapon in the New World. It is alleged that during his conquest of South America, Pizarro improved his chances of victory by presenting clothing laden with the smallpox to the natives. Pizarro is said to have presented indigenous peoples of South America with variola-contaminated clothing in the fifteenth century, and the English did the same when Sir Jeffery Amherst provided Indians loyal to the French with smallpox-laden blankets during the French and Indian War (1754–67). Native Americans defending Fort Carillon sustained epidemic casualties that directly contributed to the loss of the fort to the English. In 1763, Captain Ecuyer of the Royal Americans, out of concern that an Indian attack was possible in the near future and under the pretence of friendship, deliberately distributed two blankets contaminated with variola virus and a handkerchief from a smallpox hospital to enemy Indian forces.[10] This was followed several months later by large outbreaks of smallpox among various Indian tribes in the Ohio region. Even Napoleon used biological weapons when he attempted to force the surrender of the city of Mantua by infecting the citizens with swamp fever. A similar strategy of deliberately infecting adversaries with variola virus was used during the Revolutionary War by smallpox-immune colonists, whose vaccinations against smallpox had been made mandatory by General George Washington.[11]

The First World War

Biological warfare became more sophisticated during the 1900s—against both humans and animals. Germany, which was subject to a British blockade during the First World War, developed a broad programme of biological sabotage that was directed mainly, but not exclusively, against neutral suppliers of the Allied Powers from 1915 to 1918. The sabotage operation was the most extensive in the US during the period prior to its entry into World War I; however, Romania, Norway and Argentina were also targets. At that time, cavalry and draught animals were of crucial tactical importance on all fronts, and the German sabotage operations involved the use of biological agents to damage horses and livestock. These agents included the bacteria, *Bacillus anthracis* (causative agent of anthrax), and *Pseudomonas mallei* (causative agent of glanders in livestock).[12] Germany did not wage bacterial warfare against humans.[13]

On June 17, 1925, the Protocol for the Prohibition of the Use in War of Asphyxiating, Poisonous or Other Gases and of Bacteriological Methods of Warfare (the Geneva Protocol) was signed.[14] This was the first multilateral agreement that extended the prohibition of chemical agents to biological agents in warfare. However, the Protocol did not prohibit the manufacturing of biological weapons. As a result, a number of major States developed offensive biological weapons programmes in the years between the two world wars.

Japan

Japan had signed but not ratified the 1925 Geneva Protocol. It pursued a huge offensive biological warfare programme, which ran from 1931 to 1945. The programme was developed under the leadership of Ishii Shiro, an army medical doctor. [15] At the Ping Fan facility located south of the city of Harbin, capabilities were developed for producing kilogram quantities of bacteria that cause plague, anthrax, typhoid, cholera, dysentery and other diseases. Work was also done on viruses, rickettsia or toxin agents.[16] The operation called "The Togo Unit," was renamed Unit 731 in 1941.[17]

From 1939 to 1942, the Unit 731 carried out many field tests all over China and Manchukuo. These caused extensive human and animal losses. In 1939 and 1940 more than 1,000 water wells were contaminated with typhoid bacteria, with the result that there were several outbreaks in and around Harbin. Biological weapons operations caused a devastating outbreak of cholera in 1940 in Changchun, the capital of the puppet Manchukuo regime. Two years later, more than 130 kg of paratyphoid A and anthrax bacilli were spread over a large area in the vicinity of Nanking in central China. Epidemics raged in that region later that summer and fall. Also, plague-infested rats were let loose in densely populated areas, resulting in epidemics shortly thereafter. The frequency of these so-called field tests declined after August 1942, with only some desultory and half-hearted attacks. The reason for this decline in activity is unknown.

During the Second World War, Manchuria became the major theatre for secret Japanese biological warfare. After Japanese troops suffered heavy losses during clashes with Soviet troops on the Soviet-Manchurian and Manchurian-Inner-Mongolian borders, Ishii was able to persuade his superiors to use biological weapons. In 1939, artillery shells filled with pathogens were fired against advancing Soviet troops, even though it was known that earlier field tests with prototype shells had been failures. The results of this offensive were inconclusive. Many Japanese and Soviet soldiers later developed cholera, dysentery and plague, but it remains uncertain as to whether these diseases were caused by the biological warfare offensive or by natural outbreaks. Despite the scientific approach adopted and over 15 years of work on bio-weapons, no effective means of delivering these agents had been developed by the Japanese.[18] After the war, a number of Japanese scientists who were in American custody for having participated in the infamous Unit 731 programme were granted immunity from prosecution for war crimes on the condition that they should disclose the results of their research efforts.[19]

Germany

During the Second World War, Germany did not have any offensive biological warfare programme. Evidence suggests that it was Hitler himself who prohibited offensive biological warfare activities in Germany. The reason for this decision is not known, but it had the support of the German commanders and the scientific community as well.

The Soviet Union

Russia was hard hit by chemical weapons attacks in the First World War, suffering thousands of casualties. For this reason the Soviet Union wanted to be well prepared for possible chemical and biological weapons threats in the future. From the 1920s, the Red Army started research in biological warfare, studying a range of agents and subsequently carrying out field tests. The agents included *Bacillus anthracis*, *Clostridium botulinum* (bacterial source of botulinum toxin), *Yersinia pestis* (plague) and foot-and-mouth disease virus (to be used against animals). However, during the purges of the mid-1930s, large numbers of biological specialists were arrested and some were charged with sabotage. This loss of specialists had an effect on the Soviet biological weapons programme.[20]

Allied Forces

In 1940, a Bacteriological Warfare Subcommittee was established by the Committee of Imperial Defence in the United Kingdom for both defensive and offensive studies. The UK had ratified the Geneva Protocol in 1930, but with the reservations that it would be bound only in regard to other parties to the Protocol and that it would not be bound with respect to States and their allies who broke the prohibition. The UK reserved the right to retaliate with chemical and biological weapons. The military researchers in the UK performed tests with anthrax bombs on the Scottish island of Gruinard. Concerned that Germany might also be pursuing the development of biological weapons, the UK adopted a policy whereby the means for retaliation would be kept in readiness in the event of a Nazi attack. The UK produced five million cattle cakes (feed) contaminated with anthrax spores. These were to be dropped from planes over German farming land in order to wipe out cattle and thus deal an economic blow to the country.[21]

The UK also designed an anti-personnel biological weapon. On the basis of experiences gained during the First World War, an apparatus that could produce clouds of bacteria to be inhaled by experimental animals was developed. It was also discovered that a bursting munition could be used to create the aerosol. This was tested on Gruinard island. A modified, 30-pound, high-explosive bomb was charged with a suspension of anthrax spores and suspended from a fixed frame. Sheep were located in an arc 90-100 yards downwind. On detonation, a cloud could be seen moving downwind. Seven days later, all but two of the sheep were dead. It was later determined that the lethal effect extended some 250 yards downwind. Calculations suggested that the lethal effect was likely to extend up to 400 hundred yards downwind. The weapon was more powerful than any known chemical weapon. The Gruinard Island was so severely contaminated that it was off limits to humans and was eventually decontaminated in 1987.

The development of the bomb continued during the Second World War, in cooperation with the US and Canada. Canada's Suffield site was used for testing weapons based on anthrax and botulinum toxin. On the defensive side, Canada developed vaccines against the rinderpest virus and botulinum toxin. By the end of the war, the capabilities for anti-personnel biological warfare in the US were nearly fully developed. The Vigo production plant, which was not yet operational when the war ended, was designed to manufacture and load 500,000 four-pound anthrax bombs per month. These years saw the establishment of a massive offensive biological warfare programme, including an anti-plant biological weapons capability using fungal agents and synthetic chemicals.

During the Second World War, the Japanese were accused of using biological agents against the Soviet Union and Mongolia, against Chinese civilians from 1940 to 1944, and against Chinese troops in 1942.[22] At least 3,000 prisoners of war (including Chinese, Koreans, Mongolians, Soviets, Americans, British and Australians) are alleged to have been used as guinea pigs by Japan.[23] The Japanese, in turn, accused the Soviets of experimentation with agents of biological warfare. The Germans too accused the Allies of using biological weapons, citing the example of a widespread plague of Colorado beetles on their potato crops.

Biological Warfare Programmes after WW II

At the end of the Second World War, all the major victors (the US, the Soviet Union, the UK and Canada) had developed significant offensive biological warfare programmes. Although the French programme had been interrupted by the German invasion, France resumed its activities for the development of biological weapons soon after the war ended. All these countries continued developing biological weapons until the adoption of the Biological and Toxin Weapons Convention (BWC) in 1972.

In 1942, the US started an extensive offensive biological warfare programme,[24] under which a large number of highly infectious micro-organisms and extremely poisonous toxins were studied. The utility of biological agents was tested in the laboratory (small scale), in closed chambers (medium scale) and in the open air (large scale). After the Second World War, basic research and development activities were continued at Maryland, Fort Detrick.[25] The programme was expanded during the Korean War, when technical advances made the large-scale fermentation, concentration, storage and weaponisation of micro-organisms possible. In addition, a programme to develop countermeasures, including vaccines, antisera, and therapeutic agents to protect troops from possible biological attack, was begun in 1953. By the late 1960s, the US military had developed a biological arsenal that included numerous bacterial pathogens, toxins and fungal plant pathogens that could be directed against crops to induce crop failure and famine.[26] In addition, bio-weapons were developed for the Central Intelligence Agency using cobra venom and other toxins.[27] With regard to the development of munitions, the US started with adaptations of the burster-type bombs developed by Britain during the war, but soon extended its programme to include submunitions, gas expulsion bombs, various types of line spray tanks and highly specialised projectiles and generators, as well as insect vectors. During the Korean War, the Soviet Union, China and North Korea accused the US of waging biological warfare against North Korea and China. The US programme, however, did not weaponise contagious agents. All the programmes were terminated after President Nixon announced in 1969 that the US was unilaterally renouncing the right to possess or use biological weapons.

In the UK, some research on offensive biowarfare continued after the Second World War, but given the limited defence budget, the offensive programme ceased by 1957. Canada was cooperating with the US and Britain on research and development in the area of offensive biological weapons. Although Canada never possessed biological weapons, it assisted the British and American offensive programmes, developing vaccines and providing its site to the US for large-scale testing of chemical and biological weapons.

Iraq had signed the BWC in 1972, but it did not ratify the Convention until it was forced to do so in 1991, after it was defeated following its invasion of Kuwait. Despite Iraq's efforts to hide its biological weapons programme, the United Nations Special Commission (UNSCOM) discovered the presence of bioweapons in the country in 1995. According to the Iraqis, they began their biological programme in 1985, during the war with Iran. Iraq has declared that a total of 19,000 litres of concentrated botulinum toxin and 8,500 litres of concentrated anthrax spores were produced. Other agents were produced in smaller quantities, and research on viruses (haemorrhagic conjunctivitis viruses, rotavirus and camel pox virus) and genetic engineering of the anthrax bacillus were carried out. Work was also done on the drying of anthrax spores. In addition, testing of weaponised biological agents was carried out. Field tests of a crude dissemination device began in 1988 and this was followed by testing of more sophisticated biological bombs and spraying devices.[28] There are unconfirmed reports that when Iraq went into the 1991 Gulf war, it had some biological weapons available for use.[29]

Despite its ratification of the BWC in 1975, South Africa actively pursued an offensive biological weapons programme. The precise scope and results of the programme remain unclear, but public hearings and court documents mention research on bacterial pathogens, viral pathogens and toxins.[30] By 1985, South Africa had tested the military utility of a number of toxins. Meanwhile, the government allegedly used anthrax bacteria and botulinum toxin for assassinations, and the military is said to have used cholera bacteria to contaminate water supplies. An unsuccessful project was undertaken for the development of an anti-fertility vaccine, with the express aim of administering it to black women without their knowledge. However, no clear evidence exists of either the weaponisation or large-scale production of any pathogen or toxin, and the offensive programme was ended after the installation of the new South African government in 1994.[31]

In the latter part of the Cold War, the Soviet Union ran the largest offensive biological weapons programme of the twentieth century. It started in 1973 and ran until at least 1992, when President Yeltsin acknowledged its existence.[32] The structure of the offensive programme was very complex. Biopreparat, the civilian component, was enormous, operating in at least 20 different locations. Although supposedly a civilian enterprise, Biopreparat was directed by the military. A major Biopreparat facility was able to produce 200 kilograms of weaponised plague agent material each week. In addition to work on the well-known biological weapons agents such as those causing anthrax, tularaemia and glanders, work was done on highly lethal viruses, including Ebola virus, Marburg virus and the smallpox virus.[33]

Genetic engineering was also carried out to render the plague bacillus resistant to multiple antibiotics and to modify pathogens to disrupt physiological function. In addition, the Soviet Union carried out extensive testing of the weapons, at a major test site on Vozrozhdeniye Island in the Aral Sea. While the US Government provided finance under the Cooperative Threat Reduction programme to enhance security and retrain scientists at Russia's civilian-run bioweapons factories, the veil of secrecy surrounding military laboratories has fuelled suspicions that Russia is continuing research on offensive biological weapons.

Israel has been accused of using biological weapons in 1948. Among the charges of the alleged use of biological weapons are that Israel poisoned wells in Arab villages to prevent the Arabs from returning and induced a typhoid epidemic in the Arab town of Acre. It was recently reported that Israel has been working on biological weapons. Israel has not signed/ratified the 1972 BWC. The 1925 Geneva Protocol, acceded by Israel in 1969, does not prohibit the development, stockpiling, and production of biological weapons, though it does prohibit their use in warfare.[34]

In September 2001, one week after the terrorist attacks of 9/11, letters laced with anthrax began appearing in the US postal services. It resulted in more terror than actual mortality. In the three months following the anthrax letter ataks, five people dies of inhalation anthrax and a total of 18 others had contracted some of the disease. Over 5,000 people took broad-spectrum antibiotics, and many more people purchased antibiotics for future prophylaxis." The investigation into the anthrax attacks revealed that the US had an ongoing programme in which unspecified amounts of dried, weaponized anthrax spores for defensive testing were prepared. It is not clear what the cumulative amount of anthrax was available with the US. The total was probably in the 10s or 100s of grams of dried spores. These programmes raise concerns about the US's own compliance with the BTWC.[35] However, the US has identified countries that maintain various levels of offensive warfare capabilities or research capabilities. This list includes Russia, China, Iran, North Korea, Syria, Libya, India, and Pakistan. Most developed nations maintain some level of defensive capabilities against biological warfare and bioterrorism. Few other analysts include Egypt, Israel and Taiwan in the list of states developing bio-weapons.

In the past 40 years, there have been more than 120 incidents around the world involving the use of biological agents. Today, there are about a dozen or more rogue nations with clandestine biological weapons programmes. Only a few countries with known programmes have given them up, primarily as a direct result of a change in regime to a democratically elected pluralistic government.[36]

Biological Warfare Agents

Biological weapons are a unique class of weapons and include living micro-organisms and their toxins.[37] These biological agents represent a dangerous military threat because they are alive and are, therefore, unpredictable and uncontrollable once released. Biological warfare agents differ widely in their infectiousness, length of incubation period and lethality. Any disease-causing micro-organism could be considered a weapon.[38] A variety of micro-organisms, including bacteria, rickettsiae, viruses and toxins, were successfully weaponised by various States under their offensive biological warfare programmes. About 30 of the several hundred different pathogenic microbes that directly or indirectly afflict humans have been considered as likely biological warfare agents.

Bacteria

Bacteria are single-cell organisms that are the causative agents of anthrax, brucellosis, tularaemia, plague and numerous other diseases. They vary considerably in infectivity and lethality. The bacterium that causes tularaemia, for example, is highly infectious. The inhalation of as few as 10 organisms causes disease after an incubation period of three to five days. If not treated, tularaemia results in deep-seated pneumonia, which claims the lives of 30 to 60 per cent of victims within 30 days. Under certain environmental conditions, anthrax brucellosis, another bacterial disease, has a low mortality rate (about two per cent), but an enormous capacity to inflict casualties. The infection gives rise to fever and chills, headache, loss of appetite, mental depression, extreme fatigue, aching joints and sweating. The bacterial agent that has received the maximum attention is anthrax, the pulmonary form of which is highly lethal. The bacteria transform themselves into rugged spores that are stable under a wide range of conditions of temperature, pressure and moisture. Theoretically, one gram of dried anthrax spores contains some 10 million lethal doses.

Rickettsiae

Rickettsiae are micro-organisms that resemble bacteria in form and structure, but differ in that they are intracellular parasites that can only reproduce inside animal cells. Some examples of rickettsial diseases that might be used for biological warfare are typhus, Rocky Mountain spotted fever, Tsutsugamuchi disease and Q fever. Rickettsiae have a wide variety of natural hosts, including mammals and arthropods, such as ticks, fleas and lice. If used as biological warfare agents, however, they would probably be disseminated directly through the air.

Viruses

Viruses are intracellular parasites that are about a hundred times smaller than bacteria. They can infect humans, crops and domestic animals. Viruses consist of a strand of genetic material (DNA or RNA), surrounded by a protective coat that facilitates transmission from one cell to another. The Venezuelan equine encephalitis (VEE) virus causes a highly infectious disease that incapacitates but rarely kills. In contrast, some viruses which cause a haemorrhagic fever, such as Lassa or Ebola fever, are exceedingly virulent, killing 70 out of every 100 victims. The AIDS virus, despite its lethality, cannot be an effective warfare agent because its mean incubation period of 10 years is too slow to give it any tactical or strategic value in warfare, and because it cannot be transmitted through the air.

Fungi

Fungi do not generally cause disease in healthy humans, although the fungus *Aspergillus,* which infects by inhalation, can cause serious infections in people with a weakened immune system. A few other fungi, such as *Coccidioides immitis* and *Histoplasma capsulatum,* also infect naturally by inhalation and can cause severe pulmonary infections in susceptible individuals, but they have never been considered potential agents for biological warfare. Fungal diseases are, however, devastating to plants. Thus they might be used to destroy staple crops and cause widespread hunger and economic hardship. Some fungal pathogens that afflict plants are rice blast, cereal rust and potato blight, which can cause crop losses of 70 to 80 per cent.

Toxins

A toxin is a poisonous substance made by a living system, or a synthetic analogue of a naturally occurring poison. An enormous variety of toxins are manufactured by bacteria, fungi, marine organisms, plants, insects, spiders and animals, and more than 400 have been characterised to date. Toxins can exert their effects through three different routes—injection, ingestion and inhalation. Their potency derives from their high specificity for cellular targets. For example, many toxins bind to specific sites in nerve membranes, disrupting the transmission of nerve impulses and causing fatal respiratory paralysis. Other toxins selectively block cellular protein synthesis or other vital physiological functions. From a chemical standpoint, there are two categories of toxins: protein toxins, which consist of long folded chains of amino acids; and non-protein toxins, which tend to be small but complex molecules.

Protein Toxins

Most bacterial toxins, including those associated with cholera, tetanus, diphtheria and botulism, are large proteins. For example, various strains of *Staphylococcus aureus,* a major bacterial pathogen, secrete protein toxins that cause severe nausea, vomiting and diarrhoea lasting from one to two days. The US had developed one of these toxins, staphylococcal enterotoxin B (SEB), as a warfare agent in the 1960s. Spray-dried SEB, when disseminated through the air in aerosol form, causes a chemical pneumonia that is more debilitating than the gastrointestinal effects of the toxin when it is ingested. It can incapacitate exposed troops within hours, the recovery period being four to six days. Botulinal toxin, secreted by the soil bacterium *Clostridium botulinum,* is the most poisonous substance known. The fatal dose of botulinal toxin by injection or inhalation is about 1 nanogram (a billionth of a gram), per kg of body weight, or about 70 nanograms for an adult male. The toxin is also relatively fast-acting, causing death between one and three days in 80 per cent of victims. Attempts to weaponise botulinal toxin have failed because of extensive loss of toxicity due to dispersion.

Ricin, a plant toxin derived from castor beans, irreversibly blocks cellular protein synthesis and is lethal when inhaled in a dose of about 10 micrograms (millionths of a gram). Castor beans are widely cultivated as a source of castor oil, which has numerous legitimate industrial applications. The paste remaining after the oil has been pressed out contains about five per cent ricin, which can be purified by biochemical means. During the Second World War, several countries studied ricin as a potential agent of chemical warfare, and the British developed and tested an experimental ricin weapon known as the "W bomb," although ultimately it was not deployed.[39]

Non-Protein Toxins

Non-protein toxins are small organic molecules that often have a complex chemical structure.[40] The typical characteristics of non-protein toxins are high toxicity, the absence of antidotes, heat stability (unlike most protein toxins), resistance to other environmental factors and rapid speed of action. The initial symptoms of Saxitoxin, for example, appear within 30 seconds of ingestion, and the toxin can cause laboured breathing and paralysis in as little as 12 minutes. There is no known prophylaxis or therapy, and the lethal dose in 50 per cent of those exposed may be as low as 50 micrograms, a potency 1,000 times greater than that of the chemical nerve agents. Trichothecene mycotoxins are a family of about 100 poisonous compounds manufactured by certain strains of the mould *Fusarium* that grow on wheat, millet and barley. When ingested by people or livestock, these toxins kill rapidly dividing cells such as those of the bone marrow, skin and the lining of the gastrointestinal tract. They also block certain clotting factors in the blood, causing severe bleeding after injury. In aerosol form, about 35 milligrams of the trichothecene mycotoxin T-2 can kill a man weighing 75 kilograms. This toxin is also absorbed through the skin. Although mycotoxins are significantly less potent than the agents of chemical warfare, they are relatively easy to produce and are highly stable.

Compared to microbial pathogens, toxins offer the following tactical advantages. The most toxic toxins (e.g., botulinal toxin) are exceedingly potent, so that small, easily transportable quantities would be militarily significant for certain missions. Toxins tend to deteriorate rapidly once released into the environment, whereas anthrax spores and persistent chemical agents can contaminate soil for months or years. For this reason, territory attacked with toxin agents could be occupied more rapidly by attacking forces. Toxins are well suited to covert warfare. Whereas chemical agents leave tell-tale signs of degradation by products that persist for long periods in the environment, some toxin agents break down completely over a period of weeks or months, leaving no traces. Moreover, even fresh samples of toxin might not provide conclusive evidence of military use if the agent occurs naturally in the region where it has been employed.

Despite these operational advantages, however, toxins have drawbacks as far as their use in the battlefield is concerned. Protein toxins such as botulinal toxin decompose rapidly on exposure to sunlight, air and heat, and would thus have to be used at night. Further, they may be inactivated by the mechanical shear forces caused by passage through an aerosol sprayer. While toxins of low molecular weight such as saxitoxin and trichothecene mycotoxins, are more stable than protein toxins, they are less stable than agents of chemical warfare. Most toxins (with the exception of trichothecene mycotoxin T-2) do not penetrate the skin, nor would toxin lying on the ground create a vapour hazard. Weaponisation, therefore, requires the creation of a small-particle aerosol cloud, in which the toxin must remain airborne to be effective. The danger posed by the inhalation of protein toxins, such as botulinal toxin, can be countered effectively with modern gas masks (although a surprise or covert attack might expose personnel to lethal concentrations before they could don their masks). For conventional battlefield use, toxins offer few military advantages over chemical nerve agents. They would, however, probably be superior for small-scale clandestine operations.

Biological agents are easier and cheaper to produce than either nuclear materials or chemical warfare agents, as the necessary technology and know-how are widely available. Any nation with a modestly sophisticated pharmaceutical industry is capable of producing biological agents.[41] Despite the prohibition imposed by the Biological and Toxin Weapons Convention (BTWC) of 1975, some States continue to conduct research on and develop these weapons, which have often been characterised as the poor man's atomic bomb.

Characteristics of BW Agents

The desirable characteristics of a biological agent developed for military use include: (i) the ability to infect in small doses; (ii) high virulence, or the capacity to cause acute illness resulting in incapacitation or death, without necessitating an undue loss of potency during production, storage and transport; (iii) a short incubation period between infection and the onset of symptoms; (iv) minimal contagiousness of the disease to avoid triggering an uncontrolled epidemic that could boomerang against the attacker's population; (v) the absence of widespread immunity, either natural or acquired, to the disease in the population to be attacked; (vi) lack of susceptibility to common medical treatments, such as generally available antibiotics; (vii) suitability for economic production in militarily significant quantities from available raw materials; (viii) ease of transport, and stability under wartime field conditions of storage and delivery; (ix) ease of dissemination (e.g., as an aerosol cloud transmitted through the air); (x) ability to survive environmental stresses during dissemination (e.g., heat, light, desiccation and shear forces) long enough to infect; and (xi) availability of protection against the agent for the attacking troops, such as a vaccine, antibiotics, and/ or protective clothing and respirators.

Bioterrorism

A recent report states that the combination of a number of criteria make infectious diseases more suitable and powerful as a means of biological warfare or terrorism due to the following reasons: (i) High morbidity and potential high lethality, (ii) High infectiousness or high toxicity, (iii) Suitability for mass production and storage without loss of pathogenic potential, (iv) Suitability for wide-area delivery, and withstanding the delivery process, (v) Stability in the environment after dissemination, long enough to infect humans, and (vi) Suitability for being a biological agent, improved by genetic engineering and the weaponization process.[42] The US National Institute of Allergy and Infectious Diseases (NIAID) has composed a pathogen priority list, which contains the most likely biological warfare agents.[43] It divides the emerging infectious diseases into three categories: A, B and C. Category A consists of biological agents that pose the highest risk to national security and public health. This is based on factors such as the ease of dissemination and transmission, mortality rate, public health preparedness and the chance of public panic and social disruption. The NIAID has labeled six biological agents as category A. These are: (i) Bacillus anthracis (anthrax), (ii) Clostridium botulinum toxin (botulism), (iii) Yersinia pestis (plague), (iv) *Variola major* (smallpox) and other related poxviruses, (v) Francisella tularensis (tularemia), and (vi) Viral hemorrhagic fevers, such as Ebola.

The US Centre for Disease Control and Prevention (CDC) has designated *Yersinia pestis,* along with four other pathogens and one toxin, as a highly dangerous Category A threat agent. According to the CDC, Category A agents possess certain characteristics that add up to them being perceived as posing significant risks to national security. These characteristics are: (i) they can be easily disseminated or transmitted from person to person; (ii) the diseases they cause result in high mortality rates and have the potential for major public health impact; (iii) their appearance in a community might cause public panic and social disruption; and (iv) their prevention requires special action for public health preparedness.[44] *Yersinia pestis* is a zoonotic pathogen that is widely distributed in natural plague foci in Asia, Africa, western North America, and Eurasia. In the natural plague foci, there are more than 80 reservoirs with different kind of fleas as potential vectors and *Y. pestis* has at time been transmitted between reservoirs by infected fleas biting mammals. In many plague foci, it is possible for trained workers to capture rodents that carry fleas infected with *Yersinia pestis*. Using standardized techniques, a trained microbiologist can subsequently culture and isolate bacilli. In view of the many natural plague foci spread throughout the world, it is possible for terrorists to acquire *Yersinia pestis* bacilli from natural sources.[45] While the probability of NSAG using genetically engineered biological agent on a given city is very low, but the consequences of such an event on a thickly populated area would be very high.

Technological Development

The developments in biotechnology during the past three decades have brought out the qualitative and quantitative impact that biological warfare, or the threat of such warfare, can have on the armed forces, cities and towns. The revolution in genetic engineering and cheap new manufacturing methods have opened the way for more efficient production of biological warfare agents in much smaller facilities.[46] Such weapons could provide countries, or even small groups, with the capacity for launching a first strike with devastating results over wide areas. While most bacteria and viruses for biological warfare are developed from those occurring in nature, modern biotechnology makes it possible to create novel organisms against which vaccines or antibiotics are not effective.[47]

A United Nations study found that a 10-ton biological weapon could kill 20 per cent of the people and make another 50 per cent ill over an area of 100,000 square kilometres. These weapons of mass destruction could be produced with relatively simple technology in relatively small facilities.[48] Although advanced delivery systems are required for the employment of biological agents on a militarily significant scale against large civilian targets, isolated and sabotage attacks requiring only simple delivery could be very destructive in certain circumstances with some of these agents. Concerns have been expressed that massive attacks may alter the ecological relationship between man and lower animal. They may also unleash insect vectors of diseases previously latent. In certain cases, biological warfare aimed at animals (in order to disrupt meat, poultry and dairy production) could have important ecological consequences.
The Federation of American Scientists (1998) has summarised the potential capability of the new technology:

> (i) development of biological agents that have increased virulence and stability after deployment; (ii) ability to target the delivery of organisms to populations; (iii) protection of personnel against biological agents; (iv) production, by genetic modification, of pathogenic organisms from non-pathogenic strains to complicate detection of a biological agent; (v) modification of the immune response system of the target population to increase or decrease susceptibility to pathogens; and (vi) production of sensors based on the detection of unique signature molecules on the surface of

biological agents or on the interaction of the genetic materials in such organisms with gene probes.[49]

Techniques to Enhance Efficacy of Bioweapons

Scientific and technological advances within the field of biotechnology and synthetic biology have increased access and the likelihood of the use of infectious diseases as biological weapons.[50] Scientists and genetic engineers are considering several techniques to increase the efficacy of pathogens in warfare. These are: (1) Binary biological weapons: the technique involves inserting plasmids, small bacterial DNA fragments, into the DNA of other bacteria in order to increase virulence or other pathogenic properties within the host bacteria. (2) Designer genes: once complete genome sequencing is available, the scientists may be able to design pathogens by creating synthetic genes, synthetic viruses, and possibly entirely new organisms. (3) Gene therapy as a weapon: it involves repairing or replacing a gene of an organism, permanently changing its genetic composition. By replacing existing genes with harmful genes, this technique can be used to manufacture bioweapons. (4) Stealth viruses: these are viral infections that enter cells and remain dormant for an extended amount of time until triggered externally to cause disease. In the context of warfare, these viruses could be spread to a large population, and activation could either be delayed or used as a threat for blackmail (5) Host-swapping diseases: akin to naturally occurring West Nile and Ebola viruses, animal viruses could potentially be genetically modified and developed to infect humans as a potent biowarfare tactic. (6) Designer diseases: biotechnology may be used to manipulate cellular mechanisms to cause disease. For example, an agent could be designed to induce cells to multiply uncontrollably, as in cancer, or to initiate apoptosis, programmed cell death. (7) Personalized bioweapons: it may be possible in the near future to design a pathogen that targets a specific person's genome. This agent may spread through populations showing minimal or no symptoms; yet fatal to the intended target.[51] The biotechnology exists today for some of these possibilities and it is possible that some genetically engineered agents might have already been produced and stockpiled.[52]

Environmental Impacts of Biological Weapons

Humans are not the only target of biological weapons. These weapons might be used to attack herds of animals, crops or even a material supply that is vital for revenue. For example, if purposely introduced into a cattle farm, a bioweapon could kill all the animals. This attack could be carried out with relative ease and virtually no immediately visible signature. The usual method of controlling such widespread disease is mass slaughter of the infected animals, but this could be economically devastating for many countries. A population dependent on a staple crop such as rice could be rendered helpless by the introduction of a specific disease that devastated its unprotected rice crop.[53]

If a country's agricultural lands are attacked with biological weapons, serious economic consequences could follow.[54] Modern agricultural methods dictate that large areas be planted with genetically identical crops. This genetic homogeneity leaves entire regions susceptible to attack with an anti-plant agent to which the crop is not resistant. Entire crops could thus be wiped out during a single harvest season.[55] For instance, in 1944 and 1945, serious consideration was given to destroying the Japanese rice crop using a variety of fungus. Anti-material biological warfare might be attempted by an adversary because biological agents are hard to detect and identify and are readily concealed, and their use can plausibly be denied.[56] A purposely introduced organism that degrades specific metals and renders them useless could be devastating for a small country's economy. As technology continues to develop further, specific anti-material agents could be designed and create enormous problems.

A supply of standard biological agents for covert sabotage or attacks against broad-area targets would be relatively easy to produce and disseminate using commercially available equipment, such as agricultural sprayers. The environmental harm caused by biological weapons exceeds the damage caused by most explosive munitions.[57] The environmental harm caused by these weapons is measured by their capability to contaminate soil and water, and hence despoil an ecosystem for a prolonged period. Despite the legal ban on biological weapons, biological warfare will always be an attractive option for adversaries in future conflicts[58] and biotechnology will continue to have a profound impact on biological weapons.[59]

Biological weapons can have a primary, secondary or tertiary environmental impact.[60] In other words, they can directly degrade the environment, or their use can have an unintentional impact, or the response to an incident related to a biological weapon can have a negative environmental impact.

Environmental Effects of Biological Weapons (Primary Impacts)

In the last decade, there have been a few incidents in which biological agents have been used for bioremediation, environmental alteration and biocontrol. Mechanisms have been developed to use naturally occurring microbes, as well as specifically engineered ones, to clear up wastes, spills and contaminants. For example, microbes have been used as part of the response to oil spills.[61] Similarly, other microbes have been used to break down inorganic deposits surrounding economically important minerals and metals. Biological solutions to refining have proven more efficient and more economical than traditional industrial and chemical processes. Moreover, chemical pesticides, insecticides and fungicides have gradually been replaced with biological agents. The development of biological agents designed to destroy illicit drug crops has also been reported.[62]

Such developments have definite peaceful applications. However, they could also contribute to the development of weapons designed to have an environmental impact—either by degrading useful organic constructs, such as plastics, oils and lubricants, or by breaking down inorganic structures and machines that are in common use and often contain components made of metals, minerals, etc.

Biological agents can also be used for intentional attacks on animals and plants, which are key components of environmental stability. The direct application of agents designed to destroy illicit crops, if used with a host country's consent, might be legal, but the use of the same agent in a country without its consent might be considered contrary to the norm against the weaponisation of disease.

Unintentional Environmental Effects (Secondary Impacts)

In addition to those weapons that could intentionally target aspects of the environment, it is possible that biological weapons designed to target humans could have an indirect environmental impact. For example, some biological agents have been associated with weapons programmes because of certain biological characteristics. One such characteristic is their environmental stability. For instance, the causative organism of anthrax, *Bacillus anthracis*, has the ability to form endospores, which confer on this bacterium a virtually unprecedented capacity for environmental stability. These spores can survive for decades in environments that would lead to the degradation of most other agents. The release of anthrax bacteria into the environment can throw the future use of the contaminated land into jeopardy.[63] Allowing susceptible animals to graze on the land can lead to additional outbreaks of disease, effectively preventing agricultural uses. For similar reasons land contaminated with high concentrations of anthrax-causing spores would be unsuitable for human habitation and industrial or commercial use.

The production and development of biological weapons can also lead to environmental damage. The release of a cloud of weaponised *Bacillus anthracis* from the production plant in Sverdlovsk in 1979 had a significant environmental impact. Not only was a wide area contaminated with the bacterial spores due to the size of the plume released, but a large number of animals were also infected with anthrax. However, the authorities attempted to pass off the incident as an animal outbreak that had led to human infections.[64] The biological weapons facility can have a considerable impact on the local environment, and could affect the social and economic stability of the people in the surrounding area.

Environmental Effects of Responses to Biological Weapons (Tertiary Impacts)

The cleaning of a site contaminated by bioweapons could be a challenging task. The problems encountered during the cleaning of US postal sorting offices after only a handful of contaminated letters passed through them in 2001 demonstrates the scale of the problem.[65] Only chemicals can be used for decontamination in the case of open-air release of biological warfare agent. These chemicals are by their very nature toxic, as their role is to kill living organisms. Such agents need to be handled with considerable care so that they do not have a negative environmental impact. This could be challenging due to the amount of chemicals needed and the mechanism through which they must be used to coat all the external surfaces of structures, buildings, etc. Open-air release of biological agents may require the removal of large amounts of topsoil, which could have serious consequences for the local ecosystem. In the case of an anti-animal attack, it may be necessary to carry out large-scale culling to control the spread of disease. Disposing of the large number of carcasses can pose significant environmental problems.[66] The biological agent might seep into the water supply, contaminating rivers and streams, and lead to additional infections.

For example, the outbreak of foot-and-mouth disease in the UK in 2001 resulted in the death of over six million animals, of which approximately four million were culled as part of disease control. Disposing of these carcasses caused a series of environmental concerns. At first, the bodies were buried, but concerns were raised that the virus might seep into the water supply, contaminating rivers and streams, and lead to additional infections.[67] The mass grave for sheep caused another problem as blood began to bubble up through the topsoil. This led to a change in policy and burning of carcasses.

Thus, virtually all activities associated with biological weapons—

from their development and production, through their use to even the measures designed to respond to them and mitigate their effects—could have a significant environmental impact.

Food Security

Another environmental consideration in the context of biological weapons is the concept of food security. An attack on food animals and crops will not only have an environmental impact, but will also damage socio-political stability and have economic consequences. If a percentage of the national food production is contaminated, destroyed or removed from use, it might lead to fear and widespread panic.[68] It could result in a decrease in the population's calorific intake, an increase in political instability, and the erosion of trust and public confidence in the administration's ability to govern successfully. Food chains, a key element of the environment, are particularly vulnerable to attack with biological weapons, and this could have serious implications for human health. In the current socio-political context, the environmental implications of biological weapons are especially important.

There have been allegations that the British and the US forces have used a biological agent to cause the blight in an effort to hamper the production of and trade in opium in the Afghanistan region as these activities are essential for the continuation of the Taliban insurgency. *Pleospora papaveracea,* a fungus found commonly around the world, has been used to cause the leaf blight in poppies in the provinces of Helmand and Kandhar in south-western Afghanistan, a region estimated to produce up to 96 per cent of the country's opium. According to the Afghanistan opium survey of 2010 of the UN Office on Drugs and Crime (UNDOC), the use of the biological agent led to an estimated decrease of 48 per cent in the opium yield from 2009.[69]

Problem in Detection

A fundamental problem in countering the proliferation of biological and toxin weapons is the fact that much of the necessary know-how and technology is dual-use, with legitimate applications in the commercial fermentation and biotechnology industries. Many developing countries have acquired industrial microbiology plants for the production of fermented beverages, vaccines, antibiotics, ethanol (from corn or sugar cane), enzymes, yeast, vitamins, food colours and flavourings, amino acids and single-cell protein as a supplement for animal feeds. This global expansion of the civilian biotechnology industry, combined with the growing number of molecular biotechnologists trained in the West, has created much broader access to the expertise and equipment needed for the development of BTW agents. Sophisticated laboratories that might be used for the design of novel biological warfare agents are inexpensive compared with nuclear weapon plants. Moreover, biotechnology is information-intensive rather than capital-intensive, and much of the relevant data are available in the published scientific literature. For these reasons, it is virtually impossible for industrialised states to prevent the diffusion of weapon-relevant information to States suspected of proliferating biological weapons.

It has been estimated that more than 100 countries have the capability, if not necessarily the intent, to develop at least crude biological weapons based on standard microbial and toxin agents. In addition to the US, Russia, Western Europe and Japan, countries with an advanced commercial biotechnology infrastructure include Argentina, Brazil, Chile, Cuba, India, Israel, the People's Republic of China, Taiwan and Thailand. Cuba, in particular, has an advanced biotechnology industry that exports vaccines and reagents to other Latin American countries.

As an increasing number of developing countries become involved in commercial biotechnology, they may be tempted to explore its military potential. In addition, the legitimate use of toxins for medical therapy and biomedical research is becoming increasingly widespread. Botulinal toxin, for example, is used to treat abnormal muscle spasms, known as dystonias, through the selective paralysis of the spastic muscles. It has also been applied cosmetically to smooth wrinkles. Toxins such as ricin, when linked to antibodies that selectively target cancer cells, have shown promise in clinical trials as an anti-cancer therapy. Furthermore, saxitoxin and other exotic toxins that bind specifically to channels or receptors in nerve-cell membranes are valuable research tools in neuroscience. The inherently dual-use nature of many pathogens and toxins makes the prevention of research related to biological and toxin weapons extremely difficult. The consumption of toxins for medical therapy and research has already expanded to the level of hundreds of grams per year, and the anticipated growth of such therapies will eventually blur the distinction between medically useful and militarily significant quantities of toxins.

Biological warfare is the intentional use of micro-organisms and toxins, generally of microbial, plant or animal origin, to produce disease and/or death in humans, livestock and crops.[70] One of the main goals of biological warfare is to undermine and destroy economic progress and stability. The emergence of bio-economic warfare as a weapon of mass destruction can be traced to the development and use of biological agents against economic targets such as crops and livestock.

Unlike chemical or nuclear weapons, the components of biological warfare are found in nature. Thus, the presence of any quantity of these organisms in the environment does not necessarily connote a sinister motive. This is the main drawback, as biological warfare can always be carried out under the pretext that such traumatic occurrences are the result of natural circumstances that lead to outbreaks of diseases and disasters of either endemic or epidemic proportions.[71]

Biological weapons contain some form of bacteria, virus, or fungus. Examples include agents that cause typhoid, cholera, anthrax, smallpox, and yellow fever. However, some biological weapons contain toxins, which are dead substances made from living organisms. Examples include the botulism toxin and shellfish poison. Biological warfare agents are inherently indiscriminate and uncontrollable.

The intrinsic features of biological agents which influence their potential for use as weapons include infectivity, virulence, toxicity, pathogenicity, incubation period, transmissibility, lethality, and stability. Though almost every germ that exists has the potential to be a biological weapon, many are unsuitable for military applications since they are hard to produce, store, and disseminate effectively. Almost every biological agent deliberately used against humans, plants, or animals has the capability of causing widespread panic and adversely affecting a nation's perception of its national security. Anti-crop warfare, involving biological agents and herbicides, results in debilitating famines, severe malnutrition, decimation of agriculture-based economies and food insecurity. Several instances of the use of late blight of potato, anthrax, yellow and black wheat rusts and insect infestations with the Colorado beetle, the rapeseed beetle, and the corn beetle in the two World Wars have been documented. Defoliants were used as agents of anti-crop warfare in Vietnam. Cash crops that have been targeted in anti-crop warfare are sweet potato, soybean, sugar beet, cotton, wheat, and rice.

Advances in biotechnology are both exhilarating and frightening. Biological agents, which may have no useful or beneficial purpose today, may become tomorrow's wonder treatment. Who would have believed 30 years ago, for example, that botulinum toxin, one of the deadliest substances known to man, would one day become a beauty treatment used to temporarily wipe out facial wrinkles. Genetic engineering provides the potential for improved virulence by the incorporation of genes (i.e., specific strands of DNA) permitting the increased production of a pathogen or toxin. Thus, as much as 100 times more pathogens or toxins could be produced per cell than could be produced by naturally occurring strains. Cells that normally do not produce toxins may be altered to produce toxins for biological weapon development. Fungi in particular are attractive biological weapons because many of them can sporulate to form hardy, environmentally resistant structures that are quite easy to aerosolise. Genetic tools for the manipulation of fungal genes are increasingly available.

The biological warfare threat 50 years from now will be radically different due to revolutionary advances in the biosciences. Advancement in genetic engineering has opened the door to limitless germ weaponry. The pharmaceutical industry and numerous bio-processing industries produce large quantities of micro-organisms and employ genetics to modify microbial properties. It is hard to detect illicit research and development activities and easy to procure samples of many different bio-agents from a variety of sources. The global biotechnology industry is information-intensive rather than capital-intensive. Much of the data relevant to producing biological agents is widely available in the published literature and it is virtually impossible for the industrialised States to withhold this information from potential proliferants. Therefore, producing biological agents would be relatively easy and inexpensive for any nation that has a modestly sophisticated pharmaceutical industry. Moreover, nearly all the equipment needed for the large-scale production of pathogens and toxins is dual-use and widely available on the international market.

The devastation that could be brought about by the military use of biological agents can be gauged from the fact that throughout history, the inadvertent spread of infectious disease during war has caused far more casualties than has actual combat.[72] Even though biological warfare arouses general repugnance, it has never been conducted on a large scale and is banned by an international treaty. The biological and toxin warfare agents were stockpiled during both the World Wars and continue to be developed as strategic weapons—"the poor man's atomic bomb"—by a small but growing number of countries.[73]

Notes

1. Biological warfare (BW) is the intentional use of living organisms or their toxic products, to cause death, disability or damage in man, animals, or plants. The target is man, either by causing his sickness or death, or through limitation of his food supplies or other agricultural resources. Biological weapons may be defined as living organisms that insect their victims, causing incapacitation and often death; some can spread to other living entities, even those not initially attacked. Barry Kellman, "Bridging the International Trade of Catastrophic Weaponry," vol. 43, *Am. U. L. Rev*, 1994, pp. 762-63.

2. Recognition of the potential impact of infectious diseases on armies resulted in the crude use of filth, cadavers, animal carcasses, and contagion as weapons. These have been used to contaminate wells, reservoirs, and other water sources of armies and civilian populations under attack since antiquity, through the Napoleonic era, and into the twentieth century. *The Rise of CB Weapons: The Problem of Chemical and Biological Warfare.* 1971. Stockholm International Peace Research Institute (SPIRI), New York: Humanities Press, p. 1.
3. On October 5, 2001 an individual in Florida, USA, died after opening a letter containing the deadly anthrax bacteria. Subsequently, several more letters containing anthrax were received at the offices of Senators Daschle and Leahy and NBC headquarters in New York. These letters and others resulted in a total of five deaths and 18 infections, and caused widespread panic.
4. Kathryn McLaughlin and Kathryn Nixdorff (eds.), *Biological Weapons Reader*, The Bio-Weapons Prevention Project (BWPP), Geneva, 2009, available at: http://www.bwpp.org, accessed October 16, 2012.
5. "The Rise of CB Weapons," vol. I, 1971, in: *The Problem of Chemical and Biological Warfare*, Stockholm International Peace Research Institute (SIPRI), New York: Humanities Press.
6. E. M. Eitzen and E. T. Takafuji, "Historical overview of biological warfare," in: F. R. Sidell, E. T. Takafuji and D. F. Franz (eds.), *Medical Aspects of Chemical and Biological Warfare*, Washington DC: Office of the Surgeon General, 1997, pp. 415-23.
7. However, such incidents are usually not well documented, because there was little understanding that micro-organisms were the causative agents of infectious diseases. M. Wheelis, "Biological warfare before 1914," in: E. Geissler, J. E. van Courtland Moon (eds.), *Biological and Toxin Weapons: Research, Development and Use from the Middle Ages to 1945* (Oxford: Oxford University Press, 1999), pp. 8-34.
8. E. Geissler (ed.), *Biological and Toxin Weapons Today* (Oxford, England: Oxford University Press, 1986).
9. Recognition of the devastating impact that infectious diseases could have on an army resulted in the often crude but ingenious use of disease organisms and poor sanitation to weaken the enemy. The use of corpses of men and animals to pollute wells and other sources of water of the opposing forces was a common strategy. The fouling of water supplies continued to be used through the many European wars, the American Civil War, and into the twentieth century. In his *Memoirs*, General W. T. Sherman expressed discontent with Confederate troops, who were deliberately shooting farm animals in ponds so that their "stinking carcasses" would compromise the water supplies of the Union forces. Not only did such actions have a demoralising impact on the enemy, but the consumption of contaminated water probably also accounted for many undocumented epidemics of gastrointestinal disease.
10. L. A. Cole, *Clouds of Secrecy: The Army's Germ Warfare Tests Over Populated Areas* (Totowa, NJ: Rowman and Littlefield, 1988); *see also* F. F. Cartwright, *Disease and History* (New York: New American Library, 1974).
11. For more details on this part *see* M. Dando, *Bioterror and Biowarfare, A Beginner's Guide* (Oxford: One World Publications, 2006); K. Nixdorff, M. Hotz, D. Schilling, and M. Dando, *Biotechnology and the Biological Weapons Convention* (Munster: Agenda Verlag, 2003); E. Geissler, J. E. van Courtland Moon (eds.), *Biological and Toxin Weapons: Research, Development and Use from the Middle Ages to 1945* (Oxford: Oxford University Press, 1999); and M. Wheelis, L. Rozsa and M. Dando (eds.), *Deadly Cultures. Biological Weapons since 1945* (Cambridge: Harvard University Press, 2006).

12. The formulation of Koch's postulates and the development of modern microbiology during the nineteenth century afforded the capability to isolate and produce stocks of specific pathogens. Substantial evidence suggests that Germany developed an ambitious biological warfare programme during World War I, featuring covert operations in neutral trading partners of the Allies to infect livestock and contaminate animal feed to be exported to Allied forces. George W. Christopher, Theodore J. Cieslak, Julie A. Pavlin, and Edward M. Eitzen, "Biological Warfare: A Historical Perspective," vol. 278, no. 5, *JAMA*, August 6, 1997, pp. 412-17.
13. The 1899 Hague Convention was in operation during the First World War, which among other agreements banned the use of poison and poisoned weapons, so that biological warfare was clearly illegal. It has been speculated that the General Staff of the German Army interpreted the Hague Convention as prohibiting anti-human biological warfare only. The German sabotage efforts in the US involved such acts as painting cultures of bacteria onto the nostrils of horses purchased by the Allied Forces for shipment overseas. These acts were carried out by agents in the supplying country. Operations in Norway involved the introduction of small capillary tubes filled with the bacterial agent into sugar cubes, presumably to be fed to the animals. Kathryn McLaughlin and Kathryn Nixdorff (eds.), *Biological Weapons Reader,* The Bio-Weapons Prevention Project (BWPP), Geneva, 2009, available at: http://www.bwpp.org, accessed October 16, 2012.
14. On June 17, 1925, the Protocol for the Prohibition of the Use in War of Asphyxiating, Poisonous or Other Gases and of Bacteriological Methods of Warfare, commonly called the Geneva Protocol of 1925, was signed.
15. In 1932 Ishii set up the Epidemic Prevention Laboratory within the military medical school in Tokyo with the full support of the military. At the same time, Ishii set up in Manchukuo a small and secret subgroup, the Togo Unit, in the village of Bei-inho, 100 kilometres southeast of Harbin. Remoto Manchuduo was chosen primarily because researchers wanted to conduct medical experiments on humans using Chinese prisoners. The experimentation began as soon as the Togo Unit was established. Thus, research on defensive methods against biological weapons as conducted mainly in Tokyo, and research on offensive use and actual production of such weapons was carried out in Manchukuo. *See also* S. Harris, "The Japanese biological warfare programme: an overview," in: E. Geissler, J. E. van Courtland Moon (eds.), *Biological and Toxin Weapons: Research, Development and Use from the Middle Ages to 1945* (Oxford: Oxford University Press, 1999), pp. 127-52.
16. "Toxin" is a word that has no commonly accepted meaning in scientific literature. The 1972 Biological Weapons Convention (BWC) does not define toxins, but its *travaux preparatoires* show that the term is intended to mean toxic chemicals produced by living organisms. According to the Chemical Weapons Convention (CWC), toxic chemicals refers to any chemical that through its action on life processes can cause death, temporary incapacitation or permanent harm to humans or animals. Kim Coleman, *A History of Chemical Warfare* (New York: Palgrave Macmillan, 2005), p. 2.
17. Unit 731 was the secret biological warfare unit set up in the northeast of China following the Japanese invasion; the headquarters were on the outskirts of Harbin in Manchukuo. Unit 731 researched, developed, produced, and tested biological weapons. As part of its research programme, it experimented on humans and animals. The details of Unit 731's activities remained largely

unknown until the mid-1980s, when a number of documents concerning its activities came to light. Many of these documents were produced by the US military organisations, such as G-2 (Intelligence) in the Office of the Assistant Chief of Staff and the Office of the Judge Advocate General. Substantial parts of these records were information seized by the US occupation forces directly from former members of Unit 731 after the war, but these were never disclosed to the public. See also Malcolm R. Dando and Kathryn Nixdorff, "An Introduction to Biological Weapons," in Kathryn McLaughlin and Kathryn Nixdorff (eds.), *BWPP Biological Weapons Reader*, The Bio-Weapons Prevention Project (BWPP), Geneva, 2009, p. 2, available at: http://www.bwpp.org, accessed October 16, 2012.

18. Various methods for the dispersal of biological weapons were developed. It included the introduction of the pathogen into local water or food supply, as well as the use of airborne means. The Unit 731 had developed a bomb specifically designed for dispersing pathogens from aircraft. In 1939, the Unit introduced the typhoid-fever pathogen into the river in the local area. In 1940 and 1941 the Unit used aircraft to spread cotton and rice husks contaminated with the black plague at Changde and Ningbo, in central China, killing about 100 persons from the black plague in Ningbo. From the Japanese viewpoint, these casualties were insufficient, so they developed a bomb enabling more efficient dispersal from greater heights (thus making the process less hazardous for air crews, who would be subject to anti-aircraft fire if required to fly low over an area in order to deliver their payload). This bomb was not widely used, as it was not perfected until close to the end of the Second World War.
19. Sheldon H. Harris, *Factories of Death: Japanese Biological Warfare 1932-45 and the American Cover-up* (New York: Routledge, 1994).
20. V. Bojtzov and E. Geissler, "Military biology in the USSR, 1920-45," in: E. Geissler, J. E. van Courtland Moon (eds.), *Biological and Toxin Weapons: Research, Development and Use from the Middle Ages to 1945* (Oxford: Oxford University Press, 1999), pp. 153-67.
21. "An Introduction to Biological Weapons, Their Prohibition, and the Relationship to Biosafety," p. 3, The Sunshine Project, available at: www.sunshine-project.org, accessed September 12, 2012.
22. In October 1940, a Japanese plane supposedly scattered contaminated rice and fleas over the city of Chuhsien in Chekiang province. This event was soon followed by an outbreak of bubonic plague, a disease never recorded previously in Chuhsien. Several other mysterious flights of Japanese aircraft over at least 11 Chinese cities—with the dropping of grain (wheat, rice, sorghum, or corn), strange granules containing Gram-negative bacilli, and other materials suspected of being contaminated with the plague organism—took place through August 1942. Thousands are estimated to have been hospitalised and 700 became victims of artificially spread plague bacilli. E. Geissler (ed.), *Biological and Toxin Weapons Today* (Oxford, England: Oxford University Press, 1986).
23. In December 1949, 12 Japanese prisoners of war, including the Commander in Chief of the Japanese Kwantung Army, were tried by a Soviet military tribunal in Khabarovsk, USSR, for preparing and using biological weapons, including agents causing plague, typhoid, paratyphoid, and typhus. Major General Kawashima, former head of Unit 731's First, Third, and Fourth Sections, testified that no fewer than 600 prisoners were killed *yearly* at Unit 731. A report written by a doctor for the World War II Japanese military, which was uncovered in October 2011 in "a local office" of the National Diet Library in Kyoto Prefecture,

stated that 25,946 people were infected by the Japanese military's biological weapons during the 1937-45 Second Sino-Japanese War. The report states that the Imperial Japanese Army's Unit 731 released plague-infected fleas in six operations between 1940 and 1942 in several provinces including Jiangxi, Jilin and Zhejiang. "Report shows Japanese Imperial Army used bioweapons during Sino War," Jiji Press, October 15, 2011. *See also* S. Harris, *Factories of Death: Japanese Biological Warfare, 1932-1945, and the American Cover-up* (Revised Edition, London: Routledge, 2000).

24. *US Army Activity in the US Biological Warfare Programmes*, US Dept of the Army, Washington, DC: US Dept of the Army, February 24, 1977.
25. Tests were carried out in the anti-personnel programme both with simulant microbes and with pathogens. The programme included a research and development facility at Camp Detrick, Maryland (renamed Fort Detrick in 1956), testing sites in Mississippi and Utah, and a production facility in Terre Haute, Indiana. While the US did fill about 5,000 bombs with anthrax spores at a pilot plant at Camp Detrick, none were ever used. R. Harris and J. A. Paxman, *A Higher Form of Killing* (New York: Hill & Wang, 1982).
26. Ed Regis, *The Biology of Doom: The History of America's Secret Germ Warfare Project* (London: Henry Holt & Co., 1999); Judith Miller, Stephen Engelberg, and William J. Broad, *Germs: Biological Weapons and America's Secret War* (New York: Simon & Schuster, 2001).
27. US Senate, "Unauthorised Storage of Toxic Agents: Hearings before US Senate Intelligence Committee," 94th Cong, 1st Sess., Washington, DC: US Senate; September 16-18, 1975.
28. In August 1991, the first UN inspection of Iraq's biological warfare capabilities was carried out in the aftermath of the Persian Gulf War. The representatives of the Iraqi government informed the UN Special Commission that it had conducted research into the offensive use of biological warfare agents. Iraq had admitted to having loaded botulinum toxin (which causes muscular paralysis resulting in death) into 16 warheads, anthrax (which causes high fever and is usually fatal within two weeks) into five warheads, and aflotoxin (which causes liver cancer) into four warheads. It also admitted having filled 157 bombs with the same biological warfare agents and having conducted research on tricothecene micotoxins (which causes nausea, vomiting, and diarrhoea); wheat cover smut (which ruins food grains); haemorrhagic conjunctivitis (which causes extreme pain and temporary blindness); rotavirus (which causes acute diarrhoea that can lead to death); and camel pox (a version of smallpox). Jeffrey McNeely, "Environmental Impacts of Arms and War," in Lakshman D. Guruswamy (ed.), *Arms Control and the Environment* (New York: Transnational Publishers, Inc.), pp. 47-48.
29. Iraq is believed to have maintained a substantial stock of biological warfare agents and was researching different ways of weaponising them. Following revelations made by Lieutenant-General Hussein Kamel, a son-in-law of the Iraqi leader who defected to the United States in 1995, Baghdad admitted for the first time that it had produced biological agents. According to the Iraqi government, Baghdad produced 8,400 litres of anthrax, 19,000 litres of botulinum, and 2,000 litres each of aflatoxin and clostridium. A single gram of anthrax—roughly 1/30 oz—contains 1 trillion spores, or enough for 100 million fatal doses if properly dispersed. Iraq claimed that these agents were subsequently destroyed. Guy B. Roberts, *Arms Control without Arms Control: The Failure of the Biological Weapons Convention Protocol and a New Paradigm for Fighting the Threat of Biological Weapons*,

INSS Occasional Paper 49, March 2003, Colorado: USAF Institute for National Security Studies, pp. 20-21.

30. The South African programme, code-named Project Coast, was highly secret and operated through front companies. No publicly available document about Project Coast provides a clear picture of the nature and extent of the activities. Most of what is known about the programme came from material presented to the Truth and Reconciliation Commission, the trial of Wouter Basson (who was head of the programme), and in the personal recollections of some of the scientists who participated. The programme was initiated in 1981 by the Minister of Defence, General Magnus Malan for the South African Defence Force. The main biological weapons development facility was located north of Pretoria at the military front company Roodeplaat Research Laboratories (RRL), a complex built in 1986. Scientists involved in the work there have claimed that the main aim was to provide the military and police with covert assassination weapons for use against individuals perceived to be a threat to the apartheid government.
31. Stephen Burgess and Helen Purkitt, *The Rollback of South Africa's Biological Warfare Program,* INSS Occasional Paper, USAF Institute of National Security Studies, 2001.
32. An epidemic of anthrax occurred during April 1979 among people who lived or worked within a distance of 4 km in a narrow zone downwind of a Soviet military microbiology facility in Sverdlovsk (now Yekaterinburg, Russia). In addition, livestock died of anthrax along the extended axis of the epidemic zone out to a distance of 50 km. The facility was suspected by Western intelligence of being a biological warfare research facility, and the epidemic was attributed by Western analysts to the accidental airborne release of anthrax spores. The Soviets maintained that the epidemic was caused by ingestion of contaminated meat purchased on the black market. In 1992, Boris Yeltsin, the President of Russia, admitted that the facility had been part of an offensive biological weapons programme and that the epidemic had been caused by a non-intentional release of anthrax spores. George W. Christopher, Theodore J. Cieslak, Julie A. Pavlin, and Edward M. Eitzen, "Biological Warfare: A Historical Perspective," vol. 278, no. 5, *JAMA,* August 6, 1997, pp. 412-17 at p. 416. *See also* Jeanne Guillemin, *The 1979 Anthrax Epidemic in the USSR: Applied Science and Political Controversy,* Proceedings of the American Philosophical Society, March 1, 2002, p. 18; Jonathan B. Tucker and Raymond A. Zilinskas (eds.), *The 1971 Smallpox Epidemic in Aralsk, Kazakhstan, and the Soviet Biological Warfare Programme,* CNS Occasional Papers no. 9, August 2002.
33. Biological weapons were used for covert assassination during the 1970s. Ricin, a lethal toxin derived from castor beans, was weaponised by the secret service of the Soviet Union and deployed by the Bulgarian secret service. Metallic pellets that were 1.7 mm in diameter were cross drilled, filled with ricin, and sealed with wax intended to melt at body temperature. The pellets were discharged from spring-powered weapons disguised as umbrellas. These weapons were used to assassinate Georgi Markov, a Bulgarian defector living in London, and during an unsuccessful assassination attempt against another defector, Vladamir Kostov, in 1978. George W. Christopher, Theodore J. Cieslak, Julie A. Pavlin, and Edward M. Eitzen, "Biological Warfare: A Historical Perspective," vol. 278, no. 5, *JAMA,* August 6, 1997, pp. 412-17 at p. 416.
34. Israel's biological quest is reported to have begun as early as in 1948 when a unit dedicated to biological warfare was set up within the HEMED, the science department of the Israel Defence Forces (IDF), called the HEMED BEIT. The

unit later moved to its permanent location at Ness Ziona, outside Tel Aviv, where the Israel Institute of Biological Research (IIBR) was established in 1952. The IIBR has been at the forefront of conducting research into various aspects of biological (and chemical) warfare. It is pointed out that IIBR's capabilities and expertise are consistent with a full array of activities associated with a sophisticated BW (biological weapons) program. S. Samuel C. Rajiv, "Israel and Biological Weapons," vol. 1 no. 4, *Journal on Chemical and Biological Weapons*, July-September 2008, pp. 13-15.

35. Article I of the BTWC reads: Each State Party to this Convention undertakes never in any circumstances to develop, produce, stockpile, or otherwise acquire or retain: (1) Microbial or other biological agents, or toxins whatever their origin or method of production, of types and in quantities that have no justification for prophylactic, protective, or other peaceful purposes; (2) Weapons, equipment or means of delivery designed to use such agents or toxins for hostile purposes or in armed conflict.
36. Guy B. Roberts, "Arms Control without Arms Control: The Failure of the Biological Weapons Convention Protocol and a New Paradigm for Fighting the Threat of Biological Weapons," INSS Occasional Paper 49, March 2003, Colorado: USAF Institute for National Security Studies, p. 17.
37. The Biological and Toxic Weapons Convention, 1972, entered into force in 1975 and today has 163 member countries. It prohibits the development, production and stockpiling of weaponised disease agents such as anthrax, smallpox or plague. There are allegations that a number of countries in the world which have ratified the BWC have retained biological agents which can be used in biological warfare. On April 3, 1979, a mysterious explosion at the Soviet Institute of Microbiology and Virology in Sverdlovsk raised questions about the effectiveness of any weapons-control agreements. At least 66 persons, most of them civilians were believed to have been killed from anthrax, and many more were infected with *Bacillus anthracis*. For years, the Soviets maintained that this incident had not been due to an accidental release of anthrax from the military research facility, but instead was due to ingestion by the local residents of contaminated animal products. Controversy raged back and forth in the lay press over the incident. Finally, in 1992, the President of Russia, Boris Yeltsin, admitted that there had been an accidental airborne release of anthrax spores from the military research facility. J. R. Smith, "Yeltsin blames 1979 anthrax on germ warfare efforts," *Washington Post*, June 16, 1992. *See also* "The US Army on an anthrax buying spree: Getting ready for Bio Warfare?" *The Times of India*, New Delhi, September 6, 2005, p. 21.
38. Biological weapons may contain either replicating or non-replicating agents. Although hundreds of naturally occurring bacteria, viruses, and toxins, as well as "designer compounds," could potentially be considered agents by an aggressor, a finite number of these are actually useful as area weapons on the battlefield. The agents' utility is limited by ease of production, stability, and infectivity (bacteria and viruses), or toxicity/effectivity (toxins and other physiologically active materials). *Bacillus anthracis*, for example, is often touted as the best of bacterial agents. Stability of the spore form and ease of production are its greatest strengths as weapons material. Among viral agents, Venezuelan equine encephalitis virus can be easily grown, making it a potential incapacitating agent. The bacterial agents that cause tularaemia, Q fever, and brucellosis are infective at extremely low doses (1-10 organisms per person). Finally, the extraordinary toxicity (1,000 to 10,000 times more toxic than the nerve agents)

of the staphylococcal enterotoxins as incapacitants and the botulinum toxins as lethal agents makes them candidates for weaponisation.

39. In September 1978, the Bulgarian secret police (with technical assistance from the Soviet KGB) assassinated Georgi Markov, an exiled Bulgarian dissident living in London, by firing a tiny metal ball filled with ricin into his thigh from a pellet-gun concealed inside an umbrella; Markov died two days later.
40. Non-protein toxins include tetrodotoxin (produced by a puffer fish), saxitoxin (made by marine algae known as dinoflagellates, which are taken up and concentrated by clams and mussels), ciguatoxin and microcystin (synthesised by microscopic algae), palytoxin (made by a soft red Hawaiian coral), and batrachotoxin (secreted by poisonous frogs indigenous to western Colombia).
41. N. C. Livingstone and J. D. J. Douglass, *CBW: The Poor Man's Atomic Bomb*, Institute for Foreign Policy Analysis (Cambridge, Mass: 1984); *see also* S. Murphy, A. Hay, and S. Rose, *No Fire No Thunder: The Threat of Chemical and Biological Weapons* (New York: Monthly Review Press, 1984).
42. Erik Frinking Erik, Tim Śweijs, Paul Sinning, Eva Bontje, Christopher Frattina della Frattina, and Mercedes Abdalla, The Increasing Threat of Biological Weapons: handle with Sufficient and Proportionate Care, *The Hague* Centre for Strategic Studies, 2016, p. 6.
43. NIAID Emerging Infectious Diseases/Pathogens, *NIAID*, available at: https://www.niaid.nih.gov/topics/biodefenserelated/biodefense/pages/cata.aspx, accessed 20 June 2017.
44. Centre for Disease Control and Prevention, "Bioterrorism Agents/Diseases", 2000, available at: http://emergency.cdc.gov/agent/agentlist-category.asp.
45. *Yersinia pestis*, Biological Warfare, and Bioterrorism, *CBW Magazine*, Vol. 10, issue 1, January-June 2017.
46. There is growing, elusive, more technologically advanced set of bioweapons threats due to the increasing pace and infusion of biotechnology. "Cornell University professor says bio-weapons threat is increasing," available at: http://bioprepwatch.com/news/210908-cornell-universityprofessor-says-bioweapons-threat-isincreasing, accessed March 28, 2010. Gene-splicing techniques might facilitate weaponisation by rendering micro-organisms more stable during dissemination (e.g., resistant to high temperatures and ultraviolet radiation). Biological agents might also be genetically modified to make them more difficult to detect by immunological means and insusceptible to standard vaccines or antibiotics. At the same time, genetic engineering techniques could be used to develop and produce protective vaccines more safely and rapidly. Cloning toxin genes in bacteria makes it possible to produce formerly rare toxins in large quantities.
47. A Russian scientist claimed at a conference on biological weapons in Stockholm in May 1998 that Russia had developed a biological weapon that was a combination of anthrax and marberg virus altered to target only males, sparing women and children. D. MacKenzie, "Back to Plague us," *New Scientist*, July 25, 1998, p. 65.
48. A major biological arsenal can be built in a room of only 25 square metres, with about $10,000 worth of equipment. L. A. Cole, *The Eleventh Plague: The Politics of Biological and Chemical Warfare* (New York: W. H. Freeman, 1997).
49. Federation of American Scientists (FAS), Biological Warfare Agent Production, 1998. Available at: http://www.fas.org/nuke/intro/bw/production.htm, accessed June 23, 2011.
50. The information on the genetic composition of biological agents, the equipment for synthesizing and sequencing genomes has become more sophisticated and

easily accessible. There are number on non-profit organizations which provide free access for storing, managing and sharing research data and know-how. They share standardized genetically encoded function for free and are open to companies, institutions and individuals. Through these organizations, anyone can obtain knowledge, skills and equipment to develop biological warfare agents. Few organizations have also generated a Registry of Standard Biological Parts, from where DNA plates can be purchased. Experts envisage the possibility for the NSAGs to use commercial drones for spreading biological warfare agents. Biohacking groups are now experimenting with DNA as software they can manipulate the way hackers did with computers and the Internet. They could use these processes to create killer bugs or provide training for bioterrorists. Improvised weapons: Hell's Kitchens, *The Economist*, 21 May 2016, Print edition.

51. Foley Mackenzie, Genetically Engineered Bioweapons: A New Breed of Weapons for Modern Warfare, *Applied Sciences*, Winter 2013.
52. Ainscough Michael J., Next Generation Bio-weapons: The Technology of Genetic Engineering Applied to Biowarfare and Bioterrorism, The Counter-proliferation Paper, Future Warfare Series No. 14, Air War College, Maxwell Air Force Base, Alabama, USA, April 2002, p. 17.
53. S. Murphy, A. Hay and S. Rose, *No Fire No Thunder: The Threat of Chemical and Biological Weapons* (New York, NY: Monthly Review Press, 1984), p. 145.
54. The term "agricultural terrorism" has been used recently for the threat of a biological attack against an agricultural target, including crops and livestock, in an effort to cause widespread damage to or destruction of the target. Corrie Brown, "Agricultural terrorism: A cause for concern," vol. 5, nos. 1-2, *The Monitor*, pp. 6-8.
55. B. Gripstad (ed.), *Biological Warfare Agents* (Stockholm, Sweden: Swedish National Defence Research Institute, 1986).
56. Anti-material agents are organisms that degrade some item of material. Most of the material damage done by micro-organisms is a result of natural contamination that grows only under special conditions of temperature and relative humidity. Fungi, for example, damage fabrics, rubber products, leather goods, and foodstuffs. Some bacteria produce highly acidic compounds that cause pitting in metals; these agents could create potential problems with stockpiled material. B. Roberts (ed.), *Biological Weapons: Weapons of the Future?* (Washington, DC: The Centre for Strategic and International Studies, 1993).
57. Barry Kellman, "The Chemical Weapons Convention: A Verification and Enforcement Model for Determining Legal Responsibility for Environmental Harm Caused by War," in Jay E. Austin, and Carl E. Bruch (eds.), *The Environmental Consequences of War: Legal, Economic and Scientific Perspectives* (Cambridge: Cambridge University Press), p. 579.
58. B. Roberts (ed.), *Biological Weapons: Weapons of the Future?* (Washington, DC: The Centre for Strategic and International Studies, 1993).
59. *Towards a Food-Secure Asia and Pacific Regional Strategic Framework for Asia and the Pacific*, 2004. FAO of the United Nations regional office for Asia and the Pacific. *See also* Opi Outhwaite, "The International Legal Framework for Bio-security and the Challenges Ahead," vol. 19 (2), *RECIEL*, 2010, pp. 207-10.
60. Biological weapons can clearly have an environmental impact. This can be categorised as the intent of an attack (primary impact), an unintentional side effect of an attack (secondary impact) or an unintentional side effect of the response to an attack (tertiary impact). Kathryn McLaughlin, "Biological Weapons as an Environmental Issue," in Kathryn McLaughlin and Kathryn

Nixdorff (eds.), *Biological Weapons Reader*, The Bio-Weapons Prevention Project (BWPP), Geneva, 2009, p. 65.

61. R. C. Prince, "Petroleum spill bioremediation in marine environments," vol. 19 (4), *Critical Reviews in Microbiology*, 1993, pp. 217-42.
62. G. E. de Vries, "*Fusarium* considered to kill coca plants," vol. 5, *Trends in Plant Science*, 2000, p. 417; Sunshine Project Backgrounder No.14, Risks of Using Biological Agents to Eradicate Drug Plants, September 2005, available at http://www.sunshine-project.org/publications/bk/bk14.html, accessed January 8, 2013.
63. For example, Gruinard Island—a small island located off the North West Scottish coast was used as an anthrax field testing site by the UK government in the 1940s, which was quarantined for 48 years before decontamination attempts were eventually successful. For a brief history of the use and subsequent decontamination of Gruinard Island, *see* G. S. Pearson, "Gruinard Island returns to civil use," Vol. 1, No. 86, *ASA Newsletter*, 2001.
64. M. Meselson, J. Guillemin, M. Hugh-Jones, A. Langmuir, I. Popova, A. Shelokov and O. Yampolskaya, "The Sverdlovsk anthrax outbreak of 1979," vol. 266, *Science*, 1994, pp. 1202-1208.
65. A. Oppenheimer, "The challenge of anthrax decontamination," *Jane's News Online*, June 3, 2004. Available at http://www.andyoppenheimer.com/articles/Jane's%20Chem-Bio%20Web%20anthrax%20decon.htm.
66. Kathryn McLaughlin, "Biological Weapons as an Environmental Issue," in Kathryn McLaughlin and Kathryn Nixdorff (eds.), *Biological Weapons Reader*, The Bio-Weapons Prevention Project (BWPP), Geneva, 2009, available at: http://www.bwpp.org, accessed October 16, 2012.
67. Royal Society, "Infectious Diseases in Livestock," July 16, 2002. Available at: http://royalsociety.org/inquiry/index.html, accessed January 12, 2013.
68. J. M. Katz, V. Veguilla, J. A. Belser, T. R. Maines, N. Van Hoeven, C. Pappas, K. Hancock and T. M. Tumpey, "The public health impact of avian influenza viruses," vol. 84, *Poultry Science*, 2009, pp. 872-79.
69. UN Office on Drug and Crime and Afghanistan Ministry of Counter Narcotics, *Afghanistan Opium Survey 2010: Summary Findings*, UNDOC: Vienna, September 2010. The report of the UNDOC's analysis of the Afghanistan poppy blight has not been made public. Hart John and Peter Clevesting, "Reducing Security Threats from Chemical and Biological Weapons," *SIPRI Yearbook 2011* (Oxford: Oxford University Press), p. 403.
70. Edgar J. DaSilva, "Biological warfare, bioterrorism, bio-defence and the biological and toxin weapons convention," vol. 2, no. 3, *EJB Electronic Journal of Biotechnology*, December 15, 1999. Available at: http://www.ejb.org/content/vol2/issue3/full/2/, accessed October 17, 2012.
71. Edgar J DaSilva, "Biological warfare, bioterrorism, bio-defence and the biological and toxin weapons convention," vol. 2, no. 3, *EJB Electronic Journal of Biotechnology*, December 15, 1999. Available at: http://www.ejb.org/content/vol2/issue3/full/2/, accessed October 17, 2012.
72. John P. Heggers, "Microbial Invasion—The Major Ally of War (Natural Biological Warfare)," vol. 143, no. 6, *Military Medicine*, June 1978, pp. 390-94.
73. Jessica Eve Stem, "Will Terrorists Turn to Poison?" vol. 37, no. 3, *Orbis*, Summer 1993; *see also* The US Congress, Office of Technology Assessment, *Technology Against Terrorism: The Federal Efforts*, OTA-ISC-481 (Washington DC: US Government Printing Office, July 1991), pp. 21-22.

2 C

CHEMICAL WEAPONS

Chemical weapons are chemical agents, whether gaseous, liquid, or solid, which are employed because of their direct toxic effects on humans, animals, and plants.[1] They inflict damage when inhaled, absorbed through the skin, or ingested in food or drink.[2] Chemical agents become weapons when they are placed in artillery shells, landmines, aerial bombs, missile warheads, mortar shells, grenades, spray tanks, or any other means of delivering the agents to designated targets. Chemical warfare[3] agents cause injuries directly by irritation, burning, or asphyxiation, and indirectly by contaminating the ground so that it cannot be safely occupied, creating smoke screens to obscure operations or reduce the accuracy of an enemy's firepower, and damaging an enemy's equipment by incendiary action. They are intended for use in military operations to kill, seriously injure, or incapacitate people or destroy plants and the soil. Since World War I, several types of chemical agents have been developed into weapons. These include choking agents, blister agents, blood agents, nerve agents, incapacitants, riot-control agents, and herbicides.

Historical

Throughout history, people have used plant poisons and chemicals to kill political rivals, despotic rulers, prisoners, and even unwanted spouses.[4] The use of chemical weapons in armed conflict dates back to antiquity, when warring forces frequently poisoned the water supplies of their adversaries. For example, the Athenians poisoned the wells of their rivals as early as 600 BC. Thucydides describes that the Spartans in the Peloponnesian War in 429 BC set a large quantity of shrubs mixed with sulphur and resin on fire in order to diminish the defence of the city of Platea. However, that attempt failed because the wind had changed to the opposite direction, so that the attacker suffered a lot of losses.[5] During the Middle Ages, Genghis Khan's Mongolian forces employed chemical warfare when they catapulted burning pitch and sulfur into cities they besieged. When Belgrade was defended against the Turks in 1456, arsenic smoke clouds were used.[6]

In 1811, British naval officers observed that fumes from sulphur kilns in Sicily destroyed all vegetation and animal life for a considerable distance around the kilns. Based on this observation a memorial was presented to the Prince Regent in 1812 by the Admiralty recommending the adaptation of sulphur fumes to warfare. The Prince referred the recommendation to three commissioners. After studying the idea they rendered a favourable report. Admiral Lord Dundonald, with knowledge of the favourable report of 1812, produced a concrete plan to capture the Russian forts by suffocating the Russian garrison with sulphur fumes. However, a new committee, appointed by the English Government to examine Admiral Dundonald's scheme, concluded that the effects of sulphur fumes were so horrible that no honourable combatant would use such means. The committee, therefore, recommended that the scheme should not be adopted and that Lord Dundonald's account of it should be destroyed.[7] It was not until the siege of Sevastopol, during the Crimean War (1854-1855), that the immediate use of sulphur was contemplated.

There were several other proposals to initiate chemical warfare to assist the Allies to solve the stalemate during the siege of Sevastopol. In 1854, Lyon Playfair, a British chemist, proposed a cacodyl cyanide artillery shell for use primarily against enemy ships. The British ordnance department rejected the proposal terming it is "as bad a mode of warfare as poisoning the wells of the enemy." The value of chemicals as war weapons had attracted the serious speculations of military minds during the American Civil war, but no progress was made in his field because of the then underdeveloped state of the chemical industry.[8] John Doughty, a New York City schoolteacher, was one of the first to propose the use of chlorine as a chemical warfare agent. He envisioned a 10-inch artillery shell filled with liquid chlorine that, when released, would produce many cubic feet of chlorine gas. Doughty's plan was, however, never approved.

In 1887, the Germans apparently considered using lacrimators (tear agents) for military purposes. The French also began a rudimentary chemical warfare programme with the development of a tear-gas grenade containing ethyl bromoacetate, and proposals to fill artillery shells with chloropicrin. Two wars at the turn of the nineteenth century also saw limited use of chemical weapons. During the Boer War in 1900, British troops fired picric acid-filled shells, though it had little effect.[9] During the Russo–Japanese War (1904-1905), Japanese soldiers threw arsenal rag torches into Russian trenches.

Chemical Weapons: World War I

The First World War (1914-1918)[10] changed the face of warfare with the use of chemicals on a massive scale.[11] On the battlefield of Ypres, in Belgium, Germany launched the first large-scale use of poison gas in a surprise attack on April 22, 1915, causing 15,000 casualties and 5,000 deaths.[12] The success of the attack was more significant than the Germans expected. In May 1915, German troops released 263 tons of chlorine gas from 12,000 cylinders along a 7.5-mile line, killing 6,000 Russian soldiers at Bolimore. Two more gas cloud attacks on the same positions caused 25,000 more Russian casualties.

The same month, the British and the French began planning to retaliate with chemical weapons.[13] In the early stages of the war, the British examined their own chemical technology for battlefield use. They initially investigated tear agents, but later turned to more toxic chemicals.[14] The Allied response to the chemical attacks evolved into three general categories: (i) protective devices for the troops, (ii) toxic gases of their own, and (iii) weapons to deliver the toxic gases to the enemy lines. In September 1915, the Allied forces launched their own chlorine attack against the Germans at Loos. This initiated a deadly competition to develop better protective masks, more potent chemicals, and long-range delivery systems to disperse the agents more widely.[15] The Germans shifted to phosgene to replace the less-effective chlorine, and in July 1917, they introduced mustard agent to provide a persistent vesicant that could attack the body in places not protected by gas masks.[16] To further complicate defensive actions, both sides mixed agents and experimented with camouflage materials to prevent quick identification. As the war ground on, both sides developed new offensive agents of ever-greater potency, including phosgene and mustard gas.[17]

By the war's end, both sides had used massive quantities of chemical weapons, causing an estimated 1.3 million casualties, including 91,000 fatalities, and many of the survivors had been blinded or scarred for life.[18] On several occasions, the wind carried clouds of poison gas as far as 30 kilometres behind the front-line trenches, injuring and killing scores of noncombatants.[19] The Russian army suffered about 500,000 of these casualties, and the British had 180,000 wounded or killed by chemical arms. One-third of all US casualties in World War I were from mustard and other chemical gases, roughly the ratio for all participants combined. During the War, chemists on both sides investigated over 3,000 chemical substances for potential use as weapons. Of these only 30 were used in combat and only 12 achieved the desired military results, including mustard gas, which caused perhaps 90 per cent of all the chemical casualties from that conflict. Other choking gas agents used included chlorine, phosgene, diphosgene, and chloropicrin. The blood agents included hydrogen cyanide, cyanogen, chlorine, and cyanogen bromide. Arsenic-laced sneeze agents were also used, as were tear gases like ethyl bromoacetate, bromoacetone, and bromobenzyl cyanide. All the great powers involved had developed not only offensive chemical arms[20] but also crude gas masks and protective over-garments to defend themselves against chemical weapon attacks.

The main chemical agents used (in tons) during the First World War were as follows.[21]

	Chlorine	Phosgene	Mustard
Germany	58,100	18,100	7,600
France	12,500	5,700	2,000
Britain	20,800	1,400	500
United States	2,400	1,400	900

After the First World War, the German chemist Fritz Haber continued his work on poisonous gas under the cover of "pest control," as the Germans had been forbidden to produce gas weaponry by Article 171 of the Treaty of Versailles in 1919.[22]

The large-scale use of toxic chemicals during the First World War resulted in some 1.3 million casualties. The horrific casualties helped persuade many world leaders of the need to ban the use of chemical weapons. It inspired the international community to negotiate the 1925 Geneva Gas Protocol.[23] The Protocol banned the use in war of asphyxiating and poisonous gases but did not ban the production, acquisition, stockpiling, or transfer of such arms, and, critically, it did not contain any verification procedure to ensure compliance. Several other countries joined the treaty but reserved the right to retaliate if their enemies resorted to chemical warfare.[24]

British Garrison at Iraq

In June 1919, after the birth of Iraq,[25] a full-scale rebellion broke out and the British garrison was taken by surprise as the revolt spread throughout the lower Euphrates valley. Before the outbreak of the rebellion, the RAF had asked Churchill for permission to use chemical weapons against the Arabs as an experiment. Churchill, then Secretary of State for War, had sought the opinion of experts as to whether it would be possible to use some kind of asphyxiating bombs calculated to cause disablement against the tribes. He was informed by the military authorities that poison gas, being extremely volatile, would be more useful against the hilly Kurdish redoubts in hot and open areas. Eventually poison gas and incendiary weapons were used by the RAF, resulting in the killing of 8,000 to 9,000 Kurds and Iraqis and the collapse of the rebellion. It seems likely that Britain used the suppression of the Iraqi revolt trying out new chemical weapons. The British Air Ministry's list of available weapons for warfare in 1920 included, "phosphorus bombs, war rockets, metal crows-feet (to maim livestock), man-killing shrapnel, liquid fire and delay action bombs."[26]

Italo–Ethiopian War

During the 1935-36 Second Italo–Ethiopian War, both armies committed atrocities.[27] However, the war is remembered for Italy's successful use of chemical weapons, primarily the blister agent sulphur mustard. The use of sulphur mustard was particularly effective because the Ethiopian soldiers wore traditional light desert garb that exposed the skin. In addition, Ethiopian soldiers typically wore sandals or were barefoot. In December 1935 Italian aircraft dropped tear-gas grenades and asphyxiating gas over the Takkaze Valley in north-eastern Ethiopia. Italy controlled the air and initially dropped sulphur mustard air bombs but later shifted to the use of aerial spray tanks.[28]

Sulphur mustard air bombs reportedly caused most of the chemical weapon casualties. The use of sulphur mustard played an important role in shifting the momentum of fighting in favour of the Italian forces and in demoralising the Ethiopian forces. Its use resulted in many long-lasting, painful injuries and in a significant number of deaths. Italy also used chemical weapons in the Battle of Shire, the Battle of Maychew and in attacks on the remnants of Ethiopian forces in the Lake Ashangi region in April 1936.[29] By May 1936, Italy's army completely routed the Ethiopian army. According to Soviet estimates, about 15,000 Ethiopian casualties in the war were caused by chemical weapons.[30]

Japanese Invasion of China

The next war that drew the interest of chemical warfare experts was the Japanese invasion of China in 1937. The Japanese, in addition to their biological work, had an extensive chemical weapons programme and were producing agents and munitions in large numbers by the late 1930s. During the war with China, Japanese forces reportedly used chemical shells, tear gas grenades, and lacrimatory candles, often mixed with smoke screens. By 1939, the Japanese escalated to mustard agent and lewisite.[31] The weapons proved very effective against the untrained and unequipped Chinese troops, who retreated even when the Japanese used just smoke, thinking it was a chemical attack.[32]

World War II

By World War II, Germany and Japan had made tremendous progress in the innovation of agents toxic to the nervous system. During the war, Germany produced the G-series nerve agents, such as tabun and sarin, which also had superior dispersal characteristics. These new nerve agents were not used during the war though, and the Allies discovered them and developed countermeasures only after the conflict.[33] Japan loaded mustard agent, a mustard–lewisite mixture, and phosgene in shells and bombs and gained experience in their use during their attacks on China. They also filled hydrogen cyanide in mortar and artillery shells, and in glass grenades. Approximately 146,000 tons of chemical agents were produced by the US between 1940 and 1945. There is no record of chemical warfare among World War II belligerents other than that of the Japanese.[34] The Axis forces in Europe and the Allied forces adopted no-first-use policies, though each side was ready to respond in kind if the other acted first. Indeed, all the major powers developed extensive chemical warfare capabilities as a deterrent to their use.

The worst chemical weapons disaster of World War II was caused by the explosion of the US merchant ship *John Harvey*, which was carrying 100 tons of mustard gas during a German bombing raid of Bari, a port on the coast of Italy. More than 1,000 military personnel, and an even larger number of civilians lost their lives. Following the occupation of Germany and Japan, the Allies initiated a sea-dumping and weapons disposal programme to eliminate the large stockpiles of captured chemical agents.[35]

Post-World War II

The 1960s was a period of experimentation in using incapacitating and psychedelic agents that impaired combat performance without being lethal. During the Cold War, the UK invented the V-series nerve agents, which were weaponised by the US and the Soviet Union. V-series nerve agents are toxic in even smaller doses than G-agents and are persistent in the environment. They were considered an ideal area-denial weapon by both the western powers and the Eastern Bloc. The US had amassed a huge arsenal of chemical weapons and had begun production of a new nerve gas. In 1959, the Americans developed a new chemical weapon and designated it "VX." It was the deadliest nerve agent created after the Second World War. A small amount of VX, absorbed through the skin, could kill by severely disrupting the nervous system. In addition, the Americans developed chemical weapons delivery systems, including artillery shells, the M-23 gas landmine, the M-55 unguided gas rocket and the MK-116 "Weteye" air-dropped gas bomb. The US also developed a chemical and named it BZ, nicknamed "Agent Buzz," which caused its victims to vomit, stagger around and suffer memory lapses and hallucinations.[36] The Soviet Union continued to increase the size of its chemical stockpile during the 1970s and 1980s, and initiated a massive programme named "Foliant" to produce newer and deadlier agents. After World War II, chemical weapons were employed on a number of occasions.

Korean War

Most of the US chemical arsenals were hidden from public view and the use of chemical weapons in the Korean War[37] was never acknowledged by the American government. In June 1950, with the onset of the Korean War, the American Chemical Corps participated in its first military action since 1918. The Corps supplied the army chemical capability and defensive equipments. The chemical corps commanders favoured the use of chemical weapons particularly to offset the Korean's superior numbers. However, there was a fear that in retaliation, the Soviet Union would provide the Chinese and North Koreans with chemical warfare materials. There were allegations by the North Koreans and the Chinese that the American forces employed chemical and biological weapons on the battlefield. There are confirmed reports[38] that the American Chemical Corps did used riot control agents including CS gas, to quell riots by prisoners of war. In addition, napalm and phosphorus bombs were dropped in North Korea to incinerate every city north of the 38th parallel.[39] An official Chinese news agency reported on March 5, 1951 that in the early afternoon of February 21, two US aircraft dropped bombs charged with "poison gas of an asphyxiating type" on north Korean positions 20 miles south-east of Seoul.[40] The US also used anti-plant agents on a very minor scale in the Korean War.[41]

Vietnam War

The Vietnam War was a testing ground for new types of weaponry. In 1961, the US began the "experimental" use of the highly toxic herbicide dioxin (Agent Orange), in South Vietnam as a weapon to exterminate forests and crops. The herbicide was named "Agent Orange" after the orange bands painted on the drums it was shipped in.[42] The initial object was to undermine the economic resources of the National Liberation Front (NLF) movement.[43] The defoliation programme began with the intention of merely destroying the economic base of the NLF, but it was soon expanded into a critical aspect of the shift from ground to air power in South Vietnam. Besides destroying crops, defoliants were used to destroy the forest canopy that hid the NLF forces from detection by air.

Agent Orange penetrated the waxy covering of leaves to poison the entire plant. Other herbicides used in Vietnam were also known by their barrel colour, such as Agent Blue and Agent White. Agent Orange contained extremely toxic byproducts known as dioxins. Exposure to dioxins has been associated with severe birth defects and certain rare cancers in humans. By destroying trees and crops, the US military hoped to expose the hide-outs of the National Liberation Front and the North Vietnamese army. About 12 per cent of South Vietnam was stripped of foliage. Toxins that leaked into the land and rivers also had long-term effects on the food supply of the entire country.

Herbicides damage the soil directly. They destroy the micro-organisms that prevent erosion and improve fertility, and remove humus (decomposing vegetation on the forest floor), turning the soil into a hard, rock-like substance. It was reported that chemicals entering the Mekong River eliminated aquatic life. The damage to livestock, especially swine and poultry was severe. The interruption of food chains caused the near extinction of several rare species of wild life. Birds, bats and insects, which played an important role in pollination and dispersal of seeds in the forests were killed, by toxins as well as due to the end of a reliable food supply. This, in turn, affected the survival of the forest plants and resulted in reduced soil fertility.

Tens of thousands of the US soldiers and the Vietnamese were exposed to herbicides, which can affect people through contaminated food, poisoned water, inhaled air or by direct skin contact. The results were described by a Vietnamese: "Those who were in the sprayed areas found it difficult to breathe, difficult to stay awake, got fever and were thirsty. These symptoms hit mainly the older people, children, and pregnant women. Many vomited and had colic type pains. Others got muscle paralysis and their hands and feet became numb. Still others reported loss of hair, chest pain, pain in the back, and bleeding in the esophagus."[44] Women often suffered disturbances in the menstrual cycle and many cases of miscarriage were reported.[45] The operation that was condemned in 1964 by the Federation of American Scientists as "an unwarranted experiment in chemical warfare" nevertheless continued until the early 1970s, when it was reported that Agent Orange was causing birth defects.[46]

Official American reports stated that five million acres of land, or 12 per cent of South Vietnam, was "sterilised." In the first two months of 1969 alone, some 37 of the 44 provinces of South Vietnam were sprayed destroying more than 905,000 hectares of rice, orchards and other crops. According to Vietnamese estimates, between late 1961 and October of 1969, 43 per cent of the arable land and 44 per cent of the total forest area of South Vietnam were sprayed at least once and in many cases twice or three times with herbicides.[47] Large populated areas in the delta were sprayed as well, including the outskirts of Saigon. Approximately 70 million litres of herbicides were sprayed over the country's forests between 1962 and 1971, dousing 1.7 million hectares often several times over.[48] Over 1,293,000 people were directly contaminated.[49]

By an estimate, the US used between seven and nine million gallons of chemical defoliants in Vietnam. In September 1966, it was reported that cacodylic acid, an organic arsenic-containing compound toxic to man, was also used in Vietnam. Besides defoliants, more than 7,000 tons of other poisonous gases were used between 1964 and 1969.[50] The most common were CS-1 and CS-2; however, other gases affecting the central nervous system were also used. The US Air Force also dropped a total of 6,162,000 tons of bombs and other ordnance from 1964 to August 15, 1973. The US Navy and Marine Corps aircraft expended another 1,500,000 tons of bombs and ordnance.[51]

Table I: Major Chemical agents sprayed from the air in the Indo-China War[52]

Agent	Spray Period (approximate)	Amount sprayed (10^6 kg)	Area sprayed (10^6 ha)	Area sprayed (per cent)
Orange	1962-1970	57.0	1.6	12
White	1966-1971	22.8	0.7	5
Blue	1962-1970	10.7	0.3	2
CS	1964-1970	9.0	5.0	37
Malathion	1967-1972	3.0	6.0	44
Total	**1962-1972**	**102.5**	**13.6**	**100**

Of all the herbicides used, 75 per cent was used in South Vietnam. Mangrove forests, a vital part of the tropical ecosystem, were decimated. This led to erosion and a gradual wearing away of the shoreline. It has been estimated that more than 300,000 acres of mangrove forests were lost through the use of defoliants and napalm, severely stressing the area's mangrove ecosystem. In addition to the damage done to forests, crops were also sprayed. Following a long tradition of crop destruction aimed at breaking the will of the people, the US military often deliberately ravaged farmland, crops, stores of harvested crops, garden plots, and fruit trees.

The Vietnam War was different from the previous wars of the twentieth century in that the destruction of key components of the country's physical environment became a deliberate military strategy. The Vietnamese physical landscape was intentionally disturbed by the following three activities: (i) explosive munitions, (ii) herbicides, and (iii) land-clearing operations by specialised bulldozers called Rome Plows. Although artillery bombardment was heavily utilised in this war, it was aerial bombardment which inflicted damage to the forests and the enemy on a scale never before accomplished.[53]

After 1967, there was a recession in the overall use of chemicals in the War. Four factors were responsible for this: (i) the available commercial sources of anti-plant chemicals were becoming exhausted by the increasing military demand; (ii) a certain group within the US was becoming increasingly alarmed that anti-plant operations might undermine their agriculturally independent work by alienating farmers and other crop growers; (iii) the scientific community was expressing growing concern that the anti-plant programme might permanently distort an important sector of the Vietnamese ecology; and (iv) the view that the combat use of anti-plant chemicals was contrary to the international laws of war was gaining ground.[54]

Other Conflicts

In the early 1960s, while the US was still involved in Vietnam, chemical weapons were used in the civil war in Yemen. Egyptian military forces, participating in the civil war between royalists and republicans, used chemical weapons, such as nerve and mustard agents, in 1963, 1965, and 1967. During the Soviet intervention in the Afghan War (1978-92), chemical arms, such as mustard and incapacitating agents, were used against the Mujahideen rebels. During this lengthy conflict, frequent allegations were made of the use of a chemical known as Blue-X, which was said to cause instant immobilisation, the victim remaining in place for a number of hours before recovering. The use of other, more lethal agents was also alleged, but no definitive evidence was found.

In 1987, there were allegations of Libya using mustard munitions against rebels in Chad. The United Nations responded by sending a team of observers to Yemen, but it concluded that there was no evidence of a chemical attack.[55]

The most widespread and most open use of chemical weapons on a battlefield in recent years was by Iraq in its conflict with Iran (1980-1988). Iraq commenced a ground assault on Iran, and launched air strikes on strategic targets. However, Iranian resistance proved strong, and all Iraqi troops withdrew from the occupied portions of Iran by early 1982. Iran then initiated a series of offensives that Iraq responded to with the deployment of chemical weapons in 1983. The most infamous attack occurred on March 16, 1988 in the town of Halabja, where up to 5,000 Kurdish civilians and Iranian soldiers died from the effects of sarin nerve gas and mustard gas.[56] The continuing use by Iraq of chemical weapons and missile attacks against civilian areas, forced Iran to accept a cease-fire agreement in July 1988.[57]

The eight-year war resulted in the deaths of an estimated 600,000 Iranians and 400,000 Iraqis, created over one million refugees and cost the two countries billions of dollars. It also destroyed the once extensive date palm forests along the Shatt al-Arab estuary. However, no formal independent studies have been conducted to determine the long-term environmental impacts and risks to human health from the war.[58] At the time of the attacks, both countries were parties to the 1925 Geneva Protocol, a treaty banning the use of chemical weapons against another contracting party.[59]

After the Gulf War, the United Nations Special Commission oversaw the incineration of approximately 40,000 Iraqi chemical weapons. A bunker containing thousands of possibly war-damaged weapons was also sealed. After the US invasion of Iraq in 2003, no stockpile of chemical weapons or dedicated facilities for their manufacture was found in Iraq, contrary to US contention before the invasion. Some chemical rounds were found among the arms storage sites in Iraq, but they were thought to be left over from the Iran-Iraq War.[60] Upon becoming a signatory to the CWC in 2009, Iraq acknowledged its obligation to dispose of its remaining damaged weapons.

It has been reported that the Central Intelligence Agency (CIA), working with American troops during the occupation of Iraq, repeatedly purchased nerve-agent rockets from a secretive Iraqi seller to ensure that old chemical weapons remaining in Iraq did not fall into the hands of terrorists or militant groups. The extraordinary arms purchase plan, known as Operation Avarice, began in 2005 and continued into 2006, and the American military deemed it a nonproliferation success. It led to the United States' acquiring and destroying at least 400 Borak rockets, one of the internationally condemned chemical weapons that

Saddam Hussein's Baathist government manufactured in the 1980s but that were not accounted for by the UN inspections mandated after the 1991 Persian Gulf War.[61]

There are confirmed reports that chemical agents are still being used by States[62] and non-state actors across the world.[63] Since 2009, a large number of attacks on schoolgirls have been reported in Afghanistan. It is believed that the attacks were the work of conservative Afghan groups that oppose the education of girls which was prohibited in 2000-2001during the Taliban regime.[64] Human rights advocates have accused Turkey of using chemical weapons against the Kurds in 2010, and a German forensic expert stated that it was highly probable that eight Kurds had died due to the use of chemical substances.[65]

Between March and June 2013, a number of allegations of the use of chemical weapons in Syria were made in the media.[66] Syria itself requested the UN investigation regarding the incident of 19 March 2013 in Aleppo as the identity of the perpetrator was not clear. The General Assembly then adopted a resolution containing a demand to the Syrian authorities to refrain from using chemical weapons.[67] The Independent International Commission of Inquiry on Syria of the UN Human Rights Council reported, 'there are reasonable grounds to believe that limited quantities of toxic chemicals were used' in four incidents in different locations in March–April 2013. However, the report was unable to give any evidence to pinpoint the culprit.[68] The US, France and the UK were of the firm opinion that the governmental forces had employed the chemical weapons in Syria. Russia, in contrast, insisted that the chemical weapons were used by the opposition groups.[69] The UN team that later investigated the Ghouta Incident[70] and confirmed that 'chemical weapons have been used in the ongoing conflict between the parties in the Syrian Arab Republic, also against civilians, including children, on a relatively large scale.'[71]

Following confirmation of the use of chemical weapons in Ghouta by the UN team, an extraordinary sequence of events occurred. On 14 September 2013, Syria submitted its instrument of accession to the Chemical Weapons Convention.[72] On the same day in Geneva, Russia and the US agreed on a framework for the elimination of Syria's chemical weapons program.[73] Less than two weeks later, on September 27 in The Hague, the OPCW's Executive Council adopted a landmark decision that charted the course for a fast-tracked plan to eliminate Syria's chemical weapons based on the US-Russian agreement. Later that day in New York, the UN Security Council passed resolution 2118 endorsing the Executive Council decision.

The OPCW Executive Council decision called for the removal of all chemical weapons from Syria for destruction outside the country,[74] as well as the destruction of all production facilities in Syria.[75] Veolia, the US firm contracted by the OPCW to dispose of part of the Syrian chemical weapons stockpile completed deposal of 75 cylinders of hydrogen fluoride at its facility in Texas.[76] This completed destruction of all chemical weapons declared by the Syrian Arab Republic. Despite the delayed progression of the OPCW disarmament process, the Syrian government will maintain a small portion of its stockpile for tactical usage and for deterrence against a potential rebel offensive in major cities and in the Alawite coastal areas. The reduction of the Syrian chemical weapons manufacturing capability and stockpile has considerably reduced the potential for a major chemical attack against neighboring countries.

Chemical agents have also been used in terrorist attacks. The nerve agent sarin was used twice in Japan. The first incident, in Matsumoto in June 1994, produced more than 200 casualties, including 7 fatalities. In the second incident—in the Tokyo subway system on March 20, 1995—5,510 people were taken to medical facilities or sought medical assistance. About 20% of these were hospitalised, and 12 died. The cult that was accused of both attacks was found to have a large facility for manufacturing both chemical and biological agents.

Classification

The chemical agents developed during World War I are referred to as first-generation weapons; the nerve agents produced during World War II are called second-generation weapons; and the Cold War chemical agents (such as VX) are known as third-generation weapons. During the Cold War, the US arsenal also included CS, a riot-control agent, and BZ, an incapacitant, as well as sarin and VX. The Soviet Union had a complete chemical weapons arsenal, including "classic" agents belonging to the first, second, and third generations, all of which are now banned by the Chemical Weapon Convention (CWC). According to some interpretations, the CWC does not cover fourth-generation chemical weapons, or nontraditional agents (NTAs), such as some of the binary nerve agents known as "novichoks." There is evidence that Russia inherited NTAs from the former Soviet arsenals.[77]

Chemical warfare agents can also be classified into lethal agents and disabling agents. The former are intended either to kill or injure the enemy so severely as to necessitate evacuation and medical treatment, while the latter aim to incapacitate and cause disability from which recovery may be possible without medical aid. In addition to the known chemical warfare agents there are many toxic industrial chemicals, which although less toxic than the known chemical warfare agents, could cause great harm.[78] Post-World War I, the British adopted the following classification:[79]

Vesicants,[80] e.g., mustard gas and lewisite

Lung irritants, e.g., phosgene, chlorine and chloropicrin

Sensory irritants, e.g., diphenylchlorarsine and diphenylcyanoarsine

Lacrimators,[81] e.g., brombenzyl cyanide and xylyl bromide

Direct poisons of the nervous system, or paralysants, e.g., hydrocyanic acid gas

Gases which interfere with the respiratory function of the blood, e.g., carbon monoxide

Henry (2003) has classified chemical warfare agents into five general types: (i) Blister agents that cause blisters on the skin and damage the respiratory tract, mucous membranes and eyes; (ii) Nerve agents that disable enzymes responsible for the transmission of nerve impulses; (iii) Choking agents that damage the respiratory tract, causing extensive fluid build-up in the lungs; (iv) Blood agents that interfere with the absorption of oxygen into the bloodstream; and (v) Riot control (incapacitating) agents that rapidly produce temporary disabling effects.[82] In addition, there are plant-damaging agents like 2, 4-D, and 2, 4, 5-T.[83] Detailed characteristics of some chemical warfare agents follow.[84]

Phosgene: Phosgene does not occur naturally but since its initial preparation in the early 1800s it has become widely available in the chemical industry, where it is used as an intermediate in the manufacture of a wide range of other substances including dyes, pesticides and polymers. It is a colourless gas under ordinary conditions of temperature and pressure. Its boiling point is 8.2°C, making it an extremely volatile and non-persistent agent. Its vapour density is 3.4 times that of air. It may, therefore, remain for long periods of time in trenches and other low-lying areas. In low concentrations it has a smell resembling newly mown hay. Phosgene is readily soluble in organic solvents and fatty oils. In water, it hydrolyses rapidly, with the formation of hydrochloric acid and carbon dioxide.

Exposure to phosgene is primarily through inhalation. The lung is the main target organ and damage to it following acute exposure is proportional to the product of the concentration and duration of exposure.[85] At high concentrations skin and eye irritation also occur. Irritation of the eyes, nose and throat together with tightness in the chest occur rapidly when concentrations are greater than 3 parts per million (3 ppm). These symptoms are followed by shortness of breath and cough. Doses greater than 30ppm would damage the lungs and cause serious respiratory problems leading to death.[86] At high concentrations, the gas causes individuals to lose their sense of smell and their ability to assess danger. Phosgene was responsible for roughly 80 per cent of all deaths caused by chemical arms in World War I.[87]

Hydrogen cyanide: A rapid-acting lethal agent, hydrogen cyanide poisons by preventing individual cells from utilising oxygen. At atmospheric pressure, liquid hydrogen cyanide is colourless to yellowish brown. Not everyone can detect hydrogen cyanide at low concentrations, but those who do describe a smell of bitter almonds or marzipan. Hydrogen cyanide is widely available in the chemical industry as an intermediate and is used as a pesticide, rodenticide and fumigant. In some countries where capital punishment is still permitted, hydrogen cyanide is used to kill. The most likely route of entry is inhalation. An exposure to 60 mg/m^3 may not cause any serious symptoms, but at concentrations above 200 mg/m^3 death occurs after ten minutes. Above 2,500 mg/m^3 death is likely within one minute. As the gas is rapidly absorbed from the lungs, the symptoms of poisoning are equally rapid. Death occurs either through heart failure or failure to breathe. Hydrogen cyanide was not used much in World War I because the small munitions available at the time did not deliver sufficient casualty-inducing concentrations of the gas, which is lighter than air.

Mustard gas: Mustard gas (sometimes known as sulphur mustard) is a vesicant or blister agent.[88] It causes general tissue irritation and affects the internal functions of the body. Of the vesicant agents investigated for chemical warfare purposes, mustard gas was a favourite. First synthesised in 1860, it was developed as a chemical warfare agent during the First World War and has practically no other application. At high concentrations the gas has a pungent odour. It is slightly soluble in water, and dissolves in organic solvents and fats as well. Exposure to either the liquid or the vapour occurs mainly by inhalation and skin contact. Eye injuries are sufficient to incapacitate, and occur at concentrations of 100 mg/m^3 if the exposure occurs for one minute. Significant skin burns occur if the concentration is doubled. The estimated lethal dose by inhalation is 1,500 mg/m^3. Significant casualties from mustard gas occurred in the First World War, during the Iraq–Iran war (1980-1988) and amongst the Iraqi Kurds in 1988.

Mustard gas vapour can be carried long distances by the wind. The eyes are usually the first affected and develop a gritty feeling and appear bloodshot. This is followed by acute pain in the eyes which begin to water extensively and vision is affected. Other symptoms, such as running nose, sneezing, sore throat, coughing and hoarseness follow. Breathing problems may also develop. People are likely to complain of nausea and may vomit. Within 16-24 hours the skin begins to itch and darken in exposed areas. The armpits and genitals are vulnerable to blistering. Where there is moderate to severe exposure, large blisters filled with a clear yellow fluid develop. When this breaks, the skin is eroded and ulcers may occur. The airways can be severely damaged and the damaged tissue allows infection to set in. This may result in pneumonia which could be fatal. Sulphur mustard is absorbed and distributed through the bloodstream and affects an individual's immunity leaving them vulnerable to infections; pneumonia and septicaemia may result.

Nerve Agents: Nerve agents are mostly odourless and colourless gases. At ambient temperatures they appear as either colourless or yellow-brown liquids. They are most lethal chemicals containing organophosphate compounds that inhibit the enzymes known as cholinesterases. This affects the transmission of impulses through the nervous system and disrupts nerve function. A single drop on the skin or inhaled into the lungs can cause the brain centres controlling respiration to shut down and muscles, including the heart and diaphragm, to become paralysed. Poisoning by nerve agents causes intense sweating, filling of the bronchial passages with mucus, dimming of vision, uncontrollable vomiting and defecation, convulsions, and finally paralysis and respiratory failure. Death results from asphyxia, generally within a few minutes of respiratory exposure or within hours if the exposure was through a liquid nerve agent on the skin.[89]

In the mid-1930s chemists working for the Germans developed the first organophosphate compound with an extremely high toxicity. This came to be known as tabun (GA). As much as 12,000 tons was produced for the German army in WWII, although it was never used. Germany also invented the nerve agents, sarin (GB) in 1938; and sonam (GD) in 1944. These three German nerve agents, the G-series (for German) in US nomenclature, were all seized in large quantities by the Allies at the end of World War II. After the war the US, the Soviet Union, and a number of other States also produced these and other nerve agents as weapons.

VX, the best known of the V-series of persistent nerve agents (also the deadliest known nerve agent; "V" is for *venom*), was developed by chemists at a British government facility in 1952. Britain renounced all chemical and biological weapons in 1956 but traded information on the production of VX with the US in exchange for technical information on the production of thermonuclear bombs. In 1961, the US began large-scale production of VX. The only other countries believed to have built up VX arsenals were the Soviet Union, France, and Syria. Following the signing of the CWC in 1993, the US and Russia began the elimination of their chemical weapons stocks, a goal which they are yet to achieve.

Psycho-chemical gases, such as BZ, are incapacitating agents that attack the brain, producing hallucination and giddiness. They are not lethal. BZ was developed by the US after WWII and its chemical composition is not very well known.[90]

Tear Gas or Agent CS: CS or 2-chlorobenzalmalononitrile, is a white crystalline solid at ambient temperatures. Classed as a harassing agent, CS acts rapidly to irritate intensely the eyes and mucous membranes in the nose and throat. It can be spread as a dust cloud or in solution in an organic solvent. CS is widely available commercially as a riot-control agent. Irritation of the eye and respiratory tract occurs within a minute in some individuals at exposures as low as 0.004 mg/m^3. Marked irritation occurs at concentrations of 4 mg/m^3. These agents are favoured as riot-control agents because the lethal dose is extremely high and many, many times greater than the concentration required to cause irritation. Estimates of the lethal dose, and they are only estimates, range from 25,000 to 150,000 mg/m^3.

Recovery from harassing exposures usually occurs within about 30 minutes of the end of exposure, but may persist for longer. The major reason for the persistence of symptoms is the ineffective removal of the agents from the affected body surfaces. Solutions of CS cause severe skin irritation, the reddening of the skin occurring within a few minutes and persisting for about one hour. A delayed marked reddening (erythema) of the skin may persist for 24 to 72 hours and the skin may also blister and have a crusty look. Recovery from this more severe damage may take weeks. In those exposed to CS the chest feels sore and tight and some people try to hold their breath. Exposed skin, particularly in the nose and throat, will sting and burn after a few minutes. A few may also feel nauseated and vomit. The effects of CS make people anxious and lead to a temporary increase in blood pressure and heart rate. Those with asthma are at risk of asthmatic symptoms because of the irritation of the lungs.

The riot-control agents are banned by the CWC if used as "a method of warfare" but are allowed for domestic police enforcement. A few countries which have signed and ratified the CWC have reserved the right to use riot-control agents in certain other situations, including counterterrorist and hostage rescue operations, non-combatant rescue operations outside war zones, peacekeeping operations where the receiving State has authorised the use of force, and military operations against non-State actors initiating armed conflict.

Herbicides: Herbicides can be used to destroy enemy crops and foliage cover. They are not banned by the CWC unless they are used as "a method of warfare." However, not all the States party to the CWC consider herbicides to be chemical weapons, and these States, therefore, do not recognise their use to be banned by the treaty. For example, during the Vietnam War, Agent Orange was used extensively by the US armed forces between 1962 and 1971, to deny forest cover to the

Viet Cong and to North Vietnamese forces. Other herbicides, such as paraquat, Agent White (picloram and 2, 4-D), and Agent Blue (dimethyl arsenic acid), have also been produced to act as chemical weapons.

Toxicity of Chemical Agents

Chemical agents have a wide range of toxicity, varying from simple local irritation, such as lacrimation, to fatal systemic poisoning, as from hydrocyanic acid. The measure of the toxicity, in terms of physiological reaction, may be determined with considerable scientific accuracy, not only within the laboratory but also under the widely varying conditions encountered on the field of battle. The effects of chemical agents upon the human organism result either from internal contact, as inhalation, or from external contact with different body surfaces. In the case of agents whose vapours when inhaled produce deleterious internal reactions, it has been found that a definite relation exists between the concentration of the vapours in the air, the amount of such contaminated air that is admitted into the body, and the toxic effect produced upon the body.

Most toxic substances react chemically with the living tissues and destroy them by forming chemical combinations. The degree of intoxication or poisonous effect is proportional to the chemical reaction of the toxic substance with the tissues. This reaction is a function of three independent variables:

The time of exposure
The concentration of the toxic substance
The concentration of the living material (body tissue)

Let c = the concentration of the vapours of the toxic substance in the air, expressed in mg/m^3

v = volume of air breathed, in minutes

t = time of exposure to the contaminated atmosphere, in minutes

G = weight of the body in kg

Then the quantity of poison inhaled and generally retained in the body = ctv; and the degree of intoxication or poisoning, I = ctv/G.

Death occurs when I equals a constant critical limit, W, which is specific for each kind of animal and each toxic substance, i.e., when ctv/G = W.

In general, the amount of air inspired per minute is proportional to the body weight of the higher animals, so that the ratio v/G is constant for a given species and may be written as unity for the purposes of comparing the toxicities of gases on the same kind of animals. Then ct = W. The product ct, is called the product of morality or the lethal index of the particular toxic substance for the given animal. This product varies inversely as the toxicity of the toxic substance, i.e., the smaller the value of W, the more toxic is the substance.[91]

Environmental Concern

Historically, chemical weapons have been disposed of by land burial, open pit burning, explosion and sea dumping. Today such disposal options are prohibited under the Chemical Weapons Convention. The Convention does not apply to chemical weapons that have been either dumped at sea prior to 1985 or buried prior to 1977 (Article IV, paragraph 17) as long as they remained as such. Nonetheless, the deterioration of such munitions can pose a significant environmental threat, leading to the possible contamination of land and water. Environmental concerns may require the recovery and disposal of such obsolete munitions.

Moreover, the degradation and ageing of stockpiled chemical agents and munitions, in storage for over half a century, are also a risk and a source of constant concern. Handling and transporting munitions and containers from the storage area to the destruction facility has to be conducted in compliance with the strictest safety measures to prevent any accidental release of chemical agents which could endanger either the personnel, the civilian population or the environment. There are also inherent risks associated with the normal destruction operations, although, in most cases, they are substantially reduced by physical control safeguards within the destruction facilities. There is growing public concern on this issue regarding both the risk involved in a direct exposure, as well as the long-term low level exposure to agents, disposal and degradation products.

The protection of human health and preservation of the environment is one of the primary obligations for all States Parties under the CWC.[92] The State Parties have to maintain the highest standards during the transportation, sampling and storage of chemical weapons as well as during the destruction of chemical weapons and former production facilities. The procedure followed to fulfil these obligations must comply with national safety and environmental standards. In addition, State Parties are required to obtain the necessary environmental permits for each chemical weapons destruction facility prior to the commencement of the facility's operation. Monitoring compliance remains the responsibility of the State Party.

Effluent streams resulting from all destruction technologies, whether gaseous, liquid or solid, can vary considerably in composition and quantity, depending on the destruction technology and disposal strategy used. Before being discharged into the environment, recycled, used commercially or as landfill, effluent streams have to be treated to ensure that any remaining trace contaminants, organic or inorganic, are at acceptable levels, in compliance with national standards.[93]

Dumping at Sea

The world's oceans have always been mankind's favourite dump. In the aftermath of the two world wars, more than one million tons of CW material was dumped into the sea throughout the world. To the custodians of the material, burial at sea seemed a better solution than disposal on land.[94] At the time, a sea-bottom depository, far removed from populated areas, represented a reassuring sense of finality that land burial could not guarantee.[95] Many policymakers considered sea disposal a safer alternative in the belief that the vastness of the sea would mitigate any environmental or health risks posed by the CW agents. They expected that the agents would lose their toxicity over time through natural chemical decomposition, or if somehow released (e.g., through casing failure), would become so diluted that any remaining toxic properties would become negligible.[96] No one knows what kind of health and environmental risk these munitions pose today or will present tomorrow.

Most sea-dumping of chemical and conventional munitions started after World War I and continued throughout World War II and the Cold War and up to the 1970s, when the world began to understand the impact of these dumps on marine ecosystems and the environment in general. The NATO scientific community assessed that sea-dumped chemical munitions amounted to the total chemical arsenals reported by the US and Russia. The total amount of conventional munitions dumped at sea is believed to exceed 1,000,000 tons.

From 1918 to 1970, the US was responsible for dumping more than 350,000 short tons of surplus, damaged and captured chemical warfare (CW) material.[97] Other countries also participated in sea-dumping, especially after the Second World War, when CW material was confiscated from Germany by France, the Soviet Union, the UK and the US.[98] Each country bore responsibility for disposing of the material found in its zone. During this period, under orders of the US occupation authority, Japan also dumped CW material off its coast. The material ranged from small to massive quantities of munitions and/or canisters, and was dumped in the Atlantic, Arctic, Indian, Pacific and Southern Oceans. Obsolete, damaged or malfunctioning conventional weaponry was dumped as well.[99] Chemical reactions within these dump sites are critical issues that must be considered while assessing their impact on the marine environment and any risk that may result from seismic activities and marine operations. Standard military explosives are reactive to varying degrees, depending on the material, conditions of storage and environmental exposure. Precautions must be taken to prevent their reacting with other materials.

Munitions that have not been stored or disposed of properly may be more unstable and unpredictable in their behaviour, and more dangerous to deal with than normal munitions. This is also true of munitions that are no longer intact or have been exposed to weathering processes. Thus, sea-dumped chemical munitions, which may undergo chemical changes, are significantly more dangerous to handle than normal munitions.

Contrary to expectations, chemical weapon material has not remained at the dumping sites on the sea-bed. Dumped munitions have been found floating or washed ashore.[100] They may have been spread by trawlers, currents and tides. Sea-dumped chemical warfare material has already caused casualties, and with time, the dangers will only increase. We remain ignorant of the effects that human disturbance of the sea-bed, such as deep-sea trawling, may have on dumped chemical warfare material, and researchers have witnessed leaking containers—which is not entirely surprising considering that much of the material has sustained more than 50 years of exposure to corrosive and turbulent marine environments. In the future, more of these munitions may begin to wash up on shores and beaches of the coastal countries.[101] As marine activities increase, encounters with munitions may become the norm and complete fish stocks and their habitats may be threatened from munitions constituents such as lead azide, lead styphnate, picric acid and mercury fulminate.[102]

The fear led to an international effort to legally end the practice of sea-dumping chemical warfare material.[103] Legislation may help to ensure that there would be no increase in chemical warfare material on the seabed, but the hundreds of thousands of tons of material already dumped, may pose a latent threat to marine and human life. Chemical warfare material dumped at sea before 1985 is considered "abandoned chemical weapons" by the CWC and States Parties are not required to declare or destroy abandoned chemical weapons.[104]

The only declarations required for abandoned chemical weapons are for those buried on a State's territory after 1976.

Corroding and/or damaged containers pose too great a danger to warrant their retrieval from the sea-floor, therefore remediation (which might include recovery of the munitions or containers, in-place destruction, area quarantine or application of encapsulation devices) and clean-up efforts have not been actively pursued by any country. Instead, a handful of studies monitoring the environments around known dump sites have been performed, and new efforts, discussed in the next section, are under way.[105]

Environmental and Human Health Concerns

According to Beddington and Kinloch (2005), there are three basic types of danger that munitions dumped at sea can cause:[106]

(i) Direct physical contact with either chemical or conventional munitions resulting in threats to human health;

(ii) Contamination of marine organisms and the environment in the vicinity of dumped munitions and the consequent potential for some concentration of toxic contaminants entering wildlife and human food chains;

(iii) Spontaneous explosions which can be directly life-threatening, besides having the potential to spread material away from the dump sites thereby increasing the potential for more of it to come into direct physical contact with individuals.

There is little data on the environmental damage chemical warfare agents can cause. The risks may be higher today than when the dangers of the dumped material were first acknowledged because containment failure due to corrosion is thought to occur after 50 years. Dredging, fishing or underwater pipeline construction may speed up the degradation of containers. Also some chemical warfare agents may maintain toxic effects for longer than originally thought.[107]

Recent scientific investigations suggest that the geochemical characteristics of seawater may potentially extend the potency of some chemical warfare agents while yielding harmful degradation products from others.[108] Chemical warfare agents of low water solubility could potentially accumulate in sufficient concentrations in seawater to cause harm. It is hard to predict the danger because it is difficult to gauge lifetime and toxicity. The pH, temperature, pressure and chemical composition of marine environments can all affect dumped CW agents and all vary greatly by location. Colder water temperatures also can slow degradation and allow contamination along the seabed to persist in harmful concentrations and forms for longer periods. The effects of leaked CW agents on the environment and the local ecosystem are not clear: the potential for bioaccumulation of leaked agents in fish, for example, which could eventually enter the human food supply, is still being assessed.

Let us take the example of sulphur mustard. Because its density is greater than seawater and its solubility in water is low, if it leaks from a container, it can persist as globules on the ocean floor. The marine environment can cause chemical reactions that lead to the formation of salts on the surface of exposed or leaked sulfur mustard, perhaps prolonging its toxicity.[109] Several casualties and deaths among fishermen have resulted from exposure to such salt-encrusted sulfur mustard globules, which easily become ensnared in fishing nets. For instance, in Bari Harbour, in the Adriatic Sea, a total of 230 mustard exposure cases have been recorded recently.[110]

Conventional weapons material (and occasionally radioactive material) was often disposed of alongside chemical warfare materiel. The quantity of chemical warfare material disposed at sea, while immense, pales in comparison to the millions of tons of conventional munitions so disposed. While making any attempt at remediation efforts in the oceans, we need to be cognizant of sea-dumped radiological material—a subject that has not received enough scientific attention. Expanding the mapping of dump sites and analysing the threats they pose to include radioactive material and conventional material would be a valuable endeavour.[111]

The international community must increase its efforts to

understand the health and environmental problem posed by dumped chemical warfare munitions. Many aspects have not been sufficiently studied, and some have not been investigated at all. Three of the most urgent issues are mapping the many uncharted dump sites, the presence of chemical warfare agents in fish and any resulting effects, and the potential for reclaiming sea-dumped chemical warfare material for nefarious purposes.[112]

Marine dumped chemical munitions react differently in water depending on the agent they contain. The munition shell may break open during the dumping operation or may corrode over time, allowing the agent to leak out. Nerve agents and many other agents hydrolyse, or break down and dissolve once they come into contact with water, and are therefore rendered harmless in a relatively short amount of time. Mustard gas, however, is insoluble in water and most injuries that have occurred when fishermen come into contact with marine dumped chemical munitions have resulted from mustard gas. Phosphorous devices also present long-term problems. Dumped munitions, and in particular, the disturbance of dumped munitions by marine activities, e.g., fishing, sand and gravel extraction, dredging and dumping operations and the placement of cables and pipelines, is an important issue that should be addressed. It is essential to maintain details of the locations of all munitions dumpsites, and the areas where munitions are detected on the seabed. Any seabed activities to be undertaken within or close to these locations should be subject to a full assessment of the potential risk prior to the approval of these activities by national authorities.

A recently passed resolution by the United Nations confronts the complex issue of chemical weapons abandoned at sea.[113] The resolution calls on Member States and international organisations to cooperate more closely in assessing the environmental threats related to waste originating from chemical munitions dumped at sea. Member States have agreed to voluntarily exchange practical knowledge about the sites where chemical munitions were dumped at sea and to increase public awareness on this issue, as well as to seek the views of each other on issues related to the environmental effects of the waste. The resolution does not propose to discuss the lifting and destroying of chemical munitions.

The long-term fate of chemical weapon debris disposed of in the ocean some 50-60 years ago, now sinking into marine sediments and leaking into the ocean environment is poorly known.[114] There are a number of reasons for the decades of delay in addressing this problem. Many dumping operations were carried out secretly and it is not always clear who can be held responsible. Moreover, at the time there were no international conventions that prohibited dumping, hence assigning legal liability and responsibility is questionable. The governmental bodies of the states that carried out sea dumping operations and those bordering the dumping areas were reluctant to tackle this sensitive problem. Further, there is a lack of official records of the dumping operations, which often took place under chaotic circumstances right after WWII.[115] In addition to contamination of seawater, there have been concerns among the public that chemical weapons could wash ashore, or that they could be retrieved accidentally during dredging operations or trawl fishing along the seabed.[116]

Exposure to chemical weapons can have numerous harmful effects on human beings. Depending on the particular chemical agent, these effects can include burns and sores on the skin, vomiting, respiratory dysfunction, mental impairment, damage to the immune and nervous systems, infertility, and death. Public health advocates have questioned whether possible exposure to such substances in seawater from leaking weapons may contribute to various symptoms experienced by coastal residents, swimmers, divers, fishermen, and consumers of contaminated fish or shellfish. Marine conservationists and environmental advocates have also raised questions about the possible effects of chemical weapons agents on the marine environment, including the possible contribution to declines in populations of certain fish and other marine life in and around areas where weapons were dumped in the ocean.

Destruction of Chemical Weapons

Iraq: Under United Nations Special Commission (UNSCOM) supervision 38,537 filled and unfilled munitions, 690 tonnes of agents, 3,000 tonnes of precursor chemicals to manufacture CW agents, and thousands of pieces of production equipment and analytical instruments were destroyed in Iraq. Despite these achievements, no complete accounting of the CW programme has been possible, for two main reasons: (i) Iraq removed CW, equipment and materials from the main site of the al-Muthanna State Establishment before the first UNSCOM inspection team arrived, and no full accounting of these materials has been forthcoming.; and (ii) Iraq claims that it has destroyed 15,620 chemical munitions unilaterally, a fact and total that are so far unverified. Similarly, it provided no supporting documentation for 16,038 chemical munitions it claims to have discarded. Iraq: The UNSCOM Experience, SIPRI, Factsheet, October 1998.

Libya: Libya has already destroyed "category 1" toxins with the help of western countries. Libya's remaining stockpile of potential chemical weapons has been successfully transported abroad in an operation aimed to keeping them safe from militants. It has been confirmed by the OPCW that around 850 tonnes of industrial chemicals which could be used to produce weapons had been removed for destruction abroad.[117]

Russia: In June 2017, the Russian military, with tangible assistance from the European Union, Canada, and the US, destroyed the last warheads containing sarin, mustard, and soman gas. Experts say that only one percent of the stockpiles of chemical weapons remain to be dealt with. Russia has claimed that it will complete chemical weapons destruction by the end of 2017, a year in advance of its earlier target.[118]

The United States: From World War I to 1968, the United States produced chemical weapons as a deterrent against use of similar weapons by other countries. The amount of stockpiled chemical warfare agents in the US is thought to have reached nearly 40,000 tons by 1968. Though never used in battle, the US chemical weapons are now obsolete and deteriorating with age. The US national stockpile of lethal chemical warfare agents primarily involves six chemicals: Tabun, Sarin, VX, Sulfur-mustard, HT and Lewisite. These chemical warfare agents were stored in bulk containers or as assembled weapons and ammunition at nine sites in the United States. In **1997**, the US ratified the CWC and agreed to destroy its stockpile of aging chemical weapons (principally mustard agent and nerve agents) by April 2007. However, the final destruction deadline was extended to April 2012, at the Eleventh Session of the Conference of the States Parties to the Chemical Weapons Convention held in 2006. The US is still getting rid of its stockpile of chemical weapons and is expected to complete destruction by mid-2020.

Legacy of Agent Orange: In 2007, the US-Vietnam Dialogue Group on Agent Orange/Dioxin was established with help from the Ford Foundation. The Dialogue Group is a bi-national advocacy committee of private citizens, scientists and policy-makers. It's Vietnamese and American members include experts on toxicology, environmental clean-up, reproductive health, and comprehensive services for people with disabilities. The members of the group have traveled in Vietnam, reviewed the evidence and sought additional expertise. Their joint assessment and common understanding of the situation has led to a three-phase Plan of Action that would achieve two goals over the next ten years: (i) Clean dioxin-contaminated soils and restore damaged ecosystems; and (ii) Expand services to people with disabilities linked to dioxin, and to people with other forms of disability and to their families. Achieving these goals will require the combined efforts of governments, businesses and nongovernmental organizations. The Vietnam Red Cross estimates that up to 3 million Vietnamese adults and children have suffered adverse health effects, congenital and developmental defects. The Action Group has called upon the US to join with the Vietnamese to fund a comprehensive and humanitarian effort to resolve the legacy of Agent Orange/ dioxin in Vietnam.

Old and Abandoned Chemical Weapons

More than 65 years have elapsed since the WWII, yet the problems connected with old chemical weapons (OCW) and abandoned chemical weapons (ACW) lingers. Certain incidents of the past decades show that environmental and technical problems related to these chemical weapons pose a potent threat to humans and the environment.[119] The Centre for Non-proliferation Studies (CNS) at the Monterey Institute of International Studies has conducted a very extensive study on sea-based abandoned chemical weapons. According to the CNS there may be as many 127 such dumpsites in oceans throughout the world.[120] From 1937 to 1945, Japan employed chemical weapons against China and then abandoned large numbers of unused chemical munitions on Chinese soil. Japanese chemical weapons continue to injure and kill Chinese citizens.[121] China estimates that abandoned chemical weapons (ACW) have caused 2,000 casualties and fatalities since the end of World War II.[122] In general, ACW pose much greater hazards to civilians than military stockpiles of chemical weapons. As the locations of many ACW are not known and civilians lack an understanding of their hazards, they risk being accidentally exposed to these weapons. Since both Japan and China have ratified the CWC, the two governments need to finalise arrangements for the destruction of abandoned Japanese chemical weapons on Chinese soil.[123] With respect to the social and environmental aspects of destruction, the CWC provides, "Each State Party, during the implementation of its obligations under this Convention, shall assign the highest priority to ensuring the safety of people and to protecting the environment and shall cooperate as appropriate with other States Parties in this regard."[124] However, the CWC does not specify detailed procedures for the destruction of ACW,[125] which must be negotiated between the two sides.

The technological issues in dealing with OCW and ACW are: (i) difficulty in unearthing and identification, (ii) difficulty in differentiating between chemical ammunition and conventional ammunition; (iii) difficulty in identifying the origin of OCW; (iv) difficulty in removing active explosive charges from OCW; (v) difficulty in decontaminating complex mixtures of agents and explosives present in OCW; and (vi) unpredictability of old and abandoned CW during destruction process.[126] Moreover, the destruction is required to be carried out in a safe and environmentally acceptable manner.[127]

Notes

1. The 1993, Chemical Weapons Convention, Article II.1, defines chemical weapons as the following, together or separately: (a) Toxic chemicals and their precursors, except where intended for purposes not prohibited under this Convention, as long as the types and quantities are consistent with such purposes; (b) Munitions and devices, specifically designed to cause death or other harm through the toxic properties of those toxic chemicals specified in subparagraph (a), which would be released as a result of the employment of such munitions and devices; (c) Any equipment specifically designed for use directly in connection with the employment of munitions and devices specified in subparagraph (b). The chemical weapons, therefore, include both materials which are inherently toxic and those which are specifically designed to cause death or other harm through the action of their toxic properties.
2. http://www.britannica.com/EBchecked/topic/108951/chemical-weapon, accessed October 22, 2012.
3. Chemical warfare means the wartime use, against an enemy, of agents having a direct (toxic) effect on man, animals or plants. The use of chemical warfare agents against man, rather than animals or plants, is referred to as gas warfare, even though the substance used may be solid, liquid or gaseous. There are four main categories of chemical warfare agents: choking, blister, blood and nerve agents. One of the assets of chemical warfare is that it does not depend on extraordinary delivery systems. Chemical munitions may be adapted for delivery by almost any means—grenade throwers, artillery and aircraft. The only drawback with chemical warfare is that, once a chemical weapon has been deployed, its user has no further control over it. The chemical weapons can be very effective against troop concentrations, military facilities and highly populated civilian areas. Kim Coleman, *A History of Chemical Warfare* (New York: Palgrave Macmillan, 2005), pp. 3-5.
4. R. Harris and J. Paxman, *A Higher Form of Killing: the Secret History of Chemical and Biological Warfare* (New York, NY: Random House, 2002).
5. Nebojsa Raicevic, "The History of Prohibition of the Use of Chemicals in International Humanitarian Law," *Facta Universitatis*, Series: *Law and Politics*, vol. 1, no. 5, 2001, pp. 613-31.
6. *The Problem of Chemical and Biological Warfare*, vol. I, "The Rise of Chemical and Biological Weapons," 1971, Stockholm: SIPRI, p. 126.
7. A. A. Fries and C. J. West, *Chemical Warfare* (New York: McGraw-Hill, 1921), pp. 2-4.
8. Augustine M. Prentiss, *Chemicals in War: A Treatise on Chemical Warfare* (New York: McGraw-Hill Book Company, 1937), p. xvi. There are few examples of chemical weapons used or proposed during the course of a campaign or battle.

The Chinese used arsenical smokes as early as 1000 BC. Solon of Athens put hellebore roots in the drinking water of Kirrha in 600 BC. In 429 and 424 BC, the Spartans and their allies used noxious smoke and flame against Athenian-allied cities during the Peloponnesian War. About 200 BC, the Carthaginians used Mandrake root left in wine to sedate the enemy. The Chinese designed stink bombs of poisonous smoke and shrapnel, along with a chemical mortar that fired cast-iron stink shells. Toxic smoke projectiles were designed and used during the Thirty Years War. Leonardo da Vinci proposed a powder of sulfide of arsenic and verdigris in the fifteenth century. Jeffery K. Smart, "History of Chemical and Biological Warfare: An American Perspective," in *Medical Aspects of Chemical and Biological Warfare: The US Army Surgeon-General's Text book,* 1997, pp. 9-86, available at: http://www.bordeninstitute.army.mil/published_volumes/chembio/ch2.pdf, accessed March 29, 2012.

9. The Boer War offered the first debate among belligerents as to the use of gas. During the Boer War Great Britain employed picric acid in its shells. The result was that the shell, upon impact, would not only explode but would let off a gas called lyddite. The Boer soldiers protected themselves against lyddite by breathing through rags soaked in vinegar. General Joubert protested to Sir George White. The British replied that as the picric acid was not put in the shell solely to produce the gas, its use was not considered objectionable. The negligible tactical effect of lyddite prevented it from becoming a *cause celebre.* Major Kelly and Joseph Burns, "Gas Warfare in International Law," *Military Law Review,* July 1960 (DA Pam 27-100-9, July 1, 1960), p. 5.
10. The first large-scale use of a traditional weapon of mass destruction involved the successful deployment of chemical weapons during World War I (1914-1918). Historians refer to the Great War as the chemist's war because of the scientific and engineering mobilisation efforts by the major belligerents. The development, production, and deployment of war gases such as chlorine, phosgene, and mustard created a new and complex public health threat that endangered not only soldiers and civilians on the battlefield but also chemical workers on the home front involved in the large-scale manufacturing processes. Gerard J. Fitzgerald, "Chemical Warfare and Medical Response During World War I," available at: http://www.ncbi.nlm.nih.gov/pmc/articles/PMC2376985/, accessed October 22, 2012.
11. Although it is popularly believed that the German army was the first to use gas it was in fact initially deployed by the French. In the first month of the war, August 1914, the French forces fired tear-gas grenades (xylyl bromide) against the Germans. Nevertheless the German army was the first to give serious study to the development of chemical weapons and the first to use it on a large scale. The debut of the first poison gas however—in this instance, chlorine—came on April 22, 1915, at the start of the Second Battle of Ypres. The effects of chlorine gas were severe. Within seconds of inhaling its vapour it destroyed the victim's respiratory organs, bringing on choking attacks.
12. At the predetermined moment, German troops simultaneously opened 6,000 cylinders that had been buried along the front lines, releasing 168 metric tons of chlorine gas. The concept of creating a toxic gas cloud from chemical cylinders was credited to Fritz Haber of the Kaiser Wilhelm Physical Institute of Berlin in late 1914. Heavier than air, the greenish-gray vapour settled close to the ground, forming a dense cloud five miles wide that was carried by wing over the opposing French and Canadian trenches. As the green fog washed over them, the startled troops experienced violent nausea, asphyxiation, blindness, and agonising pain.

Within 30 minutes, the toxic gas had caused 15,000 casualties and 5,000 deaths, leading to the collapse of two entire French divisions. Jonathan B. Tucker, "From Arms Race to Abolition: The Evolving Norms Against Biological and Chemical Warfare," in Sidney D. Drell, Abraham D. Sofaer, and George D. Wilson (eds.), *The New Terror: Facing the Threat of Biological and Chemical Weapons* (Stanford CA: Hoover Institution Press, 1999), pp. 159-226. *See also* Augustine M. Prentiss, *Chemicals in War: A Treatise on Chemical Warfare* (New York: McGraw-Hill Book Company, 1937), p. 80.

13. In the aftermath of Ypres, it became apparent that lacking an offensive gas capability would impair troop morale, and the British cabinet approved the use of chemical agents. It took 5 months to plan the large-scale gas attack at Loos, which involved chlorine-filled cylinders clustered in batteries along the front rather than spaced far apart in one continuous line. The British had a major numerical advantage against the Germans, reaching 7-to-1 in some places along the front. The British commander General Douglas Haig began the offensive with a 4-day artillery bombardment by six divisions, planning to follow the bombardment with the release of 5,500 cylinders containing 150 tons of chlorine gas from the British front line.
14. In January 1915, several chemists at Imperial College successfully demonstrated ethyl iodoacetate as a tear gas to the War Office by gassing a representative. Another officer suggested using sulfur dioxide as a chemical weapon. Field Marshal Lord Kitchener, Secretary of State for War, was not interested in the concept for the army but suggested trying the navy. At the Admiralty, the idea found a sympathetic ear in Winston Churchill in March 1915. The suggestion included a plan to use a sulfur dioxide cloud against the Germans, screen the operation with smoke, and provide British troops a gas-proof helmet. Churchill declined to accept the sulfur dioxide plan but did put the officer in charge of a committee the next month to discuss the use of smoke on land and sea.
15. Possibly aware of the Allied interest in chemical weapons, the Germans also examined their own chemical technology for war applications during WWI. The Germans filled 105-mm shells with dianisidine chlorosulfate, a lung irritant, for use on the western front. To evade the 1899 international ban, the Germans also put shrapnel in the shell so the "sole" purpose was not gas dissemination. On October 27, 1914, the Germans fired 3,000 of these projectiles at the British but with no visible effects. The explosive aspect of the shells destroyed the chemical aspect. In fact, the British were apparently unaware that they were the victims of the first large-scale chemical projectile attack.
16. Mustard gas was distinguished by the serious blisters it caused both internally and externally several hours after exposure. Protection against mustard gas proved more difficult than against either chlorine or phosgene. The first large-scale mustard gas attack occurred just over a week after its first use, when the Germans attacked the British at Nieuport, resulting in over 14,000 casualties, 500 of whom died within 3 weeks. The next month the Germans fired 100,000 mustard shells, marked with a yellow cross, against the French Second Army, causing 20,000 casualties. D. K. Clark, *Effectiveness of Chemical Weapons in WWI* (Johns Hopkins University Operations Research Office, 1959), Staff Paper ORO-SP-88, pp. 99-123.
17. R. Harris and J. Paxman, *A Higher Form of Killing: the Secret History of Chemical and Biological Warfare* (New York, NY: Random House, 2002).
18. The use of mustard agent during World War I was ultimately responsible for the majority of casualties from the war. By targeting the skin, eyes, and lungs,

mustard rendered a large number of soldiers ineffective as part of the fighting force. The grotesque pattern of injury that resulted from exposure had a major psychological impact, demonstrating that a chemical weapon need not be lethal to be strategically effective. During this period, mustard agent became known as "the king of war gases." Jonathan B. Tucker, *War of Nerves: Chemical Warfare from World War I to Al-Qaeda* (New York, NY: Pantheon Books, 2006).

19. Charles E. Heller, *Chemical Warfare in World War I: The American Experience, 1917-1918,* Leavenworth Papers No. 10, Fort Leavenworth, KS: Combat Studies Institute, 1984, p. 17.
20. In November 1918, the monthly capacities of the US' Gas Offence Production Division filling plants were Augustine M. Prentiss, *Chemicals in War: A Treatise on Chemical Warfare* (New York: McGraw-Hill Book Company, 1937), p. 87:

75-mm shells	1,300,000
4.7-in shell	450,000
155-mm shell	540,000
6-in shell	180,000
Gas grenades	750,000
Smoke grenades	500,000
Stokes mortar 4-in bombs	120,000
Livens drum	40,000
Incendiary drop bombs	25,000

21. L. F. Haber, *The Poisonous Cloud: Chemical Warfare in the First World War* (Oxford: Clarendon Press, 1986), p. 170.
22. Kim Coleman, *A History of Chemical Warfare* (New York: Palgrave Macmillan, 2005), p. 40.
23. The 1925 Geneva Protocol for the Prohibition of the Use of Asphyxiating, Poisonous or Other Gases, and Bacteriological Methods of Warfare (Geneva Gas Protocol) made it illegal to employ chemical or biological weapons, though the ban extended only to those who signed the treaty.
24. Because of gaping loopholes in the 1925 Geneva Gas Protocol, all of the major combatants in WWII stockpiled large quantities of chemical weapons, which fortunately remained unused.
25. The First World War saw the break-up of empires including the Ottoman Empire whose capital Constantinople became Istanbul. Out of the remnants of that empire a series of artificial states were created which arbitrarily divided up and threw together various peoples. Under League of Nations mandates, France acquired Syria, and Lebanon and Britain procured Palestine, Jordan and Iraq. The birth of Iraq was presided over by Winston Churchill who, at the time was the British Secretary of State for the Colonies. From 1919, the population of Iraq rose up against the Hashemite ruler and his British patrons.
26. Kim Coleman, *A History of Chemical Warfare* (New York: Palgrave Macmillan, 2005), p. 44.
27. Just ten years after the 1925 Geneva Protocol had been signed, there was a massive violation of its provisions in the Italo-Ethiopian War of 1935-1936, because both Italy and Ethiopia were its signatory. It was estimated that Italy used around 700 tons of chemical agents, mostly through air forces. During those attacks, in addition to soldiers there were civilian victims as well. Reports on horrible consequences were mainly obtained from physicians, the representatives of the International Committee of the Red Cross and the journalists. John Melly, the head of a field hospital of the British Red Cross, describes the war as follows: "It is not a war, it is not even a slaughter—it is a torture of thousands of

defenceless men, women and children." R. Baudendistel, "Force versus law: The International Committee of the Red Cross and Chemical Warfare in the Italo-Ethiopian War 1935-1936," no. 322, *International Review of the Red Cross*, 1998, p. 88.

28. Lina Grip and John Hart, "The use of chemical weapons in the 1935-36 Italo-Ethiopian War," SIPRI Arms Control and Non-proliferation Programme, October 2009, available at: http://www.museobadoglio.altervista.org/docs/grip_hart.pdf, accessed October 22, 2012.
29. Despite the Geneva Protocol of 1925; which Italy had ratified in 1928, the Italians dropped mustard bombs over Ethiopia and occasionally sprayed it from airplane tanks. They also used mustard agent in powder form as a "dusty agent" to burn the unprotected feet of the Ethiopians. There were also rumours of phosgene and chloropicrin attacks, but these were never verified. Chemical weapons were devastating against the unprepared and unprotected Ethiopians. The Italian aircraft ruled the skies: Special sprayers were installed on board aircraft so they could vaporise over vast areas of territory a fine, death-dealing rain. Groups of 9, 15, or 18 aircraft followed one another so that the fog issuing from them formed a continuous sheet. It was thus that, as from the end of January 1936, soldiers, women, children, cattle, rivers, lakes, and pastures were drenched continually with this deadly rain. In order more surely to poison the waters and pastures, the Italian command made its aircraft pass over and over again. These fearful tactics succeeded. Men and animals succumbed. The deadly rain that fell from the aircraft made all those whom it touched fly shrieking with pain. All those who drank poisoned water or ate infected food also succumbed in dreadful suffering. In tens of thousands the victims of Italian mustard gas fell. The Italians attempted to justify their use of chemical weapons by citing the exception to the Geneva Protocol restrictions that referenced acceptable use for reprisal against illegal acts of war. They stated that the Ethiopians had tortured or killed their prisoners and wounded soldiers. W. Davis, *The Serpent and the Rainbow* (New York, NY: Warner Books Inc., 1985), pp. 151-52.
30. *The Problem of Chemical and Biological Warfare, Vol. 1, The Rise of CB Weapons*, Stockholm International Peace Research Institute (SIPRI) (Stockholm: Almqvist & Wiksell, 1971), p. 143.
31. Blistering agent "lewisite" was developed in 1918 by W. Lee Lewis, an American scientist of the Catholic University in Washington DC. Lewisite was similar to mustard gas in its ability to cause damage to a victim's entire body, but it was much faster acting. Following its development, the Americans built a huge production facility at Edgewood arsenal, Maryland, to manufacture lewisite in large quantity. Kim Coleman, *A History of Chemical Warfare* (New York: Palgrave Macmillan, 2005), p. 40.
32. D. J. C. Wiseman, *Special Weapons and Types of Warfare* (London, England: War Office, 1951), p. 150.
33. Most of the Germany's and Japan's chemical and biological weapons programmes did not become known until after the war. During the war, Germany produced approximately 78,000 tons of chemical warfare agents. This included about 12,000 tons of the nerve agent tabun, produced between 1942 and 1945. Germany also produced about 1,000 lb of sarin by 1945. Mustard agent, however, was the most important agent in terms of production, and the Germans filled artillery shells, bombs, rockets, and spray tanks with the agent. Phosgene, of somewhat lesser importance, was loaded in 250- and 500-kg bombs. The Germans were the greatest producers of nitrogen mustards and produced about 2,000 tons of HN-

3. This was filled in artillery shells and rockets. They also had a large number of captured chemical munitions from France, Poland, USSR, Hungary, and other occupied countries. Japan produced about 8,000 tons of chemical agents during the war. After the WW II, the US and the Soviet Union captured the stockpiles and manufacturing facilities late in the war, and they began to manufacture and stockpile these agents.

34. In *Mein Kampf*, Hitler described his own gas experience after being blinded by a mustard gas attack in Flanders at the third battle of Passchendaele: "In the night of October 13, the English gas attack on the southern front before Ypres burst loose; they used yellow-cross gas, whose effects were still unknown to us as far as personal experience was concerned. In this same night I myself was to become acquainted with it. On a hill south of Wervick, we came on the evening of October 13 into several hours of drumfire with gas shells which continued all night more or less violently. As early as midnight, a number of us passed out, a few of our comrades forever. Toward morning I, too, was seized with pain which grew worse with every quarter hour, and at seven in the morning I stumbled and tottered back with burning eyes; taking with me my last report of the War. A few hours later, my eyes had turned into glowing coals; it had grown dark around me. Thus I came to the hospital at Pasewalk in Pomerania, and there I was fated to experience—the greatest villainy of the century." A. Hitler, *Mein Kampf*, translated by J. Murphy (New York, NY: Hurst and Blackett Ltd., 1939), pp. 118-19.

35. Operation Davy Jones Locker involved sinking ships that contained German weapons in the North Sea. However, not all the German weapons were destroyed. Between 1945 and 1947, over 40,000 of the 250-kg tabun bombs, over 21,000 mustard bombs of various sizes, over 2,700 nitrogen mustard rockets, and about 750 tabun artillery shells of various sizes were shipped to the United States. In addition to disposing of the enemy stockpiles, the US also dumped the US lewisite stockpile into the sea during Operation Geranium in 1948.

36. Kim Coleman, *A History of Chemical Warfare* (New York: Palgrave Macmillan, 2005) p. 87.

37. Ibid., p. 88.

38. *The Washington Times*, August 15, 1992.

39. The 38th parallel roughly marked the line between the capitalist South Korea and the communist North Korea. The North Korean capital was a military objective for the American forces and on July 11, 1952 the US Air Force dropped 1,400 tons of phosphorus bombs and 23,000 gallons of napalm on Pyongyang, levelling more than 1,500 buildings and killing hundreds.

40. A commission of the International Association of Democratic Lawyers (IADL) also investigated and prepared a report after their visit to Korea in 1952. The report referred to four alleged uses of chemical weapons in Korean War. The first and the largest was said to have taken place on May 6, 1951 when three B-29 bombers dropped mustard gas bombs over Nampo city, causing 1,379 gas casualties of which 480 died of asphyxiation. The other incidents were said to have occurred on July 6, 1951 at Poong-Po Ri village, on August 1, 1951 at the villages of Yeng Seng Ri and Won Chol Ri, and on January 9, 1952 at Hak Seng village; available at: http://www.uwpep.org/Index/Resources_files/Crime_Reports_1.pdf, accessed November 13, 2012.

41. Chemical Warfare hearing before the subcommittee on National Security Policy and Scientific Developments, US House of Representatives, 91st Congress, Washington (November-December 1969).

42. The code name, "Purple," "Orange," "White," and "Blue," were derived from the colour of the stripe painted around the 55 gallon containers in which they were received from the United States. *Purple* and *Orange* were general purpose anti-plant chemical agents used for the destruction of broad-leaved crops, such as banana, and for the defoliation of forests and brush growth. *White* was used for longer-term forest defoliation. *Blue* was a desiccant occasionally employed for rapid defoliation, but more usually for the destruction of rice crops. Agents Purple and Blue began to be used in Vietnam in 1961, but Orange gradually replaced Purple because of its lower volatility. Agent White came into use in 1966, at a time when Orange was in short supply. However, by the end of 1967, 90 per cent of the total agent sprayed was Orange. Kim Coleman, *A History of Chemical Warfare* (New York: Palgrave Macmillan, 2005), p. 93. *See also* Le Thi Nham Tuyet and Annika Johansson, "Impact of Chemical Warfare with Agent Orange on Women's Reproductive Lives in Vietnam: A Pilot Study," vol. 9, no. 18, *Reproductive Health Matters*, November 2001, pp. 156-64.
43. In 1962 defoliants became "a central weapon" in the overall chemical and biological warfare strategy of the United States throughout Southeast Asia. Known as "Operation Ranch Hand," some of the converted C-123 cargo planes used to spray the herbicides were inscribed with the motto "Only we can prevent forests."
44. In the wake of a Vietnam War, there was worldwide concern about the environmental damage caused by US military operations in Southeast Asia. Shortly after the end of the Vietnam War, in 1975, it became clear that a disproportionate number of Vietnam veterans were coming down with non-Hodgkin's lymphoma and skin sarcomas. The Centres for Disease Control later determined that the cause of these cancers was the dioxins contained in Agent Orange. The extent of the damage to the natural environment of Vietnam as a result of the spraying was also becoming apparent. While no systematic survey of defoliated areas of Southeast Asia has been conducted, the anecdotal evidence is enormous. Mark Pery and Ed Miles, "Environmental Warfare," available at: http://www.crimesofwar.org/a-z-guide/environmental-warfare/, accessed December 13, 2011.
45. In addition to polluting the environment and causing cancers and other diseases in those directly exposed to it, Agent Orange (dioxin) has caused high rates of pregnancy loss, congenital birth defects and other health problems in their children. With an aim to explore the impact of chemical warfare on people's lives, a pilot study was undertaken in the year 2000 among 30 Vietnamese women whose husbands and/or who themselves were exposed to Agent Orange. Using the reproductive lifeline and semi-structured interviews, information was gathered on both partners' periods of exposure to Agent Orange, pregnancy outcomes, perceived health problems of children and experiences of living with handicapped children. The women had had a high number of miscarriages and premature births. About two-thirds of their children had congenital malformations or developed disabilities within the first years of life. Most of the families were poor, aggravated by impaired health in the men, the burden of caring for disabled children, and feelings of guilt and inferiority. The study concludes that at the societal level the plight of "Agent Orange families" is special and should be placed in its historical and political context. The impact over time of the largest chemical warfare in history on families and individuals in Vietnam should be highlighted, described and given a human face. Le Thi Nham Tuyet and Annika Johansson, "Impact of Chemical Warfare with Agent

Orange on Women's Reproductive Lives in Vietnam: A Pilot Study," vol. 9, no. 18, *Reproductive Health Matters*, November 2001, pp. 156-64.

46. One of the chemicals, picloram, does not decompose readily and may remain active in the environment for several years. Arthur H. Westing, "Poisoning Plants for Peace," *Friends Journal*, April 1, 1970.
47. The actual environmental impact is difficult to decipher though it is consistently reported that mangrove forests were most sensitive to the dioxin (Agent Orange) with irreversible consequences for up to 40 per cent of the population. The Vietnamese government, in cooperation with other governments and international organisations, has begun the process of inland and mangrove afforestation, though in 1993, it was estimated that it would take many more decades of industrious labour and a steady supply of international funding to recover the total area destroyed by herbicides. Pankaj Jha, "Agent Orange: Resonance on Vietnam-US," *Journal of Chemical and Biological Weapons*, October-December, 2009, p. 5.
48. The agents used consists of "Orange" (50:50 mixture of 2, 4-D and 2, 4, 5-T), used on general crops and recorded as amounting to 50 per cent of the defoliation programme; "White" 20 per cent picloram and 80 per cent isoprophalmin salt from 2, 4-D, used for 35 per cent of missions; and "Blue" (a form of arsenic) for 15 per cent of the missions; as well as the host of other agents including Phenal compounds of the type DNOC, arsenates, and earth sterilising compounds," such as Bromacil and Urox. Arthur H. Westing, *Herbicides in War: The Long-term Ecological and Human Consequences* (London: Taylor & Francis, 1984), pp. 6-7.
49. The United States Department of Defence had admitted that four and a half million acres of forest and one-half million acres of cropland were sprayed through July 1969—about 12 per cent land area of South Vietnam. The inadvertent spraying of unintended areas was also a common occurrence because of mistaken target identification, navigational errors, and wind-caused drifting of spray. Arthur H. Westing, "Poisoning Plants for Peace," *Friends Journal*, April 1, 1970.
50. *Associated Press*, January 3, 1970.
51. This tonnage far exceeded that expended in World War II and in the Korean War. The US Air Force consumed 2,150,000 tons of munitions in World War II—1,613,000 tons in the European Theatre and 537,000 tons in the Pacific Theatre—and 454,000 tons in the Korean War. Vietnam War bombing thus represented at least three times as much (by weight) as both European and Pacific theatre World War II bombing combined and about fifteen times total tonnage in the Korean War. Michael Clodfelter, *Vietnam in Military Statistics: A History of the Indochina Wars:1772-1991* (Jefferson, NC: McFarland, 1995).
52. Arthur H. Westing, *Herbicides in War: The Long-term Ecological and Human Consequences* (London: Taylor & Francis, 1984), p. 15.
53. The purpose of utilising chemicals (herbicides) in the Vietnam War, according to the US Government was to reduce the hazards of ambush by Vietcong forces. This was the first time that chemicals designed to damage or kill plants were used in war. The destruction of land may seem a trivial thing in comparison to the human slaughter every war entails, as to be of little concern. But when intervention in ecology of a region on a massive scale occurs, an irreversible chain of events is set in motion, which continues to affect the agriculture of the area and therefore the people long after the war is over. Kim Coleman, *A History of Chemical Warfare* (New York: Palgrave Macmillan, 2005), pp. 90-91.
54. Ibid., pp. 90-92.

55 Yemen Civil War: In 1962, Yemeni dissidents overthrew the monarchy and declared a republic. Royalist forces then retreated into the mountains of northern

Yemen and initiated a counter-revolt against the republican forces. Egypt recognised the new republic and sent military forces to help defeat the royalist troops, who were supported by the kingdoms of Saudi Arabia and later Jordan. Egyptian efforts to defeat the royalist forces and destroy their civilian support bases proved particularly difficult in the mountainous terrain. Apparently growing impatient with the successful royalist guerrilla tactics, the Egyptian air force allegedly dropped chemical-filled bombs on proroyalist villages to terrorise or kill not only the local inhabitants but also, possibly, the royalists who were hiding in caves and tunnels. The Egyptians denied ever using chemical warfare during their support of republican forces. M Meselson, "The Yemen," in S. Rose (ed.), *CBW: Chemical and Biological Warfare* (Boston, Mass: Beacon Press, 1968), p. 99. *See also* Pranamita Baruah, "Chemical Weapon Profile: Libya," vol. 4 (2), *Journal on Chemical and Biological Weapons*, Summer, January-June 2011, pp. 14-16.

56. On March 19, 1988, Iraqi airplanes bombed the village of Halabja, in Iraq. The inhabitants were Kurdish Iraqi citizens, a tribes-people who live in the region where the borders of Turkey, Iran, and Iraq meet. The casualties from this raid received worldwide media attention. The chemical weapons allegedly used were nerve agents, cyanide, and mustard. For more details see: http://www.opcw.org/html/global/search.html, visited November 23, 2011.
57. *Desk Study on the Environment in Iraq*. 2003. United Nations Environment Programme (UNEP), p. 52.
58. *Desk Study on the Environment in Iraq*. 2003. United Nations Environment Programme (UNEP), p. 52.
59. One of the darker chapters of the Iraq-Iran war was Iraq's use of chemical weapons against Iran and Iran's decision to employ chemical weapons (CW) in response. The use of CW by both sides created a number of dangerous precedents that continue to resonate. From a global perspective, the use of CW by Iraq and allegedly by Iran demonstrate that Third World weapons of mass destruction proliferation could potentially generate significant tactical military and strategic political benefits from the use of such instruments in conflict. Javed Ali, "Chemical Weapons and the Iran-Iraq War: A Case Study in Noncompliance," *The Nonproliferation Review*, Spring 2001, pp. 43-58.
60. In their lust to invade Iraq, the Bush administration and Tony Blair deeply discredited their own nation's moral standing, credibility and democratic ideals by outrageously misleading their own people and whipping a mass hysteria to justify the invasion of Iraq. Kim Coleman, *A History of Chemical Warfare* (New York: Palgrave Macmillan, 2005), p.130.
61. The effort was run out of the CIA station in Baghdad in collaboration with the Army's 203rd Military Intelligence Battalion and teams of chemical-defense and explosive ordnance disposal troops, officials and veterans of the units said. Many rockets were in poor condition and some were empty or held a nonlethal liquid, the officials said. But others contained the nerve agent sarin, which analysis showed to be purer than the intelligence community had expected given the age of the stock. As reported, most of the officials and veterans who spoke about the program did so anonymously because, they said, the details remain classified. According to report, the CIA declined to comment. The Pentagon, citing continuing secrecy about the effort, did not answer written questions and acknowledged its role only obliquely. Chivers C.J. and Schmitt Eric, CIA is Said to Have Bought and Destroyed Iraqi Chemical Weapons, *The New York Times*, 15 February 2015, available at: https://www.nytimes.com/2015/02/16/world/cia-is-said-to-have-bought-and-destroyed-iraqi-chemical-weapons.html.

62. It is also believed that Syria possesses sarin, VX and sulphur mustard, as well as missile and artillery shells for their delivery. US intelligence services reportedly believe that Syria possesses chemical weapons as well as delivery system. J. Solomon, "US, Israel monitor suspected Syrian WMD," *Wall Street Journal*, August 27, 2011. It has been reported that that these facilities are located in Aleppo, Damascus, Hamah and Lattakia, among other places, and that some chemical weapon production facilities are located at military sites that also store Scud missiles. US Department of State, "Daily press briefing," August 30, 2011, Available at: http://www.state.gov/r/pa/prs/dpb/2011/08/171281.htm, accessed September 15, 2011.
63. Since chemicals are integral to a number of consumer products and the chemical industry can be found in every corner of the world, the chemicals and equipment used to produce for the domestic market can be used to produce chemical warfare agents. For instance poison gas and nerve gas could be produced from chemicals used to make pesticides, fertilisers and pharmaceuticals. Similarly, flame retardant, petrol additives, paint solvents, ceramic, antiseptics can be produced from chemicals used for manufacturing Sarin; or petrol additives, hydraulic fluids, insecticides, flame retardants, pharmaceuticals, detergents, pesticides and missile fuels can be produced from Tabun. "The Chemical and Biological Weapons Threat," CIA Document, Washington DC, March 1996, pp. 9-16.
64. Afghan Taliban's campaign against female education and empowerment has reached new heights. There have been continuous unidentified poison attacks targeting several girls' schools since 2009. In April-May 2012, over a hundred schoolgirls and teachers were affected by poisoned drinking water and contaminated air at these schools. These attacks involved poisonous chemical substances and the victims had complained of headaches, nausea, vomiting, itching in the eyes following exposure. Unidentified toxic powder was used to contaminate the air in the classrooms as well as the drinking water source of these schools. Animesh Roul, "News Analysis: Chemical Substance Attacks in Afghan Schools," *Journal on Chemical and Biological Weapons*, Summer/January-June 2012, p. 7.
65. John Hart and Peter Clevesting, "Reducing Security Threats from Chemical and Biological Weapons," *SIPRI Yearbook 2011*, pp. 402-4.
66. Use of chemical weapons in the Syrian Civil War has been confirmed by the United Nations. The deadliest attacks were the Khan al-Assal attack in the suburbs of Aleppo in March 2013 and the Ghouta attack in the suburbs of Damascus in August 2013. Several other attacks have been alleged, reported and/or investigated. Prior to September 2013 the Syrian government had not publicly admitted to possess chemical weapons, although Western intelligence services believed it to hold one of the world's largest stockpiles. Patocka Jiri, Syria Conflict and Chemical Weapons: What is the Reality? Mil. Med. Sci. Lett., Vol. 85(1), 2016, p. 39-43.
67. A/RES/67/262, para 11, dated 15 May 2013.
68. Report of the Independent International Commission of Inquiry on the Syrian Arab Republic, UN Doc A/HRC/23/58, 4 June 2013, para 139.
69. 'Russia to the UN: Chemical Weapons "Clearly" Used in Syria' *CNN* (10 July 2013), edition.cnn.com/2013/07/09/world/meast/syria-russia-chemical-weapons.
70. It was reported that in Ghouta, a suburb of Syria's capital on the eastern edges of Damascus, an estimated 1,500 people died following an attack with the deadly

nerve agent sarin. In the wake of attack, social media conveyed haunting images of suffering and death on the part of innocent civilians, including many children.

71. United Nations Mission to Investigate Allegations of the Use of Chemical Weapons in the Syrian Arab Republic, *Report on the Alleged Use of Chemical Weapons in the Ghouta area of Damascus on 21 August 2013*, S/2013/553 (13 September 2013).
72. Until 14 October 2013, Syria was one of the seven non-State Parties of the Chemical Weapons Convention. In 1968, Syria acceded to the 1925 Geneva Protocol, which prohibits the use of CW, but not other activities, like production or stockpiling, which are enshrined in CWA. The Syrian government had been ambiguous in its public statements about its chemical capability and even in 2005 it said that the "Syrian Arab Republic does not possess chemical weapons, their means of delivery, or any related materials". Nevertheless, soon after the Syrian conflict started in 2011, both fractions, the Bashar al-Assad regime on one side and the Syrian opposition on the other, were accusing each other of CW use.
73. The Framework for the Elimination of Syrian Chemical Weapons, signed by US Secretary of State John Kerry and Russian Foreign Minister Sergey Lavrov.
74. Among other obligations, Article I.1(a) of the CWC bars states parties from transferring, directly or indirectly, chemical weapons to anyone. This ran counter to the US-Russia framework agreement, which sought the removal of chemical weapons from Syrian territory for accelerated destruction outside the country. In the case of Syria, given that the possessor state was not assigned the role of destroying its chemical weapons stockpile; the UN Security Council resolution 2118 allowed destruction to occur outside Syria.
75. Within three days of the Executive Council decision, a team of OPCW experts in Damascus, assisted Syrian officials to prepare an initial declaration covering some 1,300 metric tons of chemical warfare agent, as well as verifying the destruction of chemical weapons production facilities, equipment, and unfilled munitions at various sites around the country. Syria's chemical weapons were transported overland to Latakia and transferred to ships for delivery to destruction facilities at sea and on land. The most lethal chemicals, about 600 metric tons of sulfur mustard agent and methyl phosphoryl difluoride (DF), were trans-loaded and neutralized aboard the *Cape Ray* in the eastern Mediterranean. Resulting effluents from these operations, along with other toxic chemicals from Syria's weapons program, were sent for disposal to various facilities in Finland, Germany, the UK and the US. Uzumcu Ahmet, International Law and Disarmament: The Case of Chemical Weapons, The Justice Stephen Breyer Lecture Series on International Law 2014-2016, p. 24-36.
76. Destruction of Syrian chemical weapons completed, 4 January 2016, available at: https://www.opcw.org/news/article/destruction-of-syrian-chemical-weapons-completed/, accessed 30 June 2017.
77. Available at: http://www.britannica.com/EBchecked/topic/108951/chemical-weapon/274180/Banning-chemical-weapon, accessed October 22, 2012.
78. For example, the release of the chemical methyl isocyanate (MIC) in Bhopal, India, which caused thousands of deaths and even greater number of individuals with reported chronic injuries. When considering chemicals as weapons it is important, therefore, to consider not just the standard chemical warfare agents, but other toxic industrial chemicals. Alastair Hay, "Multiple Uses of Chemicals and Chemical Weapons, Toxicology of Chemical Warfare Agents," IUPAC Project, July 2007.

79. Augustine M. Prentiss, *Chemicals in War: A Treatise on Chemical Warfare* (New York: McGraw-Hill Book Company, 1937), p. 114.
80. The term vesicant agents refers to those compounds which vesicate (blister) the human and animal body on any surface, either exterior or interior, with which they come in contact. Vesicant compounds are highly toxic and produce multiple psychological effects on victim. At the outbreak of the First World War, over 70 vesicant compounds were known to science, yet only five were identified with the war. Of these two—dichlorethyl sulphide (mustard gas) and ethyldichlorarsine—were actually used; while the other three—chlorovinyldichlorarsine (lewisite), methyldichlorarsine, and dibromethyl sulphide—were not actually used in battle. Altogether about 12,000 tons of mustard gas were used in the First World War and caused a total of 400,000 casualties. Because of its low vitality, mustard gas is very persistent in the field, varying from one day in the open and one week in the woods in summer to several weeks in the woods in winter. Augustine M. Prentiss, *Chemicals in War: A Treatise on Chemical Warfare* (New York: McGraw-Hill Book Company, 1937), pp. 177, 180-81.
81. The first toxic gases employed in the First World War were the lacrimators. They cause intense, though temporary, irritation and blindness of the eyes; and are commonly known as tear gas. However, when lacrimators were employed against enclosed places, such as field fortifications, deep trenches, dugouts, etc., where vapours could accumulate, toxic concentrations could build up and serious casualties result. Brombenzyl cyanide (French) and Xylyl bromide (German) are simple lacrimators, where as Chlorpicrin (Russian) and Chloracetone (French) are examples of toxic lacrimators. Augustine M. Prentiss, *Chemicals in War: A Treatise on Chemical Warfare* (New York: McGraw-Hill Book Company, 1937), p. 129.
82. L. Henry, *Characteristics of Chemical Warfare Agents*, Stimson Centre, 2003. Available at: http://www.stimson.org/cbw, accessed May 22, 2012.
83. 2, 4-Dichlorophenoxyacetic acid (usually referred to by its abbreviation, 2, 4-D); and 2, 4, 5-T (2, 4, 5-Trichlorophenoxyacetic acid) are herbicides used in control of broadleaf weeds. B. S. Malik, "The Effectiveness of Chemical Agents," in Raja Menon (ed.), *Weapons of Mass Destruction: Options for India* (New Delhi: Sage Publications, 2004), p. 35.
84. Alastair Hay, "Multiple Uses of Chemicals and Chemical Weapons, Toxicology of Chemical Warfare Agents," IUPAC Project, July 2007.
85. Choking agents were employed first by the German army and later by the Allied forces in World War I. The first massive use of chemical weapons in that conflict came when the Germans released chlorine gas from thousands of cylinders along a 6-km (4-mile) front at Ypres, Belgium, on April 22, 1915, creating a wind-borne chemical cloud that opened a major breach in the lines of the unprepared French and Algerian units. Eventually both sides mastered the new techniques of using choking agents such as phosgene, chlorine, disphogene, chloropicrin, ethyldichlorasine, and perfluoroisoboxylene and launched numerous attacks—though without any militarily significant breakthroughs once each side had introduced the first crude gas masks and other protective measures. Choking agents are delivered as gas clouds to the target area, where individuals become casualties through inhalation of the vapour.
86. The toxic agent triggers the immune system, causing fluids to build up in the lungs, which can cause death through asphyxiation or oxygen deficiency if the lungs are badly damaged. During and immediately after exposure, there

is likely to be coughing, choking, a feeling of tightness in the chest, nausea, and occasionally vomiting, headache and lachrymation. The presence or absence of these symptoms is of little value in immediate prognosis. Some patients with severe coughs fail to develop serious lung injury, while others with little sign of early respiratory tract irritation develop fatal pulmonary oedema. There may be an initial slowing of the pulse, followed by an increase in rate. A period follows during which abnormal chest signs are absent and the patient may be symptom-free. This interval commonly lasts 2 to 24 hours but may be shorter. It is terminated by the signs and symptoms of pulmonary oedema. These begin with cough, dyspnoea, rapid shallow breathing and cyanosis. Nausea and vomiting may appear. As the oedema progresses, discomfort, apprehension and dyspnoea increase and frothy sputum develops. The patient may develop shock-like symptoms, with pale, clammy skin, low blood pressure and feeble, rapid heartbeat. During the acute phase, casualties may have minimal signs and symptoms and the prognosis should be guarded. Casualties may very rapidly develop severe pulmonary oedema. The effect of the chemical agent, once an individual is exposed to the vapour, may be immediate or can take up to three hours.

87. The ideal combat gas for use in armed conflict should meet the following tactical and technical requirements. (A) Tactical—(i) highly toxic, (ii) multiple effectiveness, (iii) non-persistency, (iv) effects of maximum duration, (v) immediate effectiveness, (vi) insidiousness in action, (vii) volatility (maximum field concentration), (viii) penetrability, (ix) invisibility, and (x) odourlessness. (B) Technical—(i) availability of raw material, (ii) ease of manufacture, (iii) chemical instability, (iv) non-hydrozable, (v) withstand explosion without decomposition, (vi) solid at ordinary temperature, (vii) melting point above maximum atmospheric temperature, (viii) boiling point as low as possible, (ix) high vapour pressure, (x) specific gravity approximately 1.5, and (xi) vapour density greater than air (the heavier the better). Phosgene came closer to meeting the above requirements than any other substance. Augustine M. Prentiss, *Chemicals in War: A Treatise on Chemical Warfare* (New York: McGraw-Hill Book Company, 1937), p. 47.

88. Blister agents were also developed and deployed in World War I. The primary form of blister agent used in that conflict was sulfur mustard, popularly known as mustard gas. Casualties were inflicted when personnel were attacked and exposed to blister agents like sulfur mustard or lewisite. Delivered in liquid or vapour form, such weapons burned the skin, eyes, windpipe, and lungs. The physical results, depending on level of exposure, might be immediate or might appear after several hours. Although lethal in high concentrations, blister agents seldom kill. Modern blister agents include sulfur mustard, nitrogen mustard, phosgene oxime, phenyldichlorarsine, and lewisite.

89. Nerve gases may be absorbed through body surface and when dispersed as a vapour, aerosol or adsorbed to dust, they are rapidly absorbed through the lungs. An exposure to concentration above 3 mg/m^3 affects vision. At higher exposures the inhibitory effects of the gases on the cholinesterase enzymes causes a wide range of symptoms including severe headache, eye pain, runny nose, tightness in the chest, wheezing, increased sweating, pronounced tiredness and weakness, rapid changes in mood and nightmares. Individuals are invariably very confused. Lethal doses of nerve agent are estimated to be about 150 mg/m^3 per minute for Tabun; and 70-100 mg/m^3 for Sarin. For VX the lethal dose is about half that for Sarin.

90. The chemical warfare agent 3-quinuclidinyl benzilate (BZ, also known as QNB) is an anticholinergic agent that affects both the peripheral and central nervous systems (CNS). It is one of the most potent anticholinergic psychomimetics known, with only small doses necessary to produce incapacitation. It is classified as a hallucinogenic chemical warfare agent. QNB usually is disseminated as an aerosol, and the primary route of absorption is through the respiratory system. Absorption also can occur through the skin or gastrointestinal tract. It is odourless. QNB's pharmacologic activity is similar to other anticholinergic drugs (e.g., atropine) but with a much longer duration of action. The onset of action is approximately 1 hour, with peak effects occurring 8 hours post exposure. Symptoms gradually subside over 2-4 days. Most of the QNB that enters the body is excreted by the kidneys, making urine the choice for detection. *The Wednesday Report*, Canada's Aerospace and Defence Weekly, available at: http://www.thewednesdayreport.com/twr/bz.htm, accessed October 23, 2012.
91. Augustine M. Prentiss, *Chemicals in War: A Treatise on Chemical Warfare* (New York: McGraw-Hill Book Company, 1937), pp. 10-12.
92. Under the provisions of the CWC, this obligation is cited repeatedly: Article IV, paragraph 10; Article V, paragraph 11; Article VII, paragraph 3; Verification Annex, Part II, paragraph 43; Part IV (A), paragraph 13; Part V, paragraph 33 (g) and paragraph 7 of Part VI of the Verification Annex.
93. Susanne Kopte, Michael Renner and Peter Wilke, "The Cost of Disarmament: Dismantlement of Weapons and the Disposal of Military Surplus," *The Nonproliferation Review,* Winter 1996, pp. 33-45.
94. A. V. Kaffka (ed.), *Sea-Dumped Chemical Weapons: Aspects, Problems and Solutions,* NATO ASI Series 7, 1995.
95. David M. Bearden, *US Disposal of Chemical Weapons in the Ocean: Background and Issues for Congress,* Congressional Research Service, 2006.
96. Geoff Plunkett, 2003, *Chemical Warfare Agent Sea Dumping off Australia,* Department of Defence, Australia, pp. 18-19.
97. The SS *LeBaron Russell Briggs* sailed for the last time on August 18, 1970. Its cargo bay held, among other materiel, more than 12,000 M55 rockets, each of which was loaded with a little less than 5 kg of sarin. US soldiers bored into the hull of the *Briggs,* allowing the incoming seawater to force it downwards. The vessel came to rest just over 5,000 m from the surface of the Atlantic Ocean, 400 km east of Cape Kennedy, Florida. The sunken ship represented the end of Operation CHASE (Cut Holes and Sink 'Em), a US Department of Defence programme that disposed of unwanted munitions at sea. Contrary to expectations, this material has not remained inert on the seabed. Dumped munitions have been found floating or washed ashore. Joshua Newman and Dawn Verdugo, "Building Awareness of Sea-dumped Chemical Weapons, Disarmament Forum: Maritime Security," available at: http://www.unidir.ch/pdf/articles/pdf-art2963.pdf, accessed October 29, 2012.
98. The US Armed Forces disposed of chemical weapons in the ocean from World War I through 1970. A total of 74 instances of disposal in the ocean were reported, of which 32 were off US shores and 42 were off foreign shores. At that time, it was thought that the vastness of ocean waters would absorb chemical agents that may leak from these weapons. Estimating the cumulative quantity of chemical weapons dumped in the ocean, and identifying all types of such weapons, is not possible because of incomplete historical records. The public concerns about human health and environmental risks, and the economic effects of potential damage to marine resources, led to a statutory prohibition on the

disposal of chemical weapons in the ocean in the early 1970s. The Congress enacted the Ocean Dumping Act, 1972, that banned the disposal of wastes in the ocean in general, including chemical weapons. The former Soviet Union, Germany, Great Britain, and France also disposed of chemical weapons in the ocean, including weapons captured during World War II. David M. Bearden, "The US Disposal of Chemical Weapons in the Ocean: Background and Issues for Congress," CSR report for Congress, January 3, 2007, available at: http://www.fas.org/sgp/crs/natsec/RL33432.pdf, accessed October 21, 2012.

99. One of the most heavily used areas for dumping of conventional and chemical warfare munitions is the Beaufort's Dyke, a 200 to 300 metres deep trench, located between Scotland and Northern Ireland. It has been estimated that over 1 million tons of munitions have been dumped in the Beaufort's Dyke since the early 1920s. Very large quantities of munitions were also dumped in the Skagerrak. It is reported that some 168,000 tonnes of ammunition were dumped in water depths of 600 to 700 metres. These munitions were dumped by sinking vessels loaded with the munitions and some 26 such vessels were dumped in the Skagerrak, south east of Arendal. One of the concerns relating to phosphorous devices is that the containers they were dumped in may now be in an advanced state of decay. John Hart, "A Review of Sea-Dumped Chemical Weapons," presented at The Environment and the Common Fisheries Policy, Threats to and Constraints on Sustainability (Greenwich Forum) January 27, 2000, The Royal Society, 6 Carlton House Terrace, London, Great Britain; Surikov and Duursma, "Dumped CW Agents in European Seas," in Egbert K. Duursma (ed.), *Dumped Chemical Weapons in the Sea—Options* (Netherlands: Dr. A. H. Heineken Foundations for the Environment, 1999).

100. The corrosion of the chemical weapon shells and rounds which were dumped five to six decades ago is progressing fast now. It is feared that major quantities of chemical agents will leak into the sea in the near future. Beyond the immediate impact of a further depletion of the world's endangered fish stocks, poisonous agents will enter the food chain via plankton. Seismic pulses have potential to damage thin skin chemical munitions, which could dramatically increase the numbers of chemical releases in an area at one time. If a dump site is disturbed enough to cause some sort of release, it could decrease the fish stock in the vicinity by approximately 70%.

101. In addition to contamination of seawater, there have been concerns among the public that chemical weapons could wash ashore, or that they could be retrieved accidentally during dredging operations or trawl fishing along the seabed. The likelihood of such events is difficult to predict. Generally, the greater the depth of disposal, the less likely that accidental retrieval or washing ashore would occur. Although ocean currents could move weapons into shallower waters and present a greater safety risk, the accumulation of sediment and marine growth could help anchor weapons to the seabed, making them less susceptible to movement. David M. Bearden, "The US Disposal of Chemical Weapons in the Ocean: Background and Issues for Congress, CSR report for Congress," January 3, 2007, available at: http://www.fas.org/sgp/crs/natsec/RL33432.pdf, accessed October 21, 2012.

102. T. Long, Introduction to sea-dumped munitions and hazardous wrecks, 2005. Available at: http://www.cnsopb.ns.ca/environment/pdf/sea/terry_longs_presentation.pdf, accessed February 28, 2012.

103. In 1946, during transport from La Serpe to Manfredonia Bay (Italy), a number of mustard bombs fell into the water. While some were recovered and dumped

further out to sea, "later, bombs were discovered floating nearby and in the harbour." A similar case occurred in the Gulf of Mexico in the same year, when a mustard bomb was recovered after having washed ashore. It was a remnant of 33 munitions that had earlier been dumped 32 km off the coast by the United States. More recently, in 1983 fishermen trawling in shallow waters (not more than 200 m) off the coast of Cape Moreton, Australia recovered a one-ton cylinder of sulfur mustard. Cases of encounters with sea-dumped CW materiel such as these intensified public fear of damage to marine and human life, as well as to coastal environments. The International Convention on the Prevention of Marine Pollution by Dumping of Wastes and Other Matter (the London Convention), 1975, prohibits the sea disposal of certain types of hazardous waste. In those countries possessing a CW materiel stockpile, more acceptable land-based chemical disposal and destruction methods have replaced sea-dumping.

104. CWC Articles III (1)(b) and IV(17).
105. E. Amato, "An Integrated Eco-toxicological Approach to Assess the Effects of Pollutants Released by Unexploded Chemical Ordnance Dumped in the Southern Adriatic (Mediterranean Sea)," vol. 149, no. 1, *Marine Biology,* (2006), pp. 17-23; G. Garnaga and A. Stankevicius, "Arsenic and Other Environmental Parameters at the Chemical Munitions Dumpsite in the Lithuanian Economic Zone of the Baltic Sea," vol. 3, no. 33, *Environmental Research, Engineering and Management* (2005), pp. 24-31.
106. J. Beddington and A. J. Kinloch, "Munitions dumped at sea: A literature review," IC Consultants Ltd., Imperial College, London, 2005. Available at: http://www.mod.uk/NR/rdonlyres/77CEDBCA-813A-4A6C-8E59-16B9E260E27A/0/ic_munitions_seabed_rep.pdf, accessed February 29, 2012.
107. Xin Zhang et al., "Geochemistry of Chemical Weapon Breakdown Products on the Seafloor: 1, 4-Thioxane in Seawater," vol. 43, no. 3, *Environmental Science and Technology* (2009), pp. 610–15.
108. If released into the marine environment, some CW agents' lifetimes are expected to be in the order of seconds to days (phosgene, cyanogen chloride), limiting their toxic effects after release. Other CW agents' lifetimes when located in deep marine environments are still relatively unknown (hydrogen cyanide). Of most concern are the nerve agents (e.g., sarin, VX), the blister agent sulfur mustard and arsenic-containing irritants, because they are predicted to persist for long periods in ocean waters. George O. Bizzigotti, et al., "Parameters for Evaluation of the Fate, Transport, and Environmental Impacts of Chemical Agents in Marine Environments," vol. 109, no. 1, *Chemical Reviews* (2009), pp. 236-56.
109. George O. Bizzigotti, et al., "Parameters for Evaluation of the Fate, Transport, and Environmental Impacts of Chemical Agents in Marine Environments," vol. 109, no. 1, *Chemical Reviews* (2009), pp. 236-56.
110. Fishermen trawling in the vicinity are most often the victims of exposure. The sulfur mustard responsible for the damage most likely came from CW materiel carried by the American freighter SS *John Harvey,* sunk by German aircraft in 1943, and CW agents dumped by US forces a few years later. The recent case of 1997 is particularly worrisome because it provides evidence that sulfur mustard remains toxic after nearly 50 years—even after having leaked into a marine environment. G. O. Bizzigotti, "Ocean Dumping of Chemical Weapons," 2005, *Noblis* <www.noblis.org>. Mustard globules caught in fishing nets near Japan account for over 100 cases of injury and 4 known deaths. Compiled from H. Kurata, "Lessons Learned from the Destruction of the Chemical Weapons of the Japanese Imperial Forces," in Jozef Goldblat (ed.), *Chemical Weapons: Destruction*

and Conversion (London, Taylor & Francis, 1980), Stockholm International Peace Research Institute, pp. 77-93.

111. Thomas Stock, "Sea-dumped Chemical Weapons and the Chemical Weapons Convention," in Alexander V. Kaffka (ed.), *Sea-dumped Chemical Weapons: Aspects, Problems and Solutions* (Dordrecht, MA: Kluwer Academic Publishers, 1995).
112. Joshua Newman and Dawn Verdugo, "Building awareness of sea-dumped chemical weapons," 2010, available at: http://www.einiras.org/pub/details.cfm?lng=en&id=119496, accessed March 4, 2012.
113. UN General Assembly Resolution A/RES/65/149 of February 10, 2011.
114. The full extent of this dumping will never be known due mainly to inadequate documentation of operations at the time of dumping and the subsequent loss or destruction of records that may have been taken. Remediation of marine chemical weapons and munitions dumpsites is technically challenging because of the nature of the material dumped and the uncertainty surrounding the quantities, type, locations and the present condition or stability of these materials. Overview of Past Dumping at Sea of Chemical Weapons and Munitions in the OSPAR Maritime Area 2010 update, OPSAR Commission, p. 4, available at: http://www.ospar.org/documents/dbase/publications/p00519_2010%20Revised%20Dumping%20at%20Sea%20of%20munitions%20and%20weapons.pdf, accessed March 4, 2010. The Convention for the Protection of the Marine Environment of the North-East Atlantic (OPSAR) entered into force on March 25, 1998. It has been ratified by Belgium, Denmark, Finland, France, Germany, Iceland, Ireland, Luxembourg, the Netherlands, Norway, Portugal, Sweden, Switzerland and the United Kingdom and approved by the European Community and Spain. In 2004, OSPAR began a programme to establish the extent of munitions dumping and to monitor the frequency of encounters. This has revealed that munitions were dumped at 148 sites and that 1,879 encounters with munitions have occurred since 2004. Around 58% of reported munitions were encountered by fishermen and 29% found on the shore. Most (76%) were removed from the sea or neutralised; 11% were returned to the sea for safety reasons.
115. P. G. Brewer and N. Nakayama, "What lies beneath: A plea for complete information," vol. 42, *Environ. Sci. Technol* (2008), pp. 1394-399.
116. David M. Bearden, *US Disposal of Chemical Weapons in the Ocean: Background and Issues for Congress*, CSR Report for Congress, updated January 3, 2007, pp. 8, 9.
117. Libya hands over last stockpile of chemical weapon ingredients, *The Guardian*, 1 September 2016.
118. Col. Gen. Valery Kapashin, a military official who heads the storage and elimination of Russia's chemical stockpiles, said the chemical weapons currently in existence will be destroyed by December 2017. Pascaline Mary, Russia's Chemical Weapon Stockpile Will Be Completely Destroyed By End of 2017, Top Moscow Official Says, http://www.ibtimes.com/russias-chemical-weapon-stockpile-will-be-completely-destroyed-end-2017-top-moscow-2437923.
119. Between the WWI and WWII the major powers, including Germany, developed and produced new chemical warfare agents and had accumulated large CW stockpiles. Since there were very few incidents of their use, the Allies seized between 270,000 and 350,000 tons of chemical ammunitions consisting of mustard gas, lewisite, adamsite, phosgene, diphosgene, and nerve agents after the WWII. Historical records show that between 288,258 to 296,103 tons of CW were discovered, destroyed, dumped or recycled on German territory

between the end of WWII and the end of 1947. According to Article 3 of the Potsdam Agreement Germany had to be demilitarised and all material should be distributed to the Allies or destroyed. One of the most favoured options those days was the disposal of these munitions by dumping at sea, as recommended by the Allied Control Commission's Standing Committee on War Material in November 1945. The information of disposal of CW at sea is not accurate. In the last two decades a number of accidents, sometimes fatal or having long-term harmful affects involving fishermen and tourists have been reported from Baltic Sea and the North Sea. There is another long-term dispute between China and Japan over finding a proper solution for the destruction of the CW stocks remaining in China, abandoned by Japan more than half century ago. Thomas Stock, "The Problem of old and abandoned chemical weapons under the Chemical Weapons Convention," in M. Bothe, N. Ronzitti and A. Rosas (eds.), *The New Chemical Weapons Convention: Implementation and Prospects* (The Hague: Kluwer Law International, 1998), pp. 204-7.

120. Pierre Waithe, United Nations resolution passed on aquatic chemical weapons, available at: http://digitaljournal.com/article/303022, accessed March 4, 2012.
121. Japan began using chemical weapons against the Chinese in 1937. By the end of 1945, Japanese chemical warfare against the Chinese had resulted in an estimated 80,000 casualties and 10,000 fatalities. The Japanese army did not use all of the chemical weapons it had brought to China and left many behind during its retreat in the closing months of the war. Tokyo feared that discovery of the stockpile of chemical munitions by the Soviet Red Army would show Japan's actions were not consistent with the Geneva Protocol banning chemical-weapons use. Accordingly, the Japanese Army sought to hide its unused chemical weapons. When the Chinese army reclaimed Japanese occupied territory, no chemical weapons were found. Subsequently a large quantity of old and toxic chemical munitions were discovered in the Tumen River in Jilin province. In 1992 China announced that 100 tons of agent and 2,000,000 chemical munitions had been abandoned on its territory. In May 1996, Shigekazu Sato of the Japanese Ministry of Foreign Affairs announced that Japanese members of a joint survey team estimated that there are 700,000 abandoned chemical munitions in Jilin province. Hongmei Deng and Peter O'Meara Evans, "Social and Environmental Aspects of Abandoned Chemical Weapons in China, A Report on Abandoned Chemical Weapons in China," *The Nonproliferation Review*, Spring-Summer, 1997, pp. 101-8.
122. Abandoned weapons have been accidentally unearthed, opened or ruptured by Chinese citizens, exposing individuals to the chemical agent. It is believed that approximately 2,000 people have been victims of abandoned weapons. Mike Bromach, *Abandoned Chemical Weapons in China: The Unresolved Japanese Legacy* (Washington: Global Green USA, May 2001), p. 22.
123. According to Chemical Weapons Convention (CWC), "For the purpose of destroying abandoned chemical weapons, the Abandoning State Party shall provide all necessary financial, technical, expert, facility as well as other resources. The Territorial State Party shall provide appropriate cooperation," CWC Verification Annex (VA), Part IV (B), paragraph 15.
124. CWC, Article VIII, paragraph 3.
125. As regards abandoned chemical weapons (ACWs), as of December 2011, 4 countries had declared that ACWs were present on their territories. It has been reported by 15 countries that they have possessed old chemical weapons (OCWs) since the CWC's entry-into-force. OCW destruction operations in 2011

were carried out in Belgium, Italy, Japan, Germany, Switzerland and the UK; while destruction operations for ACWs in China continued. *SIPRI Yearbook 2012* (Oxford: Oxford University Press).

126. Prior to actual destruction, the munitions must be recovered, identified, and disassembled—operations that are arguably more costly, hazardous, and time-consuming than the destruction process itself. In particular, munitions armed with a fuse may detonate accidentally. Hongmei Deng and Peter O'Meara Evans, "Social and Environmental Aspects of Abandoned Chemical Weapons in China," *The Non-proliferation Review,* Spring-Summer 1997, pp. 101-7.
127. The destruction of CW can produce short-term and long-term effects on human health and the natural environment. Short-term hazards mainly involve worker safety and the effects of an accidental release of agent. Long-term hazards result from the exposure of plant workers, the surrounding community, and the environment to low-level emissions and discharges from the destruction process itself. The risks to local environment are associated with the total environmental burden resulting from aqueous discharges, atmosphere emissions, and solid-waste management. Hongmei Deng and Peter O'Meara Evans, "Social and Environmental Aspects of Abandoned Chemical Weapons in China," *The Non-proliferation Review,* Spring-Summer 1997, pp. 101-7.

2 D

LEGAL CONTROL: CHEMICAL AND BIOLOGICAL WEAPONS

The history of mankind's efforts to proscribe, limit, and restrict the use of chemical and biological weapons[1] is as long as the history of the use of such weapons. **Manu Smriti,** one of the oldest and probably the most important Indian treatise on the conduct of war, urged combatants not to use poison or poisoned arrows.[2] The Greeks and Romans customarily observed a prohibition against using poison or poisoned weapons. German gunners in the late Middle Ages pledged not to use "poisoned globes" or any poison since to use such devices was considered unjust and "unworthy of a real soldier." Hugo Grotius (1583-1645), the Dutch jurist and diplomat, was of the view that it was "forbidden to kill anybody by means of poison" and that "it is not allowed to poison weapons and water."[3]

In 1675, French and German armies agreed not to use poisoned weapons against each other.[4] W. T. Sherman's memoirs contain an account of Confederate soldiers poisoning ponds by dumping the carcasses of dead animals into them. Incidents like this led to the issuance by the US Army of General Order No. 100 (Lieber Code),[5] which stated: "The use of poison in any manner, be it to poison wells, or food, or arms, is wholly excluded from modern warfare. He that uses it puts himself out of the pale of the law and usages of war." The Lieber Instructions strongly influenced the further codification of the laws of war and the adoption of similar regulations by other states.

The first international attempt to control chemical and biological weapons was made in 1874, when the International Declaration

Concerning the Laws and Customs of War was signed in Brussels. The Declaration included the prohibition of poison or poisoned arms.[6] During the First Hague Peace Appeal in 1899, the Hague Convention[7] elaborated on the Brussels accord, specifically with reference to poison gas. The Hague Gas Declaration contained an agreement "to abstain from the use of projectiles the sole object of which is the diffusion of asphyxiating or deleterious gases." Twenty-seven states became parties to this declaration, including all participants in the conference except the US. The Declaration of the Second Hague Peace Conference (1907) retained the ban against poisons.[8]

Though the use of poisonous substances as weapons of war was prohibited before the First World War, poisonous gas was used extensively in that war.[9] At the conclusion of the War, articles in various peace treaties reiterated and enlarged the prohibition embodied in the 1899 declaration. Chemical disarmament was imposed on the States which had lost the war. For instance, Article 171 of the Treaty of Versailles (1919) stated: "The use of asphyxiating, poisonous or other gases and all analogous liquids, materials or devices being prohibited, their manufacture and importation are strictly prohibited in Germany." In 1922, the Washington Treaty, signed by the US, Japan, France, Italy and Britain, prohibited the use of "asphyxiating, poisonous or other gases, and all analogous liquids, materials or devices," but it did not enter into force. The excessive use of poisonous gases in the First World War caused such abhorrence that the international community decided to prohibit the use of chemical, biological and toxin weapons in war. These efforts produced the 1925 Geneva Protocol.

The Geneva Protocol

Under the auspices of the League of Nations, the Conference for the Supervision of the International Trade in Arms and Ammunition and in Implements of War considered provisions prohibiting international trade in poisonous or asphyxiating gases.[10] The delegates to the

Convention concluded the Protocol for the Prohibition of the Use of Asphyxiating, Poisonous or Other Gases, and of Bacteriological Methods of Warfare (Geneva Protocol) on June 17, 1925.[11]

The Protocol acknowledged that the use in war of asphyxiating, poisonous or other gases, and of all analogous liquids materials or devices, had been justly condemned by the general opinion of the civilised world. The signatories to the Protocol agreed to be bound by the prohibition against the use of such arms in war and agreed to apply the Polish proposal to "extend this prohibition to the use of bacteriological methods of warfare." The Protocol also established that the prohibition "shall be universally accepted as part of international law." The inclusion of the prohibition as part of international law is significant, binding even those States that are not parties to the treaty, creating a universal standard against the first use of such weapons.[12]

Many States became parties to the Protocol subject to the reservation that it would be binding only in relation to other States bound by it and would cease to be binding if an enemy or its allies failed to respect the prohibitions embodied therein.[13] In other words, the Protocol was regarded by such States as containing not an absolute prohibition of the use of such weapons, but only an agreement not to use such weapons first.[14]

The Protocol outlawed the use of chemical as well as biological weapons in armed conflict, but was silent on the issues of research, production, development, storage, testing, and stockpiling. It was this enormous loophole that enabled nations to continue with programmes related to chemical and biological weapons. In addition, the Protocol did not address the issues of monitoring and verifying instances of non-compliance even with respect to the future use of such weapons.

Legal Control: Biological Weapons

The 1925 Geneva Protocol bans the use, but not the production, stockpiling or deployment of chemical and biological weapons.

Many States reserved the right to retaliate in kind if attacked with the prohibited weapons. The prohibition of the use of biological weapons, even in retaliation, came up during the second phase of the League of Nations Disarmament Conference in 1932-1933. The draft convention for general disarmament proposed an absolutely ban on the use of bacteriological weapons, even in retaliation. However, the conference was postponed and never reconvened. The observance of the Protocol was not strict and Italy used gas during its invasion of Ethiopia in 1935-36. After World War II, a number of biological warfare research programmes were undertaken, the largest of which were conducted by the Soviet Union and the US. The weapons developed made use of agents causing anthrax, smallpox, plague and tularaemia.[15]

In 1946, the UN General Assembly called for the disarmament of atomic and other weapons of mass destruction. In 1948, the UN Commission for Conventional Armaments included BW in its definition of weapons of mass destruction. Since 1966, the UN General Assembly has adopted several resolutions calling for the strict observance of the principles of the 1925 Geneva Protocol. Resolution 2603A (XXIV) of December 16, 1969 interprets the Protocol, declaring that it prohibits the use in international armed conflicts of: (a) Any chemical agent of warfare—chemical substance, whether gaseous liquid or solid—which might be employed because of their direct toxic effects on man, animals or plants; (b) any biological agents of warfare—living organisms, whatever their nature, or infective material derived from them—which are intended to cause disease or death in man, animals or plants, and which depend for their effects on their ability to multiply in the person, animal or plant attacked.

During the 1960s chemical and biological weapons (CBW) control and disarmament focused on the United States. At that time the US had not ratified the Geneva Protocol and was accused of using chemical weapons in Vietnam. Discussions of disarmament issues took place both in New York at the UN's First Committee and in Geneva at the Eighteen Nation Disarmament Committee (ENDC). In 1966, Hungary presented a draft resolution to the First Committee that demanded "strict and absolute compliance by all States" with the Geneva Protocol. In 1968, the UK tabled a working paper on microbiological warfare at the the ENDC, describing the principle elements of a draft convention. The working paper recommended the establishment of a competent body of experts, established under the auspices of the United Nations, to investigate allegations of breaches of the Protocol and a commitment by parties to cooperate with any investigation.[16] The principal elements in the draft convention included:[17]

1. A common understanding that any use of microbiological warfare and in any circumstances was contrary to international law and a crime against humanity and therefore a complete prohibition of use
2. A ban on the production of agents for hostile purposes while recognising the necessity of production of agents for peaceful purposes
3. A ban on the production of ancillary equipment
4. An obligation to destroy stocks of agents or equipment
5. A ban on research aimed at production of prohibited agents and equipment
6. Provisions for access by authorities to "all research which might give rise to allegations" of non-compliance
7. Openness of relevant research to international investigation and public scrutiny

The Biological Warfare Draft Convention tabled in 1969 contained very strong provisions which were watered down in the 1972 Biological Weapon Convention.[18] It prohibited the use of biological agents for hostile purposes in any circumstances and explicitly outlawed the hostile use of BW against humans, other animals, or crops. It extended the ban on use to possession and research and required parties to destroy or divert to peaceful purposes stocks of weapons agents, ancillary equipment and vectors. The draft also described the procedures for dealing with complaints of violation of the Convention, with allegations of use being treated differently from other allegations of non-compliance. Allegations of use were to be taken to the UN Secretary-General along with a recommendation for an investigation. Allegations of breaches of the Convention that did not involve use were to be taken to the Security Council along with a request for an investigation. Such requests, of course, would be subject to the veto power of the permanent members.[19]

Finally, on April 10,1972, the Convention on the Prohibition of the Development, Production and Stockpiling of Bacteriological (Biological) and Toxin Weapons and on Their Destruction (BWC) was signed in Washington, London and Moscow.[20] The BWC was the first multilateral disarmament treaty banning the production and use of an entire category of weapons. Article I of the treaty mandates several prohibitions:

Each State Party ... undertakes never in any circumstances to develop, produce, stockpile, or otherwise acquire or retain (1) microbial or other biological agents, or toxins whatever their origin or method of production or types and in quantities that have no justification for prophylactic, protective, or other peaceful purposes; (2) weapons, equipment, or means of delivery designed to use such agents or toxins for hostile purposes or in armed conflict.

In addition, the BWC enjoins participating States not to transfer any of the agents, toxins, weapons, equipment, or means of delivery to any recipient for non-peaceful purposes and otherwise not to abet the proliferation or acquisition of biological agents or weapons. The BWC also requires states that possess biological weapons to destroy them within nine months of the treaty's activation.[21] Other key provisions of the BWC are as follows:

Article III: Not to transfer, or in any way assist, encourage or induce anyone else to acquire or retain biological weapons

Article IV: To take any national measures necessary to implement the provisions of the BWC domestically

Article V: To consult bilaterally and multilaterally to solve any problems with the implementation of the BWC

Article VI: To request the UN Security Council to investigate alleged breaches of the BWC and to comply with its subsequent decisions[22]

Article VII: To assist States which have been exposed to a danger as a result of a violation of the BWC

Article X: To do all of the above in a way that encourages the peaceful uses of biological science and technology

Article I of the BWC prohibits the development or production of "microbial or other biological agents, or toxins," without further defining them. In view of this, the World Health Organisation (WHO) formulated a definition of biological agents considered to be authoritative.[23] It defined biological agents "as those that depend for their effects on multiplication within the target organism and are intended for use in war to cause disease or death in man, animals or plants; they may be transmissible or non-transmissible." The BWC (in its title and in Article I) does not explicitly prohibit "use" of biological weapons. However, the Final Declaration of the 1996 Treaty Review Conference reaffirmed that, although "use" is not explicitly prohibited under Article I of the BWC, it is still considered to be a violation of the convention.

Under Article XI of the BWC, States Parties may propose amendments to the Convention. An amendment shall enter into force for each State Party accepting the amendment when the amendment has been accepted by a majority of the States Parties to the convention. For each remaining State Party thereafter, the amendment will take effect on the date of acceptance. The Convention gives the parties a right of withdrawal, provided that notice is given to all other States Parties to the convention and to the UN Security Council three months in advance. A notice must include a statement of the extraordinary events the State regards as having jeopardised its supreme interests (Article XIII).

The BWC requires that States Parties participate in review conferences to be held at five-year intervals. The objective of these meetings is to undertake an article-by-article review of the BWC's operation, ascertaining whether the purposes of the treaty's preamble and main articles are being achieved. Each such review should take into account any new scientific and technological developments relevant to the BWC (Article XII).

The Convention embodies the principle known as the general purpose criterion under which all relevant activities are prohibited unless they can be justified as being for the peaceful purposes permitted under the Convention, including justifications relating to types and quantities of materials being used for prophylactic, protective or other peaceful purposes.

Shortcomings of the BWC

The 1972 Convention does not have provisions for monitoring and verification, implementation and enforcement. There is no formal verification regime to monitor compliance. Member States are encouraged to abide by numerous confidence-building measures (CBMs) prescribed by State Parties at various review conferences. These include domestic implementation measures, if considered necessary; consultation and cooperation among parties; lodging of complaints with the UN Security Council; and incentives, such as assistance to victims. Since 1991, there have been efforts to negotiate a verification protocol to strengthen the BWC and put in place an international mechanism to monitor compliance. The difficulties with creating such a verification regime are that any nation with a developed pharmaceutical industry has the potential to make biological weapons and that non-state have entered the field.

To cite one example of allegations of non-compliance, in 1981, the US accused the Soviet Union of supplying mycotoxins—poisonous compounds synthesised by fungi—to its Communist allies in Southeast Asia for military use against resistance forces in Laos and Cambodia. The UN Secretary-General dispatched two expert groups to the region to investigate the allegations. Both the investigations proved inconclusive, demonstrating the need to launch an investigation shortly after an alleged attack, when the forensic evidence is still fresh, and to gain full access to the affected sites and attack victims.

An additional problem is that many governments have not ratified or fully implemented national legislation and other instruments to ensure the fulfilment of their obligations. There are concerns regarding the possible misuse or negative impact of bio-defence programmes, such as their potential to provide cover for the illegal development or maintenance of biological weapons-related expertise. There is also a fear of the impact of terrorist actions, coupled with profound concern that modern economies may be particularly vulnerable to disruption from the deliberate spread of disease.[24]

Protocol to BWC

The BWC is lacking a legally binding verification mechanism for assessing state compliance.[25] Verification under the BWC poses particular problems in that every relevant public, private, government and academic facility must fall within the scope of the system and it must provide reliable enough data to display compliance convincingly. Discussion on a verification mechanism started at the Third Review Conference in 1991. The Ad Hoc Group of Governmental Experts (VEREX), was directed to study possible verification measures. VEREX laid the groundwork for the Ad Hoc Group (AHG) which became the negotiating body assigned to produce a legally binding instrument.

In 1995, a draft for the BTWC Protocol that would establish legally-binding multilateral measures to promote compliance with the Convention was prepared. It contained several important measures: (i) Annual declarations requiring states parties to identify and give brief descriptions of their bio-defence facilities and programmes, and of industrial facilities that could be used to produce microbial cultures in quantity; (ii) Random visits to declared facilities to increase confidence in the completeness and accuracy of declarations; (iii) A clarification process for cases in which a facility was not declared that another state party suspected should have been, or in which a state party questioned the accuracy of a specific declaration; and (iv) Provision for a multilateral team to be sent on short notice to investigate facilities that were suspected of being used to illegally produce microbial weapons agents, allegations of use of BW, or disease outbreaks that were suspected to be the result of accidental release of microbes from an illegal facility.

After arduous negotiations, by mid 2001 a possible consensus text had emerged. During the 24th negotiating session, the delegates expected that a final text would result from their efforts. However, the US brought that process to an end citing risks to the economic viability of its pharmaceutical and biotech industries. The US representative stated: "After extensive deliberation, the US has concluded that the current approach to a Protocol to the Biological Weapons Convention…is not, in our view, capable of… strengthening confidence in compliance with the Biological Weapons Convention … We will therefore be unable to support the current text, even with changes."

The US criticized the Protocol as inadequate to detect covert proliferation. The value of the Protocol was seen as greatly increasing the transparency of the biological industry and bio-defence activities of all countries, thus lessening unjustified suspicions. The routine visits, coupled to the possibility of an intrusive investigation to resolve specific suspicions, were thought to be a significant deterrent to all but the most determined proliferators. The Protocol was seen as an improvement in security in the short term, whose value would increase in future. The US rejection of the Protocol raises the possibility that there are new classified bio-defence programmes that are deemed too sensitive politically or technically for even the limited disclosure that the Protocol would require.[26]

Reviewing the Convention

The first[27] and second review conferences took place in Geneva from March 3 to 21, 1980 and from September 8 to 26, 1986 respectively.

The Second Conference asserted that the provisions of the BWC cover all relevant current and future scientific and technological developments and apply to all international, national and non-State actors, thereby bringing the issue of bioterrorism within the scope of the Convention. It also permitted the World Health Organisation (WHO) to coordinate emergency response measures in cases of the alleged use of biological and toxin weapons. Further, it laid down the procedure for resolving doubts about compliance, known as the Formal Consultative Process, and established an annual exchange of information, known as confidence-building measures (CBMs). The CBMs were intended to reduce ambiguities, doubts and suspicions, and improve international cooperation in the field of peaceful biological activities. An Ad Hoc Meeting of Scientific and Technical Experts was held from March 31 to April 15, 1987, to establish the precise format of the CBMs.

Prior to the Third Review Conference, a number of countries recognised the inadequacy of relying solely upon voluntary CBMs for enhancing confidence in the compliance of the BWC. In addition, other developments contributed to widening concerns about the BWC's weaknesses. A number of reports alleged that as many as ten countries possessed or were in the process of acquiring biological weapons.[28] Moreover, after the 1991 Gulf War, the UN Special Commission began to detect evidence that Iraq, then a signatory of the BWC, had a biological weapons programme. The situation in Iraq also highlighted the lack of an independent inspectorate to monitor the BWC's prohibitions.[29]

The Third Review Conference[30] asserted that the BWC covers agents relating to humans, animals and plants. It requested States to re-examine their national implementation measures; revised the format for Formal Consultative Meetings; revised the CBMs; indirectly encouraged the UN Secretary-General to conduct investigations into allegations of the use of biological and toxin weapons; and expanded upon the coordinating role of intergovernmental organisations in response to such occurrences. The Third Review Conference is remembered for the establishment of the Ad Hoc Group of Verification Experts (VEREX).[31]

The Ad Hoc Group (VEREX), examined and evaluated 21 measures that ranged from off-site surveillance of publications to on-site monitoring and inspections. VEREX evaluated each proposed verification measure according to the amount of data it could or could not provide; its ability to differentiate between activities that are prohibited and permitted under the BWC; its capability to clarify ambiguities concerning compliance; its requirements for manpower, technology, equipment, or other material; its implications for the protection of confidential business information and for the development of permitted research and scientific activities; and its financial, legal, organisational, and safety ramifications.[32] In all, VEREX met four times from March 1992 to September 1993. In its final report of September 1993, VEREX concluded that no single approach could adequately monitor the BWC. Rather, VEREX recommended a combination of means—including off-site and on-site measures—to make the BWC a more effective instrument. Off-site measures include national declarations of biological weapons defense programmes, vaccines, and facilities handling specific organisms and toxins; on-site measures include short notice-inspections and information visits to declared facilities.[33]

In September 1994, a Special Conference of BWC State Parties was convened in Geneva to discuss the findings of VEREX. This Conference called for the formation of the Ad Hoc Group to draft verification measures to be incorporated into a legally binding protocol to the BWC. In the course of its negotiations, the Ad Hoc Group was to address the creation of measures to investigate the alleged use of biological weapons, as well as the following four issues: (i) the definition of terms and objective criteria (e.g., lists of biological warfare agents and possible threshold quantities); (ii) the possible incorporation of existing and additional enhanced CBMs into the verification regime; (iii) the development of a system of measures to promote compliance with the BWC; and, (iv) the delineation of a programme for technical cooperation in the field of biotechnology for peaceful purposes.

The Fourth Review Conference established that the BWC effectively covers the use of biological and toxin weapons, and asserted that destruction and conversion activities related to existing weapons and associated facilities should take place prior to accession to the Convention.[34] It also recommended a series of specific measures to enhance the implementation of Article X. The states parties to the BWC were aware of the potential impact of new scientific and technological developments as an increasingly serious problem. Thus, during the Fourth Conference of the BTWC in 1996 these concerns were extended to genomics.[35]

The Fifth Review Conference opened in Geneva on November 19, 2001, but was suspended because of divergent positions taken by members of the Ad Hoc Group. A resumed session was held in Geneva from November 11 to 22, 2002. It was decided at this session that a series of annual meetings of experts and of States Parties would be held to discuss, and promote common understanding and effective action on a range of topics to strengthen the Convention.

In the Fifth Review Conference, the States Parties adopted a final report that included a decision to hold annual meetings of States Parties as well as meetings of experts in the years leading up to the Sixth Review Conference in 2006. These meetings were meant to bridge gaps between divergent national positions and demonstrate that States Parties could still work together to improve the functioning of the BWC. They were tasked with discussing, and promoting common understanding and effective action on a number of predetermined topics. In practice, these meetings turned out to be a much greater success than predicted. The value of the first inter-sessional process was summed up in India's opening statement to the Sixth Review Conference held in Geneva from November 20 to December 8, 2006:

> When the first inter-sessional process started, there was some scepticism about its prospects. Contrary to these forebodings,

> however, States Parties gained considerably from it. Treating the BWC regime as one of the live issues of the multilateral disarmament agenda strengthened the regime. Besides, the States Parties benefited from a most useful exchange of information and experiences on issues relevant to the effective implementation of the Convention. The knowledge creation and its dissemination, which characterised the exchanges, were enriched by the participation in the process of relevant international organisations and national public-health stakeholders.[36]

The Fifth BWC Review Conference, which many experts thought could have resolved the fate of the Ad Hoc Group, was suspended on its last day, after the US tabled a controversial proposal to terminate the Ad Hoc Group's mandate and replace it with an annual meeting of BWC States Parties. The States Parties resumed the Fifth Review Conference in November 2002, but failed to agree on any verification measures, including the proposed protocol.

The Sixth Review Conference was the most substantive review of the BWC since the Third Review Conference. It produced a final declaration which: closed a loophole on destruction deadlines for States that had signed but not previously ratified the BWC (as well as strengthening requirements for safety, security and reporting for destruction and conversion activities); established a need for national export control regimes as a means to mitigate direct or indirect transfers of relevant material; developed a basic requirement for ensuring safety and security of relevant material when used for permitted purposes; required national penal legislation and other measures to implement the BWC and called for their extraterritorial application; developed basic requirements for national education, outreach and awareness-raising activities for relevant stakeholder communities; included a commitment to develop national, regional and international capabilities for the detection and surveillance of disease; included a commitment to review national legislative and regulatory frameworks to ensure they comply with Article X and to report on how this article is being implemented; called for an efficient coordination mechanism for relevant scientific cooperation and technology transfer in the UN system; noted the increasing importance of public-private partnerships in implementing the BWC; and institutionalised the use of Arabic as an official language of future BWC meetings.

The Seventh Review Conference[37] took concrete action to strengthen the BWC, including: creating a plan of action to increase the membership of the treaty; reaching an agreement for States Parties to nominate national contact points to facilitate communications relevant to the BWC; officially endorsing the common understandings reached during the first intersessional process; establishing an Implementation Support Unit, addressing a long-standing need for institutional support for the efforts of States Parties, and tasking them with updating the reporting procedure for CBMs to take into account modern information technology; and initiating a detailed second intersessional work programme to help ensure effective implementation of the BWC until the Seventh Review Conference.

In its final declaration, the Conference reaffirmed that under all circumstances, the use of biological and toxin weapons is effectively prohibited by the Convention and reiterated the determination of States Parties to condemn any use of biological agents or toxins other than for peaceful purposes, by anyone at any time. The Conference emphasised that States must take all necessary safety and security measures to protect human populations and the environment, including animals and plants, when carrying out destruction and/ or diversion of agents, toxins, weapons, equipment or means of delivery prohibited by Article I of the Convention. Effective national export controls and other appropriate measures were called for to ensure that only authorised direct and indirect transfers relevant to the Convention took place. The Conference called upon States Parties to adopt legislative, administrative, judicial and other measures, including penal legislation, to enhance domestic implementation of the Convention, ensure the safety and security of microbial or other biological agents or toxins in laboratories, facilities, and during transportation and to prevent unauthorised access to and removal of such agents or toxins.[38]

The Eighth Review Conference was unable to reach agreement on a new, more ambitious work-plan and has left the process for the next few years (2017-2021) largely undirected.[39] The UN Under-Secretary-General and High Representative for Disarmament Affairs, Mr. Kim Won-soo had outlined four gaps in the bio-weapons regime: the 'universality gap', 'implementation gap', 'response gap', and the 'institutional gap'. He urged the states to explore new ways to address and close these gaps. Though, the conference came up with a final outcome document, it did not contain any substantive measures akin to the previous review conferences. The meeting also failed to agree upon any structural reforms in the bio-weapons regime.

Investigations

Articles VI and VII of the BWC provide a mechanism for investigating the alleged use of biological and toxin weapons and for extending assistance during such an event. Article VI states:

1. Any State Party to this convention which finds that any other State Party is acting in breach of obligations deriving from the provisions of the Convention may lodge a complaint with the Security Council of the United Nations. Such a complaint should include all possible evidence confirming its validity, as well as a request for its consideration by the Security Council.
2. Each State Party to this Convention undertakes to cooperate in carrying out any investigation which the Security Council may initiate, in accordance with the provisions of the Charter of the United Nations, on the basis of the complaint received by the Council. The Security Council shall inform the States Parties to the Convention of the results of the investigation.

Since these provisions had not been invoked so far, the final declaration of the Third Review Conference elucidated the process for lodging complaints under Article VI. The Security Council has authorised the UN Secretary-General to carry out investigations into the possible use of chemical and bacteriological (biological) or toxin weapons whenever reported by any member State. The Third Review Conference requested the Security Council to inform State Parties about the outcome of any investigation initiated under Article VI. Further, in view of Article VII,[40] the Review Conference requested that the UN and the intergovernmental organisations such as the WHO to provide timely emergency assistance whenever any State Party is exposed to the dangers of the BW. The General Assembly resolution of December 4, 1990[41] provides the mechanism for investigations of reports on the possible use of chemical and bacteriological (biological) or toxin weapons.[42]

Biological Weapons: Future Threat

The biological disarmament regime has come under growing pressure from the global spread of biotechnologies suitable for both civil and military applications, and from the revolution in genetic engineering, which has made it possible to manipulate the genetic characteristics encoded in the chemical structure of the DNA molecule. In 1973, after the publication of techniques for cutting and splicing DNA molecules across species lines, a few scientists expressed concern that these powerful methods might be applied to develop new and more dangerous biological-warfare agents.[43]

The verification of the non-production of biological weapons is inherently more difficult than that of chemical weapons, for three reasons. First, since BW agents are living micro-organisms that reproduce inside the host, they are much more potent per unit weight. Thus, whereas chemical warfare agents must be stockpiled in hundreds or thousands of tons to be militarily significant, a few kilograms of a biological warfare agent such as the anthrax bacteria could cause comparable levels of casualties. Such a small quantity of a biological warfare agent would be relatively easy to hide. Second, whereas the production of chemical warfare agents requires certain distinctive precursor materials, reactions, and process equipment and leaves behind tell-tale chemical signatures, the production of biological warfare agents involves materials and equipment that are almost entirely dual-use. As a result, it can be extremely difficult to distinguish illicit biological weapon agent production from legitimate activities permitted under the BWC, such as the production of vaccines. Third, because of the potency of biological weapon agents and the exponential rate of microbial growth, a militarily significant quantity of biological weapon agent could be produced in a matter of days in a small, easily concealed clandestine facility.

Because of the ability of pathogenic micro-organisms to multiply rapidly within the host, small quantities of a biological agent—if widely disseminated through the air—could inflict casualties over a very large area. However, the lengthy incubation period of microbial pathogens places a major limitation on their battlefield utility, except in situations of attrition warfare, sabotage attacks against command and communications facilities deep behind enemy lines, or strikes against massed troops prior to their commitment to battle. Notwithstanding the delayed effects of biological weapons, they would be suitable for use against crops, livestock, or people as a means of crippling the economy and psychological morale of a targeted country. Thus, despite the drawbacks of biological agents for tactical military use, they might be attractive as a strategic weapon, particularly for small, non-nuclear nations embroiled in regional conflicts or threatened by a nuclear-weapon state (NWS). Advances in biotechnology have made it possible to produce militarily significant quantities of pathogens and toxins rapidly and in small, easily concealable facilities.

The BWC, which established a global ban on biological weapons, complements the 1925 Gas Protocol, which prohibits the use in armed conflict of biological weapons. Biological weapons are also prohibited by customary international law.[44] Although lacking an effective verification system, the BWC provides the best complement to the Gas Protocol on juridical regulation of biological weapons. The BWC does not include any specific reference to the environment, but the prohibitions it places are of major significance to the protection of the environment. According to Dominguez-Mates (2005: 94), the BWC may be defined as the first treaty that generically refers to weapons of mass destruction and to the environment as such.[45] Article 2 of the BWC makes it mandatory to "destroy, or to divert to peaceful purposes ... all agents, toxins, weapons, equipment and means of delivery biological weapons ... to protect population and the environment."[46] However, future developments in biotechnology could create unprecedented opportunities for new violence, coercion, or subjugation.[47]

Legal Control: Chemical Weapons

The UN General Assembly, since 1966, has adopted several resolutions for the strict observance of the principles of the Geneva Protocol. In 1969, the General Assembly recognised that "the Geneva Protocol embodies the generally recognised rules of international law prohibiting the use in international armed conflicts of all biological and chemical methods of warfare, regardless of any technical developments," this included, "any chemical agents of warfare—chemical substances, whether gaseous, liquid or solid—which might be employed because of their direct toxic effects on man, animals or plants."[48]

The UN Security Council unanimously adopted Resolution 620 on August 26, 1988, condemning "the use of chemical weapons in the conflict between Iran and Iraq." The concern about the use of chemical weapons in that war led to the convening of the Paris Conference on the Prohibition of Chemical Weapons in 1989. The conference, attended by 149 states, in its final declaration reaffirmed the commitment not to use chemical weapons, and recognised the importance and continuing validity of the Geneva Protocol. It also stressed the need to conclude a Convention on the prohibition of the development, production, stockpiling, and use of chemical weapons.

Chemical Weapons Convention

The Convention on the Prohibition of the Development, Production, Stockpiling and Use of Chemical Weapons and on Their Destruction (CWC), 1997,[49] is a multilateral treaty that bans chemical weapons and requires their destruction within a specified period of time. The treaty is of unlimited duration and is far more comprehensive than the 1925 Geneva Protocol. The CWC prohibits: (i) developing, producing, acquiring, stockpiling, or retaining chemical weapons; (ii) the direct or indirect transfer of chemical weapons; (iii) chemical weapons use or military preparation for use; (iv) assisting, encouraging, or inducing other states to engage in CWC-prohibited activity; and (v) the use of riot control agents "as a method of warfare."

According to Article 1 of the CWC, "chemical weapons," means the following, together or separately:

a. Toxic chemicals and their precursors, except where intended for purposes not prohibited under this Convention, as long as the types and quantities are consistent with such purposes;
b. Munitions and devices, specifically designed to cause death or other harm through the toxic properties of those toxic chemicals specified in subparagraph (a), which would be released as a result of the employment of such munitions and devices;
c. Any equipment specifically designed for use directly in connection with the employment of munitions and devices specified in subparagraph (b).

Under the CWC, "old chemical weapons" are (i) chemical weapons which were produced before 1925; or (ii) chemical weapons produced in the period between 1925 and 1946 that have deteriorated to such extent that they can no longer be used as chemical weapons. CWC defines "abandoned chemical weapons" as chemical weapons, including old chemical weapons, abandoned by a State after January 1, 1925 on the territory of another State without the consent of the latter.[50]

The CWC is implemented by the Organisation for the Prohibition of Chemical Weapons (OPCW), which is headquartered in The Hague.

The OPCW's main functions are to carry out verification activities and ensure compliance with the treaty.[51] The CWC requires States Parties to declare in writing to the OPCW their chemical weapons stockpiles, chemical weapons production facilities (CWPFs), relevant chemical industry facilities, and other weapons-related information.[52] This must be done within 30 days of entry into force of the convention for each member State. The OPCW after receiving such declarations inspects the facilities and activities and monitors the activities of the State Parties to ensure compliance.

Obligations to destruction

After the Second World War, governments disposed of chemical weapons using methods that are primitive by today's standards.[54] The CWC requires States Parties to destroy (i) all chemical weapons, and (ii) all chemical weapons production facilities (CWPF) under their jurisdiction or control.[54] The requirement to destroy chemical weapons is based on the obligations specified in Article I and the other Articles, including obligations regarding systematic on-site verification. It takes into account the interest of States Parties for undiminished security during the destruction period; confidence building in the early part of the destruction stage; gradual acquisition of experience in the course of destroying chemical weapons; and the actual composition of the stockpiles and the methods chosen for the destruction of the chemical weapons. For the purpose of destruction, chemical weapons declared by each State Party are divided into three categories:

Category 1: Chemical weapons on the basis of Schedule 1 chemicals and their parts and components, including VX and sarin;

Category 2: Chemical weapons on the basis of all other chemicals and their parts and components, such as phosgene;

Category 3: Unfilled munitions and devices, and equipment specifically designed for use directly in connection with employment of chemical weapons.

The CWC also requires States Parties to declare CWPFs that produce or use chemicals of concern according to the convention. These chemicals are grouped into three schedules, based on the risk they pose. A facility producing a Schedule 1 chemical is considered a Schedule 1 facility. Schedule 1 chemicals and precursors pose a "high risk" and are rarely used for peaceful purposes. States Parties may not retain these chemicals except in small quantities for research, medical, pharmaceutical, or defensive use. Schedule 2 chemicals are toxic chemicals that pose a "significant risk" and are precursors to the production of Schedule 1 or Schedule 2 chemicals. These chemicals are not produced in large quantities for commercial or other peaceful purposes. Schedule 3 chemicals are usually produced in large quantities for purposes not prohibited by the CWC but have the potential to be used for other purposes. Some of these chemicals have been stockpiled as chemical weapons. The CWC also requires the declaration of facilities that produce certain non-scheduled chemicals.

Under Article 17 of the CWC, a State Party was required to start the destruction of Category 1 chemical weapons not later than two years after the Convention enters into force for the State Party. It was to destroy 1 per cent of the weapons within three years of the CWC's entry into force, 20 per cent within five years, 45 per cent within seven years, and 100 per cent within 10 years (by April 29, 2007). The OPCW could extend these deadlines due to "exceptional circumstances," but States Parties were supposed to destroy their entire stockpiles by April 29, 2012. The destruction of Category 2 and 3 weapons destruction was to start within one year after the CWC entered into force and be completed within five years after the entry into force of the Convention.[55]

Under the CWC, Member countries must use principles and methods of destruction of chemical weapons in accordance with the obligations of the Treaty.[56] However, though the CWC stipulates that the process of destruction must not harm people or the environment, and the State Parties must use safe technologies for their destruction, it fails to describe the term "safe technologies." The OPCW continuously monitors the destruction of chemical weapons at a number of chemical weapons destruction facilities around the world.[57]

Verification

The Convention establishes a coercive verification system to monitor the State Parties compliance with their obligations under the treaty. This system, which is specified in detail in the annexes to the Convention, provides for initial and thereafter annual declarations to be made by the States concerning their industrial chemical production.[59] Actual verification is carried out by inspections of three kinds: routine inspections on the basis of national declarations, challenge inspections for the sole purpose of determining facts relating to possible non-compliance with the Convention and inspections in response to an allegation that chemical weapons have been used.[60]

The CWC is one of the most far-reaching multilateral treaties for the elimination of an entire category of weapons of WMD and prevent their production or proliferation. For the first time, nations have agreed not only to forswear the use of a weapon, but also to eliminate the weapon's existence. The CWC's extensive verification regime offers the capability of monitoring a weapon's continued non-production, signifying a quantum leap in international disarmament initiatives. The CWC has a three-pronged approach. First, it specifies without qualification or condition that the use of chemical weapons, as well as their development, retention, acquisition, or transfer are absolutely prohibited. Second, it requires that the existing stockpiles and production facilities be declared and destroyed, subject to environmental, health and safety constraints, beginning within two years and completed not later than 10 years after the CWC takes effect. It also specifies: (i) the principles and methods of destruction of chemical weapons, (ii) the order of destruction and destruction deadlines, (iii) destruction plans, and (iv) the process of verification.

Third, the CWC seeks to ensure that States Parties do not initiate or resume the production and storage of chemical weapons.[62]

Old and Abandoned Chemical Weapons

Article 1 of the CWC defines the general obligations of State Parties that have abandoned chemical weapons, in the past. It provides: (i) Each State Party undertakes to destroy chemical weapons it owns or possesses, or that are located in any place under its jurisdiction or control, in accordance with the provisions of this Convention; (ii) Each State Party undertakes to destroy all chemical weapons it abandoned on the territory of another State Party, in accordance with the provisions of this Convention.

Therefore all chemical weapons produced and abandoned since January 1, 1946 have to be treated as normal chemical weapons; declared according to the provisions for declaration under Article III and IV; and destroyed under the provisions of Article IV and the verification Annex Part IV.

The CWC does not adequately cover the legal aspects of OCW and ACW.[61] During the negotiations on the CWC, the problem of OCW remained controversial. The main question was how OCW should be treated when discovered by a State Party to the Convention after its initial declaration in accordance with its obligation under Article III (Declarations). Another related issue was who should pay for the destruction of chemical weapons abandoned on the territory of another State Party.[62] When the CWC came into force, the main focus was on ensuring that once States Parties declared their chemical weapons, they destroy these weapons within a fixed time schedule and on securing a general prohibition of chemical for the future.

The CWC exclude OWC from the definition of chemical weapons and hence, exempt them from destruction regime.[63] Article II defines the main categories under the CWC, such as "chemical weapon," "toxic chemical," "precursor," "key component of binary or multi-component chemical systems," etc. Article II also defines two categories of CW related items from the past.[64]

Besides the regime for chemical weapons from the past, Articles III and IV contain two exemptions related to chemical weapons disposed by (a) land burial, and (ii) sea-dumping in the past. The exact words used are: "The provisions of this Article and the relevant provisions of Part IV of the Verification Annex shall not, at the discretion of a State Party, apply to CW buried on its territory before January 1, 1977 and which remain buried, or which had been dumped at sea before January 1, 1985."

In general the definition exempts all chemical weapons "sea-dumped" before 1985 or land-buried before 1977 from declarations under Article III and follow-up obligations under Article IV and under Part IV of the Verification Annex, as long as they remain "buried" and by assumption "sea-dumped." The CWC fails to provide any solution for the recovery and destruction of CW sea-dumped before 1985. The problem posed by OCW and ACW is serious. There are technical challenges related to their disposal and until a solution is found, leaking toxic agents from these weapons will continue to pose a risk to humans and the environment.[65]

The earlier practice of dumping of chemical weapons has been prohibited after the coming into force of the 1972 Oslo Convention for the Prevention of Marine Pollution by Dumping from Ships and Aircraft, and the London Dumping Convention of 1972. In addition, the CWC prohibits dumping of chemical weapons in any body of water, their land burial or disposal by open-pit burning.[66]

UN Security Council Resolution 1540

The proliferation of weapons of mass destruction and their means of delivery is a threat to international peace and security. Proliferation challenges have been addressed by the United Nations in a number of ways including through a process initiated by the Security Council in its Resolution 1540 (2004).[67] The Resolution 1540 is aimed at preventing non-state armed groups (NSAGs) from acquiring nuclear, biological, and chemical weapons, their means of delivery, and related materials. The resolution filled a gap in international law by addressing the risk that terrorists might obtain, proliferate, or use weapons of mass destruction. Adopted under Chapter VII of the UN Charter, Resolution 1540 formally establishes the proliferation and possession of WMD by NSAGs as "a threat to international peace and security." The resolution mirrors the approach taken under Resolution 1373 in 2001, which required all countries to adopt national counter-terrorism laws, and imposes legally binding obligations on all states to adopt appropriate effective measures to prevent the proliferation of WMD to NSAGs. The resolution includes three primary obligations:

- All States are prohibited from providing any form of support to NSAGs seeking to acquire weapons of mass destruction, related materials, or their means of delivery.
- All States must adopt and enforce laws criminalizing the possession and acquisition of such items by NSAGs, as well as efforts to assist or finance their acquisition.
- All States must adopt and enforce domestic controls over nuclear, chemical, and biological weapons, their means of delivery, and related materials, in order to prevent their proliferation.

Legally binding obligations on states under Resolution 1540 are to: (a) Refrain from providing any form of support to non-State actors that attempt to develop, acquire, manufacture, possess, transport, transfer or use nuclear, chemical or biological weapons and their means of delivery; (b) Adopt and enforce appropriate effective laws prohibiting activities involving the proliferation of such weapons and their means of delivery to non-State actors, in particular for terrorist purposes, as well any attempts to engage in such activities, assist or finance them; (c) Implement and enforce appropriate controls over related materials in order to: (i) account for and secure items in production, use, storage or transport; (ii) physically protect; (iii) detect, deter, prevent and combat the illicit trafficking and brokering through effective border controls an law enforcement efforts; (iv) control the export, transit, trans-shipment and re-export and the provision of funds and services related to such export and trans-shipment that would contribute to proliferation; and (v) penalize violations.

Resolution 1540 also emphasizes the importance of maintaining and promoting existing non-proliferation multilateral agreements, and acknowledges that the resolution does not interfere with state obligations under such treaties. It further recognizes that some countries may require assistance to meet the national implementation obligations of the resolution. As such, the resolution calls on states to make assistance available to countries in need if they are in a position to do so. The council established a committee to oversee the implementation of the resolution, initially for a period of two years. Comprised of the council's 15 members and assisted by a panel of experts, the 1540 Committee is tasked with providing awareness of the resolution and its requirements, matching assistance requests with offers, and assessing the status of implementation. States were required to report to the Committee on the actions they have taken or plan to take in order to implement the resolution within 6 months of UNSCR 1540's adoption, and the council has encouraged subsequent reports to provide additional information.

Despite the aim of preventing nuclear, chemical, and biological terrorism, resolution 1540 initially met with some resistance within the UN Security Council, with critics stressing that the resolution's focused solely on nonproliferation without adequate emphasis on disarmament. There was additional concern that the UN might use UNSCR 1540 to justify sanctions and other forms of coercion for countries that did not adequately comply with the resolution. In April 2011, the UN Security Council passed resolution 1977, extending the mandate for a period of ten years. UNSCR 1977 reaffirmed the Security Council's commitment to resolution 1540, and further emphasized cooperation with international, regional, and sub-regional organizations. It also addressed existing concerns among Council members regarding equal regional representation within the 1540 Committee.[68]

The Rome Statute and the Biological and Chemical Weapons

The Rome Statute, which established the International Criminal Court (ICC) to prosecute individuals for crimes against humanity, genocide, and war crimes, does not contain the words "biological weapon" or "chemical weapon." Article 8 of the Statute provides:[69]

1. The Court shall have jurisdiction in respect of war crimes in particular when committed as part of a plan or policy or as part of a large-scale commission of such crimes.
2. For the purpose of this Statute, "war crimes" means:
   (b) Other serious violations of the laws and customs applicable in international armed conflict, within the established framework of international law, namely, any of the following acts:
   (xvii) Employing poison or poisoned weapons;
   (xviii) Employing asphyxiating, poisonous or other gases, and all analogous liquids, materials or devices.

The provisions contained in Article 8, may refer to biological and chemical weapons implicitly, but it is unclear whether all chemical weapons are included, and whether biological weapons are included at all. The Statute is intended to encompass "the most serious crimes of concern to the international community." International law, custom, and jurisprudence show that the use of chemical and biological weapons falls within this category.

The issue of including chemical and biological weapons came up prior to the First Review Conference of the Rome Statute's in 2010. This meeting considered amendments to the Rome Statute for the first time. During a pre-conference meeting of the parties to the statute, Belgium proposed an amendment which would add chemical and biological weapons to the list of prohibited weapons. Although there was considerable support for the initiative, the amendment ultimately was not submitted to the Review Conference as time was limited and a number of issues had to be considered. Only the least controversial amendments were forwarded to the meeting. The use of biological and chemical weapons should be explicitly criminalised by the Rome Statute because they are widely recognised in the international community as serious crimes.[70] It is felt that the use of chemical and biological weapons should be explicitly prohibited by the Rome Statute to enable the ICC to adjudicate such cases as war crimes in the case of international as well as non-international armed conflicts.[71]

Recent Efforts

A number of States have adopted an informal, collaborative approach to the potential transfer of biological weapons. This initiative, known as the Australia Group (AG), meets annually to discuss ways of increasing the effectiveness of participating countries' national export licensing. The AG has developed common control lists of materials requiring licences for exports. The materials include plant pathogens, animal pathogens, biological agents and dual-use biological resources. However, applications for licences "are denied only if there is a well-founded concern about potential diversion for chemical and biological weapons' purposes."

The US and the Soviet Union had agreed bilaterally in the late 1980s to destroy their existing chemical weapons stockpiles. They had recognised that the munitions were expensive to secure and maintain, risky on account of the possibility of leakage of toxic agents, mostly obsolete without modern launch systems, open to terrorist attacks and could encourage proliferation. The US still needs a decade or more for the completion of its stockpile destruction programme.

When the Russian Federation signed the CWC in 1993 (ratified in 1997), it stated to the States Parties that it would need financial and technical support to undertake its destruction programme in a safe and timely way. To date, it has neutralised about 60 per cent of its stockpile. Several States like Belgium, France, Germany, and Italy are actively engaged in the verified destruction of OCW. However, the issue of the Japanese ACW left in China during the last century still remains unresolved.[72] In November 2012 the OPCW held its 17th annual conference in The Hague to review the recent progress in the global elimination of chemical weapons.[73]

The CWC has made an important contribution to international practice in arms control. However, the compliance and verification measures need to be made more rigorous. While certain countries can keep track of nuclear weapons programmes through satellite technology and high-altitude reconnaissance aircraft, it is extremely difficult to know about the development and storage of chemical weapons by a State or non-state actor. The issues that needed attention are: (i) destruction of existing stockpiles in an environment-friendly manner, (ii) detecting undeclared stockpiles and ensuring their destruction, (iii) monitoring chemical weapon capable countries outside the CWC regime, (iv) keeping abreast of new developments in science and chemical manufacturing, and (v) chemical terrorism.[74]

The Fourth Special Session of the Conference of the States Parties to Review the Operation of the Chemical Weapons Convention (4th CWC Review Conference) will be held in 2018. Currently approximately 95 per cent of declared CW stockpiles have been verifiably destroyed. Four states still remain outside the treaty regime (Egypt, Israel, North Korea and South Sudan). The OPCW's verification capacity and experience remain relevant in view of recent confirmed cases of CW use in Iraq and Syria, and the investigation of the assassination of Kim Jong-nam (Kim Jong-un's older half-brother) reportedly with VX at the Kuala Lumpur International Airport on 13 February 2017. The use of sarin on 4 April 2017 in Khan Shaykhun (Idlib governate) and the 6 April retaliatory US Tomahawk cruise missile strikes against the Shayrat Airfield have raised political tensions among governments at the UN Security Council, the OPCW Executive Council (EC) and elsewhere.

There is no single solution to the chemical and biological weapon problem. Whether a pathogen is used deliberately by an individual or a group to achieve political objectives by terror and violence, or it is used by a State; and whether the use of a pathogen is against humans, animals, or plants, the problem is still one that involves the deliberate use of a biological agent. The biological weapon problem represents a spectrum, and just as action at the national level cannot resolve all the security problems within this spectrum, neither can action only at the international level. A balance needs to be struck between national and international responsibilities that underpin the success of the CWC.[75] The international community must make serious attempts to harmonise, coordinate and synchronise all activities by the various stakeholders into a comprehensive international network dedicated to ensuring that all achievements in the biological sciences are used exclusively for the benefit of humankind.

Notes

1. Biological warfare is the deliberate spreading of disease amongst humans, animals, and plants. Diseases are caused when small numbers of living micro-organisms enter into the target population of humans, animals, or plants. These micro-organisms multiply, and, after an incubation period, the symptoms of the disease become apparent. In some cases, micro-organisms produce toxins—non-living toxic chemicals—that cause symptoms. Depending upon the biological agent used, the resulting disease can cause incapacitation or death of the target population.
2. The Code of Manu (*Manu Smriti*), which formed the basis for the laws, morals and customs of India and developed between BC 200 and 200 AD, also referred to the protection of war victims. Smriti means "that which has to be remembered." Unlike the Vedas, which are considered of divine origin, the Smritis are of human compositions and guide individuals in their daily conduct according to time and place. They list the codes and rules governing the actions of the individual, the community, society and the nation. The laws set forth by Manu, in *Manu Smriti*, although followed in some form even today, are not considered divine, and may be modified by society to keep up with the times. Indeed, it has been speculated that in its current form, *Manu Smriti* represents laws that have been added or modified throughout history. Available at: http://www.bharatadesam.com/spiritual/manu_smriti/manu_smriti_7.php, accessed July 24, 2012.
3. The history of mankind does not recognise the use of poisonous substances for military purposes. The use of chemical agents has been condemned for a lot of reasons. The use of poison in war was considered perfidious and inconsistent with the military chivalry. Their use has been condemned a long time ago by the ancient writers such as Philius, Ulpian, Tacitus, Claudianus and others. The Roman Senate stuck to the principle that war should be waged using weapons but not poisons. Raicevic Nebojsa, "The History of Prohibition of the Use of Chemicals in International Humanitarian Law," *Facta Universitatis*, Series: Law and Politics, vol. 1, no. 5, 2001, pp. 613-31, at p. 615.
4. The first written treaty under which the use of poison in war was limited is a Franco-German agreement of 1675 concluded at Strasbourg. Under this treaty, the use of poisoned shells was prohibited on a bilateral basis.

5. The Lieber Instructions or Code of 1863 represents the first attempt to codify the laws of war. They were prepared during the American Civil War by Francis Lieber, then a professor of Columbia College in New York, revised by a board of officers and promulgated by President Lincoln. Although they were binding only on the forces of the US, they correspond to a great extent to the laws and customs of war existing at that time. The Lieber Instructions strongly influenced the further codification of the laws of war and the adoption of similar regulations by other states. The instructions in Article 16 provide a general prohibition on use of poisons in war: "Military necessity does not admit of cruelty—that is, the infliction of suffering for the sake of suffering or for revenge, nor of maiming or wounding except in fight, nor of torture to extort confessions. It does not admit of the use of poison in any way, nor of the wanton devastation of a district." Article 70 of the Code further provided: "The use of poison in any manner, be it to poison wells, or food, or arms, is wholly excluded from modern warfare. He that uses it puts himself out of the pale of the law and usages of war."
6. The full title reads: Project of an International Declaration Concerning the Laws and Customs of War. The Project of the Declaration was adopted on July 27, 1874, at the international conference held in Brussels convened on the initiative of the Russian Emperor Alexander II. Participating in the conference were 15 European states which discussed the project submitted by the Russian Government, which was adopted with slight amendments; D. Schindlerand J. Toman, *The Law of Armed Conflicts—A Collection of Conventions, Resolutions and Other Documents,* (Geneva, 1973), pp. 3-23.
7. The First Hague Peace Conference was convened through the personal initiative of Tsar Nicholas II of Russia, with the primary objective of limiting armaments. The representatives of twenty-six States met in The Hague from May 18 to July 29, 1899, and although they failed to reach any general agreement on arms limitation, they were successful in adopting three conventions relating to the peaceful settlement of disputes, the laws and customs of war on land, and the protection of wounded, sick and shipwrecked in maritime warfare. They also adopted three declarations prohibiting the launching of projectiles and explosives from balloons, the use of projectiles diffusing asphyxiating gases, and the use of expanding bullets. The 1899 Hague Declaration 2 prohibiting the use of projectiles, whose sole objective is to diffuse asphyxiating gases, was derived from the general principle of customary law prohibiting the use of poison and materials causing unnecessary suffering. Adam Roberts and Richard Guelff, *Documents on the Laws of War* (Oxford: Oxford University Press, 2000), p. 59.
8. Article 23, Convention (IV) respecting the Laws and Customs of War on Land and Its Annex: Regulations Concerning the Laws and Customs of War on Land. The Hague, October 18, 1907.
9. In an appeal to the belligerents of February 6, 1918, the ICRC stated that: "We wish today to take a stand against a barbaric innovation ... This innovation is the use of asphyxiating and poisonous gas, which will it seems increase to an extent so far undreamed of ... We protest with all the force at our command against such warfare which can only be called criminal." Stockholm International Peace Research Institute, *The Problem of Chemical and Biological Warfare,* vol. IV, "CB Disarmament Negotiations, 1920-1970," (1974), p. 41.
10. A Polish proposal to the Conference was the first to separate biological weapons (BW) from CW. It stated that, "inasmuch as the materials used for bacteriological warfare constitute an arm that is discreditable to modern civilisation, the Polish

delegation proposes that any decisions taken by the Conference concerning the materials used for chemical warfare should apply equally to the materials used for bacteriological warfare." Prohibiting trade in poisonous chemicals and bacteriological materials, without first rejecting their manufacture or use however, proved contentious. Banning the export of these weapons materials would not halt their manufacture in states already capable of doing so, or their use in conflicts involving those states. Quoted in: *The Problem of Chemical and Biological Warfare, Volume IV: CB Disarmament Negotiation, 1920-1979*, Stockholm International Peace Research Institute (SIPRI), Stockholm: Almqvist and Wiksell, p. 60.

11. The Protocol for the Prohibition of the Use in War of Asphyxiating, Poisonous or Other Gases, and Bacteriological Methods of Warfare, Geneva, June 17, 1925. The Protocol was adopted by the International Conference on the Control of the International Trade in Arms, Munitions, and Implements of War, which had been convened by the Council of the League of Nations and met in Geneva from May 4 to June 17, 1925. The Geneva Protocol was adopted at the insistence of the US. However, it came into force, without the US's ratification.
12. N. Sims, *The Diplomacy of Biological Disarmament: Vicissitudes of a Treaty in Force, 1975-1985* (New York: St. Martins Press, 1988), p. 60.
13. Although the treaty allows States to have reservations on retaliation which renders the protocol a no-first-use agreement, it has now become accepted as customary international law binding on all countries. M. R. Dando, *Preventing Biological Warfare: The Failure of American Leadership* (Basingstoke: Palgrave, 2000), pp. 3-4.
14. Adam Roberts, *Documents on the Laws of War* (Oxford: Oxford University Press, 2000), p. 155.
15. *Weapons of Terror: Freeing the World of Nuclear, Biological and Chemical Arms*. The Weapons of Mass Destruction Commission (WMDC), final report, Stockholm, Sweden, June 1, 2006, pp. 113-14. Prior to the conclusion of the BWC and the 1993 Chemical Weapons Convention, thirty-five states reserved the right to retaliate with the prohibited weapons if another state used the weapons first against them. Nevertheless, the vast majority of States Parties did not have reservations to the Protocol. The Netherlands in 1930 and the United States in 1975 made a distinction between CW and BW and limited their retaliation reservation to CW only. Both states bound themselves not to use BW under any circumstances, even if BW were to be used against them. Marie Isabelle Chevrier, "History of BTW Disarmament," in Kathryn McLaughlin and Kathryn Nixdorff (eds.), *Biological Weapons Reader,* The BioWeapons Prevention Project (BWPP), (Geneva, 2000), p. 14.
16. The UK support for a prompt ban on the use and possession of biological weapons contained four arguments: (i) biological weapons are regarded with general abhorrence, possibly more so than any other means of waging war; (ii) it seems unlikely that development or use of biological weapons is, at the moment, regarded by any state as essential to its security; (iii) new technological developments could lead to biological weapons becoming an integral part of some states' armaments; and (iv) it would be easier to achieve a ban before such armament took place than after. Marie Isabelle Chevrier, "History of BTW Disarmament," in Kathryn McLaughlin and Kathryn Nixdorff (eds.), *Biological Weapons Reader,* The BioWeapons Prevention Project (BWPP), (Geneva, 2009), p. 16.
17. Eighteen Nation Disarmament Committee (ENDC)/231 "Working Paper on Microbiological Warfare."

18. The Convention on the Prohibition of the Development, Production and Stockpiling of Bacteriological (Biological) and Toxin Weapons and on Their Destruction (BWC) was signed in Washington, London and Moscow on April 10, 1972.
19. In September 1969 the Soviet Union responded to the UK Draft Convention by tabling its own Draft Convention prohibiting the development and production of both BW and CW. In contrast to the UK Draft Convention, the Soviet Draft combined CW and BW, excluded the explicit prohibition against use, and tabled the Convention at the UN General Assembly instead of at the Conference of the Committee on Disarmament (CCD). The US government meanwhile reviewed its CBW policies, and in November 1969 announced its decision to unilaterally terminate its offensive BW programme, to destroy its BW stocks, to place a moratorium on CW production and to submit the 1925 Geneva Protocol to the US Senate for ratification. The US also declared its intention to support the UK Draft BW Convention. In February 1970, the US extended its BW policy to toxins as well. Marie Isabelle Chevrier, "History of BTW Disarmament," in Kathryn McLaughlin and Kathryn Nixdorff (eds.), *Biological Weapons Reader*, The BioWeapons Prevention Project (BWPP), (Geneva, 2009), p. 17.
20. The 1972 Convention on the Prohibition of the Development, Production, and Stockpiling of Bacteriological (Biological) and Toxin Weapons. Hereinafter referred to as the Biological Weapons Convention or BWC. The BWC, the first multilateral disarmament treaty banning the production and use of an entire category of weapons, entered into force on March 26, 1975. Over the intervening years, increasing numbers of States joined the Convention, which currently has 164 States Parties. The BWC effectively prohibits the development, production, acquisition, transfer, stockpiling and use of biological and toxin weapons and is a key element in the international community's efforts to address the proliferation of weapons of mass destruction.
21. Biological Weapons Convention, Articles II, III and IV.
22. The BWC allows participating states to raise compliance "complaints" with the UN Security Council and requires an accused state to cooperate with any investigation to ascertain the validity of a complaint. The Security Council would initiate any non-compliance investigation (Article VI). The drawback of this approach is that any permanent member of the Security Council can veto the launch of an investigation.
23. Jozef Goldblat, The Biological Weapons Convention: An Overview, no. 318, *International Review of the Red Cross*, June 30, 1997, pp. 251-65.
24. Main problem is that most biological agents that have the potential to be used as weapons also exist in nature. Thus it may be difficult in the early stages of an outbreak to determine whether a disease has been deliberately induced or has occurred naturally. While the immediate priority following the outbreak of disease will be to respond quickly to mitigate its effects, both governments and the public need to know whether this is a natural occurrence or a man-made one for which the perpetrators must be found. Scientific advancements in biotechnology and the wide spread of facilities capable of producing biological agents make it exceedingly difficult to pinpoint potential biological threats. *Weapons of Terror: Freeing the World of Nuclear, Biological and Chemical Arms.* The Weapons of Mass Destruction Commission (WMDC), final report, Stockholm, Sweden, June 1, 2006, pp. 112-13.
25. The BTWC has no official implementation mechanism and its implementation Support Unit created in 2006 simply assists with various administrative functions and some activities that facilitate the convention's application.

26. Wheelis Mark and Malcolm Dando, On the Brink: Biodefence, Biotechnology and the Future of Weapons Control, *CBWCB*, Vol. 58, December 2002, p. 4.
27. The preparatory committee of the First Review Conference of the BWC met during July 9 to July 18, 1979 and requested two reports to be prepared for the Conference. First, the UN secretariat was asked to prepare a background paper on the compliance of the States Parties with their obligations. Second, the Depository government, the UK, the US and USSR, were requested to report on new scientific and technological developments relevant to the Convention. The success of the First Review Conference was that it kept those States Parties which had concern about its efficacy on board and demonstrated to those both inside and outside the BWC that effective action could be instigated to deal with their doubts about the compliance of the Convention. Jez Littlewood, *The Biological Weapons Convention: A Failed Revolution* (England: Ashgate, 2005), pp. 16-19. In the Final Declaration, the participants reaffirmed their support for the treaty and found that Article I of the BWC had proved sufficiently comprehensive to cover recent scientific and technological developments relevant to the Convention. Aida Luisa Levin, "Historical Outline," in Erhard Geissler (ed.), *Strengthening the Biological Weapons Convention by Confidence-Building Measures*, SIPRI, Chemical and Biological Warfare Studies, Report No. 10 (London: OUP, 1990), p. 8.
28. The British government stated in 1992 that "about 10 countries are assessed as having biological weapons programmes." Her Majesty's Stationery Office, "Statement of the Defence Estimates 1992" (London, July 1992), p. 7.
29. The Iraqi biological warfare programme disclosed to the United Nations Special Commission (UNSCOM) is said to have begun in 1975 and continued until early January 1991. Iraqi scientists worked with anthrax, botulinum toxin, *Clostridium perfringens* (gas gangrene), aflatoxin, trichothecene mycotoxin, wheat cover smut, ricin, and viruses such as the camel pox virus. Iraq produced 19,000 litres of botulinum toxin; 8,500 litres of anthrax; and 2,200 litres of aflatoxin. For delivery systems, the Iraqis developed spray tanks, remotely piloted vehicles, aerial bombs, rockets, and missiles. Graham S. Pearson, "The Threat of Deliberate Disease in the 21st Century," in Graham S. Pearson (ed.), *Biological Weapons Proliferation: Reasons for Concern, Courses of Action*, The Henry L. Stimson Centre (Washington, January 1998), pp. 25-26.
30. Held in Geneva from September 9 to 27, 1991.
31. A group of governmental verification experts (VEREX) was established at the Third Review Conference to identify and examine potential verification measures from a scientific and technical standpoint. The Final Report of VEREX concluded that there were some potential verification measures which might contribute to strengthening the effectiveness and improve the implementation of the Convention. At a Special Conference in September 1994, States Parties, on the basis of the VEREX findings, agreed to establish the Ad Hoc Group of the States Parties to the BWC in order to negotiate and develop a legally-binding verification regime for the Convention. The Ad Hoc Group was mandated to consider four specific areas, namely: definitions of terms and objective criteria; incorporation of existing and further enhanced confidence-building and transparency measures, as appropriate, into the regime; a system of measures to promote compliance with the Convention; and specific measures designed to ensure the effective and full implementation of Article X on international cooperation and exchange in the field of peaceful bacteriological (biological) activities. The Ad Hoc Group was destined to hold 24 working sessions over the next seven years. The work of the Ad Hoc Group was discussed at the Fourth

Review Conference in 1996 and the progress made thus far was welcomed. It was also decided that the Ad Hoc Group should conclude its work on the future protocol, at the latest, by the Fifth Review Conference to be held in 2001. On September 23, 1998, an Informal Ministerial Meeting of the States Parties to the BWC was held in New York at the initiative of Australia in order to demonstrate high-level political support for the negotiations. At its 24th session, July 23 to August 17, 2001, which was the last scheduled session before the Fifth Review Conference, the Ad Hoc Group was unable to conclude the negotiations on the draft protocol and could not reach consensus on the report of its work, effectively ending that effort to strengthen the BWC. Piers D. Milltee, "The Biological Weapons Convention: Content, Review Process and Efforts to Strengthen the Convention," in Kathryn McLaughlin and Kathryn Nixdorff (eds.), *Biological Weapons Reader,* The BioWeapons Prevention Project (BWPP) (Geneva, 2009), p. 23. *See also* Jez Littlewood, *The Biological Weapons Convention: A Failed Revolution* (England: Ashgate, 2005), pp. 47-62.

32. US Arms Control and Disarmament Agency, "The Biological Weapons Convention," Fact Sheet, Office of Public Affairs (Washington, D.C.: August 118, 993): 1-2.
33. United Nations, *Special Conference of the States Parties to the Convention on the Prohibition of the Development, Production, and Stockpiling of Bacteriological (Biological) and Toxin Weapons and on their Destruction: Final Report,* Document BWC/SPCONF/1, September 19-30, 1994, 14-5.
34. Held in Geneva from November 25 to December 6, 1996.
35. The Conference, conscious of apprehensions arising from relevant scientific and technological developments, inter alia, in the fields of microbiology, biotechnology, molecular biology, genetic engineering, and any application resulting from genome studies, and the possibilities of their use for purposes inconsistent with the objectives and the provisions of the Convention, reaffirms that the undertaking given by the States Parties in Article I applies to all such developments.
36. J. Prasad, Indian Statement to the Sixth Review Conference of the Biological and Toxin Weapons Convention, *Statement,* November 20, 2006. Available at: http://www.unog.ch/bwc.
37. The Seventh Review Conference was held at the United Nations Office in Geneva from December 5 to 22, 2011.
38. Under BWC, the allegations of infractions may be lodged with the UN Security Council, which may in turn initiate inspections of accused parties; however, this provision is undermined by the right of Security Council members to veto proposed inspections.
39. The Eighth Review Conference of the Biological Weapons Convention (BWC) was held in Geneva during 7-25 November 2016.
40. Article VII, BWC: "Each State Party to this Convention undertakes to provide or support assistance, in accordance with the United Nations Charter, to any Party to the Convention which so requests, if the Security Council decides that such Party has been exposed to danger as a result of violation of the Convention."
41. The UN General Assembly document A/44/561 of October 4, 1989, contains recommendations by the group of qualified experts convened pursuant to General Assembly Resolution A/RES/42/37 C for guidelines and procedures for timely and efficient investigations of reports on the possible use of chemical and bacteriological (biological) or toxin weapons. The General Assembly Resolution A/RES/45/57C of 4 December 1990, endorses the proposal for guidelines and

procedures for investigations of reports on the possible use of chemical and bacteriological (biological) or toxin weapons contained in document A/44/561. Available at: http://www.un.org/documents/ga/res/45/a45r057.htm, accessed October 19, 2012.

42. The Resolution provides that any State Party can lodge a complaint with the Security Council for a breach in Convention obligations on the possible use of chemical and bacteriological (biological) or toxin weapons. Such a complaint should include all possible evidence confirming its validity and a request for its consideration by the Security Council. The Security Council is to immediately consider the complaint lodged under Article VII, and it may request the UN Secretary-General for investigation. The States Parties are to cooperate with investigations undertaken by the Security Council or by the Secretary-General. The Security Council is to inform States Parties about the outcome of investigation undertaken. However, this procedure is not to prejudice the prerogative of States Parties to consider jointly cases of alleged non-compliance and to make appropriate decisions accordingly. BWC/MSP/2004/MX/INF.3, July 1, 2004, annexure I.
43. J. B. Petro, T. R. Plasse and J. A. McNulty, "Biotechnology: impact on biological warfare and biodefence," vol. 1, *Biosecurity and Bioterrorism: Biodefence, Strategy, Practice, and Science* (2003), pp. 161-68.
44. ICRC Customary IHL Rule 73 provides that the use of biological weapons is prohibited. There is widespread State practice in the form of military manuals and legislation to the effect that the use of biological weapons is prohibited irrespective of whether the State concerned is a party to the Biological Weapons Convention or whether it has made a "no first use" reservation to the Geneva Gas Protocol. The US Naval Handbook states that the prohibition of biological weapons is part of customary law and binds all States, whether or not they are party to the Geneva Gas Protocol or the Biological Weapons Convention. There is also national case-law (Japan, District Court of Tokyo, Shimoda case and Colombia, Constitutional Court, Constitutional Case Number C-225/95) declaring that biological weapons are prohibited, including in non-international armed conflicts.
45. Rosario Dominguez Mates, "New Weaponry technologies and International Humanitarian Law: Their Consequences on the Human Being and the Environment," in Pablo Antonio Fernandez-Sanchez (ed.), *The New Challenges of Humanitarian Law in Armed Conflicts* (Leiden: Martinus Nijhoff Publishers, 2005), pp. 91-119.
46. The UN Convention on the Prohibition of the Development, Production and Stockpiling of Bacteriological (Biological) and Toxin Weapons and on Their Destruction, 1972, Article II provides: "Each State Party to this Convention undertakes to destroy, or to divert to peaceful purposes, as soon as possible but not later than nine months after entry into force of the Convention, all agents, toxins, weapons, equipment and means of delivery specified in article I of the Convention, which are in its possession or under its jurisdiction or control. In implementing the provisions of this article all necessary safety precautions shall be observed to protect populations and the environment."
47. Morten Bremer Maerli, Relearning the ABCs: Terrorists and "Weapons of Mass Destruction," *The Non-Proliferation Review* (Summer 2000), pp. 108-19.
48. UNGA Resolution 2603 A (XXIV), dated December 16, 1969.
49. The CWC was the end-product of 20 years of negotiations. The treaty was opened for signature on January 13, 1993 in Paris, and entered into force on

April 29, 1997. To date 188 nations are party to this treaty. Two signatories—Israel and Myanmar—have yet to ratify the convention. Six States that have neither signed, or ratified or acceded to the CWC are Angola, Egypt, North Korea, Somalia, South Sudan and Syria. The CWC bans the stockpiling, transfer, production, development, and use of chemical weapons. While the CWC does not stipulate which technologies governments must use to eliminate their stockpiles, it requires that destruction be "irreversible" and safe for humans and the environment. The CWC comprises a preamble, 24 articles and three annexes on chemicals, verification and confidentiality. It is remarkable for the comprehensiveness of its provisions. Two signatories—Israel and Myanmar—have yet to ratify the convention. Six States that have neither signed, or ratified or acceded to the CWC are Angola, Egypt, North Korea, Somalia, South Sudan and Syria. Ramesh Thakur, "Introduction: Chemical Weapons and the Challenge of Weapons of Mass Destruction," in Ramesh Thakur and Ere Haru (eds.), *The Chemical Weapons Convention: Implementation, Challenges and Opportunities* (Tokyo: United Nations Press, 2007), p. 7.

50. CWC Article II, paragraphs 5 and 6.
51. There are 3 organs within the OPCW: the Conference of States Parties, the Executive Council, and the Technical Secretariat. The Conference is comprised of delegates from States Parties to the Convention (nations that have signed, ratified, and deposited their instruments of ratification with the Secretary-General of the United Nations in New York) and is the principal organ of the OPCW. The Conference makes recommendations and takes decisions on Convention-related questions, and oversees the implementation of the Convention and the activities of the other two organs. The Executive Council is the executive organ of the OPCW and is responsible to the Conference. The Council, among other functions, supervises the Technical Secretariat, cooperates with National Authorities, and considers matters regarding compliance and non-compliance with the Convention. The Technical Secretariat assists the Conference and the Council. The Secretariat, among other functions, carries out verification measures provided for in the Convention.
52. Several countries have declared chemical weapons, amounting to nearly 70,000 metric tonnes of toxic agents in 8.6 million munitions and containers. The biggest arsenals of chemical weapons that need to be destroyed are in Russia and the United States. Under CWC, other weapons-related declarations states-parties must make include: (1) Chemical weapons production facilities on their territories since January 1, 1946. (2) Facilities (such as laboratories and test sites) designed, constructed, or used primarily for chemical weapons development since January 1, 1946. (3) "Old" chemical weapons on their territories (chemical weapons manufactured before 1925 or those produced between 1925 and 1946 that have deteriorated to such an extent that they are no longer useable). (4) "Abandoned" chemical weapons (abandoned by another state without consent on or after January 1, 1925). (5) Plans for destroying weapons and facilities. (6) All transfers or receipts of chemical weapons or chemical weapons-production equipment since January 1, 1946. (7) All riot control agents in their possession.
53. The US Armed Forces have disposed of chemical weapons in the ocean from World War I through 1970. According to the US Army's report (2001), chemical weapons (chemical munitions and containers of chemical warfare agents) disposed of in the ocean included surplus and damaged bombs, rockets, projectiles, and other munitions containing chemical warfare agents, and barrels, cylinders, and other containers filled with surplus chemical warfare agents

produced for use in munitions. The public concerns about human health and environmental risks, and the economic effects of potential damage to marine resources, led to a statutory prohibition on the disposal of chemical weapons in the ocean in 1972. Department of Defence, US Army Research, Development, and Engineering Command, Aberdeen Proving Ground, Maryland, Corporate Information Office, Historical Research and Response Team, *Off-shore Disposal of Chemical Agents and Weapons Conducted by the United States*, March 29, 2001. At the end of World War II, the British authorities sea-dumped over 12,000 tons of their own chemical munitions into the English Channel. These canisters and shells are beginning to rust open with unknown consequences for marine life and humans. Phillip Knightley, "Dumps of Death," *The London Times*, April 5, 1992, pp. 26-28; Frederick Laurin, "Scandinavia's Underwater Time Bomb," vol. 17, no. 2, *The Bulletin of the Atomic Scientist* (March 1991), pp. 11-12.

54. The CWC, which was adopted in 1992 and entered into force in 1997, originally called on member states to destroy all stockpiles of banned substances by April 29, 2007. However, countries could ask for extensions of up to five years, which Russia and the US received in December 2006. At one time the United States and Russia possessed 90 per cent of the world's known chemical weapons. Unable to meet the deadline of April 29, 2012, for complete elimination of chemical weapons, the Secretary of State Hillary Rodham Clinton stated that the United States is committed to the complete elimination of chemical weapons stockpiles in the United States and around the world. She said, "To date, we have already destroyed 89 per cent of our original chemical weapons stockpile. We reaffirm our commitment to finish the job as quickly as possible in accordance with national and treaty requirements that ensure the safety of people and the protection of the environment." *Chemical Weapons Convention: Eliminating a Whole Category of Weapons of Mass Destruction*, Fact Sheet, Office of Public Liaison, Bureau of Public Affairs, US Department of State. Available at: http://www.state.gov/r/pa/pl/176872.htm, accessed August 5, 2012.
55. In 2009, India became the third State Party to complete the destruction of all chemical weapons declared to the OPCW. For details of destruction of chemical weapons please see Chapter 2C.
56. CWC, paragraph 12 of Part 4 A of the Verification Annex.
57. The OPCW also regularly inspects all former chemical weapons product facilities declared by Member States in order to verify that they are all shut down and destroyed, or converted for peaceful purposes. Most of these facilities have been either completely destroyed or converted so far. The OPCW is overseeing the destruction/conversion of the few remaining facilities. The OPCW is additionally required to monitor the destruction of chemical weapons that are old or deteriorated or that were abandoned by one country on the territory of another. Under the CWC, member countries must declare such weapons to the OPCW and undertake to destroy them. If states-parties are found to have engaged in prohibited actions that could result in "serious damage" to the convention, the OPCW could recommend collective punitive measures to other states-parties. In cases of "particular gravity," the OPCW could bring the issue before the UN Security Council and General Assembly. States-parties must take measures to address questions raised about their compliance with the CWC. If they do not, the OPCW may, inter alia, restrict or suspend their CWC-related rights and privileges (such as voting and trade rights).
58. CWC Articles III, IV.7, V.9 and VI.7-8, and Verification Annex.
59. CWC Articles IV to VI, IX and X.

60. Barry Kellman, "The Chemical Weapons Convention: A Verification and Enforcement Model for Determining Legal Responsibility for Environmental Harm Caused by War," in Jay E. Austin and Carl E. Bruch (eds.), *The Environmental Consequences of War: Legal, Economic and Scientific Perspectives* (Cambridge: Cambridge University Press, 2000), pp. 579-601.
61. Thomas Stock, "The Problem of old and abandoned chemical weapons under the Chemical Weapons Convention," in M. Bothe, N. Ronzitti and A. Rosas (eds.), *The New Chemical Weapons Convention: Implementation and Prospects* (The Hague: Kluwer Law International, 1998), pp. 203- 18.
62. Two possible solutions were always discussed: (i) to leave the responsibility for destruction of the OCW with the Party who has discovered the old weapons; and (ii) to leave the responsibility of destruction to the party which has abandoned the CW and to carry out destruction on the territory of the party which has discovered them. The negotiations in the Conference on Disarmament in Geneva were always focused on these two positions. Thomas Stock, ibid., p. 210.
63. As regards OCW, Article II (definitions), Article III (declarations) and Article IV (chemical weapons) of CWC which define clearly the exceptions from the general definition of chemical weapons, they exclude OWC from the definition of chemical weapons and hence, exempt them from destruction regime.
64. The CWC Article II, para 5: "Old Chemical Weapons" means: (a) Chemical weapons which were produced before 1925; or (b) Chemical weapons produced in the period between 1925 and 1946 that have deteriorated to such extent that they can no longer be used as chemical weapons. Para 6: "Abandoned Chemical Weapons" means: Chemical weapons, including old chemical weapons, abandoned by a State after January 1, 1925 on the territory of another State without the consent of the latter.
65. Old chemical weapons may result as left over from the two World Wars, which States parties may unwittingly not have declared upon entry into the force of CWC or may have discovered as abandoned ammunition later on. Thomas Stock, ibid., pp. 203- 18.
66. Paragraph 13, Part IV of the Verification Annex under the CWC provides: "Each State Party shall determine how it shall destroy chemical weapons, except that the following processes may not be used: dumping in any body of water, land burial or open-pit burning. It shall destroy only at specifically designated and appropriately designated and equipped facilities.
67. The United Nations Security Council Resolution 1540 was adopted on 28 April 2004.
68. In cooperation with the 1540 Committee and relevant regional and sub-regional organizations, the United Nations Office for Disarmament Affairs (UNODA) promotes and facilitates practical efforts of Member States to fully implement the key requirements of resolution 1540 (2004), including the preparation of voluntary national implementation plans, conduct of 1540 Peer Reviews and identification of effective implementation practices. In order to promote capacity-building, facilitate assistance and raise awareness, UNODA has organized or supported over 40 regional or thematic workshops held in Armenia, Belarus, Botswana, Brazil, Cambodia, China, Costa Rica, Croatia, Egypt, Ethiopia, Gabon, Ghana, India, Jamaica, Jordan, Kazakhstan, Kenya, Lithuania, Pakistan, Peru, Poland, Qatar, Republic of Korea, Serbia, South Africa, Sri Lanka, Togo, Ukraine, Vanuatu and Viet Nam.
69. Article 8, subparagraph (2)(b)(xvii) bans the use of "poison or poisoned weapons"; a prohibition first codified in 1899. Subparagraph (2)(b)(xviii), derived from the

1925 Geneva Protocol, makes the use of asphyxiating, poisonous or other gases a war crime, but not the use of biological weapons.

70. Allen Kara, Scott Spence and Rocio Escauriaza Leal, "Chemical and biological weapons use in the Rome Statute: a case for change," VERTIC Brief, February 14, 2011.
71. The prohibition on BCW use in both international and non-international armed conflicts has reached the status of customary international law, implying an international condemnation of such practices. The widespread practices by States of implementing national legislation that criminalises CBW use as a war crime shows that many countries favour the extension of this prohibition to individuals. A study undertaken by VERTIC indicates that a third of BWC parties have criminalised individuals' use of biological weapons and many others criminalise the intentional infection or intoxication of humans, plants or animals with disease-causing agents or toxins. At the Fourth Review Conference of the BWC, an understanding was reached that individuals are covered by the convention's prohibitions. In addition, many non-parties to the BWC have prohibited individual use. Many countries have some legislation dealing with biological weapons, or at least the intentional infliction of disease, in some way. There is also a clear prohibition on the use of chemical weapons by individuals; Article VII of the CWC explicitly prohibits use by individuals. Allen Kara, Scott Spence and Rocio Escauriaza Leal, ibid., p. 5. Each State must extend its penal legislation to cover activities prohibited under the biological and chemical weapon conventions. The States must provide for the extraterritorial application of these penal measures to its nationals. The ICC, in accordance with the principle of complementarity, may bring alleged criminals to justice only when a State is unable or unwilling to do so.
72. From 1937 to 1945, Japan employed chemical weapons against China. By the end of 1945, Japanese chemical warfare against the Chinese had resulted in an estimated 80,000 casualties and 10,000 fatalities. The Japanese army did not use all of the chemical weapons it had brought to China and abandoned large numbers of unused chemical munitions on Chinese soil. Japanese chemical weapons continue to injure and kill Chinese citizens. China estimates that ACW have caused 2,000 casualties and fatalities since the end of World War II. Before the negotiation of the 1993 CWC, Japan and China rarely discussed the issue of ACW. In 1991, however, the two governments became aware that the Convention would assign responsibility for destruction of ACW to the abandoning state, and initiated bilateral discussions on the legal, political, and financial aspects of this issue. The two sides also conducted several joint field surveys in China to assess the scope of the problem. Both Japan and China have ratified the CWC; as a result, the two governments must finalise arrangements for the destruction of abandoned Japanese chemical weapons on Chinese soil. Hongmei Deng and Peter O'Meara Evans, "Social and Environmental Aspects of Abandoned Chemical Weapons in China," *The Non-proliferation Review*, Spring-Summer 1997, pp. 101-07.
73. Paul F. Walker, "The Global Abolition of Chemical Weapons," aavailable at: http://www.unidir.org/pdf/articles/pdf-art3190.pdf, accessed October 26, 2012.
74. Ralf Trapp, "The Chemical Weapons Convention—multilateral instrument with a future," in Ramesh Thakur and Ere Haru (eds.), *The Chemical Weapons Convention: Implementation, Challenges and Opportunities* (Tokyo: United Nations Press, 2007), p. 25; Experts believe that Syria has and could use its chemical

and possibly biological weapons against Israel or any other neighbour in range as terror weapons. Anthony H. Cordesman, "Syrian Weapons of Mass destruction: An Overview," 2008, available at: http://csis.org/files/media/csis/pubs/080602_syrianwmd.pdf, accessed October 27, 2012.

75. Jez Littlewood, *The Biological Weapons Convention: A Failed Revolution* (England: Ashgate, 2005), p. 232.

3

CONVENTIONAL WEAPONS

The ultimate goal of all weapons systems is to destroy the target. Therefore every weapon, be it a weapon of mass destruction (WMD) or conventional, has certain adverse effects on the environment. The real risk that conventional weapons[1] pose to the environment is through indirect effects. In May 1943, for example, Royal Air Force pilots blew up a pair of German dams. The resulting flood destroyed more than 7,000 acres of farmland, inundated 125 factories, and sent water rushing through several coal mines. The US forces used a similar tactic in the Korean War. Another area of concern is the potential risk from the destruction of chemical facilities. Chemical plants today hold far larger volumes of dangerous substances than they used to, so they pose a far greater risk to the environment. Take the case of the accident at the Union Carbide plant in Bhopal (India), in 1984, when water infiltrated into a tank holding methyl isocyanate. The mixture caused an explosion that contaminated the surrounding area, killing and maiming thousands. Attacks on chemical plants using conventional weapons are a possibility and may result in serious harm to humans and the environment.

The extensive use of conventional weapons in armed conflict has been responsible for a great deal of collateral damage. Of these, explosive weapons play an important role in the military doctrines of States. The common feature of explosive weapons is that they are indiscriminate within their zones of blast and fragmentation effect, which makes their use in populated areas highly problematic. The impact of explosive weapons use in populated areas has an indiscriminate and severe humanitarian impact. Civilians within the vicinity of an explosion are likely to be killed or injured by the blast and fragmentation effects of such weapons. They may be harmed by the collapse of buildings or suffer as a result of damage to infrastructure that is vital to the well-being of the civilian population, such as hospitals and sanitation systems. The use of explosive weapons also creates unexploded ordnance that persists as a threat to civilians until it is removed.[2] For example, in Syria, explosive weapons have caused immense devastation over the last five years. Entire neighbourhoods have been levelled to the ground by shelling and bombardment with mortars and artillery shells; rockets; air-dropped bombs; and powerful improvised explosive devices (IEDs). The use of heavy explosive weapons in villages, towns and cities has been a major cause of humanitarian suffering in that conflict.[3]

There is no formal definition of the term "explosive device." In general parlance, the term denotes weapons that consist of a casing with a high-explosive filling and whose destructive effects result mainly from the blast wave (pressure effect) and fragmentation produced by detonation. Regardless of which effect applies—pressure, fragmentation or a combination of the two—high-explosive weapons can cause damage to both the biomass and the geo-mass of an ecosystem.[4] Fragmentation effects can be assumed to be more destructive in certain ecosystems than in others, especially as regards forests, where fragments embedded in trees can invite invasion by micro-organisms. Some examples of explosive weapons are mortar bombs, artillery shells, aircraft bombs, rocket and missile warheads, cluster submunitions, and other improvised explosive devices (IEDs).[5]

The pressure effect or blast wave often causes the formation of craters in the earth's crust. These craters get filled with water and act as breeding grounds for mosquitoes, increasing the risk of dengue fever and malaria. According to Westing, the Second Indo-China War of 1961-75 left a legacy of more than 20 million bomb craters as a semi-permanent feature of the landscape.[6] This applies particularly to the high-explosive weapons (HEW) such as fuel air explosives (FAE) that are pressure-maximised. An FAE produces a fuel-air mixture which causes a detonation just above the ground. The resultant evenly distributed and forceful pressure wave over a large area can reach cavities which are otherwise protected against more conventional forms of high-explosive attacks. Early FAE prototypes had the capacity to devastate vegetation and blow away trees in an area of ten square metres per kilogram of fuel. Recent research and development has greatly increased this capacity.

Conventional incendiary weapons have tremendous capabilities to cause forest fires and consequential damage to the top soil and loss of wildlife. Incendiary weapons (e.g., flame-throwers, napalm or white phosphorus) are not generally designed to produce self-spreading fires. This can however readily be the result if the target area is sufficiently susceptible to catching fire. Experiences in tropical hardwood forests have shown that vegetation will be totally destroyed within the area of the flames produced by napalm bombs. Even more dangerous to the environment are certain high-intensive incendiaries, which are specifically designed to ignite objects that are not otherwise readily susceptible to catching fire. The new high-intensity incendiary substance trietylaluminium (TEA) has, through its high level of heat radiation, an even greater ability to produce self-spreading fires. Wildfires, once started, can spread over thousands of square kilometres. A forest can smoulder during an entire winter under a blanket of snow, and succumb to full-fledged fire during the summer.[7]

This chapter deals with Depleted Uranium (DU), High-Explosive Weapons (HEW), and Incendiary weapons including Napalm and White Phosphorus (WP) which have a devastating effect on humans and the environment.

Notes

1. Conventional weapons refer to weapons that are not weapons of mass destruction. They include but are not limited to: armoured combat vehicles, combat helicopters, combat aircraft, warships, small arms and light weapons, landmines, cluster munitions, ammunition and artillery. They are the principal

tools used in all wars up to the present day. However, while they inflict serious damage to the environment, they often get less attention compared to weapons of mass destruction.

2. Explosive violence produces a distinct pattern of death and injury. Survivors of explosive weapons use tend to suffer multiple, complex, and severe wounds from the blast and fragmentation effects, and from being caught in collapsing structures. The physical and mental trauma can result in a range of debilitating long-term conditions, including lifelong disability, requiring considerable medical and public health resources. In addition, damage to social and economic infrastructure vital to the wellbeing of the civilian population caused by explosive weapons has deleterious effects on civilians. The destruction of transport facilities, markets, power, sanitation, and health infrastructure, as well as housing and shelter, impedes community access to food, clean water, health care, education, and other necessities of life. Borrie John and Maya Brehm, Enhancing civilian protection from use of explosive weapons in populated areas: building a policy and research agenda, *International Review of the Red Cross*, Volume 93, Number 883, September 2011, p. 1-28.
3. Damage to the built environment from the use of explosive weapons, Article 36, Briefing Paper, September 2013.
4. Perry J. Robinson, *The Effects of Weapons on Ecosystems*, UNEP Studies, 1979, p. 16.
5. Jonas A. Zukas and William P. Walters (eds.), *Explosive Effects and Applications* (Springer, New York, 1998), p. 9; William H. Boothby, *Weapons and the Law of Armed Conflict* (Oxford University Press, Oxford, 2009), p. 225.
6. Arthur H. Westing (ed.), *Environmental Hazards of War, Releasing Dangerous Forces in an Industrialized World* (London: PRIO/UNEP, 1990), p. 3.
7. Perry J. Robinson, *The Effects of Weapons on Ecosystems*, UNEP Studies, 1979, p. 17.

3 A

DEPLETED URANIUM WEAPONS

The 1991 Persian Gulf War exhibited one of the twentieth century's most frightening weapons. During the war, American and British forces introduced armour-piercing ammunition made of depleted uranium[1] (DU), a radioactive and toxic waste.[2] By the end of the war, nearly 300,000 kg of DU contaminated equipment and the soil on the battlefields of Saudi Arabia, Kuwait, and southern Iraq.[3] The use of a radioactive waste in ammunition heralded a dangerous trend of confusing the line between conventional and unconventional warfare. The use of DU munitions in combat, poses various short- and long-term hazards to the health of local populations, as well as to the environment.[4]

Depleted Uranium

Uranium is a heavy metal. It has a number of properties that make it a strategic material for nuclear and other weapons as well as genotoxic hazard:

(i) Radioactive isotopes: natural uranium contains the radioactive isotopes U-238 (99.28%), U-235 (0.71%) and U-234 (0.005%). Radioactive decay, combustion and nuclear reactions lead to the production of hazardous substances, thermal radiation and ionising radiation (alpha, beta and gamma). High-energy, short-range alpha particles are genotoxic, causing potentially carcinogenic and mutagenic chromosome damage.

(ii) High density: uranium has a density of 19g/cm. This is similar to that of tungsten and gold, 1.7 times the density of lead and

2.4 times that of iron. The use of uranium can increase a weapon's kinetic energy, enabling it to penetrate tanks and bunkers.

(iii) High strength: uranium forms very hard alloys with certain metals (e.g., titanium, niobium or cobalt). These alloys can be used for defensive armour, armour-piercing penetrators and high-impact warheads.

(iv) Low melting point: at 1132°C, less than half that of tungsten, uranium's melting point makes it suitable for shaped charge liners. When fired, these liners melt to form a focused jet of liquid metal that travels at very high speed to burn through metal or rock.

(v) Pyrophoric: uranium burns in air. Temperatures at explosion can reach up to 5000°C (compared with phosphorus at 900°C, napalm 1300°C and thermite at 2500°C).

(vi) Ultrafine dispersal: uranium burns to a black dust or aerosol of mainly insoluble oxides. Due to the minute size of the particles, contamination disperses widely, re-suspended by the sun, vehicles and wind.

(vii) Toxicity: uranium dust is toxic, and can cause severe skin and lung irritation and damage the kidneys. High doses can cause renal failure within days.[5]

DU is a by-product of the uranium enrichment process. It is alloyed with other metals principally to make armour-piercing ammunition and to harden armour used to shield military vehicles.[6] Armour-piercing incendiary projectiles that contain DU are designed to penetrate hard targets, such as tanks, armoured personnel carriers and concrete bunkers. The DU penetrator contains no explosive charge, rather it relies on kinetic energy. Its density and velocity allow it to bore through targets without buckling or losing much speed. The heat released when the DU comes into contact with air inside the target cause it to ignite. The crew risks death or disablement from the spalling and fire inside the target, which may explode if a vehicle's fuel tanks ignite. While the radioactive toxicity of DU is not very high, its chemical toxicity is.

When a DU projectile hits the target, dust containing particles of various sizes is formed. Most of the dust particles have been reported to be smaller than 5 µm in size which keeps them airborne for an extended period of time. They can thus spread over a large area, according to wind direction. DU dust is black and a target that has been hit by DU ammunition can often be recognised by the black dust cover in and around it. DU dust can be dispersed into the environment and contaminate the air and the ground. The deposit on the ground and other surfaces consists of pieces of the metal, fine fragments, and if the DU has caught fire, oxides of uranium. Most contamination from DU hits on armoured vehicles is limited to within about 100 metres of the target. Normally 10-35% (and a maximum of 70%) of the ammunition becomes an aerosol on impact.

Most of the penetrators that impact soft ground (e.g., sand or clay), remain intact and lie buried at a depth of about 50 cm there for a long time. Penetrators that hit armoured vehicles form an aerosol upon impact or ricochet. Bigger fragments and pieces remain intact on the ground surface, while fine fragments and dust are transported down the upper soil layer by water and soil organism. Some of the fine dust adsorbs onto soil particles, while some may be redistributed by wind and rainwater.[7]

Military Use of DU

Military services in many countries use DU in munitions and to strengthen armour in vehicles. The stockpile of DU in military arsenals is consistently growing.[8] Presently, around 17 countries have DU weapon systems in their arsenals. A non-exhaustive list includes: Bahrain, China, Egypt, France, Israel, Kuwait, Oman, Pakistan, Russia, Saudi Arabia, Taiwan, Thailand, Turkey, Ukraine, UAE, the UK and the US.[9] In addition, India is reportedly developing DU ammunition.[10] The US also uses a DU casing in the bunker busting B61-11 nuclear weapons, where the DU casing is designed to enable the nuclear warhead to penetrate the ground before detonating. Ammunition containing DU was used in the following recent conflicts:[11]

Gulf Wars (1991 and 1999)*:* More than 300 tons of DU was dropped in the aircraft rounds and tank-fired shells over an area of about 20,000 sq km in Kuwait and southern Iraq. Apparently this is the only conflict where large DU projectiles were fired from tanks. The US Air Force fired 783,514 rounds of 30 mm DU ammunition corresponding to 259 tons of DU.[12] The Army fired 9,552 DU tank rounds, corresponding to approximately 50 tons of DU and the Marine aviation expended DU ammunition corresponding to about 11 tons of DU. The UK is the only other country known to have fired DU munitions during this conflict. The UK Ministry of Defence estimates that its tanks fired less than one hundred 120 mm DU rounds, corresponding to about one ton of DU. The total adds up to 321 tons of DU.

Bosnia–Herzegovina (1995): About 10,800 DU rounds (approximately 3 tons of DU) were fired during NATO air strikes in 1994 and 1995, mainly around Sarajevo.

Kosovo (1999): According to NATO information about 31,000 rounds of DU were fired from A-10 planes, corresponding to about 10 tons of DU. A total of 112 sites close to the border of Kosovo were hit with DU ammunition.[13]

Afghanistan: The use of DU munitions by the US and its allies remains unclear. However, there are reports that DU munitions were transported to Afghanistan and were used by the US armed forces.[14] According to news reports, several US weapons that shoot DU rounds were used in combat in Afghanistan.[15] Another report said that between October 2001 and October 2002, an estimated 500 to 600 metric tons of DU ammunition was used by the US military.[16]

Iarq (2003): The Second Gulf War of 2003 was largely a US–British invasion of Iraq.[17] The US and UK have acknowledged firing 116,000kg of DU ammunition in the 2003 Iraq War. Just over 45% of this was fired by one platform, the US A-10 Thunderbolt II ground attack aircraft.[18] DU was excessively used during this war in the battle of Falluja. In an attempt to destroy the Sunni insurgents' stronghold, an airstrike destroyed up to 20 percent of Falluja's buildings and one-half to two-thirds of those remaining suffered serious damage from missiles and tank fire. When residents returned, the rubble of demolished buildings were bulldozed to the banks of the Euphrates River, a water source for most of the residents. Destroyed tanks and other DU contaminated vehicles remained all over town releasing radioactive dust into the air.[19]

Lebanon: The UNEP has examined the possible use of DU munitions during the Israel-Lebanon conflict of 2006. Thirty-two sites were visited south and north of the Litani river and more than fifty samples were taken for laboratory analysis. The dust, soil and smear samples were analysed using highly sensitive equipment; and there was no evidence of the use of depleted or natural uranium-containing weapons.[20] However, independent scientists studying samples of soil after Israeli bombing in Lebanon have shown high radiation levels, suggesting that uranium-based ammunitions were used.[21]

Syria (2012 onwards): The US has confirmed that it has fired DU ammunition in ongoing armed conflict in Syria. The US Central Command (CENTCOM) has acknowledged that DU was fired on two dates - the 18 and 23 November 2015. CENTCOM and the US Air Force had first denied DU was fired, then offered differing accounts of what happened, before finally admitting that DU had been used.[22] Between the strikes on the two dates, 5,100 rounds of 30mm DU ammunition were used by A-10 Thunderbolt II aircraft.[23] This equates to 1,524kg of DU. The US regularly states that DU ammunition is specifically used only for engaging armoured targets, in accordance with its own legal guidelines. However, evidence from a number of armed conflicts has shown that the US military has generally ignored these guidelines. An investigation has confirmed that the US used DU weapons twice in Syria, and on both occasions the targets were large convoys of fuel tankers.

The A-10's controversial DU ammunition is justified and promoted by the US on the basis of its perceived advantage against armoured vehicles. However, analysis of its use in the Balkans and Iraq clearly shows that if the political or operational decision is made to deploy the aircraft armed with its standard "combat mix" of DU

> and HEI ammunition, A-10s will attack a far wider range of targets of opportunity. It is standard practice for combat mix to be available for A-10 deployments in active conflict zones, even if it ultimately isn't used. Whatever the outcome of the armed conflict in Syria, DU contamination is now just one of many forms of environmental damage and toxic remnants of war, caused or exacerbated by the conflict. When it ends, the environment is unlikely to be a priority for anyone, be they donors or the new authorities, and it is Syria's communities and environment that will pay the cost.[24]

Besides being used in armed conflict, DU weapons have been fired during their development and testing. Two US sites used for testing DU weapons are now heavily contaminated and closed. In addition, the Nevada Test and Training Range contains a target testing area for DU weapons. Between 1976-1977 and 1982-1983, approximately 30,000 kg of DU weapons were fired from A-10 aircraft at Nevada, which has a large number of target-tanks and vehicles contaminated with DU. The UK has overseen DU weapons testing in its own territory as well as in France and the US. In 1995-1996, US aircraft shot 1,500 rounds of DU munitions at Tori Shima, an uninhabited island training range located 100 km west of Okinawa in the East China Sea. In 1999, US jets fired about 300 rounds of DU munitions during the US military exercise at Vieques, Puerto Rico.[25]

Hazards

When a DU projectile explodes, it disintegrates into particles which can contaminate the surrounding environment and be a health hazard for combatants as well as civilians. The three main routes of exposure to DU on the battlefield are through inhalation, ingestion and wounding.[26] People most likely to receive the highest doses of toxic substances are those near a target at the time of impact, and those who examine a target (or enter a tank) in the aftermath of the impact.[27]

The fraction of uranium particles (of similar size) absorbed into the blood is generally greater following inhalation than following ingestion. Uranium compounds vary in their degree of water solubility and absorption rates can vary during exposure. The fraction of DU absorbed by an individual also depends on the particle size and the environmental distribution of the DU particles. The inhalation of water soluble compounds of DU could lead to more than 20% absorption into the blood.[28]

Military personnel, civilians, post-conflict peacekeepers, and relief workers face potential DU exposure through inhalation, ingestion, embedded fragments, and/or external irradiation.[29] Troops in coated tanks receive radiation doses from the tanks' DU armour. The longer the conflict lasts, the greater is the exposure troops face. In the case of explosions, troops within the immediate vicinity of the damaged tank and rescue personnel are exposed to DU particles. Ground troops are also often exposed to contaminated vehicles after the conflict. When DU ammunition hits an object and/or catches fire, it produces small DU dust particles.

If fighting takes place in or near populated areas, civilians and relief workers may inhale DU particles long after the actual fighting ends. Those who salvage parts and goods from contaminated vehicles face additional exposure through inhalation. Small children run the risk of greater exposure to DU when they play in or near DU impact sites. Their typical hand-to-mouth activity could lead to a high rate of DU ingestion from contaminated soil, in addition to exposure through inhalation. Also, as DU munitions corrode, they leach into soil, contaminate groundwater and the entire agricultural system, which exposes an even larger population.[30]

Effect on Humans: DU particles which enter the human system can settle in the lungs, spleen, kidneys and other vital organs.[31] The effects of exposure to DU include cancer, renal damage, brain damage, chromosomal aberrations and congenital defects.[32] The two most important organ systems affected by DU are the renal and respiratory systems. Kidney toxicity can occur via inhalation of uranium dusts and aerosols. Many studies have investigated the distribution and retention of uranium in the body after inhalation or ingestion of compounds of the metal. Some of these compounds, such as uranium trioxide, dissolve rapidly in the lungs, while others, such as uranium dioxide, dissolve very slowly. When soluble uranium, for example in drinking water, is consumed, some of it is absorbed into the blood. Most of the uranium that enters the bloodstream is excreted rapidly in the urine, with about 10 per cent being retained in organs or tissues, such as bone. Studies on exposure to uranium have shown that one definite hazard is damage to the kidneys. In fact, one study found that it is possible for tank personnel as well as other armoured vehicle personnel sustaining hits from DU munitions to absorb enough DU to experience complete kidney failure within two days.

The British Royal Society published a report on the "Health Hazard of Depleted Uranium," published in 2001 to "inform the public debate."[33] According to the report, possibly the greatest risk to human health would be from lung cancer through inhaled DU dust being deposited in the soft tissues of the lung.[34] The exposure to large quantities of DU oxide would also be likely to cause an increase in the incidents of other cancers, including leukaemia, a finding that has been supported by the World Health Organisation.[35] The study highlights the increased risk to civilians, and children in particular, of developing skin cancer due to handling DU fragments found on the battlefield. The report recommended that visible remnants of penetrators should be cleared and contamination removed from areas around known penetrator impacts, especially to avoid the possibility of children being contaminated while playing in those areas. The report also recommends that water and milk supplies in affected areas should be monitored for several decades.

Ingestion of DU: DU may be ingested through crops grown in contaminated soil, products from animals grazed on contaminated pastures or contaminated water. Differences in diet may determine the intake of uranium via ingestion. DU ingestion may be significant over a period of years where the local culture dictates a preference for certain foods in which uranium has accumulated. Studies conducted by US officials clearly show that DU has entered the food chain and contaminated water sources.[36] Studies conducted by Iraqi scientists have found higher levels than that permitted by international standards for uranium-238—the major ingredient of that toxic soup called DU—in the drinking water systems of several cities and in the Tigris River. Vegetables, fish, and meat in southern Iraq are showing high levels of radiation contamination as well.[37]

The dangers posed by DU arise out of its chemical toxicity and radioactivity. The chemical toxicity of uranium is similar to that of other heavy metals, e.g., cadmium, lead or mercury and is due to its chemical affinity to proteins and formation of stable complexes with biological ligands of low molecular mass.[38] Chemical poisoning weakens the immune system and in some instances, results in acute respiratory conditions[39] and severe kidney problems. Exposure to radiation may lead to cancers, chronic fatigue syndrome (CFS), and auto-immune deficiencies.[40] In addition, genotoxic substances alter DNA, often in ways that increase the chances of genetic birth defects and cancer. A number of studies have also demonstrated a link between uranium and genetic diseases.[41] Though these risks are not well documented, anthropocentric concerns about DU weapons dominate scientific and policy literature. Scientists consider DU's most serious risk to come from heavy metal toxicity,[42] whereas environmental advocates and the public focus on DU's radioactivity.[43]

Contamination from DU and other military-related pollution is strongly suspected of causing a sharp rise in congenital birth defects and cancer cases in Iraq,[44] as well as in other nations that have been invaded by NATO and the US military forces over the past two decades. Additionally, there is a startling jump in miscarriages and premature births among Iraqi women. Many prominent doctors and scientists contend that DU contamination is also connected to the recent emergence of diseases that were not previously seen in Iraq, such as illnesses of the kidneys, lungs, and liver, as well as a total collapse of the immune system.[45]

Scientists generally agree that DU released into the environment will contaminate the soil or migrate to surface water and groundwater. Once DU enters the ground, it may remain there for years or decades. The environmental risks stem from DU's persistence in the environment, as it has an exceptionally long half-life.[46] The extent of the effects of DU on the environment will vary according to the soil, rock, water, and atmospheric conditions.[47] Small fragments of DU penetrators can be transported from their impact point in the ground to the surrounding soil by wind, water and soil organisms. They may also find their way into sources of water where they will continue to contaminate the water for billions of years. The contamination of drinking water source depends on rain, runoff, and soil composition.[48]

Unfortunately, once DU enters our environment, it may not be technically possible or economically feasible to remove it. Once we contaminate the atmosphere with uranium, we can only wait for the radioactive fallout to settle, and there are no known technologies for the removal of uranium from supplies of water such as lakes, streams, and rivers. While cleaning soil in its entirety would be impossible, the removal and/or replacement of contaminated top soil is possible. However, this would be a costly option. For example, studies have estimated that in the state of Indiana it will cost between $4 and $5 billion to clean approximately 500 acres at the former Jefferson Proving Grounds where around 152,000 pounds of DU munitions were fired in tests spanning over 25 years.[49] The cost for such a clean-up in a country such as Iraq with over 300 tons of DU used in the first Gulf War alone would easily run into the tens of billions of dollars.

The attitude of the British Ministry of Defence (MOD) towards public concern over DU during post Gulf War (1990-1991) was one of denial and non-engagement. Despite indications to contrary, it was falsely claimed that no evidence was available to show that DU posed any health or environmental risk. The MOD also stated that no further research would be undertaken on the subject as DU was considered by the British Government as innocuous, effective and necessary to protect its troops. In fact, the need and performance of DU was overstated. Despite calls from Iraq and Kuwait, no attempts were made to take responsibility for contamination. The use of DU weapons has been condemned by four resolutions in the European Parliament, including a landslide resolution in 2008, which called for a moratorium on DU's use and efforts toward a global ban. DU weapons have also been the subject of domestic ban in Belgium and Costa Rica. The British Government still refuses to recognize the potential risk from DU weapons, and is also evading responsibility for costly decontamination and potential humanitarian impact of the weapons.[50]

The UK and the US have downplayed the risks associated with the use of DU weapons, particularly when it comes to civilians. Although the UK provided a limited amount of funding for capacity building initiatives undertaken by the UNEP, the UK and the US refuse to provide critical support and funding for large-scale clean-up efforts and actively obstruct those organizations seeking to examine the impact of DU on health and environment.[51] The World Health Organization (WHO) in Iraq wanted to start a full scale investigation in 2003 to assess the health impact of DU, but calls for funding were obstructed in the UN Security Council by the US and the UK. The capacity building work by UNEP was also a slimmed down version of the initial wide scale assessment plan, which also faced opposition by the same States.

Human Rights Violations

The chemical and radiological toxicity of DU is a health hazard for combatants and for civilians living around an impacted area. Exposure to DU might also harm future generations through genotoxic effects. DU weapons violate the right to life, physical integrity, family life, and health. The right to life as contained in Article 6 of the International Covenant on the Civil and Political Rights (ICCPR) is considered to be the "supreme human right," and offers protection against arbitrary killing. The applicability of human rights to soldiers was addressed by the European Court of Human

Rights in the case of *Engel v. the Netherlands*.[52] The court held that the European Convention on Human Rights applies to civilians as well as to members of the armed forces.

DU in Military Manuals

Armed forces have drawn up precautionary guidelines to limit DU exposure for their personnel. A number of military manuals describe what DU is, how it is used and what the 'current' state of scientific understanding is when it comes to its potential health effects. Almost all the manuals label DU as potentially hazardous, although the risk from different exposures is evaluated differently. Some manuals suggest that exposure will not lead to significant health risks for most exposures in most scenarios. Each manual acknowledges the chemical and radioactive hazards of DU, and all recognize its potential health and environmental hazards. However, these manuals do not describe likely hazards to civilians who may be exposed DU in post-conflict periods. Characteristics of DU described in few military manuals are as follows.[53]

- Belgium: DU is a dense heavy metal, the toxic dust spreads on the soil near the impact zone and further, depending on the weather. DU munitions pose a radiological risk.
- Germany: DU is toxic and radioactive.
- NATO: DU is best described as a potentially toxic industrial material. Under specific combat conditions, DU can pose a risk of heavy metal toxicity. DU emits low levels of alpha, beta and gamma radiation.
- The Netherlands: No specific definition, but refers to reports written by the National Institute for Public Health and the Environment, who describe DU as 'limited chemically toxic' and a 'low level radiotoxic' material.
- United Kingdom: DU is a low specific activity radioactive material and presents two hazards, radiological and toxic.
- United States: DU is a dense, slightly radioactive metal used by the US and other armed forces in munitions, armour and other

applications. The risks associated with DU in the body are both chemical and radio-logical.[54]

Civilian DU exposure scenarios vary widely. The two primary pathways are inhalation and ingestion. Upon impact with hard targets, a proportion of the DU burns into a fine dust that can be inhaled. Dusts can be re-suspended by the wind, and thus inhaled by individuals living or working around or near the target. Other routes include ingestion by eating or drinking contaminated soil, food or water. DU rounds that miss their target may remain on the ground and oxidize, gradually polluting soils and groundwater. Thus the risks of exposure are highly dependent on the specific characteristics of the attack and the target area. For combatants, acute inhalation exposures in struck vehicles may be considerable and embedded fragments of DU have the potential to cause illness.[55]

Legal Control

The existing law on arms control bans the use of chemical and biological weapons, but there are no explicit rules or treaties that address the scope of DU weapons. Moreover, international law does not prohibit the use of nuclear or radiological weapons in an armed conflict.[56] Under international law, the defining feature of all weapons is that they are specifically designed (and/or used) to kill or injure by means of their particular characteristic property (radiological, chemical, incendiary, etc.). However DU weapons do not fit this definition.

DU weapons are not explosive devices. Nor are they used with the purpose of killing by radiation. It is also not established that they are capable of mass destruction, mass injury or mass poisoning. While armour-piercing projectiles containing DU may spread radiation as a secondary effect, it is not their primary purpose. DU weapons do not appear to meet the definition of chemical weapons set out in Article II of the CWC. DU is not among the toxic chemicals or their precursors listed in the Annex to the CWC. Nor are DU weapons specifically designed to cause death or other harm through the toxic properties of chemicals and their precursors. The chemically toxic effects of DU are a side-effect of their use. DU weapons do not fit the definition of biological weapons contained in Article I of the 1972 BWC,[57] nor can they be classified as incendiary weapons under the Protocol III of the Convention on Certain Conventional Weapons (CCW).[58]

Though it may be difficult to bring DU weapons under the purview of the legal definition of terms "radiological," "toxin," "chemical," "poison," and "incendiary," these weapons have properties of conventional weapons as well as weapons of mass destruction. DU weapons are indiscriminate and capable of causing superfluous injuries. Yuen (2003), in a working paper submitted to the ECOSOC, has recommended that DU weapons "should be considered banned, whether or not there is a specific treaty banning them," and that, "the States that have employed ... these weapons should assume their duties relative to compensation, clean-up and warning."[59]

Superfluous Injury: The 1868 St. Petersburg Declaration prohibited the use of explosives or inflammable projectiles causing superfluous injury or unnecessary suffering. The Preamble to the Declaration[60] stated that the employment of such arms would be contrary to the laws of humanity. This principle was included in the Additional Protocol I (AP I) of 1977, and Article 35 (2) accordingly provides: "It is prohibited to employ weapons, projectiles and materials and methods of warfare of a nature to cause superfluous injury or unnecessary suffering." The prohibition of causing superfluous injury or unnecessary suffering has been accorded a customary status under IHL applicable in both international and non-international armed conflict.[61] The International Court of Justice (ICJ) in its advisory opinion in the *Nuclear Weapons Case* affirmed that the prohibition of means and methods of warfare which are of a nature to cause superfluous injury or unnecessary suffering was one of the "cardinal principles" of IHL.[62]

The ICRC Commentary on Article 35 (2) of AP I, cites the example of the protection of combatants from incendiary weapons such as flame-throwers or napalm. It states that while the principle prohibiting superfluous injury or unnecessary suffering does not protect combatants from such weapons, it is generally admitted that these weapons should not be used in such a way that they will cause unnecessary suffering, which means that, in particular, they should not be used against an individual without cover.[63] Arguing along the same lines, the use of DU weapons should be prohibited if the injury or suffering caused is disproportionate to the military necessity in all cases. In the given circumstances, due to the lack of scientific information, it is difficult to state whether DU weapons cause superfluous injury or unnecessary suffering in all cases;[64] though DU has been held responsible for causing cancer and kidney damage.[65] However, according to Dan Fahey (2008), the absence of evidence should not be interpreted as evidence of absence, as there have been few long-term health studies of soldiers or civilians with confirmed DU exposure. A growing body of evidence links DU exposure with pathologies in laboratory animals and human cells, and the limited testing that has been carried out indicates that contact with high levels of DU may cause pathologies such as kidney damage and cancer.[66]

As far as military necessity is concerned, DU is a cheap and highly effective armour penetrator and its use has been justified by the US and the UK Governments.[67] However, the necessity of taking precautionary measures to protect one's own personnel from the possible effects of DU detracts from the argument of military necessity. The US government has issued detailed safety instructions to military personnel serving in operational theatres where they may be at risk of exposure to DU contamination.[68]

The US has remained silent on the adverse effects of DU weapons on civilians. However, the US Army Regulations provides for protection of military personnel from DU contaminations. It states: "In general, commanders at all levels should take prudent measures to keep radiation exposures (from Depleted Uranium or Radioactive Commodities) to all personnel as low as is reasonably achievable that is consistent with the operational risks. Radioactive material and waste will not be locally disposed of through burial, submersion, incineration, destruction in place, or abandonment without approval from overall Commanders of Major Army Commands (MACOM commander). If local disposal is approved, the responsible MACOM commander must document the general nature of the disposed material and the exact location of the disposal. The MACOM commander has the responsibility for determining the likelihood of significant exposure from contaminated equipment to any individual. Individuals that the command determines may have been exposed will be sent to a medical treatment facility for appropriate screening."[69]

Principle of Distinction: One of the most fundamental principles of IHL is the protection of civilians and civilian objects from attacks and dangers of military operations during an armed conflict. The principle requires that parties to a conflict must always distinguish between combatants and the civilian population as well as between military objectives and civilian objects; and should direct their operations only against combatants and military objectives.[70] When a DU weapon is used, the release of DU dust may contaminate soil, water, air, and plant and animal life, and through these affect human health in various ways.[71] The scientific evidence is that uranium, like other heavy metals, can enter the brain through the bloodstream. It can cause increased incidents of birth defects, childhood leukaemia and other cancers.[72]

Ramsey Clark, a former US Attorney General, and now an international human rights lawyer has argued that: "DU weapons violate international law because of their inherent cruelty and unconfined death-dealing effect. They threaten civilian populations now and for generations to come. These are precisely the weapons and uses prohibited by international law for more than a century including the Geneva Conventions and their

Protocols Additional of 1977." Clark makes an appeal to ban the use of DU weapons.[73]

The Precautionary Principle: Article 51 of AP I prohibits indiscriminate attacks "which employ a method or means of combat" of which the effects "cannot be limited as required," which certainly characterises attacks involving DU weapons.[74] Parties to armed conflicts are required to ensure that precautions are taken in planning and conducting military operations to minimise their effects on civilians.[75] In particular, Article 57(2)(a)(ii) requires military commanders to take all feasible precautions in the choice of means and methods of attack with a view to avoiding, and in any event minimising, incidental loss of civilian life, injury to civilians and damage to civilian objects. Further, Article 57(2)(a)(iii) requires parties to a conflict to refrain from deciding to launch any attack which may be expected to cause incidental loss of civilian life, injury to civilians, damage to civilian objects, or a combination thereof, which would be excessive in relation to the concrete and direct military advantage anticipated.

Parties to an armed conflict are also obliged under Article 58 of AP I, to the extent feasible, to take the necessary precautions to protect the civilian population, individual civilians and civilian objects under their control against the dangers resulting from military operations.[76] Therefore, Articles 51, 57 and 58, of AP I if taken together, provide a strong legal basis for restricting the use of DU weapons in armed conflict.

In addition, according to the Martens clause, which is a part of customary international law and AP I, the laws of war apply to weapons and methods of warfare that are not specifically mentioned in different conventions and hence, weapons could be prohibited despite the lack of a convention that bans them. This principle was originally set forth in the preamble to the Hague Convention of 1907 and shows that the drafters of the convention understood even then that technological advancement could lead to the production of new weapons which could be more destructive and inhumane than the weapons that were already banned such as expanding bullets and poison.[77] The International Court of Justice (ICJ) used this principle to find nuclear weapons illegal, despite the absence of a convention prohibiting their use.

Damage to Natural Environment: There are some key legal arguments, mainly derived from existing IHL, which support a moratorium and consequent ban on DU weapons. Article 35 of AP I, containing basic rules, prohibits the employment of methods and means of warfare which are intended, or may be expected, to cause widespread, long-term and severe damage to the natural environment. Judging by the impacts of DU in Iraq, Kosovo and Afghanistan, these weapons should fall under the category of prohibited weapons defined by Article 35, since they are suspected to have long-lasting effects on the environment.

Article 55, of AP I further states that care shall be taken in warfare to protect the natural environment against widespread, long-term and severe damage. This protection includes a prohibition of the use of methods or means of warfare which are intended or may be expected to cause such damage to the natural environment and thereby prejudice the health or survival of the population. Article 36 of AP I also obliges any State studying, developing, or acquiring a new weapon to hold a legal review of that weapon.[78] This binding law also requires signatory States to ensure that any new weapon or means of warfare does not contravene international law, thereby prohibiting the use of weapons that cause widespread, long-term damage, as is being experienced in the aftermath of the use of DU weapons in Iraq, Afghanistan and other States.

Technological developments raise the question of how to regulate warfare under conditions of uncertainty about the health and environmental effects of new weapons like DU. The precautionary principle, which encourages action on environmental problems before the cause and effect relationship of a pollutant and a potential harm has been established, offers one possible approach to the problem of scientific uncertainty with regard to new weapons systems.[79] Imported from peacetime contexts, a military precautionary principle calls for an evaluation of newly developed weapons systems.

In customary IHL, Rule 44 provides that a "lack of scientific certainty as to the effects on the environment of certain military operations does not absolve a party to the conflict from taking such precautions (to protect the natural environment and human health)."

Global Response

In January 2001, Belgium, Portugal, Norway and Finland requested that the European Parliament adopt a resolution calling for "EU members States that are also NATO members to propose that a moratorium be placed on the use of DU weapons in accordance with 'precautionary principles' and efforts be made for a global ban."[80] This was in response to the deaths from leukaemia of several veterans of Italian armed forces who had served in Kosovo.[81] The European Parliament has voted for a moratorium on DU ammunition in 2001, 2003 and 2008.[82] However, the latest European Union and United Nations resolutions have been carefully restricted to the use of DU, excluding other non-nuclear uranium weapons. By restricting debate and scientific testing to depleted uranium weapons the arms control agenda has been diverted from a third generation of undisclosed uranium weapons developed to meet more recent strategic concerns—guided weapons enhanced with un-depleted uranium. On May 22, 2008, the European Parliament issued its resolution dealing with DU, in which it reiterated "its call on all EU Member States and NATO countries to impose a moratorium on the use of depleted uranium weapons and to redouble efforts towards a global ban."[83]

ICTY Decision on *Yugoslavia v. NATO*: Yugoslavia had taken up the issue of environmental damage during the 1999 Kosovo conflict before the International Criminal Tribunal for the former Yugoslavia (ICTY), which examined its claims against NATO forces. Although the prosecutor ultimately found no basis for opening a criminal investigation into any aspect of the NATO air campaign, the ICTY did examine the question of responsibility for environmental damage and the use of DU from an environmental perspective, thereby establishing a precedent that merits attention. The Special Committee observed that Article 55 of AP I[84] "may reflect current customary law" and, therefore, may be applicable to non-Parties to the Protocol, such as France and the US.

ICJ Decision on *Yugoslavia v. NATO*: On April 29, 1999, the Federal Republic of Yugoslavia filed complaints before the International Court of Justice (ICJ) against several NATO members contending that the States had: (ii) by taking part in the use of weapons containing depleted uranium, acted in breach of the obligation not to use prohibited weapons and not to cause far-reaching health and environmental damage. Even if the Court, due to a lack of jurisdiction, could not indicate the provisional measures requested, it however added that it remained seized of those cases and stressed that its findings, at that stage, "in no way prejudged the question of the jurisdiction of the Court to deal with the merits" of the cases and left "unaffected the rights of the Government of Yugoslavia (and of the respondent States) to submit arguments regarding those questions." This articulation on the *ratione materiae* competence of the ICJ in this case suggests that the Court views cases related to environmental degradation in armed conflicts to be within its purview. As such, the decision indicates that the ICJ could be an appropriate forum for litigating such issues in the future.

In its *Nuclear Weapons Advisory Opinion*, the International Court of Justice (ICJ) noted that, "... humanitarian law, at a very early stage, prohibited certain types of weapons either because of their indiscriminate effects on combatants and civilians or because of the unnecessary suffering caused to combatants, that is to say, a harm greater than that unavoidable to achieve legitimate military objective."[85] Under IHL, the use of weapon should be in proportion to the military advantage gained. Contaminating drinking water with uranium for hundreds of years is not in proportion to what was required militarily to subdue the Iraqi forces. Contamination of agricultural lands with DU fragments comprising radioactive and chemically toxic elements having half-lives of billions of years can in no way be said to be in proportion to the military objective or advantage gained.

UN General Assembly: The UN General Assembly has also addressed the issue of DU, guided by the purposes and principles enshrined in the UN Charter and the rules of IHL.[86] The General Assembly resolution of 2007, requested the Secretary-General to submit a report on the "effects of the use of armaments and ammunition containing depleted uranium" for its Sixty-third session.[87] The General Assembly resolution 63/54 acknowledges the importance of protecting the environment and reads, in part: "humankind is more aware of the need to take immediate measures to protect the environment, any event that could jeopardise such efforts requires urgent attention to implement the required measures." The resolution also recognises "the potential harmful effects of the use of armaments and ammunitions containing DU on human health and the environment."[78] These resolutions could lead to a future codification process with regard to legal norms protecting both human health and the environment from DU weapons, thus addressing the current major gap in treaty law regarding the use of such weapons.

In 2010, the General Assembly resolution calling for DU user transparency was supported by 148 States.[89] It stated that nations using DU weapons should reveal where the weapons had been fired, when asked by affected countries. The United States, France, the United Kingdom, and Israel (the largest producers and/or having stockpiles of DU weapons) voted against the resolution, while 36 countries abstained from voting. This resolution is the strongest action taken by the international community regarding DU weapons so far. It signifies a growing international recognition of the hazards of DU contamination and of the fact that affected and poorly equipped post-conflict States require accurate information and considerable assistance to deal with the problem. The US had refused to share data on DU use in Iraq with UNEP, something that, together with security problems, ensured that they were unable to fully survey contamination in the country.

In December 2012, the General Assembly adopted a resolution calling for a precautionary approach to DU weapons. The resolution was supported by 155 States. The US, UK, France and Israel voted against it, while 27 States abstained. The resolution was informed by the UNEP's repeated calls for a precautionary approach to the use of and the post-conflict management of DU weapons. This was the fourth General Assembly resolution on the use of radioactive and chemically toxic conventional weapons that can harm human health and cause environmental contamination. The widespread opposition to the use of DU is perhaps most apparent in the increasingly well supported UN General Assembly resolutions on the issue. The UN General Assembly has backed a new on DU weapons by 151 votes to 4.[90] The resolution, which highlights the ongoing concerns of affected states and communities, health experts and civil society over the potential health risks from DU exposure, is the sixth to be adopted since 2007. The text of resolution also recognizes that countries affected by the use of DU weapons face considerable technical and financial barriers in dealing with DU contamination to internationally recognized radiation protection standards. The General Assembly resolutions cannot clear contaminations; international organizations as well as developed countries will have to come forward to tackle the post-conflict legacy of DU weapons in Iraq, Syria and elsewhere. Though non-binding, these resolutions are significant as they demonstrate an increasingly prevalent view that the use of DU weapons is unacceptable.

In UNEP's view, precaution should be backed by clean-up and decontamination, awareness raising measures to reduce the risk of civilian exposure and the long-term monitoring of contaminated sites. The resolution built on previous texts and once again included a call for greater transparency from DU users. It contained the same language as 2010's resolution which called for states to transfer quantitative and geographic data on DU usage to affected governments when requested to do so.

It has been reported that the US is actively seeking less hazardous materials and is trying to replace DU in its tank ammunition. While this decision is a positive step forward and recognition of the long-standing international opposition to the weapons, DU weapons will continue to be part of the US's arsenal for many years to come.[91] There is no evidence, whether Russia, China or Pakistan have taken any step towards banning DU weapons. However, France has been on the lookout for more "environmentally acceptable" materials for their tank ammunition for a number of years. The UK still retains one 120mm tank round in spite of longstanding domestic opposition. Iraq, the country most affected by the wartime use of DU is still struggling to deal with the legacy of contamination from 1991 and 2003. Iraq has called for assistance from the international community in dealing with DU contamination. Developed states and international organizations need to give serious thought to how such obligations could be developed.

During armed conflicts, weapons may only be used against legal military targets and for the duration of the war. Weapons may not cause undue suffering or superfluous injury and may not severely damage the environment. DU weapons cannot be used in military operations without violating these rules, and therefore must be considered illegal. Use of illegal weapons constitutes a violation of IHL and subjects the violators to legal liability for their effects on victims and the environment as well as criminal liability. The use of DU weaponry constitutes the "grave breach" of the provisions of Geneva Conventions, and hence its use constitutes a war crime or crime against humanity.[92]

Notes

1. DU is the term used for uranium that contains a very low amount of the 235U isotope, more than three times less than is found in natural uranium. DU is what remains after the element is enriched for use in nuclear power plants or in nuclear arms. DU is radioactive; a radiation dose from DU would be 60% as strong as the same dose from purified natural uranium. Uranium is the heaviest naturally occurring element and is about twice as dense as lead. Dan Fahey, "Depleted Uranium and Its Use in Weapons," in Avril McDonald, Jann K. Kleffner and Brigit Toebes (eds.), *Depleted Uranium and International Law: A Precautionary Approach* (The Hague, TMC Asser Press), pp. 3-27.
2. Depleted uranium (DU) is the by-product of uranium enrichment process—the manufacture of uranium with a concentration of highly radioactive U-235 for use in nuclear weapons and in nuclear power plants. DU, which has been depleted of its U-235 and U-234, is about 60% as radioactive as natural uranium. Most of that radiation—about 95%—is emitted as alpha particles that cannot penetrate the skin. A minute amount of beta and gamma radiation could strike deeper cell tissue were fine particles of DU inhaled or ingested, as they could easily be by any soldier or civilian in the vicinity of a recently exploded DU shell. Even low doses of low-level radiation can cause some damage to the DNA in living cells. DU is no different from natural uranium in its chemical toxicity. It is a heavy metal that, in its soluble form, accumulates in the kidneys (the primary target organ for uranium) and that, in sufficient quantities, can increase the risk of renal damage. Steve Fetter and Frank N. von Hippel, "Depleted Uranium Weapons and Acute Post-War Health Effects: An IPPNW Assessment," vol. 7, no. 1, *Medicine & Global Survival* (April 2001), pp. 43-47.
3. The US Air Force reportedly fired about 800,000 of the 30-mm DU rounds during Desert Storm. The use of DU munitions by the US Marines, Navy and British forces was relatively minor. In all, about 300 tons of DU was fired in Desert Storm. This is comparable to the amount of natural uranium that was released into the atmosphere from the US Government's Feed Materials Production Centre (FMPC) near Fernald, Ohio, between 1953 and 1977. Steve Fetter and Frank N. von Hippel, "The Hazard Posed by Depleted Uranium Munitions," vol. 8, no. 2, *Science & Global Security* (1999), pp. 125-61. See also, *Environmental Exposure Report: Depleted Uranium in the Gulf,* Office of the Special Assistant for Gulf War Illnesses, US Department of Defence; July 31, 1998; Tab F - DU use in the Gulf War. Available at: http://www.gulflink.osd.mil/du/, visited February 18, 2012.
4. The factors that determine the risk include, but are not limited to: local environmental conditions, the quantity of DU munitions shot, the number of hard targets hit by DU munitions, the proximity to water and food supplies, and the proximity to human populations. For details *see*: UNEP, Post-Conflict Assessment Unit, Depleted Uranium in Serbia and Montenegro: Post Conflict Environmental Assessment, Geneva, March 27, 2002; UNEP, Post-Conflict Assessment Unit, Depleted Uranium in Kosovo, Post-Conflict Environmental Assessment, Geneva, March 2001; J. P. McLaughlin et al., "Actinide analysis of a depleted uranium penetrator from a 1999 target site in southern Serbia," vol. 64, *Journal of Environmental Radioactivity* (2003), p. 155.
5. Williams Dai, "Under the Radar: Identifying third-generation Uranium Weapons," available at: http://unidir.org/pdf/articles/pdf-art2759.pdf, accessed February 19, 2012.

6. DU has several military applications because of its high density, its pyrophoric nature (DU self-ignites when exposed to temperatures between 600°C and 700°C and high pressures), and its property of becoming sharper, when it penetrates armour plating. United States Nuclear Regulatory Commission, "Background Information on Depleted Uranium," available at: http://www.nrc.gov/about-nrc/regulatory/rulemaking/potential-rulemaking/uw-streams/bg-info-du.html, accessed August 10, 2012.
7. *Depleted Uranium in Bosnia and Herzegovina: Post-Conflict Environmental Assessment*, United Nations Environment Programme (2003), p.17.
8. Although approximately 18 states possess or are developing DU ammunition, most DU has been shot by the UK and the US. Both States claim that the use of DU ammunition is militarily necessary on account of its superior ability to penetrate hard armour compared with tungsten (the main alternative). DU is also cheaper to purchase than tungsten and more widely available. Moreover, its density and velocity mean that pilots who air-deliver DU can shoot at a greater distance from their targets, increasing their safety. UK Ministry of Defence, *Memorandum: Gulf War Illnesses,* presented to the House of Commons Defence Select Committee on April 26, 2001 (London, HMSO, 2001), p. 37; B. Carnahan, A Military View on Depleted Uranium, in Avril McDonald, Jann K. Kleffner and Brigit Toebes (eds.), *Depleted Uranium and International Law: A Precautionary Approach* (The Hague, TMC Asser Press, 2008), pp. 99, 10410.
9. Dan Fahey, "Depleted Uranium and Its Use in Weapons," in Avril McDonald, Jann K. Kleffner and Brigit Toebes (eds.), ibid., pp. 8-9. *See also,* Depleted Uranium (DU) Hazards in Post-Conflict Environments, Geneva International Centre for Humanitarian Demining, GICHD Advisory Note, February 25, 2003; Thomas D. Williams, "The Depleted Uranium Threat," Global Research, available at: http://www.globalresearch.ca/index.php?context=va&aid=9847, accessed August 21, 2011.
10. It was suggested in a 1999 UK MoD document that India was developing DU weapons in the early 90s. If this is the case, this was most likely for India's domestically produced Arjun tank, which is fitted with a 120mm rifled gun and bespoke ammunition. Little technical information is available about this ammunition so this claim cannot be substantiated. Available at: http://www.bandepleteduranium.org/en/users, accessed November 14, 2012.
11. A. Bleise, P. R. Danesi and W. Burkart, "Properties, use and health effects of depleted uranium (DU): a general overview," vol. 64, *Journal of Environmental Radioactivity* (2003), p. 98.
12. It has been estimated that a large faction of DU bullets fired from aircraft missed their intended targets, and majority of these projectiles are still buried at various levels in the ground. Henryk Bem and Firyal Bou-Rabee, "Environmental and Health Consequences of Depleted Uranium Use in the 1991 Gulf War," vol. 30, *Environmental International* (2004), pp. 123-34.
13. Marco Durante and M. Pugliese, "Depleted uranium residual radiological risk assessment for Kosovo sites," vol. 64, *Journal of Environmental Radioactivity* (2003), pp. 237-45, at p. 238.
14. Estimates by *Jane's Defence* in 2003 suggested that the Taliban had at least 100 main battle tanks and 250 armoured fighting vehicles at the beginning of the conflict. It would be unusual if the US Army had chosen not to engage these targets with DU munitions from the air. During the operation "Enduring Freedom" in support of the Northern Alliance against the Taliban-Regime, US aircraft used, amongst others, armour-piercing incendiary munitions with a DU-

core. See: http://www.globalresearch.ca/index.php?context=va&aid=14642, accessed February 22, 2012.

15. Dan Fahey, "The Use of Depleted Uranium Munitions in Afghanistan," July 5, 2003. Available at: http://www.wise-uranium.org/dissafdf.html, visited February 22, 2012.
16. *See*, NATO, "Depleted Uranium," available at: http://www.nato.int/du/docu/d000500e.htm#3, accessed August 31, 2011; Malcolm Aitken, "Gulf war Leaves Legacy of Cancer," *British Medical Journal* 319 (1999): 401, accessed August 31, 2011; GlobalSecurity.org, "Depleted Uranium [DU] History," available at: http://www.globalsecurity.org/military/systems/munitions/du-history.htm, accessed August 31, 2011; Dan Fahey, "Depleted Uranium Weapons: Lessons from the 1991 Gulf War," available at: http://www.wise-uranium.org/dhap992.html, accessed June 28, 2011; Marc W. Herold, "Uranium Wars: The Pentagon Steps up its Use of Radioactive Munitions," available at; http://cursor.org/stories/uranium.htm, accessed August 31, 2011.
17. The US started military operation under the doctrine of pre-emptive war as President George W. Bush was determined to remove Saddam Hussein from power. Without the explicit approval of the UN Security Council, the US started the war on 19 March 2003 with airstrikes against Iraq. The following days, ground troops entered Baghdad and also headed toward oil fields and port facilities.
18. The data confirm that only 33% of the A-10s' targets were tanks or armoured vehicles, with the weapons also used against light vehicles, buildings and unmounted troops. Zwijnenburg Wim amd Doug Weir, Targets of opportunity: Analysis of the use of DU by A-10s in the 2003 Iraq War, PAX and ICBUM, August 2016. According to Dan Fahey (2003) an independent analyst, in the 2003 War, the US and the UK used ammunition containing DU to hit a wide range of targets. Although sufficient information on the quantities of the real DU ammunition used or the contaminated sites is not available, but it is believed that between 1000 to 2000 metric tons had been used to hit the tanks and armoured vehicles, buildings and sites inhabited.
19. According to the Iraqi Ministry of Environment there are hundreds of sites contaminated with nuclear radiation, while experts from the United Nations Environment Program (2005) estimated that contaminated sites are in thousands.
20. Lebanon: Post-Conflict Environmental Assessment, 2007, United Nations Environment Programme.
21. Lebanon: Rapid Environmental Assessment for Greening Recovery, Reconstruction and Reform, 2007, UNDP, p. 215.
22. The CENTCOM spokesperson later explained that the US forces wanted to ensure that trucks would be rendered completely inoperable, and that DU, rather than HEI rounds were the best way to achieve that. General Dynamics, one of the manufacturers of the A-10's 30mm ammunition family has stated that the HEI round provides fragmentation and incendiary effects for use against personnel, trucks, ammunition storage, and many other targets.
23. The 30mm DU ammunition used in both incidents was fired by A-10 aircraft, a platform notorious for the fact that the pilot cannot select between its DU and high explosive incendiary (HEI) ammunition once in flight. A-10s have been active in operations against Islamic State (IS) over Syria and Iraq since 2014, although this is the first time that DU's use has been identified in the conflict.
24. Weir Doug, Why did the US need toxic uranium munitions to destroy fuel tankers in Syria? *Ecologist*, 20 February 2017.

25. In the US, the Nuclear Regulatory Commission regulates the possession and the use of DU weapons, restricting testing of DU rounds to a few locations. The most heavily contaminated testing locations are Aberdeen Proving ground, Maryland; the newly closed Jefferson Proving Ground, Indiana; and Yuma Proving Ground, Arizona. Dan Fahey, "Depleted Uranium and Its Use in Weapons," in Avril McDonald, Jann K. Kleffner and Brigit Toebes (eds.), *Depleted Uranium Weapons and International Law*, TMC Asser Press, pp. 24-25.
26. Personnel in or near an armoured vehicle at the time these vehicles are struck by DU munitions can receive significant internal DU exposures. Recent studies have demonstrated the so-called "bystander effect," in which un-irradiated cells close to irradiated cell populations can exhibit genetic alterations. The bystander effect is predominant at low tissue doses, where few cells experience an alpha particle passage. At higher doses, recipient cells increasingly experience alpha passages themselves, with a high probability of cell killing and almost certainty of inducing other changes, thus reducing the relative effectiveness of the bystander effect. For this reason, uranium particles, which emit few alphas, would have a greater chance of inducing effects through the bystander mechanism than "hotter" particles. Alpha particle radiation is known to be a potent cause of bystander effects, particularly in the form of genomic instability and, since heavy metals can also cause instability, there is a strong case that the mixed radio-chemical exposure may be acting in this context. M. A. McDiarmid and J. P. Keogh et al., "Health effects of depleted uranium on exposed Gulf War Veterans," vol. 82, no. 2, Environ Res. (2000), p. 168. *Also see* R. Fisk, "The evidence is there. We caused cancer in the Gulf," *The Independent*, October 16, 1998.
27. International Atomic Energy Agency, "Features: Depleted Uranium," available at: http://www.iaea.org/NewsCenter/Features/DU/du_qaa.shtml#q10, accessed August 14, 2012.
28. World Health Organisation, "Depleted Uranium," available at: http://www.who.int/mediacentre/factsheets/fs257/en/, accessed August 31, 2012.
29. A. Bleise, "Properties, Use and Health Effects of Depleted Uranium: A General Overview," vol. 64, *J. Envtl. Radioactivity*, 2002, pp. 93-100.
30. Karen Hulme, *War Torn Environment: Interpreting the Legal Threshold* (Leiden: Martinus Nijhoff Publishers, 2004), p. 247.
31. "Environmental Contaminants from War Remnants in Iraq," Report: NGO Coordination Committee for Iraq, June 2011, p. 5.
32. In Southern Iraq, 34 people died of cancer in 1988; 450 died in 1998; and in 2001 there were 603 cancer deaths. In a study of 39,450 Italian military personnel previously stationed in Kosovo and Bosnia, they found a significant increase in observed cases of lymphoma. Individuals in the study showed that the rate of lymphoma was 8 times higher than the expected rate of lymphoma in average Italian citizens. Larry Johnson, "Iraqi Cancers, Birth Defects Blamed on US Depleted Uranium," *The Seattle Post*, November 12, 2002, available at: http://www.seattlepi.com/national/95178_du12.shtml, accessed August 30, 2011. *See also*: Moret Leuren, "Depleted Uranium: The Trojan Horse of Nuclear War," vol. 8, no. 2, *World Affairs*, pp. 110-35.
33. "The Health Hazard of Depleted Uranium Munitions," Part I, 2001, Policy Document 6/01, London: The Royal Society; and "The Health Hazard of Depleted Uranium Munitions," Part II, 2002, Policy Document 6/02, London: The Royal Society. Part I deals with the amount of DU to which combatant personnel may reasonably be exposed on the battlefield and radiation doses. Part II addresses the risk of toxic poisoning and environmental issues.

34. *The Health Hazard of Depleted Uranium Munitions*, Part I, 2001, Policy Document 6/01, London: The Royal Society, p. 21.
35. *Depleted Uranium: Source, Exposure and Health Effects*, 2001, Geneva: World Health Organisation, p. 84.
36. No warnings about the dangers of DU were provided by the US to coalition forces expected to encounter DU contamination on the Gulf battlefields. Combatants and support personnel were not informed of the need to check soldiers' wounds for DU contamination, or told of the requirement to don full protective suits during contact with contaminated equipment and soil. *Development of Depleted Uranium Training Support Packages: Tier I—General Audience;* US Army Chemical School; October, 1995; p. B-10. *Nuclear, Biological, and Chemical (NBC) Vulnerability Analysis;* U.S. Army Field Manual 3-14; The US Army Chemical School; July 1, 1996. The US Department of Defence also failed to warn the inhabitants of Kuwait, Saudi Arabia and Iraq about DU contamination on their lands. However, in April, 1991, the United Kingdom Atomic Energy Authority stated: "It would be unwise for people to stay close to large quantities of DU for long periods and this would obviously be of concern to the local population if they collect this heavy metal and keep it. There will be specific areas in which many rounds will have been fired where localised contamination of vehicles and the soil may exceed permissible limits and these could be hazardous to both clean up teams and the local population ..., if DU gets into the food chain or water then this will create potential health problems." *Kuwait—Depleted Uranium Contamination*, United Kingdom Atomic Energy Authority, April 30, 1991.
37. "The Case for an Immediate Ban on the Military Use of DU," presented by Damacio A. Lopez, Director, International DU Study Team, at a meeting of the European Parliament in Brussels, Belgium, on June 10, 2003, available at http://www.grip.org/bdg/g1035.html.
38. The radiological and chemical properties of DU can be compared to those of natural uranium, which is ubiquitously present in soil at a typical concentration of 3 mg/kg. Natural uranium has the same chemotoxicity, but its radiotoxicity is 60% higher. A. Bleise, P. R. Danesi, W. Burkart, "Properties, use and health effects of depleted uranium (DU): a general overview," vol. 64, *Journal of Environmental Radioactivity* (2003), pp. 93-112. Henryk Bem and Firyal Bou-Rabee, "Environmental and Health Consequences of Depleted Uranium use in the 1991 Gulf War," vol. 30, *Environmental International* (2004), p. 126.
39. The Royal Society Working Group on the Health Hazards of Depleted Uranium Munitions, "The Health Effects of Depleted Uranium Munitions: A Summary," vol. 22, *J. Radiological Protection* (2002), pp. 131-34.
40. Lesley Wexler, "Limiting the Precautionary Principle: Weapons Regulation in the Face of Scientific Uncertainty," vol. 39, no. 2, *University of California, Davis, Law Review* (2006), pp. 459-529. Available at: http://lawreview.law.ucdavis.edu/issues/39/2/articles/DavisVol39No2_Wexler.PDF, accessed February 19, 2012.
41. The US Armed Forces Radiobiology Research Institute (AFRRI) has conducted cellular and animal studies which show that DU can turn cells cancerous, cause chromosome damage, leukaemia and genomic instability. This damage can also be passed on to the next generation. "The US must stop blocking international action on depleted uranium weapons!" Available at: http://www.envirosagainstwar.org/know/read.php?itemid=12816, accessed November 15, 2012.
42. World Health Organisation, "Depleted Uranium" (January 2003), available at http://www.who.int/mediacentre/factsheets/fs257/en/.

43. As regards, radio-toxicity, U-238 is a long-lived alpha-emitter, with a weak emission of beta and gamma rays. External exposure hazards mainly regard military personnel using tanks with DU shields, while it is negligible in other occasions. The most important pathways for DU exposure are therefore in case of ingestion or inhalation. D. E. McClain, "Health effects of Depleted Uranium," Armed Forces Radiobiology Research Institute Bethesda (Maryland, USA), Report of the Science Application International Corporation, 1990. *Also see* UNEP/UNCHS BALKANS TASK FORCE: The potential effects on human health and the environment arising from possible use of depleted uranium during the 1999 Kosovo conflict, 1999, UNEP.
44. Unusually high radioactivity from DU munitions has been recorded in many areas of Iraq where there was heavy US military fire, including Baghdad city, Anbar (particularly in the cities of Falluja and Ramadi), Najaf city, Muthanna, Babil, and Basra. It has been alleged by Iraq that in the first year after DU was used, some 50,000 Iraqi children died from various diseases, most significantly cancer of the blood (leukaemia). *See*: UN General Assembly document A/56/165 dated July 3, 2001.
45. Environmental Contaminants from War Remnants in Iraq, Report: NGO Coordination Committee for Iraq, June 2011, p. 3.
46. Estimates range as high as 4.4 billion years. Ramsey Clark, "An International Appeal to Ban the Use of Depleted Uranium Weapons," in John Catalinotto and Sara Flounders (eds.), *Metal of Dishonour: How the Pentagon Radiates Soldiers and Civilians with DU Weapons* (New York: International Action Centre, 2004). Available at: http://www.iacenter.org/depleted/mettoc.htm, accessed February 20, 2012.
47. Due to the different chemical properties of different soils and rocks, the effect of DU on the environment varies. Penetrators that hit clay will remain unaffected and will not affect the surrounding soil and groundwater. If they impact on quartz sand they will weather relatively fast and may contaminate the groundwater. If the impact is in residual soils, penetrators and DU dust will weather more or less easily, depending on the type of bedrock. If the soil consists of weathered granite or acid volcanic rock, the environment will be acidic and the weathering may be fast. Acid rain will speed up the weathering. *Depleted Uranium in Kosovs: Post-conflict Environmental Assessment* (2001), UNEP, pp. 145-47; *Also see*: *Depleted Uranium in Serbia/Montenegro: Post-Conflict Environmental Assessment* (2002), UNEP.
48. Robert Thompson, "Radioactive Warfare: Depleted Uranium Weapons, the Environment, and International Law," vol. 36, *Environmental Law Reporter* (2006), pp. 10476-478.
49. US GAO, "Environmental Clean-up, Too Many High Priority Sites Impede Department of Defence's Programme," Table-3 (1994) (GAO-NSIAD-94-133) (indicating that the cost of remediation at the Jefferson Proving Grounds will be in excess of $5 billion dollars).
50. Kellay Aneaka, Managing Acceptability: UK policy on depleted uranium weapons, 2012, p. 8, available at: www.cadu.ork.uk/cadu/resources.
51. The British Government policy on environmental assessment and cleanup in Iraq appears to represent a new standard in the practice of states. The UK Ministry of Defenc (MOD) confirmed that it shot 1.9 metric tons of DU in Iraq, and promised to release the locations of DU expenditure. The MOD stated that it has no legal obligation to clean up DU contamination in Iraq.
52. The European Court of Human Rights in the case of *Engel and others v. the Netherlands*, June 8, 1976.

53. Wim Zwijnenburg, Hazard Aware: Lessons learned from military field manuals on depleted uranium and how to move forward for civilian protection norms, IKV Pax Christi, September 2012.
54. The 2015 US Manual on Law of War states that DU is used in some munitions because its density and physical properties create a particularly effective penetrating combination to defeat enemy armored vehicles, including tanks. States have regarded the use of DU weapons as consistent with their law of war obligations. Further, the US armed forces have fielded and used DU munitions. Extensive efforts have been made to study whether there are harmful health effects from exposure to depleted uranium from weapons that use it, but no such effects have been found. The US has been consistently maintaining that that there are no ill effects of DU exposure. Department of Defence Law of War Manual (2015), Para 6.5.7, page 327-328.
55. Wim Zwijnenburg, Hazard Aware: Lessons learned from military field manuals on depleted uranium and how to move forward for civilian protection norms, IKV Pax Christi, September 2012, p.11.
56. There is no international convention prohibiting nuclear weapons, and also there is no universally agreed definition of the term "nuclear weapon." Protocol III to the Modified Brussels Treaty of 1954 on the Control of Armaments defines an atomic weapon as "any weapon which contains, or is designed to contain or utilise nuclear fuel or radioactive isotopes and which, by explosion or other uncontrolled nuclear transformation of the nuclear fuel, or by radioactivity of the nuclear fuel or radioactive isotopes, is capable of mass destruction, mass injury or mass poisoning." Protocol III of the Modified Brussels Treaty, signed October 23, 1954, Annex II, paragraph I(a). Article 1(c) of the Treaty on the Southeast Asia Nuclear Weapon-Free Zone, December 15, 2012, defines a nuclear weapon as "any explosive device capable of releasing nuclear energy in an uncontrolled manner but does not include the means of transport or delivery of such device if separable from and not an indivisible part thereof."
57. Avril McDonald, "Depleted uranium weapons: the next target for disarmament?" Available at: http://unidir.org/pdf/articles/pdf-art2757.pdf, accessed October 30, 2012.
58. Protocol III of the Convention on Certain Conventional Weapons states that incendiary weapons do not include munitions designed to combine penetration, blast or fragmentation effects with an additional incendiary effect, such as armour-piercing projectiles, fragmentation shells, explosive bombs and similar combined-effects munitions in which the incendiary effect is not specifically designed to cause burn injury to persons, but to be used against military objectives, such as armoured vehicles, aircraft and installations or facilities [Article 1(1)(b)(ii)].
59. Y. K. J. Yuen and Yeung Sik, *Human Rights and Weapons of Mass Destruction, or with Indiscriminate Effect, or of a Nature to Cause Superfluous Injury or Unnecessary Suffering,* Working Paper prepared for the UN Sub-Commission on the Promotion and Protection of Human Rights, UN document E/CN.4/Sub.2/2003/35, June 2, 2003, paragraph 55.
60. 1868 Declaration of St. Petersburg (prohibiting the use of certain projectiles in wartime). The Preamble states: (i) That the only legitimate object which States should endeavour to accomplish during war is to weaken the military forces of the enemy; (ii) That for this purpose it is sufficient to disable the greatest possible number of men; (iii) That this object would be exceeded by the employment of arms which uselessly aggravate the sufferings of disabled men, or render their

death inevitable; and (iv) That the employment of such arms would, therefore, be contrary to the laws of humanity.

61. Rule 70: The use of means and methods of warfare which are of a nature to cause superfluous injury or unnecessary suffering is prohibited. Jean-Marie Henckaerts and Louise Doswald-Beck, *Customary International Humanitarian Law*, vol. I, International Committee of the Red Cross and Cambridge: Cambridge University Press, 2005, p. 237. Military manuals of Australia, Canada, Netherlands, Sweden, the UK, United States, etc., include this rule.
62. The cardinal principle of IHL prohibits the use of weapons of a nature or designed to cause (that have the effect of causing) superfluous injury or unnecessary suffering to enemy combatants. There is a minimum threshold of injury or suffering that could potentially be considered as superfluous and unnecessary, i.e., "a harm greater than that unavoidable to achieve legitimate military objectives." The International Court of Justice, *Legality of the Threat or Use of Nuclear Weapons*, Advisory Opinion of July 8, 1996, paragraphs 78 and 238.
63. Yves Sandoz, Chrisotphe Swinarski and Bruno Zimmermann (eds.), *Commentary on the Additional Protocols of 8 June 1977 to the Geneva Conventions of 12 August 1949*, International Committee of the Red Cross (Geneva: Martinus Nijhoff Publishers, 1987), p. 406.
64. Marten Zwanenburg, "The Use of Depleted Uranium and the Prohibition of Weapons of a Nature to Cause Superfluous Injury or Unnecessary Suffering," in Avril McDonald, Jann K. Kleffner and Brigit Toebes (eds.), *Depleted Uranium Weapons and International Law: A Precautionary Approach* (T. M. C. Asser Press, 2008), p. 122.
65. DU's military applications have provoked controversy since the weapon's first battlefield testing during the 1991 Gulf War. After the conflict, some persons who either did or might have come into contact with DU metal or dust, either directly or indirectly, began to exhibit a host of pathologies, which have collectively come to be known as Gulf War Syndrome. After subsequent military uses of DU in the Balkans, a range of illnesses, collectively dubbed "Balkan War Syndrome," was reported among some military personnel. None of these conditions have ever been conclusively linked with DU, and those states that consider its use militarily necessary have dismissed any suggestion that exposure to DU might be a causal factor. A growing body of evidence links DU exposure with pathologies in laboratory animals and human cells, and the limited testing that has been carried out indicates that contact with high levels of DU may cause pathologies such as kidney damage and cancer. Avril McDonald, "Depleted uranium weapons: the next target for disarmament?" *Disarmament Forum* (2008), vol. 3, p. 18.
66. Dan Fahey, "Environmental and Health Consequences of the Use of Depleted Uranium Weapons," in Avril McDonald, Jann K. Kleffner and Brigit Toebes (eds.), *Depleted Uranium and International Law: A Precautionary Approach* (The Hague, TMC Asser Press, 2008), pp. 29-71.
67. Marten Zwanenburg, "The Use of Depleted Uranium and the Prohibition of Weapons of a Nature to Cause Superfluous Injury or Unnecessary Suffering," in Avril McDonald, Jann K. Kleffner and Brigit Toebes (eds). *Depleted Uranium Weapons and International Law: A Precautionary Approach* (T. M. C. Asser Press, 2008), p. 123.
68. Though the US has been silent on the adverse effects on DU weapons on civilians, the US Army Regulations provides for protection of military personnel from DU contaminations: "In general, commanders at all levels should take

prudent measures to keep radiation exposures (from Depleted Uranium or Radioactive Commodities) to all personnel as low as is reasonably achievable that is consistent with the operational risks. Radioactive material and waste will not be locally disposed of through burial, submersion, incineration, destruction in place, or abandonment without approval from overall Commanders of Major Army Commands (MACOM commander). If local disposal is approved, the responsible MACOM commander must document the general nature of the disposed material and the exact location of the disposal. The MACOM commander has the responsibility for determining the likelihood of significant exposure from contaminated equipment to any individual. Individuals that the command determines may have been exposed will be sent to a medical treatment facility for appropriate screening." The US Army Regulation 700–48, Management of Equipment Contaminated with Depleted Uranium or Radioactive Commodities, (2002), available at: http://www.apd.army.mil/pdffiles/r700_48.pdf, accessed August 19, 2012.

69. The US Army Regulation 700–48, "Management of Equipment Contaminated with Depleted Uranium or Radioactive Commodities" (2002), available at: http://www.apd.army.mil/pdffiles/r700_48.pdf, accessed August 19, 2012.
70. Article 50, AP I: Civilians are those who do not qualify as combatants under Article 4A of Third Geneva Convention and Article 43 of AP I. Under Article 51 of AP I, the civilian population and individual civilians shall enjoy general protection against dangers arising from military operations.
71. When DU ammunition hits an object and/or catches fire, it produces small DU dust particles. If fighting takes place in or near populated areas, civilians and relief workers may inhale DU particles long after the actual fighting ends. Individuals associated with salvage of contaminated military equipments face additional inhalation exposure. Children who play near discarded war materials may experience both inhalation and ingestion exposure. In addition, as DU munitions corrode, they leach into the groundwater and contaminate agricultural systems, which expose an even larger population. Karen Hulme, *War Torn Environment: Interpreting Legal Threshold* (Leiden: Martinus Nijhoff Publishers, 2004) pp. 225-49.
72. Studies with laboratory animals have found uranium in placenta, foetus, and milk of females and in the tissues and urine of offspring fed milk from exposed females. Effects ranged from low birth weight to skeletal abnormalities for doses at which the mother exhibited signs of chemical toxicity. DU was also found in semen samples from some Gulf War veterans exposed to DU. Karen Hulme, *War Torn Environment*, pp. 239-40.
73. R. Clark, "An International Appeal to Ban the Use of Depleted Uranium Weapons," available at http://www.iacenter.org/depleted/appeal.htm.
74. Since the use of DU weapons in combat results in an uncontrolled release of depleted uranium, it is "a method or means of combat the effects of which cannot be limited," a definition of discriminate attack according to Article 51(4)(c) of AP I. When used against military objectives in urban areas, it is impossible to spatially restrict DU's spread. Considering that most DU falls within 50m of its release, but that it can travel up to 400m from the hit site immediately following an impact, any civilian within this radius runs the risk of being exposed to its radioactive and toxic effects.
75. Article 57, Additional Protocol I.
76. Article 58(c), Additional Protocol I.
77. Alyn Ware, "Depleted Uranium Weapons and International Law," in John

Catalinotto and Sara Flounders (eds.), *Metal of Dishonor: How the Pentagon Radiates Soldiers and Civilians with DU Weapons* (New York: International Action Centre, 1999), p. 198.

78. According to IHL, an explicit formulation appears in Article 36 of Protocol I additional to the Geneva Conventions, which is binding on 157 States—States are required to ensure that any new weapon, means or method of warfare does not contravene existing rules of international law. These rules prohibit weapons, means or methods of warfare of a nature to cause superfluous injury or unnecessary suffering, which have indiscriminate effects or which cause widespread, long-term and severe damage to the natural environment. The ICRC has strongly urged all States which study, develop, acquire or adopt munitions containing depleted uranium to carry out such legal reviews if they have not already done so, and would welcome an exchange of views and information on these reviews. Within alliances or groups of States, it seems particularly important that appropriate legal review mechanisms should be established on weapons, means or methods of warfare which may be used by such alliances or groups of States or that an exchange of information on national legal reviews should take place. http://www.icrc.org/eng/resources/documents/misc/57jqxp.htm, accessed January 27, 2012.

79. Principle 15 of the Rio Declaration articulates the precautionary principle in the following manner: "where there are threats of serious or irreversible damage, lack of full scientific certainty shall not be used as a reason for postponing cost-effective measures to prevent environmental degradation." UN Conference on Environment and Development, June 3-14, 1992, *Rio Declaration on Environment and Development*, U.N. Doc. A/CONF.151/5/Rev.1 (August 12, 1992).

80. Gibbons Owen Thomas, "Uses and Effects of Depleted Uranium Munitions: Towards a Moratorium on Use," *Yearbook of International Humanitarian Law*, vol. 7 (2004), p. 228.

81. Quirra is a village located in the Italian Sardinia Island, close to a big military polygon where ballistic missiles and weapons are tested. Recently, the zone has been driven to the attention of the media due to the so-called "Quirra syndrome," an apparently off-normal incidence of illnesses in that zone. The media indicated that the military use of Depleted Uranium could be a possible cause for the "Quirra Syndrome" in the population. Zucchetti Massimo, "Environmental Pollution and Population Health Effects in the Quirra Area, Sardinia Island (Italy) and the Depleted Uranium Case," available at: http://staff.polito.it/massimo.zucchetti/Quirra_JEPE.pdf, accessed February 21, 2012.

82. European Parliament resolution on the consequences of using depleted uranium munitions, January 17, 2001, Official Journal C262, pp. 167-69; European Parliament resolution on the harmful effects of unexploded ordnance (landmines and cluster submunitions) and depleted uranium ammunition, February 13, 2003, document P5_TA(2003)0062; European Parliament resolution of May 22, 2008 on (depleted) uranium weapons and their effect on human health and the environment—towards a global ban on the use of such weapons, document P6_TA(2008)0233.

83. Approved by 491 votes in favour, 18 against and 12 abstentions (total votes 521). European Parliament resolution of May 22, 2008 on DU and their effect on human health and the environment—towards a global ban on the use of such weapons, document P6_TA(2008)0233.

84. Article 55, Additional Protocol I. Protection of the natural environment: (1) Care shall be taken in warfare to protect the natural environment against widespread,

long-term and severe damage. This protection includes a prohibition of the use of methods or means of warfare which are intended or may be expected to cause such damage to the natural environment and thereby to prejudice the health or survival of the population. (2) Attacks against the natural environment by way of reprisals are prohibited.

85. International Court of Justice, *Nuclear Weapons Advisory Opinion*, para 78.
86. After the first Gulf War, the United Nations Sub-Commission on the Promotion and Protection of Human Rights (the Sub-Commission) focused on the use of DU weaponry in the War. The members of the Sub-Commission were both highly shocked and moved by the presentations on DU weaponry and as a result passed a resolution 1996/16. In 1997 the Sub-Commission adopted resolution 1997/36, in which it repeated its finding that DU weaponry is "incompatible" with existing humanitarian and human rights law.
87. In December 2007, the UN General Assembly passed its first resolution concerning DU weapons, which called on the Secretary-General to seek the views of Member States and relevant international organisations on the effects of the use of armaments and ammunitions containing DU. UN General Assembly resolution 62/30 of December 5, 2007, UN document A/RES/62/30, January 10, 2008.
88. The UN General Assembly Resolutions 63/54 of December 2, 2008, UN document A/RES/63/54, January 12, 2009. Also see resolution 65/55 (January 13, 2011) on the effects of the use of armaments and ammunitions containing DU.
89. 148 states call for transparency over depleted uranium use in UN vote, International Coalition to Ban Uranium Weapons, December 8, 2010. Available at: http://www.bandepleteduranium.org/en/a/364.html, accessed February 12, 2012.
90. The UN General Assembly resolution A/C.1/71/L.63 of 13 October 2016; the resolution was opposed only by the US, UK, France and Israel. In spite of repeated appeals from the European Parliament for progress on the topic, EU member states remained split on the resolution, with many among the 26 states still abstaining.
91. US tenders for safer penetrator materials blaming opposition to depleted uranium, available at: http://www.bandepleteduranium.org/en/us-tenders-for-safer-penetrator-materials-blaming, accessed 30 June 2017.
92. In addition to liability for damages to victims or the environment, users of DU weapons should face penal sanctions under existing humanitarian law provisions. For example, the Fourth Geneva Convention of 1949 requires that signatory States have domestic legal mechanisms for trying persons alleged to have committed serious violations of humanitarian law. Article 146 of the Fourth Convention further states that all signatory states have a duty to search for alleged violators and to bring them to its own tribunals, regardless of their nationality. Article 148 prohibits any State from absolving itself or any other State from liability for serious violations. Karen Parker, "The Illegality of DU Weaponry," available at: http://www.humanlaw.org/KPdu.html, accessed March 2, 2013.

3 B

HIGH EXPLOSIVE WEAPONS (HEW)

High explosive weapons (HEW)[1] are the largest conventional weapons. The US military used them in the Vietnam War; however, they were used extensively much later during the 1990-91 Gulf War. These bombs, delivered from either a C-130 or an MC-130 transport aircraft, are of three types: fuel-air explosives, reactive surround warheads, and slurry explosive munitions.[2]

The US Daisy Cutter bomb,[3] considered the largest of such bombs, is an example of a slurry explosive munition. The bomb's warhead contains 12,600 lb (5,700 kg) of GSX, a slurry of ammonium nitrate (the basis of nitrogenous fertiliser), highly flammable aluminium powder, and polystyrene-based soap as a thickener. Because of its cumbersome size and destruction potential, the Daisy Cutter must be uniquely deployed and detonated. It is launched on a delivery trolley and forced out of the back of a C-130 cargo plane. The plane itself must be at least 6,000 feet off the ground to avoid the bomb's massive shock wave. Once clear of the plane, the bomb releases its own parachute. Attached to one end of the bomb is a three-foot conical probe. When this probe touches the ground, the bomb is detonated. Since the bomb is detonated before the majority of it hits the ground, no crater is formed. However, the bomb inflicts heavy damage, generating excessive pressure near the point of impact,[4] and the shock waves can be felt miles away.

Some high explosive munitions made use of cluster bomb technology to scatter submunitions that contain ethylene oxide, a highly flammable material. When the submunitions explode, they disperse the ethylene oxide in the form of a fine mist or aerosol. This cloud of flammable material, which is about 60 feet in diameter and 8 feet thick, is then ignited by a secondary explosion, upon which the entire cloud explodes into a fireball. The pressure shock created is so powerful that it can knock over buildings. There is no crater, but it clears an area of about 2.5 acres.

Use in Armed Conflict

The BLU-82B/C-130 weapon system, used under the programme "Commando Vault" and nicknamed Daisy Cutter was used in Vietnam for its ability to clean out a helicopter landing zone in a forest.[5] The US military used about 14 million tons of high explosives, covering about 200,000 hectares in Vietnam. In the destruction of Iraq in 1991, the US used HEW to ignite minefields and to incinerate Iraqi personnel hiding in trenches. Eleven BLU-82Bs were dropped in five night missions during the war. The initial drops were meant to breach minefields. However, no reliable assessments of the mine-clearing effectiveness of the bombs are publicly available. Later, the bombs were dropped as much for their psychological effect as for their anti-personnel effects. Once the US realised the devastating impact of the bombs on the Iraqi troops, a new strategy was developed. A bomb would be deployed, and directly after the blast, thousands of leaflets would be dropped over the Iraqi troops with a picture of the Daisy Cutter and the words "Flee and Live, or Stay and Die!"

In Afghanistan too HEW were used for their destructive potential as well as their power to intimidate the enemy. The extremely large lethal radius combined with the visible flash and terrific sound that was audible for miles struck terror into the heads of the troops. The US air force dropped several BLU-82s to destroy the Taliban and Al Qaeda bases with their underground and cave complexes and to demoralise personnel. HEW were also used in the Battle of Tora Bora.

Massive Ordnance Air Blast (MOAB) Bomb

The BLU-82 was retired in 2008 and replaced with the more powerful Massive Ordnance Air Blast (MOAB) bomb. The MOAB bomb, often referred as the Mother of All Bombs, is a large-yield conventional bomb developed for the US military. Development of the MOAB bomb began in 2002, and it was successfully field-tested twice in 2003. The MOAB bomb, which weighs 21,000 lb, is a GPS-guided munition with fins and inertial gyro for pitch and roll control. It uses 18,000 lb of H6, a mixture of RDX (cyclotrimethylene trinitramine), TNT, and aluminium, and produces a very large explosive blast, with lesser fragmentation effects due to a thin-walled aluminum casing. Due to its size, it is expected to be delivered from either an MC-130 Talon II or "Slick" C-130 Hercules by way of a parachute.

The MOAB weapon is based upon the same principle as the BLU-82 Daisy Cutter, except that it is larger and has a guidance system. It is expected to produce a tremendous explosion that would be effective against hard-target entrances, and soft-to-medium surface targets. The size of the explosion will make it effective for landing zone clearance and mine and beach obstacle clearance. Injury or death to persons will primarily be caused by blast or fragmentation.

On 13 April 2017, the US Air Force dropped the largest non-nuclear bomb, the MOAB (GBU-43/B), in Achin district of Nangarhar province of Afghanistan. The bomb was used against "tunnel complex" used by the Islamic State's Afghanistan affiliate. It was claimed that the bomb killed nearly 100 terrorists. Designed for destroying underground targets but not itself a deep-earth penetrator weapon, the GBU-43/B has the explosive yield of more than 11 tons of TNT. The massive bomb is dropped from air force planes and detonates before reaching the ground, resulting in an enormous blast radius. The psychological effect on survivors or observers is considered an added impact of the weapon. The US claims that MOAB weapon is consistent with IHL. Only the Massive Ordnance Penetrator GBU-57, which has never been used in war, is a larger conventional weapon.[6] Since the original development of MOAB bomb, Russia has tested its own "Father of All Bombs" or FOAB which it claims to be four times more powerful than the MOAB.

The term 'explosive weapon' has not yet been formally defined in international law. It represents weapons that generally consist of a casing with a high-explosive filling and whose destructive effects result mainly from the blast wave and fragmentation produced by detonation. For example, mortar bombs, artillery shells, aircraft bombs, rocket and missile warheads, cluster sub-munitions, and improvised explosive devices (IEDs) fall within this category.[7] According to Boothby (2009) weapons falling into his category are 'missiles, bombs and artillery' as these weapons typically employ a warhead with an explosive fill such that a combination of blast and fragmentation which provides the damaging effect of the weapon.[8] There is evidence that they are increasingly used in armed conflict. They can be air-delivered, ground service ordnance, or improvised explosive devices.[9]

Environmental Effects

Enhanced blast-munitions (e.g., the Daisy Cutter) are effective against "soft" targets, including human beings, animals and crops, and targets open to the atmosphere, including un-reinforced buildings. Trees are blown away and all exposed humans, farm animals and wildlife within 1,300 feet of the explosion are killed. Although the Daisy Cutter is not a nuclear weapon, its use has caused controversy because of its terrifying and utterly destructive nature. No plant or animal life survives in the immediate area where the bomb is dropped, and there is only a 50 per cent chance of survival in the surrounding 25 acres. The ignition of the gases consumes the oxygen in the immediate vicinity of the blast so that personnel taking shelter in underground bunkers are asphyxiated. The explosion may also cause a wildfire. The total impact is so terrifying that it is now used as psychological weapon.[10]

HEW cause unnecessary suffering that is disproportionate to the military advantage that may be reasonably expected to be gained. These weapons are also indiscriminate and have a "high capacity to damage the social and economic infrastructure upon which civilian populations rely." The destruction of houses, transport facilities, markets, and power, sanitation and health infrastructure has profound implications for the communities' access to food, health care, clean water and other necessities of life. In addition, these weapons leave behind explosive remnants that continue to pose a threat to civilians and cause ongoing harm long after use and negatively impact socio-economic development.

Notes

1. "Strike Warfare," US Naval Academy, available at: www.usna.edu/training/prorefcent/FallProbook/06_Strike.doc.
2. The BLU-82 (BLU stands for Bomb Live Unit) uses conventional explosive ammonium nitrate and aluminium, incorporating both agent and oxidiser. In contrast, fuel-air explosives (FAE) consist only of an agent and a dispersing mechanism, and take their oxidisers from the oxygen in the air. FAEs generally run between 500 and 2,000 pounds (225 and 900 kg); making an FAE the size of a daisy cutter would be difficult because the correct uniform mixture of agent with ambient air would be difficult to maintain if the agent were so widely dispersed. Thus, the conventional explosive of a daisy cutter is more reliable than that of an FAE, particularly if there is significant wind or thermal gradient.
3. It earned its nickname "The Daisy Cutter" because of the circular pattern of destruction that it left after detonation. A daisy cutter is a type of fuse designed to detonate an aerial bomb at or above ground level. The fuse itself is a long probe affixed to the weapon's nose, which detonates the bomb if it touches the ground or any solid object. The purpose for a daisy-cutter fuse is primarily to maximise blast damage on the surface of a target. A bomb with a conventional fuse will often be driven deeply into the ground by the force of its impact, limiting the range of its blast. A bomb with a daisy-cutter fuse will detonate before it has a chance to penetrate the ground, allowing its energy to spread over a larger area. For this reason daisy-cutter fuses are often used to clear foliage and vegetation, such as for the purpose of creating Landing Zones for helicopters.
4. In a daisy cutter explosion the pressure reaches about 70 kg/sq cm (1,000 psi) at the centre and affects an area typically reported to be the size of several football grounds.
5. In the Vietnam War, BLU-82 was nicknamed "Commando Vault" and was originally used to instantly vaporise large, unwanted swaths of jungle so that the clearings could be used for artillery emplacements and helicopter landing zones. The area vaporised by a bomb is somewhere between 26,000 and 240,000 square metres. The USAF used large, high-explosive "daisy cutter" bombs (up to 15,000 pounds) to clear landing zones for helicopters. These bombs, extracted by parachute from C-130s, exploded a few feet above the ground and cleared enough area in the jungle for 1 or 2 helicopters to land. The ordnance allowed

engineers to establish suitable landing zones quickly in enemy territory and contributed substantially to the rapid movement of troops into and out of Laos. December 1, 1970-May 14, 1971; Vietnam Campaigns: November 15, 1961-January 28, 1973. Available at: http://www.c-7acaribou.com/history/medals/Vietnam_Campaigns.pdf, accessed January 17, 2013.

6. US drops largest ever non-nuclear bomb on Isis affiliate in Afghanistan, military says, available at: https://www.theguardian.com/world/2017/apr/13/us-military-drops-non-nuclear-bomb-afghanistan-islamic-state, accessed 10 June 2017.
7. The United Nations Secretary-General's report of 2012 on the protection of civilians in armed conflict provides an illustrative list: "Explosive weapons include artillery shells, missile and rocket warheads, mortars, aircraft bombs, grenades and improvised explosive devices". Security Council, Report of the Secretary-General on the Protection of Civilians in Armed Conflict, UN document S/2012/376, 22 May 2012, paragraph 35.
8. William Boothby. 2009. *Weapons and the Law of Armed Conflict*, Oxford: Oxford University Press, Oxford, 2009, p. 225.
9. Wille Christina, The Implications of the Reverberating Effects of Explosive Weapons Use in Populated Areas for Implementing the Sustainable Development Goals, UNIDIR, 2016, pp. 28.
10. Regardless of which effect applies—pressure, fragmentation or a combination of the two—high explosive weapons can cause serious damage to both the biomass and the geo-mass of an ecosystem. J. Perry Robinson, *The Effects of Weapons on Ecosystems*, UNEP Studies, 1979, p. 16. Fragmentation effects can be assumed to be more destructive in certain ecosystems than in others, especially as concerns forests, where fragments embedded in trees can invite invasion by fungous micro-organisms. Pressure effects often cause crater formations in the earth's crust. These craters will either be filled with water or converted to dams or remain as open sores in nature. In High Explosive Fragmentation (HEF) weapons—munitions consist of high explosive filler, which upon detonation produces rapidly expanding gases that shatter the metal casing. As a result, fragments of metal and debris fly outwards from the point of explosion with substantial force. The deployment of HEF munitions can cause significant disruption to transport, agriculture and forestry. B. S. Levy, C. Lee and B. S. Shahi, "The Environmental Consequences of War," in B. S. Levy and V. W. Sidel (eds.), *War and Public Health* (New York: Oxford University Press, 1997), pp. 51-62.

3 C

INCENDIARY WEAPONS

Incendiaries are chemical substances used to set fire on enemy materials in war. Fire has a long history in warfare. Flame and incendiary weapons are among the oldest known to man. It has been employed by belligerents to drive out enemy forces taking cover in forests, swamps or other forms of natural cover. The idea of using incendiaries in battle dates back to early Biblical times when armies attacking and defending fortified cities threw upon each other burning oils and flaming fireballs consisting of resin and straw. The Old Testament narrates ancient employment of scorched land warfare. Sun Tzu, in *The Art of War*, has described incendiary warfare: "There are five ways of attacking with fire. The first is to burn soldiers in their camp; the second is to burn stores; the third is to burn baggage trains; the fourth is to burn arsenals and magazines; the fifth is to hurl dropping fire among the enemy."

In *History of the Peloponnesian War*, Thucydides has described how the Spartans used the first known flame-thrower against the Athenians in 429 BC during the War.[1] The first flame projector consisted of a hollow tree trunk to the lower end of which was attached a basin filled with glowing coals, sulfur, and pitch. A bellows blew the flame from the tree trunk in the form of a jet, setting fire to enemy fortifications and aiding the besiegers in the capture of the city. The next recorded use of incendiaries was by the Trojan king, Aeneas, about 300 BC. He made use of fire compositions consisting of pitch, sulfur, tow, resinous wood, and other highly inflammable substances which were easily ignited and hard to extinguish. The incendiary composition was poured burning into pots, which were fired from the walls of besieged cities upon the attacking troops below. Little later the Romans hurled from catapults crude iron latticework bombs, about two-feet diameter, filled with highly inflammable materials. These were ignited and thrown as flaming projectiles upon the enemy fortifications. Later incendiary arrows were used as a means of setting fire to the wooden forts sheltering enemies. The greatest impetus to the use of incendiaries in war came with the introduction of "Greek Fire," which was said to have been invented by the Syrian, Callinicus, about 600 AD. The exact formula of "Greek Fire" has never been definitely established.[2]

During the Siege of Malta in 1565, a variety of incendiaries were employed by the defenders. These included: small earthen pots filled with incendiary mixture; trumps made of hollowed wood or metal filled with incendiary; firework hoops filled with a mixture of inflammable substances or gunpowder. These devices had considerable effect on the invading Turkish troops, whose long white robes easily caught fire during war.[3]

From the beginning of the modern times down to the First World War, incendiaries were not extensively employed. The introduction of firearms caused armies to engage in battle at such distances that they could not be effectively reached by the incendiaries. The use of incendiary weapons increased with the industrialisation and the advent of the military airplane. They greatly increased the field of application of incendiaries, as it became possible to reach large and vulnerable targets at practically any point in the theatre of war. Air-delivered incendiary devices were employed first on May 31, 1915, when the German Zeppelin LZ38 bombed London with incendiary bombs and high-explosive grenades. In 1915, more than 70% of the munitions dropped on London by Zeppelins were incendiaries. The following year, on October 21, 1916, 22 German Gotha bombers attacked London with high explosive bombs and ten-pound incendiary bombs. During WWI, both sides were quick to recognise the value of incendiary munitions in aerial attacks on industrial facilities. High explosive bombs could cause some structural damage to a building, but anti-materiel incendiaries proved more effective to do substantial damage to manufacturing or other industrial equipment. Throughout WWI, all the principal belligerents engaged in the development of incendiary armaments, particularly aviation drop bombs.

Incendiaries are of four types. The first includes the thermite or thermate (TH) weapons whose incendiary agents are based on mixtures of powered ferric oxides, of granular aluminum, of barium nitrate or of triethylaluminium. The primary use of these incendiaries has been anti-materiel. The second concerns weapons that are similar to thermites and contain magnesium agents (MG)[4] while the third encompasses weapons with incendiary agents based on combustible hydrocarbons, including the various classes of oils and thickened gasoline, such as napalm. Thickened oil incendiaries are more effective against "soft" targets. The last includes weapons designed to deliver white phosphorus (WP).[5] While more than 180 models of incendiary weapons exist, the effects of those with two types of chemical substances—napalm and white phosphorus—exemplify the specific humanitarian problems the incendiary weapons present.[6] In this chapter, these two incendiary weapons, namely, napalm and white phosphorus, have been discussed.

Napalm

"Napalm" is a combination of the names of two of its constituents: napthenic acid and palmitic acid. It is a thickening/gelling agent generally mixed with petroleum or a similar fuel for use in an incendiary device, against buildings and as an anti-personnel weapon. Napalm B is the modern version, and is chemically distinct from its predecessor Napalm.[7] It is a mixture of polystyrene and benzene, used as a thickening agent to make jellied gasoline. One of the advantages of this new mixture is its increased safety during handling and storage. The original napalm usually burned for 15 to 30 seconds while napalm B can burn for up to 10 minutes. During combustion, Napalm rapidly deoxygenates the available air and generates large amounts of carbon monoxide and carbon dioxide. Unlike explosive bombs and bullets, napalm is more dangerous because it flows and spreads very effectively. For example, it can form a river of burning liquid that can flow into hidden underground trenches.

Napalm: Use in War

Napalm was used first during the Second World War. In December 1941, when Pearl Harbour was attacked, the US had no incendiary bombs, but by December 1945, the stockpile of napalm bombs had reached a quarter billion. One firebomb could affect a 2.5 square km area. On March 10, 1945, the US accomplished the greatest military victory in history when napalm-firebombs killed about 84,000 residents of Tokyo in a few hours. Napalm bombs incinerated 66 of Japan's 68 largest cities.[8] In the later stages of the war, large numbers of napalms were dropped over targets in Germany and Japan.[9] They had killed far more Germans and Japanese, and flattened much more urban landscape, than did the two atomic bombs dropped over Hiroshima and Nagasaki.[10]

Napalm played a major role in the Korean War. The US forces used a large amount of napalm, killing millions of innocent civilians due to the indiscriminate bombing of non-military targets. It is estimated that the US dropped approximately 7000,000 lb of napalm over Korea. In 1952, an average daily bombing included 70,000 gallons of napalm bombs.[11] High-altitude bombers and dive-bombers were used to drop napalm on enemy tanks and soldiers.

During the Vietnam War, napalm weapons were also used as a part of strategy of area denial. The US dropped about 400,000 tons of Napalm-B on Vietnam and used forest fire as a weapon of warfare. A great effort was made to destroy villages, crops, and the cover provided by a large area of forest, by defoliation, burning and finally by scraping away vegetation with bulldozers.[12] In other operations, growing crops were destroyed in the fields by bombing, burning and spraying with chemicals or by combinations of these methods. Mechanised flame-throwers on land vehicles and river boats were also used for the destruction of crops and forests. The use of mechanised flame-throwers was very successful against dug-in positions, particularly when the positions were in dense thickets or scrub growth. It has been reported that greater quantity of incendiary munitions has been used in South Vietnam than in any other country in any other war. Many civilian casualties resulted from these incendiary munitions.[13]

The US also used napalm in the North Vietnam. In 1967, the numbers of civilian casualties from burns in the southern part of North Vietnam were about 13%. It is reported that the US had used magnesium-thermite incendiary cluster bombs in some attacks on North Vietnam. The US estimated that about 52,000 civilians had died from air strikes by the time bombing halted in 1968.[14] The most successful use of fire as a weapon in Vietnam was a large fire in the U Minh area, in Southwest Vietnam. The estimates of final effects of fire as a military weapon in U Minh area were:[15]

- 75 to 85 per cent of the true forest destroyed
- 50 per cent of various outlying swamps destroyed
- Hundreds of tons of ammunition, rice and petroleum products destroyed
- 100 to 200 Viet Cong killed or incapacitated while either fighting the fire or by rockets and air strikes in the area
- The probable dislocation of large quantities of supplies and ammunition and the relocation of several major Viet Cong headquarters and rear service areas
- The increased opportunity for aerial reconnaissance of the area
- The lack of lumber and possible food shortage for the local populace
- The increased danger of floods in areas adjacent to the forest since there is no longer tree or underbrush to provide watershed

Although the Vietnam War produced numerous images of bombs exploding and their aftermath, none of them is as well-known as that of Phan Thi Kim Phuc, taken by Associated Press photographer, Nick Ut.

> Kim Phuc was 9 years old when her village was napalmed by American forces. In the famous picture, Kim Phuc and a group of children are running, fleeing their village. Phuc is naked, screaming because napalm is burning her body. Upon realising how hurt she was, Ut took Kim Phuc to a hospital. She survived but after enduring extensive third-degree burns and 17 operations. In her late teens and early 20s, the Vietnamese government used Kim Phuc as a propaganda tool, forcing her to speak to reporters from abroad. Eventually, she and her husband fled to Canada. She was also a United Nations Goodwill Ambassador. Ut's photograph, winner of a Pulitzer Prize that year, leaves a painful reminder about the horror of napalm in the Vietnam War. It is one of the most widely seen photos from the war.

The use of napalm in Vietnam galvanised the antiwar movement in the US. During the 1960s Dow Chemical was the leading manufacturer of polystyrene, and became contractor to produce napalm for the US military. The orders were to be filled in 25-million-pound lots. Napalm was relatively easy to make. It required a simple mixing of the ingredients—gasoline, benzene, and polystyrene. Dow set up a small production line and tankage system combining the three chemical ingredients at its Torrance, California plant. With a small group of workers, Dow met its napalm contracts over the next four years. However, Dow Chemical was no stranger to weapons production and government contracting. From WWI on, Dow did what the government asked, and repeatedly served as its wartime chemist and producer of munitions, strategic materials, and weapons—from mustard gas in WWI to plutonium triggers for nuclear weapons during the Cold War and beyond. But in the Vietnam War of the 1960s, it was napalm that made Dow a target of activist protests, which manufactured napalm for the US government from 1965 to 1969.

With the extension of the Indo-China War to Cambodia, incendiary means of warfare like napalm and flame-throwers were used in Cambodia. Between April 1970 and March 1973, the US air force dropped an estimated 78,000 tons of napalm on Cambodia targets. In addition the Khmer (Cambodian) air force had used napalm, dropping it from their propeller-driven fighter bombers.

During the Israel-Arab conflicts, incendiary weapons of various kinds have been used by both the states. In June 1947, Israeli aircraft dropped incendiary and high explosive bombs on Amman. On the ground improvised incendiary grenades and flame-throwers were used by the Israelis against the Syrians. It has been reported that the Israeli use of napalm in 1956 was a contributory factor for victory, as the Egyptian soldiers were not prepared for it. During the war of June 1967, Israel made extensive use of napalm against Egyptian soldiers fighting in the Sinai desert. In February 1968, Israeli aircraft attacked villages and refugee camps along the River Jordan with napalm, causing casualties amongst soldiers and civilians alike. This also resulted in about 70,000 people fleeing towards Amman. In August 1968, Israeli planes carried out a napalm attack on Jordan killing 28 people, including 22 civilians. During the "War of Attrition" in 1969-70, Israeli aircraft dropped napalm bombs and delayed-action fragmentation bombs over the heavily populated Nile delta region. During the war of October 1973, napalm weapons were used by both sides.

In Yemen, during the period of prolonged civil war (1962-1969), reportedly napalm was used between Royalist forces and the armed forces of the new military government. During 1969, there were allegations of the use of napalm by the Iraqi government against Kurds, who were fighting an intermittent war for autonomy. There have been allegations of sporadic uses of napalm in Angola, Chad, Mozambique, Peru, South Africa and Venezuela, during the period between the 1960s and 1970s, however, most of the allegations were denied by the parties to conflict.[16]

During the destruction of Iraq in 1991, the US Air Force used 500 lb fire bombs called MK-77. They dropped about 250,000 lb of these napalm bombs to weed out Iraqi troops and to deliberately ignite the oil-filled trenches that they had constructed to stop US tanks. Although the US military claims it has not used napalm in Afghanistan or the war in Iraq, some experts believe this distinction is simply a semantic one. They contend that while the old form of napalm was not used, a similar, reformulated compound, also a jelled incendiary substance, has been used, most notably in the form of the MK-77 bomb.[17]

In August 2003, a report appeared in the *San Diego Union–Tribune* stating that the US forces had employed firebombs earlier that year against Iraqi troops. The report cited various US Marine Corps officers, who had fought in Iraq, stating American helicopters and jets had dropped these incendiary bombs at approaches to the Saddam canal and the Tigris river bridge. This news was followed by a denial by the Pentagon officials stating that the US had removed napalm from the service in the 1970s[18] and had destroyed its stockpiles in 2001. It was claimed that the Marines had dropped "Mark-77 firebombs," which are substantially different from Napalm in their chemical make-up and effects. While "firebombs" employ a kerosene-based fuel with some benzene, a mixture of gasoline and benzene was used in the 1970s US versions of napalm bombs. The latest mixture was said to make the most recent versions of the Mark-77 firebombs less harmful to the environment. However, the similarity between the chemical composition of the two bombs showed that the Mark-77 bombs were indeed napalm. There was no difference in the impact and the use of Mark-77 and napalm. Both bombs were made for the same purpose, both were designed to kill as many humans as possible, attack bunkers and spread fire.

Napalm Burns

The extensive tactical use of napalm in the Pacific theatre in WWII, in Korea, in Indo-China War and elsewhere resulted in a high mortality amongst the persons affected. The thickened oily incendiary components of napalm are intended to cause burns by direct adhesion of the burning agent to the body; and by combustion of clothes, houses, vegetation and other material. Burning hydrocarbon fuels produce thick-black smoke, high heat, and carbon monoxide unless there is very good ventilation. Thus the casualty effects of napalm are due to a variety of causes. The exposure to burning hydrocarbon fuel in an enclosed space with good ventilation may lead to death within two minutes at 600°C and five to six minutes at 250°C. Death may take place due to two reasons: (i) Systematic hypothermia (heatstroke) resulting from the overheating of blood during its circulation through the superficial network of blood vessels; and (ii) Prevention in the rate of respiration by severe burning of the mouth and pharynx, followed by an obstructive oedema of the pharynx, trachea and lungs. In case ventilation is bad, the hydrocarbon fuel will burn more slowly, increasing the danger of death from carbon monoxide or other toxic fumes. Thus, inhalation of flame, hot vapours, carbon monoxide and unburned hydrocarbons can produce casualties. Burning napalm uses up large quantities of oxygen, and in confined areas there is a possibility that the level of oxygen may sink below that required to support life.[19] Compared with single penetrating weapons such as low velocity bullets, napalm must be regarded as an exceptionally cruel weapon of war.[20]

Napalm-B, being very sticky, cannot easily be removed from skin. Versions of Napalm-B containing white phosphorus even burns underwater (in case there is trapped oxygen in folds of cloth) so even jumping into the water bodies does not help the individuals. The victim either dies from severe burns, from the effects of the prolonged intense heat (heat stroke), or possibly from carbon monoxide and phosphorus poisoning from the fumes given off. The burns caused by napalm are tough for doctors to treat.

Napalm bombs generate carbon monoxide while simultaneously removing oxygen from the air. The air in the bombing area can be 20 per cent or more carbon monoxide. This effect occurs because napalm partially combusts the oxygen in the air, turning CO_2 (carbon dioxide) into CO (carbon monoxide). In some cases, people have been boiled to death in rivers made hot by the heat of napalm bombs.

In a study carried out in Vietnam, it was reported that 35% of the persons affected by napalm died immediately, i.e., within 15 to 20 minutes of exposure. Those who survived the initial infliction of serious burns faced a variety of potentially fatal complications for months. A further 21.8% died in hospitals, making a total fatality to 56.8%.[21] In another study it was reported that 62% of affected persons died before the healing of their wounds. The victims whose lives were saved were faced with varying degrees of physical disability, characterised by ugly scars and contractions. Reconstructive surgery to treat such conditions requires a long service of operations over several years and is unlikely to be available to ordinary people in most societies during armed conflict.[22]

Napalm's Effects on the Environment

When dropped from an aircraft, single napalm "bomb" is capable of completely destroying an area covering thousands of square metres. Although one of napalm's early uses was agricultural, it was found that it destroyed crabgrass by burning the invasive species' seeds while preserving other, necessary grasses. It has largely proved destructive toward the environment. Fires caused by napalm also cause widespread damage. In Vietnam, the US military took advantage of this fact by deploying napalm to destroy forests that North Vietnamese soldiers relied on for cover. The extensive use of napalm in Vietnam, along with Agent Orange, herbicides and a variety of unexploded landmines and munitions, have contributed to the country's ongoing environmental and public health problems.

During the Vietnam War, fire was used as weapon in the Plain of Reeds; the largest submerged area in all of Vietnam, covering nearly 2 million acres in the Mekong Delta. These wetlands were home to hundreds of thousands of birds such as cormorants, egret, herons, ducks, storks and cranes, and a variety of wetland grasses, lotuses, and water lilies. Large freshwater tarpon also found homes in the region. Wild mammals like tapir, bear and the gibbon lived in the vast wetlands, among them numerous species endangered elsewhere. The area was also covered with mighty cajeput trees, reaching up to 60 feet tall at times. Floating rice was abundant and provided a vital source of food to the rural population.

The US military constructed canals through the Plain of Reeds, resulting in the drying of mangrove marshland. This made the upper eight inches of soil barren and useless. Sulfur then rose to the surface of the dry soil, creating sulfuric acid. The Plain of Reeds thus could not support fish, floating rice or the bird and other wildlife population. Napalms were then used to destroy the cajeput forests, turning it into a waste land.[23] The Southeast Asian wildlife was greatly impacted by the war. In addition to the loss of habitat caused by aerial bombing, use of defoliants, land clearing, and fires, animals caught in the crossfire were frequent casualties during the decades of war.[24] Although made differently than in the past, napalm is still used by the US military for combat operations.

White Phosphorus

White phosphorus (WP) is a flare- and smoke-producing agent and an incendiary agent that is made from a common allotrope of the chemical element phosphorus.[25] WP has both military and nonmilitary applications. For non-military purposes WP is used in fireworks, food additives, fertilizers, and cleaning compounds. The main utility of WP munitions is to create smokescreens to mask movement from the enemy. In contrast to other smoke-causing munitions, WP burns quickly causing an instant bank of smoke. As a result of this, WP munitions are very common—particularly as smoke grenades for infantry; loaded in defensive grenade dischargers on tanks and other armoured vehicles; or as part of the ammunition allotment for artillery or mortars. In addition to its incendiary effect on materiel, WP has been proved very effective in use against personnel. When scattered from overhead burst of grenades and trench-mortar bombs, the WP rained down in flaming particles, which stuck to clothing and could not be brushed off or quenched. The larger particles quickly burned through clothing and produced painful burns that were slow and difficult to heal. WP burns quite fiercely and can also set fuel, ammunition, and other combustibles on fire; and can function as an anti-personnel weapon[26] with the compound capable of causing serious burns or death. WP can cause injuries and even death in three ways: by burning deep into tissue, by being inhaled as a smoke, and by being ingested. Extensive exposure by burning and ingestion is fatal.

When phosphorus burns in air, it first forms phosphorus pentoxide. The pentoxide is extremely hygroscopic and quickly absorbs even minute traces of moisture to form liquid droplets of phosphoric acid. Because of the great weight efficiency of WP smoke, it is particularly suited for applications where weight is highly restricted, such as hand grenades and mortar bombs. An additional advantage for hand smoke grenades—which are more likely to be used in an emergency—is that the WP smoke clouds form in a fraction of a second. Because WP is also pyrophoric, most munitions of this type have a simple burster charge to split open the casing and spray fragments of WP through the air, where they ignite spontaneously and leave a trail of rapidly thickening smoke behind each particle. WP is used in bombs, artillery, and mortars, short-range missiles which burst into burning flakes of phosphorus upon impact. WP weapons are controversial today because of their potential use against civilians.[27]

Military Use

The armed forces have a legitimate requirement for substances that can be used to illuminate a battlefield at night or to provide cover during daylight, to mark a target, to assist in range-finding or to set fire to material targets such as ammunition or fuel stores. WP is suitable for many of these task and can be used in five different ways: (i) Use of bursting WP for creation of a smoke screen/as an obscurant: WP almost instantaneously produces a dense white smoke that can obscure military movements. (ii) Use of WP burster rounds for illumination: WP can be used to illuminate a battlefield at night. Illumination can be achieved in two ways: First, WP flares can be attached to parachutes and, second, rounds can be designed to burst in the air and eject burning WP. (iii) Use of WP for marking a target: This function may include marking for assisting in range-finding and/or in preparing subsequent strikes from the air or the ground. (iv) Use of WP for "flushing out" combatants: WP rounds are fired into confined spaces where enemy combatants are taking cover, in order to drive them out and then rendering them *hors de combat* with other weapons. The tactic is often referred to as "shake and bake", and was applied by the US military in Fallujah in 2004. Pentagon spokesman Lt Col Barry Venable has described the use of WP in Fallujah in the following manner: "When you have enemy forces that are in covered positions....one technique is to fire a white phosphorus round into the position because the combined effects of the fire and smoke—and in some cases the terror brought about by the explosion on the ground—will drive them out of the holes so that you can kill them with high explosives." (v) Use of WP for incendiary purposes, i.e., setting fire to persons or objects.[28]

WP: Use in Armed Conflict

The use of WP has been increasing since WWI, because it produced both obscuring smoke and incendiary effects and could be classified either as smoke or incendiary projectiles. The British Army introduced the first factory-built WP grenades in late 1916. In the Second World War, WP mortar bombs, shells, rockets and grenades were used extensively by the US and the UK, and to a lesser extent by Japanese forces, in both smoke-generating and anti-personnel roles. WP was widely credited by Allied soldiers for breaking up German infantry attacks and creating havoc among enemy troop concentrations during the latter part of the war. Incendiary bombs were used extensively by the German, British and US air forces against civilian populations and targets of military significance in civilian areas (London, Hamburg,

Dresden, Area bombing etc).[29] Late in the war, some of these bombs used WP in place of magnesium as the igniter for their flammable mixtures.

WP munitions were used extensively in Korea, Vietnam and later by Russian forces in Chechnya. It was alleged that during the Iraq-Iran War (1988), the Saddam Hussein regime used WP as well as chemical weapons scheduled in the CWC. It has been reported that during April and November 2004, the US used WP weapons in Fallujah, Iraq.[30] Despite the US's claim that WP has only been used for legitimate purposes (illumination and smoke) in Iraq, there have been numerous allegations and accounts by members of the US military, war correspondents, and Iraqi civilians that WP has been used as an anti-personnel weapon against Iraqi combatants and civilians within urban areas.[31]

During the 2006 Israel-Lebanon conflict, Israel stated that it had used WP shells "against military targets in open ground" in south Lebanon; and claimed that the use of WP weapons was under the rules of international law. There have been numerous reports that Israeli phosphorus munitions have injured and killed many civilians in Lebanon. During the 2008-09 conflict, Israel used WP munitions in Gaza. It was reported that shells exploded over populated civilian areas, including a crowded refugee camp and a United Nations school where civilians were seeking refuge.[32] The ICRC also confirmed the use of WP weapons by Israel in Gaza. There were also confirmed reports that the US-NATO coalition forces used WP munitions in Afghanistan as a number of civilians sustained WP burns injuries in the US-Taliban clashes near Bagram. Recently the US has accused the Taliban of using WP in improvised explosive devices (IEDs) in civilian areas in Afghanistan, as well as in mortar and rocket attacks against US forces.[33] However, the Taliban denied using or possessing WP munitions.[34] Other conflicts in which the use of WP munitions has been documented or alleged includes Somalia[35] and Sri Lanka.[36]

Afghan insurgents have also used and stockpiled WP munitions. Abandoned ordnance in Libya, including incendiary weapons, has posed an ongoing threat to civilians.[37] There have been allegations that in November 2012, Myanmar police used WP on monks and other demonstrators who were protesting against a mining project in north-western Myanmar.[38] In 2016, the Saudi Arabia-led coalition in Yemen used artillery-delivered WP munitions.

The US-led coalition has used artillery-delivered white phosphorus against Islamic State (ISIS) forces in Syria and Iraq. In early 2017, US Marine artillery deployed to Syria in support of the operation to retake Raqqa, an operation in which Syrian Democratic Forces (SDF) were also participating. The use of WP weapons poses a high risk of horrific and long-lasting harm in crowded cities like Raqqa and Mosul and any other areas with concentrations of civilians. According to Human Rights Watch, WP munition should never be used as an incendiary weapon to attack personnel or materiel in populated areas, even when delivered from the ground. Allegedly, an internet cafe in Raqqa was recently hit by white phosphorus, killing around 20 people.[39]

Effects of WP on Humans

WP can cause serious injuries and extensive exposure can be fatal. Incandescent particles from a WP weapon can produce extensive, deep second and third degree burns because WP has the tendency to stick to the skin. Burning WP is difficult to extinguish and tends to reignite unless fully smothered. It also gives off phosphorus pentoxide, which can cause chemical burns, and, on contact with water, phosphoric acid, which is corrosive. Smoke inhalation can cause temporary discomfort. Signs and symptoms include irritation of the eyes and the respiratory tract; abdominal pain, nausea, and jaundice; anaemia, cachexia, pain, and loosening of teeth, excessive salivation, and pain and swelling of the jaw; skin and eye burns.

Phosphorus burns carry a greater risk of mortality than other forms of burns due to the absorption of phosphorus into the body through the burned area, resulting in liver, heart and kidney damage, and in some cases multiple organ failure. The WP weapons are particularly dangerous to exposed people because white phosphorus continues to burn unless deprived of oxygen or until it is completely consumed. In some cases, burns are limited to areas of exposed skin because the smaller WP particles do not burn completely through personal clothing before being consumed.[40] WP burns from exploding munitions are often associated with other injuries such as lacerations, fragment wounds, traumatic amputations of one or more digits, and fractures of long bones.[41]

The common assertion by the armed forces has been that WP is primarily an incendiary device and any subsequent injury as a result of exposure to WP, most likely to be skin and tissue burns, are a secondary effect due to the heat produced by burning phosphorus rather than a direct chemical interaction with an individual's physiology. However, this premise is based on the most immediate, superficial injuries that may result from exposure and does not take into account the systemic and long-term effects that could arise from inhalation, oral or dermal (skin) exposure.

The story of eight-year-old Razia exemplifies the civilian suffering caused by white phosphorus. A white phosphorus shell ripped through the Afghan girl's home in the Tagab Valley of Kapisa in June 2009. The Associated Press reported that the attack left Razia's skin burned to a scaly red, her hair would never grow back, and most of her left ear was burned off. When she reached the operating room, white powder covered her skin, the oxygen mask on her face started to melt, and flames appeared when US military doctors attempted to scrape away the dead tissue. A related Associated Press video about Razia's treatment in the hospital vividly illustrates the horrific nature of her burns, which, if she lives, will cause long-term disfigurement as well as short-term agony. A US military spokeswoman with NATO's security force said that officials could not be certain whether it was their own round or an enemy round that hit Razia's house, noting that "either scenario is possible and equally regrettable" and that the harm to Razia "could have been NATO's fault."[42]

Effect on Environment

Chemical residues from ordnance detonations have potential adverse ecological consequences in addition to threats to human population. When WP munitions are used, the phosphorus breaks up into minute particles which are dispersed over a large area. Toxicological studies on WP indicate that it is extremely toxic to fish and it is difficult to set maximum safe levels. The incipient lethal level in water is probably less than 1 ppb for most fish. Phosphorus poisoning appears to be cumulative and irreversible. Furthermore, WP can be passed on to humans since a considerable portion, 25 per cent or more, remains in the muscle of the fish after processing, storage, and cooking.

The knowledge of the environmental effect of WP on aquatic species is derived from studies initiated in the late 1960s in response to a massive fish kill caused by wastewater discharged from factory manufacturing elemental phosphorus in Placentia Bay.[43] Once in the water, the particles settle into the sediment, where they are available to be consumed by aquatic organisms and waterfowl. WP is very toxic to waterfowl, and may be magnified up the food chain.[44] WP can persist indefinitely as a solid underwater. However, if it is warm and dry, it will sublime to non-toxic phosphate species. WP reacts with water and the main product of the hydrolysis is phosphine (PH_3). The other reaction product in the reaction is hypophosphorous acid (H_3PO_2). Hydrolysis reactions will directly compete with oxidation reactions. PH_3 is a toxic gas with a maximum permissible concentration of 0.3 ppm for humans. It has an immediate off-gassing and is rapidly biologically degraded in wet soil. It is not expected to accumulate in aqueous or soil environments. Eventually, it will be oxidised to oxyphosphorus compounds.

Phosphorus-pentoxide, also known as phosphoric oxide, is the major breakdown product of WP combustion in the presence of excess air. Phosphorus-pentoxide is responsible for the dense white cloud generated during a WP munition burst. It cannot be further oxidised, but it will react with atmospheric moisture to form polyphosphorus acids. The WP degradation rate is independent of the concentration.

If solid WP is buried in soil, the rate of oxygen diffusion will determine the rate of WP transformation. Factors that affect the oxidation rate of WP in soil are (i) the presence of a surface oxide layer that builds up on a WP particle, (ii) the surface area of the WP, and (c) the depth at which the WP is buried. Other factors that determine the persistence of these particles include sediment porosity, moisture content, and temperature. In soils or sediments where the partial pressure of oxygen is low, oxidation will be very slow and WP will be persistent.[45]

WP is not generally designed to produce self-spreading fires. This can however readily be the result if the target area is sufficiently susceptible to catching fire.[46] WP munitions can lead to burning of forests, crops and vegetation. It may result in increased air pollution; loss of biodiversity in forest ecosystems; land degradation, including the loss of the water capacity and soil fertility of forest and other wooded land due to organic matter mineralisation and soil erosion; and increase in wind erosion due to windbreak destruction.[47] Environmental concerns and contamination of agricultural lands with WP is presented in Table below.[48]

Path-way	**Origin**	**Issue of Environmental Concern**
Air	Rapid reaction with oxygen to produce relatively harmless chemicals within minutes.	The reaction with oxygen releases heat and facilitates the burning of the vegetation cover. Breathing WP for short periods may cause coughing and irritation of the throat and lungs.

Water	WP reacts with oxygen within hours or days. In water with low oxygen content, it may degrade to a highly toxic compound called phosphine, which evaporates to the air and is eventually oxidised into less harmful chemicals.	WP can build up slightly in the bodies of fish that live in contaminated lakes or streams. The increasing phosphorus concentrations in surface waters raise the growth of phosphate-dependent organisms, such as algae. These organisms use large amounts of oxygen and prevent sunlight from entering the water. This makes the water fairly unlivable for other organisms.
Soil	WP may stick to particles and be changed within a few days to less harmful compounds.	In deep soil or sediments with little oxygen, WP may remain unchanged for many years.

Incendiary Weapons: Legal Control

IHL permits the use of weapons to incapacitate enemy combatants but has intervened to prohibit weapons on the grounds of humanity, because their effects go beyond what is military necessity. When considering the lawfulness of a particular weapon or its use, one has to consider, first, whether it has been banned or regulated by an existing treaty and, if not, secondly, whether it has been banned or regulated by general principles of the law of armed conflict.[49]

Before 1939, incendiary weapons were generally regarded as illegal and inhumane, in the same category as weapons, such as mustard gas, which cause chemical burns. However, the question of illegality was totally ignored during the Second World War, and practice of States during this period made the use of incendiary weapons legal. While there is no specific prohibition in IHL on the use incendiary weapons against combatants, a few States placed certain restrictions in their military manuals on the use of these weapons. In 1932, the Disarmament Conference of the League of

Nations concluded that keeping in view the inherent cruelty in use and the suffering which it causes, incendiary weapons cannot be regarded as a military necessity.[50]

In October 1972 the UN Secretary General's report on "Napalm and other Incendiary weapons and All Aspects of Their Possible Use" was published.[51] The report brought out social and economic consequences of incendiary warfare. In particularly, it highlighted the marked disparity between the abilities of the developed world and the underdeveloped countries, both to inflict and repair the economic damage that may result from incendiary attack. The report also pointed out that production of incendiary weapons of even greater destructiveness was continuing and there was a possibility of its subsequent proliferation to an increasing number of States. The report concluded that the destruction caused by incendiaries was often indiscriminate and more damaging to civilian population than to the military. Following the publication of the report, the General Assembly, in November 1972, denounced the use of napalm and other incendiary weapons in armed conflict. It also requested the Secretary-General to make the report widely available.[52] The General Assembly in its 27th session in December 1972, adopted a resolution on general and complete disarmament in which it deplored the use of napalm and other incendiary weapons in armed conflicts. The resolution, passed by 99 votes in favour and none against, exhibited that the international society was averse to the use of incendiary weapons in armed conflict.

UN Convention on Conventional Weapons (CCW)[53]

During the discussions in the 1970s, many States were in favour of a total prohibition on the use of incendiary weapons, including against combatants. The legislation of several States prohibited the use of incendiary weapons altogether. At the CCW preparatory conference in 1979, Austria, Egypt, Ghana, Jamaica, Mexico, Romania, Sudan, Sweden, Switzerland, Togo, Venezuela, Yugoslavia, and Zaire put forward a proposal prohibiting all uses of incendiary weapons.

However, during the discussions at the Conference, when it became clear that a total prohibition on incendiary weapons would not command consensus, a number of States tried to achieve a prohibition of their use against combatants with limited exceptions, such as when they were under armoured protection or in field fortifications. Since Protocol III[54] to the CCW was to be adopted by consensus, this prohibition was not included in the Protocol.[55]

Definition of incendiary weapons is contained in Article 1(1) of Protocol III: "Incendiary weapon means any weapon or munition which is primarily designed to set fire to objects or to cause burn injury to persons through the action of flame, heat, or a combination thereof, produced by a chemical reaction of a substance delivered on the target." Subparagraph (a) of Article 1(1) contains non-exhaustive forms that incendiary weapons can take such as flame-throwers, fougasses, shells, rockets, grenades, mines and bombs. The inclusion of the phrase "primarily designed" in the definition, rules out the qualification as incendiary of any weapon designed to deliver incendiary agents the primary purpose of which is not to set fire to objects or to cause burn injuries. In other words, the infliction of the above effects must be the prime military utility of any weapon which is to fall within the scope of the Protocol.[56] Article 1(1)(b) provides that "Incendiary weapons do not include: (i) munitions which may have incidental incendiary effects, such as illuminants, tracers, smoke or signalling systems; (ii) munitions designed to combine penetration, blast or fragmentation effects with an additional incendiary effect, such as armour-piercing projectiles, fragmentation shells, explosive bombs and similar combined-effects munitions in which the incendiary effect is not specifically designed to cause burn injury to persons, but to be used against military objectives, such as armoured vehicles, aircraft and installations or facilities."

The incendiary weapons are subject to the limitations stipulated by Protocol III and to those promulgated with respect to all weapons by the customary principles of IHL. Article 2 of Protocol III makes provisions for the protection of civilians and civilian objects. It states:

1. It is prohibited in all circumstances to make the civilian population as such, individual civilians or civilian objects the object of attack by incendiary weapons.
2. It is prohibited in all circumstances to make any military objective located within a concentration of civilians the object of attack by air-delivered incendiary weapons.
3. It is further prohibited to make any military objective located within a concentration of civilians the object of attack by means of incendiary weapons other than air-delivered incendiary weapons, except when such military objective is clearly separated from the concentration of civilians and all feasible precautions are taken with a view to limiting the incendiary effects to the military objective and to avoiding, and in any event to minimising, incidental loss of civilian life, injury to civilians and damage to civilian objects.
4. It is prohibited to make forests or other kinds of plant cover the object of attack by incendiary weapons except when such natural elements are used to cover, conceal or camouflage combatants or other military objectives, or are themselves military objectives.

Although, Protocol III has been ratified by 114 countries, incendiary weapons have continued to be in use during in armed conflict.[57] A total of 29 countries have produced 182 different types of incendiary weapons which include air-dropped bombs, ground-launched rockets, mortars, and artillery projectiles of varying sizes.[58] These weapons have caused serious injuries to human beings and have been responsible for extensive damage to the environment. Incendiary weapons are indiscriminate; they can start fires and cause casualties over a large area without distinguishing between soldiers and civilians, and military targets and civilian objects. For example, a single typical 155 mm artillery round spreads 116 white phosphorus wedges over an area with a radius of up to 125 metres. Each wedge burns at about 815°C (1500°F) and produces a thick chemical smoke. These wedges ignite whatever they touch in their broad footprint, burning civilians and setting fire to buildings. As a result, use of incendiary munitions in populated areas severely endangers civilians.

The definition of "incendiary weapon" in Protocol III is too narrow because it does not clearly cover multi-purpose incendiary munitions. The purpose of CCW is to protect human beings from weapons that are excessively injurious or that have indiscriminate effects. Accordingly, the language of Protocol III should focus on how incendiary weapons actually affect people—the cruel nature of the injuries they cause and their tendency to injure soldiers and civilians without distinction—regardless of the purpose for which weapons are primarily designed.

Article 1 of Protocol III provides a loophole for such munitions in two ways: it encompasses only munitions "primarily designed" to set fires or cause burn injuries, and it provides exceptions for munitions with incendiary effects that are "incidental." This definition allows multi-purpose, and widely used, incendiary munitions such as WP to escape regulation. For example, militaries describe M825E1 155 mm artillery projectile rounds as smoke munitions, Protocol III could be read to exclude them from its purview. These rounds have caused serious harm to civilians when used in or near populated areas. The restrictions on the use of incendiary weapons made by Article 2 of the Protocol III are not sufficiently rigorous. They include exceptions that too often permit attacks that could endanger civilians. While the article prohibits attacks in populated areas with air-delivered incendiary weapons, it permits the same kinds of attacks with ground-launched models under certain circumstances.

WP as Chemical Weapon

There is also a debate on whether WP should be considered a chemical weapon[59] and thus be outlawed by the CWC.[60] The CWC has a much broader scope of application than any previous regime. Under Article 1, each State Party undertakes "never under any circumstances ... to use chemical weapons," or "to develop, produce, otherwise acquire, stockpile or retain chemical weapons, or transfer, directly or indirectly, chemical weapons to anyone." Likewise, a State may not "engage in any military preparations to use chemical Weapons" or "assist, encourage or induce, in any way, anyone to engage in any activity prohibited to a State Party under this Convention." States are also required to destroy their current (and abandoned) chemical weapon stockpiles, and any current or former production facilities. The phrase "never under any circumstances" emphasises the comprehensive and totally binding character of the prohibitions. Geographically, the prohibitions possess a universal character, applying to the activities of State Parties everywhere. The wording is such that it covers international and non-international armed conflicts, regardless of whether the parties recognise each other. Furthermore, State Parties are required to adopt penal legislation to enforce the convention and extend that legislation extraterritorially to all persons holding their nationality. Reservations to the articles of this treaty are not permitted.

The CWC is meant to prohibit weapons that are "dependent on the use of the toxic properties of chemicals as a method of warfare" (Article II). The Convention defines a "toxic chemical" as a chemical "which through its chemical action on life processes can cause death, temporary incapacitation or permanent harm to humans or animals" (Article II). A study by the US Army Centre for Health Promotion and Preventive Medicine states that continued exposure to the vapours of WP can lead to bronchitis, persistent coughing, severe burns, weakness, anemia, loss of appetite, and possibly pneumonia. There is no mention in CWC Article II(2) of how long the exposure to the chemical would have to be, in order for the relevant effects to occur. Therefore, the definition in this article is wide enough to cover WP smoke.[61]

If used as part of an incendiary weapon, WP would fall within the controls of Article 2 of Protocol III. The definition of incendiary weapons excludes weapons having incidental incendiary effects as well as combined-effects munitions. Therefore, the use of incendiary weapons against military objectives, such as fortified military positions may be perfectly legitimate, even if that has horrible consequences for the enemy military personnel inside.[62]

When WP is used to produce smoke for camouflage movement, which does not require or does not intend to use the toxic properties of WP, it is not forbidden by the CWC. However, if the toxic properties of WP are specifically intended to be used as a weapon, then it would be prohibited under the CWC. The CCW Protocol III prohibits the use of all air-delivered incendiary weapons against civilian populations, or for indiscriminate incendiary attacks against military forces co-located with civilians. WP bombs and shells are essentially incendiary devices, but can also be used as an offensive anti-personnel flame compound capable of causing serious burns or death.[63]

General Principles of IHL

IHL does not ban WP munitions either as an "obscurant" to hide military operations or as an incendiary weapon. Its use, however, remains regulated by the rules of IHL on the conduct of hostilities, restrictions that limit the use of weapons to minimise harm to civilians and civilian property.[64] IHL also places restrictions on the means and methods of warfare by parties to an armed conflict and requires them to respect and protect civilians and captured combatants. The fundamental tenets of this law are "civilian immunity" and "distinction."[65] Besides, Article 23 of the Hague Regulations 1907 prohibits employment of "poison or poisonous weapons." If we consider its incendiary, poisonous and chemical effects, the incendiary weapons needs to be banned under customary IHL.[66]

IHL prohibits indiscriminate attacks. Indiscriminate attacks are of a nature to strike military objectives and civilians or civilian objects without distinction. Examples of indiscriminate attacks are those that are not directed at a specific military objective or that use weapons that cannot be directed at a specific military objective. Thus, if a party launches an attack without attempting to aim properly at a military target, or in such a way as to hit civilians without regard to the likely extent of death or injury, it would amount to an indiscriminate attack. Prohibited indiscriminate attacks also include area bombardment, which are attacks by artillery or other means that treat as a single military objective a number of clearly separated and distinct military objectives located in an area containing a concentration of civilians and civilian objects.[67] Also prohibited are attacks that violate the principle of proportionality. Disproportionate attacks are those that are expected to cause incidental loss of civilian life or damage to civilian objects that would be excessive in relation to the concrete and direct military advantage anticipated from the attack.[68]

Humanitarian law requires that the parties to a conflict take constant care during military operations to spare the civilian population and to "take all feasible precautions" to avoid or minimise the incidental loss of civilian life and damage to civilian objects.[69] These precautions include doing everything feasible to verify that the objects of attack are military objectives and not civilians or civilian objects,[70] and giving "effective advance warning" of attacks when circumstances permit.[71] IHL does not prohibit fighting in urban areas, although the presence of civilians places greater obligations on warring parties to take steps to minimise harm to civilians. Forces deployed in populated areas must avoid locating military objectives near densely populated areas,[72] and endeavour to remove civilians from the vicinity of military objectives.[73] Belligerents are prohibited from using civilians to shield military objectives or operations from attack. "Shielding" refers to purposefully using the presence of civilians to render military forces or areas immune from attack.[74] However, even if one party considers opposing forces responsible for having located legitimate military targets within or near populated areas, it is not relieved from the obligation to take into account the risk to civilians when conducting attacks.

There is evidence of State practices that view the anti-personnel use of WP as prohibited under IHL. The UK's official policy is not to use it as an anti-personnel weapon.[75] Although the Israelis were reported to have used WP as an anti-personnel weapon, the official position of Israel was that they do not use WP in that way. Likewise, in response to allegations of illegal WP use in Iraq, the Russian Duma (Senate) issued a statement condemning the use of phosphorus bombs under any circumstances and stated that such bombs are banned by international treaties even "under cover of noble aims of the fight against terrorism." The US Environmental Protection Agency (EPA) describes white phosphorus as "extremely toxic to humans."[76] A number of countries have also stated publicly that WP is only used for the purpose of screening and/or illumination and not as an anti-personnel weapon.

While use of WP might be legal as an illuminator or smoke screen, its legality may shift when used in the confines of a cave, bunker, or foxhole, to flush out individuals. Indeed, WP not only has the potential of causing superfluous injuries and unnecessary suffering through painful chemical burns, but also has the potential of asphyxiating or suffocating the occupants of an enclosed space on account of the burst of yellow flames and thick smoke produced upon its contact with oxygen, as its chemical reaction continues until the material is consumed or the oxygen is depleted entirely. Peter Kaiser, spokesman for the Organisation for the Prohibition of Chemical Weapons (OPCW) has described the prohibited uses of WP as those military purposes that are dependent on the chemical's toxicity.[77] While it is true that weapons are meant to kill and maim, IHL recognises that some weapons, uses, and tactics are strictly prohibited because they violate core principles of IHL.[78]

Role of the ICRC

In November 2011, during the Fourth Review Conference of the CCW, States parties actively took on the issue of incendiary weapons for the first time since the adoption of Protocol III to CCW in 1980. The Conference noted the concerns raised by a few State parties relating to the use of incendiary weapons, however, there was no agreement on these issues.[79] At the Review Conference, the ICRC, expressed grave concerns and noted, "Recent reports of the use of weapons with incendiary effects in densely populated areas, and the humanitarian impact of such use, highlight the relevance of this issue and the dangers that exist for the civilian population." As a result, there is a need to examine "the adequacy of protections provided under Protocol III of the CCW." On WP in particular, the ICRC emphasised not only the "horrific burns" of this substance, but also the difficulty in treating the burns and the risks flammable remnants pose for medical personnel. The ICRC concluded that "the protections afforded to civilians and civilian objects by Protocol III warrant a review."[80]

The ICRC study on customary IHL[81] has two rules concerning incendiary weapons. Rule 84 states that if incendiary weapons are used, particular care must be taken to avoid, and in any event to minimise, incidental loss of civilian life, injury to civilians and damage to civilian objects. Rule 85 prohibits the anti-personnel use of incendiary weapons, unless it is not feasible to use a less harmful weapon to render a person *hors de combat*. The use of the words "particular care" in Rule 84 further enhances the requirement for a clear distinction. It is a reminder to military commander, towards the use of incendiary weapons and protection of civilians.[82] It addition, the UN Secretary-General's Bulletin of August 6, 1999 prohibits the employment of incendiary weapons by the armed forces engaged in UN peacekeeping operations.[83]

Several States (for example Austria, Denmark, Egypt, Ghana, Indonesia, Jamaica, Mexico, Norway, Romania, Sweden, Venezuela, Yugoslavia and Zaire) have specified the few restricted situations in which incendiary weapons may be used, namely when combatants are under armoured protection or in field fortifications. The military manuals of a few States (Australia, Canada and New Zealand) provide that incendiary weapons may not be used in a way that would cause unnecessary suffering; while the military manuals of Belgium, Colombia and Sweden make the point that the use of incendiary weapons against combatants is prohibited because it causes unnecessary suffering.[84]

The British Manual of the Law of Armed Conflict (2004) prohibits direct use of WP weapons against personnel. It states: It is prohibited 'in all circumstances to make any military objective located within a concentration of civilians the object of attack by air-delivered incendiary weapons'. Subject to that, the use of incendiary weapons, including incendiary bombs, napalm, and flamethrowers, against military objectives is not prohibited under customary or treaty law. Although these weapons can cause severe injury to personnel, their use is lawful provided the military necessity for their use outweighs the injury and suffering which their use may cause. Use of weapons such as napalm and flamethrowers against combatant personnel is not dealt with specifically in the CWC or any other treaty. Such uses are governed by the unnecessary suffering principle so that they should not be used directly against personnel but against armoured vehicles, bunkers, and built-up emplacements, even though personnel inside may be burnt. The same applies to WP, which is designed to set fire to targets such as fuel and ammunition dumps or for use to create smoke, and which should not be used directly against personnel.[85] The US Department of Defence, Law of War Manual (2015) does not prohibit the use of WP as an antipersonnel weapon. It however states that such use must comply with the general rules for the conduct of hostilities, including the principles of discrimination and proportionality. In addition, feasible precautions to reduce the risk of harm to civilians must be taken. [86]

CCW Protocol III allows the use of incendiary munitions in ways harmful to civilians due to definitional loopholes and narrow regulations. In addition, the Protocol's key regulations apply only to use in populated areas and are weaker for ground-launched than for air-dropped munitions. Regardless of their type, targeting, and delivery mechanism, however, incendiary munitions cause cruel and lasting injury to people. The munitions produce exceptionally painful thermal and respiratory burns, which can lead to complications such as shock, infection and asphyxiation.[87] People who survive often suffer long-term physical and psychological damage.[88] Protecting human beings from the cruel and often indiscriminate effects of incendiary weapons requires a total prohibition on the use of incendiary weapons.[89]

Notes

1. Stockholm International Peace Research Institute (SIPRI), *Incendiary Weapons* (The MIT Press, 1975), pp. 15-18.
2. Augustine M. Prentiss, *Chemicals in War: A Treatise on Chemical Warfare* (New York: McGraw-Hill Book Company, 1937), pp. 248-51.
3. The Ottoman Turks never attempted to besiege Malta again. The failure of the siege denied Turkish forces control of Western Mediterranean and prevented their plans to conquer Southern Europe. The Great Siege of Malta was one of the most decisive victories in military history, changing the course of history and preventing the Western expansion of Turkish power. E. Bradford, *The Great Siege: Malta 1565* (UK: Penguin Books, 1964).
4. The metal incendiaries are characterised by high burning temperatures and the tendency to splatter small particles of molten or burning metal on the victim. These small particles may cause small but deep burns. Such burns are uncommon in civilian life and normally occur amongst workers in munition factories. Magnesium burns produce ulcers which are small at first but gradually enlarge to form extensive lesions. The deeper part of the lesions is usually quite irregular. Tissue destruction may be increased by the formation of small bubbles of hydrogen in the wound. Burning thermite produces particles of iron which at the temperature of combustion are molten. Therefore, while not actually burning, the drops of molten iron are capable of causing small, deep burns until they cool and solidify. The Stockholm International Peace Research Institute (SIPRI), *Incendiary Weapons* (Cambridge: The MIT Press, 1975), p. 150.
5. W. Hays Parks, "The Protocol on Incendiary Weapons," *International Review of the Red Cross*, 1990, vol. 279, pp. 544-45.
6. The Human Suffering Caused by Incendiary Munitions, Memorandum to Convention on Conventional Weapons Delegates, Human Rights Watch and Harvard Law School's International Human Rights Clinic March 2011, p.2.
7. The new Napalm-B was not made from naphthenic and palmitic acids (the source of the original napalm name) and was called super-napalm, made of 33 per cent gasoline, 21 per cent benzene and 46 per cent polystyrene. Napalm-B was considered safer to those who deploy the weapon. One of Napalm-B's safety features was that it was rather difficult to ignite, decreasing the chances of an accidental ignition. Thermite, a chemical mixture that burns at very high temperatures, is often used with a fuse to ignite Napalm-B.
8. Robert Neer, "The Role of Humiliation and Dignity for the History of the Use of Napalm in War." Available at: http://www.humiliationstudies.org/documents/NeerNY09meeting.pdf, accessed January 20, 2013.
9. Napalm bombardment has two principal effects: fire and asphyxiation. During the Second World War, troops found Japanese shelters which had been struck by napalm bombs in which all the occupants were dead without having been burned at all. These soldiers had died, apparently without pain, and with an expression of fright and surprise frozen on to their faces; they had been instantaneously and massively poisoned by carbon monoxide. The only way

to escape the asphyxiating effects of napalm is to flee into the open air—where the direct destruction by burning from flaming splashes is greatest. In a strike zone it is almost impossible to escape the effects of napalm by taking shelter, for one cannot hold one's breath for the time it takes napalm to burn off. The carbon monoxide poisoning paralyses the will and robs the victim of the ability to move.

10. J. R. McNeill, "The Global Environmental Footprint of the US Military," in Charles E. Closmann (ed.), *War and the Environment: Military Destruction in the Modern Age* (USA: Texas A&M University Press, 2009), p. 19.
11. Napalm was proving to be a top "all-purpose weapon" in Korea; an average of 70,000 gallons were employed each day against enemy personnel and supply lines. Stephen Endicott and Edward Hagerman, *The United States and Biological Warfare* (Indiana University Press, 1988), p. 63.
12. Several experimental attempts to burn forests in Vietnam were made by the US military under the direction of the Advance Research Projects Agency of the Department of Defence. A number of attempts were made to initiate fire-storms in forest areas, using magnesium incendiary bombs dropped by B-52 strategic bombers, following defoliation of the trees by chemicals. In addition to air and naval bombardment, land based artillery was also used to keep the fires going. A large number of civilians lost their homes and means of livelihood in these experiments and large areas of forests, estimated to be 100,000 acres, were burned. The Stockholm International Peace Research Institute (SIPRI), *Incendiary Weapons* (Cambridge: The MIT Press, 1975), pp. 57-58.
13. Ibid., p. 59.
14. Ibid., p. 61.
15. According to a US Forest service report declassified in 1983, the Joint Chiefs of Staff had requested in late 1965 that a programme be developed to "determine the feasibility of dehydrating jungle growth to the point where such material would support combustion, and to initiate development of operational means for determining the specific conditions under which there is the greatest possibility of destroying jungle or forest growth by fire." Susan D. Lanier-Graham, *The Ecology of War: Environmental Impacts of Weaponry and Warfare* (New York: Walker and Company, 1993), pp. 33-34.
16. The Stockholm International Peace Research Institute (SIPRI), *Incendiary Weapons* (Cambridge: The MIT Press, 1975), pp. 67-68.
17. Jacob Silverman, *How Napalm Works*, available at: http://science.howstuffworks.com/napalm4.htm, accessed January 23, 2013.
18. It has been reported that the American officials lied to British ministers over the use of "internationally reviled" napalm-type firebombs in Iraq. Colin Brown, Deputy Political Editor, "US lied to Britain over use of napalm in Iraq war," available at: http://www.cwalocal4250.org/news/binarydata/Napalm.pdf, accessed January 20, 2013.
19. The Stockholm International Peace Research Institute (SIPRI), *Incendiary Weapons* (Cambridge: The MIT Press, 1975), pp. 151-52.
20. Ibid., p. 155.
21. J. Takman (ed), *Napalm* (Stockholm: Raben and Sjorgren, 1967), pp. 16-25.
22. The Stockholm International Peace Research Institute (SIPRI), *Incendiary Weapons* (Cambridge: The MIT Press, 1975), p. 154.
23. Susan D. Lanier-Graham, *The Ecology of War: Environmental Impacts of Weaponry and Warfare* (New York: Walker and Company, 1993), pp. 35-36.
24. There are eleven rare species of mammals found only in Southeast Asia. Of these,

four species are now in danger of extinction, and several others are threatened. The red-shanked douc langur, a small monkey, is one of the species not found elsewhere in the world, and is threatened. In addition the pleated gibbon, Owston's civet, and the kouprey are all endangered in their last remaining habitat in the world. John Lewallen, *Ecology of Devastation: Indochina* (Baltimore, Penguin Books, 1971).

25. Phosphorus is the chemical element (symbol P and atomic number 15) and is commonly found in inorganic phosphate rocks. Due to its high reactivity, phosphorus is never found as a free element in nature on Earth. Elemental phosphorus exists in two major forms—white phosphorus and red phosphorus. The first form of phosphorus to be discovered (white phosphorus in 1669) emits a faint glow upon exposure to oxygen—called "light-bearer" (Latin *Lucifer*), referring to the "Morning Star," the planet Venus. Phosphorus compounds are widely used in explosives, nerve agents, friction matches, fireworks, fertilisers, pesticides, toothpaste and detergents. Phosphorus has several forms (allotropes) which have strikingly different properties. Red phosphorus is an intermediate phase between white and violet phosphorus. Another form, scarlet phosphorus, is obtained by allowing a solution of white phosphorus in carbon disulfide to evaporate in sunlight. Black phosphorus is obtained by heating white phosphorus under high pressures (about 12,000 atmospheres). "Phosphorus," *Encyclopaedia Britannica*, 2008, Encyclopedia Britannica Online, available at http://www.britannica.com/eb/article-9059785, accessed February 25, 2012.
26. WP could also be used as an anti-personnel weapon. In cases where enemy forces are in covered positions and high explosive artillery rounds are not having any impact, one technique is to fire a WP round into the position because the combined effects of the fire and smoke—and in some cases the terror brought about by the explosion on the ground—will drive them out of the holes so that the enemy can be killed with high explosives. US Forces Used "Chemical Weapon" in Iraq, *The Independent* (London), November 16, 2005.
27. White phosphorus (WP) is formed by quickly cooling the vapours distilled from phosphate rock. When pure, it is a waxy solid, has specific gravity of 1.8, melts at 44°C and boils at 287°C. It is chemically very active and combines readily with oxygen in the air, even at room temperature. The greater the surface exposed to the air, the more rapid is the reaction. Upon oxidation the phosphorus becomes luminous and in a few minutes bursts into vigorous flames that can only be quenched by complete submersion in water. Augustine M. Prentiss, *Chemicals in War: A Treatise on Chemical Warfare* (New York: McGraw-Hill Book Company, 1937), p. 234.
28. Christensen Stian Nordengen, Regulation of White Phosphorus Weapons in International law, Brussles: Torkel Opsahl Academic E-Publisher, 2016, p. 7-8.
29. The use of incendiary weapons against civilians was banned in the 1980 Convention on Certain Conventional Weapons Protocol III.
30. The United States' use of white phosphorus during the Iraq War resulted in considerable controversy among critics of the war. The US Department of Defence (DoD) spokesman stated that WP "was used as an incendiary weapon against enemy combatants," though not against civilians. In November 2005, the DoD, however, admitted that they have used [phosphorus shells] very sparingly in Fallujah, for illumination purposes; and WP was used for producing obscuring smoke, which is legal and does not violate the Chemical Weapons Convention (CWC). The US Department of State website carried an addendum in November 2005, replacing the previous statement with the comment: We have learned that

some of the information we were provided [in the above paragraph] is incorrect. White phosphorus shells, which produce smoke, were used in Fallujah not for illumination but for screening purposes, i.e., obscuring troop movements and, according to an article in US *Field Artillery* magazine (Capt. James T. Cobb, "The Fight for Fallujah," March 2005), "as a potent psychological weapon against the insurgents in trench lines and spider holes ..." The article stated that US forces used WP rounds to flush out enemy fighters so that they could then be killed with high explosive rounds. The munitions used included ... white phosphorous (WP, M110 and M825), with point-detonating (PD), delay, time and variable-time (VT) fuses. The article claimed: "WP proved to be an effective and versatile munition. We used it for screening missions at two breeches and, later in the fight, as a potent psychological weapon against the insurgents in trench lines and spider holes when we could not get effects on them with HE. We fired "shake and bake" missions at the insurgents, using WP to flush them out and HE to take them out." Article available at: http://www.tradoc.army.mil/pao/ProfWriting/2-2AARlow.pdf, accessed February 27, 2012.

31. The use of WP in Fallujah was in violation of a number of international treaties and customary obligations binding upon the US armed forces. The WP smoke was used in a manner inconsistent with the US obligations under the CWC, being used as a precursor chemical and as a riot control agent as a method of warfare. It thus amounted to the use of a chemical weapon. The US also violated its obligations under the customary rules regarding the use of an indiscriminate incendiary weapon in a mixed civilians and combatant setting. Roman Reyhani, "The Legality of the Use of White Phosphorus by the United States Military During the 2004 Fallujah Assaults," vol. 10, *Journal of Law and Social Change* (2007), p. 45. *See also:* Joseph D. Tessier, "Shake & Bake: Dual-Use Chemicals, Contexts, and the Illegality of American White Phosphorus Attacks in Iraq," vol. 6, no. 2, *Pierce Law Review*, 2007, pp. 323-63.
32. The Human Rights Watch published a 71 page report titled *Rain of Fire: Israel's Unlawful Use of White Phosphorus in Gaza* (2009) and claimed Israel's usage of the weapon was illegal. The report concludes that the Israel Defence Forces (IDF) repeatedly exploded white phosphorus munitions in the air over populated areas, killing and injuring civilians, and damaging civilian structures, including a school, a market, a humanitarian aid warehouse and a hospital.
33. The Associated Press, *US accuses Afghan militants of using phosphorus*, May 11, 2009. Available at http://www.guardian.co.uk/world/2009/may/11/taliban-phosphorus-attacks-afghanistan; accessed March 23, 2011. *Afghan Commandos Kill 18 Enemy Fighters in Helmand Province*, US Department of Defence, 5/20/2009. Available at http://www.defenselink.mil/news/newsarticle.aspx?id=54429, accessed March 23, 2012.
34. Sayed Salahuddin, *Afghan Taliban deny using white phosphorus*, Reuters, May 12, 2009. Available at:http://www.alertnet.org/thenews/newsdesk/ISL473840.htm, accessed March 25, 2012.
35. Mark Turner and Barney Jopson, "US, Ethiopia accused over Somalia," *The Financial Times*, July 21, 2007. Available at: http://www.ft.com/cms/s/0/2bbc3932-3c60-11dc-b067-0000779fd2ac.html?nclick_check=1, accessed August 4, 2102.
36. Nicolas Revise, *On the operating table, evidence of Sri Lanka's brutal war*, Agence France-Presse (AFP), May 10, 2009. Available at: http://reliefweb.int/rw/rwb.nsf/db900sid/MYAI-7RW633?OpenDocument&query=white%20phosphorus, accessed March 9, 2012.

37. According to Human Rights Watch leaking drums of napalm powder were found abandoned at a military depot in Benghazi alongside casings and igniters for napalm bombs. Abandoned ordnance in general endangers civilians, particularly children. *Libya: Abandoned Weapons, Landmines, Unexploded Ordnance,* Human Rights Watch, April 5, 2011, available at: http://www.hrw.org/features/libya-abandoned-weapons-landmines-unexploded-ordnance, accessed June 24, 2012.
38. "Myanmar police used white phosphorus," *The Hindu,* February 2, 2013. Available at: http://www.thehindu.com/news/international/myanmar-police-used-white-phosphorus/article4369882.ece.
39. The US-led coalition has stated that as matter of policy it cannot publicly discuss the use of specific munitions, but admits to using white phosphorus in its operation in Iraq and Syria. Further, a spokesperson for the US-led coalition in Iraq and Syria stated, "in accordance with the law of armed conflict, white phosphorus rounds are used for screening, obscuring and marking in a way that fully considers the possible incidental effects on civilians and civilian structures."Iraq/Syria: Danger From US White Phosphorus, Take All Needed Measures to Minimize Civilian Harm, Human Rights Watch, June 14, 2017, available at:https://www.hrw.org/news/2017/06/14/iraq/syria-danger-us-white-phosphorus, accessed 30 June 2017.
40. Initial dermal exposure to burning WP will immediately result in local tissue destruction of the outer layers of the skin. Depending on the quantity and size of WP particles an individual is exposed to, burn damage can continue beyond the superficial layers of the skin, penetrating deep into muscle tissue and on occasion as far as any underlying bone, until the burning WP is extinguished due to a lack of oxygen. I. J. MacLeod and A. P. V. Rogers, "Use of White Phosphorus and the Law of War," vol. 10, *Yearbook of International Humanitarian Law,* 2007, pp. 89-90.
41. The Stockholm International Peace Research Institute (SIPRI), *Incendiary Weapons* (Cambridge: The MIT Press, 1975), p. 158.
42. *Incendiary Weapons: Government Positions and Practices,* Memorandum to Convention on Conventional Weapons Delegates Human Rights Watch and the Harvard Law School International Human Rights Clinic, April 2012, p. 5.
43. D. Burrows and J. C. Dacre, (1973), Mammalian toxicology and toxicity to aquatic organisms of white phosphorus and "phossy water," a waterborne munitions manufacturing waste pollutant—a literature evaluation, Final comprehensive Report AD-777 901, Associated Water and Air Resources Engineers, Inc., Nashville, TN.
44. One of the United States Army training ranges was closed in 1989 due because WP residues were poisoning ducks and swans. During examination it was found that detonated projectiles containing WP in the shallow ponds of the wetland impact area, left sand-size particles of WP that were subsequently ingested by dabbling ducks. A few milligrams of WP were found lethal to waterfowl and thousands of waterfowl were poisoned. As a result of these findings, the US army banned training with WP in areas that had wetlands. NATO: "Environmental Impact of Munition and Propellant Disposal," Final Report of Task Group AVT-115, pp. 3-18 and 19. Available at: http://natorto.cbw.pl/uploads/2010/2/$$TR-AVT-115-ALL.pdf, accessed February 21, 2012.
45. Yilda B. Rivera, Robert Jones and R. Mark Bricka, "Diffused Air Aeration as a Treatment Technology for the Remediation of White Phosphorus-Contaminated Soils," available at: http://www.bvsde.paho.org/bvsaidis/puertorico/xxi.pdf, accessed February 21, 2012.

46. Ove Bring, *Arms Control and International Environmental Law,* Stockholm Institute for Scandinavian Law, pp. 397-417. Available at: http://www.scandinavianlaw.se/pdf/39-18.pdf, accessed May 20, 2011.
47. Fruit orchards in South Lebanon were affected by Israeli bombs and were burned by white phosphorus. Since fruit crops would need several years to produce and bring in a return on farmers' investment, it is anticipated that farmers will shift to cash crops, which lead to rapid return on investments. Such changes in the cropping pattern would negatively affect both the environment and the socio-economic equilibrium in South Lebanon. The cultivation of cash crops would result in a higher depletion of water resources with a higher risk of seawater intrusion, an increase in the use of chemicals (fertilisers, pesticides), higher levels of soil salinity, loss of soil fertility, and enhanced land degradation. *Lebanon: Rapid Environmental Assessment for Green Recovery, Reconstruction and Reform, 2006,* UNDP, 2007, pp. 6-16.
48. ATSDR (Agency for Toxic Substances and Disease Registry), "Toxicological Profile for white phosphorus" (Atlanta, GA: US Department of Health and Human Services, Public Health Service, 1997).
49. I. J. MacLeod and A. P. V. Rogers, "Use of White Phosphorus and the Law of War," vol. 10, *Yearbook of International Humanitarian Law,* 2007, p. 79.
50. There has been support for a blanket ban on incendiary weapons in particular for decades. During the League of Nations Conference for the Reduction and Limitation of Armaments (Geneva 1932-1934), the Special Committee on chemical, bacteriological and other weapons proposed prohibiting incendiary bombs.
51. *Napalm and Other Incendiary Weapons and All Aspects of Their Possible Use,* United Nations 1972, Report of the Secretary-General, A/8803, October 9, 1972 and A/9207.
52. UN General Assembly, Res. 2932 A (XXVIII), November 29, 1972. The resolution was passed by 99 nations in favour, none against and 15 nations abstaining (Australia, Belgium, Canada, France, Greece, Israel, Italy, Japan, Luxemburg, the Netherlands, New Zealand, Portugal, South Africa, the US and the UK).
53. The 1980 UN Convention on Prohibitions or Restrictions on the Use of Certain Conventional Weapons Which May Be Deemed to Be Excessively Injurious or to Have Indiscriminate Effects (CCW). The CCW, sometimes referred to as the "Inhumane Weapons Convention," was established with the intent of saving innocent civilians from the effects of armed conflict and limiting the suffering caused by conventional weapons. There are five protocols included to the CCW: the First Protocol (1980) restricts fragmentation weapons; the Second Protocol (1980) limits landmines; the Third (1980) prohibits incendiary weapons; the Fourth (1995) bans blinding laser weapons, and other weapons designed to cause permanent blindness to its victims; and the Fifth Protocol (2003) minimises the effects of explosive remnants of war (ERW) in post-conflict situations.
54. Protocol on Prohibitions or Restrictions on the Use of Incendiary Weapons (Protocol III), October 10, 1980.
55. Jean-Marie Henckaerts and Louise Doswald-Beck, *Customary International Humanitarian Law,* vol. I (International Committee of the Red Cross and Cambridge: Cambridge University Press, 2005), p. 290.
56. W. H. Boothby, *Weapons and the law of armed conflict* (Oxford: Oxford University Press, 2009), p. 201.
57. Lebanon became the 114th country to ratify CCW Protocol III on 5 April 2017. Iraq, Russia, and the US are parties to the Protocol III.

58. The list of countries include Argentina, Australia, Austria, Belgium, Bosnia, Brazil, Chile, China, Czech Republic, Egypt, France, Greece, India, Iraq, Israel, South Korea, Netherlands, Pakistan, Romania, Russia, Serbia, Singapore, South Africa, Spain, Thailand, Turkey, the UK, and the USA. *Ammunition Handbook 2007-2008 and Air Launched Weapons* (Issue 44), Jane's Information Group.
59. There are a number of similarities between the military uses of incendiary and chemical agents: (i) Both incendiaries and chemical agents may be used as weapons of mass destruction, as strategic area weapons; (ii) Both may be used on the battlefield as tactical area weapons, either for their direct casualty effects, or in order to enhance the effectiveness of conventional muntions; and (c) Both may be used for penetrating confined areas (buildings, tunnels and bunkers). Mixing various munitions, such as fragmentation, high explosive, napalm and phosphorus bombs, has been widely practised as a means of mutually enhancing the effectiveness of the weapons. Another possible combined use of chemical and incendiary agents is to desiccate an area of vegetation. Grass and weeds in particular become highly inflammable after this treatment. O. L. Forman and D. W. Longrace, "Fire potential increased by weed killers," *Fire Control Notes*, vol. 31 (3), 1970, pp. 11-12.
60. CWC has been ratified by 188 States, including the US, the UK, Russia, Iran, India, and Pakistan. The ban on use of chemical weapons is total. They may not even be used in internal security operations. The ban on riot control agents applies in international armed conflicts. The definition of chemical weapons is complicated, but in essence they are weapons consisting of or containing toxic chemicals or their precursors. A toxic chemical is one which, through its chemical action on life processes, can cause death, temporary incapacitation or permanent harm to humans or animals. Some such chemicals are listed in schedules to the convention.
61. Christensen Stian Nordengen, Regulation of White Phosphorus Weapons in International law, Brussles: Torkel Opsahl Academic E-Publisher, 2016, p. 17.
62. I. J. MacLeod and A. P. V. Rogers, "Use of White Phosphorus and the Law of War," vol. 10, *Yearbook of International Humanitarian Law*, 2007, p. 95.
63. I. J. MacLeod and A. P. V. Rogers, "White Phosphorous and the Law of War," in Timothy L. H. McCormack (ed.), *Yearbook of International Humanitarian Law*, vol. 10, 2007, TMC Asser Press, pp. 76-97.
64. "Unnecessary" in this context means suffering which is not necessitated by legitimate military requirements. The International Court of Justice has attached great importance to it as one of the cardinal principles of humanitarian law. According to the court's formulation, "it is prohibited to cause unnecessary suffering to combatants: it is accordingly prohibited to use weapons causing them such harm or uselessly aggravating their suffering." However, the meaning of unnecessary suffering is important. The court explained that this meant: "a harm greater than that unavoidable to achieve legitimate military objectives." *Advisory Opinion on the Legality of the Threat or Use of Nuclear Weapons of 8 July 1996*, 110 ILR, p. 163, at p. 207. Rule 85, *Customary International Humanitarian Law*, International Committee of the Red Cross (ICRC), Cambridge: Cambridge University Press, 2005. Various armed forces prohibit the use of incendiary weapons where it would cause unnecessary suffering. See US Army, Field Manual 27-10 (1956) (the use of incendiary weapons is not a violation of international law. They should not, however, be employed in such a way as to cause unnecessary suffering to individuals) sec. 36; UK Ministry of Defence, The Manual of the Law of Armed Conflict, white phosphorus "should not be used

directly against personnel" (Oxford: Oxford University Press, 2004), p. 112.

65. Additional Protocol I Articles 48, 51(2), and 52(2).
66. While the use of WP as a smoke signal or flare is uncontroversial, direct use against enemy soldiers is problematic. This is a result of blurred boundaries: "burning," a chemical reaction with oxygen, is the hallmark of incendiary weapons, while those due to "chemical effects" signify a chemical weapon. Due to this blurred boundary, many armies do not use WP in its anti-personnel role against areas which may have civilians. If WP is used as a weapon based on its toxic properties it may constitute a violation of several conventions, in spirit if not in letter.
67. Articles 51(4) and 51(5) of Additional Protocol I enumerate five kinds of indiscriminate attacks: those that (i) are not directed at a "specific military objective," (ii) cannot be directed at "a specific military objective," (iii) have effects that violate the Protocol, (iv) treat separate urban military objectives as one (carpet bombing), or (v) violate the principle of proportionality.
68. Additional Protocol I, Article 51(5)(b). The expected danger to the civilian population and civilian objects depends on various factors, including their location (possibly within or near a military objective), the accuracy of the weapons used (depending on the trajectory, the range, environmental factors, the ammunition used, etc.), and the technical skill of the combatants (which can lead to random launching of weapons when combatants lack the ability to aim effectively at the intended target). ICRC, Commentary on the Additional Protocols, p. 684.
69. Additional Protocol I, Article 57. The ICRC Commentary to Protocol I states that the requirement to take "all feasible precautions" means, among other things, that the person launching an attack is required to take the steps needed to identify the target as a legitimate military objective "in good time to spare the population as far as possible." ICRC, Commentary on the Additional Protocols, p. 682.
70. If there are doubts about whether a potential target is of a civilian or military character, it "shall be presumed" to be civilian. Additional Protocol I, Article 52(3). The warring parties must do everything feasible to cancel or suspend an attack if it becomes apparent that the target is not a military objective.
71. Additional Protocol I, Article 57(2).
72. Additional Protocol I, Article 58(b).
73. Additional Protocol I, Art. 58(a).
74. Additional Protocol I, Art. 51(7).
75. The UK Ministry of Defence Manual proposes as the "correct criterion is whether the use of a weapon is of a nature to cause injury or suffering greater than that required for its military purpose. In deciding the legality of use of a specific weapon, therefore, it is necessary to assess: (a) its effects in battle; (b) the military task it is required to perform; and (c) the proportionality between factors (a) and (b)," UK Ministry of Defence, *The Manual of the Law of Armed Conflict*, Oxford: Oxford University Press, 2004, para 6.2 and 6.21. The UK government has asserted that the use of WP during combat is strictly reserved for screening purposes and that advantage is not taken of its incendiary capabilities. BBC News "WP: weapon on the edge" available at: http://news.bbc.co.uk/1/hi/world/americas/4442988.stm, accessed February 24, 2012.
76. US Environmental Protection Agency, "Phosphorus," available at: http://www.epa.gov/ttn/atw/hlthefwhitepho.html.
77. Paul Reynolds, *White Phosphorus: Weapon on the Edge*, BBC News, November

16, 2005, available at: http://news.bbc.co.uk/2/hi/americas/4442988.stm, accessed February 27, 2012. *See also:* Toxicological Profile for White Phosphorus, Science International, Inc., US Department of Health and Human Services, September 1997. Available at: http://www.atsdr.cdc.gov/toxprofiles/tp103.pdf, accessed February 28, 2012.

78. Joseph D. Tessier, "Shake & Bake: Dual-Use Chemicals, Contexts, and the Illegality of American White Phosphorus Attacks in Iraq," vol. 6, no. 2, *Pierce Law Review*, 2007, pp. 323-63.
79. CCW Fourth Review Conference Final Document (Part II), CCW/CONF.IV/4/Add.1, Geneva, November 14-25, 2011, available at: http://daccess-dds-ny.un.org/doc/UNDOC/GEN/G11/652/03/PDF/G1165203.pdf?OpenElement, accessed July 27, 2012, p. 9.
80. Statement of Louis Maresca, Legal Adviser, Arms Unit, Legal Division, International Committee of the Red Cross, Fourth Review Conference of States Parties to the CCW, Geneva, November 16, 2011. Available at: http://www.unog.ch/80256EDD006B8954/(httpAssets)/C77CB1DD06229E70C1257967003BC545/$file/MCI_ICRC_ProtocolIII.pdf, accessed May 12, 2012.
81. Jean-Marie Henckaerts and Louise Doswald-Beck, *Customary International Humanitarian Law,* vol. I, International Committee of the Red Cross and Cambridge: Cambridge University Press, 2005.
82. However, according to Boothby (2009) the general principle of distinction as specified in Article 57(2)(ii) of the 1977 Additional Protocol I, requires the attacker to take all feasible precautions□to avoid damage to civilian persons or objects. It is difficult to see how the demand for particular care in using incendiary weapons can exceed the demand for taking all feasible precautions. W. H. Boothby, *Weapons and the law of armed conflict* (Oxford: Oxford University Press, 2009), p. 206.
83. UN Secretary-General's Bulletin on the observance by United Nations forces of IHL, UN Doc. ST/SGB/1999/13.
84. Sweden's 1991 IHL manual of 1991 provides: "There is a need to supplement the present CCW Protocol III so that the agreement constitutes a *complete prohibition of incendiary weapons*. In this way, protection of civilians could be further enhanced, and this should be extended to cover combatants." Jean-Marie Henckaerts and Louise Doswald-Beck, op. cit., p. 290.
85. The British Manual of the Law of Armed Conflict (2004), para 6.12 page 110-112.
86. The US Department of Defence, Law of War Manual, June 2015, p. 384.
87. As the international community has prohibited the use of blinding lasers, dum-dum bullets, and poison gas to protect soldiers, States parties should prohibit the use of incendiary weapons, to protect military personnel and other combatants. *Strengthening the Humanitarian Protections of Protocol III on Incendiary Weapons,* Memorandum to Convention on Conventional Weapons (CCW) Delegates, Human Rights Watch and the Harvard Law School, August 2011.
88. Bonnie Docherty, "Statement on the Civilian Harm Caused by Incendiary Weapons" at CCW Meeting, March 30, 2011, available at: http://www.hrw.org/news/2011/03/30/statement-civilian-harm-caused-incendiary-weapons, accessed January 23, 2013.
89. *Incendiary Weapons: Government Positions and Practices,* Memorandum to Convention on Conventional Weapons Delegates, Human Rights Watch and the Harvard Law School International Human Rights Clinic, April 2012, p. 20.

4

PROHIBITED CONVENTIONAL WEAPONS

Restrictions on certain weapons have existed for thousands of years. Ancient codes of war prohibited means or methods of warfare, considered barbarous, treacherous or inhumane. In the past, this process has continued by laying down specific prohibitions on certain types of weapons. The St. Petersburg Declaration of 1868 stipulated that nations should not employ arms which aggravate the sufferings of the wounded or render their death inevitable. When the dumdum bullet was invented a few years later, it was considered contrary to the 1868 Declaration. The Hague Conference in 1899, therefore, banned the use of dumdum bullet during international armed conflict.

The 1899 and 1907 Conferences at The Hague adopted conventions which also restricted the use of submarine contact mines and prohibited the use of poison or poisoned weapons as well as the use of projectiles diffusing asphyxiating or deleterious gases. It was followed by the ban on the use of "asphyxiating, poisonous or other gases and bacteriological method of warfare" by the 1925 Geneva Gas Protocol. The increased cooperation among the States in the area of weapons of mass destruction (WMD) ensured ban on "biological" and "chemical" weapons in 1972 and 1993 respectively. The trend continued and a treaty banning anti-personnel landmines was signed in 1997. The State Parties to the UN Convention on Certain Conventional Weapons (CCW),[1] in 2003, adopted the Protocol on Explosive Remnants of War (ERW).[2] In 2008, the States signed a treaty banning the use, development and trasfer of "cluster munitions,"[3] as the weapon was held responsible for killing and maiming of civilians, and obstructing economic and social development in the affected areas.

However, all States have not agreed on the ban on the weapons like anti-personnel landmines (APM), cluster munitions or recognised the serious post-conflict humanitarian problems caused by explosive remnants of war (ERW). These States, on the other hand, have justified retaining these conventional weapons in their arsenal, though they have been criticised for causing unnecessary suffering or having indiscriminate effects. This criticism of weapons has been disseminated in the reports prepared by the United Nations, the International Committee of the Red Cross (ICRC), the Stockholm International Peace Research Institute (SIPRI) and a few other international NGOs.[4]

The use of APM has been banned because it is indiscriminate and inhumane and violates basic principles of IHL. The law imposes certain restrictions on the use of means and methods of warfare.[5] IHL dictated that the armed forces must distinguish between civilian and military targets and that the injuries inflicted should be proportionate with military objectives. APM fail both the discrimination and the proportionality tests. They are indiscriminate because a landmine is triggered by its victim, whether military or civilian. Landmines are inhumane because they inflict brutal injuries and have disastrous long-term consequences. The ICRC has estimated that as many as 27,000 people are either killed or severely injured by anti-personnel landmines every year. The overwhelming majority of these victims are civilians because most landmines remain active in the ground long after the cessation of armed conflict—in some cases for up to 60 years or longer.[6] Modern arms technology has produced green-camouflage APM devoid of metal, which are difficult to detect and remove, and remain functional after a long period of time.[7]

Cluster munitions have been a significant weapon in world's arsenals. However, their use has drawn sharp criticism for its impact on civilian populations. These weapons have been used extensively in Southeast Asia, Yugoslavia, Gulf Wars, Iraq, Afghanistan and

Syria. The main problem with cluster munitions is that large number of submunitions fail to detonate, and the failure rate can go up to 30%. These submunitions are difficult to detect, and remain explosive hazards for decades, killing innocent civilians including children. The ICRC estimates that in Laos alone, 9 million to 27 million unexploded submunitions remained after the conflict, resulting in over 10,000 civilian casualties to date.

In a post-conflict scenario, ERW are to be found in many shapes and sizes, from small fuse detonators to large free-fall bombs, or missiles, weighing up to hundreds of kilograms. They are devices that usually come in metal casings designed to fragment into many tiny pieces and embed themselves at high velocity into surrounding people or objects when detonated. The explosive from ERW can cause massive trauma and death to humans in a wide radius, depending on weapon yield and intervening obstacles. Because they are devices that have failed to function as intended,[8] individual items of unexploded ordnance (UXO) are unpredictable. Over time, the condition of an item of ERW becomes even more unpredictable because of physical degradation from humidity and change of temperature. ERW could also be radioactively contaminated.[9] The impact of AMP, cluster munition and ERWs on children has been serious. In 2013, there were 1,112 child casualties in 39 states and three other areas from landmines, victim-activated improvised explosive devices (IEDs), cluster munition remnants, and other ERW. Of this total, 333 children were killed and 779 were injured.[10]

In this chapter two specific conventional weapons, anti-personnel landmines (APM) and cluster munitions, as well as the threats posed by ERW are covered.

Notes

1. The Geneva Conventions for the protection of the victims of war were adopted in 1949. These Conventions were updated in 1977 by two Additional Protocols. Although these agreements contributed to the advancement of IHL, they had certain limitations in view of subsequent arms developments. The drafting of the Additional Protocols also provided an opportunity to take another look at matters connected with the prohibition of weapons and to clarify the

relationship between IHL and disarmament. The basic rules of IHL governing methods and means of combat did not automatically impose any prohibitions or restrictions on the use of specific weapons. Therefore, an attempt was made to prohibit or restrict the use of certain conventional weapons which were deemed to be particularly inhuman. This led to the adoption of the 1980 UN Convention on Prohibitions or Restrictions on the Use of Certain Conventional Weapons which May be Deemed to Be Excessively Injurious or to Have Indiscriminate Effects, also known as the "Convention on Inhumane Weapons."

2. The term explosive remnants of war (ERW), is used to describe the explosive threat to the community in a region at the end of an armed conflict or at the beginning of a period of stability. ERW are generated in a number of ways and present a variety of hazards due to the diverse types of ammunition used. The explosive threat could be from (i) Mines and unexploded military ordnance contamination of the ground; (ii) Abandoned armoured fighting vehicles (AFV); (iii) Small arms and light weapons (SALW), including limited ammunition and explosives in the possession of civilians and non-State actors; and (iv) Abandoned and/or damaged/disrupted stockpiles of ammunition and explosives. Each of the above categories affects a population seeking to return to a normal lifestyle, depending on factors such as the density of the ERW, civilian awareness of the dangers of ERW, and the extent to which some civilians will deliberately interact with the ERW. *Explosive Remnants of War (ERW): A Threat Analysis,* The Geneva International Centre for Humanitarian Demining (GICHD), Geneva, 2002.
3. The Convention on Cluster Munitions (CCM) is the latest attempt by the international community to ban an indiscriminate weapon and humanise an armed conflict. Frustrated with the efforts of the UN to ban cluster munitions under CCW process, a number of CCW members—led by Norway—initiated negotiations in 2007 outside of the CCW to ban cluster munitions. On May 30, 2008, they reached an agreement to ban cluster munitions. The US, Russia, China, Israel, Egypt, India, and Pakistan did not participate in the talks or sign the agreement. During the Signing Conference on Oslo from December 3-4, 2008, 94 states signed the convention and four of the signatories ratified the convention at the same time. France, Germany, and the UK were among the 18 NATO members to sign the convention on later dates. The CCM, inter alia, bans the use of cluster munitions, as well as their development, production, acquisition, transfer, and stockpiling. The convention does not prohibit cluster munitions that can detect and engage a single target or explosive submunitions equipped with an electronic self-destruction or self-deactivating feature.
4. For example, The International Campaign to Ban Landmines (ICBL) is a global network in over 100 countries that works for a world free of anti-personnel landmines, where landmine survivors can lead fulfilling lives. The Campaign was awarded the Nobel Peace Prize in recognition of its efforts to bring about the 1997 Mine Ban Treaty.
5. Article 35 (1), Additional Protocol I to the Geneva Conventions of 1949.
6. Special Brochure: "Landmines Must be Stopped," International Committee of the Red Cross, Geneva, 1995, p. 4.
7. Ove Bring, "Arms Control and International Environmental Law," available at: http://www.scandinavianlaw.se/pdf/39-18.pdf, accessed October 30, 2012.
8. The reasons for explosive ordnance failure can include: production faults; poor storage (damp, too hot or too cold conditions will adversely affect the explosive composition, meaning higher failure rates); rough handling; bad firing drills (for example, failure to set electronic time fuzes properly); incorrect launch profiles

(for example, air-delivered weapons dropped too low may not have time to arm themselves properly); poor strike angles (a munition impacting at too shallow an angle may lead to fuze failure); terrain types (for example, soft ground increases the risk of fuze failure); heavy precipitation (some fuzes may initiate early due to the resistance caused by rain, leading to submunition deployment at the wrong time); and the interaction with other items of ordnance. *Explosive Remnants of War: A Global Survey*, Landmine Action 2003, pp. 8-9.

9. Today, most of the ERW in Iraq are radioactively contaminated. Kadhim Al-Muqdadi and Nadhir Al-Ansari, "The waste of wars in Iraq: Its nature, size and contaminated areas," available at: http://www.ltu.se/cms_fs/1.85152!/file/2.3%20Almuqdadi%20and%20Alansari%201.pdf, accessed February 17, 2013.
10. The Impact of Mines/ERW on Children, Landmine and Cluster Munition Monitor, Fact Sheet, November 2014.

4 A

ANTI-PERSONNEL LANDMINES

Landmines have been widely used in armed conflicts since their invention. Despite concerted efforts by various humanitarian organisations,[1] to put an end to their use, landmines continue to be placed. In modern times, since the first reported explosive landmines were invented and used in American Civil War, they have been used on a large scale in the two World Wars. In the Cold War era, landmines, in particular anti-personnel landmines (APMs), were widely used in the wars in Korea, Vietnam, Angola, Cambodia, Ethiopia, Mozambique, Nicaragua, Iraq, Somalia, Sudan, Caucasus, Gulf Wars, and the former Yugoslavia.

The unique characteristic of a mine is in its time-delayed explosive function, allowing it to remain inactive until hit by a victim. This unique and inexpensive property has led mines to be used intensively during conflicts to block enemies and opposition forces from accessing large pieces of land. Landmines are victim-activated and indiscriminate in their targets and impact. Mines emplaced during a conflict against enemy forces can still kill or injure decades later. Whoever triggers a mine, whether a soldier, a child, a woman, a farmer, or an animal, becomes its victim.[2]

Due to their widespread use in armed conflict, landmines have become one of the most significant social, economic and environmental problems of humanity. Restricting access to land, roads and water supplies, landmines have been responsible for the displacement of persons and the stagnation of infrastructure development in every region of the world. Besides causing physical harm, death, and psychological duress, they have also caused land

and soil degradation, loss of biodiversity and severe limitations to agricultural productivity.

Military use

Landmines are usually designed to attack either tanks or vehicles (anti-tank mines) or people (APMs). The main characteristic of a mine is that it is designed to be victim-actuated, which means it will detonate or explode through the "presence, proximity or contact" of its victim (a person or a vehicle) with it or its fusing mechanism. Anti-tank mines usually contain between 2 and 9 kg of explosive, and their fusing mechanism requires a pressure of about 100-300 kg to activate it. APMs are smaller, with 10-250 g of explosive, and detonate under about 5-50 kg of pressure.

There are different kinds of APMs, depending on the damage they cause. These are: (i) blast mines that cause mainly serious injuries to the feet and legs, and can often result in amputations; (ii) fragmentation mines that separate on detonation into hundreds of smaller parts, and can be spread over an area of up to 50m. Some of these mines first jump to a height of between 1-1.5m before explosion and can also cause injuries at the level of the stomach of an adult or the head of a child; and (iii) smart mines having self-destruction mechanism. After a certain time, the smart mines destroy themselves. However, there is nothing smart in these mines as they too, cannot distinguish between civilians and soldiers. Newer types of mine can be activated by proximity rather than contact pressure, but the principle of victim activation remains the same.[3] Landmines can be laid by hand, but they can also be remotely delivered by helicopter, aircraft or artillery.[4]

Historical: The predecessors of today's APM were non-explosive devices such as traps, concealed spikes and stakes that were employed by ancient armies. In the tactical defensive, the use of concealed spikes and stakes was almost identical to that of contemporary landmines. They were used by armies to enhance fortifications in static defence or to change the terrain to their advantage, often in the face of a stronger enemy. The concept of landmines can be traced back 2,000 years, making it one of the oldest weapon systems in existence. In 52 BC, in the campaign to suppress a Gallic uprising against Roman domination, Julius Caesar created elaborate defensive fortifications around the town of Alesia to meet simultaneous threats. The purpose was to provide protection for the defenders while forcing the attackers to negotiate obstacles and concealed obstructions. The use of obstacles as a "force multiplier" exhibited that defence was a superior form of combat. It increased the time and resources required to clear a breach, and provided a buffer zone for defenders who remained out of range of attacking weapons.[5] The use of concealed traps and caltrops to pierce the feet of attacking soldiers or the hooves of horses, camels and elephants became a feature of war throughout the ages.

The introduction of gunpowder for military purposes led to the gradual improvement of landmines. During the thirteenth century, the first self-contained APM was employed by the Chinese against Mongol invaders. These APM could be activated with either a pressure or pull-firing device. However, these devices were highly vulnerable to dampness and required frequent maintenance.[6]

During the American Civil War (1861-1865), the development of electrical initiation systems along with improved manufacturing techniques greatly improved the reliability of landmines. Confederate forces used landmines in an attempt to redress the imbalance between the competing armies. Pressure-operated mines were deployed in belts to create or enhance defensive positions, or individually to inflict casualties and create caution. The use of landmines continued as the war progressed. The total number of landmines used during the Civil War was probably less than 20,000, resulting in a few hundred casualties.

During colonial expeditions, the British Army used landmines in the Sudan campaign (1884-1888) and the Boer War (1899-1902). Landmines were employed during the Russo-Japanese War (1902-1904) to defend trenches. These included electrically initiated, vibration and pressure sensitive mines; however, many of the landmines failed to explode.

World War I and II: Despite the massive scale of the First World War, the use of APM was not widespread. Machine guns, artillery and barbed wire were used successfully to stop massed infantry advances. Modern landmines were used to free summits or mountain flanks from enemy forces during the War. During the Second World War, APM were used to surround anti-tank mines to protect them from removal and eventually they were used as weapons in their own right. The Germans incorporated landmines into the overall tactical setting to ensure a higher kill ratio. Landmines were laid according to several principles: they were marked and recorded, covered with small arms fire, used to enhance other obstacles (ditches and wire), and mixed fields of anti-tank and APM was laid. Tactical (in front of defensive positions), nuisance (along lines of communication), random (at positions likely to be occupied by enemy), and dummy minefields were employed.

During the War, APM were always covered with fire, normally from both small arms and anti-tank weapons. Often, the Germans would wait until the enemy had infiltrated well inside the minefield before opening fire. This tactic was very effective as it mutilated and maimed enemy troops. The German S-mine was probably the most feared and respected device encountered by Allied troops in World War II. The Germans were able to engineer and produce mines following a number of fundamental principles: they were reliable, economical, simple, durable and used standardised sizes and interchangeable parts to ensure compatibility.[7] Throughout the war, mines had caused the Allies considerable anxiety.

Post-World War II: Since 1945, mine designs have concentrated on effectiveness, size, detectability, logistical effort and speed of laying. Modern refinements in technology, including synthetic materials and electronics, have contributed to the evolution of APM.[8] Advances in mine technology accelerated, and Korea and Vietnam became testing grounds for new generations of weapons, including the APMs. The US in the early 1960s, used remotely delivered APM, to stop the flow of troops and supplies from North Vietnam to South Vietnam through Laos and Cambodia.[9]

During the UN operation in Korea (1951-53), the US, Canadian, British, Australian, New Zealand, Turkish, Chinese, North and South Korean forces used primarily APMs, because of the preponderance of North Korean and Chinese infantry. In one incident Australian forces suffered 5 casualties when they entered an unmarked and unrecorded minefield, which were laid by the Canadians around an outpost. Minefield marking suffered considerably as a result of Chinese artillery bombardment and heavy rains. The UN-laid APMs were regularly used as a source of mines and explosives by the Chinese.

The war in Vietnam (1958-1975) provided a test case for the successful use of APM against a superior enemy who was on the offensive. APM and booby traps were a consistent problem for the US Army. Although the war was won due to a number of factors, APM slowed advancing troops, and, in combination with the dense jungle, made movement difficult. The Viet Cong took APM out of their traditional role, and used them as offensive weapons to attack and harass their opponent. The use of APM and booby traps had an adverse effect on the US military, as they were forced to allocate manpower and resources to mitigate the threat posed by mines. As a result, APM and booby traps caused up to 11% of the US casualties and about 15% were wounded in action (compared to less than 4% in the Second World War and Korea). Most of the US casualties occurred during road clearing operations.

The French, North Vietnamese, South Vietnamese, Americans or Australians did not maintain records of their minefields, especially those dropped from the air. In general, mines were not marked, especially the many tons of mines and submunitions dropped on the Ho Chi Minh trail in Viet Nam, Cambodia and Laos.[10] In the end, stealth, dispersion, concealment and simplicity countered superior technology and manpower.[11]

The mine warfare carried out by both parties during the India-Pakistan Wars (1947-48, 1965, 1971), was unique in the way in which it was conducted. These wars were also remarkable for the restraint and responsibility shown by both sides. A very small number of mines were laid during these wars to protect certain installations. In all three cases, mine warfare was conducted by well-trained and disciplined soldiers. Minefields were carefully mapped, and maps were made available by both parties after the conflict, allowing the early removal of the mines and the return of the land for agriculture. The limited nature of the wars and their short duration ensured that the mine problem remained relatively small, and both parties had the resources to clear the mines almost immediately after each confrontation.[12] During its face-off with Pakistan in 2002, India laid APMs along its western border. This was one of the largest landmine-laying operations anywhere in the world in those years. By the end of the year, more than 80 Indian army personnel had lost their lives and many more were injured in mine-laying. Civilian casualties in mine explosion were also high.[13]

During the Arab-Israeli Wars of 1967 and 1973, the Israeli, Egyptian and Syrian armies laid minefields on their borders. Though, the Israeli army handed over its minefield maps, casualties were sustained by both Egyptian and Israeli soldiers after the cease-fire. The UN disengagement forces also suffered casualties, during mine clearance operations.

On gaining independence in 1980, Zimbabwe inherited over 1.5 million APM, scattered in eight minefields running 766 km along her borders with Zambia and Mozambique. The oldest had been laid around the Kariba Power Station before 1963 by the Rhodesian federal government following a dispute over control of the facility with the emerging nationalist government in Northern Rhodesia (now Zambia). The rest were intended as barriers against guerrilla infiltration during the war of liberation, beginning in 1974.[14] These mines have been responsible for the killing of about 100 innocent civilians and maiming of more than 500 individuals.

Civil Wars in Mozambique, Angola, Bosnia, Croatia and other countries significantly increased the spread of these weapons. In Cambodia, it was estimated that approximately six to ten million landmines have been laid between 1983 and 1992, compared to a population of eight million to nine million inhabitants. Bosnia and Croatia had a combined figure of between two-and-a-half million and four-and-a-half million landmines, and included some of the world's most difficult mines to detect and many of the mines were neither marked nor mapped.[15]

In the war in Afghanistan, the Soviets laid between 30-50 million mines, including many non-metallic mines that were extremely hard to detect. The Soviets also made extensive use of booby traps that were air dropped or scattered outside plotted minefields. It is estimated that these mines killed and maimed between 25,000 and 50,000 Mujahideen soldiers and civilians. The Mujahideen also made extensive use of APM, many of which were retrieved from Soviet minefields or supplied from external sources. Today, Afghanistan is one of the most heavily mined countries in the world. Over 530 sq km area of Afghanistan have now been identified as contaminated by mines and UXOs.[16]

During the Iran-Iraq war (1980-1989), both parties used APM. Breaching of minefields was at times carried out, in the absence of modern means, by "martyrs," including children, who stormed across minefields to open the way for professional forces. Few of the mines used by either side were marked or mapped, but they have not been cleared. The mines left from the Iran-Iraq war in Kurdistan were also used by the Iraqi government for deliberate harassment of the civilian population.[17]

During the Operation Desert Storm (1992), after the capture of Kuwait, the Iraqi armed forces laid an estimated 9 million mines on the beaches to the east and in protective mine belts to the south and west. These mine belts mainly contained mixed APM and anti-tank mines. Most of the mines were laid in patterns, and on the surface, but they soon became partially or totally covered by sand.[18]

These mines failed to slow, much less stop, the Coalition's ground attack because the Iraqis were reluctant to aggressively patrol and defend their barriers, they placed too much emphasis on artillery, and they did not deploy effective anti-armour capability in forward areas. In addition, the Coalition had enough equipment to penetrate minefields and barriers without extensive dismounting, and had a decisive advantage in fire, air support and mechanisation during the operation. Landmines introduced in Kuwait have caused significant short- and long-term damage to the environment, resulting in soil erosion, destruction of vegetation and topsoil and negatively impacting wildlife.

The years of conflict in Bosnia-Herzegovina (1992-1995) have left areas of major contamination, with an estimated 3-6 million mines remaining uncleared, including some sophisticated APMs. Mines were used by all parties to the conflict, most of which were of former Yugoslav manufacture and primarily made of plastic. In 1997, the United Nations Mine Action Centre (UNMAC) estimated that there were over 30,000 mined areas in Bosnia and Herzegovina, littered with some 750,000 mines. Most minefields were unmarked and posed a threat in the post-war environment. The mines prevented refugees and displaced persons from returning to their pre-war communities. They were also used for the protection of private properties. The effect of landmines in Bosnia and Herzegovina was widespread and had its impact at all levels of society. The mines contaminated fertile agriculture land, severely reducing food production. Due to the presence of landmines, rehabilitation activities like restoration of water supply and the resumption of the logging industry remained affected for nearly two years after the end of hostilities.[19]

The area close to the border between Eritrea and Ethiopia is presently heavily affected by mines laid in the 1998-2000 war between the two countries. Ethiopia currently suffers from problems related to UXO, as well as landmines, and ten of its eleven districts have UXO and APM problems, although APM problems are concentrated in areas bordering Eritrea, including Tigray and Afar.[20]

Forces of the Islamic State (ISIS) fighting the government of Iraq have used victim-activated improvised mines, including explosive booby-traps, extensively since 2014. Boko Haram militants have allegedly been laying unspecified types of landmines in Nigeria since mid-2014. The government of Ukraine has stated that since 2014, it had not used APM in the conflict and accused Russian forces of laying landmines in Ukraine. In September 2016, Ukraine's Department of Defence reported that pro-Russian separatists had laid POM-2 APM including improvised mines in its territory. In July 2016, South Korea's Yonhap News Agency alleged the use of mine by North Korea in the demilitarized zone (DMZ) between the two countries.

In 2015, there was a sharp rise in the number of people killed and injured by APM, improvised mines, and other ERW. It has been reported that in 2015, there were 6,461 mine/ERW casualties, of which at least 1,672 people were killed. This sharp increase in casualties was due to more casualties recorded in armed conflicts in Libya, Syria, Ukraine, and Yemen. The increase also reflects greater availability of casualty data, particularly from unique systematic surveys of persons injured in Libya and Syria in 2015.

APM has also been used by the police forces, insurgent groups and warlords for purposes of population control and terrorism. Recovered mines have even been used by civilians to protect their own property.[21] During internal armed conflicts, APM have been deployed by irregular forces against government troops in Northern Ireland, Spain, India and Sri Lanka.

The new use of APM by NSAGs in conflicts in Ukraine and Yemen and continued large-scale use of victim-activated improvised mines across Afghanistan, Iraq, Nigeria, Pakistan, Syria, and Yemen is particularly disturbing. According to Pakistan, NSAGs in Baluchistan and the Federally Administered Tribal Areas (FATA) have used APM and victim-activated explosive devices. These victim-activated mines are often referred to as improvised explosive devices (IEDs) or booby-traps.[22]

Military Necessity

During conventional warfare, up until the time of the Gulf Wars, landmines were mainly used by armies as defensive weapons, to create protective obstacles, often in conjunction with other natural obstacles such as hill features or river lines. These obstacles, which are frequently linked in the form of an obstacle belt, are normally designed to delay the enemy advance by breaking up its attack formations and canalising them into areas where they can be attacked by other weapons such as artillery, tank guns, rockets and ground attack aircraft. Where a large-scale assault of armoured forces is intended, minefields usually consist of anti-tank mines; however APM have often been laid amongst them to prevent the enemy from hand-lifting the mines during an assault on the minefield.

In a study undertaken by the ICRC, it has been reported that APM are not indispensable weapons of high military value and they do not necessarily offer any military advantage. Their use in accordance with military doctrine is time-consuming, expensive and dangerous and has seldom occurred under combat conditions. Landmines are not needed by a modern army. While in the past they may have protected borders and slowed advancing troops, now most armies are mobile and can get through a minefield in less than 30 minutes. Modern motion detection equipment, night detection technology and strategically placed guns can protect military installations, borders and other areas better than landmines.[23]

A number of authoritative analysts have concluded that APM have proven to be weapons of severely limited utility. General Sagren (1994), Commander-in-Chief of the Swedish Army, has stated "APM are not of vital importance to the Swedish national Defence." British General Sir Hugh Beach testified to the House of Commons in 1995: "where 'Regular military use' is concerned there is no case known where APM as such have influenced a campaign, a battle or even a skirmish in any decisive way."[24] Former US Marine Corps Commandant Alfred Gray has opined: "I know of no situation in the Korean War, nor in the five years I served in Southeast Asia, nor in Panama, nor Desert Shield-Desert Storm where our use of mine warfare truly channelised the enemy and brought him into a destructive pattern. I'm not aware of any operational advantage from the broad deployment of the APM. It is only a delaying element that does not stop the creation of the breach or the subsequent attack. It can therefore be argued that the APM has become less relevant to modern armoured warfare."[25]

Mines used to protect military camps are considered to have a certain deterrent value while at the same time, they create a number of specific problems. In order to prevent easy infiltration they need constant monitoring, as do other minefields. They need constant maintenance because the minefield is regularly damaged by heavy precipitation, erosion of the soil (especially when chemical means are used to keep down vegetation), enemy attacks and frequent incursions by animals. Dead animals mean that the mines they detonated are no longer active; moreover the carcasses begin to rot and cause both a stench and a health hazard. Since soldiers have to enter these areas regularly to clean up the mess and replace the mines, accidents are not uncommon.

The Dangers of Landmines

It is believed that each year 2-5 million new mines are put in the ground, adding to "one of the most widespread, lethal and long-lasting forms of pollution" the world has ever known.[26] It is estimated that 20 new mines are laid for every mine that is cleared. Landmines are produced as "weapons of war," but in fact only 10 per cent of landmine victims are soldiers. The United Nations has reckoned that landmines are at least ten times more likely to kill or injure a civilian after a conflict than a combatant during hostilities. In 1994, the United Nations had projected that if the use of mines were stopped immediately it would take about 1,100 years and $33 billion dollars to clear, at current rates, those already in place.[27] They are also long-lasting. No estimate has been given for the "life" of a mine; however, mines laid in Libya and Europe during World War II are still active and causing casualties over 50 years later. Modern plastic-cased mines, which are stable and waterproof, are likely to remain a hazard for many decades. The presence of landmines in a country is one of the most socially, environmentally and economically damaging legacies of war that the world is facing today. According to Landmine Monitor Report 2016:

- In 2015, there were 6,461 mine/IED casualties, of which at least 1,672 people were killed, marking a 75% increase from casualties recorded for 2014.
- The vast majority of recorded landmine/IEDs casualties were civilians (78%) and children accounted for 38% of all civilian casualties.
- Non-state armed groups (NSAG) mostly used improvised explosive devises (IEDs) and booby traps, which are banned by the Mine Ban Treaty as they explode due to the presence, proximity, or contact of a person.
- Sixty-four states and areas are contaminated by antipersonnel mines as of October 2016. This includes 36 States Parties to the Mine Ban Treaty, 24 states not party, and four other areas.
- Massive antipersonnel mine contamination (more than 100 km^2 total per country) is believed to exist in Afghanistan, Angola, Azerbaijan, Bosnia and Herzegovina, Cambodia, Chad, Croatia, Iraq, Thailand, Turkey, and in the area of Western Sahara.

Consequences of Landmines

APM stand out from other weapons of warfare, because of their very persistent, undiscriminating and uncontrolled nature. The global landmine calamity has transcended both humanitarian and sociological concerns to bring about environmental damage. But unfortunately, it is also one of the least studied and documented environmental problems.[28] In scale, the landmine crisis is global, affecting many countries in Africa, the Americas, Asia and Europe. However, the problem is ultra-hazardous to the environment and development of a number of developing nations. A third of all developing countries are experiencing some form of landmine crisis.[29]

Impact on Human Life

Landmines remain a daily threat to the community. APMs cannot distinguish between civilians and soldiers. They continue to kill and maim civilians long after the fighting has ceased. Vast areas of valuable land are put out of use, destroying livelihoods. Communities can be affected for decades after the end of an armed conflict. Of all continents, Africa is the most severely affected by landmines,[30] and 22 countries are facing this problem. Fifteen countries in Asia are affected by landmines,[31] 11 in Europe and 8 in the Americas.

Landmines continue to maim and kill civilians long after hostilities have officially ceased. Even decades after cease-fire children, farmers, nomads, herders, returning refugees and internally displaced persons continue to fall victim to landmines. Mine blast injuries place a tremendous immediate burden on health care resources. According to a recent report, nearly 500,000 people live with injuries inflicted by mines. Many victims are both severely handicapped and unable to afford the rehabilitation and the other services that they need. Victims are often not economically productive, and may have lost their economic value to the community. The conflict in Syria has caused the largest displacement crisis of our time. These refugees, asylum seekers, returnees, and internally displaced person (IDPs) remain especially vulnerable to landmines when they are leaving, entering, or staying in countries contaminated by these explosive hazards. Syrian refugees today encounter risks due to landmine and ERW contamination along Syria's border areas.[32]

Improvised Explosive Devices (IED)

Improvised Explosive Devices (IEDs) threaten security, stability, humanitarian operations, and sustainable development in communities around the world. There has been a marked increase in the unlawful use of improvised explosive devices (IEDs), particularly by NSAGs and rogue individuals.[33] Such IED attacks deliberately target concentrations of civilians to achieve a maximum effect of lethality, terror and societal disruption; and they currently occur globally on a scale of hundreds per month. Casualties from IED attacks have been very high. During the period from 2011 to 2015 IED there have been more than 6,300 recorded IED explosions, resulting in over 105,000 casualties. The majority of IED attacks occur in populated areas, causing harm overwhelmingly to civilians.[34] In the period 2011-2015, 82 per cent of recorded casualties were civilians.[35]

IEDs have recently been used from India to the United States of America, from Norway to Turkey, from Colombia to Belgium and from the Russian Federation to Thailand. The countries most affected by IED attacks are Afghanistan, Iraq, Nigeria, Pakistan and Syria. In addition to violating international humanitarian law, the use of IEDs against civilians affects the entire spectrum of their human rights, including the rights to life, physical security, education and health.

The United Nations has defined an IED as, "A device placed or fabricated in an improvised manner incorporating explosive material, destructive, lethal, noxious, incendiary, pyrotechnic materials or chemicals designed to destroy, disfigure, distract or harass. They may incorporate military stores, but are normally devised from non-military components.[36] The term "improvised" can be misleading in the sense that some IED users and networks have quite sophisticated production capabilities. They may include chemical, biological, radiological, incendiary or even nuclear elements.[37]

IED makers strive continuously to alter the characteristics, functioning or delivery context of a device. IEDs generally consist of a switch, power source, initiator, container and explosives. Initiation methods include time-controlled, command-initiated, radio-controlled, and victim-operated systems. Main charges can be drawn from commercial or military explosives. Casings can range from soda cans, plastic bags, pressure cookers and shoeboxes to suicide vests, gas cylinders and trucks. In some instances, booby traps meet the definition of an IED as well.

IED components can be sourced from conventional munitions, such as artillery shells, mortar bombs and landmines, which are found in government and non-state actor stockpiles and abandoned military positions, and in explosive remnants of war both in conflict areas and where active hostilities have ceased. The components are easily available and include fertilizer, bleach (peroxide), nail polish remover, brake fluid, herbicides, disinfectants and cleaning solvents. Their trade, transfer and storage are not subjected to a strict scrutiny and regulation as compared to storage and transfer of munitions. Commercial explosives and detonators for mining and construction are also sought-after components. IEDs may be packed with additional materials, such as nails or ball bearings, to enhance fragmentation. Enhancements may also include copper plates, which can threaten the integrity of armoured vehicles and pose a particular threat to the police and military personnel. IEDs can be statically deployed or hand-launched, delivered by vehicle, boat, aircraft, or rocket launcher or by mail or strapped to a person or animal.

Impact on Environment

The impacts of APM on soil, flora and fauna, and people are felt at different levels of the ecological system, whether the mines have detonated or not. The ways in which landmines cause land degradation are broadly classified into five groups: access denial, loss of biodiversity, micro-relief disruption, chemical contamination, and loss of productivity.

Access denial: It is estimated that globally, landmines have denied access to or degraded 900,000 sq km of land.[38] The fear of presence of even a single APM can deny people access to land that they desperately need for agriculture, water supply or to undertake conservation measures, and for technical teams engaged in pest control. Landmines have been used in large quantities around arable lands in Lebanon, Angola, Mozambique, Cambodia; pasturelands in the Sinai, Kuwait and Iraq; forests in Nicaragua and the demilitarised zone between North and South Korea; coastal areas in Kuwait and

Egypt; borders, infrastructures (bridges, roads, electrical installations, canals and water sources) and nearby commercial and public centres in Vietnam, Zimbabwe, Eritrea and Ethiopia; and residential areas in Serbia. One study has shown that the detonation of UXO in the Vietnamese province of Quang Tri has drastically reduced soil productivity. According to estimates, rice production per hectare has decreased 50 per cent in this area. Access denial restricts development activities. When landmines restrict access to arable or pastoral lands, the people who depended on those lands are pushed to use or abuse marginal resources, or move into refugee camps or urban centres, depending on the availability of alternatives.

Biodiversity loss: Landmines can threaten biodiversity in affected regions by destroying vegetation cover during explosions or demining, and when animals fall victim. They also pose an extra burden for threatened and endangered species. Landmines have been blamed for pushing various species to the brink of extinction. Many of the biodiversity loss hotspots of the world are severely affected by landmines. A large number of species are threatened or endangered due to many factors, including the presence of landmines in their habitat or migratory paths. Moreover, landmines are used for poaching endangered species of wildlife.[39]

In Bosnia and Croatia, where landmines are still common, brown bears are regular victims. In India, rare species such as barking deer, clouded leopard, snow leopards, and Royal Bengal tigers have been killed by landmines. In Libya, gazelles are reported to have disappeared from sites that were mined during World War II. Mines also threaten rare and endangered species. They have killed elephants in Africa and Sri Lanka, pushed snow leopards to the brink of extinction in Afghanistan, and killed a few silver-backed mountain gorillas in Rwanda. Native tigers are threatened by landmines in Cambodia. In Tibet, rare species of clouded leopard, barking deer, snow leopard, and Royal Bengal tiger have been reported as casualties of landmines—either maimed or killed. In the Democratic Republic of the Congo, rebel forces tested some fields for the presence of landmines by herding cattle across them.[40]

After 25 years of civil war, which ended with a peace agreement signed in April 2002, Angola's parks and reserves have been reduced to just 10% of their 1975 wildlife population levels. This has been the result of a combination of deforestation, habitat loss, and soldiers hunting for food and poaching for tusks. Elephants, black rhinos, and buffalos are among those which have been slaughtered for these purposes. Poaching is an increasingly attractive pursuit for guerrilla fighters who use it as a way to generate income for the purchase of weapons and other equipment. Angola's national wildlife reserves were abandoned throughout the conflict, and the countryside has been virtually depopulated. There have been reports of antelopes and elephants killed by landmines during the civil war in Angola.[41]

Landmines also introduce poisonous substances into the environment as their casings corrode and decay. Mines commonly use 2, 4, 6-trinitrotoluene (TNT) and RDX, which can leach into the surrounding soil and water as the metal or timber casings disintegrate. These substances and the compounds derived from them are soluble in water, have long-life, are carcinogenic and toxic, even in small quantities. TNT and RDX are lethal to mammals, aquatic micro-organisms, and fish.

Micro-relief disruption: Landmine detonation causes damage to the soil's stability by shattering the soil structure, and causing local compaction, and increasing the susceptibility of soil to erosion. Deterioration of soil structure due to explosion, compaction or burning can be a slow and insidious progression, but their combination results in long-term changes that have significant, sustained impacts on moisture availability, erodibility and productivity of the land. When a 250 g APM is detonated, it can create a crater with a diameter of approximately 30 cm. The explosion would result in the removal and displacement of topsoil while forming a raised circumference around the crater and compaction of soil into the side of the crater.[42] The level of the impact can vary depending on the physical conditions of the soil; the type and composition of the explosive and how many landmines detonate in the vicinity. The impact is greater in dry, loosely compacted and exposed desert soils but is less severe in humid soils that have vegetation or physical protection. Micro-relief disruption can also occur during demining operations affecting biochemical and physical quality of the soil.

Chemical contamination: Landmines interfere with the ability of the soil system to serve as a geochemical sink for contaminants (i.e., act as a natural buffer to control the exchange of elements between the atmosphere, hydrosphere and biota). Depending on density of mines per unit area; the type and composition of the mine; and the length, amount and degree of exposure of resources to the mines, landmines can pose a serious pollutions threat, accumulation of non-biodegradable toxic waste of casings or unexploded remnants. Moreover, after conflicts, many regions are left with a massive volume of exploded and unexploded ordinances that ruin the aesthetic quality of the area.

Landmines are made of metal, timber or plastic casing and are filled with trinitrotoluene (TNT), RDX or Cyclonite, or tetryl. Landmines can also introduce other non-biodegradable and toxic waste, such as DU. These compounds have been known to leach into soil and underground water as casings of the mines disintegrates.[43] Specific contaminants have unique consequences and the effects depend on many complex factors. Many of the organic and inorganic substances and compounds that are derived from the explosives are long-lasting, water-soluble and toxic even in small amounts. The contamination can be delivered directly or indirectly into soil, water bodies, micro-organisms and plants with drinking water, food products or during respiration. These pollutant compounds can leach into subterranean waters and bioaccumulate in the organs of land animals, fish and plants. Their effects can be mortal to some mammals and aquatic macro- and micro-organisms by acting as a nerve poison to hamper growth.[44] Lead toxicity from landmines can be harmful even at very small amounts, and its effects rise with increasing concentration. In human beings lead toxicity can result in kidney damage, sterility, miscarriage, and birth defects. Moreover, high levels of mercury can result in neurological disorder; while cadmium can cause kidney failure and softening of bones leading to fracture.[45]

Loss of productivity: Landmines affect resource productivity whether they have detonated or not. Low availability of land (access denial), degradation of the soil (micro-relief disruption, chemical contamination), combined with loss of flora and fauna add up to land degradation and subsequent reduction in productivity. Landmines have restricted agricultural production on a land area equivalent to 6 per cent of the 1,474 million ha of land cultivated globally.[46] One study has shown that the detonation of UXO in the Vietnamese province of Quang Tri has drastically reduced soil productivity. According to estimates, rice production per hectare has decreased 50 per cent in this area. When people cannot get access to their land resources because it is no longer safe to enter it, a whole host of problems are created. Land degradation leads to many complex socio-politico-economic problems, including exploitation of available resources beyond their ecological carrying capacity, unemployment, poverty, and social marginalisation.

Demining and Land-degradation

The demining[47] operations to alleviate the impact of landmines are conducted in ways that cause degradation and, in some instances, irreversible damage to the environment. Due to the lack of an effective environmental management system, three environmental issues surface during demining operations. These issues are: (i) conservation of soil and erosion control; (ii) preservation of vegetation and natural wildlife; and (iii) limiting the adverse effects of human presence.[48]

Major challenge faced by the mine-action community is the balancing act of removing mines from the ground while simultaneously protecting the contaminated soil from further damage. Many mine removal and disposal methods can ultimately have an unfavourable effect on the environment, particularly on fragile soil structures. Clearance operations are divided into three main varieties: manual demining, mine-detection dogs and mechanical-demining systems. These three types are used interchangeably and cooperatively, creating an integrated methodology capable of confronting most mine-clearance challenges. However, improper implementation and management of these methods can severely compromise soil integrity. Irreversible damage to soil quality and structure can be devastating to local communities, especially those dependent on the land for survival. For example, a 2002 study conducted in Africa described the deterioration of soil fertility as being "a major biophysical cause of low per capita food production."[49]

Landmines are clandestine weapons; they are most effective when well-hidden. When available, their users rely on the natural cover provided by vegetation. This presents a serious problem for mine-clearance teams: While the removal of vegetation is necessary to allow for the safe removal of mines, indiscriminate vegetation clearance can have drastic effects on the environment. Because manual deminers and mine-detection dog teams require a clear view of the ground in order to safely detect and dispose of hidden explosives, vegetation clearance is often the first step of the physical demining process. The Environmental Impact Assessments (EIA) is generally not considered vital to the demining. The impacts of demining on vegetation and wildlife are similar to those imposed on the soil. Demining operations may also damage the natural habitats of insects and wildlife and affect areas of historical or cultural significance. In the process of clearing Iraqi minefields, bomb disposal units ploughed up large areas of the desert, tearing up and damaging fragile and slow-growing vegetation and destroying habitat for numerous animal species.

Demining activities also influence biodiversity in many ways. Domesticated animals are frequently used for mine clearance purposes, especially dogs, sheep and cattle.[50] These animals are let loose in minefields as easy and fast means of clearance. Furthermore, demining operations demand clearing all the vegetative cover, including forests from mine-suspected areas, usually by using fire. The result is removal of litter that plays crucial roles in infiltration, protecting soil from erosion and the impact of rain drops, and providing organic matter that is important to biota and stability of soil's structure.

The humanitarian-demining process involves more than just detection, removal and disposal of explosive remnants of war. Demining implies a much wider range of related activities, "including technical survey, mapping, clearance, marking, post-clearance documentation, community mine-action liaison and the handover of cleared land."[51] Each activity is time-consuming, often requiring a prolonged human presence in the mine-affected area.

For longer demining projects, the construction of temporary support facilities is required and often occurs in the vicinity of mine-affected areas as location is critical during facilities mobilisation. When choosing a location, the obvious priority is that it be safe, isolated from the threats posed by the mine-affected area. Extensive clearance of existing vegetation, such as might occur during the creation of access routes, often results in difficulties with natural vegetation recovery, yielding an unnecessary loss in the area's biodiversity. Human waste materials are also potentially harmful to the environment. Regular maintenance of mechanical-demining equipment often results in hazardous by-products, including toxic oils and fuels. If mishandled or improperly discharged, these materials could have substantial adverse impact on local water supplies by way of natural runoff.

The quick and effective methods for demining can sometimes result in equally deplorable situations. Land once arable can become infertile, unable to provide much-needed agricultural resources. Although motivated by the best of intentions, certain actions may ultimately prove to be more harmful than any number of landmines could be.[52]

APM and Economic Growth

APM slow repatriation of refugees and displaced people, or even prevent it altogether. They hamper the provision of aid and relief services and threaten, injure and kill aid workers. Medical treatment for landmine victims, where available, is costly, burdening an already overstretched health-care system. Communities are deprived of their productive land: farm land, orchards, irrigation canals and water points may be no longer accessible. Mines also cut off access to economically important areas, such as roads, electricity pylons and dams. A landmine incident may cost a family their breadwinner. Vocational training and support are often not available so many survivors struggle to make a living after their accident. On the flipside, a mine-affected country stands to gain international assistance for mine clearance and victim assistance once they ban landmines and join the Mine Ban Treaty. Donor governments are understandably reluctant to fund demining in countries until they have given up landmines altogether.

Landmines and demining both accelerate environmental damage by several mechanisms: fear of mines denies access to abundant natural resources and arable land; populations are forced to move preferentially into marginal and fragile environments in order to avoid minefields; this migration speeds depletion of biological diversity; and landmine explosions disrupt the essential soil and water processes. The limited productive land that is available is over-cultivated, which contributes to long-term underproduction, as minerals are depleted from the soil. Furthermore, landmines introduce poisonous substances into the environment as their casings erode. In spite of intensive efforts at clearance and deactivation of landmines, millions of hectares remain under interdiction in Europe, North Africa and Asia. In Libya one-third of its land mass is considered contaminated by landmines and unexploded munitions from World War II. When these mines explode, in addition to causing serious injury and death to humans, domestic animals and wildlife, they shatter soil systems, destroy plant life and disrupt water flows, accelerating ecosystem disruption.

Landmines kill livestock and cause serious loss. In Libya between 1940 and 1980, mines and other UXO have killed more than 125,000 camels, sheep, goats, and cattle. There were about 264,000 goats and sheep killed in Afghanistan, at a value of about $ 31.6 million dollars. The total direct cost of damage caused by mines to animals was about $ 155 million.[53] In subsistence pastoral and agricultural societies where livestock possession is an important wealth, the economic and social impacts of livestock losses can be devastating.

Interactions between natural disasters and buried landmines slow attempts to define areas and protect populations. For instance, the floods in Mozambique in 1999 and 2000 displaced the hundreds of thousands of APM left from the civil war. Landmines have been placed by non-state actors with complete disregard to IHL to mark, map, monitor and remove them. Hence, the majority of the victims of APM explosions are civilians engaged in daily farming or foraging activities. The countryside of Kosovo was rimmed and internally laced with landmines laid by all sides. After years of international efforts to remove them, an estimated 750 suspected minefields still remain.[54]

APM have long-term negative repercussions on national development. In Libya, according to a United Nations study, about 27 per cent of the total arable land is unusable. It is still covered by minefields dating back to WW II, more than 65 years ago. In northern Iraq, according to UN Department of Humanitarian Affairs, some 17 per cent arable land is infested with mines, and in border areas this figure rises to 50 per cent.[55]

The Mine Ban Treaty

The 1997 Convention on the Prohibition of the Use, Stockpiling, Production and Transfer of Anti-Personnel Mines and on their Destruction (Mine Ban Treaty) came into force on March 1, 1999.[56] Since the treaty has entered into force, the States are no longer required to sign it; rather they may become bound without signature through accession. According to Article 16 (2), the treaty is open for accession by any State that has not signed. Treaty comprehensively bans the use, production, stockpiling, and transfer of anti-personnel mines, and requires states to destroy their stockpiles within four years and to clear all mined areas within 10 years. As on July 31, 2017, there are 162 States Party to the treaty.

The Mine Ban Treaty had a significant impact on worldwide use, production and trade of APM. Its use among the States is rare and by the non-State armed groups is declining. Production of APM has ceased in States and the legal trade in these weapons is virtually non-existent. There are 34 non-signatory countries including China, India, Russia and the US;[57] and some of these countries have large stockpiles of APM. According to Landmine Monitor's estimates, 12 States are still producing mines or retaining the right to do so;[58] while 3 governments (Israel, Libya and Myanmar) are still laying landmines.

The 1996 Amended Protocol on Prohibitions or Restrictions on the Use of Mines, Booby Traps and Other Devices (Protocol II), to the 1980 CCW provides more restrictive regulation of the use of landmines. The Amended Protocol obliges parties (including non-State parties covered by the AP II to the 1949 Geneva Conventions) to clear landmines as soon as possible after the cessation of hostilities. Each party to a conflict is responsible for all mines deployed by it and must undertake to clear, remove, destroy, or maintain them under the terms of the Protocol.[59] In particular, the Amended Protocol stipulates that the deployment of all landmines, booby traps, and other such devices must be registered, while remotely delivered anti-personnel mines must be equipped with self-destruct and self-deactivation mechanisms and detectable. It also prohibits the use of mines, booby traps, and other such devices that explode when detected with magnetic equipment.[60] The two regimes, the Mine Ban Treaty and CCW Protocol II operate independently at present. The 1949 Geneva Conventions only address the issue of mine clearance, expressly prohibiting the forcible use of prisoners of war for such purposes.[61]

The use of IEDs is governed by IHL and by international human rights law. The only existing directly relevant legal instrument that explicitly mentions IEDs is the Protocol on Prohibitions or Restrictions on the Use of Mines, Booby Traps and Other Devices as amended on 3 May 1996 (Amended Protocol II) to the Convention on Prohibitions or Restrictions on the Use of Certain Conventional Weapons Which May Be Deemed to Be Excessively Injurious or to Have Indiscriminate Effects. During an armed conflict, the CCW Protocol II [62] prohibits the use of "devices that are designed or of a nature to cause superfluous injury or unnecessary suffering", "against the civilian population as such or against individual civilians or civilian objects" or in an "indiscriminate" manner.[63]

The UN has an important role to play in addressing both the security and humanitarian impacts of IEDs. The UN has shown deep concerns at the humanitarian and development problems caused by APM, IED and ERW, which have serious and lasting social and economic consequences for the populations in affected countries, and negatively affect the delivery of humanitarian assistance. The Secretary General has urged the states having the capacity, as well as the UN systems and other organizations and institutions involved in mine action, to support mine-affected States by providing:

- Assistance to establish and develop national mine action capacities;
- Support for national programmes, in cooperation with the relevant bodies of the UN system and relevant regional, governmental and NGOs, to reduce the risks posed by APM, IED and ERW, taking into consideration the different needs of women, girls, boys and men;
- Reliable, predictable, and timely contributions for mine action activities, including those relating to rapid response in humanitarian emergencies, victim assistance and mine risk education, especially at the local level, as well as through relevant national, regional and global trust funds, including the Voluntary Trust Fund for Assistance in Mine Action;

- Necessary technical, financial and material assistance to locate, remove, destroy and otherwise render ineffective minefields, mines, IED, booby traps, and ERW in accordance with international law;
- Technological assistance to promote user-oriented scientific research and development of mine action techniques and technology which are effective, sustainable, appropriate and environmentally sound.[64]

Customary Obligations

Although the use of landmines is not prohibited by custom, the parties to armed conflict have certain obligations under customary IHL in the use of APM. The ICRC report on Customary IHL states the following restrictions on the use of APM: (i) when landmines are used, particular care must be taken to minimise their indiscriminate effects (Rule 81); (ii) a party to conflict using landmines must record their placement, as far as possible (Rule 82); (iii) at the end of active hostilities, a party to the conflict which has used landmines must remove or otherwise render them harmless to civilians or facilitate their removal (Rule 83).[65] Thus the ICRC study finds two unique customary IHL principles on the use of landmines: (i) the obligation to record their placements, and (ii) obligation to remove them at the end of hostilities.

According to UNICEF, APM and UXO violate nearly all articles of the Convention of the Rights of the Child: a child's right to life, to a safer environment in which to play, to health, clean water, sanitary conditions and adequate education.[66]

In 1997, the United Nations Mine Action Service (UNMAS) was established within the Department of Peacekeeping Operations to be the UN's focal point on landmine related matters. UNMAS is responsible for the strategic management and coordination of all UN activities in the area of humanitarian mine action to ensure an effective, proactive and coordinated response to the problems of landmines and ERW, including cluster munitions. UNMAS is to develop policy related to the mines issue, assess and monitor the global landmine threat, identify needs, and develop appropriate responses in light of that determined threat.[67]

India is a party to CCW and its five Protocols and remains committed to the CCW objective of progressively strengthening the principles of IHL while striking balance between addressing humanitarian concerns and military necessity of State. India supports the vision of a world free of the threat of landmines and committed to the eventual elimination of antipersonnel landmines. India has discontinued the production of non-detectable anti-personal landmines and observes a moratorium on their transfer. We are also contributing to international demining and rehabilitation efforts. India supports the UN Register on Conventional Arms and UN report on Military Expenditures…..and has strong and effective national export control governing the transfer of conventional weapons which conform to the highest international standards.[68]

The Ottawa Mine Ban Treaty now has 162 States Parties. It provides the framework for eradicating antipersonnel landmines through its comprehensive prohibitions and requirements that States Parties clear mined areas within 10 years, destroy stockpiles within four years, and provide victim assistance. There is a need for universalisation of the treaty and strict compliance with its implementation for the destruction of stockpiles and the clearance of contaminated areas. The UNGA Resolution 70/55 has called for universalisation and full implementation of the Mine Ban Treaty, through the continued implementation of the action plan for the period 2014–2019.[69] The resolution was adopted by a vote of 168 states in favour, none against, and 17 abstentions. This is the highest number of affirmative votes for the annual resolution. A core of 14 states not party abstained from consecutive Mine Ban Treaty resolutions: Cuba, Egypt, India, Iran, Israel, Myanmar, North Korea, Pakistan, Russia, South Korea, Syria, Uzbekistan, the US, and Vietnam.

To build confidence in the Treaty, the States should immediately conclude a binding agreement to destroy stockpiles of APM, being held by them. Demining operations have potential to damage the environment in which they are conducted. The national mine action authorities and the organisations involved in demining operations must ensure that their operations are not only carried out in a safe, effective and efficient manner, but also in a manner that minimises impact on the environment.[70] In order to promote the social integration of mine survivors especially amputees, the government and non-governmental organisations should address their psycho-social needs. A landmine is a morally outlawed weapon and should never be used again.

Notes

1. In the late 1980s a former British army sergeant went to Afghanistan to begin agricultural development programmes but discovered that such work was impossible because of mines and subsequently founded the Mines Advisory Group, one of the first NGO humanitarian mine clearance programmes. In the summer of 1991, the Vietnam Veterans of America Foundation (VVAF) opened its first prosthetics clinic in Cambodia and soon recognised that providing prosthetic devices alone did not solve the mine infestation of that country. Medico International joined with VVAF to launch an advocacy campaign to ban landmines. About the same time, Human Rights Watch Asia Division and Physicians for Human Rights issued "Landmines in Cambodia: The Coward's War," and jointly called for a ban on anti-personnel landmines. Handicap International became more of an advocacy organisation after years of assisting landmine victims in the field and launched its campaign to "Stop the Coward's War" with a petition calling for greater restrictions on mines use. Handicap International, Human Rights Watch, Medico International, Mines Advisory Group, Physicians for Human Rights and Vietnam Veterans of America Foundation issued their "Joint Call to Ban Anti-personnel Landmines," and hosted the first NGO-sponsored international landmines conference in May 1993. These six groups became the ICBL's steering committee and Jody Williams of the VVAF became its coordinator. Humanitarian actors Jody Williams and Rae McGrath were awarded a Nobel Peace Prize in 1997 for founding The International Campaign to Ban Landmines. Jody Williams and Stephen Goose, "The International Campaign to Ban Landmines," in Maxwell A. Cameron, Robert J. Lawson and Brian W. Tomlin (eds.), *To Walk Without Fear—The Global Movement to Ban Landmines* (Oxford: Oxford University Press, 1998), pp. 20-47.
2. Heshmati Almas and Nabaz T. Khayyat. 2013. *Socio-Economic Impacts of Landmines in Southern Kurdistan*, Cambridge Scholars Publishing, pp. 350.
3. The majority of landmines used during and shortly after World War II had metal casings, but the development of stable and durable plastics in the 1950s and 1960s led to their common use as casing material. These improved plastics are now used in the fusing mechanisms as well; a modern, light, AP blast mine may contain so little metal that it is almost impossible to detect by an electronic mine detector, which senses the small amounts of metal in a mine. The growing difficulty in detecting mines has led to proposals that a minimum quantity of metal be used in every mine, to make it easier to locate using conventional mine-clearance techniques. *Anti-personnel Landmines: Friend or Foe?* A study of the

military use and effectiveness of anti-personnel mines, Geneva: International Committee of the Red Cross, March 1996.

4. Technological advances have made landmines more dangerous for civilians and more difficult, if not impossible, to detect. Greater numbers of mines can be laid more rapidly than ever before. Furthermore, as landmines have become more sophisticated, mine clearance technologies have developed very slowly. Plastic mines contain very little metal content, and are virtually impossible to detect with traditional metal detectors. Mines with electronic sensors are often capable of identifying the numbers of passers-by before they explode, but they do not distinguish between soldiers and civilians, and between children and adults. Civilians are frequently maimed or killed if they are near the epicentre of an explosion at the time of self-detonation. *Landmines, The Problem,* International Campaign for a Ban on Landmines, available at: www.icbl.org, accessed February 12, 2012.
5. Lawrence Keppie, *The Making of the Roman Army: From Republic to Empire,* Norman, University of Oklahoma Press, pp. 89-94; Major William C. Schenck, "The Origins of Military Mines, part I," vol. 58, *Engineer,* July 1998, p. 50.
6. Major William C. Schenck, "The Origins of Military Mines, part I," vol. 58, *Engineer,* July 1998, p. 52.
7. C. E. E. Sloan, *Mine Warfare on Land* (London: Brassey's Defence Publishers, 1986), pp. 34-36.
8. Landmines are cheap to manufacture and have simple technology. Modern technology has produced mines which are small and camouflaged; the absence of metal parts makes them nearly impossible to detect with technical instruments, and they remain functional after a long period of time. For example, the Chinese-made Type 72A has only one moving part, and there is no precision technology required for its manufacturing. It is also easy to store landmines, as compared to more complicated weapons. It requires just a shovel to emplace an AP mine. In military parlance, landmines act as "force multipliers" in that they can help a small defending force defeat a larger attacking force, and can do so more cost effectively than other weapons. The International Campaign to Ban Landmines (ICBL) has estimated that it takes as low as $ 3 to make an APM. However, it may cost $ 1,000 to clear this mine. The simplicity and cost-effectiveness of mines is also a major factor in explaining the widespread use of mines throughout the numerous countries that are now dealing with the mine contamination problem.
9. The most commonly remotely delivered or scatterables APM by the US were the US BLU-43 and BLU-44 nicknamed "dragon tooth" because of their needlelike shape. They were the forerunners of the Soviet PFM-1, or "butterfly" mines, used extensively in Afghanistan. *Human Rights Watch Arms Project,* 1993, p. 17.
10. In Cambodia, the ICRC has estimated that there were approximately six to ten million landmines compared to a population of eight million to nine million inhabitants. While the majority of those mines were believed to have been laid between 1983 and 1992, Cambodian officials and NGOs reported in 1996 that landmines continued to be laid. *Landmines in the Killing Fields: The Carnage Continues—Cambodia,* 1996, Geneva, International Committee of the Red Cross. Pol Pot, whose regime was responsible for the deaths of some 1.7 million Cambodians between 1975 and 1979, purportedly called landmines his "perfect soldiers." They never sleep. They wait, with limitless patience. Although weapons of war, landmines are unlike bullets and bombs in two distinct ways. First, they are designed to maim rather than kill, because an injured soldier requires the help of two or three others, reducing the enemy's force. Second, when a war ends,

landmines remain in the ground, primed to explode. Only 25 per cent of landmine victims around the world are soldiers. The rest are civilians—boys gathering firewood, mothers sowing rice, girls herding goats. Mark Jenkins, "The Healing Fields," vol. 221, no. 1, *National Geographic,* January 2012, pp. 96-113.

11. Mike Croll, *A History of Landmines* (Barnsley: Leo Cooper, 1998), p. 108.
12. *Anti-personnel Landmines: Friend or Foe?* A study of the military use and effectiveness of anti-personnel mines, March 1996, Geneva: International Committee of the Red Cross, pp. 29, 41.
13. In January 2002, as the build-up along the border began, the army acquired land belonging to about 350 villages in Firozpur district for laying landmines or constructing fortifications. Thousands of villagers had to migrate from their villages because of mine laying. There were a number of incidents in which villagers were hurt and disabled because of the landmines. In Ganganagar district, three girls bathing in a canal were injured by a mine blast. The mines had been washed down into the canal. Later as the temperatures began rising in Rajasthan, the army was forced to evacuate villagers living near densely mined areas as the high temperatures were triggering off the mines. The mining exercise caused large-scale dislocation and returning villagers were not sure that their fields and grazing pastures had been entirely demined. It is evident from the experience of last two decades mine-laying examples that the social and human cost of landmines use are just too high. Historical evidence has shown that when mines are used on a large scale, they have little or marginal effect on the outcome of hostilities. At best, they have a marginal, tactical value under very specific conditions. They may delay or slow down at attack, but not prevent it. Singh Shubha, "Step out of dangerous terrain," *Hindustan Times,* New Delhi, May 19, 2003.
14. *Anti-personnel Landmines: Friend or Foe?* A study of the military use and effectiveness of anti-personnel mines, March 1996, Geneva: International Committee of the Red Cross, pp. 30-31.
15. Shawn Roberts and Jody Williams, *After the Guns Fall Silent: The Enduring Legacy of Landmines* (Washington DC: Vietnam Veterans of America Foundation, 1995), p. 193.
16. An area of about 149 sq km has been identified as priority one, or areas which have immediate impact on people's lives (residential areas, commercial areas, agricultural land, irrigation canals, roads and grazing areas). *Afghanistan has 10 million landmines.* Human Rights Watch Report, available at: http://www.hrw.org/legacy/backgrounder/arms/landmines-bck1011.htm, accessed January 12, 2013.
17. The Iraqi government is reported to have used mines as weapons of terror in Kurdistan, where many villages had their fields sown with APM. *Hidden Death—Landmines and Civilian Casualties in Iraqi Kurdistan,* Human Rights Watch—Middle East, October 1992, p. 1.
18. *Anti-personnel Landmines: Friend or Foe?* A study of the military use and effectiveness of anti-personnel mines (Geneva: International Committee of the Red Cross, March 1996), pp. 35-36.
19. *The Silent Menace: Landmines in Bosnia and Herzegovina* (Geneva: International Committee of the Red Cross, 1997), pp. 5-6.
20. The 2007 Landmine Monitor reports on Eritrea and Ethiopia, available at www.icbl.org. *See also:* Christopher Harland, "Anti-Personnel Landmines: Balancing Military Utility and the Humanitarian Cost," *CLAWS Journal,* Summer 2008, pp. 236-48.

21. Paul Davies and Nic Dunlop, *War of the Mines: Cambodia, Landmines and the Impoverishment of a Nation* (London: Pluto Press, 1999), p. 19.
22. Landmine Monitor 2016, International Campaign to Ban Landmines – Cluster Munition Coalition (ICBL-CMC), pp. 112.
23. *Anti-personnel Landmines: Friend or Foe?* A study of the military use and effectiveness of anti-personnel mines (Geneva: International Committee of the Red Cross, March 1996).
24. Evidence put before the UK Parliamentary Foreign Affairs Committee by General Sir Hugh Beach, Hansard, March 30, 1995, Appendix 38, p. 385. Beach was a Royal Engineer who served inter alia in north-western Europe in WWII where mines were heavily used. His last appointment was as Master General of the Ordnance which included responsibility for procurement of all land warfare equipment, including mines.
25. In the Gulf war, mines may have given the Iraqi Army a false sense of security as regards the strength of their defensive positions around Kuwait, whereas when the ground war began most minefields were simply bypassed. Where it was necessary to pass through them, the Coalition forces used tank-mounted ploughs and armoured hoses, and breached the Iraqi minefields where and when they wanted to with apparent ease. It could hardly be claimed that the many AP mines laid by Iraqi were "force multipliers." In addition, certain terrains are particularly unsuitable for minefields because the mines can move considerable distances and therefore do not create the intended obstacle, for example in areas of shifting sands or steep terrain.
26. "Assistance in Mine Clearance," Report of the UN Secretary-General, document A/49/357, September 6, 1994.
27. Mine removal is a lengthy and expensive business. Landmines can be blithely spread at rates of over 1,000 per minute, but it may take a skilled expert an entire day just to clear by hand 20-50 square metres of mine-contaminated land. See: http://www.unicef.org/graca/mines.htm.
28. A. A. Berhe, "The Contribution of Landmines to Degradation," vol. 18, *Land Degradation & Development*, 2007, p. 1.
29. Ibid., p. 4.
30. The list of mine-infested States reads like the history of recent conflicts: Angola, Afghanistan, Bosnia-Herzegovina, Cambodia, Croatia, Ethiopia, Iraq, Mozambique, Rwanda, Somalia, Sudan and Yugoslavia. Each year 2-5 million new mines are put in the ground, adding to "one of the most widespread, lethal and long-lasting forms of pollution" the world has ever known. *Anti-personnel Landmines: Friends or Foe;* A study of the military use and effectiveness of anti-personnel mines, Geneva: ICRC, March 1996, p. 9.
31. In Sri Lanka, the war is over but the country is now busy fighting a new type of war to unearth hundreds of thousands of landmines, unexploded and abandoned ordnance and improvised explosive devices (IEDs) scattered all over the war ravaged North and East Provinces. The two provinces are not yet safe to live and people eke out economic and development activities. The situation on the ground reflects the brutality of the war. In September 2010 The National Strategy for Mine Action in Sri Lanka was shared among mine action stakeholders by the government: according to estimation done by the Sri Lankan Army 1.6 million landmines have been laid in Sri Lanka of which 366,870 mines have been cleared through military demining and humanitarian demining. Further, this leaves the country with an estimated number of 1.23 million mines still to be cleared. The Government of Sri Lanka with the support of the international community

has started a large-scale humanitarian demining programme with the goal of creating a mine and explosive remnants of war (ERW) free environment in support of resettlement and development programmes. It has targeted a mine threat free Sri Lanka in 2020 and this means it will take at least another eight years to clear the land. See: http://www.asiantribune.com/news/2010/10/31/banning-landmines-sri-lanka-looking-it-socio-economic-political-perspectives.

32. In Turkey, it was reported that refugees from Syria were trapped in the extensive border minefield across from Syria. The exact number of people killed and injured by landmines in the border minefields was not known due to a lack of accurate reporting. However, there were at least 12 Syrian civilian casualties reported at the Turkish-Syrian border in the month of September 2014 alone. Reports also indicate that since January 2015, dozens of refugees returning to Kobane from Turkey have been killed or injured by mines/ERW, IEDs, and booby traps inside Syria.Landmines/ERW, Refugees, and Displacement, Briefing Paper, World Refugee Day 2015, Landmine and Cluster Munition Monitor,20 June 2015, p. 3.
33. The threat of IED attacks is a global problem. In recent years IEDs have become a common weapon of choice and they are widely employed in conflict situations mainly characterized by asymmetry (such as insurgencies, rebellions, or armed violence against government or foreign forces) where the main perpetrators are either organized armed groups or individual non-state actors.
34. IED attacks deliberately target civilian objects, including airports, markets, police stations, schools, public transit, commercial hubs, nightclubs, courts, political gatherings and sports venues, to ensure infliction of the greatest amount of civilian harm. In addition to producing large-scale carnage, such attacks can impede commerce, contribute to internal displacement and refugee flows, obstruct humanitarian responses and civil society activity, and disrupt the provision of health care, education and sanitation and the practice of governance.
35. Countering the threat posed by improvised explosive devices, Report of the Secretary-General, UN Doc. A/71/187 dated 25 July 2016.
36. UN International Ammunition Technical Guidelines (IATG), Glossary of Terms, Definitions and Abbreviations, 2011; NATO also uses nearly identical definition for IED.
37. Finaud Marc, Addressing Improvised Explosive Devices: Options and Opportunities to Better Utilize UN Processes and Actors, The United Nations Institute for Disarmament Research, 2015, p.13.
38. A. A. Berhe, "The Contribution of Landmines to Degradation," vol. 18, *Land Degradation & Development* (2007), p. 5.
39. Mines destroy flora and damage the soil structure, reducing soil productivity. Mines cause irreversible damage to ecosystems, including prolonged direct damage to soil through shattering and displacement, destruction of soil structure, and increased vulnerability of soil to water and wind erosion. The disruption to the soil structure further exacerbates the erosion problem, which leads to an increased sediment load in the drainage system. Increased sedimentation in coastal waters can adversely affect fish and prawn habitats. C. Torres-Nachon, *Environmental Aspects of the International Crisis of Anti-personnel Landmines and the Implementation of the 1997 Mine Ban Treaty: Thematic Report*, Landmine Monitor Report 2000, New York: International Campaign to Ban Landmines.
40. Paul Carr, "'Shock and Awe' and the Environment," vol. 19, *Peace Review: A Journal of Social Justice*, pp. 335-42. Available at: http://www.paulrcarr.net/assets/files/articles/en/PeaceReviewmanuscript_NEW-july222010.pdf, accessed May 22, 2011.

41. There is speculation that the populations of cranes, pelicans and other migratory birds were affected by US air strikes on Afghanistan. The birds migrate from Siberia and other central Asian states through to Pakistan, which has reported a record low number of incoming birds. Bombing and troop activities are thought to have driven the birds away from their usual travel route, causing them to die of exhaustion or starvation. A. Gangwar, *Impact of War and Landmines on Environment*, 2003, Centre for Environment Education, Himalaya, available at: http://www.mtnforum.org/resources/library/ganga03a.htm, accessed January 12, 2011. The refugees and internally displaced people also contribute to loss of biodiversity when they hunt animals for food or when they destroy their habitat in order to make shelters for themselves. K. Troll, *The Impact of Anti-Personnel Landmines on the Environment* (Geneva: United Nations Institute for Disarmament Research, 2000).
42. United Nations General Assembly document UNGA/A/38/383, 1983.
43. B. Gray, "Landmines: the most toxic and widespread pollution facing mankind." A Colloquium, Towards Ottawa and Beyond—Demining the Region: The Environmental Impacts. July 14-17, 1997, International Campaign to Ban Landmines and University of Sydney.
44. In laboratory experiments with rats, TNT and RDX were found to be carcinogenic, causing tumours in the bladder and male reproductive systems, and congenital defects, skin irritation, and disruption of the immunological system. K. Troll, *The Impact of Anti-Personnel Landmines on the Environment*, United Nations Institute for Disarmament Research: Geneva, 2000.
45. Agency for Toxic Substances and Disease Registry (ATSDR) 1999a. Toxicological Profile for Mercury. US Department of Health and Human Services, Public Health Service: Atlanta, GA; ATSDR. 1999b. Toxicological Profile for Cadmium. US Department of Health and Human Services, Public Health Service: Atlanta, GA.
46. Food and Agriculture Organisation 1997. Production Yearbook (vol. 48). Food and Agriculture Organisation: Rome.
47. Mine action refers to a range of activities including mine identification, contamination demarcation, removal, land release, risk education, victim assistance and rehabilitation, stockpile elimination, and advocacy to end the trade and use of mines. Demining operations are a part of mine action activities.
48. Anthony Morin, "Demining and the Environment: A Primer, Mine Action Information Centre," available at: http://maic.jmu.edu/journal/11.2/feature/morin/morin.htm, accessed June 26, 2011.
49. P. Sanchez, "Soil Fertility and Hunger in Africa," *Science*, 2002, vol. 295, pp. 2019-20. Available at http://www.scienceonline.org/cgi/reprint/295/5562/2019.pdf, accessed August 10, 2011.
50. Demining hazardous areas is hugely important and is currently accomplished through the use of mechanical devices, such as hand-held metal detectors, and with the help of animals, such as specially trained dogs. APOPO has recently begun using giant African pouched rats (*Cricetomys gambianus*) as mine detectors. The rats are nocturnal burrowing natives of sub-Saharan Africa. They are pests in the wild and are sometimes hunted and eaten. They can live up to eight years; the adults reach body lengths of 25-45 cm and they weigh 1-2 kg, making them considerably lighter than dogs, and it is therefore substantially more unlikely for them to detonate the mines with their weight. APOPO's rats are born and trained in Morogoro, Tanzania. Pups are handled regularly to socialise them; they are then trained to sniff the ground and to pause when they smell 2, 4, 6-trinitrotoluene (TNT), which is the main explosive charge in

most mines. The training takes about 250 days (three times less than the time required to train mine detection dogs); it starts in a laboratory, where the rats learn in long metal cages to stop at holes above TNT. They then learn to locate perforated balls containing TNT that are buried in sandy soil. The final stages of training occur on a large simulated minefield. All throughout the training and the detection process, the rats' correct behaviour is reinforced through positive operant conditioning, with rewarding treats like smashed banana bits.

51. M. Habib, "Mechanical Mine Clearance Technologies and Humanitarian Demining," 2002. Available at http://www.demine.org/SCOT/Papers/Habib.pdf, accessed February 11, 2011.
52. C. Torres-Nachon, *Environmental Aspects of the International Crisis of Anti-personnel Landmines and the Implementation of the 1997 Mine Ban Treaty*, Landmine Monitor Report 2000, International Campaign to Ban Landmines, available at: http://www.icbl.org/lm/2000/appendices/environment.html, accessed February 12, 2012. See: TN 10.10 01, Environmental Management during Mine and UXO Clearance Operations, version 1.0.
53. N. Andersson, C. P. da Sousa and S. Paredes, Social cost of land mines in four countries: Afghanistan, Bosnia, Cambodia, and Mozambique. *British Medical Journal* 311: 718-721. A. A. Berhe, "The Contribution of Landmines to Degradation," vol. 18, *Land Degradation & Development*, 2007, p. 10.
54. In 1992, Bosnia and Herzegovina became independent of Yugoslavia and immediately afterwards entered into war as a consequence of the instability in the wider region of the former Yugoslavia. During this war numerous landmines, originating mostly from the former Yugoslavian People's Army, were deployed to secure borders and to restrict enemy movement. Some areas have been mined after the war; mostly to prevent the return of refugees. Minefields can still be found across most parts of the country, since they were laid along conflict lines that often changed. The war ended in the winter of 1995, and the country is still trying to cope with the problem of landmines more than seventeen years after the war. Bosnia-Herzegovina has signed the 1997 Mine Ban Treaty dealing with the prohibition on the use, stockpiling, production, and transfer of anti-personnel mines and on their destruction.
55. *Anti-Personnel Landmines: Landmines Must be Stopped*, Mines Overview 1996, Geneva: ICRC, p. 10.
56. The 1997 Anti-Personnel Mine Ban Convention (Mine Ban Treaty) bans the use, stockpiling, production and transfer of anti-personnel mines. It also establishes a framework for action, including the obligation to destroy stockpiles of anti-personnel mines within four years, and to be mine-free within 10 years of joining the Convention. The Mine Ban Treaty was negotiated outside of the normal UN multilateral disarmament framework mainly because the CCW failed to secure a ban on anti-personnel mines during the negotiations to amend the CCW Protocol on Prohibitions or Restrictions on the Use of Mines, Booby-Traps and Other Devices (the amended instrument became known as Amended Protocol II) during 1995 and 1996. It ultimately led to a comprehensive ban signed by more than 130 countries and to the 1997 Nobel Peace Prize for the International Campaign to Ban Landmines and its coordinator Jody Williams.
57. The countries are: Armenia, Azerbaijan, Bahrain, China, Cuba, Egypt, Finland, Georgia, India, Iran, Israel, Kazakhstan, Kyrgyzstan, Laos, Lebanon, Libya, Micronesia, Mongolia, Morocco, Myanmar, Nepal, North Korea, Oman, Pakistan, Russia, Saudi Arabia, Singapore, South Korea, Sri Lanka, Syria, Tonga, United Arab Emirates, the US, Uzbekistan and Vietnam. Militaries of these

countries are reluctant to suddenly forfeit a useful weapon, on humanitarian grounds alone, that has been part of their doctrine and procedures for decades.

58. The Mine Ban Convention: Progress and Challenges in the Second Decade, Geneva: ICRC, August 2011, p. 5. The Monitor identified 12 producers of anti-personnel mines (the same number as reported in 2010 and the lowest total ever): China, Cuba, India, Iran, Myanmar, North Korea, Pakistan, Russia, Singapore, South Korea, the United States, and Vietnam. Available at: http://www.the-monitor.org/index.php/publications/display?url=lm/2011/es/Major_Findings.html.

59. Protocol II specifically restricts the use of landmines, providing among other things that: (i) Mines may be directed only against military objectives. Indiscriminate use of mines and all feasible precautions must be taken to protect civilians; (ii) remotely delivered mines may not be used unless their location is accurately recorded or each one is fitted with an effective self-destruct or self-neutralising mechanism. (iii) record must be kept of the locations of planned minefields, and the parties to conflict should also endeavour to keep records of the locations of other minefields laid during the hostilities. (iv) at the end of hostilities, the parties must try to reach an agreement, both among themselves and with other states and organisations, on taking the necessary measures to clear minefields.

60. There were significant flaws in Protocol II: (i) it did not restrict the use of long-lived mines (dumb mines) that are likely to cause civilian casualties long after the conflict has ended; (ii) there was no requirement that mines be detectable; as a result many plastic landmines could escape detection by standard mine detection equipment, thus posing serious risk to mine-clearance personnel, civilians and peacekeeping personnel; (iii) it was applicable only in international armed conflicts; and (iv) the exceptions in some provisions were so vague that they actually undermine the substantive obligations. For example, Article 5 (2) provided: if the circumstances do not permit, the parties do not have to give effective advance warning. The combinations of exceptions, limitations, loopholes, and admonitory clauses rendered this treaty ineffective. Norman B. Smith, "A Plea for the Total Ban on Landmines by International Treaty," vol. 17, *Loyola of Los Angeles International and Comparative Law Journal* (1995), p. 527. Amended Protocol (1996) improves Protocol II in many ways, not only in terms of IHL, but also international law on disarmament and arms control, and to a large extent deletes flaws in Protocol II. The scope of application was extended to situations referred to in Article 3 common to the four Geneva Conventions of 1949, namely, armed conflicts not of an international character. Lijiang Zhu, "A Test of International Humanitarian Law on Landmines in Recent Conflicts: Problems and Possible Solutions," in M. J. Matheson and D. Momtaz (eds.), *Rules and Institutions on International Humanitarian Law Put to the Test of Recent Armed Conflicts* (Leiden/Boston: Martinus Nijhoff Publishers, 2011), pp. 662-63.

61. Article 52 of Geneva Convention III dealing with the Protection of Prisoners of War provides that unless volunteer, no prisoner of war may be employed on labour which is of an unhealthy or dangerous nature. The removal of mines or similar devices is considered as dangerous labour under Article 52.

62. CCW Protocol on Prohibitions or Restrictions on the Use of Mines, Booby Traps and Other Devices as amended on 3 May 1996 (Amended Protocol II) to the Convention on Prohibitions or Restrictions on the Use of Certain Conventional Weapons Which May Be Deemed to Be Excessively Injurious or to Have Indiscriminate Effects. CCW Protocol V: Protocol V on Explosive Remnants of War.

63. Prohibition includes the devices that are attached to or associated with: internationally recognized protective emblems, corpses or graves, medical facilities or transportation; object intended for children, food or beverage; objects of a religious character; historic monuments, works of art or places of worship, animals or their carcasses;" "in any city, town, village or other area containing a similar concentration of civilians in which combat between ground forces is not taking place or does not appear to be imminent, unless: (a) such weapons are placed on or in close vicinity of a military objective, or (b) measures are taken to protect civilians from their effects, for example, the posting of warning sentries or the issuing of warnings"; operational information exchange and following the cessation of active hostilities, other devices are to be cleared. A few experts are of the view that a number of other instruments may have relevance to IEDs, including the Anti-Personnel Landmine Ban Convention, the Convention on Cluster Munitions, the Rome Statute, the International Convention for the Suppression of Terrorist Bombings, the Chemical and Biological Weapons Conventions, and UN Security Council resolution 1540.
64. Assistance in Mine Action, The General Assembly Doc A/RES/70/80 dated 15 December 2015.
65. Jean-Marie Henckaerts and Louise Doswald-Beck, *Customary International Humanitarian Law*, vol. I: Rules, International Committee of the Red Cross and Cambridge University Press, Cambridge, 2005.
66. http://www.unicef.org/graca/mines.htm.
67. UNMAS's responsibility is to coordinate the mine-related activities with 13 other UN departments, including Department of Disarmament Affairs; Office for the Coordination of Humanitarian Affairs, Office of the United Nations High Commissioner for Refugees, United Nations Children's Fund, United Nations Development Programme, United Nations Office for Project Service, World Food Programme, Food and Agriculture Organisation, the World Health Organisation and World Bank. UNMAS is to ensure that there is UN assistance in the creation of sustainable national capacities and in the implementation of overall programmes. UNMAS provides direct support and assistance to 17 programmes. For further details see: http://www.mineaction.org/overview.asp?o=22.
68. Statement by Ambassador DB Venkatesh Varma, Permanent Mission of India to the CD, 26 October 2015.
69. The UN General Assembly resolution A/RES/70/55 dated 11 December 2015.
70. In order to provide the mine action community, with consistent and globally relevant International Mine Action Standards (IMAS), the United Nations Mine Action Service (UNMAS), and the Geneva International Centre for Humanitarian Demining (GICHD) with the support of the mine action community represented through the IMAS Review Board has developed an IMAS on the protection of environment. 2009 Meeting of Experts of the States parties to CCW Protocol V, paper presented by the Geneva International Centre for Humanitarian Demining on clearance, removal or destruction of ERW, pursuant to Article 3 of the Protocol.

4 B

CLUSTER MUNITIONS

Cluster munitions (the terms "cluster munitions" and "cluster bombs" are used interchangeably) consist of a container that releases submunitions, or bomblets, while in flight.[1] It can be delivered by several means,[2] which results in a shower of small explosives covering a large area.[3] These munitions were designed to attack multiple targets, wide-area targets like airfields, industrial plants, ammunition storage houses as well as small or fast-moving targets like personnel, tanks or surface-to-air missile sites. The original idea behind using cluster munitions was to compensate for aiming imprecision with free-falling unitary munitions against single targets which could not be easily hit. A large number of free-falling explosive sub-munitions, when delivered over a wide area, increases the probability of hitting the target. The military value of cluster munitions is seen in the capability to deliver a higher number of explosives against the targets over a larger area within a shorter period of time. This reduces exposure to enemy counter-attack as well as the number of firing platforms, ammunition and personnel required.[4] Cluster munitions, however, in their last six decades of existence have caused extensive harm to civilians and the environment.

The Convention on Cluster Munitions (CCM),[5] which bans the weapons, defines a cluster munition as "a conventional munition that is designed to disperse or release explosive submunitions each weighing less than 20 kilograms, and includes those explosive submunitions." Although the Convention sets 20 kilograms as the maximum weight for submunitions, in practice submunitions are much smaller. Usually the size of tennis balls or soda cans and weighing only a few kilograms, submunitions are more akin to hand grenades than other bombs. The cluster munitions could be of the following kinds:

- Incendiary: Incendiary cluster bombs are intended to start fires, just as conventional incendiary bombs (also called firebombs). They are specifically designed for this purpose, with submunitions of white phosphorus or napalm, and they often include anti-personnel and anti-tank submunitions to hamper firefighting effects.
- Anti-tank: Most anti-armour munitions contain shaped charge warheads to pierce the armour of tanks and armoured anti-personnel cluster bombs use explosive fragmentation to kill troops and destroy soft (unarmoured) vehicles.
- Anti-personnel cluster bombs use explosive fragmentation to kill troops and destroy soft (unarmoured) targets.
- Anti-runway: Anti-runway submunitions such as the British JP 233 are designed to penetrate concrete before detonating, allowing them to shatter and crater runway surfaces.
- Mine-laying: When submunition-based weapons are used to disperse mines, their submunitions do not detonate immediately, but behave like conventional landmines that detonate later. The submunitions usually include a combination of anti-personnel and anti-tank mines.
- Leaflet dispensing: The LBU-30 is designed for dropping large quantities of leaflets from aircraft. (Dispensing leaflets from the air is a common propaganda tactic in wartime.) Enclosing the leaflets within the bomblets ensures that the leaflets will fall on the intended area without being dispersed excessively by the wind.

A cluster munition could be a dual purpose improved conventional munition which can be used against both personnel and material targets, including armour. Although small in size, the bomblets of cluster munitions are powerful and versatile, often delivering anti-personnel fragmentation, armour-piercing shape charges, and incendiary effects in the same compact package. The multiple effects of the submunitions are designed to achieve the intended uses of cluster munitions; they are deployed against troop formations, vehicle convoys, airfields, anti-aircraft weapons, and other targets that combine personnel and light armour.[6]

Development and Use of Cluster Munitions

Ordnance designed to target multiple targets with a single discharge can be traced back to the grape and canister shot used by artillery crews before the invention of explosive shells. Cluster munitions were developed in the twentieth century and German and Soviet forces used them on the Eastern Front in the Second World War. The Germans also used them in the bombardment of Britain.[7] However, the weapon saw its first widespread use in Cambodia, Laos and Vietnam.[8] Since the Vietnam War, cluster munitions have been used by over twenty States, as well as some non-state actors. Cluster munitions were used in the first Gulf War,[9] the Balkans, Chechnya,[10] the conflict between Ethiopia and Eritrea, Afghanistan, Iraq,[11] and in Israel's conflict in Lebanon, as well as in over a dozen other instances. The Russian military has recently used cluster munitions in Georgia. It has been reported that globally, 34 countries[12] have produced over 210 different types of cluster munitions.[13] The US remains a leader in the use and development of cluster munitions. Currently, all four branches of the American military employ cluster munitions. These included artillery projectiles, aerially delivered bombs, rockets, and surface-to-surface and air-to-surface missiles.[14]

Cluster Munitions: Use and Footprint of Damage

In 1943, the German Air Force dropped SD2 submunitions (butterfly bombs) on the British port of Grimsby. Only around one-quarter of the 1,000 submunitions dropped exploded on impact or within half an hour. These killed 14 people and ignited numerous fires. The rest of the bomblets lay unexploded on roads and roofs and caught in trees and hedges. Within an hour of the air raid "all clear" signal, another

31 people were killed and many more injured as they interacted with these bomblets. Despite immediate action by the authorities it took more than 10,000 hours of work over the next 18 days to clear the submunitions and re-open the port.[15]

The US has used cluster munitions extensively in Cambodia, Laos and Vietnam in the 1960s and 1970s. According to Handicap International, at least 26 million submunitions were delivered in Cambodia by some 80,000 cluster munitions between 1969 and 1973; at least 260 million submunitions were delivered in Laos by over 414,000 cluster bombs between 1965 and 1973; and nearly 97 million submunitions were dropped in Vietnam by over 296,000 cluster munitions between 1965 and 1973. The Soviet forces air-dropped and rocket delivered large quantities of cluster munitions during their invasion and occupation of Afghanistan from 1979 to 1989.

In the first Gulf War (1991-92), the US used 47,167 cluster bombs containing over 13 million submunitions. In 1999, the US, the UK, and the Netherlands used 1,765 cluster bombs containing 195,000 submunitions in the former Yugoslavia. In Afghanistan during 2001-02, the US used 1,228 cluster bombs containing 248,056 submunitions, while in Iraq during 2003, the US and UK forces used 13,000 cluster bombs having 1.8 to 2.0 million submunitions. US-made cluster munitions, having over four million cluster submunitions, were used by Israel, in its 2006 conflict with Hezbollah in Lebanon. In 2011, Thai forces fired artillery-delivered cluster munitions into Cambodia during border clashes near the Preah Vihear temple; while the Libyan government forces used MAT-120 mortar-fired cluster munitions, RBK-250 cluster bombs with PTAB-2.5M submunitions.[16]

The Syrian government forces have used 13 types of cluster munitions, including aircraft, and ground-launched rockets, while IS forces have used at least one type of cluster munition. Cluster munition attacks increased after Russia began its joint military operation in Syria in September 2015, including the use of types not seen used before in Syria. Evidence of continued use of cluster munitions persists to date and they have been used at as many as

300 locations in 10 of 14 of Syria's governorates. There is evidence that unexploded submunitions have been used by NSAGs in Syria as improvised explosive devices.[17] A Saudi Arabia-led coalition of states that began attacking Ansar Allah forces in Yemen on 25 March 2015 has used CBU-105 Sensor Fuzed Weapons, CBU-58 and CBU-87 bombs, and M26 and Astros rockets. In addition, ground-launched cluster munitions have been used, however, the user is not known. There is credible evidence that two types of cluster munition rockets were used in Nagorno-Karabakh in April 2016. Armenia and Azerbaijan denied using cluster munitions while accusing each other of use. The Sudanese Air Force was responsible for cluster munition attacks in Southern Kordofan in 2015 using RBK-500 AO-2.5 RT cluster bombs. In 2015, both Ukrainian government forces and opposition groups backed by Russia used cluster munition rockets in eastern Ukraine.[18]

Recent estimates show that 98 percent of cluster bomb casualties are civilians. This percentage is based on statistical evidence drawn from 13,306 recorded and confirmed cluster submunition casualties in the following countries/regions: Afghanistan, Albania, Bosnia and Herzegovina, Cambodia, Chad, Chechnya/Russian Federation, Croatia, Eritrea, Ethiopia, Iraq, Israel, Kosovo, Kuwait, Lao People's Democratic Republic, Lebanon, Montenegro, Nagorno-Karabakh/Azerbaijan, Serbia, Sierra Leone, Sudan, Syria, Tajikistan, Vietnam, and Western Sahara/Morocco.[19]

Cluster munitions, like other unguided ordnance, have the potential to miss their targets, thus harming civilians and their properties. A perfectly executed strike aimed at military objectives can result in significant collateral damage if the target is located in close proximity to civilians.[20] The cluster munitions are also infamous for their high dud rates. Many explosive submunitions when dispersed, fail to detonate as designed, becoming *de facto* landmines that kill and maim indiscriminately long after the conflict has ended. Generally, some percentages of all ordnance are faulty, leaving unexploded ordnance (UXO) on the battlefield. Official estimates, including those supplied by manufacturers, state that the failure rate of submunitions is about 5 per cent, meaning these weapons are just as likely to be duds as any other bombs. However, estimates of dud rates in practice are much higher, ranging from 10 to as high as 30 per cent.[21] Battlefield conditions differ significantly from manufacturer testing conditions, accounting for these increased failure rates. The stress of flying, particularly takeoffs and combat manoeuvring, is likely to increase dud rates. Moreover, many of the cluster munitions used in combat are stockpiled for years, even decades, increasing the chances of failure. Some submunitions, such as the armour piercing varieties that must land properly to explode, may fail to explode if they land at an angle. Terrain can also increase dud rates, for example, soft surfaces like desert sand and jungle marshes may not provide the resistance needed to detonate the bombs. Submunitions with parachutes can become entangled in tree limbs. As a result of high dud rates, thousands of unexploded submunitions disperse on battlefields.[22]

The size of the "footprint," the area covered by the submunitions, varies based on several factors, including release altitude, wind, and number of submunitions. Roughly most cluster munitions are designed to have a footprint at least the size of a football field, and often larger. When multiple cluster munitions are deployed in tandem, the area multiplies. For example, the US Army's Multiple Launch Rocket System can fire 12 rockets together, creating a footprint of the size of 60 football fields. A fully loaded B-52 bomber, delivering 40 cluster bombs in a "carpet bombing" attack, can cover over 27,000 football fields. Multiple cluster munitions can also be targeted at the same point, increasing the saturation of submunitions within the footprint. Although some cluster munitions have precision guidance systems, the vast majority are unguided. The same factors that affect the size of the footprint affect the accuracy of the weapon as a whole—the location of the footprint can vary by distances as large as the footprint itself.[23]

Unexploded submunitions are more harmful than other unexploded bombs. For example, an unexploded 500-pound bomb is larger in size and easily identifiable. The small size of the submunitions creates two significant problems. First, they are difficult to detect and can lay hidden in mud, water, and even on treetops and can remain active for years. Even today, submunitions released during the Vietnam War are killing and maiming farmers in Southeast Asia. The widespread distribution of easily hidden submunitions makes clearance difficult, and can render areas uninhabitable for years after the conflict has ended. In this regard, cluster munition duds are like active APM.

The governments do not care about the effects of failed submunitions in the post-conflict period. For instance, the British armed forces used a large number of cluster bombs in the Gulf, Kosovo and Afghanistan. In reply to a question raised by a parliamentarian about what reviews have been undertaken by the Ministry of Defence regarding the civilian casualties caused by unexploded cluster submunitions, the reply was: "No such review and assessments have been undertaken."[24]

Effect on Environment and Population

Cluster munitions can affect very wide areas of land. Once deployed, hundreds of submunitions can spread over an area that is often the size of a football field. This means that even when aimed at military targets, submunitions may disperse into nearby civilian areas. Cluster bombs endanger the civilian population in two principal ways. First, if dropped on a military target in a populated area, cluster bombs, because of their enormous footprint and destructive power, can kill or wound a large number of innocent civilians and damage infrastructure necessary for daily life. Secondly, dud submunitions can remain dangerous years after launch and a slight vibration can detonate them. At least in some models, the passage of time makes the cluster bomb more dangerous, as the fuzing mechanism deteriorates.

Even visible submunitions are problematic. Their appearance is similar to humanitarian aid packages, thus exacerbating the problem. Besides being dangerous to human and environment, cluster munitions create barriers to socio-economic development. In Afghanistan, unexploded submunitions killed a number of civilians due to confusion between unexploded American BLU97s, which are yellow, and air dropped yellow food-aid parcels.[25]

Because cluster munitions litter civilian areas such as fields where people farm and roads on which people travel to work, they have a devastating impact on the ability of civilians to earn a livelihood or to rebuild their homes post-conflict. Farming can be heavily affected by the presence of explosive remnants of cluster munitions. Contaminated land diminishes the capacity of communities to feed themselves. Because explosives can penetrate below the surface of the soil, making them impossible to see, farmers are particularly at risk. Cattle and other animals can also fall victim to these weapons, further reducing a community's means of subsistence. Cluster munitions use and contamination also have an impact on the economy in a variety of ways. Aside from the damage to infrastructure and property, livelihood activities are interrupted or limited because of this damage or the lack of safe access to resources. When these factors are assessed in their totality, it becomes clear that they cause indiscriminate and long-term harm that is difficult for civilians to avoid. There is abundant evidence that civilian lives and livelihoods may not only be endangered during armed conflicts but also tampering with submunition duds may maim or kill civilians.[26]

Effect on Refugees and IDPs

Besides direct threat of injury or death, the use of cluster munitions and the resulting contamination exacerbates the difficulties faced by refugees and IDPs. The resettlement of IDPs and returnees can be complicated if the land is contaminated. There are instances when IDP camps have been struck with cluster munitions.

Effect on Children

Children are one of the main victims of cluster munitions.[27] It has been reported that 92% of the casualties caused by cluster munitions are civilians, among those half of them were children. The bright coloured unexploded submunitions attract children, who think they are toys and pick them up, often resulting in death or amputation. This is mainly because of the nature of children to be curious, inexperienced and to explore their environment. Young children are often not aware of the danger cluster munition remnants pose or are unable to read warning signs which makes them even more vulnerable. The consequences of an explosion are much worse for children because of their small bodies and the closeness of the vital organs to the detonation. This often leads to the death of children or permanent disabilities caused by serious injuries of the limbs.[28]

Violation of IHL

Cluster munitions imprecision and high failure rate are major concerns as they violate principles of IHL. The Fourth Geneva Convention of 1949 codifies a set of rules that protect not only civilians, but all non-combatants, including prisoners of war, wounded and sick enemy soldiers, and shipwrecked sailors, regardless of belligerent status. The Convention does not directly protect the environment; however, it provides a list of rules implying that the States engaging in armed conflict may be held accountable for environmental damage. Article 53 of the Convention provides, "any destruction by the Occupying Power of real or personal property … is prohibited, except where such destruction is rendered absolutely necessary by military operations." Article 147 further states that "grave breaches" of the Convention include "extensive destruction ... of property, not justified by military necessity and carried out unlawfully and wantonly." Thus, wanton damage to the environment may be prosecuted under the Fourth Geneva Convention.

Cluster munitions are regulated as a weapon in armed conflict under IHL, which includes the Additional Protocol I (AP I) to the Geneva Conventions of 1949. Regardless of whether a State Party has signed AP I or not, many of its provisions constitute customary international law, and therefore apply to any party in armed conflict.

AP I specifically prohibits employment of "methods or means of warfare which are intended, or may be expected, to cause widespread, long-term, and severe damage to the natural environment."[29]

There are four principles set forth in AP I that are vital to appropriately applying IHL to cluster munitions. The first principle, expressed in Article 48 of AP I, presents the rule of distinction, "In order to ensure respect for and protection of the civilian population and civilian objects, the Parties to the conflict shall at all times distinguish between the civilian population and combatants and between civilian objects and military objectives and accordingly shall direct their operations only against military objectives."

Article 51 of AP I lay out the basic rule against making civilians and civilian populations the object of attack.[30] The second principle, expressed in Article 51 (4), presents the rule against indiscriminate attacks, "Indiscriminate attacks are prohibited. Indiscriminate attacks are (a) those which are not directed at a specific military objective; (b) those which employ a method or means of combat which cannot be directed at a specific military objective; or (c) those which employ a method or means of combat the effects of which cannot be limited as required by this Protocol; and consequently, in each such case, are of a nature to strike military objectives and civilians or civilian objects without distinction."[31]

Article 51(5) goes on to define indiscriminate attacks, which consist of "an attack[32] by bombardment by any methods or means which treats as a single military objective a number of clearly separated and distinct military objectives located in a city, town, village or other area containing a similar concentration of civilians or civilian objects."

The third principle, also expressed in Article 51 (5) (b), presents the rule of proportionality, "It is prohibited to launch an attack which may be expected to cause incidental loss of civilian life, injury to civilians, damage to civilian objects, or a combination thereof, which would be excessive in relation to the concrete and direct military advantage anticipated." The fourth principle, contained in Article

57, emphasises the rule on feasible precautions. It states, "In the conduct of military operations, constant care shall be taken to spare the civilian population, civilians and civilian objects. All feasible precautions must be taken to avoid, and in any event to minimise incidental loss of civilian life, injury to civilians, and damage to civilian objects."

Provisions contained in Article 55 (1) and (2) serve to discourage States from conducting operations against particular targets, the destruction of which would result in environmental damage. Article 55(2) appears to be unique in its outright ban on attacks against the environment in particular situations.

The use of a weapon that violates any of the above principles violates IHL. An application of these principles to the effects of cluster munitions indicates that the weapons and methods of deployment violate IHL.[33] Furthermore, the toy-like appearance of the submunitions violates Protocol II to the Convention Prohibiting Certain Conventional Weapons (CCW). Article 7 of Protocol prohibits the use "in all circumstances" of "booby traps which are in any way attached to or associated with … children's toys …"[34]

Two international tribunals recently have found defendants liable for civilian deaths caused by cluster munitions. In 2004, the Eritrea-Ethiopia Claims Commission (EECC) held Eritrea liable for the deaths of civilians killed in cluster munition strikes on Mekele, Ethiopia on June 5, 1998. The 1998, lethal cluster bomb attack on Mekele by Eritrean aircraft at the outbreak of hostilities with Ethiopia killed scores of civilians and fanned the flames of the conflict. On June 12, 2007, the International Criminal Tribunal for the Former Yugoslavia (ICTY) held the former president of the now defunct Republic of Serbian Krajina (RSK),[35] criminally liable for deaths and injuries resulting from cluster munition rocket attacks on Zagreb, Croatia on May 2-3, 1995.[36] Both the EECC and the ICTY held that commanders should act to prevent future strikes when they have fore knowledge about the adverse humanitarian effects of weaponry in actual combat usage. The ICTY also held the defendant liable for the death of one person and the injury of another by dud submunitions.[37]

Although it took two and half years to clear Kosovo, the population can never be assured that all the submunition duds, in fact, have been cleared. Unlike mines, cluster bombs cannot be precisely marked and often hide themselves in mud, underbrush, trees, bodies of water, and even house roofs. As a practical matter, therefore, large portions of the land of Kosovo and Serbia will be forever environmentally damaged, prejudicing the health of the population. In other theatres of war, for example, Laos, civilians are still dying from Vietnam-era cluster bombs dropped over fifty years ago.

Cluster munitions are present in all regions: countries from Africa, the Americas, Asia, Europe, and the Middle East have used, produced, stockpiled, and transferred them, and some countries have transferred them to non-state armed groups.[38] Their widespread use and stockpiling represent a continued threat to civilians, particularly to children, who are disproportionately likely to be harmed by cluster munitions.[39]

Cluster Munitions Convention

The issue of legal control of cluster munitions was initially discussed within the framework of the 1980 Convention on the Prohibitions or Restrictions on the Use of Certain Conventional Weapons Which May Be Deemed to Be Excessively Injurious or to Have Indiscriminate Effects (CCW). The CCW and its five Protocols seek to prohibit and restrict the use of certain conventional weapons that are considered to cause excessive injuries and unnecessary suffering, or to have indiscriminate effects. The CCW itself does not contain specific limitations on the use of certain weapons, and is instead confined to general provisions such as its scope, entry into force and structure. It is only a framework convention and has separate protocols each regulating specific types or categories of conventional weapons.

A modified version of Protocol II (Amended Protocol II), which strengthened the rules of landmines, booby traps and other devices (besides putting greater emphasis on anti-personnel landmines), was adopted on May 3, 1996. In a further amendment to Article 1 of the CCW on December 21, 2001 during the Second Review Conference, the scope of existing Protocols (up to Protocol IV) was extended to cover internal conflicts. During the Review, the States Parties also agreed to the elaboration of the proposals concerning the problems of explosive remnants of war (ERW) and the adoption of a new protocol to the CCW.[40]

However, during the Review Conference, no consensus could be reached on binding measures relating to the procurement, stockpiling, or the actual use of the weapons with a view to avoiding ERW as far as possible. No decision on banning or regulating cluster munitions was taken at the Conference. The lack of substantive action on banning cluster munitions frustrated a number of States. Norway therefore, called on States, the ICRC and international NGOs to develop a legally binding instrument on cluster munitions outside the CCW framework. The Conference on Cluster Munitions was held in Oslo and on February 23, 2007, 46 participating States signed the Oslo Declaration committing themselves to a future legally binding instrument banning cluster munitions.[41] The Convention entered into force 1 August 2010. The United Nations Secretary-General is the depository for the treaty. To date 119 states have joined the convention, of which 101 are States Parties and remaining 18 are signatories that have yet to ratify.

The CCM[42] is a humanitarian and disarmament instrument, and bans the use, production, transfer, and stockpiling of cluster munitions and establishes post-conflict remedial measures designed to minimize harm to civilians. The convention has the potential to eliminate deaths and injuries from this type of weapon in the future. It is the first weapons treaty to identify non-state armed groups (NSAGs) as potential users and suggests, in its preamble that states parties have a duty to prevent them from acting contrary to the convention.[43] The CCM offers new solutions for changing warfare and the welfare of civilians caught in it. It has a few unique features.

First, it advances the key components of IHL: the principles of discrimination and proportionality. Second, it strengthens IHL by articulating stronger obligations on states that use cluster munitions. Third, it reinforces the linkages between IHL and international human rights law. Thus, the CCM not only demonstrated the crystallisation of IHL norms; it also strengthened their content and the likelihood of its implementation by providing detailed obligations.[44]

Article 1 of the Convention obliges every State party never under any circumstances to (i) Use cluster munitions; (ii) Develop, produce, otherwise acquire, stockpile, retain or transfer to anyone, directly or indirectly, cluster munitions; or (iii) Assist, encourage or induce anyone to engage in any activity prohibited to a State Party under this Convention.

This CCM does not apply to mines and munitions designed to dispense flares, smoke, pyrotechnics or chaff for an air defence role. The Convention also does not cover a munition or submunition designed to produce electrical or electronic effects. The following cumulative criteria do not qualify as cluster munitions and fall outside the scope of the prohibition:

(i) Each munition contains fewer than ten explosive submunitions;
(ii) Each explosive submunition weighs more than four kilograms;
(iii) Each explosive submunition is designed to detect and engage a single target object;
(iv) Each explosive submunition is equipped with an electronic self-destruction mechanism; and
(v) Each explosive submunition is equipped with an electronic self-deactivating feature.

Given the technical nature of the weapon, a number of definitions have been included in Article 2 of the Convention. These include, "explosive submunition," "failed cluster munition," "unexploded submunition," "abandoned cluster munitions," "cluster munition remnants," "self-destruction mechanism," and "self-deactivating."

Each State Party, under Article 3 undertakes to destroy or ensure the destruction of all cluster munitions as soon as possible but not later than eight years after the entry into force of this Convention. State Party is to ensure that destruction methods comply with applicable international standards for protecting public health and the environment. The transfer of cluster munitions to another State Party for the purpose of destruction is permitted.

Under Article 4, State Parties undertake to clear and destroy, or to ensure the clearance and destruction of cluster munition remnants located in contaminated areas under their jurisdiction or control, as soon as possible after the Convention has entered into force, but not later than 10 year after the end of the active hostilities, or 10 years after the Convention has entered into force for that party. The States parties are also obliged to take certain measures to ensure that the local population will not become a victim of cluster munition remnants.

The CCM advances stronger standards for the key IHL principles of discrimination and proportionality by elucidating the ways in which cluster munitions violate these principles. One of the most important principles of the law of armed conflict is the requirement that parties to a conflict must discriminate between military targets and civilians. The Convention also places the responsibility on user states. This is provided in Article 4.4, which articulates that a state party is "strongly encouraged" to clear the remnants of cluster munitions that it has used or abandoned before the treaty has entered into force. It provides:

> This paragraph shall apply in cases in which cluster munitions have been used or abandoned by one State Party ... and have become cluster munition remnants that are located in areas under the jurisdiction or control of another State Party ... (a) In such cases, upon entry ... the former State Party is strongly encouraged to provide ... assistance to the latter State Party ... to facilitate the marking, clearance and destruction of such cluster munition remnants. (b) Such assistance shall include, where available,

> information on types and quantities of the cluster munitions used, precise locations of cluster munition strikes and areas in which cluster munition remnants are known to be located.

Article 4.4 (b) also strongly encourages States to share information vital for timely and comprehensive clearance, including the "types and quantities of the cluster munitions used, precise locations of cluster munition strikes and areas in which cluster munition remnants are known to be located."

Because user states are in the best position to provide such information, this provision addresses the information gap that often hinders efficient and effective clearance following a cluster munitions strike. The information-sharing component of Article 4.4 (b) builds on existing international law, such as the annex of the CCW Protocol V on Explosive Remnants of War, which denotes the recording and sharing of such information with the "parties in control of the affected area" as best practices. Because information-sharing should also be undertaken regarding cluster munitions used or abandoned prior to the treaty's entry into force, the CCM provides for effective solutions to decades-long problems.

Article 6 of the Convention contains detailed provisions on international cooperation and on providing and receiving assistance. In order to enhance transparency, States Parties must report to the UN Secretary-General, as the Depository, about the different aspects and elements of implementation of the Convention.

Another way the CCM strengthens international legal norms is by integrating aspects of IHL and international human rights law. It contains many references to human rights law. For example, Preamble to CCM makes commitment for "ensuring the full realisation of the rights of all cluster munition victims" and to "the Convention on the Rights of Persons with Disabilities" which, *inter alia,* requires that States Parties to the Convention undertake to ensure and promote the full realisation of all human rights and fundamental freedoms of all persons with disabilities.

The Preamble recognises "the need to provide age- and gender-sensitive assistance to cluster munition victims and to address the special needs of vulnerable groups," thus incorporating such human rights sub-fields as children's rights, gender-specific rights, and the rights of other vulnerable groups—a category broad enough to refer to multiple groups, such as refugees and those made vulnerable by ethnic, religious, or other types of persecution.

A cluster munition victim has been defined in Article 2,[45] and victim assistance has been dealt in Article 5.1 of the Convention. It makes references to "applicable IHL and human rights law" when obligating State Parties to care for "cluster munition victims in areas under its jurisdiction or control." Obligations to provide assistance span to remedies typically considered social and economic in nature, such as "medical care, rehabilitation and psychological support, as well as ... social and economic inclusion." This article further requires State Parties to adapt their laws and create timely national plans and budgets to achieve victim assistance; additionally, such laws and plans are to be incorporated "within the existing national disability, development and human rights frameworks and mechanisms."[46] In this sense, the victim assistance provisions of the CCM mirror the traditional human rights and responsibilities model, in which states have human rights obligations to persons within their jurisdiction or territory. The Convention demonstrates that IHL, when it takes a long-term view of a weapon's effect, merges with the duties incumbent in human rights, including the social and economic duties states have to all persons within their jurisdiction. In doing so, the CCM advances the meaning and content of both IHL and international human rights law. Applicable international law includes the Convention on the Rights of Persons with Disabilities and the Mine Ban Treaty. Other instruments with relevant provisions that could support the implementation of the victim assistance obligations of the Convention on Cluster Munitions include the Convention on Conventional Weapons (CCW), the Convention on the Rights of the Child, the Convention on the Elimination of all Forms of Discrimination against Women, and the International Covenant on Civil and Political Rights.

The humanitarian impact of cluster munitions is dependent on the degree to which people are brought into contact with them. Thus, the impact in one country, or even one area of a country, will not be the same as in another. It depends, among other things, on the level of contamination, the terrain, land use, population density, common economic activities and resources, and the level of development. Impact also varies over time as these factors change. While it may be difficult to quantify the scale of contamination and its effects, the use of cluster munitions in the last six decades has demonstrated that it disrupts lives and societies. Cluster munitions, like any other mechanical device can malfunction, resulting in unexploded submunitions. Thus, given that they are used in the hundreds, thousands, or even millions, contamination is almost unavoidable. Contamination impedes post-conflict recovery and development as infrastructure, property and resources are rendered unusable or unsafe. Clearance operations may cost millions of dollars and can require decades of effort. The poor are most exposed and susceptible to the threat of cluster munition contamination because they have fewer alternatives. The only source of income—agriculture land available to them is contaminated—and they either take their chances by using the land or by attempting to clear the land themselves. Whenever cluster munitions are used, they continue long after to maim and kill indiscriminately and to disrupt families and communities, economies and countries.

Rarely in human history has a weapon become so stigmatised that a large sector of the international community decides that it must be completely banned in spite of opposition from powerful user states.[47] A number of military analysts have argued that since the majority of the world's significant military powers are not signatories to the Oslo Treaty the agreement must be more symbolic than enforceable international law. However, critics of cluster munitions hope the treaty will gain moral authority and stigmatise the use of the weapons resulting in the reduced use of the munitions.[48]

The Convention does not prohibit cluster munitions that can detect and engage a single target or explosive submunitions equipped with an electronic self-destruction or self-deactivating feature. This exemption permits sensor-fused or "smart" cluster submunitions.[49] Article 23, Paragraph 3 of the Convention permits States Parties to engage in military cooperation and operations with non-States Parties. It states:

> Notwithstanding the provisions of Article 1 of this Convention and in accordance with international law, States Parties, their military personnel or nationals, may engage in military cooperation and operations with States not party to this Convention that might engage in activities prohibited to a State Party.

The text does not prohibit "military cooperation and operations" with States not party to the Convention and which may use cluster munitions in a joint operation. Since cluster munitions cause unintended casualties among the civilian population long after the conclusion of the hostilities, the military should also have contingency plan for cleaning up unexploded munitions and submunitions.

The First Review Conference of the Convention on Cluster Munitions (CCM) was held in Dubrovnik, Croatia, from 7-11 September 2015. A total of 95 countries attended the meeting (61 States Parties, nine signatories, and 25 non-signatories) in addition to UN agencies and the ICRC. President of the First Review Conference, Croatia's Prime Minister Zoran Milanovic, in his opening address called on all countries to reject the use of cluster munitions and adopt the CCM. During the meeting, Colombia ratified the convention, while Cuba made an announcement committing to accede. States Parties adopted a progress report reviewing implementation since entry into force and an action plan. States Parties also adopted the "Dubrovnik Declaration" committing to end the harm caused by cluster munitions" and "ensure that cluster munitions remain a stigmatized weapon by working for a world free of the suffering, casualties and socio-economic impacts caused by the weapons. The Declaration's firm statement that "We condemn any use of cluster munitions by any actor" was adopted without amendment.

On 11 December 2015, Croatia and 36 co-sponsors introduced UNGA Resolution 70/54 on the implementation of the Convention on Cluster Munitions.[50] The non-binding resolution calls for full implementation of the Convention on Cluster Munitions and urges states outside the convention to join as soon as possible. It was the first UNGA resolution on the convention to be adopted by a vote. The resolution affirmed that in cases not covered by the CCM, or by other international agreements, civilians and combatants remain under the protection and authority of the principles of international law, derived from established custom, from the principles of humanity and from the dictates of public conscience.

It is widely acknowledged that cluster munition is outdated and counterproductive for modern militaries. Cluster munitions are also poor defensive weapons, leaving behind a large number of explosive submunitions that would endanger a State's own population. The political cost of using cluster munitions has become very high given the CCM's powerful stigmatising force. There is a hope that every country in the world would ratify the Convention to eliminate the problem posed by the cluster munitions.

Notes

1. The US Air Force describes cluster munitions as follows: "Cluster bombs, or CBUs, are used to attack area targets such as concentrations of military personnel, vehicles or armour. Among other things, the use of cluster munitions reduces the risks to aircrews and equipment by reducing the number of sorties required to effectively attack such military objectives. A CBU munitions consists of a canister-type dispenser containing submunitions, that disperse in the air after the dispenser opens. The submunitions, in general, arm after dispersal and detonate upon impact ... One dispenser of submunitions may cover an oblong or rectangular area on the ground measuring several hundred feet in length. The dispersal pattern is determined by the type of CBU, the dispenser spin rate (if the particular CBU uses spin to dispense the submunitions), and release parameters." Air Force Operations and the Law, The Judge Advocate General's Department, United States Air Force, First Edition, 2002, p. 296.
2. Today's cluster munitions can be delivered by aerial bombs, artillery shells, artillery rockets, and cruise missiles. The primary weapon, or dispenser, carries

scores, even hundreds, of submunitions. At a predetermined point prior to reaching the target, the dispenser releases the submunitions, dispersing them in the air and blanketing the target area. As the submunitions fall to the earth, their explosive mechanisms become armed, usually by rapid spinning or the deployment of small parachutes. Once armed, the submunitions explode either shortly before landing, on contact, or shortly after landing. The submunition casings are often scored to create a fragmentation pattern of uniformly shaped projectiles, rather than irregular shards of metal. These fragments make submunitions powerful anti-personnel weapons, capable of killing or seriously wounding anyone standing within 150 metres of the explosion. Each submunitions essentially acts similar to a powerful variant of the hand grenade. Many submunitions are designed to serve multiple purposes, and thus contain directional charges designed to penetrate armour or an incendiary element, such as zirconium, which burns at a very high temperature. The anti-armour submunitions usually must land in a particular manner to detonate, in order to ensure that the charge fires in the right direction. Thus, they are usually stabilised by parachutes in their descent. Daniel Joseph Raccuia, "The Convention on Cluster Munitions: An Incomplete Solution to the Cluster Munition Problem," vol. 44, no. 2, *Vanderbilt Journal of Transnational Law* (March 2011), pp. 472-76.

3. Virgil Wiebe, "Footprints of Death: Cluster Bombs as Indiscriminate Weapons under International Humanitarian Law," vol. 22, *Mich J. Int'l L.*, 2000, pp. 85-89.
4. Geneva International Centre for Humanitarian Demining, "A Guide to Cluster Munitions," 2nd ed., June 2009, p. 23, available at: http://www.gichd.org/fileadmin/pdf/publications/Guide-to-Cluster-Munitions-June2009.pdf, accessed January 22, 2012.
5. To protect civilians from the effects of cluster munitions, Norway and other like-minded countries initiated a fast-track diplomatic process in 2007 aimed at creating a new international treaty. Working in partnership with UN agencies, the ICRC, and civil society grouped under the Cluster Munition Coalition (CCM), the Oslo Process resulted in the adoption in May 2008 of the Convention on Cluster Munitions. After 30 states ratified, the CCM entered into force on August 1, 2010. It prohibits the use, production, transfer, and stockpiling of cluster munitions. The Convention also requires destruction of stockpiled cluster munitions within eight years, clearance of cluster munition remnants within 10 years, and assistance to victims, including those killed or injured by submunitions as well as their families and affected communities.
6. Article 2 (2), Convention on Cluster Munitions (CCM), 2008. The CCM also lists three exceptions to the general definition, excluding anti-aircraft weapons and countermeasures, munitions with electrical or electronic effects, and ordnances that carry fewer than ten submunitions and have specific safeguards that mitigate the negative externalities that led to the treaty's creation.
7. Cluster munitions have been used in combat since World War II, when Soviet forces dropped cluster munitions on German tanks and Germany dropped cluster munitions on the port of Grimsby in the UK. Mark Hiznay, "Operational and Technical Aspects of Cluster Munitions," in UN Inst. for Disarmament Research, vol. 4, *Disarmament Forum*, 2006, pp. 15-25, available at: http://www.unidir.org/pdf/articles/pdf-art2530.pdf.
8. During the 1961-75 Vietnam War cluster bombs were used by the USA as area-denial and anti-personnel weapons. A total of roughly 1.5 million cluster bombs used in the conflict contained 750 million bomblets, dropped onto portions of Viet Nam, Laos and Cambodia over a period of about a decade. The initial appeal of

cluster munitions during the Vietnam War was this ability to blanket large areas with just a few bombs. American aircrews put them to use in attacking enemy anti-aircraft positions. Because today's sophisticated guidance systems were not yet in existence, hitting a relatively small target with a unitary bomb was a difficult task that often required an aircraft to fly low, making it more susceptible to anti-aircraft fire. Cluster munitions offered a solution to this problem. By covering a wide area with small but powerful bomblets, they increased the margin of error when aiming at small targets and allowed attacking planes to maintain safer altitudes. The same properties that made the bombs useful in attacking small singular targets offered advantages in attacking troop columns and vehicles—not only was accuracy less of a concern than with a unitary bomb, but the ability to engage multiple targets at once increased the weapons' utility. Responding to political pressure, American commanders also used cluster munitions in situations where they had previously been using napalm. Eric Prokosch and Earnst Jan Hogendoorn, "Anti-personnel Weapons," in Ilkka Taipale (ed.), *War of Health? A Reader* (New York: Zed Books, 2002), p. 71.

9. In 1991, Allied forces delivered approximately fifty million simple-fuse and parachute-fuse submunitions in Iraq. Mark Hiznay, "Operational and Technical Aspects of Cluster Munitions, in UN Institute for Disarmament Research," vol. 4, *Disarmament Forum,* 2006, pp. 15-25, available at: http://www.unidir.org/pdf/articles/pdf-art2530.pdf.
10. NATO forces, primarily the US and British, used cluster munitions extensively in the 1999 aerial bombing campaign over Kosovo.
11. The US recently made extensive use of cluster munitions in Iraq and Afghanistan. Karl C. Ching, "The Use of Cluster Munitions in the War on Terrorism," vol. 31, *Suffolk Transnational Law Review,* 2007, pp. 127-40.
12. Thirty-four states manufacture or have manufactured cluster munitions. These are Argentine, Belgium, Brazil Bulgaria, Canada, Chile, China, Egypt, France, Germany, Greece, India, Iran, Iraq, Israel, Italy, Japan, North Korea, South Korea, the Netherlands, Pakistan, Poland, Romania, Russia, Serbia & Montenegro, Singapore, Slovakia, South Africa, Spain, Sweden, Switzerland, Turkey, the UK, and the US. *The Human Rights Watch Regional Fact Sheet Report,* April 2008.
13. Nout van Woudenberg and Wouter Wormgoor, "Cluster Munitions Convention: Around the World in One Year," in Tim McCormack (ed.), *Yearbook of International Humanitarian Law,* vol. 11, 2008, The Netherlands: TMC Asser Press, pp. 391-406.
14. The US CBU-87 has been designed for use against troop concentrations, materiel and armour. Each dispenser contains 202 submunitions or bomblets. The bomblets have no self-destruct or other safety feature should they fail to operate as intended. The UK air-delivered cluster bomb, the RBL 755 contains 147 bomblets and produces an area of effect of roughly one hundred metres by two hundred metres. *Working Paper on the Military Utility of Cluster Munitions,* prepared by the United Kingdom Delegation to the Conventional Weapons Convention Group of Governmental Experts Meeting in Geneva, March 2005.
15. Colin King, *Explosive Remnants of War: Submunitions and Other Unexploded Ordnance,* ICRC, August 2000, pp. 10–11.
16. *Cluster Munition Monitor,* 2012, p. 17.
17 Use of Cluster Munition in Syria, technical briefing Note, Human Rights watch, 4 April 2014.
18. Cluster Munition Monitor 2016, International Campaign to Ban Landmines – Cluster Munition Coalition (ICBL-CMC), August 2016, p. 58-60.

19 Circle of Impact: The Fatal Footprint of Cluster Munitions on People and Communities, Handicap-International, May 2007.

20. The use of cluster munitions almost inevitably results in explosive remnants of war (ERW) since it must be assumed that some of the submunitions do not explode on impact are, therefore, left unexploded at the cessation of hostilities. Nout van Woudenberg and Wouter Wormgoor, "Cluster Munitions Convention: Around the World in One Year," in Tim McCormack (ed.), *Yearbook of International Humanitarian Law*, vol. 11, 2008,The Netherlands: TMC Asser Press, pp. 391-406.

21. A number of factors influence submunition reliability. These include delivery technique, age of the submunition, air temperature, landing in soft or muddy ground, getting caught in trees and vegetation, and submunitions being damaged after dispersal, or landing in such a manner that their impact fuzes fail to initiate. Submunitions lacking a self-destruct capability (duds or dumb munitions) are of particular concern because they can remain a hazard for decades, thereby increasing the potential for civilian casualties.

22. The reasons of high rate of failure are: storage of weapons, loading, airspeed, wind conditions, terrain, angle of submunitions impact and drop height. Brian Rappert, *Controlling the Weapons of War: Politics, Persuasion and the Prohibition of Inhumanity* (London: Routledge, 2006), p. 148.

23. Daniel Joseph Raccuia, "The Convention on Cluster Munitions: An Incomplete Solution to the Cluster Munition Problem," vol. 44, *Vanderbilt Journal of Transnational Law*, 2011, pp. 465-97.

24. Brian Rappert, *Controlling the Weapons of War: Politics, Persuasion and the Prohibition of Inhumanity* (London: Routledge, 2006), p. 149.

25. *Explosive Remnants of War (ERW): Warnings and Risk Education*, Geneva International Centre for Humanitarian Demining, Geneva, Switzerland, May 2003.

26. According to Article 1 of the Convention on the Rights of Child and based on the principle of majority, incorporated in most of the international legal systems, a child is defined as "human being below the age of eighteen years unless, under the law applicable to the child, majority is attained earlier."

27. In contrast to APM, which are aiming at injuring individuals, cluster munitions contain larger charges, made to kill, and hence putting children at a greater risk to die. Victims may suffer from amputation of one or several limbs, fragmentation injuries, the loss of senses such as vision, hearing and touch, burns, internal injuries such as spinal cord damages and serious traumas in various body parts for instance the chest, the abdomen, craniofacial regions as well as upper and lower limbs. Aigner Helena, Consequences of Cluster Munitions on the rights of the child, *ICL Journal*, Vol. 10, pp.56,

28. Cluster munitions have a humanitarian impact on civilian populations at the time of use and post-conflict. There is an immediate danger of injury or death to civilians during cluster munition strikes, especially in built-up areas. After hostilities have ceased, unexploded submunitions pose a threat to the population, with the potential to cause death or physical and psychological trauma, and disrupt economic activities and daily life. The fear of such dangers, and the resulting influence on behaviour, can have real effects on the well-being of individuals and communities. Submunitions can prevent or hinder the peace-building and development efforts. Unexploded cluster munitions also pose a physical threat to humanitarian workers and peacekeepers. Collectively, prior to any destruction activities, 24 States Parties possessed 1.09 million cluster munitions and 143

million submunitions. *The Humanitarian Impact of Cluster Munitions*, Geneva: United Nations Institute for Disarmament Research, 2008, p. 1.

29. Article 35 (c), AP I. Nicholas G. Alexander, Comment, Airstrikes and Environmental Damage: Can the United States Be Held Liable for Operation Allied Force?" vol. 11, *COLO. J. INT'L ENVTL. L. & POL'Y* (2000), pp. 471-98.
30. The provision is also applicable during the non-international armed conflicts under Article 13(2) of 1977 Additional Protocol II to the Geneva Conventions of 1949.
31. The Israeli use of cluster munitions during their invasion of Lebanon in 2006 was condemned by Amnesty International calling it "indiscriminate and disproportionate." Mounting civilian casualties, apparently caused by the Israeli use of CMs during the last few days of the conflict, resulted in an investigation by the UN Human Rights Council. The investigation produced a report that accused Israel of the improper use of CMs, resulting in human rights violations. Jan Egeland, a member of the UN Council, said "what is shocking and completely immoral is 90% of the cluster bomb strikes occurred in the last 72 hours of the conflict, when we knew there would be resolution." Excessive civilian casualties in the conflict resulted in calls for international regulation on the use and production of CMs. *Lieutenant Colonel Michael O. Lacey,* "Cluster Munitions: Wonder Weapon or Humanitarian Horror?" *The Army Lawyer*, May 2009, pp. 28-33.
32. Defenders of using cluster bombs might argue that the prohibition in Article 51(5) applies only to "attacks." The Additional Protocol I, however, defines "attacks" broadly: "Attacks mean acts of violence against the adversary, whether in offence or in defence." This definition of attacks applies to any land, sea or air warfare which may affect the civilian population, individual civilians, or civilian objects on land. Thomas Michael McDonnell, "Cluster Bombs Over Kosovo: A Violation of International Law?" Pace Law Faculty Publications, Paper 282. Available at: http://digitalcommons.pace.edu/lawfaculty/282, accessed March 23, 2012, p. 85.
33. Joseph Anzalone, "The Virtue of a Proportional Response: The United States Stance Against the Convention on Cluster Munitions," vol. 22, *Pace Int'l L. Rev.*, 2010, pp. 183-211.
34. Presumably, the designers of the submunition did not intend it to be attractive to children. The bright colour presumably is used to help clearance crews find dud submunitions. The small parachute serves an important orienting and arming function. Under general principles of criminal law, however, an actor may still be considered to have acted intentionally when he or she hopes that an injury will not occur yet knows to a practical certainty that it will. Thus, even though neither the designers, who made the submunitions, nor the Generals who ordered their use, nor the pilots who delivered these bombs may have intended the harm, they would still be acting intentionally because they knew that it is practically certain that a deadly device made to look like a toy will be picked up by children. Thomas Michael McDonnell, *Cluster Bombs over Kosovo: A Violation of International Law?* Pace Law Faculty Publications, Paper 282, p. 82. Available at: http://digitalcommons.pace.edu/lawfaculty/282, accessed March 23, 2012.
35. In 1995, Milan Martic was the President of the Republic of Serbian Krajina (RSK), an area in what is now Croatia.
36. *Prosecutor v. Martic*, Case No. IT-95-1 I-T, Judgment, 456-73 (June 12, 2007), available at http://www.un.org/icty/martic/trialc/judgement/mar-tcjud07O6I2e.pdf, accessed March 22, 2011.

37. Virgil Wiebe, "For Whom the Little Bells Toll: Recent Judgments by International Tribunals on the Legality of Cluster Munitions," vol. 35, issue 4, *Pepperdine Law Review*, 2008, pp. 895-966. Available at: http://digitalcommons.pepperdine.edu/plr/vol35/iss4/2, accessed April 29, 2012.
38. Human Rights Watch, "Flooding South Lebanon: Israel's Use of Cluster Munitions in Lebanon in July and August 2006," available at http://www.hrw.org/reports/2008/lebanon0208/lebanon0208web.pdf6. The Report states that at least fourteen countries have used cluster munitions, at least thirty-four have produced them, at least seventy-six stockpile them, and that they have been used in at least thirty countries and territories and have been transferred by at least thirteen states to at least sixty other states and non-state armed groups.
39. Press Release, UNICEF, "UNICEF Highlights the Horrific Impact of Cluster Munitions on Children as Governments Meet to Decide on Treaty Banning the Weapon" (May 19, 2008), available at: http://www.unicef.org/media/media_43982.html, accessed January 22, 2012.
40. The CCW has five protocols: The 1980 Protocol I on Non-Detectable Fragments; the 1980 Protocol II on Prohibition or Restrictions on the Use of Mines, Booby Traps and Other Devices; the 1980 Protocol III on the Prohibition or Restrictions on the Use of Incendiary Weapons; the 1995 Protocol IV on Blinding Laser Weapons; and the 2003 Protocol V on Explosive Remnants of War.
41. Nout van Woudenberg and Wouter Wormgoor, "Cluster Munitions Convention: Around the World in One Year," in Tim McCormack (ed.), *Yearbook of International Humanitarian Law*, vol. 11, 2008, The Netherlands: TMC Asser Press, pp. 391-406.
42. The text of the Convention on Cluster Munitions (CCM) was completed on May 30, 2008. The Convention was opened for signature at a signing conference in Oslo on December 3, 2008 and entered into force on August 1, 2010—six months after its ratification by 30 States parties. A total of 111 countries have signed or acceded to the Convention on Cluster Munitions as of July 31, 2012, of which 75 are States Parties legally bound by all of the convention's provisions. The CCM is an example of an agreement based on the principle that, even if a given weapon delivers some military advantage, it should still be limited or banned because the humanitarian consequences of use outweigh any military benefit.
43. Docherty Bonnie, Breaking New Ground: The Convention on Cluster Munitions and the Evolution of International Humanitarian Law, Human Rights Quarterly, Volume 31, Number 4, November 2009, pp. 934-963.
44. Jessica Corsi, "Towards Peace Through Legal Innovation: The Process and the Promise of the 2008 Cluster Munitions Convention," vol. 22, *Harvard Human Rights Journal*, 2009, pp. 145-57.
45. According to Article 2 (1) CCM, "all persons who have been killed or suffered physical or psychological injury, economic loss, social marginalisation or substantial impairment of the realization of their rights caused by the use of cluster munitions are termed as 'victims.' They include those persons directly impacted by cluster munitions as well as their affected families and communities."
46. The Convention on Cluster Munitions requires that States Parties with cluster munition victims implement the following victim assistance activities: (i) Collect relevant data and assess the needs of cluster munition victims; (ii) Coordinate victim assistance programmes, including by designating a government focal point; (iii) Develop a national plan, budget, and time frames for implementation; (iv) Report and monitor obligations regarding implementation; (v) Consult with

and actively involve cluster munition victims; (vi) Provide adequate assistance, including medical care, rehabilitation, psychological support, and social and economic inclusion for victims; (vii) Implement national legislation according to the principles of international law; and (viii) Provide assistance that is gender- and age-sensitive as well as non-discriminatory. Article 5, CCM.

47. Jessica Corsi, "Towards Peace Through Legal Innovation: The Process and the Promise of the 2008 Cluster Munitions Convention," vol. 22, *Harv. Human Rights Journal*, 2009, pp. 145-57.
48. Liz Sly, "Can the Cluster Bomb Be More Than a Symbol?" *Chi. Trib.*, December 3, 2008, available at http://archives.chicagotribune.com/2008/dec/03/nation/chi-lebanon-cluster_slydec03.
49. In an ideal world, there would be an inexhaustible supply of perfectly precise weapons which technology would allow to be targeted individually against every kind of military objective in all circumstances and which would operate with absolute reliability on all occasions. Technology does not yet permit us to achieve this high standard, and not all States are at the same stage in this development process. William Boothby, *Cluster Bombs: Is There a Case for New Law*, Programme on Humanitarian Policy and Conflict Research, Harvard University, Occasional Paper Series, Fall 2005, no. 5, p. 44.
50. UN General Assembly Resolution UN Doc A/RES/70/54 dated 11 December 2015.

4 C

EXPLOSIVE REMNANTS OF WAR

Combatants have a wide range of ammunition and explosives available to them. These may include small arms ammunition, pyrotechnics, grenades, mortar ammunition, projectiles, landmines, guided missiles, free flight rockets, aircraft bombs, and unmanned aerial vehicles and "cruise" missiles. Even when properly targeted, however, many explosive weapons fail to function as designed. These explosive munitions that have been fired, dropped or otherwise delivered during the war but have failed to explode as intended or have been abandoned by the warring parties on the battlefield are termed as explosive remnants of war (ERW).[1]

ERW pose serious threat to humanity and environment. For instance, at the end of the Second World War, Poland's territory was saturated with unexploded mines, missiles and other explosives of warfare. These ERW prevented the economic utilisation of nearly 20,000 sq km for more than five years. Explosion from war remnants killed nearly 4,000 persons, including 3,000 children, and injured over 8,000, of which nearly 7,000 were children.[2] Unexploded ordnance left over from the Vietnam War has killed more than 42,000, while some 62,000 people have been injured in the country since the conflict ended in 1975.[3]

Nearly every armed conflict in modern times has left behind large amounts of explosive remnants.[4] ERW found in conflict affected areas may vary in size from hand grenades the size of an apple to large aircraft bombs weighing more than 1,000 kg. Although they have failed to function as intended, ERW can sometimes require only the slightest disturbance to detonate. They remain unpredictable in behaviour, and their age and appearance can be deceptive. For instance, lethal explosives from the First World War found in France and Belgium, are often found to be in perfect working order.[5] Two apparently identical items of ordnance might behave very differently when handled, depending on what has happened to that item before it is discovered.

ERW are a persistent problem and a deadly threat that kill and injure large numbers of men, women and children who disturb or tamper with them.[6] As these weapons often take years and even decades to clear, their presence can hinder reconstruction, the delivery of humanitarian aid, farming and the return of people displaced by the fighting.[7] It is estimated that at least 80 countries and 10 territories are affected by ERW.[8]

Explosive Remnants of War

Until 2003, Explosive Remnants of War (ERW) was used as a broad term for explosive ordnance (such as mortar bombs, grenades, cluster submunitions and air-dropped bombs) which have not exploded and are left as a hazard in the post-conflict environment.[9] This resulted from ordnance being fired but failing to explode (unexploded ordnance—UXO) or from ordnance stores being abandoned during the fighting (abandoned explosive ordnance—AXO). The 2003 CCW Protocol V on Explosive Remnants of War defines ERW as "unexploded ordnance and abandoned explosive ordnance."[10] The term "unexploded ordnance" means explosive ordnance that has been primed, fused, armed, or otherwise prepared for use and used in an armed conflict. It may have been fired, dropped, launched or projected and should have exploded but has failed to do so. The term "abandoned explosive ordnance" means explosive ordnance that has not been used during an armed conflict, that has been left behind or dumped by a party to an armed conflict, and which is no longer under control of the party that left it behind or dumped it. Abandoned explosive ordnance may or may not have been primed, fused, armed or otherwise prepared for use.[11]

ERW can be generated in many ways and present a variety of hazards due to the diverse types of ammunition used. In the post-conflict situation, the battlefields are often littered with explosive debris. The explosive threat from the debris can be divided into four categories (i) mine and unexploded military ordnance (UXO), (ii) abandoned armoured vehicles (AFV), (iii) small arms and light weapons (SALW), and (iv) abandoned, damaged/disrupted stockpiles of ammunition and explosives.[12]

Toxic Munitions Constituents

Munitions, explosives and other military use materials contain a range of potentially hazardous elements and compounds. Common metal constituents in small and light weapons ammunition include lead (Pb), copper (Cu), mercury (Hg), antimony (Sb) and tungsten (W). Out of these, lead makes up 95-97 per cent of the metallic components of military ammunitions and grenades. Energetic materials recognised as being toxic are also prevalent in munitions.[13] Whether solid, liquid or vaporised, these substances have the potential to lead to environmental contamination and may negatively affect human health depending on dose, duration and route of exposure.

Metals generally adhere to soil or partially dissolve in water, where they may be transported to deeper layers, and can end up in biota. Only one metal, i.e, Hg volatilizes in elemental form at room temperature, other metals are not volatilized, unless methylated/alkylated. Because they do not break down in the environment, heavy metal contamination can result in long-term risks for public health and the environment as a whole. Explosive substances undergo varying types of chemical and biochemical transformation, depending on the compounds involved and environmental and microbial conditions, this makes predicting their environmental fate and subsequent health risks complex. Most explosive compounds are relatively persistent in the environment. TNT may be transformed by sunlight or microbial action into compounds more toxic than itself. The majority of the particulate explosives are not very mobile in the environment, and absorbed materials provide an ongoing source of groundwater contamination. Particulate explosives adsorbed to soil particles may be spread over a wide area as wind-blown dust. The degradation of explosives is affected by many factors, such as the presence of oxygen, light and microorganisms. For nitramines that end up in the environment, such as RDX and HMX, the half-life is generally hundreds of days.

Many of the heavy metals, energetic compounds, and some of their decomposition products, such as DNTs and amino-DNTs that have been used in the Syrian conflict have been proven to be carcinogenic, genotoxic or mutagenic. Acute or chronic exposure to some has also been associated with respiratory problems, skins problems, or other detrimental effects on the organs, and scenarios in which civilians could be exposed to a range of toxic munitions residues in Syria are commonplace. Civilians or combatants can be exposed directly or indirectly to these substances, be it through ingestion of contaminated soil, food or water or by inhalation of toxic fumes, dust or particles.

Global impact of ERW

ERW and Mines Other Than Anti-Personnel Mines (MOTAPM) present hazardous contamination in almost all post-conflict environments. Wherever explosive ordnance has been used in armed conflict, some ERW contamination is generated. In a survey, it has been identified that more than 80 countries or disputed territories world over contain some level of ERW contamination.[14] There are a number of countries, for example Belgium, Germany, Greece, Latvia, Lithuania, the Netherlands, Slovakia, Slovenia and the UK, that have a residual ERW problem, as a result of WWI and WWII. Today, at least 24 countries and territories in sub-Saharan Africa appear to suffer negative socio-economic effects from the presence of ERW. They are posing significant problems in several countries in the Central and South Americas, including Nicaragua. Due to prolonged armed conflict in Asia and the Pacific, nineteen countries including

Afghanistan, Iraq, Nepal, Pakistan, Sri Lanka and Vietnam[15] have been affected by ERW. It has also caused socio-economic effects in 13 countries and territories in Europe, and at least 7 in Central Asia. Seventeen countries and territories in the Middle East and North Africa experience socio-economic impacts from ERW or mines. A few serious situations of ERW contamination are discussed in greater detail.[16]

Kuwait: Wide desert and coastal areas of Kuwait were contaminated with mines and ERW, as a result of the 1990-1991 Gulf War. Despite massive demining operations that employed foreign contractors following the war, mines still remain in some areas, particularly along the natural sand corridors.[17] According to a 2009 United States Overseas Security Advisory Council report, "unexploded bombs, mines, and other ordnance from the 1991 Gulf War remain present in some desert areas in Kuwait." Unexploded ordnance has also been discovered in piles of sand used at construction sites, including at Camp Arifjan, the largest US military base in the country.[18] In the west, southeast, and north of the country, ERW are still found under oil lakes as a consequence of the destruction of Kuwaiti oil wells by Iraqi forces in 1991. Bubiyan Island, off the northeast coast of Kuwait, was used for military exercises and is also contaminated with ERW.[19] The Kuwait Institute for Scientific Research (KISR) holds the most comprehensive information on ERW casualties covering the period from August 1990 to 2002. Its records show that ERW and mines killed 204 people and injured 1,201 during this period.[20]

Sri Lanka: Civilians in Sri Lanka have a very different relationship with ERW compared to landmines. Mines are treated with respect and known/marked minefields avoided. Due to the more random nature of ERW, there is a greater risk of unintentional interaction with it. Most incidents of explosion have occurred when people interacted with ERW, either out of curiosity or deliberately due to economic needs. It also happened while clearing land, collecting firewood and water, tending animals or because they were in proximity to ERW.

Afghanistan: Afghanistan still has to clear what remains of the hundreds of thousands of decades-old mines and explosive remnants dating as far back as the 1979-89 war with the Soviet Union and the subsequent factional fighting, even as newer explosives take lives on a daily basis. The ongoing conflict is restricting the movements of demining crews, civilians are being killed and maimed by homemade roadside bombs planted by insurgents, as well as unexploded ordnance left behind by coalition forces around bases they abandoned. According to UN Mine Action Service, Afghanistan has successfully carried out one of the world's largest demining efforts over several decades, removing nearly two million items of explosive material, more than 700,000 antipersonnel mines and more than 29,000 antitank mines. The efforts have resulted in a 65 percent reduction in casualties caused by mines and explosive remnants since 2001. Further, the programme to remove unexploded ordnance (UXO) and ERW in and around the city of Mosul could cost $50 million.[21]

Lebanon: All regions of Lebanon have been significantly affected by ERW due to its various conflicts, including the civil war (1970-1990), two Israeli invasions and its 18-year occupation, the US bombing campaign (1983) and Israeli bombardments in 2006. The 2006 conflict, in which Israel bombarded southern Lebanon with 4 million cluster munitions in the space of 2 months resulted in 1/4 of Lebanon's arable land contaminated; up to 1/3 of the Lebanese population were affected; and the economic costs of lost livelihoods, mine action activities and casualties were estimated at between USD 150 and 230 million.

Iraq: Iraq is one of the most landmine and ERW contaminated regions in the world, with an estimated 18 million mines laid during the Iran-Iraq war and an additional 1 million planted prior to the US-led invasions in 1991 and 2003. These US-led invasions also utilised cluster bombs and other weapons which dispersed an estimated 52 million submunitions primarily across southern Iraq, but also some in Kuwait and in the Kurdistan Region of Iraq. According to the Iraqi government, the primary risks are posed to the development of Iraq's oil fields, tourism and agricultural sectors, however, casualties from ERW and landmines are likely underreported. Several of the Syrian refugee camps established on or near former military installations also face risk of UXO contamination. Mine action group has cleared and destroyed about 60 UXO from Domiz camp and 1,200 UXO from the Bajet Kandela transit camp site, which received Syrian refugees. Due to ongoing contamination around the camps and the limited awareness among Syrians, refugees are at high risk of being affected by ERW and land-mines. The Syrian conflict driven by the Islamic State and other Iraqi opposition groups in Anbar and northern Iraq are also leaving UXO threats.

Turkey: Since the 1950s, the Syria-Turkey border has been mined by the Government of Turkey (GoT). Turkey's borders with Bulgaria, Georgia and Greece have also been mined, although the GoT has reported that these borders have been cleared of mines. In addition, during the 1980s and 1990s conflict, both the GoT and the Kurdistan Workers' Party (KPP) laid mines in southeastern Turkey. In March 2013, the GoT had identified over 3,500 contaminated areas, with about 20% of the areas located near military infrastructure, and a further 350 areas suspected to be contaminated. 90% of the identified contamination is located along the Syrian border. In 2003, the governments of Syria and Turkey reportedly agreed to demine the border between the 2 countries and in 2009, the GoT passed a law to demine its side of the border. Since the conflict erupted in Syria, these demining efforts have been halted. Turkey is also affected by ERW, particularly due to fighting near the Syria-Turkey border and in the southeast as a result of the conflict with the KKP.

Libya: Even brief conflicts can give rise to major ERW crises. For instance, at the end of the 2011 international armed conflict, Libya found itself contaminated by a large amount of unexploded and abandoned ordnance. The country was already enduring the effects of unexploded landmines laid during the desert battles of World War II, and of contamination resulting from armed conflicts with its neighbours in the 1970s and 1980s. In 2012, clearance organizations destroyed more than 240,000 pieces of ERW in Libya.

Syria: Syria's major cities—Damascus, Homs, and Aleppo—are still affected by fighting between government forces and armed groups, in addition to the bombing by the international coalition led by the Americans or by the Russian air force. Significant proportions of bombs do not explode on impact and are embedded in the ground or in buildings. These cities will have a high density of explosive remnants which will pose a threat to civilians in highly populated urban areas. The international community will have to launch an unprecedented clearance operation in Syria. According to Handicap International, it may take at least 30 years to clear these contaminated areas with high concentrations of ERW.[22] While the physical and humanitarian impacts of explosive weapons, such as mortars, missiles, barrel bombs and IEDs, have been highly visible and documented throughout the conflict in Syria, the unexploded remnants of these weapons and landmines have received limited attention. Intense fighting in urban areas likely involves the use of a variety of small and medium calibre munitions, explosives from mortars, artillery rounds, bombs, RPGs, and surface-to-surface and air-to-surface missiles. Low-order detonations, i.e., not fully detonated bombs, can result in the leaking of explosives such as RDX, DNT and TNT, contaminating soil, surface water and groundwater. The intensive use of explosive munitions and information limitations throughout the conflict means that it will take decades of rigorous clearance efforts, as ERW are buried among rubble and debris.

ERW contamination in urban areas in Syria, where conflict is in the sixth year may require decades of clearance efforts. In the due course of time, ERW and landmines will also migrate due to flooding or erosion, particularly in soft, sandy soil, thereby further spreading the contamination risk. Prior to 2011, Syria experienced some ERW contamination, with high concentration of mines and ERW in the occupied Golan Heights and Quneitra governorate, as well as in other areas due to various con-flicts with Israel. Between 2011 and

2012, the number of victims of ERW/mines increased significantly due to significant population movements along the borders. The ongoing conflict in Syria has left many cities and towns littered with damaged and destroyed military hardware, including tanks and armoured vehicles. The conflict has seen the deployment of a wide range of weapons by all parties. The use of massive quantities of munitions from North Africa, Europe, Russia as well and Asia is likely to leave a serious environmental footprint in Syria.[23]

Many rural areas in Syria have suffered the same fate due to constant fighting between a multitude of armed groups. Whenever there's a lull in the fighting, displaced families try to move back to their homes. In order to survive, they often try to remove explosive devices themselves from their homes, immediate environment, and fields. This is highly dangerous, because these people are generally not aware of the dangers posed by explosive remnants of war and improvised explosive devices (IEDs). These devices such as 'barrel bombs',[24] large oil drums, gas cylinders, and water tanks, filled with high explosives such as RDX, TNT and scrap metal for fragmentation effects have also been used in Syrian conflict. Hundreds of attacks have been reported in Aleppo and in several other towns in Syria, such as Daara, Darayya, Idlib and Homs, resulting in the death and injury of thousands of civilians. There are not enough local, trained, monitored, and coordinated teams to guarantee the safety of people who have moved back to their homes. It is unlikely that the Syrian countryside will ever be entirely cleared of ERW, just like parts of northern and eastern France and Belgium, where shells left over from World War I and II are still found every year.[25]

ERW victims are predominantly male; this is mostly related to the division of labour. It has resulted in economic implications for the family and community as a whole as the principal breadwinner is killed or disabled. Although women are not at high risk from ERW, they bear the burden of the long-term consequences, looking after a disabled husband or child, while continuing household works without effective social support. Many have to assume the responsibilities of head of household and earn an income, breaking cultural constructions. Death or injury has serious economic implications for households. The internal armed conflict has affected the country and government support has been minimal. Continuing death and injury from ERW has impeded resettlement, rehabilitation and delayed people from rebuilding their lives and livelihoods.[26]

ERW also affects schools, community centre, places of worship and cemeteries, preventing people from returning to normal everyday lives. This may create frustration and anger that could result in violence, endangering the peace process. Though most ERW may not be harmful to the environment as such, detonated explosives are toxic. Once detonated, ERW can be toxic and contaminates soil and water through secondary exposure.[27]

ERW and Children

Many innocent civilians, including children have lost their lives and limbs by disturbing or inadvertently coming into contact with ERW. It poses a greater risk to children than APM: children are at risk when they are involved in economic activities such as collecting firewood or playing in an area infested with ERW. They also deliberately tamper with ERW out of curiosity when they do not recognise it as a dangerous munition, or to demonstrate bravery.

In 2009, a total of 3,956 new casualties from ERW and victim-activated improvised explosive devices (IEDs) were recorded in 64 countries. It was discovered that children made up more than half of all casualties in 14 countries: Afghanistan, Chad, Eritrea, Georgia, Guinea-Bissau, India, Jordan, Kuwait, Mali, Mozambique, Nepal, Philippines, Somalia, Somaliland, and Sudan. In some countries, child casualties, particularly due to ERW, were on the rise again after several years of decreases, for example, in Afghanistan. In Chad, children made up 95% of all casualties. In the Philippines, child casualties, accounting for more than 50% of all casualties, were identified for the first time since 2005. In Bosnia and Herzegovina, the number of child casualties was the highest since 2004. In Eritrea, overall casualty figures decreased significantly in 2009, but the number of child casualties remained consistent and increased to 76% from 50% of civilian casualties in 2008. The vast majority of child casualties were boys (80%). In many countries, child survivors have to end their education prematurely due to the long period of recovery and the accompanying financial burden of rehabilitation.[28]

ERW in Sri Lanka posed a greater risk to children than landmines: children have been at risk when involved in economic activities, or while deliberately tampering with ERW out of curiosity. Children under 18 years of age make up a significant proportion of ERW victims in Sri Lanka. In the Jaffna peninsula, during the year 2000, 78% of ERW victims were children.

Children made up nearly one-third of civilian deaths in Operation Cast Lead, which ended on 18 January 2009 following 23 days of aerial and artillery bombardment and land operations in Gaza. In 2010, instances of the use of explosive weapons continued, particularly in the border area with Israel as well as the coastal area, resulting in child casualties. In Afghanistan, Pakistan, Somalia, Syria and Yemen the ongoing use of explosive weapons still constitutes a significant threat to children. In Afghanistan, children make up almost 50% of all casualties from unexploded ordnance. On 27 April 2009, 12 children were killed when a bomb hidden in a football exploded near the compound wall of a girls' school in Dir, in Pakistan's Khyber Pakhtoonkhwa Province. The UN Secretary-General's 2010 annual report on Children in Armed Conflict stated that during 2009 explosive weapons were responsible for child casualties in 13 of the countries.[29]

Socio-economic Impact

The presence of explosive remnants of war in post-conflict communities has undeniable socio-economic impacts. The most obvious socio-economic impacts of ERW are the deaths and injuries they cause.[30] The survivors of ERW are often economically and socially marginalised. Their ability to support their families and contribute productively to local community life is reduced, adversely affecting agriculture and other economic activities. Continuing incidents from ERW may also sustain and reawaken feelings that create tension and possible violence, again affecting the ceasefire.

There is strong evidence that, like APM, threat from ERW compounds the existing developmental problems of affected communities by modifying their social and economic patterns. The presence of ERW prevents the use and rehabilitation of community infrastructure and resources including housing, water and irrigation, schools and villages, clinics and markets and the roads. Clearance activities are often needed before they can be used or repaired. ERW presence dissuades the inhabitants of affected communities from certain types of land use, or makes exploitation of local resources less efficient. Ultimately, land denial not only affects economic productivity; it can also produce wholesale change in traditional social and economic practices.

ERW and other military debris have value as an economic resource in many poor communities. It can provide access to cash within communities where this is otherwise rare. For those on the margins of society, ERW can be the mainstay of their economic survival. This leads people to undertake high-risk activities to locate and scrap ERW, a major cause of accidents in Laos, Eritrea, Guinea-Bissau and Chad.

Besides having the highly visible impacts on mortality and morbidity, the presence of ERW alienates a population's access to critical agricultural, forestry and pastoral resources, which are necessary for restoring livelihoods. ERW also delays the return of the IDPs and the refugees. The land rights situation becomes critical in the conflict-torn States affected by ERW, where land access can be denied or disrupted for years or even decades. ERW contamination not only leaves a profound social, economic and political footprint on the locations where they are located, but their presence also has significant repercussions on larger, adjacent areas.[31]

ERW is not only a post-conflict threat in war-torn societies, it can also affect adjacent countries or territories not directly involved in conflict. Laos and Cambodia are the two examples of "spill-over" of ERW threat. Although not directly involved in conflict between North Vietnam and the US, huge quantities of ordnance were dropped on both countries during the 1960s and 1970s by the US to interdict the Ho Chi Minh Trail. As a result, very large numbers of ERW of almost every type of air-delivered ordnance, including large high explosive bombs continue to pose a severe threat to communities within Laos and Cambodia, as well as Vietnam.[32] To a lesser extent, similar phenomena have occurred in the vicinity of Central Africa. While most fighting in recent years has been centred on the Democratic Republic of the Congo, troop movements and fighting have sometimes strayed into adjoining countries. While this has not resulted in high casualties, but has created impediments to land use, infrastructure development and activities such as livestock grazing and hunting.[33]

The Dangers from ERW

The dangers posed by ERW and their impact on affected communities are the following:[34]

- Injuries or deaths can take place at a distance from the explosion, depending on the ordnance involved; the danger area can vary from a few metres to several hundred metres.
- Items of UXO could be more powerful and lethal than anti-personnel mines; depending upon the kind of the ordnance, UXO incidents may result in a greater proportion of deaths than incidents involving mines.
- When UXO accidents do not involve deaths, they typically result in severe wounds, such as fragmentation injuries to the abdomen and chest, which often include damage to vital organs, amputation of limbs, and loss of vision or hearing.
- ERW are generally found on the surface, and more visible, resulting in a higher interaction of people. However ERW can also be found sub-surface where clearance can be difficult, for example, aircraft bombs can be found buried up to several metres.

- ERW are unpredictable and can be detonated at any time under a variety of stimuli: by pressure, by hit or kick or by simple touch. ERW often respond differently to the same action: an item of UXO can explode after being kicked once or it may explode after ten kicks.
- Unlike mines, it is difficult to identify the reason for the failure of ERW.

Environmental Impact

ERW contamination denies the safe use of agricultural land. It renders large tracts of agricultural land unusable, wreaking environmental and economic devastation. Refugees returning to their conflict ravaged countries face this life-threatening obstacle to rebuilding their lives. Many people leave the land and drift to the towns; while the poorest elements of society in ERW affected countries, take risks to survive. ERW can even prevent tourism by denying access to cultural heritage sites.

Wild elephant populations are also affected by ERW and landmines as they roam in search of food. In a number of cases, elephants working for humans are injured in remote areas and are unable to be helped for many days. The emotional and physical distress that the elephants experience is often accompanied by the emotional distress of the handler who is dependent on the elephant's well-being for sustenance. In many cases, the injured elephants need to be put down as a result of the inherent difficulty in finding veterinary help and keeping the wounds and amputations of an elephant clean. In Sri Lanka, according to wildlife veterinarians, as many as 10 elephants were killed or injured each year by ERW or landmines.[35]

Removal of ERW

Once a conflict is over, the stockpiles of unexpended ammunition pose serious hazard as abandoned ordnance deteriorates over time and it becomes difficult to relocate them. This is particularly true with poor quality or old ammunition, which further deteriorates in high temperature. There is an additional problem where stocks of abandoned ordnance include small arms and their ammunition, which can be plundered by armed gangs at the end of an armed conflict.[36]

ERW and their clearance have a serious impact on land rights in countries recovering from armed conflict. Apart from the highly visible impacts on mortality and morbidity, the presence of ERW alienates a population's access to critical agricultural, forestry and pastoral resources, necessary for restoring livelihoods. ERW also delay the return of displaced populations, thwart the reconstruction of infrastructure, and disrupt land and property restitution and security.[37]

In order to ensure that removal or the destruction of ERW causes minimum impact on the local environment, following is recommended.[38]

1. ERW should be disposed of in a manner that minimises environmental impact, avoids contamination of the land and water and has minimal affect on flora and fauna. In cases where ERW are to be destroyed in situ and there is a risk to property or infrastructure, protective works must be used.
2. Debris, rubble, wire and other remains of obstacles removed from a demining worksite must be disposed of in accordance with local waste management regulations.
3. Demining organisations must not obstruct or divert the natural flow of watercourses unless absolute necessary for the operation. They must consult the local community before undertaking diversions.
4. Demining organisations must ensure that the impact of demining on air quality (smoke, dust and toxic fumes) is minimised and the local communities and authorities are explained about the scope and duration of degradation.
5. Burning of vegetation should be avoided, however when it is inescapable, proper procedures and control measures should

be applied. Burning should not to be undertaken during night hours, and it should not be started unless there are sufficient firefighting arrangements.

6. Stockpile destruction must be planned and conducted in a manner that minimises the impact to the environment. If required by the national authorities, "environmental impact assessment," be undertaken.
7. Rubbish from the site must be disposed of at approved dumping sites. Rubbish pits must be located away from watercourses and wells, so as not to contaminate groundwater. Human waste should not be discharged into watercourses or onto the soil surface.
8. Demining organisations must ensure that advance planning is undertaken to prevent any spills of fuel, oil and lubricant (FOL). FOL storage facilities should not contaminate the soil or groundwater.
9. Toxic or hazardous waste products of demining operations must be disposed off under the directions of national authorities.
10. International standards must be observed while transporting hazardous, toxic or flammable materials.
11. While demining is undertaken in areas of cultural or historical importance, demining organisations must take all possible steps to prevent damage to these sites. Where human remains are encountered, action in accordance with IHL be undertaken.
12. Environmental incidents must be reported to the national authority as soon as practicable after the incident occurred.
13. On completion of demining operations, equipment, surplus materials, and waste must be removed.
14. As far as possible, local community should be involved in demining operations.

The CCW Protocol V on ERW

The Protocol V to CCW on ERW is a major achievement of IHL. The Protocol does not apply to landmines, booby-traps and other similar devices, which are covered by earlier IHL instruments, specifically the Anti-Personnel Mine Ban Convention and Amended Protocol II of the Convention on Certain Conventional Weapons. It does, however, apply to unexploded or abandoned cluster munitions, for those States that are not party to the 2010 Convention on Cluster Munitions. It strengthens the law in areas where no specific rules previously existed. The Protocol was adopted in 2003 to address one of the deadliest threats faced by civilians in post-conflict situations.[39] It establishes new rules that require the parties to a conflict to clear ERW, to take measures to protect civilians from the effects of these weapons and to assist the efforts of international and non-governmental organisations working in these areas.

The Preamble to Protocol manifests the willingness of the States Parties to observe generic preventive measures, through voluntary best practices specified in a Technical Annex of the Protocol. The Protocol is applicable on the land territory including internal waters of High Contracting Parties.[40] It deals only with the ERW from conventional weapons and does not address the post-conflict problems arising from the use of biological, chemical or nuclear weapons.

The Protocol is applicable in both international and non-international armed conflicts.[41] Article 1(3) states that the Protocol will apply to the situations arising from the conflicts referred to in paragraphs 1 to 6 of Article 1 of the CCW as amended on December 21, 2001. This is a reference to the amendment adopted by the Second CCW Review Conference that extends the scope of application of CCW Protocols I-IV to non-international armed conflict. The amendment stipulated that the scope of application for other CCW protocols would be determined on a case-by-case basis. Article 1(4) clarified that the Protocol's main operative provisions apply to ERW produced after the Protocol's entry into force for the relevant State.

Article 3 of the Protocol establishes rules on clearance of ERW. It provides that explosive munitions, other than landmines, must be cleared once the fighting has ended. Each State Party and party to armed conflict is responsible for the clearance of these remnants in the affected territory under its control [Article 3 (1)]. In cases where a user of explosive ordnance which has become ERW, does not exercise control of the territory, the user is to provide assistance, to facilitate the marking and clearance of the ERW in territory outside their control that have been produced during military operations. Such assistance may be technical, material, financial or in the form of personnel. It may be provided directly to the party in control of the territory where the explosives are found, or through a third party such as the United Nations, international agencies or NGOs. Under Article 3(3), after the cessation of active hostilities, the State Parties and party to an armed conflict shall take the following measures in affected territories under their control, to reduce the risks posed by ERW: (i) survey and assess the threat posed by ERW; (ii) assess and prioritise needs and practicability in terms of marking and clearance, removal or destruction; (iii) mark and clear, remove or destroy ERW; and (iv) take steps to mobilise resources to carry out these activities. This responsibility relates to the clearance of ERW immediately after the end of active hostilities and does not mean after the conclusion of a formal peace agreement. Clearance is to begin as soon as feasible in affected areas and must not wait for a formal declaration of peace between the parties.

Recording and Sharing of Information

The lack of information on the used or abandoned ordnance in an armed conflict is an important detriment to effective removal or destruction of ERW. The immediate transmission of such information by the parties to an armed conflict can significantly improve an organisation's ability to respond swiftly to ERW. Article 4 of the Protocol accordingly stipulates that State Parties and parties to an armed conflict must record and retain information on the use or abandonment of explosive ordnance "to the maximum extent possible and as far as practicable." Parties are subsequently required to share this information without delay after the cessation of active hostilities with other parties, the UN or other organisations involved in risk education or the marking and clearance of contaminated areas.

The information that the parties to an armed conflict are expected to record are listed in the Protocol's Technical Annex. These include the types and amounts (number) of explosive ordnance used; the areas targeted with these weapons; the types, amount and location of abandoned explosive ordnance; and the general location where unexploded ordnance is known to exist or is likely to be found. The Annex also provides details of the information that should be transmitted to the other parties and relevant organisations. The Technical Annex sets out voluntary best practices and its contents are not legally binding. However, as parties to the armed conflict are bound by Article 4 to record, retain and transmit information to facilitate the rapid removal of explosive remnants of war as well as risk education, the article's effective implementation will require that the information recorded matches the specifications in the Technical Annex.[42]

Precautions to Protect Civilians and Humanitarian Organisations

Article 5 of the Protocol stipulates that the parties to an armed conflict must take all feasible precautions in the territory under their control to protect civilians and civilian objects from the effects of ERW. Article 5 specifically provides:

> High Contracting Parties and parties to an armed conflict shall take all feasible precautions in the territory under their control affected by explosive remnants of war to protect the civilian population, individual civilians and civilian objects from the risks and effects of explosive remnants of war. Feasible precautions are those precautions which are practicable or practicably possible, taking into account all circumstances ruling at the time, including humanitarian and military considerations. These precautions may include warnings, risk education to the civilian population, marking, fencing and monitoring of territory

affected by explosive remnants of war, as set out in Part 2 of the Technical Annex.

As regards minimising the effects of ERW on the operations of humanitarian organisations, Article 6 states that the High Contracting Parties and parties to a conflict must protect such organisations from the effects of ERW. It also states that each party must provide information on the location of ERW to humanitarian organisations involved in demining operations.

Assistance and Cooperation

Under Article 7, State Parties facing problems posed by existing ERW have the right to seek and receive assistance from other States and relevant organisations in dealing with them. At the same time, each High Contracting Party, having expertise in ERW is required to provide assistance, where necessary and feasible. The qualifications in this article; "where appropriate," and "as necessary and feasible," show that this provision was intended to be a flexible one and was not meant to be absolutely binding for the parties.[43] Article 10 establishes that High Contracting Parties will consult and cooperate with each other on all issues related to the Protocol's operation.

Article 9 mandates State Parties to implement generic preventive measures aimed at minimising the occurrence of ERW. It includes a range of activities taken before the use of explosive ordnance (EXO) to ensure that weapons will explode as intended. A number of general best practices are listed in Part 3 of the Protocol's Technical Annex. They include standards for munitions manufacturing, storage, transport and handling, and the training of personnel. Article 11 promotes compliance with the Protocol and stipulates that a State Party must issue appropriate instructions and procedures and make sure that its personnel receive training consistent with the Protocol's provisions. It also requires State Parties to work bilaterally, through the UN or through other international procedures, to resolve any problems that may arise in the Protocol's interpretation or application.

There are certain shortcomings in the Protocol. It contains many qualifying phrases in its key provisions. These include phrases such as "where feasible" and "as soon as feasible." These phrases, if abused, could undermine the effectiveness of the Protocol. It is felt that it would be difficult to implement the Protocol's operational provisions in situations where there was not sufficient goodwill between the parties to the conflict. However, there are opposing views[44] that such clauses were intended to provide a degree of flexibility to deal with the practical difficulties and complexities that the governments and armed forces often face in post-conflict situations.

Explosive weapons play an important role in the military doctrines of states. While using weapons during an armed conflict is a military decision, modern combat operations have introduced a dilemma: what to do with ERW that remain after a conflict ends. ERW constitute a serious and persistent problem for humanity. Such weapons not only threaten the post-conflict safety of civilians and military personnel but can also be a major impediment to economic development. With the adoption of the ERW Protocol, the Anti-Personnel Mine Ban Treaty and the Convention on Cluster Munitions, the international community has created a comprehensive framework for addressing the threat posed by explosive weapons left on the battlefield. However, the goal of protecting civilians and affected communities will be reached only when these instruments have achieved universal acceptance and become normal practice for governments, armed forces and NSAGs.

Notes

1. The reasons for explosive ordnance failure could include: (i) production defects; (ii) improper storage (adverse climatic conditions can affect the explosive composition, meaning higher failure rates); (iii) rough handling; (iv) inadequate firing drills (for example, failure to set electronic time fuses properly); (v) incorrect launch profiles (for example, air-delivered weapons dropped too low may not have time to arm themselves properly); (vi) poor strike angles (a munition impacting at too shallow an angle may lead to fuse failure); (vii) terrain types (for example, soft ground increases the risk of fuse failure); (viii) heavy precipitation (some fuses may initiate early due to the resistance caused by rain, leading to submunition deployment at the wrong time); and (ix) interaction

with other items of ordnance.

2. These deaths and injuries were reported during the periods 1945 to 1975. Bengt Anderberg, submission at UNITAR symposium in Geneva, May 1981. Publication No. UNITAR/EUR/81/WR/20, 1981.
3. US forces used 15 million tons of bombs and ammunition during the war and an estimated 800,000 tons of unexploded ordnance still contaminates 20% of the country's area. It may take more than 100 years to clear the contaminated area. Vietnam War ammo has killed 42,000 since. *The Times of India*, June 30, 2009. Available at: http://timesofindia.indiatimes.com/World/Rest-of-World/Vietnam-War-ammo-has-killed-42k-since/articleshow/4718385.cms.
4. Louis Maresca, "A New Protocol on Explosive Remnant of War: The History and Negotiation of Protocol V to the 1980 Convention on Certain Conventional Weapons," vol. 86, no. 856, *International Review of the Red Cross*, December 2004, pp. 816-17.
5. Every year we handle approximately 250 tons of ammunition from these wars. Within these 250 tons, some 20 tons are doubtful ammunitions which could be chemical shells from WWI. Michel Lambrechts, quoted in Mine Action Information Centre Journal, 2000. Available at: http://maic.jmu.edu/journal/4.2/Features/ww2/ww2.htm, accessed March 31, 2012.
6. The explosive weapons produce a distinct pattern of death and injury. Survivors of explosive weapons use tend to suffer multiple, complex, and severe wounds from the blast and fragmentation effects, and from being caught in collapsing structures. The physical and mental trauma can result in a range of debilitating long-term conditions, including lifelong disability, requiring considerable medical and public health resources. Evidence suggests a consistent pattern of harm to civilians from the use of explosive weapons in places such as towns, cities, and other areas in which civilians congregate. John Borrie and Maya Brehm, "Enhancing civilian protection from use of explosive weapons in populated areas: Building a policy and research agenda," vol. 93, no. 883, *International Review of the Red Cross*, September 2011, pp. 809-36.
7. Louis Maresca, "A New Protocol on Explosive Remnant of War: The History and Negotiation of Protocol V to the 1980 Convention on Certain Conventional Weapons," vol. 86, no. 856, *International Review of the Red Cross*, December 2004, pp. 815-35.
8. ERW continue to pose a threat to people in over 80 countries. Accidents involving these weapons occur on an almost daily basis, resulting in deaths and severe injuries. Despite the positive fact that the number of accidents is declining, almost 500,000 survivors of accidents involving landmines and unexploded ordnance devices continue to require assistance. Jan Schulz, "Victim Assistance: An Introduction," *Explosive Remnants of War—Challenges for Victim Assistance*, Conference Document, 2009, Handicap International. *Also see: Explosive Remnants of War: A Global Survey*, Landmine Action, 2003, London.
9. Legally, if stockpiles are under national control, they would not be defined as ERW as they are not abandoned. In case ordnance is stored by non-state actors and then abandoned, it could be considered ERW. The key is that they are explosive and not under the control of the party that left them behind or dumped them.
10. The Protocol V on Explosive Remnants of War to the 1980 Convention on Certain Conventional Weapons (CCW) was adopted in November 2003. In addition, ERW could include armoured fighting vehicles (AFV), damaged military transports, and crashed aircrafts. The threat posed by abandoned AFV can be

complex, involving many explosive components which need to be considered while clearing ERW. It may include (i) surrounding mines and unexploded ordnance; (ii) depleted uranium fragments; (iii) explosive reactive armour; (iv) smoke dischargers; (v) unstable stocks of internally stowed ammunition; and (vi) access denial devices and booby traps. If the AFV were abandoned in a defensive position, there is a possibility of the presence of infra-red and target decoys in the immediate area, which have an associated UXO threat. Abandoned AFVs are, in themselves, ERW and, because of their attraction to children and the curious, need to be given a high priority for clearance. The clearance of armoured fighting vehicles (AFV) could be one of the most technically complex and demanding operations.

11. Article 2, CCW Protocol V on Explosive Remnants of War.
12. Adrian Wilkinson, *Explosive Remnants of War (ERW)—A Threat Analysis* (Geneva: Geneva International Centre for Humanitarian Demining, 2002), p. 5.
13. These include dinitrotoluene (DNT), trinitrotoluene (TNT), hexahydrotrinitrotriazine (RDX) and octahydrotetranitrotetrazocine (HMX). Other toxic substances often found in weapons include solid or liquid propellants for various types of rockets and missiles, such as hydrazine, whilenitroglycerin (NG), nitroguanidine (NQ), nitrocellulose (NC), 2,4-dinitrotoluene (DNT), and various perchlorate formulations are employed in missile, rocket, and gun propellants.
14. *ERW and Mines other than APM: Global Survey 2003-2004*, Landmine Action, March 2005, London, UK, p. 6.
15. Vietnamese territory was heavily bombarded and the Vietnamese government estimates that there still are 300,000 tons of unexploded ordnance around, two per cent of the bombs, landmines and artillery shells fired by US forces during the war. Approximately 16,478 million square metres of land remain contaminated by ERW and mines. This equates to about five per cent of Vietnam's total landmass. Little data is currently available indicating exactly the number of casualties. The Ministry of Labour, Invalids and Social Affairs (MOLISA) estimated in a 1999 report that ERW and mines had killed at least 38,248 people since 1975, with at least another 64,064 additional people injured. Both the Vietnamese and American governments estimate that about 2,000 new ERW and mine casualties occur each year. *Explosive Remnants of War: A Global Survey*, Landmine Action, 2003, p. 44.
16. *Explosive Remnants of War: A Global Survey*, Landmine Action, 2003, London.
17. *Landmine Monitor Report 2009*, pp. 514-17.
18. US Overseas Security Advisory Council, "Kuwait 2009 Crime & Safety Report," February 12, 2009, available at: www.osac.gov.
19. *Landmine Monitor Report 2007*, p. 481.
20. *Landmine Monitor Report 2002*, p. 686.
21. Mujib Mashal, Left-Behind Explosives Taking Deadlier Toll on Afghan Children, UN Says, *The New York Times*, 6 February 2017.
22. Protecting Syrians Form Explosive remnants of War, Handicap International, available at: http://www.handicap-international.us/protecting_syrians_from_explosive_remnants_of_war, accessed 30 June 2017.
23 Wim Zwijnenburg and Kristine te Pas, Amidst the debris: A Desktop study on the environmental and public health impact of Syria's conflict, PAX, October 2015, pp. 84.
24. Barrel bombs come in different shapes and sizes. As they tend to contain a large amount of explosive material, and due to the difficulty of delivering them

accurately to a target, barrel bombs tend to have wide area effects. Like other explosive weapons with wide area effects, such as heavy artillery shells, rockets and aircraft bombs, their use in populated areas is highly problematic. As they are improvised weapons, the effects of any particular barrel bomb are very hard to foresee, making it impossible to adequately assess the risk of harm to civilians and prevent that harm. Besides causing enormous damage and human suffering, these barrel bombs often fail to detonate. Unexploded bombs can result in exposure of civilians to the toxic substances used in the device. These barrel bombs could weigh up to 1500 kg. Wim Zwijnenburg and Kristine te Pas, Amidst the debris: A Desktop study on the environmental and public health impact of Syria's conflict, PAX, October 2015, pp. 84.

25. Many European countries are still removing weapons used in the Second World War. For example, in 2012 alone, the explosive ordnance disposal unit of the Hungarian Defence Force destroyed more than 45,000 pieces of ERW left over from that conflict. Belarus, Poland and Russia also continue to clear large amounts of World War II ordnance. Explosive Remnants of War, International Committee of the Red Cross, Geneva, Switzerland, December 2014.
26. Large-scale destruction of homes, cultivations, roads, schools, and hospitals in in the Vanni region of Sri Lanka in 2009 was caused by explosive weapons. Report of the Secretary-General's Panel of Experts on Accountability in Sri Lanka, March 31, 2011, available at: www.un.org/News/dh/infocus/Sri_Lanka/POE_Report_Full.pdf, visited July 22, 2011.
27. Explosive Remnants of War: ERW in Sri Lanka, Landmine Action, May 2003.
28. Accessible inclusive or special education is seldom available and further hindered by the lack of appropriate training for teachers. In addition, insufficient awareness of disability issues among teachers and fellow pupils can lead to discrimination, isolation and the inability to participate in certain activities. This is a de-motivating factor for child survivors to stay in school. As a result, education rates among child survivors are lower, while school drop-outs are more frequent, which results in diminished employment prospects later on. Impact of Mines/ERW on Children, *Landmine and Cluster Munition Monitor: Fact Sheet*, November 2010.
29. UN Secretary-General, Annual Report on Children and Armed Conflict, UN Doc. S/2010/181, 13 April 2010, paragraph 48. The figures included in the report are 131 deaths from airstrikes, 128 deaths from IEDs and 55 deaths from mines. The 13 countries listed are Afghanistan, Chad, Iraq, Lebanon, Myanmar, Nepal, occupied Palestinian territory (OPT), Somalia, Colombia, India, Philippines, Sri Lanka and Yemen.
30. It is usually difficult for the local population to coexist with ERW contamination without either accidental exposure to risks or some form of deliberate engagement with the ordnance in an effort to manage the risks they are facing. ERW contamination also contributes to a general atmosphere of insecurity and fear in many post-conflict communities. ERW accidents do occur from people accidentally striking items while farming or building fires above buried ordnance, a significant proportion of accidents occur because people deliberately interact with ordnance that they find. *Explosive remnants of war and mines other than anti-personnel mines: Global Survey 2003-2004*, Landmine Action, March 2005, London, UK, pp. 8-9.
31. Once violence ends, displaced persons often seek to re-establish their homes and livelihoods, creating a surge of land and property problems, which can be exacerbated by the enduring presence of ERW. Depending on the size of the

displaced population and the duration of displacement and conflict, land and property issues can quickly become one of the primary features of a post-war phase. The re-establishment of ownership, use and access rights to land after a war ends is often very difficult as people try to reclaim what they lost. Failure to effectively address these problems can serve as the basis for renewed conflict and armed confrontation. Jon Unruh and Alexandre Corriveau-Bourque, "Volatile Landscapes: the Impact of Explosive Remnants of War on Land Rights in Conflict Affected Countries," issue 18, *Journal of Peace, Conflict & Development*, December 2011, pp. 8-11.

32. *Explosive Remnants of War: A Global Survey*, Landmine Action, 2003.
33. *Explosive Remnants of War and Mines other than Anti-personnel Mines: Global Survey 2003-2004*, Landmine Action, London, 2005.
34. *Explosive Remnants of War (ERW): Warnings and Risk Education*, Geneva International Centre for Humanitarian Demining, Geneva, Switzerland, May 2003, pp. 9-10.
35. On April 4, 2011—International Mine Awareness Day—while many advocates for mine removal were celebrating the inclusion of 10 more states to the Mine Ban Treaty, two elephants were killed in Sri Lanka by landmines. This comes after a decision made by the Sri Lankan government to relocate the Sri Lankan Nature Conservatory to a former war zone containing as many as 1.5 million active landmines; proving even more that elephant safety depends on the actions taken and decisions made by humans in affected regions. Windy Borman, *Sri Lanka Moves Elephants Into Former War Zone, Landmines Remain*, January 10, 2011, The Eyes of Thailand, available at: http://www.eyesofthailand.com/2011/01/10/sri-lanka-elephants-landmines/; Windy Borman, *2 Elephants Step on Landmines in Sri Lanka on International Mine Awareness Day*, April 4, 2011, The Eyes of Thailand, available at: http://www.eyesofthailand.com/2011/04/04/2-elephants-step-onlandmines-in-sri-lanka-on-intl-landmine-awareness-day/.
36. Robert Keeley, "Understanding Landmines and Mine Action," September 2003, p. 6.
37. Jon Unruh and Alexandre Corriveau-Bourque, "Volatile Landscapes: the Impact of Explosive Remnants of War on Land Rights in Conflict Affected Countries," *Journal of Peace, Conflict & Development*, issue 18, December 2011, pp. 7-25.
38. Explosive ordnance disposal (EOD) is the term used to describe the specific technical procedure for the detection and disposal of items of unexploded ordnance. The EOD procedure depends upon the type of terrain and variety of munitions that are likely to be in the affected area. Where items are buried underground metal detectors have to be used to locate the ordnance. The actual disposal procedure usually involves the destruction of unexploded ordnance using an explosive charge. Sometimes UXO has to be destroyed where it is since moving the item may be dangerous and could result in its premature detonation; at other times UXO is gathered in a central location to be destroyed in a "bulk demolition" (many items simultaneously). Large items such as aircraft bombs, particularly if they are close to vital infrastructure, are disposed of by a dismantling process sometimes involving the removal of the explosives for disposal elsewhere. *Explosive Remnants of War: ERW in Sri Lanka*, Landmine Action, May 2003, p. 24.
39. The CCW Protocol V on Explosive Remnants of War was adopted in November 2003 and entered into force on November 12, 2006. As on July 31, 2017, it has been ratified by 92 States.
40. Article 1 (2) Protocol V on Explosive Remnants of War, 2003.

41. As a result of its application to non-international armed conflicts, the Protocol refers to "High Contracting Parties" and "parties to an armed conflict." The former is the equivalent of "States Parties," i.e., States that have formally ratified or acceded to the Convention and the Protocol. The phrase "parties to an armed conflict" is a reference to non-State actors (i.e., organised armed groups) and is the formula used in Amended Protocol II to the CCW, which also applies to non-international armed conflicts. As used in Protocol V, "parties to an armed conflict" does not encompass States involved in a conflict that have not ratified or otherwise expressed their consent to be bound by the Protocol. Such States are not bound by it. Louis Maresca, "A New Protocol on Explosive Remnant of War: The History and Negotiation of Protocol V to the 1980 Convention on Certain Conventional Weapons," vol. 86, no. 856, *International Review of the Red Cross*, December 2004, p. 824.
42. Louis Maresca, "A New Protocol on Explosive Remnant of War," p. 824.
43. Ibid., p. 830.
44. Ibid., p. 834.

5

WEAPONS AND THE LAW

Most weapons are capable of causing environmental harm of some kind, even though environmental harm may not be intended. The availability of weapons of mass destruction and the change in the nature of warfare have increased the scale of environmental harm resulting from armed conflict. When nuclear weapons were dropped on Hiroshima and Nagasaki in August 1945, the international community voiced little concern over the environmental catastrophe unleashed by the nuclear radiation. This may have been due to their failure to understand the fragile nature of the environment and the inter-relationship between human activities and the environment.

In the Vietnam War, the US forces directly targeted and manipulated the environment. They used chemicals (herbicides and other chemical agents) to destroy forests, vegetation, and croplands. They also cleared almost three-quarters of a million acres of forests using heavy tractors (Rome Plows), in order to prevent the North Vietnamese and Viet Cong from using the vegetation as cover. In addition, the Air Force used chemical agents to increase rainfall so as to soften the surface of roads, to reduce enemy mobility and to divert men and material from military operations to attend to the muddied roads. The impact of the US military operations in Vietnam generated domestic and international concern over the legality of weapons in armed conflict. Till then, the word "environment" had not appeared in any IHL treaty.

The laws of war are aimed at preventing belligerents from making unrestrained use of weaponry. The most effective regulatory modes available are those promulgated by disarmament instruments.

These agreements provide for the prohibition of a particular weapon per se, outlawing not only its use but its possession, stockpiling and ultimately its production as well.[1] Another category of instruments constraining the means of warfare available to the States encompasses treaties that prohibit the use of a particular category or class of weapons. This category can be further divided into two subcategories; the first stipulates an obligation of no first use, and the second, an absolute duty to refrain from use even in case the adversary has breached its own obligation in this respect. A third type of weapons control instrument includes agreements which impose limitations on the use of means of warfare without, however, prohibiting them in all circumstances. Finally, the employment of all weapons in both international and non-international armed conflicts is subject to certain constraints stemming from three principles of conventional and customary IHL and more specifically from the principles of chivalry,[2] superfluous injury or unnecessary suffering, and distinction.

Following the carnage of the Second World War, the ICRC convinced the international community to adopt the four Geneva Conventions in 1949, laying down the normative framework for the protection of victims of armed conflict. In particular, the fourth Convention on the Protection of Civilian Persons in Time of War, relates to the protection of the environment, albeit indirectly. Article 53 of the Convention provides that "any destruction by the Occupying Power of real or personal property belonging individually or collectively to private persons, or to the State, or to other public authorities, or to social or cooperative organisations, is prohibited, except where such destruction is rendered absolutely necessary by military operations."

In 1972, the international community banned bacteriological weapons through the adoption of the Convention on the Prohibition of Development, Production and Stockpiling of Bacteriological (Biological) and Toxin Weapons and on their Destruction. In 1970s, with the adoption of ENMOD[3] and AP I,[4] international standards for assessing damage to the environment during armed conflict were agreed upon for the first time. AP I, containing two specific provisions on environmental damage was negotiated at the Diplomatic Conference on the Reaffirmation and Development of IHL Applicable in Armed Conflict. Since then, there have been only piecemeal efforts to impose restriction on certain weapons considered indiscriminate and affecting the environment adversely. Out of the eight weapons discussed in Chapters 2 to 4 of this book, five have been specifically banned by international treaties. However, all these treaties do not enjoy international acceptance.

The principles of IHL, customary and soft laws, and treaties that restrict inhuman and indiscriminate weapons have been covered in this chapter. The provisions for the review of new weapons before their induction and the responsibility of a military commander towards the protection of the natural environment during an armed conflict have also been discussed.

I. Legal Restrictions

A. Principles of IHL

The core principles of IHL[5] include the principles of distinction, proportionality, military necessity, and humanity—all of which have a bearing on environmental protection during armed conflict.

Distinction. It stipulates that the parties to a conflict must distinguish at all times between combatants and civilians. Parties may not attack civilians and civilian objects and may direct attacks against only military objectives.[6] According to Richard (1992), to be lawful, weapons and tactics must clearly discriminate between military and non-military targets, and be confined in their application to military targets.[7] The purpose of this requirement is to ensure respect for and protection of the civilian population and civilian objects. However, this principle has certain weaknesses. It protects the environment to the extent that the civilian environment is linked to the natural environment, and presumes that a clear distinction can be made between civilian and military environments. It imposes no limit on attacks on the environment surrounding a military objective.

Proportionality. The principle states that even if there is a clear military target, it must not be attacked, if the risk of civilians or civilian property being harmed is greater than the expected military advantage.[8] A military target is an object that contributes effectively to the military operation. Thus, to be lawful, weapons and tactics must be proportional to the military objective. The proportionality principle places limits on belligerents in choosing methods and tactics of warfare by the belligerents.[9] It requires that a comparison be made between two elements, the military target and the environmental effects. Prior to destroying a natural resource site by military activity, the military authority should weigh the expected environmental harm against the military benefits expected to be gained. If the environmental damage outweighs the military advantage, the military operation should be avoided.[10]

Military Necessity. Military necessity justifies the infliction of suffering upon an enemy combatant, but only that much suffering is justified as is necessary to bring about the submission of the enemy. No more force should be used to carry out a military operation than is necessary in the circumstances. To be lawful, weapons and tactics involving the use of force must be reasonably necessary to the attainment of their military objective. No superfluous or excessive application of force is lawful, even if the damage done is confined to the environment, thereby sparing people and property.[11] The principle of military necessity ensures the minimisation of human and environmental loss, especially when an armed conflict is taking place between a developed armed force and a developing one, such as the war in Afghanistan, between the NATO/the US armed forces and the Taliban armed forces.[12]

Humanity. The 1868 Declaration of St. Petersburg was the first to introduce limitations on the use of weapons of war. It codified the customary principle, still valid, prohibiting the use of weapons to cause unnecessary suffering.[13] To be lawful, no weapon or tactic can be validly employed if it causes unnecessary suffering to its victims, whether by way of prolonged or painful death or by causing severe fright or terror. Accordingly, weapons and tactics that spread poison or disease or cause genetic damage are generally illegal per se, as they inflict unacceptable forms of pain, damage, death and fear. All forms of deliberate ecological disruption would appear to fall within the ambit of this overall prohibition.[14]

Customary international law principles of military necessity, humanity and proportionality may in certain circumstances, operate so as to protect certain areas from damage in specific conditions. However, there are several difficulties in relying purely on these principles. They are so fraught with vagaries and uncertainties that they may not be able to provide sufficient guidance to the military commander on the ground. Indeed by their nature, it is often possible to evaluate the legality of a particular action on an *ex post facto* basis—after the possibly reversible environmental damage has occurred.[15]

B. The Martens Clause

The Martens Clause[16] responds to the fundamental purpose of humanitarian law: the preservation of humanity. It originally appeared in the Preamble to the 1989 Hague Convention II Respecting the Laws and Customs of War on Land, as:

> Until a more complete code of the laws of war has been issued, the High Contracting Parties deem it expedient to declare that, in cases not included in the Regulations adopted by them, the inhabitants and the belligerents remain under the protection and the rule of the principles of the law of nations, as they result from the usages established among civilised peoples, from the laws of humanity, and the dictates of the public conscience.

The Martens Clause has proved to be of fundamental importance in providing a minimum legal standard to govern the conduct of all persons in times of armed conflict when no other international law is applicable. Specialists in humanitarian law are not in agreement over the interpretation of the Martens Clause.[17] In a restricted sense, the Clause serves as a reminder that customary international law continues to apply even after the adoption of a treaty norm. However, the Martens Clause covers only civilians and belligerents without any explicit reference to the environment.[18] It is doubtful whether the terms in the Clause, such as "public conscience," which are undefined, would offer any significant protection to the natural environment during an armed conflict.

C. Customary IHL

The origin of IHL, in fact, lies in the customs and usages followed by armies to minimise the miseries of war from ancient times. Customary law consists of the rules which, as a result of state practice over a period of time, have become accepted as legally binding.[19] In 2005, after extensive research and consultation among experts, the ICRC released its study on customary IHL, containing 161 rules.[20] The ICRC study extends the principles of distinction, proportionality and military necessity to the natural environment, and emphasises the importance of taking a precautionary approach in the absence of scientific certainty about the likely effects of a particular weapon on the environment. In addition, the rules expressly prohibit the use of means of warfare that are intended or can be expected to cause significant damage to the environment, requiring Member States to consider the likely environmental repercussions of their military methods.[21]

The protection of the natural environment is governed by Rules 43, 44 and 45. Rule 43 states that the general principles on the conduct of hostilities—distinction, military necessity, and proportionality—apply to the natural environment as well. There are three parts to the rule:

> **Rule 43:** The general principles on the conduct of hostilities apply to the natural environment:

> **A.** No part of the natural environment may be attacked, unless it is a military objective.
>
> **B.** Destruction of any part of the natural environment is prohibited, unless required by imperative military necessity.
>
> **C.** Launching an attack against a military objective which may be expected to cause incidental damage to the environment which would be excessive in relation to the concrete and direct military advantage anticipated is prohibited.
>
> **Rule 44:** Methods and means of warfare must be employed with due regard to the protection and preservation of the natural environment. In the conduct of military operations, all feasible precautions must be taken to avoid, and in any event to minimise, incidental damage to the environment. Lack of scientific certainty as to the effects on the environment of certain military operations does not absolve a party to the conflict from taking such precautions.
>
> **Rule 45:** The use of methods or means of warfare that are intended, or may be expected, to cause widespread, long-term and severe damage to the natural environment is prohibited. Destruction of the natural environment may not be used as a weapon.

Rule 43 recognises the civilian status of the environment and appears uncontroversial, at least in the context of international armed conflict. The inclusion of the word "part" gives a notion that every "part" of the environment is protected. Rule 44 requires the states to give "due regard" not only to the protection of the natural environment, but also to its preservation, thus going beyond the scope of Article 55 of AP I.[22]

The phrase "due regard" contained in the first part of Rule 44, relates to standard to be applied to prevent trans-boundary environmental harm. According to Koppe (2014), this is related to the general obligation of each state not to allow knowingly its territory to be used for acts contrary to the rights of others state.[23] This obligation is based on a general duty of care similar to the one binding private individuals and legal persons under the tort law. The general obligation contained in the first sentence becomes operational through the second sentence of Rule 44. A duty of care for the environment or an obligation to use methods or means of warfare with due regard for the environment during armed conflict entails that states must take all feasible precautions in the conduct of military operations to avoid, and minimize incidental damage to environment. An obligation to take all feasible precautions to avoid or minimize damage to environment is further enforced through the third sentence of Rule 44. It states that lack of scientific certainty does not absolve a party to the conflict from taking such precautions. Since there is no lack of scientific certainty as to the effects on the environment of the use of nuclear weapons, third sentence of the Rules is not relevant to nuclear weapons.

Considering the scale and duration of the ongoing Syrian conflict, it is beyond doubt that the targeting decisions, the widespread damage to populated areas, the vast quantity of weapons and munitions expended and the breakdown of environmental services and governance will have caused grave environmental damage in Syria. The damage to Syria's environment and the immediate and long-term risks that this damage may pose to Syria's civilian population, clearly demonstrate that environmental protection during conflict is a humanitarian issue. Yet environmental damage during conflict suffers from low prioritisation throughout the UN system.

State practice shows that the protection to be accorded to the environment during armed conflicts stems not only from the application to the environment of the rules protecting civilian objects, but also from a recognition of the need to provide particular protection to the environment as such. The extensive development of international law to protect the environment over the last few decades has been motivated by the recognition of the unprecedented degradation of the natural environment by mankind. The general need to protect the environment during armed conflict has been recognised in some military manuals, official statements and reported practice.[24]

Causing widespread, long-term and severe damage to the environment is an offence under the legislation of numerous States. The prohibition of widespread, long-term and severe damage to the natural environment is incorporated in the UN Secretary-General's Bulletin on IHL to be observed by the UN peacekeepers.[25]

In principle, there is no difference between the enforcement of treaty law and customary international law, as both are sources of the same body of law. However, in case of violation, IHL can be enforced through diplomatic means, including measures adopted by international organisations, such as the UN Security Council. It may also be enforced by national and international courts and tribunals, for example, by the trial of an individual responsible for a violation. On the other hand, customary IHL rules applicable to IAC are largely unenforceable and often disregarded. The main reasons being that the legal regime relies exclusively on broadly construed principles with little substantive details and is thus questionable.

D. Treaty Provisions

I. The Convention on the Prohibition of Military or Other Hostile Use of Environmental Techniques (ENMOD), 1976

The ENMOD Convention came in response to the environmental modifications made by the US during conflicts in Vietnam, Laos, and Cambodia in the 1960s and 1970s. The ENMOD Convention is a short document consisting of a preamble, ten articles, and a set of four understandings in an annex. It prohibits use of environmental modification techniques[26] as a method of warfare. States are also prohibited from assisting others in the hostile use of environmental modification. The basic obligation imposed upon States is set out in Article I (1) which states: "Each State Party to this Convention undertakes not to engage in military or any other hostile use of environmental modification techniques having widespread, long-lasting or severe effects as the means of destruction, damage or injury to any other State Party." Also, Parties undertake not to assist, encourage or induce any State, group of States or international organisation to engage in such activities. Some environmental manipulation is permitted. For example, armies may use herbicides or other means to denude the perimeter of military bases in order to reduce the chance of sneak attack.[27]

The ENMOD Convention has been the object of much criticism. In particular Article 3, which authorises the use of environmental modification techniques for peaceful purposes, is considered as vague. This leaves open the possibility that prohibited uses of such techniques may be substituted for peaceful ones.[28] ENMOD also does not outlaw development and testing of hostile environmental modification techniques, nor does it include verification mechanisms for identifying attempts by Parties to develop such techniques. The Convention does not include a system of compensation for damages resulting from breach of its obligations as it lacks provisions for penalising State Parties that breach its provisions. A State party can be held responsible, but not liable. Liability and redress, therefore, must be sought through other international legal instruments. To date, ENMOD has been ratified by only 74 State Parties. The UN General Assembly has called for global ratification on several occasions, but without much success.[29]

II. The 1977 Additional Protocol I Relevant to the Protection of Victims of International Armed Conflicts (AP I)[30]

AP I represents a considerable development of IHL regarding environmental protection in times of armed conflict.[31] It recognises that environmental protection is necessary to human health and survival and contains two important provisions relating to protection of the environment and limitation on ecological destruction during IAC. Articles 35 and 55 of AP I contain explicit provisions for environmental protection.

Article 35 establishes the basic rules regarding environmental protection. It forbids the use of weapons and methods of warfare that may cause unnecessary injury to humans or the environment. Article 35 (3), which appears under the heading "Basic Rules," states, "It is prohibited to employ methods or means of warfare which are intended, or may be expected, to cause widespread, long-term and severe damage to the natural environment." Article 35(3) strengthens the protection of the environment by stating that "it is prohibited to employ methods of warfare which are intended, or may be expected, to cause widespread, long-term, and severe damage to the natural environment". By placing subparagraph 3 in the Article dealing with the well-established 'Basic Rule', the Protocol raises the restraint on wartime damage of the environment to a new level. In addition, Article 36 obligates parties to ensure that any new means or method of warfare comply with the existing international law.

Article 55, which appears in part IV on the Protection of the Civilian Population, states:

Protection of the natural environment

1. Care shall be taken in warfare to protect the natural environment against widespread, long-term and severe damage. This protection includes a prohibition of the use of methods or means of warfare which are intended or may be expected to cause such damage to the natural environment and thereby to prejudice the health or survival of the population.
2. Attacks against the natural environment by way of reprisals are prohibited.

The obligation of "protection" in Article 55(1) suggests that states parties must take positive steps to guard, defend the environment and keep it safe from damage. The obligation of protection could, therefore, include a wide range of actions; (a) undertaking a rigorous environmental assessment to evaluate potential environmental harm to a particular attack scenario, including a full appraisal of the environmental effects of proposed weapons, as well as risks to particular kinds of environment; (b) the alteration of an attack scenario to avoid potential environmental harm; and (c) calling off a planned attack due to the potential environmental harm.[32]

Article 55 must be interpreted as a "governing principle" that requires that the effects (or consequences) of permitted actions do not result in escalating damage or cause expressly prohibited widespread, long-term and severe damage to the natural environment. The scope of Article 55 thus extends beyond that of Article 35 in so far as it concerns issues relating to the health or survival of the civilian population.

The provisions of both, AP I and the ENMOD place a limit upon the mindless mayhem that normally accompanies war. However, a number of military activities potentially devastating to the environment remain insufficiently regulated. For example, collateral damage from weapons does not appear to be covered under either AP I or the ENMOD. Second, even intentional, direct damage to the environment is permissible if it is not covered specifically by the prohibitions. In Hulme's opinion (2010: 681), "the real gem hidden behind Article 55 (1), is not the prohibition of means and methods causing widespread, long-term, and severe damage, but the obligation on states parties to take 'care' to protect the environment against such harm."[33]

III. The UN Convention on the Prohibitions or Restrictions on the Use of Certain Conventional Weapons (CCW), which May Be Deemed to Be Excessively Injurious or to Have Indiscriminate Effects, 1980[34]

The CCW and its five protocols deal with specific conventional weapons. The Preamble to the CCW reiterates Article 35 (3) of AP I, which address environmental damage in IAC. It declares: "it is prohibited to employ methods or means of warfare which are intended, or may be expected, to cause widespread, long-term and severe damage to the natural environment." Because it links human injury to environmental injury, the CCW also provides collateral environmental protection while recalling "the general principle of the protection of the civilian population against the effects of hostilities." By seeking to avoid direct and indirect injuries to civilian population from the weapons of war, the Convention also seeks to protect the environment.

Protocol III of the CCW on Prohibitions or Restrictions on the Use of Incendiary Weapons, which consists of only two articles,[35] plays an important role by stipulating that "it is prohibited in all circumstances to make the civilian population as such, individual civilians or civilian objects the object of attack by incendiary weapons." Article 2(4) of the Protocol directly addresses environmental protection, as it prohibits "making forests or other kinds of plant cover the subject of an attack by incendiary weapons except when such natural elements are used to cover, conceal, or camouflage combatants or other military objectives, or are themselves military objectives."[36] Finally, Protocol V on Explosive Remnants of War (ERW), which was adopted in 2003, is the first international legal instrument dealing with the problem of unexploded and abandoned ordnance, and sets out guidelines for indirect protection of the environment in the post-conflict situations.

Rome Statute of the International Criminal Court

The Rome Statute contains a provision directly protecting the environment and penalizing attacks on it, even when humans are not affected. According to Article 8(b)(iv) of the Statute, a war crime is committed by intentionally launching an attack in the knowledge that such attack will cause incidental loss of life or injury to civilians or damage to civilian objects or widespread, long-term and severe damage to the natural environment which would be clearly excessive in relation to the concrete and direct overall military advantage anticipated. The Rome Statute requires both intention and knowledge of the outcome rather than either intention or expectation as set forth in the Additional Protocol I of 1977. In addition, for the act to qualify as a war crime, the damage to the natural environment must be clearly excessive in relation to the military advantage anticipated. Criminal responsibility will therefore extend to only those who order operations with the knowledge that widespread, long-term, and severe damage will occur. However, pursuant to Article 28 of the Rome Statute, a commander or superior who "knew, or owing to the circumstances, should have known" that those under his or her command and/or control were committing environmental crimes and "failed to take all necessary and reasonable measures within his or her power to prevent or repress their commission" is subject to prosecution. Indeed, commanders or superiors will be criminally responsible even if they merely fail to "submit the matter to the competent authorities for investigation and prosecution". However, there is a serious lacuna in the Rome Statute.

The Rome Statute defines a crime against humanity as any of a number of specified acts committed as part of a wide-spread or systematic attack directed against any civilian population, with knowledge of the attack.[37] These include: (i) persecution against any identifiable group or collectivity on political, racial, national, ethnic, cultural, religious, gender ...., or other grounds that are universally recognized as impermissible under international law, in connection with any act referred to in this paragraph or any crime within the jurisdiction of the Court; (ii) Other inhumane acts of a similar character intentionally causing great suffering, or serious injury to body or to mental or physical health.[38] The term 'persecution' is defined for the purpose of Article 7(1) of the Rome Statute as the intentional and severe deprivation of fundamental rights contrary to international law by reasons of the identity of the group or collectively. The intentional or deliberate destruction of a habitat or access to safe or clean water could in certain circumstances represent a breach of fundamental rights of the individuals within a targeted group. Thus theoretically, the terms of Article 7(1)(h) of the Rome Statute could be extended to certain acts of intentionally targeting the environment during an armed conflict.[39]

The Office of the Prosecutor (ICC) has recently declared that it would prioritize crimes that result in the "destruction of the environment", "exploitation of natural resources" and the "illegal dispossession" of land. In view of the Office of the Prosecutor, it does not amount to formal extension of the jurisdiction of the court, but it would assess existing offences, such as crimes against humanity, in a broader context. The 2016 ICC's policy paper on case selection and prioritization declares: "The office [of the prosecutor] will give particular consideration to prosecuting Rome Statute crimes that are committed by means of, or that result in, inter alia, the destruction of the environment, the illegal exploitation of natural resources or the illegal dispossession of land." According to policy paper, land-grabbing has become increasingly common worldwide, with national and local governments allocating private companies tens of millions of hectares of land in the past 10 years. The terrible impacts of land-grabbing and environmental destruction have been acknowledged at the highest level of criminal justice, and private sector actors could now be put on trial for their role in illegally seizing land, flattening rainforests or poisoning water sources.[40]

E. The ICRC Guidelines for military manuals and instructions on the protection of the environment in times of armed conflict

Concerned by the extensive damage caused to the environment during the Gulf War, the International Committee of the Red Cross (ICRC), issued "Guidelines for military manuals and instructions on the protection of the environment in times of armed conflict" in 1994.[41] The guidelines were drawn from existing international legal obligations and from State practice concerning the protection of the environment against the effects of armed conflict. In the recommending note, the ICRC stated:

> To the extent that the Guidelines are the expression of international customary law[42] or of treaty law binding a particular State, they must be included in military manuals and instructions on the laws of war. Where they reflect national policy, it is suggested that they be included in such documents.

Specific rules on the protection of the environment:

1. Destruction of the environment not justified by military necessity violates international humanitarian law. Under certain circumstances, such destruction is punishable as a grave breach of international humanitarian law.
2. The general prohibition on destroying civilian objects, unless such destruction is justified by military necessity, also protects the environment.
3. In particular, States should take all measures required by international law to avoid:
   (a) Making forests or other kinds of plant cover the object of attack by incendiary weapons except when such natural elements are used to cover, conceal or camouflage combatants or other military objectives, or are themselves military objectives;
   (b) Attacks on objects indispensable to the survival of the civilian population, such as foodstuffs, agricultural areas or drinking water installations, if carried out for the purpose of denying such objects to the civilian population;
   (c) Attacks on works or installations containing dangerous forces, namely dams, dykes and nuclear electrical generating stations, even where they are military objectives, if such attack may cause the release of dangerous forces and consequent severe losses among the civilian population and as long as such works or installations are entitled to special protection under Protocol I additional to the Geneva Conventions;
   (d) Attacks on historic monuments, works of art or places of worship which constitute the cultural or spiritual heritage of peoples.
4. The indiscriminate laying of landmines is prohibited. The location of all pre-planned minefields must be recorded. Any unrecorded laying of remotely delivered non-self-neutralising landmines is prohibited. Special rules limit the emplacement and use of naval mines.
5. Care shall be taken in warfare to protect and preserve the natural environment. It is prohibited to employ methods or

means of warfare which are intended, or may be expected, to cause widespread, long-term and severe damage to the natural environment and thereby prejudice the health or survival of the population.

6. The military or any other hostile use of environmental modification techniques having widespread, long-lasting or severe effects as the means of destruction, damage or injury to any other State party is prohibited. The term "environmental modification techniques" refers to any technique for changing—through the deliberate manipulation of natural processes—the dynamics, composition or structure of the Earth, including its biota, lithosphere, hydrosphere and atmosphere, or of outer space.
7. Attack against the natural environment by way of reprisals are prohibited for States party to Protocol I additional to the Geneva Conventions of 1949. States are urged to enter into further agreements providing additional protection to the natural environment in times of armed conflict.
8. States are urged to enter into further agreements providing additional protection to the natural environment in times of armed conflict.
9. Works or installations containing dangerous forces, and cultural property shall be clearly marked and identified, in accordance with applicable international rules. Parties to an armed conflict are encouraged to mark and identify also works or installations where hazardous activities are being carried out, as well as sites which are essential to human health or the environment.
10. Sates shall respect and ensure respect for the obligations under international law applicable in armed conflict, including the rules providing protection for the environment in times of armed conflict.
11. States shall disseminate these rules, making them known as widely as possible in their respective countries, and include them in their programmes of military and civil instruction.

12. In the study, development, acquisition or adoption of a new weapon, means or method of warfare, States are under an obligation to determine whether its employment would, in some or all circumstances, be prohibited by applicable rules of international law, including those providing protection to the environment in times of armed conflict.
13. In the event of armed conflict, the parties thereto are encouraged to facilitate and protect the work of impartial organisations contributing to preventing or repairing damage to the environment, pursuant to special agreements between the parties concerned or, as the case may be, the permission granted by one of them. Such work should be performed with due regard to the security interests of the parties concerned.
14. In the event of breaches of rules of international humanitarian law protecting the environment, measures shall be taken to stop any such violation and to prevent further breaches. Military commanders are required to prevent and, where necessary, to suppress and to report to competent authorities breaches of these rules. In serious cases, offenders shall be brought to justice.

The ICRC had concluded that existing law, if properly implemented, was capable of providing adequate protection.[43] The UN General Assembly, decided in its 49th session not to formally approve them but rather, to invite states to "give due consideration" to their incorporation into military manuals and instructions.[44]

F. UNGA Resolutions

The UN General Assembly resolutions have made a significant contribution to the framing of international law towards the protection of environment during armed conflict. In 1969, following reports of the use of chemical agents such as herbicides by the US in the Vietnam War, the UN General Assembly passed a resolution declaring that the 1925 Gas Protocol prohibits the use of the following in armed conflicts:

(a) Any chemical agents of warfare, i.e., chemical substances, whether gaseous, liquid or solid—which might be employed because of their direct toxic effects on man, animals or plants.

(b) Any biological agents of warfare, i.e., living organisms, whatever their nature, or infective material derived from them, which are intended to cause disease and death in man, animals or plants, and which depend for their effects on their ability to multiply in the person, animal or plant attacked.[45]

The UN General Assembly, in its Resolution of February 9, 1993, stated that "destruction of the environment, not justified by military necessity and carried out wantonly is clearly contrary to existing international law."[46] Resolution A/RES/50/7(M) specifically recognises the importance of considering environmental safeguards in treaties and agreements regarding disarmament, and further highlights the detrimental environmental effects of the use of nuclear weapons, as well as "the positive potential implications for the environment of a future comprehensive nuclear-test-ban treaty."[47]

Guided by the purposes and principles enshrined in the Charter of the United Nations and the rules of IHL, the General Assembly has also addressed the issue of depleted uranium (DU). The Resolutions of 2007 and 2009 could eventually lead to the codification in treaty law of norms protecting human health and the environment from DU armaments, thus addressing the current major gap in treaty law regarding the use of such weapons.[48]

II. Responsibility of a Military Commander

All military activities including operations have negative environmental consequences, though of differing degrees of effects on the environment. To cite a few examples, (i) compaction, erosion, and contamination of soils by bombs and missiles and their hazardous and toxic residues, (ii) land degradation by the passage of heavy military vehicles, (iii) land and water pollution from military wastes, landmines, unexploded ordnance, and radioactive dust, (iv) defoliation, deforestation, and land degradation from routine military activities, (v) contamination of surface waters and groundwater from improper handling of oil wastes, (vi) atmospheric emissions and resulting air pollution from military equipment and vehicles, (vii) direct and collateral killing of animals and plants and loss of habitat, (viii) degradation and destruction of protected natural areas, and (ix) noise pollution.

An armed conflict may result in the damage and destruction of water storage and distribution systems, waste treatment facilities, sewer systems, croplands, pasturage, marine fisheries, power grid systems and so on, disrupting and destroying the social and economic infrastructures of human communities. It may cause the dislocation of human populations resulting in overcrowding and the spread of infectious diseases. Many environmental impacts linger long after a war ends, and can lead to further negative impacts as demographic and economic frontiers expand into remaining natural areas and fragile land- and waterscapes.[49]

Military commanders can play an important role for the protection of natural environment, both during times of peace and armed conflict. In all military systems, the power to command and the duty to obey are of central importance. As part of their responsibility for ensuring operational effectiveness, commanders build effective team relationships within their units, thus fostering team spirit and a climate of mutual trust and respect.[50] According to the doctrine of command responsibility, applicable in times of armed conflict, commanders can be held responsible for the deeds of their subordinates if they knew or should have known that their subordinates were engaging in impermissible conduct and if they failed to prevent or punish such conduct.[51] Commanders also have a duty not to issue improper or illegal orders to their subordinates. The military legal systems of several countries define "an illegal order" and dictate that subordinates must not execute illegal orders given by their commanders.[52] Examples include the use of illegal or banned weapons in armed conflict to harm the natural environment, or an order to kill another soldier without a reason.

There are two main reasons why a military commander must be concerned about the environment. First, the environment can affect the health and safety of soldiers. Second, the environment can affect the ability of commanders to accomplish their mission and achieve national objectives.[53] Military commanders can minimise the adverse effects of military activities on the environment.[54] Environmental contamination due to poor management of hazardous materials can affect the health of soldiers, particularly when camps are located improperly or soldiers are not trained to handle the potentially hazardous materials they encounter. Hazardous wastes or materials stored at military camps can also be used against soldiers.

The prolonged deployment of armed forces and their increased involvement in post-conflict activities have increased the importance of environmental considerations in military operations. Environmental considerations like conservation of water, sanitation and hazardous waste management are important factors for achieving overall military objectives during operations, reconstruction, and post-conflict situations. If not properly addressed, environmental considerations can increase the costs of an operation and make it more difficult for the military to sustain a mission. National and international laws protect the environment and could make military units liable for not following the prescribed standards.

Military commanders usually view the environment as a resource to be exploited for tactical, strategic, or economic reasons. However, they have a responsibility towards the environment in both peace and war.[55] Peacetime responsibilities are founded on the commander's professional responsibility as an agent of the State and the domestic laws related to environmental protection. Wartime responsibilities stem from IHL and relate to the well-established rules against harming non-combatants and destroying works of art and objects of historical or cultural value.[56]

The peacetime responsibilities of a commander could include conservation of the land entrusted to his care.[57] A commander must ensure the maintenance of air and water quality, management of hazardous substances, waste and sewage, protection of wildlife, conservation of soil, etc. It may be impossible for him to protect the environment from the adverse effects of the training of troops. For instance, the use of weapons and war machinery may result in the destruction of vegetation, erosion of soil and loss of wildlife. However, a commander can prevent the wanton destruction of vegetation and terrain, the killing of wildlife, and the intentional dumping of hazardous wastes. Once training is over, he must take measures to repair environmental damage as far as possible. This could include planting trees, filling in fighting positions, removing contaminated soil, trash, and removing unexploded ordnances, and cleaning up fuel spills.

While the peacetime responsibilities of a military commander may include protecting the ecological fragile area under his use and care, wartime responsibilities for the environment are more difficult to justify. Military necessity overrides environmental concerns during a conflict. Following orders, winning battles, and protecting one's own troops are a military commander's primary responsibilities, and much of combat will require killing (at least indirectly) animals and plants, disrupting community and ecosystem structures, and causing land, water, and air pollution.[58] What would be the consequences, say, if a military commander does not allow his forces to open artillery fire towards a forested area where his adversaries have taken position, in order to save an endangered species? Alternative methods of war may result in losing the battle and a few of his soldiers.[59]

The protection of the environment during armed conflict can be derived from the traditional "just war" theory.[60] One of the primary tenets of this theory is that warfare is a fight between combatants. A combatant is a person who can harm you; and everyone else is a non-combatant and poses no threat. The natural environment must be regarded as a non-combatant, and it must not be attacked.[61] A military commander can certainly prevent destruction of crop and food stuff, poisoning of water supply, flooding of land, killing of wildlife, destruction of forests,[62] removal of vulnerable natural resources, etc. No doubt a military commander has a very difficult task in an armed conflict. He must fight to win while protecting the rights of non-combatants and the lives of his soldiers. The responsibility for environmental protection is an added burden on his shoulders. However, military commanders at various levels can take positive steps to prevent wanton destruction of the environment during armed conflict.[63]

In order to protect the environment during conflicts and undertake ecological restoration and rehabilitation in post-conflict situations, it is necessary for military commanders to be well-trained in various aspects of the environmental conservation. They must be aware of the adverse effects of various weapons and tactics on the natural environment and must not use weapons and methods that have the potential to devastate large areas of the biosphere. Commanders, subordinate leaders, and soldiers must understand their individual duties and responsibilities towards environmental protection and become environmental stewards. Environment education must be an essential component of military training manuals so that military commanders and their subordinates understand the basic environmental management responsibilities that apply to their work area or assigned duties.

Figure 1: Interaction between deployed forces and the environment[64]

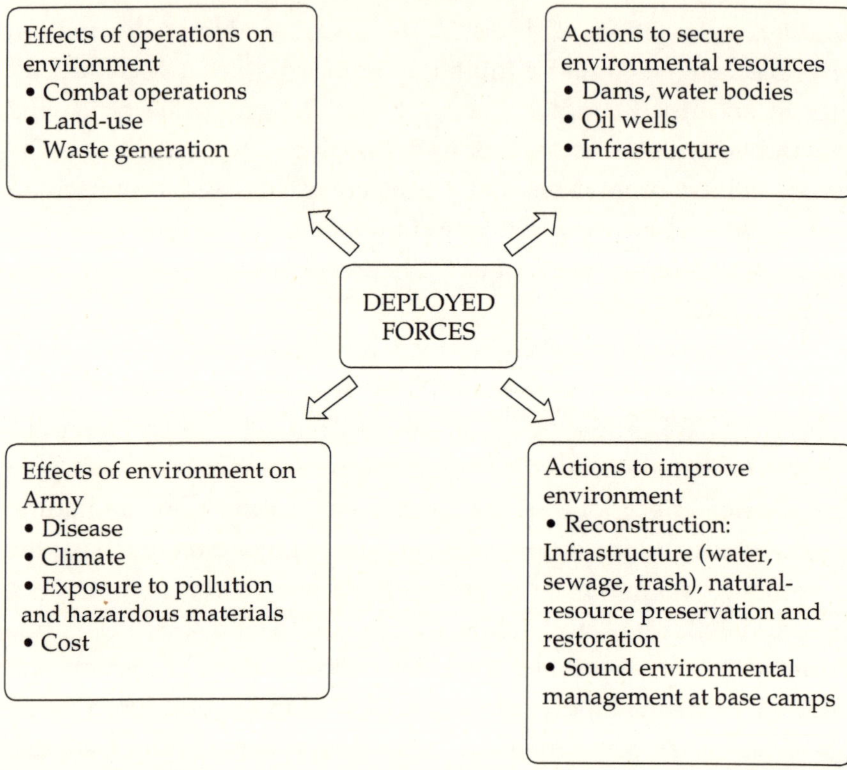

Environmental damage is an inescapable consequence of military operations; however, military technology has made it possible to minimise the damage. It is no longer necessary to obliterate terrain to achieve the desired military effect. Wanton employment of military weaponry can produce three primary environmental effects:[65]

(i) Unnecessary impacts are environmental damages that military necessity cannot justify. For example, Iraqi forces committed wanton acts during the Persian Gulf War when they set Kuwaiti oil fields ablaze and fouled the Persian Gulf by releasing crude oil. A few legal commentators are of the view that Iraq had military reasons for these actions. However, the advantage gained was not proportional to the environmental damage caused.

(ii) Collateral damage results from military actions used to achieve strategic, operational, or tactical objectives. For example, damaging enemy targets (such as ammunition stockpiles or wastewater treatment plants) can release hazardous substances that cause unintended casualties long after the battlefield/area of operations is secured. Commanders must weigh the military value of an operation against collateral damage.

(iii) Modification of the environment includes using environmental modification (ENMOD) techniques on the atmosphere, oceans, or land masses and associated water systems to cause widespread, long-lasting, or severe damage to human life, natural or economic resources, or other assets. ENMOD may include river diversion, destruction of oil wells on the seabed, weather modification and or large-scale burning or defoliation of vegetation.

A military commander must identify ways to protect the natural environment while executing the full range of missions by (i) considering the environment in planning and decision-making in conjunction with other essential considerations of national policy; (ii) using environmental risk assessment and environmental management principles to integrate environmental considerations into mission performance; (iii) instilling an environmental ethic amongst the rank and file; and (iv) understanding the linkages between environmental protection issues and safety and health of the troops as well as non-combatants' protection. Military environmental protection is the application and integration of all aspects of natural environmental considerations as they apply to the conduct of military operations.[66]

Good environmental practices during military operations and in post-conflict situations can reduce the financial liabilities of the armed forces and the government. In many cases, the contractors employed by the military remove hazardous wastes from camps and dump them in other inappropriate locations. Members of the local population may bring claims against the military for damages related to the environment. Illegal dumping by contractors and poor waste management practices by soldiers may cause diplomatic problems with host nations, in the case of overseas deployment. Financial liabilities can also arise from claims brought by an army's own soldiers who believe they were exposed to hazardous substances.[67]

III. Legal Review of New Weapons

The development and procurement of weapons and weapon systems by a State and their intended use during an armed conflict need to be consistent with the State's treaty obligations. Before acquiring, developing or modifying a weapon, a State must ensure its possession and intended use in armed conflict are consistent with international law. Article 36 of AP I, states, "In the study, development, acquisition or adoption of a new weapon, means or method of warfare, a High Contracting Party is under an obligation to determine whether its employment would, in some or all circumstances, be prohibited by this Protocol or by any other rule of international law applicable to the High Contracting Party." The States Parties to AP I are therefore, obliged to determine the legality of a new weapon whenever they adopt, acquire, or develop it. All States bound by customary international law are also under an obligation to ensure that in acquiring new weapons, they comply with those rules.[68] The aim of Article 36 is to prevent the States from incorporating such weapons into their arsenal as would violate international law, and imposing restrictions on their use if this violates international law in some circumstances.[69]

Scope of Article 36

Article 36 of AP I refers to weapons, and means or methods of warfare. The material scope of the legal review[70] under Article 36 is, therefore, very broad. It would cover: (i) weapons of all types, be they anti-personnel or anti-material, lethal, non-lethal or less lethal, and weapon systems; (ii) the ways in which these weapons are to be used pursuant to military doctrine, tactics, rules of engagement, operating procedures and countermeasures; (iii) all weapons to be acquired, be they procured further to research and development on the basis of military specifications, or purchased off-the-shelf; (iv) a weapon which the state intends to acquire for the first time, without its necessarily being new in a technical sense; (v) an existing weapon which is modified in a way that alters its function, or a weapon which has already passed a legal review but is subsequently modified; and (vi) an existing weapon where a State has joined a new international treaty which may affect the legality of the weapon.[71]

The obligation to review the legality of new weapons implies at least two things: (i) A State should have in place some form of permanent standing mechanism that can be activated at any time when it is developing or acquiring a new weapon; (ii) Such a procedure should be made mandatory for the authority responsible for developing or acquiring new weapons. Other than these minimum procedural requirements, a State is free to decide the other specific necessities of its review mechanism.[72] When in doubt as to whether the device or system proposed for study, development or acquisition is a "weapon," legal advice should be sought from the weapons review authority.

Article 36 is complemented by Article 82 of AP I, which requires that legal advisers be available at all times to advise military commanders on IHL and "on the appropriate instruction to be given to the armed forces on this subject." Both provisions establish a framework for ensuring that the armed forces will be capable of conducting hostilities in strict accordance with IHL, through legal reviews of planned means and methods of warfare.

In order to ensure that the new weapon adheres to IHL, a few States have constituted expert committees to determine: (i) the purpose of the new weapon; (ii) the factors which favour the introduction of the new weapons; (iii) the damage mechanism of the new weapon (blast, fragmentation, etc.); (iv) whether the new weapon is specifically designed to cause injury to personnel; (v) the human injuries that the new weapon is capable of inflicting; (vi) what other weapons, if any, would be capable of fulfilling the same purpose as the new weapon; (vii) whether the new weapon has been adopted by the armed forces of other States or by other agencies in the country or overseas and, if so, by which one; and (viii) whether evaluation data concerning the new weapon are available from the armed forces of other States or from other agencies.[73] Having a "national mechanism" to review the legality of new weapons is especially relevant in view of the emergence of new technologies, such as directed energy, incapacitants, behaviour-change agents, acoustics and nanotechnology.[74]

AP I does not impose any obligation on the States for conducting a review in a specific way. However, in assessing the legality of a particular weapon, the reviewing authority must examine not only the weapon's design and characteristics (the means of warfare), but also how it is to be used (the method of warfare), bearing in mind that the weapon's effects will result from a combination of its design and the manner in which it is to be used. All States, whether or not they are party to the AP I, must assess the lawfulness of their new weapons in order to ensure that they are able to comply with their customary legal obligations during armed conflicts and other situations of violence.[75]

The ICRC has called on States to establish mechanisms and procedures to determine the conformity of weapons with international law. In particular, the 28th Conference declared: "In the light of the rapid development of weapons technology and in order to protect civilians from the indiscriminate effects of weapons and combatants from unnecessary suffering and prohibited weapons, all new weapons, means and methods of warfare should be subject to rigorous and multidisciplinary review."[76] However, very few States not party to AP I have adopted formal weapons review procedures as there is no obligation on States to disclose their conclusions about the legality of a weapon.

The UK Ministry of Defence has recently published the result of the legal review of its depleted uranium (DU) anti-armour tank rounds, known as CHARM3, the only munition of the UK's arsenal manufactured using DU. Legal review is undertaken routinely in respect of weapon systems brought on to the UK inventory following the State's ratification of AP I, on January 28, 1998. The legal review process under Article 36 of AP I required the use of CHARM3 to be considered in the light of certain key legal principles, namely: (i) Whether it is prohibited by any specific treaty provision; (ii) Whether it is of a nature to cause unnecessary suffering or superfluous injury; (iii) Whether it is capable of being used discriminately; (iv) Whether it will cause long-term, widespread and severe damage to the natural environment; (v) Current and possible future trends in IHL.

The review committee reported that in view of the scientific studies, and the continuing military imperative underpinning the retention of CHARM3 as a weapon system, the use of CHARM3 does not offend the principle prohibiting superfluous injury or unnecessary suffering in armed conflict. It also held that the crew training, weapon design and automated targeting systems indicate that CHARM3 is capable of being used discriminately. Further, where DU ordnance residues have existed, in the aftermath of an armed conflict, annual potential radiation doses have been shown by scientific study to be well below the annual doses received by the general population from sources of natural radiation in the environment and far below the reference level recommended by the International Atomic Energy Agency as a criterion to determine whether remedial action is necessary. "Inevitably an environmental footprint will be left by use of DU munitions ... will not have significant risk of any long-term damage to the environment." The weapon review committee concluded that CHARM3 was capable of being used lawfully by the UK Armed Forces in an international armed conflict. The use of CHARM3 would be limited to a war fighting role, specifically in tank battles, and likely therefore to be employed only in exceptional and limited circumstances.[77] Perhaps the UK has downplayed the potential health risks posed by exposure to DU.[78]

For States manufacturing weapons for self-use or export, the review should be undertaken at the stage of the conception/design of the weapon, and thereafter at the stages of its development and testing. For States purchasing weapons, the review should take place at the stage of the study of the weapon proposed for purchase. The purchasing State remains under an obligation to conduct its own review of the weapon after acquisition. When State made technical modifications to an existing weapon, the review of the proposed modification should take place at the earliest stage.[79] After a weapon has been incorporated into the arsenal of a State, further legal review may be needed if there is any change in law.

The ICRC has recently drawn up *A Guide to the Legal Review of New Weapons, Means and Methods of Warfare*,[80] which has been prepared in consultation with about 30 military and international law experts, including government experts from 10 countries. It makes suggestions on the substantive and procedural questions to be considered while engaging in such a review. The Guide reflects the ICRC's interpretation of the subject, based on the text of Article 36 of AP I, the ICRC's Commentary on the AP, statements of international conferences and the practice of six States which have established their weapons review procedures.

Conclusion

Concern for environmental damage during armed conflict came to the fore only in the 1970s. The rules of IHL adopted by the international community before that offered no real environmental protection. IHL was designed to ameliorate human suffering, and any environmental benefit was secondary. Even when the international NGOs condemned the use of weapons of mass destruction (biological, chemical and nuclear weapons) they had no intention of going into the question of environmental protection. Most IHL provisions are subject to constraints, such as the "necessity of war" used in Article 23 (1)(g) of the 1907 Hague Convention IV or "necessary by military operations" used in Article 53 of the Fourth Geneva Convention of 1949. Thus, military necessity has been used as a part of the legal justification for using weapons (on legitimate military targets) that may have adverse or even terrible consequences for civilians and civilian objects. Large-scale environmental destruction has taken place during armed conflicts under the pretext of military necessity. For example, the US has justified the use of DU weapons in Iraq and Afghanistan.

Recent conflicts have demonstrated that even those IHL rules that are applicable to the protection of the environment during armed conflict are largely unenforceable and often disregarded. Limitations in application and enforcement mechanisms hinder the effectiveness of these provisions. In addition, a lack of synergy and coherence between the existing provisions of IHL has created a series of prohibitions riddled with loopholes. The absence of effective punishments for environmentally destructive conduct reinforces the ineffectiveness of the current system in preventing environmental harm due to combat.[81]

According to Bothe (2010: 569), there are three main shortcomings in the existing body of IHL relating to the protection of the environment during armed conflict: (i) the definition of impermissible environmental damage is both too restrictive and unclear; (ii) there are legal uncertainties regarding the protection of elements of the environment as civilian objects; and (iii) the application of the principle of proportionality where harm to the environment constitutes "collateral damage" is problematic. These gaps present specific opportunities for clarifying and developing the existing framework. Some of the inadequacies of IHL could be addressed by the application of international environmental law to armed conflict.[82]

Notes

1. The Convention on the Prohibition of the Development, Production, Stockpiling and Use of Chemical Weapons and on their Destruction (CWC), 1993 is the most successful treaty in this regard.
2. The prohibition of treacherous acts during combat.
3. Motivated by military use of environmental modification techniques in the 1960s and 1970s (particularly by the US) which went against basic principles of

IHL like discrimination and proportionality, the Convention on the Prohibition of Military of Other Hostile Use of Environmental Techniques (ENMOD), was adopted by the UN General Assembly in 1976 and entered into force in October 1978. Today, almost 37 years after ENMOD was negotiated, the treaty is all but forgotten and only 76 countries have ratified the agreement. Twenty were required to bring it into force. Parties to ENMOD have met only twice, in 1982 and 1992. Despite the fact that, ENMOD was recognised as a flawed treaty, no international civil society group has seriously tried to fix it.

4. Protocol Additional to the Geneva Conventions of August 12, 1949, and relating to the Protection of Victims of International Armed Conflicts (Protocol I), June 8, 1977 (AP I).
5. The principles of IHL are a source of law on their own. Statute of the International Court of Justice (ICJ), Article 38.
6. Military objectives are members of the armed forces, other persons taking a direct part in hostilities, and "those objects which by their nature, location, purpose or use make an effective contribution to military action and whose total or partial destruction, capture or neutralisation, in the circumstances ruling at the time, offers a definite military advantage." IHL prohibits attacks "of a nature to strike military objectives and civilians or civilian objects without distinction." Additional Protocol I, Articles 51(3), (4) and 52.
7. Richard D. Tarasofsky, "Legal Protection of the Environment During International Armed Conflict," *Netherlands Yearbook of International Law,* vol. XXIV, 1993, p. 27.
8. The concept of proportionality is described in Article 22 of 1907 Hague Regulations IV.
9. The proportionality principle is contained in Articles 35 (2), 51(5)(b), and 57(2) (a) and (b) of the Additional Protocol I to the Geneva Conventions of 1949.
10. Michael D. Diederich, "Law of War and Ecology, A Proposal for a Workable Approach to Protecting the Environment through the Law of War," vol. 136, *Mil. Law Rev.* (1992), p. 137.
11. Richard Falk, "The Environmental Law of War: An Introduction," in Glen Plant (ed.), *Environmental Protection and the Law of War: A "Fifth Geneva" Convention on the Protection of the Environment in Time of Armed Conflict* (John Wiley & Sons, 1992), p. 84.
12. The Committee Established to Review the NATO Bombing Campaign Against the Federal Republic of Yugoslavia was of the view that the environmental impact of that bombing campaign was "best considered from the underlying principles of the law of armed conflicts such as necessity and proportionality." Committee Established to Review the NATO Bombing Campaign Against the Federal Republic of Yugoslavia, Final Report. Available at: http://www.icty.org/x/file/Press/nato061300.pdf, accessed September 12, 2012.
13. Fleck Dieter, *The Handbook of International Humanitarian Law* (Oxford: Oxford University Press, 2009), p. 23.
14. The British Manual of Military Law (2004) defines military necessity as: "The principle whereby a belligerent has the right to apply any measures which are required to bring about the successful conclusion of a military operation and which are not forbidden by the laws of war." Put another way, a state engaged in an armed conflict may use that degree and kind of force, not otherwise prohibited by the law of armed conflict, that is required in order to achieve the legitimate purpose of the conflict, namely the complete or partial submission of the enemy at the earliest possible moment with the minimum expenditure

of life and resources. The Manual further provides that the humanity forbids the infliction of suffering, injury, or destruction not actually necessary for the accomplishment of legitimate military purposes. The principle of humanity is based on the notion that once a military purpose has been achieved, the further infliction of suffering is unnecessary. The principle confirms the basic immunity of civilian populations and civilian objects from attack because civilians and civilian objects make no contribution to military action.

15. Richard G. Tarasofsky, "Protecting Specially Important Areas during International Armed Conflict: A Critique of the IUCN Draft Convention on the Prohibition of Hostile Military Activities in Protected Areas," in Jay E. Austin and Carl E. Bruch (eds.), *The Environmental Consequences of War: Legal, Economic and Scientific Perspectives* (Cambridge: Cambridge University Press, 2000), p. 568.
16. The Martens Clause is so called after Friedrich von Martens, the Russian delegate who chaired the 11th meeting of the Second Committee of the Second Commission of the First Hague Peace Conference of 1899. The inclusion of the Martens Clause in that document affirmed its importance again in protecting civilian populations and combatants as they comprise a substantial part of the environment. Its wording is reflected in articles and preambles in a number of subsequent treaties, including the four Geneva Conventions of 1949, the 1977 Additional protocols I and II, and the 1980 UN Convention on Certain Conventional Weapons (CCW). The relevance of this clause to environmental protection has been widely accepted. Adam Roberts, "The Law of War and Environmental Damage," in Jay E. Austin and Carl E. Bruch (eds.), *The Environmental Consequences of War: Legal, Economic and Scientific Perspectives* (Cambridge: Cambridge University Press, 2000), p. 52.
17. The Martens Clause broadens the range of applicable norms governing conduct during armed conflict beyond those that are laid out in the treaty instruments. In essence, where gaps exist in the international framework governing specific situations (including, for instance, the relationship between armed conflict and the environment), the Martens Clause stipulates that States should respect a minimum standard as established by the standards of "humanity" and the "public conscience." The Martens Clause is generally considered to constitute a foundational principle of IHL and core principle protecting the environment in the absence of other provisions in treaty or customary law. *Protecting the Environment During Armed Conflict: An Inventory and Analysis of International Law* (November 2009), UNEP, p. 12.
18. Nada Al-Duaij, *Environmental Law of Armed Conflict* (New York: Transnational Publishers, 2004), p. 95.
19. Many of the rules of IHL are considered part of customary international law and, therefore, mandatory for all parties to an armed conflict. The advantage of customary law is that it is not necessary for a State to formally accept a rule in order to be bound by it, as long as the overall State practice on which the rule is based is accepted as law. Article 38 of the Statute of the International Court of Justice (ICJ) lists custom as a source of international law, describing it as "evidence of a general practice accepted as law." Statute of the International Court of Justice, Article 38, June 26, 1945.
20. Jean-Marie Henckaerts, "Study on Customary International Humanitarian Law: A contribution to the understanding and respect for the rule of law in armed conflict," *International Review of the Red Cross*, vol. 87, no. 857, March 2005, pp. 175-212. The 161 rules have been catalogued in six parts: (i) Principle of distinction, (ii) specifically protected persons and objects, (iii) specific methods

of warfare, (iv) weapons, (v) treatment of civilians and persons *hors de combat*, and (vi) implementation. Of the 161 rules identified, 159 apply in international armed conflicts and 149 in non-international armed conflicts. Although key States such as Israel, India, and the United States are not party to AP I, they recognise many of the Protocol's provisions as reflective of the customary law of armed conflict.

21. *Protecting the Environment During Armed Conflict: An Inventory and Analysis of International Law*, November 2009, UNEP, p. 23.
22. The words "due regard" and "preservation" have not been defined. The authors of the study have not adhered to the language used in IHL, and have extended the scope of the laws resulting in a questionable "rule" of customary international law. Major J. Jeremy Marsh, "*Lex Lata* or *Lex Ferenda?* Rule 45 of the ICRC Study on Customary International Humanitarian Law," vol. 198, *Military Law Review*, Winter 2008, p. 135.
23. Koppe Erik V., "Use of nuclear wepons and protection of the environment during international armed conflict", in Nystuen Gro, Stuart Casey-Maslen and Annie Golden Bersagel (Ed.), *Nuclear Weapons under International Law*, Cambridge: Cambridge University Press, 2014, pp. 247-268.
24. For example, the military manuals of Australia, South Korea and the United States.
25. Secretary-General's Bulletin: Observance by United Nations forces of international humanitarian law, UN Document ST/SGB/1999/13, dated August 6, 1999. Section 6 of the Bulletin provides: 6.1. The right of the United Nations forces to choose methods and means of combat is not unlimited. 6.3. The United Nations force is prohibited from employing methods of warfare which may cause superfluous injury or unnecessary suffering, or which are intended, or may be expected to cause, widespread, long-term and severe damage to the natural environment. Available at:http://www1.umn.edu/humanrts/instree/unobservance1999.pdf, accessed September 12, 2012.
26. Historical examples of hostile modification of environment would include the spreading of salt by the Romans in the fields of Carthage in 146 BC. A more recent example is the near extermination of the bison in the United States during the nineteenth century. Critical resources for indigenous peoples of the North American plains, bison were hunted to near extinction by immigrants from the Eastern parts of the US. The elimination of the bison assisted the campaign of the US government to extinguish Native American land rights and remove native peoples to reservations. By destruction of the bison, basic environmental resources were denied to Native Americans. Many Native Americans were forced to choose between capitulation or starvation and freezing. As a result, immigrants were rewarded with land and US sovereignty was extended to new areas.
27. An attached understanding to Article II in ENMOD contains a list of events that could be caused by environmental modification techniques. This includes: Earthquakes, tsunamis, an upset in the ecological balance of a region, changes in weather patterns (clouds, precipitation, cyclones of various types and tornadic storms), changes in climate patterns, changes in ocean currents, changes in the state of the ozone layer and changes in the state of the ionosphere.
28. Antoine Philippe, "International Humanitarian Law and the Protection of the Environment in Time of Armed Conflict," no. 291, *International Review of the Red Cross*, November-December 1992, p. 522.
29. ENMOD is neither a Convention that prosecutes wartime environmental

damage as such nor a Convention that bans the use of certain weapons, but rather an effort to restrict the use of certain techniques in armed conflict such as those that had been employed by the US military in Vietnam. Julian Wyatt, "Law-making at the Intersection of International Environmental, Humanitarian and Criminal Law: The Issue of Damage to the Environment in International Armed Conflict," vol. 92, no. 879, *International Review of the Red Cross*, September 2010, p. 611.

30. The United States' widespread use of heavy munitions; incendiary weapons; herbicides; anti-personnel chemicals; weather manipulation; and bombing raids against dams, dykes, and seawalls, during the Vietnam War had serious environmental effects. The international community objected to these measures, kindling controversy over their employment. The result of the controversy was Protocol I to the 1949 Geneva Conventions of 1949. It advanced additional restraints on the means and methods of waging war and was perhaps the first significant development of IHL since 1907. Michael Diederich, "Law of War and Ecology: A Proposal for a Workable Approach to Protecting the Environment through the Law of War," vol. 136, *Military Law Review*, Spring 1992, pp. 137-60.
31. The negotiations of Additional Protocols I and II to the Geneva Conventions took place against the backdrop of various wars of national liberation—including the Vietnam War—that raised serious questions regarding the protection of civilian populations and the environment. Growing environmental awareness, as well as concern over military tactics employed during these wars, led to the inclusion of two provisions in AP I that explicitly addressed environmental harm. The AP I has been ratified by 172 States, the US, China, India and a few other major powers have consistently refused to do so.
32. Karen Hulme, "Taking Care to Protect the Environment against Damage: A Meaningless Obligation," *International Review of the Red Cross*, vol. 92, no. 879, September 2010, p. 681.
33. Karen Hulme, "Taking Care to Protect the Environment against Damage: A Meaningless Obligation," *International Review of the Red Cross*, vol. 92, no. 879, September 2010, pp. 675-69.
34. AP I is noteworthy for containing the key provisions of IHL specifically addressing the environment. In addition, there are a number of articles which indirectly offer environment protection. Many restate principles expressed elsewhere in the law. For instance, Article 35(1) mirrors the St. Petersburg Declaration and Hague IV in reiterating the principle that "the right of the Parties to the conflict to choose methods and means of warfare is not unlimited." Similarly, Article 35(2) prohibits the causation of superfluous injury or unnecessary suffering, and, as noted, the Martens Clause is found in Article I of Additional Protocol I. Michael N. Schmitt, "Humanitarian Law and the Environment," vol. 28 (3), *Denv. J. International Law & Policy* (2000), pp. 265-323.
35. Article 1 defines certain terms like "incendiary weapons," "military objectives," "civilian objects," and "feasible precautions." Article 2 deals with the protection of civilians and civilian objects.
36. Article 2 (4) CCW Protocol III grants the armed forces the right to ignore the protection of natural resources if they are "used to cover, conceal or camouflage combatants or other military objectives, or are themselves military objectives." Nada Al-Duaij, *Environmental Law of Armed Conflict* (New York: Transnational Publishers, 2004), p. 294.
37. Rome Statute, Article 7(1).
38. Rome Statute, Article 7(1) (h) and (k).

39. Freeland Steven. 2015. *Addressing the Intentional Destruction of the Environment during Warfare under the Rome Statute of the International Criminal Court,* Cambridge: Intersentia, p. 202.
40. ICC, The Officer of the Prosecutor: Policy Paper on Case Selection and Prioritization, 15 September 2016.
41. Available at: http://www.icrc.org/eng/resources/documents/misc/57jn38.htm, accessed July 2, 2012.
42. The rules grounded in Articles 35 (3), 55 and 56 of AP I, though included in the ICRC's text cannot be regarded as having customary status. William H. Boothby, *Weapons and the Law of Armed Conflict* (Oxford: Oxford University Press, 2009), p. 100.
43. Hans-Peter Gasser, "For Better Protection of the Natural Environment in Armed Conflict: A Proposal for Action," vol. 89 (3), *American Journal of International Law* (1995), pp. 637-45.
44. William H. Boothby, *Weapons and the Law of Armed Conflict* (Oxford: Oxford University Press, 2009), p. 99.
45. UN GA Res. 2603 A, U.N. GAOR, 24th Sess., U.N. Doc. A/7890 (1969).
46. UNGA Resolution 47/37 (February 9, 1993). The resolution did not, however, identify specific gaps in the existing international legal framework, and consequently did not recommend developing or strengthening particular measures.
47. Among the recent objects under consideration by the General Assembly in relation to armed conflict and the environment was Resolution 63/211 (December 19, 2008) on the oil slick on Lebanese shores caused by the bombing of the El-Jiyeh power plant during the 2006 war. The resolution emphasises "the need to protect and preserve the marine environment in accordance with international law."
48. Since 2007, the UN General Assembly has adopted two resolutions aimed at assessing both the human and environmental impacts of depleted uranium armaments. UNGA Resolutions 62/30 of December 2007 and 63/54 of January 2009 request the Secretary-General to produce reports on the issue. UNGA Resolution 63/54 clearly acknowledges the importance of protecting the environment and reads, in part, that because "humankind is more aware of the need to take immediate measures to protect the environment, any event that could jeopardise such efforts requires urgent attention to implement the required measures." The resolution also recognises "the potential harmful effects of the use of armaments and ammunitions containing depleted uranium on human health and the environment."
49. Mark Woods, "The Nature of War and Peace: Just War Thinking, Environmental Ethics, and Environmental Justice," in Michael W. Brough, John W. Lango and Harry van der Linden (eds.), *Rethinking the Just War Tradition* (USA: State University of New York Press, 2007), p. 19.
50. The Russian Federal Law, for example, provides: Commanders ... in peacetime and wartime are solely responsible for constant combat and mobilisation readiness; the successful fulfilment of combat tasks; education; military discipline; law and order; the moral and psychological condition of military personnel; the safety of military service; the condition and safety of military equipment and military stocks; pecuniary, technical, financial, and everyday maintenance; and medical service. Art. 27.2 of Federal Law No. 76-FZ of May 27, 1998 on the Status of Military Personnel.
51. Additional Protocol I, Article 87: Duty of Commanders

1. The High Contracting Parties and the Parties to the conflict shall require military commanders, with respect to members of the armed forces under their command and other persons under their control, to prevent and, where necessary, to suppress and to report to competent authorities breaches of the Conventions and of this Protocol.
2. In order to prevent and suppress breaches, High Contracting Parties and Parties to the conflict shall require that, commensurate with their level of responsibility, commanders ensure that members of the armed forces under their command are aware of their obligations under the Conventions and this Protocol.
3. The High Contracting Parties and Parties to the conflict shall require any commander who is aware that subordinates or other persons under his control are going to commit or have committed a breach of the Conventions or of this Protocol, to initiate such steps as are necessary to prevent such violations of the Conventions or this Protocol, and, where appropriate, to initiate disciplinary or penal action against violators thereof.

52. The Lithuania law states: Illegal orders are orders that force military personnel to contravene the military oath; that violate national laws, principles, and norms of international law; or that force military personnel to serve other persons or group of persons beyond official military duties.
53. David E. Mosher, Beth E. Lachman, Michael D. Greenberg, Tiffany Nichols, Brian Rosen and Henry H. Willis, *Green Warriors: Army Environmental Considerations for Contingency Operations from Planning Through Post-Conflict*, RAND Corporation, 2008, p. 5.
54. Colonel Frank R. Finch, "This Land in Our Land: The Environmental Threat of Army Operations," in Richard J. Grunawalt, John E. King and Ronald S. McClain (eds.), *Protection of the Environment During Armed Conflict* (Newport, Naval War College, International Law Studies, 1996), vol. 69, p. 113.
55. At the time of active hostilities, military commanders tend to accumulate and use all the firepower they can, both to accomplish their assigned missions and to protect their troops from harm. Sometimes they use more force than necessary, or cause excessive collateral damage because of poor planning, flawed intelligence, enemy deception, computer glitches, or other equipment failure.
56. Major Merrit P. Drucker, "The Military Commander's Responsibility for the Environment," vol. 11 (2), *Environmental Ethics (1989)*, p. 1. Available at: http://isme.tamu.edu/JSCOPE88/Drucker88.pdf, accessed September 23, 2012.
57. Conservation includes two types of resource management: controlled use and preservation. Controlled use focuses on managing military land to ensure long-term natural resource productivity. Preservation focuses on protecting natural and cultural resources (to include endangered species) by maintaining them in their current state. Renewable resources, such as timber or training land, require controlled use. Non-renewable resources, such as historic monuments or endangered species, require preservation. The military must balance these demands in a responsible effort to conserve natural resources and still maintain readiness. Paras 1-32. Environmental Protection and Military Operations, FM 3-100.4, June 15, 2000; The US Department of the Army.
58. Mark Woods, "The Nature of War and Peace: Just War Thinking, Environmental Ethics, and Environmental Justice," in Michael W. Brough, John W. Lango and Harry van der Linden (eds.), *Rethinking the Just War Tradition* (USA: State University of New York Press, 2007), p. 18.
59. According to Major Drucker: "if we accept the view that the environment

and its inhabitants all have inherent worth, then we need to give genuine consideration to the well-being of all plants, animals and persons. In addition to exercising due care, I think commanders should take at least minimal risk with their soldier's life to protect the environment. The amount of risk he should allow is difficult to specify, and is a situational variable. Each commander will have to decide in each case. When he decides, the commander must weigh his moral responsibilities to achieve victory, protect his soldiers, and protect non-combatants. The proposition that commanders could take extraordinary efforts to protect the environment, sacrificing their soldiers' lives in the process, seems both irrational and immoral." Major Merrit P. Drucker, "The Military Commander's Responsibility for the Environment," vol. 11 (2), *Environmental Ethics (1989)*, pp. 135-52. Available at: http://isme.tamu.edu/JSCOPE88/Drucker88.pdf, accessed September 23, 2012.

60. The environment might be more effectively protected by building environmental considerations via the just war tradition (JWT). Armed humanitarian interventions are of central importance within the JWT today given their increasing occurrence and due to the fact that the vast majority of armed conflicts in the world are intrastate as opposed to interstate wars between separate nation-states. If humanitarian interventions can be justified on grounds of ending human rights abuses, rescuing people threatened with massacre, and/or stopping acts that shock our moral conscience, can such interventions constitute a just cause to protect the environment? Might armed environmental interventions be justified to protect, for example, environmental entities such as the Amazon rainforest or the endangered mountain gorillas of central Africa? Mark Woods, "The Nature of War and Peace: Just War Thinking, Environmental Ethics, and Environmental Justice," in Michael W. Brough,, John W. Lango and Harry van der Linden (eds.), *Rethinking the Just War Tradition* (USA: State University of New York Press, 2007), pp. 22-28.

61. According to Drucker, the environment should be treated as a non-combatant because: (i) it is not a fighting combatant and poses no direct threat to combatants, (ii) it is like other non-combatants that did not choose to be involved with combat fighting, and (iii) it is similar to non-combatant chaplains and medical personnel that do not participate in killing but instead heal and nurture people. Merrit Drucker, "The Military Commander's Responsibility for the Environment," vol. 11, *Environmental Ethics* (1989), pp. 146-47.

62. When in your war against a city you have to besiege it a long time in order to capture it, you must not destroy its trees, wielding the axe against them. You may eat of them, but you must not cut them down. Are trees of the field human to withdraw before you into the besieged city? Only trees which you know do not yield food may be destroyed; you may cut them down for constructing siege works against the city that is waging war on you, until it has been reduced.— Deuteronomy 20:19-20. *The Torah: A Modern Commentary*, 1983, vol. V, New York: Union of American Hebrew Congregations.

63. "Everyone must protect and conserve the natural environment as an individual responsibility. Seemingly minor infractions by individuals, particularly in cumulative effect, can have major effects on human health and natural habitat— or upon operating budgets. Leaders must set the example as well as to strictly enforce environmental policy and regulations. Environmental responsibility involves all of us. The environmental ethic must be part of how we live and how we train." General Dennis Reimer, 1995, Chief of Staff, US Army.

64. Adapted from: David E. Mosher, Beth E. Lachman, Michael D. Greenberg,

Tiffany Nichols, Brian Rosen and Henry H. Willis, *Green Warriors: Army Environmental Considerations for Contingency Operations from Planning Through Post-Conflict*, RAND Corporation, 2008, p. 3.

65. "Environmental Considerations in Military Operations," FM 3-100.4, MCRP 4-11B, The US Department of the Army, dated June 15, 2000, Paras 4-13 to 4-18.
66. "Environmental Considerations in Military Operations," FM 3-100.4, MCRP 4-11B, The US Department of the Army, June 15, 2000, p. vi.
67. There is increasing worldwide support for a DU ban. Italian government has agreed to pay Euro 170 m compensation damage for personnel exposed to DU weapons in the Balkans. Available at: http://www.bandepleteduranium.org/en/overview, accessed March 2, 2013.
68. According to Boothby, this is the logical interpretation of the stipulation in Article 3 of the Hague Convention IV, 1907, that states are responsible for all acts of the armed forces. William H. Boothby, *Weapons and the Law of Armed Conflict* (Oxford: Oxford University Press, 2009), p. 341.
69. *A Guide to the Legal Review of New Weapons, Means and Methods of Warfare: Measures to Implement Article 36 of Additional Protocol I of 1977*. Geneva: ICRC, 2006, p. 4. In 2006, in order to assist States, the ICRC prepared the Guide in consultation with military and international law experts from ten countries. Available at: http://www.icrc.org/eng/assets/files/other/icrc_002_0902.pdf, accessed March 15, 2011.
70. The UK "Joint Service Manual of the Law of Armed Conflict," Joint Service Publication-383, 2004, paragraph 6.20, provides: "This obligation is imposed on all states party, not only those that produce weapons. To this end each state is required to have effective review procedures operating in accordance with the rules of international law but there is no requirement that the findings from these proceedings should be published. In the UK the weapons review process is conducted by the Ministry of Defence in a progressive manner as concepts for new means and methods of warfare are developed and as the conceptual process moves towards procurement. Qualified legal staff contributes to the weapon development process. The review process takes account not only of the law as it stands at the time of the review but also attempts to take account of likely future developments in the law of armed conflict."
71. *A Guide to the Legal Review of New Weapons, Means and Methods of Warfare: Measures to Implement Article 36 of Additional Protocol I of 1977*. Geneva: ICRC, 2006, pp. 9-10.
72. Kathleen Lawand, "Reviewing the legality of new weapons, means and methods of warfare,"vol. 88, no. 864, *International Review of the Red Cross*, December 2006, p. 927.
73. Multidisciplinary expertise is important, given the wide range of factors that must be considered during the review; in particular the reviewing authority must have a technical understanding of the reliability and accuracy of the weapon in the light of the prohibition of the use of indiscriminate weapons, and a medical understanding of the effects of weapons on health in the light of the prohibition of the use of weapons of a nature to cause superfluous injury or unnecessary suffering. Medical expertise is especially important when faced with technologies that have effects different from those with which surgeons are generally familiar, notably effects other than those of explosive or projectile force, such as changes in body chemistry, electromagnetic energy, etc. Kathleen Lawand, "Reviewing the legality of new weapons, means and methods of

warfare," vol. 88, no. 864, *International Review of the Red Cross*, December 2006, pp. 925-30.

74. Under NATO guidelines, states have an obligation to check the legality of Non Lethal Weapons (NLW). This legal review should at least include the following elements for analysis:
Is the new NLW lawful? New NLW should not violate this principle. However, new technologies such as directed energy weapons, laser technologies or electrical devices must be carefully reviewed for their human effects, both in the short term and in the long term. A multidisciplinary approach including legal, military, technical and medical expertise is recommended.
Is the new NLW indiscriminate in its effect? The obligation to discriminate between combatants and civilian persons and objects is a fundamental principle of the law of armed conflict. Weapons with indiscriminate effects are prohibited. Every weapon system must be able to be controlled in such a way as to be directed at a lawful military objective.
Specific rules of law. The individual review of specific technologies is necessary. There is no legal impediment to the development of new weapons. Specific new weapons might be impacted by one or several of the IHL conventions. For example, new NLW based on toxic chemicals will be governed by the 1993 Chemical Weapons Convention. They will need to be developed with this Convention in mind. Additionally, each nation is to ensure respect for domestic law (e.g., labour law).
Finally, the military commander has to ensure the legality of the use of the new weapon at the time of employment. This includes the following issues: (i) Is the target a lawful military objective? And (ii) Are there civilians or civilian objects in the vicinity of the military objective? If so, precautions have to be taken to minimise excessive damages to civilians or civilian objects.
NATO: Guidelines for Legal Review of NLWs, available at:http://ftp.rta.nato.int/public//PubFullText/RTO/TR/RTO-TR-SAS-040///TR-SAS-040-ANN-C.pdf, accessed August 20, 2012.
75. Reviewing the legality of new weapons, means and methods of warfare is not a novel concept. The first international instrument to refer to the legal assessment of emerging military technologies was the 1868 St. Petersburg Declaration. The Declaration addresses the development of future weapons in these terms, "The Contracting or Acceding Parties reserve to themselves to come hereafter to an understanding whenever a precise proposition shall be drawn up in view of future improvements which science may effect in the armament of troops, in order to maintain the principles which they have established, and to conciliate the necessities of war with the laws of humanity." Undertaking legal reviews of new weapons is of particular importance today in light of the rapid development of new weapons technologies. In conducting reviews, a State must also consider the prohibitions or restrictions on the use of specific weapons, means and methods of warfare pursuant to customary international law. *A Guide to the Legal Review of New Weapons, Means and Methods of Warfare: Measures to Implement Article 36 of Additional Protocol I of 1977* (2006), Geneva: ICRC.
76. The International Conference of the Red Cross and Red Crescent in the 27th (1999) and the 28th Conference (2003) called on the States to establish mechanisms and procedures to determine the conformity of weapons with international law. Final Goal 2.5 of the Agenda for Humanitarian Action adopted by the 28th International Conference of the Red Cross and Red Crescent (2003).
77. The Review report of July 12, 2012, available at: http://www.

bandepleteduranium.org/en/docs/192.pdf, accessed August 20, 2012.

78. Since the 1991 Gulf War, concern over the health and environmental effects of depleted uranium (DU) weapons has continued to grow. DU is an extremely dense metal made from low-level radioactive waste. Weapons containing DU is principally used by the US, but also by other countries such as Britain, in defensive military armour, conventional munitions, and some missiles. The Royal Society, the UK's national science academy, predicts that soldiers and civilians exposed to high DU levels may be at increased risk for kidney damage and lung cancer. Unfortunately, a DU clean-up and monitoring programme, necessary to confirm suspected health threats, is on hold until coalition forces agree to reveal where and how much DU was used in Iraq. "Royal Society calls on coalition forces to reveal where DU has been used in Iraq," *The Royal Society*, 2003, May 29, 2003, http://www.royalsoc.ac.uk/news/.
79. "A Guide to the Legal Review of New Weapons, Means and Methods of Warfare: Measures to Implement Article 36 of Additional Protocol I of 1977," vol. 88, no. 864, *International Review of the Red Cross*, December 2006, pp. 951-52.
80. *A Guide to the Legal Review of New Weapons, Means and Methods of Warfare: Measures to Implement Article 36 of Additional Protocol I of 1977*. 2006. Geneva: ICRC.
81. Meredith DuBarry Huston, "Wartime Environmental Damage: Financing the Cleanup," vol. 23, *U. Pa. J. Int'l Econ. L.* (2000), p. 908.
82. Michael Bothe, Carl Bruch, Jordan Diamond, and David Jensen, "International Law Protecting the Environment during Armed Conflict: Gaps and Opportunities," vol. 92, no. 879, *International Review of the Red Cross*, September 2010, pp. 569-92.

6

CONCLUSION AND RECOMMENDATIONS

Weapons[1] include anything used to gain an advantage over an adversary or to place an adversary at a disadvantage. Down the ages, they have undergone an evolutionary change from stones to clubs and maces, to bows and arrows, to swords, to guns, aircraft and missiles to nuclear weapons. In the last hundred years or so, not just weapons, but the method of armed conflict too has undergone striking changes. All these changes had a direct as well as a collateral impact on the natural environment.

Though biological and chemical weapons have been a part of the military arsenal since hundreds of years, the twentieth century saw them developed into lethal weapons capable of mass destruction and suitable for various kinds of delivery systems, including aerial bombs, artillery shells, sprayers, and missile warheads. One of the gravest dangers associated with such weapons is that the material required for their production is widely available, making it more difficult to curb their development and use through normal mechanisms. Biological and chemical weapons are suited to the goals and modus operandi of terrorist organisations, which function by sowing fear and panic and demoralising a population. Indeed, global terrorist organisations such as Al Qaeda have declared that they will not hesitate to use biological and chemical weapons, and there is evidence of their attempts to obtain them.[2]

There is no dispute over the fact that the use of nuclear weapons poses extraordinary risks to the environment. The destructive power of nuclear weapons cannot be contained in space or time. They have the potential to destroy all civilisation and the entire ecosystem of the planet.[3] Depleted Uranium (DU) weapons, though far less destructive, pose a variety of health and environmental risks. The two most cited concerns stem from DU's chemical toxicity and radioactivity. Chemical toxicity is common to all heavy metals, many of which are used on the battlefield and in everyday life, for example lead. The chemical toxicity of DU may weaken the immune system and cause respiratory and kidney problems, while radiation may lead to cancers, chronic fatigue syndrome, and auto-immune deficiencies. In addition, DU may also be genotoxic. Genotoxic substances alter the DNA, often in ways that increase the chances of genetic birth defects and cancer.[4] Generally, the longer the conflict, the greater is the exposure.[5] Also, as DU munitions corrode, they leach into the soil and contaminate groundwater and agricultural systems, which exposes a large section of the population to the harmful effects of DU. Since DU has an exceptionally long half-life (estimates range as high as 4.4 billion years), it persists in the environment for very long.[6]

Cluster munitions can be delivered by aerial bombs, artillery shells, artillery rockets, and cruise missiles. At a predetermined point prior to reaching the target, the dispenser releases hundreds of submunitions, dispersing them in the air and blanketing the target area. These submunitions are powerful anti-personnel weapons, capable of killing or seriously wounding anyone, civilian and combatant alike. Landmines, in particular APM, have become one of the most significant social, economic and environmental problems. Unexploded ordnance, be they landmines, cluster bombs or other conventional explosive ordnance, render land uninhabitable even after a war is over. For civilians who have no choice but to use the land, these weapons can go on killing and maiming decades later. An array of chemical pollutants, such as heavy metals, acids and alkalis are often left behind after troops leave the battle arena.

During the Second World War, incendiary weapons became a popular means of burning cities. They killed many more people, and flattened much more urban landscape than did the two atomic bombs dropped over Hiroshima and Nagasaki. In March 1945, the US accomplished the greatest military victory in history when napalm-firebombs killed about 84,000 residents of Tokyo in a few hours. These weapons incinerated 66 of Japan's 68 largest cities over subsequent weeks. More recently they were used by the US in Iraq (1991), NATO forces in Afghanistan (2003-2011), Israel in Gaza and Lebanon (2006-2008), and Ethiopia in Somalia (2007). Recently, the US-led coalition has used artillery-delivered white phosphorus against Islamic State forces in Syria and Iraq.

Nuclear, chemical, and biological weapons present a threat to life itself; but short of that apocalypse, modern weapons can cause or hasten a host of environmental disasters, such as deforestation and erosion, global warming, desertification, and holes in the ozone layer. The devastating effects of military weapons on the environment were reflected in the wars of the twentieth century—World War I and II, the Korean and Vietnam Wars, the Cambodian Civil War, Gulf Wars I and II, the Kosovo Conflict, the Afghanistan War and in the recent Syrian conflict..

Legal Control

International humanitarian law related to the regulation of weapons has its origins in antiquity, when war was conducted with extreme cruelty, but considerations of humanity placed certain restraints on the weapons and methods of waging war. For instance, the Code of Manu, developed in India during the sixth century BC, prohibited the use of poison or other inhumane weapons in warfare. Manu's Code laid down rules such as: "When the king fights with his foes in battle, let him not strike with weapons concealed in wood, nor with arrows that are barbed, poisoned, or the points of which are blazing with fire." In AD 600, the Saracens, as a result of the promulgation of rules of war based entirely on the Koran, outlawed the use in war of burning arrows, the incendiary weapons of the time.

In 1625, Hugo Grotius' treatise, *The Law of War and Peace,* made a significant contribution to the regulation of weaponry. It articulated the important principle that restraint should be observed in war. This fundamental principle finds place in the St. Petersburg Declaration of 1868 which states, "The only legitimate object which States should endeavour to accomplish during war is to weaken the military force of the enemy; that for this purpose, it is sufficient to disable the greatest possible number of men." The principle was also reflected in Article 22 of the "Regulations respecting the laws and customs of war on land" annexed to the 1899 Hague Convention II and the 1907 Hague Convention, which provides that "the right of belligerents to adopt means of injuring the enemy is not unlimited." The principle that weapons causing "unnecessary suffering" must be avoided is also set forth in the Hague Regulations, Article 23, sub-paragraph (e).[7]

The bitter experience of the widespread use of chemical weapons during World War I, led the major powers to come together to prohibit the use of asphyxiating, poisonous, or other gases and of bacteriological methods of warfare through the Geneva Gas Protocol (1925). The use of nuclear weapons in World War II prompted the international community to take steps to protect civilian populations through the adoption of the Fourth Geneva Convention of 1949. In 1972, the prohibition of bacteriological weapons found in the 1925 Gas Protocol was expanded through the adoption of the Convention on the Prohibition of Development, Production and Stockpiling of Bacteriological (Biological) and Toxin Weapons and on their Destruction (BWC).[8] The States Parties to the BWC agreed "never in any circumstances to develop, produce, stockpile or otherwise acquire or retain" these weapons. The BWC requires the destruction or diversion to peaceful purposes of "all agents, toxins, weapons, equipment and means of delivery," and prohibits State Parties from transferring biological weapons to others and from assisting or encouraging others to acquire biological weapons capability.

In the wake of the environmental devastation caused by the US military in Vietnam, two specific international treaties related to the environment were negotiated. The ENMOD Convention of 1976 was the first instrument specifically focusing on the protection of the environment in armed conflict.[9] The 1977 Additional Protocol I (AP I) to the Geneva Conventions of 1949 was the second instrument to provide direct protection to the environment during international armed conflict. It did so through two provisions: Article 35—basic rules, and Article 55—dealing with the protection of the natural environment. These provisions prohibited the employment of means or methods of warfare which are intended, or may be expected, to cause widespread, long-term and severe damage to the natural environment, and thereby prejudice the health or survival of the population. The Protocol also required that care should be taken during armed conflict to protect the natural environment from widespread, long-term and severe damage. Attacks against the natural environment by way of reprisals were also prohibited.

The 1980 Conventional Weapons Convention (CCW) relates to environmental damage during armed conflict. Its preamble reaffirms the AP I prohibition of the use of methods or means of warfare "which are intended, or may be expected, to cause widespread, long-term and severe damage to the natural environment." Its Protocol III on incendiary weapons is of significance, as also Protocol V of 2003 which addresses the post-conflict humanitarian problem caused by the explosive remnants of war (ERW). Article 2.4 of Protocol III provides that "it is prohibited to make forests or other kinds of plant cover the object of attack by incendiary weapons except when such natural elements are used to cover, conceal, or camouflage combatants or other military objectives, or are themselves military objectives."

In 1993, the international community expanded the restraints on chemical weapons by adopting the Convention on the Prohibition of the Development, Production, Stockpiling and Use of Chemical Weapons and on Their Destruction (CWC). The CWC provides that the States Parties must refrain from any use or military preparation for the use of chemical weapons, as well as undertake never to "assist, encourage, or induce, in any way, anyone to engage in any activity prohibited to a State Party." Like the BWC, it also obligates Parties not to develop, produce, or otherwise acquire chemical weapons, and requires them to destroy their stockpiles and production facilities, an obligation which the US and Russia are yet to fulfil.

The destruction of chemical agents and munitions under the CWC is a herculean task. The official cost estimates for destroying the US chemical weapons arsenal have been rising, amid continuing public concern over the safety of storing, transporting and incinerating chemical agents. As costs have risen, the projected completion dates have been extended. With severe budget constraints, the Russian Federation has also experienced enormous difficulties in fulfilling its CWC obligations in a timely manner, as have other countries that produced such weapons on a large scale.

The 1997 Ottawa Convention on the Prohibition of the Use, Stockpiling, Production and Transfer of Anti-Personnel Mines and on their Destruction came into effect in March 1999. The treaty is comprehensive and the States Parties undertake "never under any circumstances" to use, develop, acquire, retain, or transfer anti-personnel mines, or to assist or encourage anyone else to do so. Parties are also under an obligation to destroy their existing stockpiles, and reservations to the treaty are impermissible. The 2008 Convention on Cluster Munitions, the latest weapon regulation treaty, is a comprehensive document, not only banning the indiscriminate weapon but also dealing with the care and assistance to be given to the victims.

In spite of the agreements relating to the ban of specific weapons, armed conflicts continue to take a toll not only in terms of casualties of war but also by causing damage to homes and infrastructure, displacement of people and destruction and degradation of the environment. The problem is that these instruments are only binding on the States that have signed them, unless they are deemed reflective of customary international law. Judging by the practice so far, it seems difficult to make any of these provisions applicable under customary international law applicable against some of the most militarily active States, which have refused to ratify these agreements.

At present, there are 174 parties to AP I, but these do not include the US, Israel, Iraq, and Iran; which are some of the most militarily active States. The ENMOD Convention has been ratified or acceded to by only 76 States. The 1997 Ottawa Anti-personnel Landmine Ban Treaty has not been signed by China, India, Iran Israel, Pakistan, Poland, Russia, Saudi Arabia, Somalia, Sri Lanka, UAE, the US, and Vietnam; while the Convention on Cluster Munitions (CCM) has been ratified by only 101 States.[10]

International law does not outlaw most classes of conventional weaponry, even though some of them are capable of producing devastating effects on the environment. Entire cities have been fire-bombed or flattened and large numbers of civilians have been killed by non-nuclear bombs, but such weapons have not been treated as illegal.[11]

As regards nuclear weapons, their development and maintenance will continue to consume enormous human and financial resources. Annual worldwide investment in nuclear weaponry will probably exceed the level of resources needed to eliminate acute malnutrition on a global scale.[12] Technological development raises another difficult question of how to regulate new weapons under conditions of uncertainty about their effect on health and environmental effects.

The preamble to the UN Charter seeks to save succeeding generations from the scourge of war. We have to ensure that the weapons of today do not end up damaging or destroying the natural environment. Besides, we are using scarce natural resources for the manufacture of weapons, the storage, deployment, and retirement of which also have an adverse impact on human health and the natural environment.[13]

In case the existing body of IHL is unable to provide protection to the environment, it is for us to look towards other legal regimes which are dynamic and relevant. IHL and international environmental law share common values. The larger composite principle of these bodies of law is the same: conservation of the environment. The former limits destruction, while the later limits exploitation. Both protect man. The objective is the protection of resources for common use and exploitation; maintenance of the regenerative capacity of the environment; and promotion of the well-being of all. In addition, human rights laws provide guidance on State conduct affecting the environment and natural resources during armed conflict.[14] Keeping in view that the environment continues to lack effective protection during armed conflicts, the following recommendations may be made to protect it from the impact of specific classes of weapons.

Weapons of Mass Destruction: The Biological Weapons Convention (BWC) is a comprehensive treaty and specific prohibitions apply in relation to biological/bacteriological weapons.[15] Under the BWC, the States Parties must refrain from and prevent activities prohibited under the Convention and must consult with each other to solve problems regarding the application/interpretation of the Convention. The Preamble to the CWC reveals its purpose.[16] It aims to make progress towards the "prohibition and elimination of all types of weapons of mass destruction." The CWC imposes a comprehensive ban on activities associated with manufacturing, transporting, storing, and deploying chemical weapons, including all programmes related to such weapons, and the destruction of existing stockpiles as well as weapons abandoned by States on the territory of other States. The BWC and CWC are bona fide disarmament treaties, requiring parties to ban the use of certain types of weapon and destroy any existing stockpiles of the prohibited types of weapons.[17] Hopefully, in due course of time, non-signatory States would accede to the BWC and CWC, and meet their treaty obligations.

The UN General Assembly's first resolution of 1946 identified the goal of the elimination from the national armaments of atomic weapons and all other weapons adaptable to mass destruction. The attempt to ban atomic weapons is based on the premise that all countries deserve equal security. In the last week of March 2017, history was made at the United Nations in New York, when diplomats from about 130 countries started formal talks on an international treaty to ban nuclear weapons. The goal was towards fulfillment of a long-standing demand that all countries deserve equal security; and to declare it illegal for any country to produce, possess, stockpile, deploy, threaten to use, or use nuclear weapons. None of the nuclear weapon countries were present at the meeting.[18]

The General Assembly on 7 July 2017 has adopted the Treaty on the Prohibition of Nuclear Weapons. It is the first multi-lateral legally binding instrument for nuclear disarmament to have been negotiated in 20 years. It is based on principles and rules of IHL, in particular the principle that the right of parties to an armed conflict to choose methods or means of warfare is not unlimited, the rule of distinction, the prohibition against indiscriminate attacks, the rules on proportionality and precautions in attack, the prohibition on the use of weapons of a nature to cause superfluous injury or unnecessary suffering, and the rules for the protection of the natural environment. The treaty recognises that any use of nuclear weapons would be contrary to the rules of international law applicable in armed conflict, in particular the principles and rules of international humanitarian law. Further, a legally binding prohibition of nuclear weapons constitutes an important contribution towards the achievement and maintenance of a world free of nuclear weapons, including the irreversible, verifiable and transparent elimination of nuclear weapons. Article 1 of the treaty states:

Each State Party undertakes never under any circumstances to:

(a) Develop, test, produce, manufacture, otherwise acquire, possess or stockpile nuclear weapons or other nuclear explosive devices;

(b) Transfer to any recipient whatsoever nuclear weapons or other nuclear explosive devices or control over such weapons or explosive devices directly or indirectly;

(c) Receive the transfer of or control over nuclear weapons or other nuclear explosive devices directly or indirectly;

(d) Use or threaten to use nuclear weapons or other nuclear explosive devices;
(e) Assist, encourage or induce, in any way, anyone to engage in any activity prohibited to a State Party under this Treaty;
(f) Seek or receive any assistance, in any way, from anyone to engage in any activity prohibited to a State Party under this Treaty;
(g) Allow any stationing, installation or deployment of any nuclear weapons or other nuclear explosive devices in its territory or at any place under its jurisdiction or control.[19]

The treaty contains 20 articles which are not subject to reservations. The treaty will be open for signature to all states at UN headquarters in New York on 20 September 2017, and enter into effect after it has been ratified by at least 50 states.

Conventional Weapons: The obligation to ensure the legality of weapons of war is not new. Article 1 of the Hague Convention II of 1899 obligated States parties to issue instructions to their armed forces, which were to conform to the rules contained in the Annex to that Convention. This included Article 23 (e), which prohibited the employment of "arms, projectiles or material of a nature to cause superfluous injury." The three conventional weapons discussed in the book, viz., DU, high explosives (HEW), and incendiaries (napalm and white phosphorus), violate this basic rule formulated 110 years ago. DU is a highly toxic, radioactive weapon that can lead to environmental contamination and harm the health of humans. What is more, the contamination persists long after the conclusion of hostilities. There has been an appeal to ban the use of DU weapons.[20] Keeping in view the harmful effects of DU, the use of such weapons must be discontinued forthwith. Disarmament efforts have reaped a number of notable successes over the past years. The international community must adopt a treaty to ban DU weapons.

High explosive weapons (HEW) are capable of causing serious damage to the biomass as well as the geomass of an ecosystem. They cause unnecessary suffering that is disproportionate to the military advantage reasonably expected to be gained from their use. They are also indiscriminate and leave a large footprint. HEW need to be banned and replaced by the other weapons, which are less destructive to humanity. According to Greenwood (2006: 796), in deciding whether the use of a particular weapon or method of warfare contravenes the unnecessary suffering principle, the crucial question is whether other weapons or methods of warfare available at the time would achieve the same military goal as effectively while causing less suffering or injury.[21] Protocol III to the CCW, allows the use of incendiary munitions due to loopholes in definitions and regulations. In view of the human suffering and environmental damage caused by the cruel and devastating effects of incendiary weapons, it is necessary that international community ban the military use of napalm and WP weapons, which go beyond incapacitation by making medical treatment extremely difficult.

Prohibited Weapons: The Ottawa Anti-Personnel Mine Ban Treaty has been ratified by 162 States.[22] Every year, there is a UN General Assembly Resolution in support of the total ban on anti-personnel landmines. There is a need for the universalisation of the treaty to end the suffering caused by anti-personnel landmines.

The use of cluster munitions has drawn sharp criticism for their impact on civilian populations. In the ongoing civil war in Syria, there have been allegations of the use of cluster munitions by the armed forces against civilian protesters. Cluster munitions violate the principles of proportionality and distinction, embodied in AP I. They leave behind a large number of dangerous unexploded ordnance. Such remnants kill and injure civilians, obstruct economic and social development, and have other severe consequences that persist for decades after use. The 2008 Convention on Cluster Munitions (CCM)[23] addresses the humanitarian consequences and unacceptable harm to civilians caused by cluster munitions, and has been ratified by 101 States so far. A universal ratification of the Convention is required for placing a complete ban on "indiscriminate" and "dumb" cluster munition weapons.[24]

The adoption of Protocol V to the CCW represents a considerable step in addressing the hazards posed by ERW. The threat to civilians from ERW can be reduced with the incorporation of self-destruction and self-neutralisation mechanisms in submunitions. The States involved in armed conflict as well as the UN must provide technical, material and financial assistance to facilitate the removal of ERW from the affected areas. The States Parties in a position to do so must provide assistance to help affected parties to reduce the threat posed by these ERW.[25] There is need for universal ratification of the treaty; at the time of writing, there were only 71 States Parties to Protocol V.

A complete ban on indiscriminate weapons would prevent superfluous injuries and unnecessary suffering to both combatants and civilians; and decrease the adverse impact on the natural environment. Historically, banning a weapon has not guaranteed its total destruction. Regardless of the intrusiveness of the legal instrument applied, the States can always develop and/or maintain a hidden arsenal. However, banning will ensure that the weapon is, at least, outside the reach of regular combat units when a bitter conflict erupts, making it impossible for the alleged arsenal to be used other than as a last resort.[26] The additional recommendations addressed to the international community and the States are as follows:

1. Weapons that destroy the environment or make it uninhabitable should be banned by the international community. Whilst it is recognised that most weapons have some damaging effect on the environment, a clear threshold should be defined at the international level, so that weapons that cause destruction beyond this threshold can be outlawed. Such a ban should include future research, testing, possession and use of the weapons.
2. An international agency should be established to ensure the protection of the environment in times of armed conflict. This

should preferably be a part of the UN and have the powers to prosecute nations, organisations and individuals for crimes against the environment committed during armed conflict. It should also have the ability to monitor the activities of combatants to ensure compliance with international law, and to secure compensation where there has been a breach.

3. International non-governmental organisations, like the ICRC, have the potential to influence the States about the legitimacy of the possession or the use of weapons in question; they must make serious efforts to persuade leaders of the States to abandon the use of weapons responsible for the degradation of the environment.
4. A State guilty of using banned weapons, including the waging of environmental warfare or the wanton destruction of the environment not justified by military necessity, should be made responsible for any unjustified environmental damage which results.
5. The States should make environmental protection during armed conflicts a centrepiece of the military doctrine; and must outlaw the military use of any weapon or device that would have long-lasting deleterious effects on people or the natural environment.
6. The States must formulate an environmental management system (EMS)[27] for military weapons and activities.[28]
7. The States must conduct an honest critical review of the legality of new weapons before deploying them, taking into account the technical, military, health, environmental, and humanitarian issues involved.
8. The sites for the storage of armaments must be selected by the armed forces, keeping in view health and safety of the residents of the locality and the ecology of the area.
9. Areas that suffer environmental damage through their use for military purposes, such as artillery ranges, armoured vehicle

practice, sea and aerial bombardment and conventional weapons testing, should be subject to environmental audit and environmental impact assessment.[29]

10. Military personnel should be educated in international and national "best environmental practice" and environmental laws. Military manuals should contain clear instructions in this regard.
11. The use of explosive ordnance in training and operations can result in contamination by munitions that fail to operate correctly. These unexploded ordnance (UXO) must be recorded by the armed forces, and deactivated at regular intervals.
12. Military commanders, while planning an operation should not use the environment itself as a weapon. The destruction of large areas of natural habitat or the poisoning of waterways, for instance, should be prohibited. Military investigation systems should not be maintained as exclusive criminal investigation for grave breaches of IHL.
13. Commanders at all levels must promote the protection of environment by their subordinates and incorporate the concept of pollution prevention into all military activities by promoting reuse, recycling, best available techniques and processes substitution, and improved operational efficiency.
14. Demilitarised weapons and munitions, no longer required in national inventories should be recycled. This includes anti-personnel landmines, small arms and light weapons, chemicals, cluster munitions, ammunition containing WP, DU and tungsten.[30]

During an armed conflict, some environmental impacts are unavoidable. However, these could be reduced or even prevented if the right actions are taken in the right places and at the right times. An environment-conscious State, its leaders and military commanders must shun weapons inflicting unnecessary suffering, injury and destruction. The armed forces of all States must agree to adopt a standard set of norms to serve as a definitive guide in protecting the environment during armed conflict.[31]

Notes

1. Weapons: A weapon may be a shock weapon, held in the hands, such as the club, mace, or sword. It may also be a missile weapon, operated by muscle power, mechanical power, or chemical power (as with the rocket and missile and such guns as the cannon, rifle, and pistol). Weapons may also be classified as conventional, destroying by kinetic energy (bullet) or by chemical energy (bomb and grenade). The unconventional category comprises nuclear weapons, such as the atomic bomb and thermonuclear bomb, as well as weapons of chemical warfare and biological warfare. Weapon System: Weapons could also be operated with the help of computer, and could be called weapon system. The weapon system can be classified into two (i) strategic weapon system and (ii) tactical weapon system. The strategic weapon system is designed to strike an enemy at the source of his military, economic, or political power. In practice, this means destroying a nation's cities, factories, military bases, transportation and communications infrastructure, and seat of government. Strategic weapons system uses atomic or thermonuclear devices, because only these weapons have sufficient explosive power to destroy, with relative ease and quickness, the entire war-making capability of a nation. The term strategic weapons system refers not merely to the explosive devices themselves but rather to the complex delivery systems that enable these warheads to reach their targets. Tactical weapons system integrates tactical weapons with electronic equipment for target acquisition, aiming, or fire control or a combination of such purposes. Tactical weapons are designed for offensive or defensive use at relatively short range with relative immediate consequences. They include weapons used for anti-tank assault, anti-aircraft defence, battlefield support, aerial combat—i.e., air-to-air or air-to-ground attack missiles, or naval combat. *The Encyclopedia Britannica*: 2010.
2. David Friedman, "Biological and Chemical Weapons Control in the Middle East," vol. 19, no. 3, *Non-proliferation Review*, November 2012, available at: http://cdn.www.inss.org.il.reblazecdn.net/upload/(FILE)1352263831.pdf., accessed February 22, 2013.
3. Weeramantry (1987) has given 11 reasons to establish that the use of nuclear weapons is illegal and a crime against humanity. These are: (i) causation of indiscriminate harm to combatants and non-combatants, (ii) aggravation of pain and suffering, (iii) violation of law of humanity, (iv) contradiction of the principle of proportionality, (v) nullification of a return to peace, (vi) destruction of the ecosystem, (vii) the extermination of population and the decimation of mankind, (viii) the possibility of extinction of the human race, (ix) intergenerational damage, (x) the express prohibition of asphyxiating gases and analogous materials, and (xi) destruction and damages to neutral states.
   C. G. Weeramantry, *Nuclear Weapons and Scientific Responsibility* (USA: Longwood Academic Wolfeboro, 1987), pp. 84-96.
4. Lesley Wexler, "Limiting the Precautionary Principle: Weapons Regulation in the Face of Scientific Uncertainty," vol. 39, *University of California, Davis* (2006), p. 471.
5. A. Bleise et al., *Properties, Use and Health Effects of Depleted Uranium (DU): A General Overview*, vol. 64, *Journal of Environmental Radioactivity* (2002), pp. 93, 99-100.
6. Ramsey Clark, "An International Appeal to Ban the Use of Depleted Uranium Weapons," in John Catalinotto and Sara Flounders (eds.). *Metal of Dishonour: How*

the Pentagon Radiates Soldiers and Civilians with DU Weapons (USA: International Action Centre, 1999), pp. 21, 22.

7. The authentic French version and the English translation of the Article 23 differ in some respects. The authentic French of the Hague Regulation text uses the term "superfluous injury" (maux superflus), the phrase "unnecessary suffering" used in English translation has acquired a relevance of its own through the practice of States. The English version would be narrower if its contents were taken to add a subjective element to the original rule. In conformity with the authoritative French text, the principle must be stated to be that—irrespective of the belligerent's intention—any means of combat are prohibited that are apt to cause unnecessary suffering or superfluous injury. *Weapons that May Cause Unnecessary Suffering or Have Indiscriminate Effects*, Report on the Work of Experts, 1973, Geneva: ICRC, p. 12.
8. Today, 165 states are members of the BWC. Twelve states, including Egypt and Syria, have signed but not ratified it, and nineteen states, including Israel, have neither signed nor ratified it.
9. It is neither a Convention that prosecutes wartime environmental damage as such nor a Convention that bans the use of certain weapons, but rather an effort to restrict the use of certain techniques in armed conflict such as those that had been employed by the US military in Vietnam. Julian Wyatt, "Law-making at the Intersection of International Environmental, Humanitarian and Criminal Law: The Issue of Damage to the Environment in International Armed Conflict," *International Review of the Red Cross*, vol. 92, no. 879, September 2010, pp. 593-646.
10. For instance, the US military currently employs DU in both anti-tank ammunition and protective tank armour. DU weapons were used by the US in huge amounts in Afghanistan to wipe out Al Qaeda fighters hiding in mountain caves. The exact quantity of the DU used in Afghanistan as well as its location has not been not revealed, however, it is estimated that at least 500 tons of DU shells were dropped in Afghanistan and Iraq War. Dai Williams, "Mystery Metal Nightmare in Afghanistan?" (2002), available at: http://www.eoslifework.co.uk/u231.htm, accessed September 2, 2012; Katsuma Yagasaki, "Depleted Uranium Shells, The Radioactive Weapons—Perpetuation of War Damage by Radiation," available at:http://www.ratical.org/radiation/DU/KYagasakiOnDU.pdf, accessed September 4, 2012; Lesley Wexler, "Limiting the Precautionary Principle: Weapons Regulation in the Face of Scientific Uncertainty," vol. 39, *University of California, Davis* (2006), pp. 459-529 at pp. 468-69.
11. C. G. Weeramantry, *Nuclear Weapons and Scientific Responsibility* (USA: Longwood Academic Wolfeboro, 1987) p. 29.
12. David C. Gompert, "Approaching the Nuclear Future," in David C. Gompert et al. (eds.), *Nuclear Weapons and World Politics: Alternatives for the Future* (New York: McGraw-Hill Book Company, 1977), pp. 3-4.
13. Jayantha Dhanapala, "The Environmental Impacts of Manufacturing, Storing, Deploying, and Retiring Weapons," Symposium Paper, National Energy-Environment Law and Energy Policy Institute, The University of Tulsa, College of Law Tulsa, Oklahoma, December 9, 1999.
14. *Protecting the Environment During Armed Conflict: An Inventory and Analysis of International Law*, November 2009, UNEP, p. 48.
15. The BWC has been ratified by 165 States.
16. The CWC has been ratified by 188 States.
17. Davis S. Jonas, "General and Complete Disarmament; Not Just for Nuclear

Weapons States Anymore," vol. 43, *Georgetown Journal of International Law*, Spring 2012, pp. 587-634.

18. Zia Mian and M.V. Raman, Ending nuclear lawlessness, *The Hindu*, 13 April 2017.
19. Draft text of treaty: UN General Assembly resolution A/CONF.229/2017/L.3/rev.1 dated 7 July 2017.
20. DU weapons are an unacceptable threat to life, a violation of international law and an assault on human dignity. To safeguard the future of humanity, we call for an unconditional international ban forbidding research, manufacture, testing, transportation, possession and use of DU for military purposes. In addition, we call for the immediate isolation and containment of all DU weapons and waste, the reclassification of DU as a radioactive and hazardous substance, the clean up of existing DU-contaminated areas, comprehensive efforts to prevent human exposure and medical care for those who have been exposed. R. Clark, *An International Appeal to Ban the Use of Depleted Uranium Weapons*, available at http://www.iacenter.org/depleted/appeal.htm, accessed February 23, 2013.
21. C. Greenwood, "The Law of War: International Humanitarian Law," in M. Evans (ed.), *International Law* (Oxford: Oxford University Press, 2006), p. 796.
22. The Convention on the Prohibition of the Use, Stockpiling, Production and Transfer of Anti-Personnel Mines and on Their Destruction, commonly referred to as the Mine Ban Treaty, was adopted on September 18, 1997 and entered into force on March 1, 1999. It has been ratified by 166 States. The major States not party to the Treaty include: China, Egypt, Finland, India, Israel, Pakistan, Russia and the US.
23. The Convention on Cluster Munitions has been ratified by 77 States.
24. The 2008 CCM has placed a ban on the weapons, however, the major states that use the weapons, including the US, have not joined the Convention. The US remains a leader in the use and development of cluster munitions. Although the US Department of Defence maintains that the cluster munitions currently in its arsenal are legal, the Pentagon has adopted a policy intended to reduce the harm the weapons cause to civilians. The policy calls for the cluster munitions stockpile to have a dud rate of less than 1 per cent by 2018. International pressure can ensure that the US adopt a policy of gradual reduction of cluster munitions from its arsenal. Even in the absence of customary prohibitions on cluster munitions, the US while employing the weapon is under an obligation by the customary rule of proportionality to take all necessary steps to prevent cluster munitions from indiscriminately causing civilian casualties. Eitan Barak, "None to be Trusted: Israel's Use of Cluster Munitions in the Second Lebanon War and the Case for the Convention on Cluster Munitions," vol. 25, *AM. U. INT'L L. REV.*, 2010, pp. 423-83.
25. States Parties are required to provide assistance with: (i) marking and clearance, removal and destruction of ERW; (ii) risk education to civilian populations; (iii) related activities; (iv) care and rehabilitation and social and economic reintegration of ERW victims; and (v) contribution to relevant trust funds. CCW Protocol V, Article 8 (1)(2) and (3). The assistance may be given through the United Nations, relevant organisations including the ICRC.
26. Eitan Barak, "None to be Trusted: Israel's Use of Cluster Munitions in the Second Lebanon War and the Case for the Convention on Cluster Munitions," vol. 25, *AM. U. INT'L L. REV.*, 2010, pp. 423-83.
27. T. B. Ramos, I. Alves, R. Subtil and J. J. de Melo, "Environmental performance policy indicators for the public sector: The case of the defence sector," vol. 82,

Journal of Environmental Management (2007), pp. 410-32.

28. The term "military activities" has been used to include (i) the active use of weapons in armed conflict, civil disturbances, civil war and low-intensity war; (ii) weapon development, production, testing, storage, transport and disassembly and disposal, and military training; and (iii) the prevalence of military oriented attitudes and practices within a nation or in the world (militarism). G. S. Shahi and V. W. Sidel, "The Impact of Military Activities on Development, Environment, and Health" in G. S. Shahi et al. (ed.), *International Perspectives on Environment, Development, and Health* (New York: Springer Publishing Company, 1997), p. 283.
29. In at least 19 States—Bangladesh, Croatia, Denmark, Finland, India, Indonesia, Iran, Malaysia, Maldives, the Netherlands, Norway, Pakistan, Poland, South Africa, Sri Lanka, Sweden, Thailand, the US and Vietnam—national legislations apply equally to the military and civil sectors during peacetime. In Switzerland, Serbia/Montenegro, Germany and the UK, the governments have expressly exempted their armed forces from wholly or partly having to comply with national environmental standards. NATO has recently developed a set of detailed environmental guidelines for armed forces during peacetime, and has suggested that these would be appropriate for any State to adopt. Arthur H. Westing, "In Furtherance of Environmental Guidelines for Armed Forces During Peace and War," in Jay E. Austin and Carl E. Bruch (eds.), *The Environmental Consequences of War: Legal, Economic and Scientific Perspectives* (Cambridge: Cambridge University Press, 2000), pp. 173-74.
30. Obsolete military equipments and weapons could be recycled. For examples: valuable metal could be extracted for commercial use; chemicals could be used as fertiliser; steel from weapons could be turned into manhole covers, piping and reinforcing rods for the building industry; the bodies of demilitarised missiles could be turned into water tanks; demilitarised explosives could be converted to commercial use; demilitarised WP could be converted into Phosphoric Acid for commercial use; and plastic landmine bodies could be converted into children's toys and plastic piping.
31. For example, the *US Navy Commander's Handbook on the Law of Naval Operations*, July 2007, is one of a few military manuals that address the protection of the environment during armed conflict as a separate subject: "It is not unlawful to cause collateral damage to the natural environment during an attack upon a legitimate military objective. However, the commander has an affirmative obligation to avoid unnecessary damage to the environment to the extent that it is practicable to do so consistent with mission accomplishment. To that end, and as far as military requirements permit, methods or means of warfare should be employed with due regard to the protection and preservation of the natural environment. Destruction of the natural environment not necessitated by mission accomplishment and carried out wantonly is prohibited. Therefore, a commander should consider the environmental damage which will result from an attack on a legitimate objective as one of the factors during targeting analysis;" Para 8.4.

BIBLIOGRAPHY

Abijola, B. "Protection of the Environment in Times of Armed Conflict." In N. Al-Nauimi and R. Meese (eds.), *International Legal Issues Arising Under the United Nations Decade of International Law*. The Hague: Martinus Nijhoff Publishers, 1995.

Afghanistan: Post-Conflict Environment Assessment. United Nations Environment Programme (UNEP), 2003.

Ahmed, Usman and Raghav Thapar. Security Council Resolution 1887 and the Quest for Nuclear Disarmament. *Michigan Journal of International Law*, vol. 33, Spring 2012, pp. 587-625.

Ainscough Michael J., Next Generation Bio-weapons: The Technology of Genetic Engineering Applied to Biowarfare and Bioterrorism, The Counter-proliferation Paper, Future Warfare Series No. 14, Air War College, Maxwell Air Force Base, Alabama, USA, April 2002.

Al-Duaij, Nada. *Environmental Law of Armed Conflict*. New York: Transnational Publishers, 2004.

Alexander, Nicholas G. "Airstrikes and Environmental Damage: Can the United States be Held Liable for Operation Allied Force?" *Colorado Journal of International Environmental Law and Policy*, vol. 11, no. 2, 2000, pp. 471-98.

Alfredson, Gudmundur. "Human Rights and the Environment." In David Leary and Balakrishna Pisupati (eds.), *The Future of International Environmental Law*. Tokyo: United Nations University Press, 2010, pp. 127-46.

Anti-personnel Landmines—Friend or Foe? A study of the military use and effectiveness of anti-personnel mines. Geneva: ICRC, 2007.

Antoine, Philippe. "International Humanitarian Law and the Protection of the Environment in Time of Armed Conflict." *International Review of the*

Red Cross, no. 2915, November-December 1992, pp. 517-37.

Arkin, William M. "Cyber Warfare and the Environment." *Vermont Law Review*, vol. 25 (3), 2000-2001, pp. 779-91.

Armed Conflict and the Environment. Report of the Committee on the Environment, Council of Europe, Doc 12774, October 17, 2011.

"Assessment of the Environmental Impact of Military Activities During the Yugoslavia Conflict." Prepared by: The Regional Environmental Centre for Central and Eastern Europe, June 1999. Available at: http://www.grip.org/bdg/pdf/g1691.pdf.

Asthana, Vandana and A. C. Shukla. "Environmental Consequences of Armed Conflict in South Asia." *South Asian Journal*, October-December 2008, pp. 79-91.

August, Robert M. "Environmental Damage Resulting From Operation Enduring Freedom: Violations of International Law?" *ELR News & Analysis*, vol. 33, 2003, pp. 10668-81.

Austin, Jay E. and Carl E. Bruch (eds.), *The Environmental Consequences of War: Legal, Economic and Scientific Perspectives*. Cambridge: Cambridge University Press, 2000.

Australian Defence Force. "Environmental Management." Appendix 4, Defence Annual Report 2009-2010, pp. 310-15.

Benjamin, Paul. "Green Wars: Making Environmental Degradation a National Security Issue Puts Peace and Security at Risk." *Policy Analysis*, no. 369, April 20, 2000.

Bergstrom, Margareta. "The Release in War of Dangerous Forces from Hydrological Facilities." In Arthur H. Westing (ed.), *Environmental Hazards of War: Releasing Dangerous Forces in an Industrialized World*. New Delhi: Sage, 1990.

Berhe, A. A. "The Contribution of Landmines to Land Degradation." *Land Degradation & Development*, vol. 18, 2007, pp. 1-15.

Biswas, Asit K. "Scientific Assessment of the Long-term Environmental Consequences of War." In Jay E. Austin and Carl E. Bruch (eds.), *The Environmental Consequences of War: Legal, Economic and Scientific Perspectives*. Cambridge: Cambridge University Press, 2000, pp. 303-15.

Blank, Laurie and Amos Guiora. "Teaching an Old Dog New Tricks: Operationalizing the Law of Armed Conflict in New Warfare." *Harvard National Security Journal*, vol. 1, 2010, pp. 45-85.

Bleise, A., P. R. Danesi and W. Burkart. "Properties, Use and Health Effects of Depleted Uranium: A General Overview." *Journal of Environmental Radioactivity*, vol. 64, 2003, pp. 93-112.

Bodansky, Daniel. *Legal Regulation of the Effect of Military Activity on the Environment.* Berlin: Erich Schmidt Verlag, 2003.

Bondarenko, B. B. and Kasyanenko. "Military Pollution—Chemical Waste." In *War or Health? A Reader.* Edited by Ilkka Taipale, P. Helena Makela and Kati Juva. London: Zed Books, 2001, pp. 426-30.

Boothby, Bill. "The Law of Weaponry—Is It Adequate?" In *International Law and Armed Conflict: Exploring the Faultlines; Essays in Honour of Yoram Dinstein.* Edited by Michael Schmitt and Jelena Pejic. Martinus Nijhoff Publisher, 2007, pp. 297-316.

Boothby, William H. *Weapons and the Law of Armed Conflict.* Oxford: Oxford University Press, 2009.

Borrie, John. *Unacceptable Harm: A History of How the Treaty to Ban Cluster Munition Was Won.* Geneva: United Nations Institute for Disarmament Research, 2009.

Borrie John and Maya Brehm, Enhancing civilian protection from use of explosive weapons in populat-ed areas: building a policy and research agenda, *International Review of the Red Cross,* Volume 93, Number 883, September 2011, pp. 1-28.

Bothe, M., K. J. Partsch and W. A. Solf. *New Rules for Victims of Armed Conflicts.* Hague: Martinus Nijhoff, 1982.

Bothe, Michael, Carl Bruch, Jordan Diamond and David Jensen. "International Law Protecting the Environment during Armed Conflict: Gaps and Opportunities." *International Review of the Red Cross,* vol. 92, no. 879, September 2010, pp. 569-92.

Bothe, Michael. "Environmental Destruction as a Method of Warfare." *Disarmament,* vol. XV, no. 2, 1992, pp. 101-61.

———. "The Protection of Environment in Times of Armed Conflict." In

German Yearbook of International Law, vol. 34, 1991.

Bouvier, Antoine. "Protection of the natural environment in time of armed conflict." *International Review of the Red Cross*, no. 285, December 1991, pp. 567-78.

———. "Recent Studies on the Protection of the Environment in Time of Armed Conflict." *International Review of the Red Cross*, no. 291, November-December 1992, pp. 554-66.

Bradford, E. *The Great Siege: Malta 1565*. UK: Penguin Books, 1964.

Brauer, Jurgen. *War and Nature: The Environmental Consequences of War in a Globalized World*. London: AltaMira Press, 2011.

Breitegger A. 2012. *Cluster Munitions and international law: Disarmament with a human face?* Routledge.

Briggs, Chad M. et al. "Environmental health risks and vulnerability in post-conflict regions." *Medicine, Conflict and Survival*, vol. 25, no. 2, April-June 2009, pp. 122-33.

Bring, O. *Arms Control and International Environmental Law*. Stockholm Institute for Scandinavian Law, pp. 397-417. Available at: http://www.scandinavianlaw.se/pdf/39-18.pdf.

———. "Regulating Conventional Weapons in the Future: Humanitarian Law or Arms Control?" *Journal of Peace Research*, vol. 24, Oslo, 1987, pp. 275-86.

Bruch, Carl E. "All's Not Fair in (Civil) War: Criminal Liability for Environmental Damage in Internal Armed Conflict." *Vermont Law Review*, vol. 25, no. 3, 2000-2001, pp. 695-752.

Bull, John M. R. "Decades of Dumping Chemical Arms Leave a Risky Legacy, Special Report," Part 1 & 2. *Daily Press*, October 30 and 31, 2005. Available at: http://www.dailypress.com/news/dp-02761sy0oct30,0,5136883,full.story.

Bunker, Alice Louise. "Protection of the Environment During Armed Conflict: One Gulf Two Wars." *RECIEL*, vol. 13 (2), 2004, pp. 201-13.

Butts, Kent Hughes. "Why Military is Good for the Environment." In Kakonen Jyrki (ed.), *Green Security or Militarized Environment*. USA: Dartmouth, 1994.

Caggiano, Mark J. T. "The Legality of Environmental Destruction in Modern Warfare: Customary Substance Over Conventional Form." *B.C. ENVTL. AFF. L. REV.*, vol. 20, 1993, p. 479.

Caron, David D. "The Place of Environment in International Tribunals." In Jay E. Austin and Carl E. Bruch (eds.), *The Environmental Consequences of War: Legal, Economic and Scientific Perspectives.* Cambridge: Cambridge University Press, 2000.

Carr, Paul. "'Shock and Awe' and the Environment." *Peace Review: A Journal of Social Justice*, vol. 19, pp. 335-42. Available at: http://www.paulrcarr.net/assets/files/articles/en/PeaceReviewmanuscript_NEW-july222010.pdf.

Carus, W. Seth. *Defining "Weapons of Mass Destruction,"* Centre for the Study of Weapons of Mass Destruction, Occasional Paper, no. 8. Washington, DC: National Defence University Press, January 2012.

Casey-Maslen Stuart (ed.). 2014. *Weapons Under International Human Rights Law*, Cambridge: Cambridge University Press.

Cave, Rosy. *Explosive Remnants of War in Sri Lanka.* London: Landmine Action 2003. Available at: http://www.landmineaction.org/resources/ERW_Sri_Lanka.pdf.

Chambers, W. Bradnee. "Towards an Improved Understanding of Legal Effectiveness of International Environmental Treaties." *Georgetown International Environmental Law Review*, vol. 16, Spring 2004, pp. 501-30.

Chamorro, Susana Pimiento and Edward Hammond. *Addressing Environmental Modification in Post-Cold War Conflict*, Occasional Paper. USA: The Edmonds Institute. Available at: http://www.edmonds-institute.org/pimiento.html, accessed May 23, 2011.

Christensen Stian Nordengen, Regulation of White Phosphorus Weapons in International law, Torkel Opsahl Academic EPublisher, Brussels, 2016, pp. 62.

Cieslak, Theodore J. and Fred M. Heretig. "Medical Consequences of Biological Warfare: The Ten Commandments of Management." *Military Medicine*, vol. 166, no. 12, pp. 11-12.

Closmann, Charles E. (ed.). *War and the Environment: Military Destruction in the Modern Age*. USA: Texas A&M University Press, 2009.

Cluster Munition Monitor: 2016, International Campaign to Ban Landmines – Cluster Munition Coalition (ICBL-CMC), August 2016.

Cohan, John Alan. "Modes of Warfare and Evolving Standards of Environmental Protection under International Law of War." *Fla. J. Int'l L.*, vol. 15, 2002-03, pp. 481-539.

Coleman, Kim. *A History of Chemical Warfare*. New York: Palgrave Macmillan, 2005.

Compton, J. A. F. *Military Chemical and Biological Agents: Chemical and Toxicological Properties*. Caldwell, NJ: Telford Press, 1988.

Daehler, Curtis C. and S. K. Majumdar. "Environmental Impacts of the Persian Gulf War." In S. K. Majumdar, G. S. Forbes, E. W. Miller and Schmalz (eds.), *Natural and Technological Disasters: Causes, Effects and Preventive Measures*. The Pennsylvania Academy of Science, 1992 pp. 329-36.

Dahl, Arne Willy. "Environmental Destruction in War." *Disarmament*, vol. XV, no. 2, 1992, pp. 113-27.

Damgaard Ciara. 2008. *Individual Criminal Responsibility for Core International Crimes*, Berlin: Springer.

Desgagne, Richard. "The Prevention of Environment Damage in Time of Armed Conflict: Proportionality and Precautionary Measures." In Horst Fischer and Avril McDonald (eds.), *Yearbook of International Humanitarian Law*, vol. 3, 2000, pp. 109-29.

DeWeerdt, Sararh. "War and the Environment." *World Watch*, vol. 21 (1), January-February 2008.

Diederich, Michael. "Law of War and Ecology: A Proposal for a Workable Approach to Protecting the Environment through the Law of War." *Military Law Review*, vol. 136, Spring 1992, pp. 137-60.

Dill Janina, *Applying the Principle of Proportionality in Combat Operations*, Oxford Institute of Ethics, Law, and Armed Conflict, University of Oxford, Policy Briefing, December 2010.

Dinstein, Yoram. "Protection of the Environment in International Armed Conflict." In J. A. Frowein and R. Wolfrum (eds.), *Max Planck Yearbook of the United Nations Law*, vol. 5, pp. 523-49. Available at: http://www.mpil.de/shared/data/pdf/pdfmpunyb/dinstein_5.pdf.

Docherty Bonnie, Breaking New Ground: The Convention on Cluster Munitions and the Evolution of International Humanitarian Law, *Human Rights Quarterly*, Volume 31, Number 4, November 2009, pp. 934-963.

Dogra, Bharat. "How destructive can these weapons be." *The Statesman*, New Delhi, December 17, 2009.

Dominguez-Mates, Rosario. "New Weaponry technologies and International Humanitarian Law: Their Consequences on the Human Being and the Environment." In Pablo Antonio Fernandez-Sanchez (ed.), *The New Challenges of Humanitarian Law in Armed Conflicts*. Leiden: Martinus Nijhoff Publishers, 2005, pp. 91-119.

Draulans, Dirk and Ellen van Krunkelsven. "The impact of war on forest areas in the Democratic Republic of Congo." *Oryx*, vol. 36, no. 1, 2002, pp. 35-40.

Drucker, Major Merrit P. "The Military Commander's Responsibility for the Environment." *Environmental Ethics*, vol. 11 (2), 1989, pp. 135-52.

Drumbl, Mark A. "Waging War Against the World: The Need to Move from War Crimes to Environmental Crimes." In Jay E. Austin and Carl E. Bruch (eds.), *The Environmental Consequences of War: Legal, Economic and Scientific Perspectives*. Cambridge: Cambridge University Press, pp. 620-46.

Drumbl, Mark A. "Waging War Against the World: The Need to Move from War Crimes to Environmental Crimes." *Fordham International Law Journal*, vol. 22, issue 1, 1998, pp. 122-53.

Dudley, Joseph P. et al. "Effects of War and Civil Strife on Wildlife and Wildlife Habitats." *Conservation Biology*, vol. 16, no. 2, April 2002, pp. 319-29.

Dycus, Stephen. "Nuclear War: Still the Gravest Threat to the Environment." *Vermont Law Review*, vol. 25 (3), 2000-2001, pp. 753-71.

El-Baz, Faronk and R. M. Makharita. *The Gulf War and Environment*. USA: Gordon & Breach Science Publishers, 1994.

Enemark, Christian. *Biological Weapons: An Overview of Threats and Responses*. Working Paper no. 379. Canberra: Strategic and Defence Studies Centre, 2003.

Environmental Contaminants from War Remnants in Iraq, NGO Coordination Committee for Iraq, June 2011, available at: http://reliefweb.int/sites/reliefweb.int/files/resources/images...unitionsHumanHealthinIraq.pdf.

Falk, Richard. "The Inadequacy of the Existing Legal Approach to Environmental Protection in Wartime." In Jay E. Austin and Carl E. Bruch (eds.), *The Environmental Consequences of War: Legal, Economic and Scientific Perspectives*. Cambridge: Cambridge University Press, 2000.

Fidler, David P. "War and Infectious Diseases: International Law and the Public Health Consequences of Armed Conflict." In Jay E. Austin and Carl E. Bruch (eds.), *The Environmental Consequences of War: Legal, Economic and Scientific Perspectives*. Cambridge: Cambridge University Press, 2000.

Finger, Matthias. "Global Environmental Degradation and the Military." In Kakonen Jyrki (ed.), *Green Security or Militarized Environment*. USA: Dartmouth, 1994.

Fleck, Dieter (ed.). *The Handbook of International Humanitarian Law*. Oxford: Oxford University Press, 2008.

Fort, Timothy L. and Cindy A. Schipani. *Ecology and Violence: The Environmental Dimensions of War*. William Davidson Institute Working Paper no. 698, May 2004.

Freeland Steven. 2015. *Addressing the Intentional Destruction of the Environment during Warfare under the Rome Statute of the International Criminal Court*, Cambridge: Intersentia.

Freeland, Steven. "Human Security and the Environment: Prosecuting Environmental Crimes in the International Criminal Court." Available at: http://law.anu.edu.au/anzsil/conferences/2004/proceedings/freeland.pdf.

Furitsu, Kastumi. *Hazard of Uranium Weapons to Health and Environment*, Report to the Workshop Towards a Ban of DU, Organised by the International

Coalition to Ban Uranium Weapons (ICBUW) in cooperation with the International Peace Bureau (IPB), Geneva, November 9, 2005.

Gander, T. J. *Nuclear, Biological and Chemical Warfare*. London: Ian Allan Ltd., 1987.

Gangwar, Abdhesh. "Impact of War and Landmines on Environment, Centre for Environmental Education." Available at: http://archive.mtnforum.org/rs/ol/counter_docdown.cfm?fID=1409.pdf.

Garrett, Benjamin C. and John Hart. *Historical Dictionary of Nuclear, Biological and Chemical Warfare*. USA, Maryland: The Scarecrow Press, 2010.

Gasser, Hans-Peter. "For Better Protection of the Natural Environment in Armed Conflict: A Proposal for Action." *American Journal of International Law*, vol. 89 (3), 1995, pp. 637-45.

———. "Guidelines for Military Manuals and Instructions on the Protection of the Environment in Times of Armed Conflict." *International Review of the Red Cross*, no. 311, 1993, pp. 230-37.

Geib, Robin. "Poison, Gas and Expanding Bullets: The Extension of the List of Prohibited Weapons at the Review Conference of the International Criminal Court in Kampala." In M. N. Schmitt et al. (eds.), *Yearbook of International Humanitarian Law*, vol. 13, 2010, pp. 337-52.

Gibbons, Owen Thomas. "Uses and Effects of Depleted Uranium Munitions: Towards a Moratorium on Use." In *Yearbook of International Humanitarian Law*, vol. 7, 2004, pp. 191-232.

Gibson, Sarah. "Polluters as Perpetrators of Person Crimes: Charging Homicide, Assault, and Reckless Endangerment in the Face of Environmental Crime." *Journal of Environmental Law and Litigation*, vol. 25, 2010, pp. 511-58.

Gill, Terry D. and Dieter Fleck (eds.), *The Handbook of the International Law of Military Operations*. Oxford: Oxford University Press, 2010.

Gilman, Ryan. "Expanding Environmental Justice after War: The Need for Universal Jurisdiction over Environmental War Crimes." *Colo. J. Int'l Envtl. L. & Pol'y*, vol. 22, no. 3, 2011, pp. 447-71.

Goldblat, Jozef. "The Mitigation of Environmental Disruption by War: Legal Approaches." In Arthur H. Westing (ed.), *Environmental Hazards of War: Releasing Dangerous Forces in an Industrialized World*. New Delhi: Sage, 1990, pp. 48-60.

———. "Laws of Armed Conflict: An Overview of the Restrictions and Limitations on the Methods and Means of Warfare." *Bulletin of Peace Proposals*, vol. 13, Oslo, 1982, pp. 127-33.

Gopal, Sriram and Nicole Deller. *Precision Bombing, Widespread Harm; Two Case Studies of the Bombings of Industrial Facilities at Pancevo and Kragujevac During Operation Allied Force, Yugoslavia 1999*. Institute for Energy and Environmental Research, November 2002. Available at: http://www.ieer.org/reports/bombing/pbwh.pdf.

Grace, Charles S. *Nuclear Weapons: Principles, Effects and Survivability*. London: Brassey's, 1994.

Granoff, Jonathan. "Nuclear Weapons, Ethics, Morals, and Law." *Brigham Young University Law Review*, vol. 4, 2000, pp. 1413-1442. Available at: http://www.gsinstitute.org/gsi/docs/gran_12-9-00.pdf.

Grunawalt, Richard J., John E. King and Ronald S. McClain (eds.), *Protection of the Environment During Armed Conflict*. Newport, Naval War College, International Law Studies, 1996, vol. 69.

Guidelines for Military Manuals and Instructions on the Protection of the Environment in Times of Armed Conflict. *International Review of the Red Cross*, no. 311, March-April 1996, pp. 230-37.

Guruswamy, Lakshman D. and Suzette R. Grillot. *Arms Control and the Environment*. Ardsley, New York: Transnational Publishers Inc., 2001.

Haavisto, Pekka. "Kosovo War: First Environmental Impact Assessment." In Ilkka Taipale, P. Helena Makela and Kati Juva (eds.), *War or Health? A Reader*. London: Zed Books, 2001, pp. 447-51.

Haber, L. F. *The Poisonous Cloud: Chemical Warfare in the First World War*. Oxford: Clarendon Press, 1986.

Halle, Silja (ed.). *From Conflict to Peace-building: The Role of Natural Resources and the Environment*. UNEP, 2009, p. 50.

Hancock, Jan. *Environmental Human Rights: Power, Ethics and Law*. USA:

Ashgate, 2003.

Harland, Christopher. "Anti-Personnel Landmines: Balancing Military Utility and the Humanitarian Cost." *CLAWS Journal*, Summer 2008, pp. 236-48.

Harrell, Eben. "Regional Nuclear War and the Environment." *Time Magazine*, January 22, 2009. Available at: http://www.time.com/time/health/article/0,8599,1873164,00.html.

Hay, Alastair W. "Defoliant: The Long-term Health Implications." In Jay E. Austin and Carl E. Bruch (eds.), *The Environmental Consequences of War: Legal, Economic and Scientific Perspectives*. Cambridge: Cambridge University Press, 2000.

Henckaerts, Jean-Marie. "Towards Better Protection for the Environment in Armed Conflict: Recent Developments in International Humanitarian Law." *RECIEL*, vol. 9 (1), 2000, pp. 13-19.

Henckaerts, Jean-Marie and Louise Doswald-Beck. *Customary International Humanitarian Law*, vol. I. International Committee of the Red Cross and Cambridge: Cambridge University Press, 2005.

Hiskes, R. P. "The Right to a Green Future: Human Rights, Environmentalism, and Intergenerational Justice." *Human Rights Quarterly*, vol. 27, no. 4, 2005, pp. 1346–1364.

Hosmer, Alicia Watts, Colby E. Stanton and Julie L. Beane. "Intent to Spill: Environmental Effects of Oil Spills Caused by War, Terrorism, Vandalism, and Theft." Paper presented at International Oil Spill Conference, 1997. Available at: http://www.iosc.org/papers/01058.pdf.

Hourcle, Laurent R. "Environmental Law of War." *Vermont Law Review*, vol. 25 (3), 2000-2001, pp. 653-93.

Hulme, Karen. "A Darker Shade of Green: Is it time to Ecocentrise the Laws of War." In Noelle Quenivet and Shilan Shah-Davis (eds.), *International Law and Armed Conflict: Challenges in the 21st Century*. TMC Asser Press, 2010, pp. 142-60.

———. "Taking Care to Protect the Environment against Damage: A Meaningless Obligation." *International Review of the Red Cross*, vol. 92, no. 879, September 2010, pp. 675-69.

War Torn Environment: Interpreting the Legal Threshold. Leiden: Martinus Nijhoff Publishers, 2004.

Hupy, Joseph. "The Environmental Footprint of War." *Environment and History*, vol. 14, no. 3, August 2008, pp. 405-21.

Incendiary Weapons. Stockholm International Peace Research Institute (SIPRI), The MIT Press, 1975.

International Committee of the Red Cross. *Expert Meeting on Humanitarian, Military, Technical and Legal Challenges of Cluster Munitions*. Conference Report, Montreux, Switzerland, April 18-20, 2007.

Jensen, Eric Talbot and James J. Teixeira. "Prosecuting Members of the US Military for Wartime Environmental Crimes." *The Georgetown International Environmental Law Review*, vol. 17, 2004-2005, pp. 651-71.

Jensen, Eric Talbot. "The International Law of Environmental Warfare: Active and Passive Damage During Armed Conflict." *Vanderbilt Journal of Transnational Law*, vol. 38 (1), 2005, pp. 145-85.

Jha U. C. and Ratnabali K. 2017. *The Law of Armed Conflict: An Introduction*, New Delhi: Vij Books India Pvt Ltd.

Jongerden, Joost et al. "Forest Burning as a Counter-Insurgency Strategy." 2006. Available at: http://www.joostjongerden.info/ForestBurning_website.pdf.

Kazi Reshmi. 2013. *Nuclear Terrorism: The New Terror of the 21st Century*, Institute for Defence Studies and Analyses, New Delhi, pp. 56-57.

Kellman, Barry. "The Chemical Weapons Convention: A Verification and Enforcement Model for Determining Legal Responsibility for Environmental Harm Caused by War." In Jay E. Austin and Carl E. Bruch (eds.), *The Environmental Consequences of War: Legal, Economic and Scientific Perspectives*. Cambridge: Cambridge University Press, 2000.

Kile Shannon N. and Kristensen Hans M., Trends in World Nuclear Force, 2016, SIPRI, Factsheet June 2016.

King Coli, Elke Hottentot and Berengere Lenoir, *A Guide to Cluster Munitions* (Third Edition), Geneva International Centre for Humanitarian Demining (GICHD), Geneva, May 2016, pp. 236.

Kiss, Alexandre. "International Humanitarian Law and the Environment."

Environmental policy and Law, vol. 31, no. 4/5, 2001, pp. 223-31.

———. "State Responsibility and Liability for Nuclear Damage." *Denv. J. Int'l L.& Pol'y*, vol. 35 (a), 2006, pp. 67-83.

Koppe Erik V., "Use of nuclear wepons and protection of the environment during international armed conflict", in Nystuen Gro, Stuart Casey-Maslen and Annie Golden Bersagel (Ed.), *Nuclear Weapons under International Law*, Cambridge: Cambridge University Press, 2014, pp. 247-268.

Koplow, David A. "Green Chemistry: Dismantling Chemical Weapons While Protecting the Environment." In Lakshman D. Guruswamy (ed.), *Arms Control and the Environment*. New York: Transnational Publishers, Inc., 2001, pp. 143-57.

Koppe, Erik. *The Use of Nuclear Weapons and the Protection of Environment During International Armed Conflict*. USA, Oregon: Oxford and Portland, 2008.

Kristensen H.M. and McKinzie M.G., Nuclear arsenals: Current developments, trends and capabilities, *International Committee of the Red Cross*, Vol. 97, No. 899, 2015, pp. 563-599.

Kritsiotis, Dino. "The fate of nuclear weapons after the 1996 advisory opinions of the world court." *Journal of Armed Conflict Law*, 1996, pp. 95-119.

Kumar, Manoj. "Challenges for the Indian Military: Managing Ozone Depleting Substances." *AIR POWER Journal*, vol. 5, no. 2, Summer 2010, pp. 117-31.

Landmine Monitor 2016, International Campaign to Ban Landmines – Cluster Munition Coalition (ICBL-CMC), pp. 112.

Landmine Monitor Report 2006: Toward a Mine-Free World. ICBL, 2006.

Lanier-Graham, Susan D. *The Ecology of War: Environmental Impacts of Weaponry and Warfare*. New York: Walker and Company, 1993.

Larsson, Marie-Louise. "Legal Definitions of the Environment and of Environmental Damage." Stockholm Institute for Scandinavian Law. Available at: http://www.scandinavianlaw.se/pdf/38-7.pdf.

Leibler, Anthony. "Deliberate Wartime Environmental Damage: New

Challenges for International Law." *California Western International Law Journal*, vol. 23, no. 1, 1992-1993, pp. 67-137.

Lewis, Jeff. "Unexploded Ordnance and the Environment—a Legacy of Past Practices." *Canadian Military Journal*, vol. 10, no. 4, 2009, pp. 46-52.

Lijiang, Zhu. "A Test of International Humanitarian Law on Landmines in Recent Conflicts: Problems and Possible Solutions." In M. J. Matheson and D. Momtaz (eds.), *Rules and Institutions on International Humanitarian Law Put to the test of recent Armed Conflicts*. Leiden/Boston: Martinus Nijhoff Publishers, 2011, pp. 653-93.

Littlewood, Jez. *The Biological Weapons Convention: A Failed Revolution*. England: Ashgate, 2005.

Lopez, Aurelie. "Criminal Liability for Environmental Damage Occurring in Time of Non-International Armed Conflict: Rights and Remedies." *Fordham Environmental Law Review*, vol. 18, 2006-2007, pp. 247-48.

Low, Luan and David Hodgkinson. "Compensation for Wartime Environmental Damage: Challenges to International Law After the Gulf War." *Virginia Journal of International Law*, vol. 35, no. 2, 1995, pp. 405-83.

Luck, Edward C. *Environmental Emergencies and the Responsibility to Protect: A Bridge Too Far*. American Society of International Law, Proceedings of the 103rd Annual Meeting, March 25-28, 2009, Washington, DC, pp. 32-38.

Majeed, Abeer. *The Impact of Militarism on the Environment: An Overview of Direct & Indirect Effects*. Canada: Physicians for Global Survival, 2004.

Malich Gregor, Robin Coupland, Steve Donnelly and Johnny Nehme, Chemical, biological, radiological or nuclear events: The humanitarian response framework of the International Committee of the Red Cross, *International Review of the Red Cross*, Vol. 97, No. 899, 2015, pp. 647-661.

Mannion, A. M. *The Environmental Impact of War and Terrorism*. Geographical Paper no. 169, Department of Geography, University of Reading, Whiteknights, UK, 2003.

Manual on International Law Applicable to Air and Missile Warfare. Harvard University, Program on Humanitarian Policy and Conflict Research (HPCR), Bern, 2009.

Marauhn, Thilo. "Environmental damage in times of armed conflict not really a matter of criminal responsibility?" *International Review of the Red Cross*, no. 840, 2000, pp. 1029-1036.

Marauhn, Thilo, Georg Nolte and Andreas Paulus. "Possible Future Trends in International Humanitarian Law." *Human Rights Journal*, vol. 28, no. 3-6, August 31, 2007, pp. 65-75.

Matheson, Michael J. "The Environmental Effects of Nuclear Weapons and the 1996 World Court Opinion." *Vermont Law Review*, vol. 25 (3), 2000-2001, pp. 773-77.

Mathien, Timothy R. "Environmental Protection and the Law of Armed Conflict: A Study of Current Provisions and a Recommendation for the Future." *The Bowdoin Forum: Journal of International Affairs*, vol. VIII, Spring 2005, pp. 37-65.

Matousek, Jiri. "The Release in War of Dangerous Forces from Chemical Facilities." In Arthur H. Westing (ed.), *Environmental Hazards of War: Releasing Dangerous Forces in an Industrialized World*. New Delhi: Sage, 1990, pp. 30-37.

McDonald, Avril, Jann K. Kleffner and Brigit Toebes (eds.), *Depleted Uranium Weapons and International Law: A Precautionary Approach*. T. M. C. Asser Press, 2008.

McEwan, A. C. "Environmental Effects of Underground Nuclear Explosions." In Jozef Goldblat and David Cox (eds.), *Nuclear Weapon Tests: Prohibition or Limitation*. SIPRI, Oxford: Oxford University Press, 1988.

McLaughlin, Kathryn and Kathryn Nixdorff (eds.), *Biological Weapons Reader*. The Bio-Weapons Prevention Project (BWPP), Geneva, 2009. Available at: http://www.bwpp.org.

McNaught, L. W. *Nuclear Weapons and Their Effects*. London: Brassey's Defence Publishers, 1984.

McNeely, Jeffrey A. "Conserving Forest Biodiversity in Times of Violent Conflict." *Oryx*, vol. 37, no. 2, April 2003, pp. 142-52.

———. "Environmental Impacts of Arms and War." In Lakshman D. Guruswamy (ed.), *Arms Control and the Environment*. New York:

Transnational Publishers, Inc., 2001, pp. 41-58.

———. "War and Biodiversity: An Assessment of Impacts." In Jay E. Austin and Carl E. Bruch (ed.), *The Environmental Consequences of War: Legal, Economic and Scientific Perspectives*. Cambridge: Cambridge University Press, 2000.

Miguel, Edward and Gerard Roland. "The Long-run Impact of Bombing Vietnam." *Journal of Development Economics*, vol. 96, 2011, pp. 1-15.

Misak, Raafat and Omar, S, Environmental Damages from Minefields, *Journal of ERW and Mine Action*: Vol. 11, Issue 2, 2007, pp. 40-42.

Mitchell Eleanor and Maresca Louse, The human costs and legal consequences of nuclear weapons under international humanitarian law, *International Committee of the Red Cross*, Vol. 97, No. 899, 2015, pp. 612-645.

Moret, Leuren. "Depleted Uranium: The Trojan Horse of Nuclear War." *World Affairs*, vol. 8, no. 2, pp. 110-35.

Morin, Anthony. "Demining and the Environment: A Primer, Mine Action Information Centre." Available at: http://maic.jmu.edu/journal/11.2/feature/morin/morin.htm.

Moxley, Charles J., John Burroughs and Jonathan Granoff. "Nuclear Weapons and Compliance with International Humanitarian Law and the Nuclear Non-Proliferation Treaty." *Fordham International Law Journal*, vol. 34, 2011, pp. 595-697.

Murray, Richard R. and Kellye L. Fabian. "Compensating the World's Landmine victims: Legal Liability and Anti-Personnel Landmine Producers." *Seton Hall Law Review*, vol. 33, 2003, pp. 303-69.

Nanda, Ved P. "International Environmental Norms Applicable to Nuclear Activities, With Particular Focus on Decisions of International Tribunals and International Settlements." *Denv. J. Int'l L & Policy*, vol. 35 (1), 2006, pp. 47-65.

Nystuen Gro, Stuart Casey-Maslen and Annie Golden Bersagel (Ed.). 2014. *Nuclear Weapons under International Law*, Cambridge: Cambridge University Press.

Patocka Jiri, Syria Conflict and Chemical Weapons: What is the Reality? Mil.

Med. Sci. Lett., Vol. 85(1), 2016, pp. 39-43.

Paxman, J. and R. Harris. *A Higher Form of Killing: The Secret Story of Chemical and Biological Warfare*. New York: Hill and Wang, 1982.

Percival, Robert V. "Liability for Environmental Harm and Emerging Global Environmental Law." *Maryland Journal of International Law*, vol. 25, 2010, pp. 37-63.

Peterson, Ines. "The Natural Environment in Times of Armed Conflict: A Concern for International War Crimes Law?" *Leiden Journal of International Law*, vol. 22, issue 2, 2009, pp. 325-43.

Peytrignet, Gerard. "Protection of the Natural Environment in Time of Conflict: Overview of the State of International Humanitarian Law and the Position of the ICRC." Available at: http://www.bibliojuridica.org/libros/4/1985/15.pdf.

Plant, Glen. *Environmental Protection and the Law of War: a fifth Geneva Convention on the protection of the environment in the time of armed conflict*. London, New York: Belhaven, Press, 1992.

Polkinghorne, Michael and James Cockayne. "Dealing with the Risks and Responsibilities of Landmines and their Clearance." *Fordham International Law Journal*, vol. 25, issue 5, 2001, pp. 1187-1204.

Poll, Letetia van der and Ashraf Booley. "In Our Common Interest: Liability and Redress for Damage Caused to the Natural Environment During Armed Conflict." *Law, Democracy & Development*, vol. 15, 2011, pp. 1-43.

Prentiss, Augustine M. *Chemicals in War: A Treatise on Chemical Warfare*. New York: McGraw-Hill Book Company, 1937.

Protecting the Environment During Armed Conflict: An Inventory and Analysis of International Law. UNEP, November 2009.

Rappert, Brian. *Controlling the Weapons of War: Politics, Persuasion and the Prohibition of Inhumanity*. London: Routledge, 2006.

Reichberg, Gregory and Henrik Syse. "Protecting the Natural Environment in Wartime: Ethical Considerations from the Just War Tradition." *Journal of Peace Research*, vol. 37, no. 4, 2000, pp. 449-68.

Reyhani, Roman O. "The Protection of the Environment During Armed Conflict." *Missouri Environmental Law and Policy Review*, vol. 14, no. 2,

2007, pp. 323-38.

Roberts, Adam. "The Law of War and Environmental Damage." In Jay E. Austin and Carl E. Bruch (eds.), *The Environmental Consequences of War: Legal, Economic and Scientific Perspectives*. Cambridge: Cambridge University Press, 2000.

———. *Documents on the Laws of War*. Oxford: Oxford University Press, 2002.

———. "Environmental Destruction in the Gulf War." *International Review of the Red Cross*, no. 291, November-December 1992, pp. 538-53.

Richard, Moyes (ed.). *Explosive Remnants of War and Mines Other than Anti-Personnel Mines: Global Survey 2003-2004*. Landmine Action, 2005.

Robinson, J. P. Perry. "Difficulties Facing the Chemical Weapons Convention." *International Affairs*, vol. 84, no. 2, 2008, pp. 223-39.

Roscini, Marco. "Protection of the Natural Environment in the Time of Armed Conflict." In Md. J. H. Bhuiyan, Louise Doswald-Beck and A. R. Chowdhury (eds.), *International Humanitarian Law—An Anthology*. Nagpur: LexisNexis Butterworths, 2009, pp. 155-79.

Sadik, M. and J. C. McCain. *The Gulf War Aftermath: An Environmental Tragedy*. Springer, 1993.

Saillan, Charles de. "Disposal of Spent Nuclear Fuel in the United States and Europe: A Persistent Environmental Problem." *Harvard Environmental Law Review*, vol. 34, 2010, pp. 461-519.

Sand, Peter H. "International Environmental Law After Rio." *EJIL*, vol. 4, 1993, pp. 377-89.

Sassoli, Marco. "State Responsibility for Violations of International Humanitarian Law." *International Review of the Red Cross*, vol. 84, no. 846, June 2002, pp. 401-33.

Scheetz, Lori. "Infusing Environmental Ethics into the Space Weapons Dialogue." *Georgetown International Environmental Law Review*, vol. 19, no. 1, Fall 2006, pp. 57-82.

Schmitt, Michael N. "Humanitarian Law and the Environment." *Denv. J. International Law & Policy*, vol. 28 (3), 2000, pp. 265-323.

———. "Investigating Violations of International Law in Armed Conflict."

Harvard National Security Journal, vol. 2, 2011, pp. 31-84.

———. "Green War: An Assessment of the Environmental law of International Armed Conflict." *Yale Journal of International Law*, vol. 22, no.1, Winter 1997, pp. 1-109.

Schofield, Timothy. "The Environment as an Ideological Weapon: A Proposal to Criminalize Environmental Terrorism." *Boston College Environmental Affairs Law Review*, vol. 26, issue 3, 1999, pp. 619-47.

Schwabach, Aaron. "Environmental Damage Resulting From the NATO Military Action Against Yugoslavia." *Columbia Journal of Environmental Law*, vol. 25, no. 1, 2000, pp. 117-40.

Schwabach, Aaron. "Law Regarding Protection of the Environment During Wartime, International Law and Institutions," pp. 1-7. Available at: http://www.eolss.net/Sample-Chapters/C14/E1-36-02-04.pdf.

Shambaugh, J., J. Oglethorpe and R. Ham with contributions from S. Tognetti. *The Trampled Grass: Mitigating the Impacts of Armed Conflict on the Environment*. Washington, DC: Biodiversity Support Program, 2001.

Shelton, Dinah and Alexandre Kiss. "Martens Clause for Environmental Protection." *Environmental Policy and Law*, vol. 30, no. 6, 2000, pp. 285-86.

Sidel, Victor W. "The Impact of Military Preparedness and Militarism on Health and Environment." In Jay E. Austin and Carl E. Bruch (eds.), *The Environmental Consequences of War: Legal, Economic and Scientific Perspectives*. Cambridge: Cambridge University Press, 2000, pp. 426-43.

Sieg, Richard. "A Call to Minimize the Use of Nuclear Power in the Twenty-first Century." *Vermont Journal of Environmental Law*, vol. 9, 2008, pp. 305-73.

Skons, Elisabeth. *The Costs of Armed Conflict*. Stockholm International Peace Research Institute Project on Military Expenditure and Arms Production. Pp. 169-90. Available at: http://www.conflictrecovery.org/bin/SIPRI-Costs_of_Armed_Conflict.pdf.

Smith, D. *Trends and Causes of Armed Conflicts*. Berlin: Berghof Research Center for Constructive Conflict Management. Available at: http://www.berghof-handbook.net/smith/final. pdf.

Solf, Waldemar A. "Article 55: Protection of the Natural Environment." In Michael Bothe, Karl Josef Partsch and Waldemar A. Solf, *New Rules for Victims of Armed Conflict: Commentaries on the Two 1977 Protocols Additional to the Geneva Conventions of 1949*. The Hague: Nijhoff, 1982.

Stenhouse, M. J. and V. I. Kirko. *Defence Nuclear Waste Disposal in Russia: International Perspective*. NATO ASI Series, Disarmament Technologies, vol. 18. London: Kluwer Academic Publishers, 1998.

Stephen, Dale. "Human Rights and Armed Conflict—The Advisory Opinion of the International Court of Justice in the Nuclear Weapons Case." *Yale Human Rights & Development L. J.*, vol. 4, 2001, pp. 1-24.

Stone, Christopher D. "The Environment in Wartime: An Overview." In Jay E. Austin and Carl E. Bruch (eds.), *The Environmental Consequences of War: Legal, Economic and Scientific Perspectives*. Cambridge: Cambridge University Press, 2000.

Sundaram, Vinothine. "Fighting a Chemical War: The Environmental Impact of War on Iraq and Its Neighbouring Regions." Available at: http://www.cwru.edu/med/epidbio/mphp439/Chemical_War.pdf.

Tarasofsky, Richard G. "Legal Protection of the Environment During International Armed Conflict." *Netherlands Yearbook of International Law*, vol. XXIV, 1993, pp. 17-79.

"The Continuing Environmental Threat of Nuclear Weapons: Integrated Policy Responses." *EOS*, vol. 88, no. 21, May 22, 2007, pp. 228-31. Available at: http://climate.envsci.rutgers.edu/pdf/RobockNwEos2007EO210012.pdf.

The Manual of the Law of Armed Conflict. UK Ministry of Defence. Oxford: Oxford University Press, 2004.

The Military Impact on the Human Environment, SIPRI Yearbook, 1978, pp. 43-68.

Thompson, Robert. "Radioactive Warfare: Depleted Uranium Weapons, the Environment, and International Law." *Environmental Law Reporter*, vol. 36, 2006, pp. 10474-10486.

Toon, Owen B., Alan Robock and Richard P. Turco. "Environmental Consequences of Nuclear War." *Physics Today*, December 2008, pp. 37-42.

Tranquillo, Nicoletta. *Green Casualties of War: The need for international protection of the environment during armed conflicts and the case of the war between Israel and Lebanon in 2006*. Sweden: Lund University, 2007. Available at: http://www.lumes.lu.se/database/alumni/05.07/thesis/Nicoletta_Tranquillo.pdf.

UNEP Report of the International Meeting on Environmental Norms and Military Activities. UNEP/Env.Law/Mil/IG/1/2, December 10, 2009.

United Nations Environment Programme (UNEP), and United Nations Centre for Human Settlements (UNCHS). *The Kosovo Conflict: Consequences for the Environment and Human Settlements*. Geneva, Switzerland: UNEP and UNCHS, 1999.

Uzumcu Ahmet, International Law and Disarmament: The Case of Chemical Weapons, The Justice Stephen Breyer Lecture Series on International Law 2014-2016, pp. 24-36.

Verwey, Wil D. "Observations on the Legal Protection of the Environment in Times of International Armed Conflict." *Hague Yearbook of International Law*, vol. 7, 1994, pp. 35-52.

———. "Protection of the Environment in Times of Armed Conflict: In Search of a New Legal Perspective." *Leiden Journal of International Law*, vol. 8 (1), 1995, pp. 7-40.

"Vietnam and US in joint venture to clean up Agent Orange damage." June 17, 2011. Available at: http://www.guardian.co.uk/world/2011/jun/17/vietnam-us-agent-orange-damage.

Walsh, Nicolas E. and Wendy S. Walsh. "Rehabilitation of landmine victims—the ultimate challenge." *Bulletin of the World Health Organization*, vol. 81 (9), 2003, pp. 665-70.

Wantuck, Marnie. "Broken Arrows: Movement Towards Complete Prohibition of Nuclear Weapons through International Environmental Law." Editorial, *Vermont Journal of Environmental Law*, 2005. Available at: http://www.vjel.org/editorials/ED10048.html.

"War and the Environment." *World Watch Magazine*, vol. 21, no. 1, January/February 2008. Available at: http://www.worldwatch.org/node/5520.

Weapons of Mass Destruction and the Environment. Stockholm International Peace Research Institute (SIPRI). London: Taylor & Francis Ltd., 1977.

Weisberg, Barry. *Ecocide in Indochina: The Ecology of War.* San Francisco: Canfield Press, 1970.

Weir Doug, Why did the US need toxic uranium munitions to destroy fuel tankers in Syria? *Ecologist,* 20 February 2017.

Westing, Arthur H. "Environmental Protection form Wartime Damage: The Role of International Law." In N. P. Gleditsch et al. (eds.), *Conflict and Environment.* Netherlands: Kluwer Academic Publishers, 1997, pp. 535-53.

———. *Herbicides in War: The Long-term Ecological and Human Consequences.* London: Taylor & Francis, 1984.

———. "In Furtherance of Environmental Guidelines for Armed Forces During Peace and War." In Jay E. Austin and Carl E. Bruch (eds.), *The Environmental Consequences of War: Legal, Economic and Scientific Perspectives.* Cambridge: Cambridge University Press, 2000.

Wexler, Lesley. "Limiting the Precautionary Principle: Weapons Regulation in the Face of Scientific Uncertainty." *University of California Davis,* vol. 39, 2006, pp. 459-529.

What Rights for Mine Victims? Reparation, Compensation: From Legal Analysis to Political Perspectives. France: Handicap International, April 2005.

William Boothby. 2009. *Weapons and the Law of Armed Conflict,* Oxford: Oxford University Press.

Woolf Amy F., Non-strategic Nuclear Weapons, Congressional Research Service, February 23, 2015.

Yemelyanenkov, Aleksander and Andrei. "Military Pollution—Nuclear Waste." In Taipale Ilkka, P. Helena Makela and Kati Juva (eds.), *War or Health? A Reader.* London: Zed Books, 2001, pp. 416-19.

York, Christopher. "International Law and the Collateral Effects of War on the Environment: The Persian Gulf." *South Africa Journal of Human Rights,* vol. 7, 1991, pp. 269-90.

Yuzon, Ensign Florencio J. "Deliberate Environmental Modification Through the Use of Chemical and Biological Weapons: 'Greening' the

International Laws of Armed Conflict to Establish an Environmentally Protective Regime." *AM. U. INT'L L. & POL'Y*, vol. 11, no. 5, 1996, pp. 793-846.

Yves, Sandoz, Christophe Swinarski and Bruno Zimmermann (eds.), *Commentary on the Additional Protocols of 8 June 1977 to the Geneva Conventions of 12 August 1949*. ICRC, Geneva and Martinus Nijhoff, 1987.

Zia Mian and M.V. Raman, Ending nuclear lawlessness, *The Hindu*, 13 April 2017.

Zirojevic, Mina, Milos Markovic and Milan Pocuca. "Nuclear and Biological terrorism Implication on Environment." *The Review of International Affairs*, vol. LXII, no. 1144, 2011, pp. 97-108.

Zwijnenburg Wim amd Doug Weir, Targets of opportunity: Analysis of the use of DU by A-10s in the 2003 Iraq War, PAX and ICBUM, August 2016.

INDEX

F

G